Best wishes.

*To Cyrus Vance and Thorvald Stoltenberg
and all those from the UN and the EU
who worked with us in the
International Conference on the Former Yugoslavia*

Balkan Odyssey

DAVID OWEN

Victor Gollancz
London

First published in Great Britain 1995
by Victor Gollancz
An imprint of the Cassell Group
Wellington House, 125 Strand, London WC2R 0BB

A catalogue record for this book is
available from the British Library.

ISBN 0 575 06251 7

Illustrations

Photographs between pages 138 and 139:
p. i, Colton/Saba/Katz; p. iii, *Private Eye*; p. iv, top and bottom, David Ludlow;
p. v, top, L. Bianco, bottom, David Ludlow; p. vi, Paul Lowe/Magnum; p. vii,
top, Josef Koudelka/Magnum, bottom Roger Hutchings/Network;
p. viii, James Nachtwey/Magnum.

Photographs between pages 266 and 267:
p. i, David Ludlow; p. ii, top, Martin Mayer/Network, bottom, Jenny
Matthews/Network; p. iii, top, Sasy Laurent/Gamma, bottom, Shone/Gamma;
p. v, top, L. Bianco, bottom, Arturo Mari/Vatican Photographic Service;
p. vi, top and bottom, David Ludlow; p. vii, top, Paul Lowe/Magnum,
bottom, David Ludlow; p. viii, Pava/Zamur/Gamma.

All other photographs are from David Owen's private collection.

Map 3:
Ante Markotic, Ejup Sijencic, Asin Abdurahnanovic
(Bosnia-Herzegovina: Altermedia NUB, 1991).

Designed and typeset by Production Line, Minster Lovell, Oxford
Maps by Hardlines, Charlbury, Oxford
Printed and bound in Great Britain by Butler & Tanner Ltd,
Frome, Somerset

Contents

Acknowledgements

I AM INDEBTED to many people in addition to those to whom I have dedicated *Balkan Odyssey*. In particular, to Norbert Both, who was my research assistant for one year, funded by the University of Sheffield from the Basil Hicks Lecture Endowment; also to Gillian Bromley, an independent editor brought in by Sean Magee, the Commissioning Editor, and Katrina Whone, the Managing Editor, of Victor Gollancz. Their efforts have enhanced this book and without them it would never have been possible for it to have been written and produced in the necessarily short time-scale.

In my own office, I cannot thank enough Maggie Smart, Ruth Martin, Ruth Best, Charles Scott Armstrong, Craig McMillan, Henry Johnson, Alex Gordon-Brander and Harry Willis Fleming for their work on the manuscript and the production and design of the CD-ROM which accompanies this book. Vanessa Glyn Jones, Gemma Hirst and Debbie have been invaluable.

I am also grateful to David Ludlow, Herb Okun, Paul Szasz, Laura Silber and Drenka Willen of Harcourt Brace for their helpful comments on the text.

Dramatis Personae

Abdic, Fikret Leader of Muslim faction in Bihac; Muslim member of Bosnia-Herzegovina Presidency

Ahrens, Geert: ICFY Chairman of Nationalities and Minorities Working Group; formerly member of EC Peace Conference on Yugoslavia

Ahtisaari, Martti President of Finland 1994–; ICFY Chairman of Bosnia-Herzegovina Working Group 1992–4

Akashi, Yasushi UN Secretary-General's Special Representative for former Yugoslavia, 3 December 1993–October 1995

Akmadzic, Mile Bosnian Croat leader; Prime Minister of Bosnia-Herzegovina 1992–3

Albright, Madeleine US Permanent Representative to the UN 1993–

Annan, Kofi UN Secretary-General's Special Representative for former Yugoslavia, October 1995–

Babic, Milan Croatian Serb leader

Bartholomew, Reginald US Special Envoy to former Yugoslavia 1992–3

Bildt, Carl ICFY Co-Chairman of Steering Committee 1995–; former Prime Minister of Sweden

Boban, Mate Leader of the Bosnian Croats 1992–4

Boras, Franjo Bosnian Croat leader; member of Bosnia-Herzegovina Presidency

Boutros Ghali, Boutros UN Secretary-General 1992–

Briquemont, Francis UNPROFOR Commander for BH, 1993

Broek, Hans van den EU Commissioner for External Affairs; former Dutch Foreign Minister

Buha, Aleksa Bosnian Serb leader specializing in foreign affairs

Bulatovic, Momir President of Montenegro

Bush, George President of the USA 1989–93

Carrington, Peter Chairman of EC Peace Conference on Yugoslavia 1991–2

Charette, Hervé de Foreign Minister of France 1995–

Chirac, Jacques President of France 1995–

Christopher, Warren US Secretary of State

Churkin, Vitaly Russian Special Envoy to former Yugoslavia 1993–4

Claes, Willy Secretary-General of NATO 1994–; Foreign Minister of Belgium until 1994

Clinton, Bill President of the USA 1993–

Cosic, Dobrica Serbian writer; President of the FRY (Serbia and Montenegro) 1992–3

Cot, Jean Commander of UNPROFOR in former Yugoslavia 1993–4

Cutileiro, José Secretary-General of WEU; chaired negotiations on Bosnia-Herzegovina in EC Peace Conference 1992

Demirel, Suleiman President and former Prime Minister of Turkey

Dole, Robert US Senator; Republican majority leader in Senate 1995–

Draskovic, Vuk Leader of the Serbian opposition party SPO

Eagleburger, Lawrence US Secretary of State 1992–3

Eide, Kai ICFY negotiator between the Croatian government and the leaders of the Croatian Serbs

Frasure, Robert, the late US Special Envoy to former Yugoslavia and US representative on Contact Group 1994–5

Galbraith, Peter US Ambassador to Croatia 1993–

Ganic, Ejup Vice-President of Bosnia-Herzegovina; Yugoslav member of Bosnia-Herzegovina Presidency; SDA leader; Vice-President of Croat–Muslim Federation of BH 1994–

Gligorov, Kiro President of Former Yugoslav Republic of Macedonia

Goldstone, Richard Chief Prosecutor, Yugoslav War Crimes Tribunal

Granic, Mate Croatian Foreign Minister 1993–

Hadzic, Goran Croatian Serb leader

Hall, Peter ICFY deputy to Lord Owen 1992–3; member of EC Peace Conference on Yugoslavia; former UK Ambassador to Yugoslavia

Hannay, David UK Permanent Representative to the UN; retired 1995

Helveg Petersen, Niels Foreign Minister of Denmark 1993–

Holbrooke, Richard US Assistant Secretary of State 1994–

Hurd, Douglas UK Secretary of State for Foreign Affairs; retired 1995

Izetbegovic, Alija President of Bosnia-Herzegovina; founding leader of SDA

Janvier, Bernard Commander of UNPROFOR in former Yugoslavia 1995–

Jovanovic, Vladislav Former Foreign Minister of FRY; former Foreign Minister of Serbia

Juppé, Alain Prime Minister of France 1995–; Foreign Minister of France 1994–5

Karadzic, Radovan Leader of the Bosnian Serbs

Kinkel, Klaus Foreign Minister of Germany

Kljujic, Stjepan Croat member of Bosnia-Herzegovina Presidency, removed by Boban 1992, reinstated 1994

Kohl, Helmut Chancellor of Germany

Koljevic, Nikola Bosnian Serb leader; former Serb member of Bosnia-Herzegovina Presidency

Kooijmans, Peter Foreign Minister of The Netherlands 1993–4

Kozyrev, Andrei Foreign Minister of Russian Federation

Krajisnik, Momcilo Bosnian Serb leader; former President of the Assembly of Bosnia-Herzegovina

Lake, Anthony US National Security Adviser

Lanxade, Jacques French Chief of Defence Staff

Lapresle, Bertrand de Adviser to Carl Bildt; UNPROFOR Commander in former Yugoslavia 1994–5

Ludlow, David Special Assistant to Lord Owen 1992–4; representative of ICFY Co-Chairmen on Contact Group 1994

Major, John Prime Minister of the United Kingdom

Manning, David UK representative on Contact Group 1994

Martic, Milan Leader of the Croatian Serbs

Masset, Jean-Pierre ICFY deputy to Lord Owen 1993–4

Mazowiecki, Tadeusz UN Special Rapporteur on human rights in former Yugoslavia 1992–5

Mérimée, Jean-Bernard French Permanent Representative to the UN until 1995

Mierlo, Hans van Foreign Minister of The Netherlands 1994–

Milosevic, Slobodan President of Serbia

Mitsotakis, Constantine Prime Minister of Greece until 1994

Mitterrand, François President of France until 1995

Mladic, Ratko Commander of the Bosnian Serb army

Morillon, Philippe Commander of UNPROFOR in Bosnia-Herzegovina 1993

Nambiar, Satish Commander of UNPROFOR in former Yugoslavia 1992–3

Ogata, Sadako UN High Commissioner for Refugees

Okun, Herbert ICFY Deputy to Cyrus Vance 1992–3

Panic, Milan Prime Minister of FRY (Serbia and Montenegro) 1992

Papoulias, Karolos Foreign Minister of Greece

Perry, William US Defense Secretary

Plavsic, Biljana Bosnian Serb leader; former member of Bosnia-Herzegovina Presidency

Poos, Jacques Foreign Minister of Luxembourg

Powell, Colin Chairman of US Joint Chiefs of Staff to 1994

Ramcharan, Bertie Director of ICFY Secretariat

Redman, Charles US Special Envoy to former Yugoslavia 1993–4; member of Contact Group

Renwick, Robin UK Ambassador to the US; retired 1995

Roberts, Ivor Chargé d'Affaires, UK Embassy, Belgrade, 1994–

Robinson, Michael Chargé d'Affaires, UK Embassy, Belgrade, 1992–4
Rose, Michael Commander of UNPROFOR in Bosnia-Herzegovina 1994–5
Rugova, Ibrahim Leader of the Kosovar Albanians
Sacirbey, Muhamed Foreign Minister of Bosnia-Herzegovina 1995–; BH Permanent Representative to the UN 1992–5
Sarinic, Hrvoe Head of President Tudjman's office; former Croatian Prime Minister
Sédouy, Jacques-Alain de ICFY deputy to Lord Owen 1994–5; French representative on Contact Group
Seselj, Vojislav Leader of Serbian Radicals and leader of Serb militia
Shalikashvili, John US Chairman of Joint Chiefs of Staff; former SACEUR
Silajdzic, Haris Prime Minister of Bosnia-Herzegovina; former Foreign Minister of Bosnia-Herzegovina
Smith, Rupert Commander of UNPROFOR in Bosnia-Herzegovina 1995–
Solana, Javier Foreign Minister of Spain
Sommaruga, Cornelio President of the International Committee of the Red Cross
Steiner, Michael German representative on Contact Group
Stojanovic, Svetovar Personal adviser to FRY President Cosic
Stoltenberg, Thorvald ICFY Co-Chairman 1993–
Susak, Gojko Croatian Minister of Defence
Szasz, Paul ICFY legal adviser; representative of ICFY Co-Chairmen on Contact Group; former deputy head of UN legal department
Tarnoff, Peter US Under-Secretary of State for Political Affairs
Thomas, Charles US Envoy to former Yugoslavia 1994; member of Contact Group
Tudjman, Franjo President of Croatia
Vance, Cyrus Personal Representative of UN Secretary-General to former Yugoslavia 1991–2; Co-Chairman of ICFY Steering Committee 1992–3; former US Secretary of State
Wahlgren, Lars Eric Commander of UNPROFOR in former Yugoslavia 1993–4
Wilson, John UNPROFOR liaison officer on ICFY
Woerner, Manfred, the late Former NATO Secretary-General
Yeltsin, Boris President of Russian Federation
Zotov, Alexandr Russian Special Envoy to former Yugoslavia 1994–
Zubak, Kresimir Bosnian Croat; President of the Croat–Muslim Federation 1994–

Chronology of Events

1992

3 Sept First meeting of ICFY Steering Committee, Geneva

9–12 Sept Co-Chairmen visit Zagreb, Sarajevo and Belgrade

12–13 Sept Lord Owen at EC Foreign Ministers' informal meeting, Brocket Hall

14 Sept UNSCR 776 authorizes additional UNPROFOR deployment

16 Sept Co-Chairmen meet Ibrahim Rugova, leader of Kosovar Albanians

18–19 Sept First meetings of ICFY Working Group on Bosnia-Herzegovina with parties

18 Sept Mr Vance meets Chairman of Arbitration Commission, Robert Badinter

22–3 Sept Co-Chairmen meet Greek Prime Minister Mitsotakis, Athens

25–6 Sept Co-Chairmen visit Banja Luka

28 Sept Co-Chairmen visit Belgrade

29 Sept Co-Chairmen meet President Izetbegovic, Geneva

30 Sept Presidents Tudjman and Cosic meet with Co-Chairmen, Geneva

3 Oct Lord Owen briefs Council of Europe

5 Oct Lord Owen addresses Council of Europe Assembly

9 Oct UNSCR 781 establishes no-fly zone over Bosnia-Herzegovina

10 Oct Co-Chairmen meet Foreign Minister Kozyrev, Moscow

13 Oct Lord Owen negotiates with Bosnian Serb leader Karadzic on grounding of aircraft

13–14 Oct First round of ICFY-brokered talks in Pristina; Mr Vance briefs UN Security Council on ICFY developments, New York

16 Oct Co-Chairmen meet Macedonian President Gligorov, Geneva

17 Oct Co-Chairmen meet FRY Prime Minister Panic, Geneva

19 Oct Presidents Cosic and Izetbegovic meet with Co-Chairmen, Geneva

20 Oct Second meeting of Presidents Tudjman and Cosic with Co-Chairmen, Geneva

21 Oct Co-Chairmen meet with President Izetbegovic

24 Oct Lord Owen meets Irish Prime Minister Reynolds, Dublin

28 Oct New constitutional proposals for Bosnia-Herzegovina, Geneva

28–30 Oct Co-Chairmen visit Belgrade, Zagreb, Pristina, Tirana, Skopje and Podgorica

31 Oct Lord Owen meets Italian Foreign Minister Andreatta, Rome

4 Nov Co-Chairmen meet Turkish Prime Minister Demirel, Ankara

5 Nov Co-Chairmen meet Bosnian Foreign Minister Silajdzic and Bosnian Serb leader Karadzic

6 Nov Lord Owen at European Parliament Foreign Affairs Committee, Brussels

7 Nov Co-Chairmen meet Former Yugoslav Republic of Macedonia President Gligorov

9 Nov Lord Owen at EC Foreign Affairs Council, Brussels

11–14 Nov Co-Chairmen address UN Security Council, New York

19–20 Nov Co-Chairmen visit UNPAs in Croatia

25 Nov Lord Owen meets Spanish Prime Minister Gonzales, Madrid

28–9 Nov Co-Chairmen pay private visit to President Tudjman, Brioni

30 Nov–2 Dec Co-Chairmen at Organization of the Islamic Conference Foreign Ministers' meeting, Jeddah

4 Dec Lord Owen meets NATO Secretary-General Woerner and Belgian Foreign Minister Claes, Brussels

11 Dec UNSCR 795 authorizes deployment of UNPROFOR contingent to Macedonia

14 Dec Lord Owen attends CSCE Council of Ministers in Stockholm

16 Dec Ministerial meeting of ICFY Steering Committee, Geneva

17 Dec Co-Chairmen meet Presidents Tudjman and Izetbegovic, Zagreb; Lord Owen meets Abdic, Velika Kladusa

18 Dec Mr Vance meets UN Secretary-General Boutros Ghali and Security Council, New York; meets President Bush and Secretary of State Baker, Washington

18–22 Dec Lord Owen visits Sarajevo, Kiseljak and Pale

19 Dec Mr Vance meets US President-elect Clinton's foreign policy advisers, Washington

27 Dec Co-Chairmen meet Presidents Tudjman and Izetbegovic, Geneva; meet Foreign Minister Kozyrev, Geneva

28 Dec UN Secretary-General Boutros Ghali and Co-Chairmen meet Presidents Tudjman, Izetbegovic and Cosic

29 Dec Lord Owen meets Croatian Defence Minister Susak, Zagreb

30 Dec Lord Owen meets President Milosevic and Karadzic, Belgrade

31 Dec Mr Vance and UN Secretary-General Boutros Ghali visit Sarajevo

1993

2–4 Jan Co-Chairmen convene plenary meeting on Bosnia-Herzegovina, Geneva

5–6 Jan Co-Chairmen visit Belgrade and Zagreb

7 Jan Co-Chairmen meet President Gligorov of Former Yugoslav Republic of Macedonia, Geneva

10–12 Jan Second plenary session on Bosnia-Herzegovina, Geneva

13 Jan Lord Owen meets President Mitterrand, Paris

15 Jan Co-Chairmen meet Presidents Tudjman and Izetbegovic, Zagreb

20–1 Jan Co-Chairmen visit Sarajevo and Zagreb

23–30 Jan Third plenary session on Bosnia-Herzegovina, Geneva

31 Jan Lord Owen reports to the Presidency of the EC, Brussels

1 Feb Co-Chairmen meet US Secretary of State Christopher

11 Feb Co-Chairmen meet Karadzic

18 Feb Co-Chairmen meet US envoy Bartholomew and Russian envoy Churkin

22 Feb Co-Chairmen meet Greek Foreign Minister Papaconstantinou

23 Feb Co-Chairmen meet Macedonian Deputy Prime Minister Crvenkovski

2 Mar Co-Chairmen meet President Izetbegovic, Akmadzic, Boban and Karadzic, New York

3 Mar President Izetbegovic signs military agreement for peace in Bosnia-Herzegovina

8 Mar Lord Owen at EC Foreign Affairs Council, Brussels

11 Mar Co-Chairmen meet President Mitterrand, Foreign Minister Dumas and President Milosevic, Paris

21 Mar Lord Owen meets Karadzic, New York

22 Mar Co-Chairmen meet permanent members of the Security Council, New York

24 Mar Co-Chairmen hold separate talks with President Izetbegovic, Karadzic and Boban, New York

25 Mar At plenary session on Bosnia-Herzegovina, President Izetbegovic and Boban sign the VOPP, New York

2 Apr Mr Stoltenberg to succeed Mr Vance, 3 May

5 Apr Lord Owen at EC Foreign Affairs Council, Luxembourg

12 Apr Co-Chairmen meet Croat and FYROM Foreign Ministers, New York

17 Apr UNSCR 820 imposes financial sanctions on FRY

21 Apr Lord Owen meets Presidents Cosic and Milosevic, Karadzic and Mladic, Belgrade

22 Apr Lord Owen meets President Gligorov, Skopje; meets Prime Minister Mitsotakis, Athens

23 Apr Lord Owen meets President Gligorov, Skopje; meets President
Bulatovic, Podgorica; meets President Milosevic, Belgrade

24 Apr Lord Owen meets Karadzic, Krajisnik and Mladic, Belgrade;
meets Presidents Izetbegovic and Tudjman, Zagreb; meets Milosevic
and Karadzic, Belgrade

25 Apr Lord Owen holds talks with UNPROFOR Force Commander
General Wahlgren to discuss implementation of the Vance–Owen Peace
Plan

26 Apr Lord Owen meets Foreign Minister Kinkel, Bonn; meets President
of the EC Council of Ministers Helveg Petersen, Copenhagen

27 Apr Lord Owen meets Prime Minister Balladur and Foreign Minister
Juppé, Paris

1–2 May Plenary session on Bosnia-Herzegovina, Athens; Karadzic signs
VOPP

5 May Lord Owen meets NATO Secretary-General Woerner, Brussels

6 May UNSCR 824 designates towns including Sarajevo as 'safe areas'

7 May Lord Owen and Mr Stoltenberg meet, London

10 May Lord Owen at EC Foreign Affairs Council, Brussels

16 May Co-Chairmen meet Foreign Minister Kozyrev, Moscow

18 May Co-Chairmen meet Izetbegovic and Tudjman, Medjugorje

19 May Co-Chairmen meet Admiral Boorda and General Shalikashvili,
Naples

20 May Co-Chairmen visit Minsk and Kiev

22 May US, UK, France, Russia and Spain launch Joint Action
Programme, Washington

25 May UNSCR 827 establishes Yugoslav War Crimes Tribunal

26 May Lord Owen meets Spanish Foreign Minister Solana, Geneva

2 June Co-Chairmen meet President Tudjman, Zagreb

3 June Co-Chairmen meet President Izetbegovic, Sarajevo; meet Karadzic,
Pale

4 June UNSCR 836 enforces protection of 'safe areas'

8 June Lord Owen at EC Foreign Affairs Council, Luxembourg

9 June Co-Chairmen meet UN Secretary-General Boutros Ghali, Paris;
meet President Milosevic, Belgrade

10–11 June Co-Chairmen meet Albanian President Berisha, Tirana; meet
President Bulatovic, Podgorica; meet President Milosevic, Belgrade

14 June Co-Chairmen meet Chancellor Kohl and Foreign Minister Kinkel,
Bonn

16 June Co-Chairmen meet Presidents Milosevic, Tudjman and Izetbegovic

18 June UNSCR 844 provides for implementation of 'safe areas'
Resolution and for reinforcement of UNPROFOR

19 June Lord Owen meets Prime Minister Major, London

22 June Lord Owen at European Council, Copenhagen

23 June Co-Chairmen meet members of the Bosnia-Herzegovina Presidency, Geneva; meet Presidents Milosevic, Tudjman and Bulatovic, and Karadzic and Boban, Geneva

28 June Co-Chairmen meet Karadzic and Boban and members of the Bosnia-Herzegovina Presidency, Geneva

8 July Co-Chairmen meet President Milosevic and members of Draskovic's party (SPO)

9 July Lord Owen meets President Tudjman and Croatian Defence Minister Susak, Zagreb; Mr Stoltenberg meets President Milosevic, Belgrade

10 July Co-Chairmen meet President Tudjman and Bosnia-Herzegovina Presidency, Zagreb

12 July Mr Stoltenberg meets UN Secretary-General Boutros Ghali and UN Security Council and OIC representatives, New York

19 July Lord Owen at Foreign Affairs Council, Brussels

26 July Co-Chairmen have dinner with President Izetbegovic, Geneva

27–30 July Plenary session on Bosnia-Herzegovina; Co-Chairmen meet Presidents Milosevic, Tudjman, Izetbegovic and Bulatovic, and Karadzic and Boban, Geneva

3 Aug Co-Chairmen meet Presidents Milosevic, Tudjman, Izetbegovic and Bulatovic, Geneva

11 Aug Charles Redman replaces Reginald Bartholomew as US Special Envoy to former Yugoslavia

20 Aug Co-Chairmen issue package containing the constitutional papers and maps agreed upon during negotiations

31 Aug Co-Chairmen meet Presidents Izetbegovic, Milosevic, Tudjman and Bulatovic, also Karadzic and Boban, Geneva

11 Sept Lord Owen attends EC Foreign Ministers' informal meeting, Alden Bissen

17 Sept Co-Chairmen meet President Izetbegovic and Krajisnik; Muslim–Serb joint statement issued; Co-Chairmen meet Turkish Foreign Minister Cetin, Istanbul; meet President Gligorov, Skopje; visit UNPROFOR on border with Serbia

18–19 Sept Co-Chairmen visit Neum area; meet President Tudjman, Split

20 Sept Co-Chairmen meet Presidents Milosevic, Bulatovic, Tudjman and Izetbegovic, and Karadzic and Boban, on HMS *Invincible*

22 Sept Co-Chairmen at North Atlantic Council meeting, Brussels

29 Sept Bosnian Assembly votes for HMS *Invincible* peace plan, but rejects map

4 Oct Co-Chairmen at Foreign Affairs Council, Luxembourg

11 Oct Lord Owen meets Foreign Minister Kinkel, Bonn

15 Oct Lord Owen meets His Holiness the Pope and Foreign Minister Andreatta, Rome

17 Oct Co-Chairmen meet President Milosevic and Foreign Minister
Jovanovic, Belgrade

21 Oct Lord Owen meets Foreign Minister Kooijmans, The Hague

25 Oct Lord Owen meets Foreign Minister Papoulias, Athens

26 Oct Lord Owen briefs Foreign Affairs Council, Luxembourg

28–31 Oct Mr Stoltenberg in Zagreb and Belgrade

11 Nov Lord Owen meets Croatian Defence Minister Susak, London

17 Nov Lord Owen meets President Mitterrand, Paris

18 Nov Co-Chairmen meet Silajdzic, Karadzic and Boban, Geneva

22 Nov Lord Owen attends FAC, attended by Generals Cot and
Briquemont

29 Nov EC Foreign Ministers meet Presidents Milosevic, Bulatovic,
Tudjman and Izetbegovic, and Karadzic and Boban, Geneva

3 Dec Mr Akashi appointed UN Secretary-General's Special
Representative for former Yugoslavia

6 Dec Lord Owen attends FAC, Brussels

9 Dec Co-Chairmen meet President Milosevic and Karadzic outside
Belgrade

10 Dec Lord Owen briefs EC Directorate-General for External Affairs,
Brussels

21 Dec Co-Chairmen meet Presidents Milosevic, Bulatovic, Tudjman and
Izetbegovic, and Karadzic and Boban, Geneva

22 Dec Co-Chairmen and EU ministers meet Presidents Milosevic,
Bulatovic, Tudjman and Izetbegovic, and Karadzic and Boban, Brussels

1994

8 Jan Co-Chairmen meet Presidents Izetbegovic and Tudjman, Petersberg

18 Jan All-party negotiations commence, Geneva

28 Jan Lord Owen meets Prime Minister Major, London

31 Jan–1 Feb Co-Chairmen meet Foreign Minister Kozyrev, Moscow

5 Feb Marketplace mortar attack, Sarajevo

7 Feb Lord Owen at Foreign Affairs Council, Brussels

10–13 Feb Plenary session on Bosnia-Herzegovina, Geneva

16 Feb Lord Owen at Foreign Affairs Committee, European Parliament,
Brussels

1 Mar Agreement in principle on Croat–Muslim Federation

17 Mar Co-Chairmen at meeting for signature of Croat–Muslim
Federation Agreement, Washington

18 Mar Presidents Izetbegovic and Tudjman, Bosnian Croat leader Zubak
and Bosnian Prime Minister Silajdzic sign draft constitution of
Croat–Muslim Federation; Presidents Izetbegovic and Tudjman sign
letter of intent on Confederation, Washington

26 Mar Lord Owen at EU Foreign Ministers' meeting, Ioannina, Greece

27 Mar Lord Owen meets President Milosevic outside Belgrade

13–14 Apr Co-Chairmen meet General Rose, Churkin, Redman and President Izetbegovic, Sarajevo; meet Karadzic and Mladic, Pale

18 Apr Lord Owen at EU Foreign Affairs Council, Luxembourg

20 Apr Co-Chairmen meet Foreign Minister Kozyrev

26 Apr First meeting of officials of Contact Group, London

29 Apr Co-Chairmen meet Churkin, Oslo

13 May First meeting of Contact Group ministers plus EU Troika

16–19 May Co-Chairmen in Belgrade and Zagreb

31 May Bosnian Constituent Assembly unanimously elects Kresimir Zubak and Ejup Ganic as President and Vice-President respectively of Croat–Muslim Federation

7 June Co-Chairmen meet Martic, President of the Croatian Serbs, Geneva

24–5 June Co-Chairmen at EU Summit, Corfu

25 June Co-Chairmen meet President Gligorov, Skopje; then visit Belgrade and Zagreb

5 July Second Contact Group ministerial meeting, Geneva

18 July Lord Owen at EU Foreign Affairs Council, Brussels

30 July Third Contact Group ministerial meeting, Geneva

13 Aug Mr Stoltenberg meets Karadzic, Pale

29 Aug Lord Owen meets President of the EU Council of Ministers Kinkel, Bonn

4 Sept Co-Chairmen meet President Milosevic, Belgrade

5 Sept Co-Chairmen meet President Bulatovic, Podgorica; drive to Prevlaka and Dubrovnik

6 Sept Co-Chairmen meet President Tudjman, Zagreb; fly to Knin

10–11 Sept Lord Owen at EU Foreign Ministers' informal meeting, Usedom, Germany

27 Sept Co-Chairmen meet President Milosevic, Belgrade

28 Sept Co-Chairmen meet Prime Minister Horn, Budapest

30 Sept Lord Owen meets Foreign Minister Kozyrev, New York

4 Oct Lord Owen at EU Foreign Affairs Council, Luxembourg

6 Oct Lord Owen attends European Parliament Foreign Affairs Committee, Brussels

12 Oct Co-Chairmen meet Foreign Minister Kozyrev, Moscow

13 Oct Co-Chairmen meet President Tudjman, Zagreb

14 Oct Co-Chairmen meet President Milosevic, Belgrade

19 Oct Co-Chairmen and Foreign Ministers Granic (Croatia) and Jovanovic (FRY) hold undisclosed meeting

26 Oct Co-Chairmen meet President Milosevic, Belgrade; meet President Tudjman, Zagreb

27 Oct Co-Chairmen meet Croatian government delegation headed by
Sarinic and Krajina Serb delegation headed by Mikelic

31 Oct Lord Owen at EU Foreign Affairs Council, Luxembourg

3 Nov Co-Chairmen meet Sarinic and Mikelic, Knin

4 Nov Co-Chairmen meet Croatian Foreign Minister Granic and FRY
Foreign Minister Jovanovic, Zagreb

9 Nov Co-Chairmen meet President Milosevic, Belgrade

15 Nov Co-Chairmen resume economic talks with Sarinic and Mikelic,
Belgrade

25 Nov Co-Chairmen meet President Tudjman, Zagreb; meet President
Milosevic, Belgrade; meet President Tudjman again, Zagreb

2 Dec Co-Chairmen at economic agreement signing ceremony with
Sarinic and Mikelic, Zagreb; at third Contact Group ministerial
meeting, Brussels

6 Dec Co-Chairmen meet President Milosevic and Mikelic, Belgrade

23 Dec Lord Owen meets President Milosevic and Mikelic, Belgrade

1995

2–4 Jan Co-Chairmen meet Martic, Mikelic and Babic, Knin; meet
President Milosevic, Belgrade; meet Sarinic, Zagreb

10 Jan Co-Chairmen meet Sarinic, Zagreb; meet President Milosevic and
Mikelic, Belgrade

23 Jan Lord Owen at EU Foreign Affairs Council, Brussels

30 Jan Lord Owen meets Foreign Minister Juppé, Paris

2 Feb Co-Chairmen meet President Milosevic, Belgrade; meet President
Tudjman, Zagreb; meet French officials, Paris

6 Feb Lord Owen at EU Foreign Affairs Council, Brussels

14 Feb Co-Chairmen meet Foreign Minister Agnelli, Rome

15 Feb Co-Chairmen meet President Milosevic, Belgrade

16 Feb Co-Chairmen meet Foreign Minister Kozyrev, Moscow

23 Feb Mr Stoltenberg meets UN Secretary-General Boutros Ghali, New
York

6 Mar Co-Chairmen meet President Milosevic, Belgrade

7 Mar Co-Chairmen meet Sarinic, Zagreb

16 Mar Lord Owen meets Foreign Minister Solana, Madrid

20 Mar Mr Stoltenberg meets President Milosevic, Belgrade

23 Mar Co-Chairmen meet President Milosevic and Mikelic, Belgrade

24 Mar Lord Owen meets Prime Minister Major, London

18 Apr Co-Chairmen meet President Milosevic, Belgrade

27 Apr Lord Owen meets Foreign Minister Papoulias, Athens

4 May Lord Owen meets Foreign Minister Kinkel, Bonn

5 May Lord Owen meets Foreign Secretary Hurd, London

22 May Co-Chairmen visit President Ahtisaari, Helsinki

23 May Co-Chairmen visit Chancellor Vranitzky, Vienna

29 May Lord Owen at EU Foreign Affairs Council, Brussels; Co-Chairmen at fourth Contact Group ministerial meeting, The Hague

31 May Lord Owen announces decision to step down as Co-Chairman in House of Lords, London

5 June Co-Chairmen meet President Tudjman, Zagreb; meet President Milosevic, Belgrade

9 June Lord Owen meets President of the EU Council of Ministers Juppé, Paris

13 June Lord Owen at his last Steering Committee with successor Carl Bildt, Geneva

List of Acronyms and Terms

APC Armoured personnel carrier

ARRC Ace Rapid Reaction Corps

Badinter Commission EC Peace Conference and ICFY Arbitration Commission

BiH Bosnia and Herzegovina

Bosniacs Old label for mainly Bosnian Muslims, recently revived by the 'Muslim Bosniac Organization' and used in constitution for Croat–Muslim Federation of Bosnia-Herzegovina

BSA Bosnian Serb army

CFSP Common Foreign and Security Policy (European Union)

Chetniks Serb nationalist movement founded in the nineteenth century which fought against the Germans, the Ustashas and the Partisans during the Second World War; during the wars from 1991 used by Croats and Muslims as a contemptuous term for Serbs

CINCSOUTH Commander in Chief South (NATO)

COHA Cessation of hostilities agreement

COREU Official telegrams between EC/EU capitals

CSCE/OSCE Conference on Security and Cooperation in Europe; now Organization on Security and Cooperation in Europe

DS Democratic Party (Serbia)

EC European Community

ECMM European Community Monitoring Mission

EC Peace Conference EC Peace Conference on Yugoslavia, 1991–2

EU European Union (from 1 November 1993)5

European Council Meeting of EC/EU heads of government

FAC Foreign Affairs Council: meeting of EC/EU Foreign Ministers

Federation of Bosnia-Herzegovina Croat–Muslim Federation established under Washington Accords, March 1994

FRY Former Republic of Yugoslavia (Serbia and Montenegro)

FYROM Former Yugoslav Republic of Macedonia (provisional name in UN)

HDZ Hrvatska Demokratska Zajednica: the Croatian Democratic Union (Croatia, Bosnia-Herzegovina)

HV Hrvatska Vojska: the Croatian army

HVO Hrvatsko Vijece Odbrane: the Croatian Defence Council (the army of the Bosnian Croats)

ICFY International Conference on the Former Yugoslavia

ICRC International Committee of the Red Cross

JA Acronym used in diplomatic circles for Yugoslav army, the army of Serbia and Montenegro and successor to the JNA

JAP Joint Action Programme launched by US, UK, France, Russia and Spain, May 1993, Washington

JNA Jugoslovenska Narodna Armija: the Yugoslav People's Army

NAC North Atlantic Council

NATO North Atlantic Treaty Organization

NDH Nezavisna Drzava Hrvatska: the Independent State of Croatia, the Second World War fascist state run by the Ustasha leader Ante Pavelic

NFZ No-fly zone

OIC Organization of the Islamic Conference

Opstina District of local government in Bosnia-Herzegovina

OSCE Organization for Security and Cooperation in Europe; formerly CSCE (see above)

Partisans Tito's army during the Second World War, which fought against the Germans, Ustashas and Chetniks

PFP Partnership For Peace: NATO cooperation arrangements with former Warsaw Pact members

RS Republika Srpska: the Bosnian Serb Republic

RSK Republika Srpske Krajine: the Republic of Serbian Krajina

Sabor Parliament of Croatia

SACEUR Supreme Allied Commander, Europe (NATO)

SAM Sanctions Assistance Mission

SDA Stranka Demokratske Akcije: the (Muslim) Party of Democratic Action

SDS Srpska Demokratska Stranka: the Serbian Democratic Party (Bosnia-Herzegovina, Croatia)

SHAPE HQ Supreme Headquarters Allied Powers Europe (NATO)

SPO Srpski Pokret Obnove: the Serbian Renewal Movement (Serbia)

SPS Socialisticka Partija Srbije: the Socialist Party of Serbia

SRS Srpska Radikalna Stranka: the Serbian Radical Party

Tanjug Yugoslav press agency

UN United Nations

UNCRO United Nations Confidence Restoring Operation (successor of UNPROFOR in Croatia)

UNHCR United Nations High Commissioner for Refugees

UNMO United Nations Military Observer

UNPA United Nations Protected Area (Croatia)

UNPROFOR United Nations Protection Force (Croatia, Bosnia-Herzegovina, Macedonia)

UNSCR United Nations Security Council Resolution

Ustashas Movement led by the Croatian fascist Ante Pavelic, head of the NDH, the Croatian puppet state of Nazi Germany; used during the wars from 1991 by Serbs and Muslims as contemptuous term for Croats

VOPP Vance–Owen Peace Plan

WEU Western European Union

YWCT Yugoslav War Crimes Tribunal, formally entitled the International Tribunal for the Prosecution of Persons Responsible for Serious Violations of International Humanitarian Law Committed in the Territory of the Former Yugoslavia since 1991

Z4 Plan Zagreb Four Plan: plan by the US and Russian ambassadors to Croatia and two ICFY ambassadors

Introduction

NOTHING IS SIMPLE in the Balkans. History pervades everything and the complexities confound even the most careful study. Never before in over thirty years of public life have I had to operate in such a climate of dishonour, propaganda and dissembling. Many of the people with whom I have had to deal in the former Yugoslavia were literally strangers to the truth.

This is an account of how the international community tried to cope with the break-up of the former Yugoslavia. It is not a history of how the war started, or even of how the war developed, although I keep referring to that history for its impact on the present day. My vantage point is that of a negotiator who became involved in the autumn of 1992, after the war in Bosnia-Herzegovina had already taken a very heavy toll. A negotiator inevitably starts with an inbuilt bias towards achievable solutions. I tried to be impartial; I was not neutral, nor did I pretend to be neutral about ethnic cleansing, crimes against humanity, racial prejudice or religious intolerance. My task, as Co-Chairman of the Steering Committee of the International Conference on the Former Yugoslavia (ICFY) established by the London Conference of 26–7 August 1992,[1] first with Cyrus Vance and later with Thorvald Stoltenberg, was to search at all times for a just and peaceful settlement. Not a just settlement alone, for sadly every year of war in the former Yugoslavia made that harder to achieve, but at least a settlement which would roll back much of the Serb territorial advance in Bosnia-Herzegovina and allow many of those ethnically cleansed in Croatia as well as Bosnia-Herzegovina to return to their homes. The more speedily a settlement was reached, the greater the chance would be of reversing ethnic cleansing. The killing and maiming made it impossible to justify waiting until the fighting petered out into an exhausted peace. The penalties for delay – permanent ethnic division, lives lost and a population disabled in body and in spirit with fewer and fewer displaced people and refugees ready to return to their homes – always had to be costed against the price of an unfair peace.

By the summer of 1992 the first war in the disintegration of Yugoslavia, the Serb–Croat war of July 1991–January 1992, had reached an uneasy truce. The second war, the war between the Bosnia-Herzegovina government forces and the Bosnian Serbs in Bosnia-Herzegovina which flared up in April 1992, had reached the stage where over 65 per cent of the country was in the hands of the Serbs. After the London Conference Declaration of Principles[2] at the end of August 1992, the UN Security Council authorized a humanitarian intervention in Bosnia-Herzegovina,[3] adding this task to that of the United Nations Protection Force (UNPROFOR) already operating under a peace-keeping mandate in Croatia.[4] The primary task of this new force of 7,000 was to help feed the population of Bosnia-Herzegovina through the coming winter of 1992–3. In Geneva the ICFY was to establish, as quickly as it could, the framework for pursuing a negotiated settlement through a United Nations–European Union political initiative involving in its Steering Committee thirty-one countries.[5] The Steering Committee of the Conference was chaired by Cyrus Vance, representing the UN Secretary-General, Boutros Boutros Ghali, and myself, representing the six-monthly rotating Presidency of the European Community (later, after ratification of the Maastricht Treaty, the European Union).

I have tried to provide the background information to the events which shaped the decisions taken within the UN Security Council, the EC/EU, NATO, the ICFY and the Contact Group of France, Germany, Russia, the UK and the US, and also bilaterally between states, and to make them easily available not just through the medium of the written word in this conventional printed book but also electronically, with television footage, sound, pictures and very detailed documentation, on a CD-ROM. Any reader who becomes involved in a particular aspect of the story as it unfolds can in addition use the CD-ROM at home or at a place of study to bring up on the screen all detailed references. This way anyone can check prejudices and judgements against the documentary evidence.

My wish to support statements with facts in this way stems from the complexity and controversy that surround the break-up of Yugoslavia. The present-day leaders of the nationalist parties in the former Yugoslavia lived their formative years under Communism in Tito's Yugoslavia, where truth was valued far, far less than in the Western democracies. It is not sufficient to explain away the frequently broken promises, the unobserved ceasefires merely as the actions of lying individuals. They were also the product of South Slavic history, particularly its most recent phase of exposure to Communism.

I hope this book will help readers to discover and understand the complexities of international diplomacy, learn about the UN Security Council, sense how the Foreign Affairs Council of the European Union actually works, appreciate the complex role of the armed forces who serve the UN, see how the UN relates to NATO and the United Nations High Commissioner for Refugees (UNHCR) to bring help to people suffering the consequences of war. Techniques of negotiating, variously in Geneva, Sarajevo, Pale, Zagreb or Belgrade, will also become apparent.

War is often a proving ground of personality; for good or ill, it highlights the underlying nature of individuals and groups, and it is in that sense all-revealing. In Yugoslavia, the most distinctive feature of the fighting has been its callousness, evident in one episode after another: the three-month pulverizing of Vukovar and the wanton shelling of Dubrovnik by the Yugoslav People's Army (JNA) and Serb militias; the selective destruction of houses on ethnic grounds, predominantly by Serbs, but also by Croats and Muslims; the long Serb siege of Sarajevo; the destruction by Croat forces of the historic bridge in Mostar, perhaps the greatest architectural monument in the former Yugoslavia; the conditions in some prison camps; the widespread raping of women and the peculiar defiling of the bodies of the dead. Physical callousness of action, moreover, was only one side of the coin: leaders who had had no experience of democracy also displayed a callousness of mind in which the people's view never seemed to come anywhere near the conference table, despite much consulting of assemblies and the holding of referenda in circumstances of dubious democratic validity.

History points to a tradition in the Balkans of a readiness to solve disputes by the taking up of arms and acceptance of the forceful or even negotiated movement of people as the consequence of war. It points to a culture of violence within a crossroad civilization where three religions, Orthodox Christianity, Islam and Roman Catholicism, have divided communities and on occasions become the marks of identification in a dark and virulent nationalism. All wars bring evil to the surface, but the peculiar ferocity of civil wars is well chronicled throughout history. The fact that the wars in the former Yugoslavia contained elements both of a war of secession and of civil war only added to the difficulty of forming objective judgements.

Many lessons are being drawn from the break-up of the former Yugoslavia, some prematurely and precipitately. Day-by-day commentators, often on the basis of little experience of what has actually happened in the region, draw profound implications for Europe generally, European–American and European–Russian relations, NATO, the EU, the UN and Christian–Muslim relations. For some people the alleged failures of the EU over Yugoslavia are an indictment of the whole concept of European unity, a powerful refutation of the arguments for a single foreign policy with majority voting, let alone a United States of Europe; for others, the experience has heightened their demands for an integrated European defence capability and foreign policy for a United States of Europe. Many see in the ambivalence of US positions over the former Yugoslavia the necessity for an independent West European defence organization; for others, it only strengthens the case for greater cohesion and solidarity within NATO. There are obviously important lessons to be learnt and part of my reason for writing this account now and bringing together all this source material is the hope that it will enlighten such debates.

1

Mission Impossible?

THE PHONE RANG on the afternoon of Wednesday 29 July 1992 as I sat in my London office at 20 Queen Anne's Gate looking out on St James's Park across Birdcage Walk, one of the most peaceful scenes in inner London. It was a young researcher from the BBC radio programme *Today*, asking if I would come on the next morning to talk about the Serbian prison camps in Bosnia-Herzegovina. He was more persuasive than most but I was not keen. I had just come back from visiting Zimbabwe and I had finished an anthology of poetry, called *Seven Ages*,[i] which was due to be published before Christmas. I had deliberately kept out of politics since leaving the House of Commons before the general election in April of that year. Though I had decided to go to the House of Lords, this was to emphasize that I was never going back into party politics. As a Peer of the Realm I no longer had even the right to vote. I had become a crossbencher sitting as an independent Social Democrat and had no interest in recycling my political career in the House of Lords. I was intent on forging a new career and on taking up one or two of the offers I had had involving international business and in developing the work of a small charity, Humanitas. I had no wish, then, to be dragged in by the BBC to comment on the former Yugoslavia, an area of policy of which I had deliberately steered clear; but surprisingly I weakened slightly and suggested he might call after six that evening, when I would be back home.

The researcher had mentioned in particular the *Guardian* story on the camps which I had read with shock that morning but had not fully absorbed, and so I read the *Guardian* exposé again with more attention. It was a horrifying tale and as I read it I became angry. I had been growing increasingly restless about the inaction of the Western democracies over Yugoslavia but wary of involving myself. The last serious discussion I had had on Yugoslavia had been with Douglas Hurd at the end of May at a mutual friend's house, sipping a pre-lunch drink on the grass, when he had asked me straight out if I would put British troops into Bosnia-Herzegovina;

my reaction had been to say no – stay clear of becoming a combatant but bring EC diplomacy and UN peacekeeping together.

I asked myself that Wednesday evening two months later whether anything had changed. I was still against putting in troops on the ground, but the revelations coming in from the camps showed that we were witnessing grotesque abuses of humanitarian law and that the Bosnian Serb leadership was failing to act to curb them despite the clamour of world condemnation. Though the evidence was still patchy, all my instincts told me that what we were hearing and seeing was just the tip of an iceberg and I feared that, as over the humanitarian disaster that faced the Kurds a year before, Western governments were deliberately shutting their eyes and blocking their ears. My role as chairman of Humanitas, a charity that I had set up to build on the findings of the Independent Commission on International Humanitarian Issues, to which I had contributed in 1983–8, was my one exception to withdrawal from political activity and I had been particularly interested in humanitarian intervention since Humanitas had sponsored a conference on the issue, so I was already mentally engaged in analysing what could be done in Bosnia.

The same young man from the BBC rang that evening, this time even more persuasive. Without much enthusiasm I said I would be interviewed. So I pondered the whole issue afresh and turned my mind back to the history. At the start of the fighting I had dipped into, rather than re-read, Rebecca West's account of her travels through Yugoslavia in the late 1930s.[ii] On every page I had found a labyrinth of history, weaving a complexity of human relations that seemed to bedevil the whole region. I glanced at her book again and also at Fitzroy Maclean's *Eastern Approaches*,[iii] for I was keen to establish how many German divisions the Yugoslav partisans really had tied down. Some were talking about twenty-five or even thirty-six divisions, whereas the truth was probably nearer to six divisions, or some 90,000–100,000 men.

I was no stranger to Yugoslavia, for I had travelled there more extensively than in any other country in Europe, except France. As a student I had read with fascination the writings of Milovan Djilas, the Partisan leader and friend of Tito who had denounced Communism in the 1950s. During my time as Foreign Secretary the main concern about Yugoslavia had been what would happen to it when Tito died, which actually happened in 1980 – the year after I left office. Yet no one could forget that the First World War had been triggered in Sarajevo, and ominously the best of the futuristic scenarios on the start of a Third World War, by General Sir John Hackett,[iv] had taken Yugoslavia as its focus.

We all learnt at school that on 28 June 1914 the heir to the Habsburg throne, Archduke Franz Ferdinand, was assassinated while visiting Sarajevo. Yet I suspect I am not alone in never realizing that the visit was made with

deliberate Austrian provocation on Serbia's National Day, comparable –
according to the historian A. J. P. Taylor – to sending a member of the
British royal family to Dublin on St Patrick's Day at the height of the
troubles. On 23 July the Austrian government, knowing that the assassination had been done by a Bosnian Serb with the nationalist motive of
achieving a greater Serbia, sent a threatening and humiliating ultimatum to
the Serbian government. The British Foreign Secretary, Sir Edward Grey,
offered to mediate and attempted to persuade the German government to
restrain the incompetent militarists in Vienna. Despite the Serbian government accepting virtually every demand and satisfying Kaiser Wilhelm sufficient for him to comment 'every reason for war disappears', on 28 July
Vienna declared war and the Austro-Hungarian armies started to bombard
Belgrade. Within six weeks Grey was declaring 'the lamps are going out all
over Europe,' and a war which claimed 8 million lives in Europe had begun.

　　Serbia, Britain, France and Russia were now allies. The Croats and
Bosnians were within the Austro-Hungarian Empire, whose army in 1915
pushed down to Istanbul, defeating the Serbs. The Serbian army retreated
from Kosovo across the mountains to the Adriatic, where King Peter formed
a government in exile on Corfu. A Yugoslav Committee set up by exiled
Habsburg Slavs in London campaigned for a united South Slav state to be
founded after the war; and when the Austro-Hungarian Empire disintegrated,
the political life of the Kingdom of Serbs, Croats and Slovenes began, on 1
December 1918. It was renamed Yúgoslavia in 1929, as literally the country
of the South Slavs. Yet in 1918 many of its inhabitants were not South Slavs
but Germans, Hungarians, Albanians, Romanians, Turks and Greeks. There
were three religious groups – Serbian Orthodox, Roman Catholic and
Muslim; six customs areas, five currencies, four railway networks, three
banking systems and for a time two governments, in Zagreb and Belgrade.

　　The Serbian-dominated Parliament of the new state never accommodated
Stjepan Radic's Croat Peasant Party, the biggest political party in Croatia,
and the nationalism of Radic's supporters was further inflamed when he
was assassinated in that very Parliament by a Serb delegate in 1928.
Parliamentary democracy did not take root and a royal dictatorship took
over under King Alexander from 1929 to 1934, until his assassination by a
Macedonian gunman hired by the Fascist Croatian leader, Ante Pavelic. A
Regency Council was then formed headed by Prince Paul, who in the late
1930s did attempt to introduce democratic reforms and to reconcile the
Croats. These efforts led to an agreement between the Serbian politician
Cvetkovic and the leader of the Croat Peasant Party Macek in 1939, which
gave a large degree of autonomy not only to Croatia itself but also to Croat-
inhabited areas in Bosnia-Herzegovina. Meanwhile, within the Yugoslav
Communist Party Josep Broz, known later to the world by one of his
aliases, Tito, was rising to become General Secretary by early 1939.

Even before the start of the Second World War Croat separatism had been fed and financed by Mussolini's Fascist government. On 25 March 1941 an agreement was signed with Hitler in Vienna, linking Yugoslavia with the tripartite Pact; two days later Prince Paul was deposed in a coup d'état by predominantly Serbian officers from the armed forces. The British Prime Minister Winston Churchill, desperate for allies in the battle against Nazi Germany, appealed to the heart and to history in his broadcast to the people of Yugoslavia on 13 April: 'Serbs, we know you. You were our allies in the last War, and your arms are covered with glory. Croats and Slovenes, we know your military history. For centuries you were the bulwark of Christianity. Your fame as warriors spread far and wide on the Continent.'

In April 1941 Germany attacked Yugoslavia and the German Luftwaffe bombed Belgrade, killing between 5,000 and 17,000 civilians.[v] Hitler proceeded rapidly to dismember Yugoslavia, giving parts of it to Nazi Germany's allies Hungary, Romania and Bulgaria. The Nazis also endorsed the creation of the Independent State of Croatia (NDH), which included Bosnia-Herzegovina, divided into German and Italian spheres of influence, with the Croat Fascist Pavelic as its puppet ruler. Over the next few years Pavelic and his armed Ustashas committed atrocities and massacres of an unspeakable kind. Later Nuremberg judged what happened to the Serbs at the hands of the Croats and the Germans as genocide. No one knows exactly how many Serbs were killed. The Serbs say three-quarters of a million; the Germans 350,000. Whatever the number, it is hard to deny that these killings are an essential part of the background to the wars of disintegration in the former Yugoslavia. A good short history of Yugoslavia says that the Croatian government attitude to the Bosnian Muslims in the early 1940s was ambivalent.[vi] Although there were cases of Ustasha atrocities against Muslims, there were also other incidents where Muslims were encouraged by the authorities to massacre Serbs. There were Muslim SS units but there were also Muslims who fought with Tito's Partisans.

The world has never recognized sufficiently clearly that a long and bloody civil war went on in Yugoslavia throughout the Second World War, and the reason for this ignorance is that the existence of that civil conflict was deliberately suppressed by Tito, both during and after the war. Tito wanted to concentrate on the Partisan victory over Fascism and felt that to dwell on the Yugoslav civil war would detract from this victory and make it harder to weld the country together. It was Tito who ordered the Croat-run extermination camp at Jasenovac, near the Sava river, where many thousands of Serbs, Jews and Gypsies were murdered, bulldozed down after the war; and not until 1960 did he allow a museum and memorial centre to be built there. In total, of the 1.7 million Yugoslavs killed during the Second World War, about 1 million were slain by fellow Yugoslavs. For the Allies during the war the crucial question was to encourage the Yugoslavs to expend their energies not on fighting themselves but on fighting Hitler's and Mussolini's forces; hence they too somewhat glossed over the existence of the civil war.

In 1942 Britain supported the Serbian nationalist resistance leader, Colonel Draza Mihailovic, but by early 1943 it seemed the Allies had been backing, in war effort terms, the wrong horse and Churchill switched to Tito. At the Tehran Conference of 28 November 1943 Churchill told Stalin and Roosevelt that Tito was doing 'much more' for the Allied cause than Mihailovic and that the Balkan theatre was one of the areas 'where we could stretch the enemy to the utmost'.[vii] Differences between the UK and US over Yugoslavia are not a new phenomenon. On 6 April 1944, learning that the Americans were about to send an intelligence mission to Mihailovic at the very moment when Britain was withdrawing the last of its support, Churchill cabled Cairo to delay 'by every reasonable means' any arrangements to fly the American mission into Yugoslavia, 'the greatest courtesy being used to our friends and Allies in every case, but no transportation'.[viii] Churchill also cabled Roosevelt that same day to warn that dispatching an American mission 'will show throughout the Balkans a complete contrariety of action between Britain and the United States'.[ix]

There are many mistaken myths about Tito, one of which is that he was not a true Communist. When Churchill met Tito on 12 August 1944 at Naples he told him he could not tolerate Allied war material being used against rival Yugoslavs. The records show that Tito reassured Churchill that 'he had no desire to introduce the Communist system into Yugoslavia, if only for the reason that it was to be expected that most European countries after the war would be living under a democratic system from which Yugoslavia could not afford to differ.' Tito was, of course, lying – confirmation, if one needed it, that the sort of outright mendacity we have all seen over the last few years from politicians in the former Yugoslavia is not a new factor.

Some retrospective criticism has been made of Churchill's decision to back Tito and thereby Communism. However, given the information available to him at the time, there was no other choice for Churchill to make. Mihailovic did talk with the Germans and after the war was tried and sentenced to death for collaboration. We now know, however, that Tito's Partisans were also talking to the Germans. It is important to recall that Mihailovic was posthumously given the Legion of Merit in 1948 by President Truman after a US Commission had fully exonerated him, albeit in an atmosphere deeply antagonistic to Tito's Communist Yugoslavia.

Yugoslavia did not liberate itself to the extent that its propaganda and history books claim. The British historian Michael Howard writes: 'Though it is unfashionable to say so, it was liberated by Marshal Tolbukhin's Third Ukrainian Army, which by the end of 1944 occupied about one-third of Yugoslav territory.'[x]

It is another carefully fostered myth about Tito that he rebelled against Stalin. It was in fact Stalin who first isolated Yugoslavia because he felt Tito and Yugoslavia were getting above themselves. 'I will shake my finger and there will be no more Tito,' said Stalin. Moscow's decision came on 27 March 1948, in Tito's words 'as if a thunderbolt had struck me'. He thought of himself as a loyal Soviet Communist. It was then that disillusionment, disengagement and non-alignment started.

Both the British Foreign Secretary Ernest Bevin and the US Truman administration decided in the autumn of 1948, at the start of the Cold War period, to keep Tito 'afloat' to weaken Moscow and show that a Communist government could exist without Stalin's support. Britain again fostered the romantic image of Tito as Partisan leader. From then until his death in 1980 Western democratic governments found it convenient to take Tito at face value. Western aid and loans financed the absurdly large Yugoslav army long after any remote threat of Soviet invasion had gone.

The cult of Tito's personality inside Yugoslavia was in part matched outside the country. Tito's role in the Non-Aligned Movement cleverly pointed to an apparent 'third way', as did his economic self-management programme and encouragement of tourism. In reality, Communism failed in Yugoslavia as it failed everywhere else in Europe; but in Yugoslavia there was Tito's world prestige to cover that failure, and the lifestyle of the privileged elite masked a much lower average standard of living.

Long before Tito died many had predicted division and disarray to follow; that it did not come as soon as forecast lulled people into believing that the old nationalisms had been forgotten. In truth, Croatian, Serbian and Slovenian nationalism was just suppressed, though Serbian nationalism was in part assuaged by Serbian dominance in the higher ranks of the army and among the administrators in Belgrade. When in 1990 elections were held in all six republics – the first proper elections since 1927 – it was the nationalist parties that everywhere received the strongest support through the ballot box. In retrospect the West should have recognized an inevitable trend and encouraged an ordered and negotiated path to nationhood for Slovenia and Croatia, with Serbia, Montenegro, Macedonia and Bosnia-Herzegovina perhaps emerging as a modern democratic Yugoslavia. Both Kiro Gligorov and Alija Izetbegovic would have been content with a lesser degree of independence than Croatia and Slovenia. But the prevailing wisdom was 'no fragmentation': Gorbachev was still striving to keep the Soviet Union together, and Czechoslovakia and Yugoslavia were discouraged from splitting up their territory.

Could NATO have stopped the Serb–Croat war when it broke out in 1991? The answer must be yes, but at a risk of military lives that no democratic leaders were prepared to ask of their people. The military advice was clear: ground troops would have to be used and there would be casualties. President

Map 1 Yugoslavia 1945–1991

Bush knew better than anyone that the Vietnam syndrome had not been eradicated by the success of his military intervention over Kuwait. He no doubt remembered Beirut in 1983 and how rapidly President Reagan had pulled out the US Marines, part of a multilateral force, after more than 200 were killed by a terrorist bomb. Body-bag counts, as we saw in 1993 in Somalia, still figure in US public opinion's measure of whether their forces should or should not be serving in foreign lands.

The main strategic concern associated with the wars in former Yugoslavia is the fuse line which runs from Sarajevo to the Sandzak Muslims to the Albanians in Kosovo (both within Serbia), to the Albanians in Macedonia, to Albania itself, and then to Greece and to Turkey. This powder keg could have ignited in 1991 and then again in 1992 after the appalling rapidity with which the Serb ethnic cleansing campaign developed in Bosnia-Herzegovina in the spring and summer of that year. Greek–Macedonian disagreements have only added to the tension. There is a real risk of Turkey and Greece being on opposite sides in any Balkan war, particularly one which brings the Serbs and the Albanians into confrontation. Such a wider war would affect the vital interests of the EU as well as NATO and the US. The US has an active involvement in the region, with ships stationed in Greece and planes in Turkey. In the battle to reverse the Iraqi invasion of Kuwait, Turkey was of critical strategic importance. Not for nothing did President Bush warn Belgrade that any ethnic cleansing of Albanians in Kosovo risked US intervention, a pledge reiterated by President Clinton and helpfully reinforced by putting some US troops into Macedonia as part of the UN's preventive deployment. Albanian secessionist demands and the Serbian removal of the autonomy granted to Kosovo by Tito constitute an explosive mix.

Had NATO intervened from the air in the autumn of 1991 against the Yugoslav JNA, it could have moderated the worst excesses of the war. There would have been far less overt military deployment, for example along the Zagreb–Belgrade autoroute – Tito's 'Highway of Brotherhood and Unity' – and around cities like Vukovar. There would, very likely, have been continued fierce Serb–Croat village-to-village fighting, for that form of combat is effectively untouchable from the air; but it was not strategically vital to stop such fighting, particularly if air power had been able to protect the strategic road down the Dalmatian coast. If NATO forces had attempted to move in on the ground, in areas like Knin in the Krajina, a Serb stronghold, they would have found it hard to pacify them and would have risked being locked into a conflict – possibly a long one – with the Serbs. But NATO action from the air could probably have stopped the three-month Serb shelling of Vukovar, and NATO action from the sea the short spell of shelling of Dubrovnik.

Could the Europeans in NATO have acted militarily in 1991 without the US? Regrettably, the answer is no. The Germans were excluded from military participation, in part because of constitutional restrictions that were themselves a product of Germany's role in the Second World War, an involvement which also ruled out Italy. Turkey and Greece were felt to be mutually excluded, while France and Britain were never ready to put ground forces into a combatant role in what they felt was a civil war of far greater complexity than was, or ever could be, presented on television news bulletins. The UN came into Croatia in early 1992 to keep a negotiated peace.

Despite all the history, despite my reluctance to see British forces involved in a combatant role, I tried to re-examine the diplomatic caution and the military obstacles and face up to the stark decision that had to be made – at what point should we say that enough was enough? First, we had watched the shelling by the JNA and Serb militias of Vukovar, then Dubrovnik; later, the Serb shelling of Sarajevo; and now we were discovering what were being described, not unreasonably, as Serb concentration camps. The more I read and thought it all through the more I judged that John Major, as Prime Minister, should call for an international threat of air strikes in relation to the Serbs in a fashion not dissimilar to the 'safe haven' initiative which I had urged him to take over the Kurds the previous year.

I began to search for a limited form of military action which could make the Serbs stop practising ethnic cleansing in their war against the Muslims and come out in favour of a military standstill. The prison camps were in western and northern Bosnia, not in the mountains that covered most of Bosnia-Herzegovina. The associated military installations could easily be reached from NATO airfields based in surrounding countries and, given the flat terrain, action from the air against Serb military targets could in my view have been as surgical as in the desert flatness of Iraq. I had followed the arguments for and against military intervention in the former Yugoslavia with care and I genuinely felt that here, unlike in Sarajevo, there was an opportunity for limited action for a humanitarian purpose which did not set NATO on an automatic escalator to putting in ground troops. Moreover, the UN was then not yet involved on the ground, except for a small contingent of 300 to keep Sarajevo airport open who would need to be removed or reinforced before any strike action, as would UNHCR and other aid workers. The risk was to the Muslims in these camps for, following air strikes, many could have been massacred by undisciplined militia and vengeful local people; also, Sarajevo might have been taken by the Serbs.

What I did not know is that on Sunday 26 July Governor Bill Clinton, campaigning in the US presidential election against the incumbent George Bush, had authorized his campaign office in Little Rock, Arkansas, to issue a little-noticed policy statement on the fighting in Bosnia-Herzegovina, saying: 'The United States should take the lead in seeking United Nations Security Council authorization for air strikes against those who are attacking the relief effort. The United States should be prepared to lend appropriate military support to that operation.' Looking back, Clinton's views then were identical to mine. He went on: 'We should make clear that the economic blockade against Serbia will be tightened, not only on weapons but also on oil and other supplies that sustain the renegade regime of Slobodan Milosevic. European and US naval forces in the Adriatic should be given authority by the UN to stop and search ships that might be carrying contraband heading for Serbia and her ally, Montenegro.' Clinton also called for international action to charge people 'with crimes against humanity under international law – as we should have done long ago in the case of Iraq.'

For the White House press spokesman, Marlin Fitzwater, this was an opportunity for Bush to attack Clinton on an issue after Iraq on which the presidential team felt their candidate was strong. While Bush said nothing, Vice-President Dan Quayle began to point up Bush's experience in foreign policy and contrast it with Clinton's inexperience. Increasingly, Yugoslavia became a factor in the US election campaign. An old friend of mine, Johnny Apple, wrote a detailed and perceptive analytical article in the 28 July edition of the *New York Times* entitled 'Campaign Shifts to a New Turf', describing Clinton's foreign policy team as being divided along hawk-and-dove fault-lines that first emerged in the Vietnam War and as fearful of seeming soft on Communism and other foes of the United States. He reminded his readers that Clinton had spoken out on Bosnia, several times taking a more aggressive posture than Bush, and cited an interview on 25 June in which he professed willingness to see US participation in a multilateral military force that would 'shoot its way into' Sarajevo airport, if necessary, to make it safe enough for a steady airlift of relief supplies. But on the evening of 29 July in London I was unaware of any of this and was only to discover it when I arrived in the United States a few days later.

It is not hard for me to see how these underlying attitudes coloured much of the policy ambivalence of President Clinton towards the Balkans over the next few years. We both started from the same basic position and in some ways we both trod the same painful learning curve, albeit at a different pace and along different paths. The biggest difference between us was that Clinton's foreign policy advisers took a long time to grasp the implications of the UN humanitarian intervention in Bosnia-Herzegovina after October 1992. Some of them did adjust, while others appeared never to accept that UN deployment in vulnerable areas like Srebrenica, Zepa, Gorazde and Bihac inhibited widespread intervention from the air and that these UN forces would have to leave these parts of Bosnia-Herzegovina before a lifting of the arms embargo could be considered and supportive strikes started.

Next morning, 30 July, there was an emotive article in the *Daily Express* about the situation in the camps, drawing analogies with the Nazi concentration camps. In the BBC *Today* studio I called on John Major to act and to use NATO air power to *impose* a ceasefire.[6] Immediately afterwards, I dictated a letter to John Major over the phone to my secretary, and sent the final version by fax direct to No. 10 Downing Street, the *Evening Standard* and the Press Association, all before nine o'clock in the morning. It said:

Dear Prime Minister

  Almost a year ago I wrote to you about the then threatened genocide of the Kurds in Northern Iraq. At that time the world community was wringing its hands and saying that nothing could be done. Fortunately you overrode the advice of the fainthearts, and championed the safe haven policy enforced by allied military power outside Iraq and then reinforced by a military presence inside Iraq.

  It is a sad commentary on our world that a situation even worse in humanitarian terms has now developed in what was Yugoslavia. Over the last few days the world has read authenticated reports of concentration camps being established and sealed wagon trains transporting Muslim families in which children have died. It is not an exaggeration to say that we are witnessing, 50 years on, scenes in Europe that mirror the early stages of the Nazi holocaust under the dreadful description of 'ethnic cleansing'.

I urge you not to accept the conventional wisdom that nothing can be done militarily to stop the escalation of fighting and the continuation of such grotesque abuses of human rights. I no longer think it is even possible to wait until the peace conference which you have called in London. Lord Carrington's mission on behalf of the European Community, for all his immense personal efforts, cannot deliver the sort of peacemaking not just peacekeeping that is now so urgent. Only the United Nations has both the experience and the authority to impose international order. But the European Community cannot simply transfer responsibility to the UN Secretary-General without simultaneously putting at the disposal of the UN the command and control, personnel and military equipment, of NATO to enforce a peace.

The first essential step is to stop by threat of force the use or movement of any military aircraft, tanks, armoured vehicles or artillery in the former territory of Yugoslavia. It is perfectly within the power of NATO to enforce such an immediate ceasefire. Satellite and air reconnaissance could pinpoint any unauthorized military activity and retaliatory air strikes could be mounted from NATO airfields that ring Yugoslavia or by planes flying from aircraft carriers. This could be implemented within hours, not even days, once the requisite authority has been got from the UN Security Council.

I believe that a few of the bigger cities currently under attack such as Sarajevo and Gorazde should be reinforced by air with troops acting under the authority of the UN, if necessary initially parachuting men and materials in to secure air communications. If these actions were taken within days then Bosnia would not be completely overrun by Serb and Croatian forces and a peace settlement could then be negotiated. If no action is taken now there will be virtually nothing left of Bosnia for the Muslim population to negotiate about. What is even more dangerous, military activity could then start in Kosovo and that is bound to provoke Albania and take the conflict outside the confines of what was once Yugoslavia.

The situation is of course moving very rapidly and this has been recognized by the UN Secretary-General in his most recent request for authority to control civilian entry into UN protected areas in Yugoslavia and to exercise immigration and custom functions at their borders. These are 'quasi-governmental' functions and will necessarily grow rapidly in the next few weeks. In my judgement this only stresses the need for a much clearer line of political authority and makes it urgent that the present separate functions between the European Community

*dealing with the diplomacy of peace and the UN dealing with peace-
keeping should end. Nevertheless I cannot stress enough that that should
not be an excuse for the European Community to step back. The
European Community should be doing far more to enforce UN
sanctions and should overcome any residual anxiety it may have about
using the sophisticated proven and trusted command and control of
NATO.*

*The one thing the world will not forgive, as August approaches, is if
the morally outrageous happenings in Yugoslavia become victim of the
governmental holiday period.*

A few hours later my letter was on the front page of the London *Evening
Standard*, together with an editorial.[xi] I feared that the London Conference
due at the end of August was a defusing device, a diplomatic way of
reducing the pressure to act – a mere delaying tactic. I had thought about
talking to Stephen Wall, the Prime Minister's private secretary, the previous
evening but I did not want to compromise his or my position as we were
due to have lunch together the next day. By noon it was clear that I had
lobbed a political hand grenade into the Whitehall/Westminster nexus; press
interest was immediate, triggering a reaction on *The World at One*, and I
agreed to write for the *Daily Mail*.[xii]

Over lunch Stephen Wall and I talked about one subject: Yugoslavia. We
are old friends and when I was Foreign Secretary Stephen was one of my
private secretaries dealing with Africa and Europe. Imaginative, immensely
thorough and hard-working, since then he had served as private secretary
to three other Foreign Secretaries, Geoffrey Howe, John Major and Douglas
Hurd, before going to No. 10 Downing Street. We normally agreed on
major issues: but on this occasion we were at opposite poles. Patiently he
explained the fears of the Chiefs of Staff of being sucked into a combatant
role in what was essentially a civil war. We began a debate about the potential of air power that was to continue over the next few years. We did not
agree, but he undoubtedly dented some of my arguments. For instance, I
was conscious that I did not have a good answer to the question what
NATO's response should be if Bosnian Serb soldiers, who were in some
instances operating outside the formal command structure, ignored NATO
air strikes and continued ethnic cleansing, killing Muslim prisoners. What
if the Serbian air force at Banja Luka shot down one of the attacking
NATO aircraft? What should NATO's response be if the Serbs took
hostages from the many voluntary humanitarian organizations operating in
the field? What would we do if the Serbs closed the airfield in Sarajevo, then
operated by the UN for humanitarian relief flights? What if the Serbs
responded by shelling Sarajevo in much the same manner and intensity as
they had shelled Vukovar?

It was clear that, whereas I had come new to the subject, Stephen had been living the issue daily for many months. His questions obviously reflected much thought in Whitehall and in Washington. He told me the views of President Bush's National Security Adviser, Brent Scowcroft, with whom he was in constant touch. Scowcroft was a former US Air Force general and a former military attaché to the US Embassy in Belgrade, a fluent Serbo-Croat speaker and therefore someone whose views could not be ignored. I was being brought face to face with the harsh choices that accompany power and can be all too easily ignored by protest. Unlike the situation a year before when I had written to the Prime Minister to urge the use of air power to save the Kurds, an intervention welcomed by Stephen who had used my letter to push hard for a positive response within Whitehall, now he was clearly disappointed with my logic and thought I was being self-indulgent and not facing the real issues of government honestly. It was a good discipline for me, for he put me back in the Foreign Secretary's seat and did not allow me the luxury of playing to the gallery. We parted after what diplomats would call a vigorous exchange of views.

That afternoon Donald Trelford, the editor of the *Observer*, rang and said he wanted me to write for his op ed page that Sunday. Now feeling more cautious, I said I needed more time to think my position through and instead opted for an interview as being less time-consuming and less committing.[xiii] Andrew Gimson, my godson, rang and said he was writing an article on Yugoslavia for the *Sunday Telegraph*,[xiv] and we talked the subject through in some detail. He reminded me that the Balkans was the issue that had inspired Gladstone to return to the battleground of British politics, and how Benjamin Disraeli, after the Congress of Berlin, had despaired of bringing order to Serbia, Bosnia and Herzegovina.[xv] I reiterated what was becoming a familiar mantra about not wanting to be sucked back into politics and preparing for an international business career. But Andrew also quoted with some passion Otto von Bismarck's saying that 'the Balkans were not worth the healthy bones of a single Pomeranian grenadier.' I was to discover that it was this view which was held by all the key governments when it came to committing troops on the ground in Bosnia-Herzegovina and which ensured that international diplomacy without military power was the hallmark of every attitude and action towards the former Yugoslavia.

On Monday morning I started to write an article for *The Times* and did an interview for ITN's lunchtime programme. Just prior to the ITN interview I had been given John Major's reply.

Dear David
   Thank you for your letter of 30 July about the appalling tragedy in Bosnia.

I fully understand why you should feel strongly about this issue: we all do. That is precisely why we have launched the London Conference on 26 August. This will be a major effort to mobilize international pressure on all the former Yugoslav parties and in particular the Serbs to abandon their wholly unacceptable use of force. This will be the first time that the UN's and EC's efforts have been so closely coordinated. The Secretary-General will be fully involved both in the conference itself and in the follow-up work which will stem from it. There is no question of the summer lull leading to a slackening of effort on Yugoslavia. On the contrary, we shall be intensifying our efforts over the next three weeks. We have begun wide-ranging consultations to make sure that no momentum is lost in the peace process.

We do not believe that this is the time to think in the terms you suggest of a military solution. We could not unite the international community behind such a policy. In practice we see real difficulties over proposals to use either air power or ground forces in the way you suggest. We have of course professionally studied the military implications which are more serious than you suggest. Air power would be unlikely to be enough. The numbers of forces involved, the likely length of operations and the level of casualties (civilian as well as military) would all be higher than you suggest. We are not dealing with an orthodox war, a single enemy, a front line, or clearly identifiable targets. Nor do I detect any support in Parliament or in public opinion for operations which would tie down large numbers of British forces in difficult and dangerous terrain for a long period.

I do not rest on that. We have to look all the time at fresh possibilities. We already have army officers helping to keep the peace in Croatia as EC monitors, a UN force sharing that task on a bigger scale and ensuring help for Sarajevo, and naval action in support of sanctions. There may well be other ways in which armed forces may become useful, and I do not exclude such developments. What we cannot sensibly undertake is an operation which would begin with an ultimatum but might lead to a commitment to some form of international protectorate in Bosnia-Herzegovina, sustained indefinitely by military force. We will focus our efforts on humanitarian help for victims of the conflict (we have contributed nearly £30 million) and on intensified pressure on all the parties to halt the fighting and negotiate seriously. This may take time. But this is all the more reason for tackling these tragic issues energetically and systematically, as we are doing.

Afraid that I could be criticized for being away on holiday at this critical juncture, since I was scheduled to leave the next day for the US, I rang

David Stephen, my old political adviser in the Foreign Office who was now in the UN writing speeches for the Secretary-General, to see if he could fix an appointment with Boutros Boutros Ghali on Thursday when I could come into New York from my wife Debbie's family home at St James, Long Island. I also rang Cy Vance at his New York law firm to see if he would be free for lunch that day.

On the plane crossing the Atlantic on Tuesday 4 August I read my article in *The Times*, with an accompanying cartoon. It respected John Major's position but disagreed with the government's objections to any aggressive military response and challenged the Whitehall mood that there was nothing that could be done. In fairness, John Major's letter had kept the door slightly ajar in case public opinion demanded more action, and his government's arguments against the use of aircraft could not be easily dismissed. I had to admit also that there was a large element of bluff in my strategy, which relied on the judgement that after a few accurate air sorties the Serb heavy guns would stop retaliating on Sarajevo and that after a few Serb planes had been shot down they would remain grounded and the movement of troops and equipment in convoys on the roads would stop. What if NATO's bluff were called by the Serbs? It would be an immense humiliation if NATO air power were insufficient.

I pondered on all this flying to the US and read the first of Anthony Lewis's many articles on the former Yugoslavia on the op ed page of the *New York Times* for Monday 3 August. I had known Tony since he was that paper's London correspondent in the late 1960s; whatever he wrote I engaged with his arguments, even if I did not agree with them. This piece, entitled 'Yesterday's Men', started: 'The men were taken from the village at gunpoint and forced into freight cars. As many as 180 were jammed, standing, into boxcars measuring 39 by 6 feet. They were kept that way for three days, without water or food, as the train moved slowly across the countryside. Nazis transporting Jews in 1942? No, Serbs transporting Muslim Bosnians in 1992: one glimpse of the worst racial and religious bestiality Europe has known since World War II.' Castigating the Bush spokesman, Marlin Fitzwater, for denouncing Clinton's call for meaningful action to stop such Serbian atrocities, he wrote that it reminded him of Prime Minister Neville Chamberlain explaining in 1938 why Britain should not care about Nazi designs on Czechoslovakia: it was, Chamberlain said, 'a quarrel in a faraway country between people of whom we know nothing'. The article went on to accuse President Bush of being 'a veritable Neville Chamberlain in refusing to face the challenge in Yugoslavia. He has dithered, deferred to a Europe that was looking to him for leadership, refused to call for the international military action that everyone knows is the only way to stop the Serbian aggression.' This was vintage Tony writing – passionate, emotional and committed. 'President Bush compared Saddam

Hussein to Hitler. I am against such analogies because they cheapen the Holocaust. But if that one is to be used, it better fits the Serbian leader, Slobodan Milosevic, the inventor of "ethnic cleansing".' This was even more emotional than my *Daily Mail* article, but I shared almost all his sentiments at that time, even his withering remarks about talk of the 'political compli- cations in Yugoslavia'. Little did I realize that it would fall to me to have to relate to and understand those very complications.

On Wednesday 5 August I woke up to a fine summer's day on Long Island. Yugoslavia was however not far away. In a back number of the *New York Times* of 28 July I read for the first time the detail of Bill Clinton's stance. It was clear that the public mood in the US was responding to stories about the Serb detention camps more strongly than was the case in Britain. There was also in the newspapers the first hint of a State Department cover- up, with allegations that they had known much earlier about what was likely to be happening to Muslim prisoners. That day Governor Clinton, campaigning in Illinois, had said again, 'I would begin with air power against the Serbs to try to restore the basic conditions of humanity,' and on the same platform Senator Gore said, 'the Europeans have been a little timid about doing something to stop this mass murder,' a theme which he was to develop further.

On Thursday 6 August over lunch in New York I had a fascinating discussion on Yugoslavia with Cy Vance. He told me that Boutros Boutros Ghali had asked him that morning to be his special representative for a new standing conference that was to be set up following the London Conference. He asked me whether I felt he should accept. It was rather like when I saw him the day he resigned as US Secretary of State, just after he had been to see President Carter in the White House.[xvi] He was questioning himself by asking me questions. Were the Europeans really committed to reversing ethnic cleansing? What did Douglas Hurd and John Major really think about the Conference? I explained about the reaction to my letter calling for intervention from the air, and though Cy did not comment much on the substance he clearly believed that even such limited military action would not work. I advised him to accept the Secretary-General's request only if he was sure he would not be made a prisoner of policies that involved accepting the status quo, partitioning Bosnia-Herzegovina and acquiescing in a Greater Serbia. He was clearly adamant that ethnic cleansing had to be to a great extent reversed and that as far as possible no territory taken as a result of force should be conceded to the Serbs. It was almost certain from what Cy said that the Conference would be a joint UN–EC venture. I already felt it was vital to involve the UN and that the EC had no longer much of a role on its own. Cy, in passing, mentioned that he was not sure how strongly Peter Carrington was committed to staying with the negotia- tions and how nice it would be if I could be involved, but I joked that I was persona non grata with the British government after my recent call for military action. As I left he said it would be pleasant for us to get together with Debbie and his own wife Gay, and I said there was a chance that we might be in New York Tuesday evening before flying out to Salt Lake City on Wednesday morning.

I then met Boutros Ghali for an interesting thirty-minute talk. Cy had briefly mentioned problems between the UN Secretary-General and the UK permanent representative, David Hannay, and in a recent interview Boutros had referred to himself as being seen as a 'wog', a British colonial term of disparagement, so it was kind of him to see me, a retired British politician. People do not often feel neutral about Boutros. He has his fans and his critics: I am a fan. I have known his three predecessors – U Thant, Kurt Waldheim and Perez de Cuellar – and of the four he is the most intelligent, the liveliest and the bravest. His is one of the most exacting jobs in the world, for there is little of the back-up which most heads of state receive. It has always been difficult to avoid being dictated to by the permanent members of the Security Council, and since the collapse of the Soviet Union there is a new danger of the Secretary-General and other senior UN officials becoming too subservient to the United States. It is to Boutros Ghali's credit that he has kept his independence of mind and of action, albeit at the price of being subjected at times to savage and unwarranted criticism.

When I arrived back at the railway station that night, Debbie explained that Cy had rung and they had fixed dinner for Tuesday. Debbie's intuition was: 'He wants something, David. This is not just a social occasion.'

Over the weekend I read myself into American attitudes to the crisis in the former Yugoslavia. Leslie Gelb, who had been with Cy Vance at the State Department and whom I knew and respected, had written an article in the *New York Times* on Thursday 6 August entitled 'False Humanitarianism', which predicted future events:

> *The Bush Administration seeks a much narrower focus for the London conference – to strengthen humanitarian relief efforts. Administration officials want to expand these efforts beyond Sarajevo. This will require land convoys, which in turn will require protection. The Administration will support giving UN relief units some firepower for self-protection. It will also grudgingly consider providing the convoys with air cover, but neither London nor Paris is enthusiastic about that.*
>
> *The effect of such an American focus on relief will be to preclude discussion of wider UN military action. And Washington is not alone in this stratagem. No UN Security Council member seems prepared to cross the line from humanitarian relief to combat. Russia even seems ready to veto proposals to do so.*

In New York in the early evening on Tuesday 11 August I saw the Bosnian government's representative to the UN, Muhamed Sacirbey, for what proved to be the first of many meetings. He is an attractive, intense but hard-nosed young man, at that time desperately trying to represent his country out of his own law offices, his desk and floor piled high with files. Clearly no professional diplomat, he was angered – as he had every right to be – by the world's lack of response to his country's plight. Margaret Thatcher's people were coming to see him later that evening. While he liked much of what had been reported to him of what I had said, he did not agree when I reiterated that I could not see any way in which the UN arms embargo would or should be lifted. While I admitted that it was discriminatory against the Muslims now in 1992 as it had been against the Croats in 1991, in that the Serbs in Bosnia had large supplies of equipment and ammunition, no Security Council, I argued, could be seen to fuel the fire by lifting the ban. I also distanced myself from the idea of attacking Serbian bridges on the border or doing anything to take the battle outside the borders of Bosnia-Herzegovina, as he had suggested in a powerful article in the *New York Times* a few days before. We parted on good terms and I felt for him, representing a new country in such a desperate situation, a basic sympathy which has never left me. He was to develop into a strong representative with a brilliant sense of public relations, putting, as he was bound to, a spin and a slant on his government's actions which often made life difficult for me in the negotiations. But he was always more astute in his political judgement than many in the New York diplomatic community would give him credit for. His direct line to President Izetbegovic allowed him to circumvent his Foreign Minister, which did not endear him to his colleagues but made him a more powerful representative to deal with. Despite some harsh criticism of me over the years I remain an admirer of what he is doing for his country now as Foreign Minister.

At dinner with Gay, Debbie and me in the River Club that evening, Cy went straight to the point. He was flying to London by Concorde on Thursday for a meeting with Peter Carrington to plan the London Conference. David Hannay would be there as well. Carrington had said on the telephone that he wanted to appoint an 'alternate' for himself as Chairman, and had suggested another Conservative politician, whose name Cy had difficulty in recalling. Cy saw this as a sign that Carrington wanted out, and he even suspected that it was a device to get out since Carrington would expect Cy to refuse such an arrangement. Cy wanted to be in a position to suggest my name if this happened. Would I agree?

Over the weekend I had occasionally wondered what I would say to this question, so I had already weighed up the counter-argument about needing to gain experience of international business quickly and not waiting until I was too old to start a new career. But I never took the possibility very seriously because I thought my views on Yugoslavia would exclude me from consideration. I knew Cy did not share my opinions on using air power, but I suspected there was not a single European head of government who shared them either. The emphasis now being put on a humanitarian initiative by President Bush was itself a recognition that he was not ready to use US military power to dislodge the Serbs. The question was whether to go on being a voice in the wilderness over Yugoslavia or join in the quest for peace. Cy was a man I deeply respected, he shared all of my passion in wanting to reverse ethnic cleansing and it would be a delight to work with him again. My saying yes on the spot was not a snap answer but a considered judgement. All the same, I felt less certain than Cy that Peter Carrington would opt to go, and I gave a strong warning that Douglas Hurd might not want me to replace him if he did.

Early in the morning of Monday 17 August Cy rang me in Colorado to say that he had heard from Peter Carrington that Douglas Hurd was keen for me to do the job. I told Cy what I had heard from Stephen Wall about John Major's positive attitude to my appointment. It was now looking very likely that the UK, which held the EC Presidency, would put me forward and the big question in my mind was whether the French would agree. I felt they might not like another British chairman. Peter Carrington had been offered the job by the Dutch when they held the EC Presidency and there was no automatic right for the post to be filled by the UK. And although my strongest card was Cy Vance's support, this might be less of an advantage with the French, for they would be suspicious of anything that smacked of an Anglo-American axis. I sensed it would all need careful handling, so, as I was about to depart for a few days river-rafting, I rang the ever cool-headed Stephen Wall and said that if the news broke of any approach to the EC while I was out of reach, he and Maggie Smart, my personal assistant who had formerly been my diary secretary in the Foreign Office, together could authorize any statement they felt right to the press. I blessed the fact that I had two people who knew me so well that I could safely rely on them to reflect my views. We then packed a few belongings into waterproof kitbags and boarded the bus for the journey to the launching place on the Colorado river. At 10.00 a.m. we stepped on to our rubber raft and pushed off for a memorable five days away from civilization.

I cannot say I had no cares in the world, and from time to time I mulled over the Yugoslavian situation and pondered: what if I was offered the job? Only international, not domestic, politics could have tempted me to give up being a private citizen. Objectively the prospect had moved from an unlikely possibility to a probability. On the raft family and friends teased me about the way I pronounced Herzegovina, and indeed, so bad is my ear for pronunciation that it took all of that time to get it right.

On Friday 21 August we arrived at Lake Powell, feeling like astronauts:

that part of America is like a moonscape and we had not heard a radio broadcast or seen a newspaper for five days. On the landing stage I called Stephen Wall to find out what had happened. His news was that the Prime Minister and Douglas Hurd had agreed on my candidature and my name had gone forward to the EC. The response from the other European governments so far was very positive, though the French were grumbling that I was anti-Serb, so while it was not yet definite it was more likely than not that I would be appointed. Interestingly, and somewhat magnanimously, in view of my criticism of their recognition of Croatia and Bosnia, I was told the German government was in favour of my appointment.

Early on Monday 24 August we arrived back in London. Douglas Hurd rang me up and said he was delighted I had agreed to serve; he warned me that there were dangers ahead with the French, but thought it was likely they would be overcome.

On Tuesday 25 August I went into my office at the beginning of three difficult days when everyone was speculating almost to the point of assuming I was going to get the job, and yet I did not know for certain and heard little from anybody. It was hard to act normally. The French were in trouble with their public opinion over their referendum on the Maastricht Treaty, and Mitterrand was allegedly inviting John Major to appear with him on a television programme; from that position it seemed hard for the French to say no to my appointment. Peter Carrington gave a press conference to confirm the BBC story in the one o'clock news that he was going and said I was going to replace him. Douglas Hurd's private secretary confirmed that their intention was to announce my appointment on Thursday evening at the close of the London Conference and Douglas rang to say we might need to discuss a form of words to cover my previous statements about use of air power which still worried the French. On BBC's *Newsnight* the leader of the Bosnian Serbs, Dr Radovan Karadzic, criticized my appointment as EC mediator, saying: 'it would not be right or advisable to nominate him to that job and I think that the Serbian side in Bosnia-Herzegovina would have a very hard time dealing with him.'

On Wednesday 26 August there was an excellent editorial in the *Guardian* entitled 'Carrot or Stick Needed for Serbia', saying: 'What is absolutely certain is that, unless Lord Carrington's successor can be delivered from the problem he faced, that of possessing neither stick nor carrot, we can expect no end to the tragedy of the South Slavs.'

On Thursday 27 August I was rung by the Egyptian Embassy to ask Debbie and me to a dinner that night for Boutros Ghali. I accepted on the condition that my appointment had been announced by then. Shortly after 6.00 p.m. I heard that I had been appointed. Douglas Hurd rang with a quick confirmation of my appointment and invited me to the EC Foreign Ministers' informal weekend meeting at Brocket Hall on 12–13 September.

Then the Foreign Office News Department rang to ask for a press statement. As I began to work through all the details I became ever more dubious about accepting a salary from the British government, from whom it would have to come since they were holding the Presidency. I had no wish to be seen as a British diplomat or civil servant and preferred not to accept the 'Queen's shilling'. Cy Vance had assured me that our task would only last for six months, and in the moral mess that was the former Yugoslavia it seemed better for me to be totally independent and not profiting in any way from the misery and despair of it all, so I refused a salary.

When we arrived at the Egyptian Embassy for dinner Boutros Ghali and Cy Vance were still involved with John Major in a press conference and the French Minister of Defence, Joxe, was there waiting. We had a long chat on the use of air power, both of us being very worried about Serbian air activity, and he was far from ruling out enforcing a no-fly zone over Bosnia-Herzegovina. I was rather encouraged, because I wanted to persuade the French to put some steel behind our diplomacy. But Joxe's view was not that of President François Mitterrand, as I discovered when I saw him in Paris a few days later. Mitterrand specifically warned me of the dangers of aggressive force against the Serbs and ruled out air strikes.

Eventually Cy and Boutros Ghali arrived with their wives and we went in to dinner. Very astutely I was placed next to Cy. Whether he had asked or our hostess had guessed we would have much to talk about I do not know, but it was sophisticated diplomacy. He did not hide his utter delight that I was on the team and said he had not dared to telephone me but had just kept his fingers crossed while repeatedly asking whether there were any obstacles to my appointment. He wanted to start the Geneva Conference in five days' time and was flying back to New York the next day. Boutros was very warm about my appointment and full of praise for John Major's chairmanship of the Conference. The Turkish Foreign Minister, who was also present, wanted NATO force to be used and was cogent as to why. The French Foreign Minister Roland Dumas came in late; he was very civil throughout our short conversation and I sensed no animosity over my appointment. The Ambassador made a good speech and Cy replied gracefully. Many were clearly surprised to learn from his references to me how close we were. We agreed that I would come and meet the Prime Minister of the Federal Republic of Yugoslavia (FRY: Serbia and Montenegro), Milan Panic, at his hotel the next morning.

That night I sensed that the Vance–Owen team was back in harness – fifteen years from when we had started developing Anglo-American policy towards southern Africa together, and thirteen years from when Cy had rung me on the Friday morning after Labour had lost the general election. Since then we had kept in constant touch, and had continued to work together on the Palme Commission. We were a natural blend: he cautious, methodical, at times legalistic but brave and moral; I more innovative, mercurial, more lateral-thinking but less experienced. After the post-mortem on the 1987 general election and my period as joint party leader with David Steel I had begun almost to believe those who said that it was impossible for me or perhaps any two people to work in partnership in a political leadership role – and yet I knew it was not true. I felt the old compatibility and the added strength of two minds; and while Cy was older his vitality, far from being impaired, seemed even greater. Thereafter he kept up a cracking pace that at times left me reeling and many of the hard-working younger members of our team in Geneva exhausted.

On Friday 28 August Stephen Wall rang over breakfast to make an appointment for me to see the Prime Minister that morning. I had already arranged to see David Gillmore, the Permanent Secretary at the Foreign Office, over a sandwich lunch and to meet Paul Sizeland, Peter Carrington's private secretary, who would try to fix a meeting with some of the EC Foreign Ministers who were still in London, in particular the German, Klaus Kinkel. In Cy's hotel room the first person I met was Herbert Okun, with whom I had done a television programme on the UN and human rights a few months earlier. Cy told me he was to be his deputy and it came as a very pleasant surprise to know we would be working together in Geneva. He proved a joy to work with, providing excellent support and advice, and was a fund of wisdom, precision and good judgement.

Prime Minister Panic, whom I had never met, was flanked by the former US Senator Birch Bayh, who was acting as his legal adviser, and another American, the former US Ambassador to Belgrade. My first reaction to Panic was ambivalent. Part of me was a bit dismissive, and yet another part liked his ebullience and frankness. I kept saying to myself: 'this guy is head of a large pharmaceutical company and you cannot do that if you are a mere buffoon,' but many thought he was something of an unguided missile. Certainly he was unlike any Prime Minister I had ever met before or was likely to meet again. Always eager to please, he offered an opportunity of fresh Serb thinking and an effervescent mind in the midst of the many old Communists still in power in Belgrade.

Since No. 10 Downing Street was being painted I went to Admiralty House to see the Prime Minister, and we walked out into the courtyard for a photocall – which produced the front cover illustration for the satirical magazine *Private Eye*, as a mirror image of the picture with us shaking our left hands and speech bubbles from John Major's mouth saying 'I'm afraid it's a lost cause' and from mine replying 'then I'm your man.' Most of the morning's press comment, while favourable to me personally, was not in the least optimistic about the task ahead. John Major and I had a good chat during which he pressed me quite hard to take a salary on the basis that he could not always appoint people of independent means like Peter

Carrington, and I doubt he understood my somewhat confused objections. He made no attempt to hide the immense difficulties ahead. Then he asked me what I thought of our permanent representative to the UN, Sir David Hannay, and since I knew of his recent clash with Boutros Ghali I was conscious that I might lose him in New York if I said anything critical. I remembered David Hannay from when he dealt with energy in the Foreign Office – quick, bright, interested in detail; I was sure I could work with him and said so. He never gave me any cause to change that judgement. Exceptionally good at drafting and making sense of Security Council decisions, he and his French counterpart Ambassador Mérimée were able to check and counter most of the erratic and irresponsible actions contemplated in the Security Council.

I then drove to Queen Elizabeth Hall and met Klaus Kinkel, the German Foreign Minister, whom I found friendly, informal and direct. Despite differences on policy I always enjoyed working with him. He was very conscious that since Germany was constitutionally prevented from deploying troops for the UN effort in Bosnia-Herzegovina he had to be very careful not to advocate policies that could lead to other countries' servicemen losing their lives. It was a sensitive stance to adopt and needed courage to maintain as the German press were strong advocates of a more aggressive policy. I found him at all times a man with genuinely liberal instincts, but he did not have the knowledge in foreign affairs, or authority within his party, of Hans-Dietrich Genscher. I decided then and there that I would not spend time on public finger-pointing about German support for premature recognition of Croatia and Bosnia or the rights and wrongs of EC policy hitherto. My task was to keep the twelve member states together, and the best way to do that was to look forward.

I adopted a somewhat similar attitude in public towards the causes of the wars in the former Yugoslavia. It was enough to deal with present outrages and future peace. What should have been done before the dissolution of Yugoslavia was an interesting but very divisive question. Also, the facts were not all as I had first thought. While the terms 'aggressor' and 'victim' were being brandished as weapons in a propaganda war, the true situation was obviously far more complex than that dichotomy implied – and anyhow, they were terms better avoided publicly by a negotiator.

I saw Cy Vance again for a quick chat, while we appeared together for the cameras. Then I talked to Martti Ahtisaari, whom Cy had asked to come over. He was going back to Finland, where he was the diplomatic head of the Ministry of Foreign Affairs, to consult and give us an answer on whether or not he would join us in Geneva. Martti I knew from 1978 over Namibia, since when he had successfully led the UN operation for Namibian independence, and Cy and I had worked with him when we were representing our countries in the Namibia Contact Group then comprising the US, the UK, France, Germany and Canada. We needed his experience badly; he became our anchorman in Geneva in negotiations with the parties in Bosnia-Herzegovina and made an invaluable contribution. He was elected as President of Finland in 1994.

At the Foreign Office I saw Sir David Gillmore as arranged. With him was Jeremy Greenstock, the head of policy on the former Yugoslavia, who opened up immediately to say they had a problem over heavy weapons. Apparently Dr Karadzic had signed an agreement with Douglas Hogg accepting UN supervision and control of heavy weapons handed in by the Serbs. But the British government was embarrassed by Cabinet decisions which did not allow our troops assigned to the UN for humanitarian purposes to be tasked with supervising and controlling these heavy weapons. I had already been told by Cy that neither he nor Boutros was aware of the agreement before it had been signed and that they believed that it was a promise that Karadzic had no intention of fulfilling. Moreover, the UN believed the deal was quite unenforceable, for there were no troops mandated to do the job. I told them I would try to sort it out.

The Foreign Office agreed that Maggie Smart would in effect return to the diplomatic service and would be my link with London and my private office in Geneva. In view of my refusal to take a salary they offered a generous Geneva-based expense allowance. I had told the Prime Minister that I would give the Conference all the time it needed until the New Year and then I would need to look at whether I should continue, but I would not leave them in the lurch. Cy Vance had told Boutros Ghali that he would live in Geneva until the end of January and that at the most he would give the Conference six months.

That afternoon Cy and I gave a press conference in Queen Elizabeth Hall. We were warned beforehand that the Foreign Office was saying to journalists that it was for the two Co-Chairmen to set the clock for the collecting of heavy weapons. But Cy had not even yet seen the Karadzic letter on heavy weapons and apparently Boutros Ghali was also denying to journalists that he had seen it. So much for what the UK press was calling the main achievement of what was meant to be a joint UN–EC conference. Cy was clearly irritated and refused to give any clue or timetable in response to journalists' questions. He had earlier warned me to avoid using the word 'ceasefire' if at all possible, and we both stressed the hard road ahead. Cy was asked if he thought this more difficult than the Camp David negotiations and he said with much emphasis: 'this is more difficult because the fighting is more severe, it is more brutal, the situation has been completely out of control. The ability to control the fighters is not in the hands of the government the way it was at the time of the Middle East negotiations.' Then he left to catch a plane to New York and I saw Douglas Hurd.

There was an element of *déjà vu* in returning to the office where I had worked from 1977 to 1979, and for the first time I saw in the outer office my photo up in the rogues' gallery of former Foreign Secretaries. Douglas was very friendly and informative. I then had a meeting to discuss the heavy weapons issue with Marrack Goulding, the UN Under-Secretary. Heavy weapons control was clearly a major problem for the UN. No one in the room had any idea of what was the definition of a heavy weapon, a question which had apparently not even been touched on with Dr Karadzic; whatever they were, precisely, Goulding doubted whether UNPROFOR would be able to supervise them without a new mandate from the Security Council. His intelligent assistant, Shashi Tharoor, felt that this was certainly the case and asked who was going to pay for this new task; the UN officials made it clear that Boutros Ghali would insist on the Europeans paying for what he had already described as a 'rich man's war'. It was my first encounter with the gap between the rhetoric about peace and the practical grinding realities of peacekeeping on the ground.

I asked for arrangements to be made to visit as many European capitals as possible, starting on Monday before the Conference opened in Geneva on the Thursday, and then drove with my family to our home in Buttermere. Once there, I did little else but read about Yugoslavia. We drove back to London on Sunday via Peter Carrington's Buckinghamshire farm for tea. Peter was relaxed as ever, but as he talked about the way he had been treated by the European Foreign Ministers a hard edge came into his voice. There was no doubt he saw the EC recognition decision in December 1991 as a betrayal, and as he chronicled the story I wondered aloud what they could do to me, only for him to chortle: 'don't worry, there's nothing left for them to do.' His comments about the various Balkan leaders were unprintable but I was surprised that there was not much to choose between them on his scale of perfidy. He, even more than the press over the weekend, emphasized the scale of the problem facing me. Almost everyone believed that not much could be done to halt the fighting. The task was being labelled 'mission impossible'.

2

Establishing the Conference

THE INTERNATIONAL CONFERENCE on the former Yugoslavia (ICFY) began in continuous session on the morning of Thursday 3 September 1992. Cy Vance had flown in from New York overnight and I had flown in from Rome; we met at the airport for an impromptu press conference. I had learnt much in my previous three days' travelling. I had been to Belgium (to see the European Commission), the Netherlands, Denmark, Portugal, France and Italy. Many background documents had been collected for me to read on the plane. One of the most interesting was Lord Carrington's concise statement to the London Conference on the opening day,[7] which gave much of the history of the negotiations; I had supplemented it with his statement to the parties after the first six months of the Conference on Yugoslavia (the Hague Conference) which the EC had set up in September 1991 under the chairmanship of Lord Carrington.[8] The speeches and conclusions of the London Conference provided a condensed but depressing introduction.[9] In Paris I had talked to the Dutch Ambassador to France, Henry Wijnaendts,[i] who had been the EC envoy to what was then still Yugoslavia and Co-ordinator of the EC Peace Conference. He has since written an interesting account of the EC's mediation efforts in the second half of 1991.[10]

The Netherlands had held the EC Presidency from the outbreak of the war in July until December 1991, and in consequence of my visit to the Hague I discovered that on 13 July 1991, when the Slovenian and Croatian declarations of independence were just eighteen days old, the Dutch government had suggested to the other EC member states that the option of agreed changes to some of the internal borders between the Yugoslav republics might be explored.

The Presidency continues to feel that it is necessary to reconcile the various principles of the Helsinki Final Act and the Charter of Paris which may apply to the situation in Yugoslavia. It considers it especially important that selective application of principles be avoided. The principle of self-determination e.g. cannot exclusively apply to the existing republics while being deemed inapplicable to national minorities within those republics.

The following should be seen as a very tentative attempt on the part of the Presidency at structuring our discussion on the future of Yugoslavia, with a view to developing a common position which may serve as guidance for possible Troika involvement in the Yugoslav negotiating process.

1 *We seem to agree that it is not possible for Yugoslavia to continue to exist with its present constitutional structure intact. The joint declaration of Brioni clearly states that a new situation has arisen in Yugoslavia.*

2 *It is equally difficult to imagine that Yugoslavia could peacefully dissolve into six independent republics within their present borders. Both Serbia and Serbian elements in the federal administration – not least the JNA – have made it plain that they will never tolerate the emergence of an independent Croatia with 11 per cent Serbs within its borders.*

3 *A loosely structured Yugoslavia consisting of six sovereign republics is not likely to assuage these Serbian concerns either. The higher the degree of sovereignty for Croatia, the greater the need for solid guarantees for the Serbian minority in Croatia. The looser the federal structure, the more difficult it will be to supply such guarantees.*

4 *The foregoing seems to point in the direction of a voluntary redrawing of internal borders as a possible solution.*

It is clear that this option would entail daunting problems. In the first place it is impossible to draw Yugoslavia's internal borders in such a way that no national minorities would remain. Many minorities reside in relatively small pockets or even in isolated villages. On the other hand it cannot be denied that, if the aim is to reduce the number of national minorities in every republic, better borders than the present ones could be devised.

As soon as one starts to think in terms of independent republics, however, the first principle of Helsinki should apply, which means that the frontiers of Yugoslavia's constituent republics can only be changed 'in accordance with international law, by peaceful means and by agreement'. According to recent press reports secret negotiations are allegedly being conducted between President Tudjman of Croatia and President Milosevic of Serbia on the establishment of new borders between these

two republics. The Presidency has not been able to obtain a confirma-
tion of these reports, but it should be clear that the Twelve could never
agree to a redrawing of Yugoslavia's borders in which the federal
government is not involved and the rights of other republics (such as e.g.
Bosnia-Herzegovina with, to be sure, 33 per cent Serbs and 18 per cent
Croats, but in addition to that no less than 47 per cent Muslims) are
ignored.

This example shows why unilateral declarations of independence of
individual republics cannot solve Yugoslavia's problems and why it
continues to be necessary to aim for a comprehensive solution which
involves all republics and the federal government. This does not imply a
continued insistence on the unity of Yugoslavia: the Twelve can accept
any solution that results from a peaceful process and is based on general
agreement.

Incomprehensibly, the proposal to redraw the republics' boundaries had
been rejected by all eleven other EC countries. The first ground for objection was that it would open a Pandora's box; but the Organization of
African Unity, while against changes to the map of Africa, is defending the
boundaries of states already recognized by the UN. Secondly, it was considered out of date to draw state borders along ethnic lines. Thirdly, it was
thought that republic boundaries could not be redrawn in view of the large
numbers of separate 'pockets' where there were ethnic majorities not
geographically connected. It is true that there could not have been a total
accommodation of Serb demands; but to rule out any discussion or opportunity for compromise in order to head off war was an extraordinary
decision. My view has always been that to have stuck unyieldingly to the
internal boundaries of the six republics within the former Yugoslavia,
namely Serbia, Croatia, Slovenia, Bosnia-Herzegovina, Montenegro and
Macedonia, before there was any question of recognition of these republics,
as being the boundaries for independent states, was a folly far greater than
that of premature recognition itself. The refusal to make these borders
negotiable greatly hampered the EC's attempt at crisis management in July
and August 1991 and subsequently put all peacemaking from September
1991 onwards within a straitjacket that greatly inhibited compromises
between the parties in dispute. There are no easy parallels with other
countries, but the Slovak–Czech division by agreement on 1 January 1993
shows that there is an alternative to staying locked in a loveless, even antagonistic, marriage. All over the world there are peoples who believe that their
nationality would be better expressed by living in an independent state
separate from that in which they are living. On the other hand, in Spain
and Britain two democratic EU governments have withstood terrorism over
many years in order to prevent forced change in the boundaries of their

countries. The armed intervention in Chechnya by Russia to prevent secession and the shelling of Grozny raise fundamental questions not dissimilar
to those involved in the disintegration of Yugoslavia.

No country is the same as any other: nations' histories are different,
peoples have diverse attitudes. There can be no universal solution, but a
blanket ban on any boundary changes, particularly to internal boundaries,
is as hard to sustain as a belief that boundaries can be in a permanent state
of flux.

The main reason why Slovenia had an easy time fighting off the Yugoslav
National Army in the ten-day war in 1991 was that the JNA were not
allowed to fight. There was no territorial dispute between Slovenes and
Serbs, because Slovenia consisted of more than 90 per cent Slovenes with
their own language and there was no significant Serb minority. There are
indications that the Slovenian leadership passed on to President Milosevic
an offer for a deal under which Slovenia would stay neutral in the dispute
between Serbs and Croats if it were allowed to secede from Yugoslavia.[ii] By
contrast, in Croatia there were substantial areas where there had been Serb
majorities for centuries. As Misha Glenny explains:[iii]

> Following Tudjman's victory in the April elections, Milosevic was
> increasingly willing to raise the spectre of the right of all Serbs to live in
> a single state, should Tudjman attempt to take Croatia and its 600,000-
> strong Serbian minority out of Yugoslavia. Milosevic's chosen weapon,
> the Serb minority in Croatia, was a dangerous club to brandish. The two
> presidents, Milosevic and Tudjman, began pulling and grabbing this
> excessively sensitive group of people like two small children arguing
> over a toy. Every time Croatia and Slovenia pushed their claims for
> independence, Milosevic simply said that Croatia could go but without
> the regions where Serbs live.

Amazingly, neither before, during or after the Serb–Croat war did EC
mediation touch on these territorial questions: all that was offered was a
level of autonomy for Serbs living within the republic of Croatia. Map-
making apparently was too sensitive an issue to contemplate. For the EC it
was a question of either keeping Yugoslavia together or separating it into
independent countries divided by the republican boundaries determined in
most particulars in 1945. But what were these boundaries?

Milovan Djilas, who during the Partisan war was given by Tito the main
responsibility for designing the administrative boundaries of the republics
and autonomous provinces within post-war Yugoslavia, never made any
secret of the fact that sometimes they were made quickly 'during a march'
without the fullest consideration, and were often arbitrary and driven by
political expediency;[iv] and he confirmed to me personally that they were

never intended to be international boundaries. Because the 1939 Cvetkovic–Macek Agreement had given the Croatian nation control over substantial parts of Bosnia-Herzegovina, many Croats, not least Franjo Tudjman, never in their hearts accepted the 1945 boundary between Croatia and Bosnia-Herzegovina. Similarly, the Serb-inhabited areas of northern Dalmatia, Lika, Kordun, Banja, Slavonia and Baranja, which together made up the Military Frontier territory, Krajina, between the Habsburg and Ottoman empires, areas which had been ruled from Vienna but not from Zagreb, resisted incorporation into Croatia. This resistance was particularly strongly felt after 1945, for the inhabitants had been subjected to genocide by the Croat Ustashas during the Second World War. Very few commentators in 1995 understood or acknowledged that when the Croatian government attacked the Krajina they were not 'retaking' or 'reoccupying' this land, for the Serbs had inhabited it for more than three centuries. At most the Croats were reclaiming territory.

The Communist leaders did consider forming an autonomous province from these Serb areas in Croatia. According to Djilas the idea was rejected both because of the region's odd intestine-like shape and because of the number of Croats living there.[v] To the Communist Partisan leaders, nationalism was a product of capitalism. Croat and Serb national ambitions, Albanian and Hungarian minority feeling as well as Muslim identity would, they thought, weaken with the development of socialism; brotherhood and unity would weld a nation of Yugoslavs.

Milovan Djilas died in Belgrade in 1995. Fortunately for me, I had visited him at his home some months previously and we had discussed the present troubles. He had been a more important influence on my thinking in the 1960s than Alexander Solzhenitsyn or other famous Eastern bloc dissidents. His writings were regularly reviewed during the late 1950s and 1960s in *Encounter*, a literary and political magazine which I read with delight every month to offset the diet of facts which is the least attractive part of being a medical student. To my generation in Britain the Yugoslav Partisans had an aura of glamour, conferred on them above all by Fitzroy Maclean through his book *Eastern Approaches*. Djilas' dissent had therefore a relevance to me personally and an air of dash and romance to it. I knew he was a tough Montenegrin but it did shock me when I discovered many years later that he had negotiated on behalf of Tito's Partisans with the German occupying forces – the very crime for which the royalist Serb Mihailovic had been executed by the Partisans after the war.

While talking to Djilas, a vague memory had stirred of a short story of his which I had read. Going back through old copies of *Encounter*, I found it in the April 1962 edition. It was called 'War', and is about a peasant couple who tried to smuggle their sole surviving son out of the battle zone in a coffin; when discovered by soldiers he is summarily shot, still in the coffin, as a deserter. At the age of twenty-four I remember being shocked by the brutal nature of the writing but I now recognize that it represents many Yugoslavs' basic attitude to war. As Djilas writes: 'War has no mind, and it cannot tell what could or could not at any moment be of value to the opposing side; for this reason, the wisest course of action in war becomes the destruction of absolutely everything – houses and cultivated plots, bridges and museums, and naturally, first and foremost, human beings and their livelihood.' Even museums. We have seen this with Serbs deliberately shelling the Oriental Library in Sarajevo and with Croats defacing the Jasenovac memorial to the genocide against the Serbs committed by the Croat Ustashas in the Second World War.

It is the frankness of Djilas' writing about his own past ideological commitments that is so refreshing. There is no trace of self-justification. 'One cannot be a Communist and preserve an iota of one's personal integrity,' he wrote in *Encounter* in December 1979 in 'A Conversation with Milovan Djilas'. Maybe if Djilas' advocacy of democracy had been given the hearing it deserved in the 1950s and implemented in the 1960s, the present Serb–Croat, Serb–Muslim and Muslim–Croat wars could have been avoided. Although democracy puts a high value on self-determination, it also fosters a spirit of compromise and consensus. It was the absence of this spirit in Yugoslavia in 1990 that made for the bitterness and bloody-minded intransigence that accompanied the state's disintegration. Even democracies will defend the integrity of their country and use force to check seces- sionism; but consideration of when to fight, when to compromise, is the essence of democratic leadership, as we saw in the peaceful break-up of Czechoslovakia. Perhaps if that negotiated divorce had occurred earlier, it would have influenced Yugoslavia and at least made the EC more open to boundary changes.

Djilas wrote in June 1967 in *Encounter*:

What brought and held different Yugoslav nationalities together was the common fear of foreign aggression or imperialism, the Turkish and Habsburg Empires in the first place, then Nazi Germany and Fascist Italy; later for a while Stalin's Russia. But now there are no such threats; nobody has any designs on this country. It is only natural that the Slovenes, the Croats, the Macedonians and so on are seeking to affirm their own identity and cultural independence. If Togo can be a state on its own, they ask, why not us?

Clear signs of a yearning for freedom under Tito occurred with the 1971 'Croatian Spring' initiated by Croatian nationalists and reformers. It was suppressed, though Tito was reluctant to use the Yugoslav army.[vi] So it is a great mistake to believe that Slovenian, Serbian and Croatian nationalism were creatures of the collapse of Communism. Nationalistic feelings were stirring well before Milosevic and Tudjman personally revived and fanned them in the 1980s. What ignited them was the rapid collapse of Yugoslavian Communist authority amid the fading of Tito's legacy. Television and newspaper stories refighting the 1942–5 civil war revived the emotional memories and folklore of the Ustasha horrors, of Chetnik behaviour and of Partisan revenge.[11]

Democracy for Yugoslavia, which Djilas championed in the 1960s, would, I believe, have hastened its break-up, which is one of the reasons why Tito was against it. Yet the inevitable recognition of nationhood would have been tolerated far better in a democratic environment. The problem in Yugoslavia in the 1980s was that the consensual model for holding the constituent nations together relied on authoritarian rule. As authoritarian rule and real, democratic consensus are mutually exclusive, Tito's mechanisms became ever more useless. Ambitious politicians stayed within the republics to build their careers. Those who went to Belgrade had less and less influence in their regional capitals. The 1990 elections elected newly minted nationalist governments in Croatia and Slovenia, committed to independence.

The extent to which a Yugoslav identity was developed and a genuine multi-ethnic culture established under Communist rule will long be argued. This identity, like the constitution, was sadly never underpinned by democracy. On Europe's television sets in 1989, when Holland played a friendly football match against Yugoslavia in Zagreb, we saw how even sport could not keep a Yugoslav identity alive: the crowd turned their backs on the Yugoslav players, booed the Yugoslav national anthem and cheered for the Dutch team throughout the match. However, it is beyond dispute that a Yugoslav identity was developed in parts of the former Yugoslavia and the valiant struggle to keep a multi-ethnic identity alive in besieged Sarajevo will for many always be a benchmark for what might have been. Yet life in cosmopolitan Sarajevo, Tuzla or Mostar was not necessarily representative of life in other parts of Bosnia-Herzegovina. There is disagreement as to how well integrated and multi-ethnic its peoples' lives had actually become and the evidence is patchy. Some believe that not much has changed since Ivo Andric, who won the Nobel Prize for his book *Bridge on the Drina*, wrote in a short story, 'Letter Dated 1920', that 'Bosnia is a country of fear and hate.' In this story, written as a love letter to what he believed was his divided country, he tackled this question of not being able to face the reality of their own divisions. 'Perhaps your greatest tragedy is that you do not even realize how much hate lies behind your love, your enthusiasm, your tradition, your piety.' Born in 1892 of Croatian parents near Travnik, he was criticized by many Sarajevan intellectuals for painting too harsh a picture of what he called his 'dark country'. Those intellectuals wanted the

world to know the tolerant side of Bosnia-Herzegovina; they were proud
that it was the crossroads of civilizations, where the Muslim, Orthodox and
Catholic religions mingled, home to Serbs, Croats, Bosnians, Jews and
Gypsies. Certainly it was that Bosnia-Herzegovina which inspired the
London Declaration of Principles, enjoining Cyrus Vance and me to try to
keep the citizens of this newly recognized country together in one state.
Despite the cynics, in 1992 it was a task I genuinely believed to be desirable
and achievable; and I still believe that had the Clinton administration
supported the Vance–Owen Peace Plan, we would have been able to carry
it out.

In the many letters of congratulations on my appointment there were
some very useful nuggets of advice. In all wars the personalities of the
leading figures do much to determine the character and the intensity of the
conflict, and one letter from an old friend who knew how I liked to get into
the minds of those with whom I was going to negotiate contained extracts
of the writings of three key figures, Presidents Cosic, Izetbegovic and
Tudjman, which I read eagerly.[12]

Alija Izetbegovic was born in 1925 and educated as a lawyer. He is one
of the most enigmatic of all the political personalities in the former
Yugoslavia. Of the six Presidents of the former Yugoslav republics, he is the
only one who has never been a Communist, and it showed in the way he
talked and thought. A question often asked is whether Izetbegovic is an
Islamic fundamentalist. The answer is difficult to give in terms of 'yes' or
'no'. He is, I am sure, a deeply religious man; which allows him to take a
long view of the war as a struggle for minds as well as territory; but as to
whether he is a fundamentalist, very few know for certain. If he is, he hides
it behind a self-disciplined portrayal of himself as a secular politician, as any
dissenter learnt to do in Tito's Yugoslavia. I found that Izetbegovic's
deepest feelings became apparent from time to time when he openly
agonized – unlike some Muslim leaders – over whether to accept the
compromises in various peace settlements. He had two loyalties, to multi-
ethnic Bosnia and his own Muslim party, but it was religion that gave him
an inner certainty and composure. As with many people who have spent
time in prison for their beliefs, there is an inner toughness and a
surrounding hard shell which is difficult to penetrate. In personal contact I
always liked him and wanted to help him; as I got to know him I found
him a perplexing personality: I would go out of my way to talk informally
to him over a meal, but he kept himself to himself and was easiest to
approach through his son or daughter, both delightful people who were part
of his political entourage.

My favourable appraisal of Izetbegovic is not shared by others who have
also spent long hours negotiating with him. Some feel he is the most
difficult of all the people they had to deal with in the former Yugoslavia,

manipulative and untrustworthy, and that his closest advisers are shadowy fundamentalists who play on his chronic indecisiveness and make him hold out against any compromise; and yet in fairness he has had by far the most difficult position to defend and sustain. He built and rallied his much weaker army over three years and clung on to the legitimacy of his role as President of a country that has never known peace since being independent. At the same time he convinced the world that he speaks for the majority, not just for the largest group, namely the 44 per cent Bosnian Muslims, but for all those who had lived in what many believed was but a volcanic peace in Bosnia-Herzegovina even prior to the declaration of independence.

Europe has good reasons to honour and respect the Muslim religion and the many people who practise it and have done so over many centuries within our nation-states. There are however mutual misunderstandings which I fear the war in Bosnia-Herzegovina has done much to perpetuate. Sadly, in part it is a religious war, an aspect which has been heightened as the war proceeds and the ideology of Communism has appeared ever more broken-backed, and its practitioners discredited.

Dobrica Cosic had been put into the role of President of Serbia and Montenegro – the rump state of Yugoslavia – by Milosevic in June 1992 in an attempt to regain the support of the intelligentsia who had moved away from Milosevic. Cosic was a novelist of distinction and his writing had been very influential in buttressing the respectability of the Serb nationalists.

Both Cosic and Izetbegovic were dissenters under Tito. Cosic actually protested publicly when Izetbegovic was imprisoned by Tito for his political beliefs. As I grew to know them both I became more and more interested in gauging how their respective Orthodox and Muslim faiths influenced their political stance. The Serb Orthodox Church was important to Cosic, but for its national identity; I never felt that he was a religious person. Visiting him in his house in Belgrade and having a meal with him and his wife, I felt Serbian history and heartbeat were more important than religion. For Izetbegovic the reverse seemed to be the case: his religion was his life, and history did not intrude. There were no outward and visible signs that he was a Muslim. He, his son and his daughter dressed and acted as Europeans. He wanted to be President, by democratic decision, of a Muslim state accepting full multi-ethnic participation in that state. Yet he did not appear to comprehend how inflammatory it was to some Serbs and Croats for him to visit Libya in March 1991 to arrange a $50 million loan, and in July to ask that Bosnia-Herzegovina, while still part of Yugoslavia, should be an observer at the meetings of the Organization of the Islamic Conference.

Cosic, Izetbegovic and Tudjman are nationalists if nationalism is defined as 'simply the determination of a people to cultivate its own soul, to follow the customs bequeathed to it by its ancestors, to develop its traditions according to its own instincts'.[vii] But is their nationalism a more malignant force than this? Serbian and Croatian nationalism, as it developed in the latter half of the nineteenth century, carries with it an inherent tendency to cross over into racial and religious discrimination and to ignite passions that feed on violence. Bosnian Muslim nationalism has historically been more benign, but the party Izetbegovic leads, the SDA, became ever more intolerant under the pressures of war. It was a reflection of Izetbegovic's pre-war view that the state was a means to an end, not an end in itself, that he opposed the break-up of Yugoslavia, was reluctant to press for an independent Bosnia-Herzegovina and was against recognition being granted to Croatia and Slovenia. Once nationalism had found independent expression in Croatia and Slovenia, he felt he had to establish Bosnia's independence from Serbia. Izetbegovic knew that this would lead to bloodshed. In his *Islamic Declaration* he warned that 'the Islamic renaissance cannot be imagined without people prepared for enormous personal and material sacrifice.'[viii]

I have often wondered whether Izetbegovic might have found it easier to negotiate with the Serbs if he had not been a devout Muslim. An economic technocrat like Gligorov aroused less paranoia. Gligorov managed to negotiate the withdrawal of the JNA from its bases in Macedonia early in 1992 with all its arms and equipment and its dignity intact. Of course, there were fewer Serbs in the Macedonian Republic and no Croats; and the Serbs were anxious to avoid having to fight on all their borders. But the absence of deeper religious conflict between the Macedonians and the Serbs was also a factor.

Nationalism, we all know, is a powerful force and when linked to religion it can gather even greater strength. It is however too simple to see nationalism as the fount of all evil. Fascism in 1940 was countered and fought by the UK when an international response was lacking, so national pride and independence cannot be lightly decried. The essential safeguard against the more extreme passions of nationalistic feeling is to set it on the bedrock of a true democracy. Yet nationalists often practise a manipulated democracy buttressed by highly selective referenda. Nationalism becomes authoritarian when people are not able to hold their leaders genuinely to account and to vote them out of as well as into office in fair and free elections. Nationalists who are in a minority within a multinational state need a fair measure of geographical or functional autonomy to express their nationhood in their day-to-day living and in familiar customs and traditions. Without that satisfaction nationalism finds its outlet in secessionism, and people are then prepared to fight for independence. It was clear that by 1992 the challenge facing us in the ICFY was to devise forms of decentralization and autonomy in Bosnia-Herzegovina, in Croatia and in Kosovo that would contain the legitimate nationalism of Croatian and Bosnian Serbs,

Bosnian Croats, Bosnian Muslims and Kosovar Albanians, and ensure respect for Albanians living in Macedonia.

Our first priority in Geneva at a meeting of the Steering Committee was to settle the financing of the Conference and the membership of its six working parties, and to start building a secretariat from scratch. From the start we had the full backing of the Swiss government and the Geneva canton. As for the Palais des Nations, quite apart from its marble-halled grandeur and the wonderful view over Lake Geneva to Mont Blanc, there are excellent facilities for a conference, with the capacity to expand quickly to absorb numerous delegates and press and then contract down to a small secretariat. Yet sometimes, as I wandered at night through the deserted art deco halls, I felt haunted by the 1930s and wondered whether Yugoslavia would do to the UN what Abyssinia did to the League of Nations. Sometimes I would go past the main Council Chamber and, looking up at the inscription on the wall outside, draw comfort from the words of one of my predecessors as Foreign Secretary, Robert Cecil: 'Be just and fear not.'

The calm of Geneva was shattered for us the moment we arrived with the news that an Italian air force plane carrying humanitarian relief supplies into Sarajevo had been shot down over an area controlled by forces of the Bosnian Croat army (HVO). The territory contained some Bosnian government (mainly Muslim) forces, but the UN felt it most unlikely to have had any Bosnian Serb forces. Suspicion fell on the Croats, but what surprised me was that the senior people in the UNHCR who controlled the flights and UNPROFOR's senior officers all refused to rule out the possibility that the very people who would gain most from the relief supplies, the Muslims, might be responsible for shooting down the plane. Up until then I had no idea that their past conduct had given grounds for any such suspicion. It was later thought that the Italian aircraft had been shot down by a Stinger hand-held ground-to-air missile which had been used to considerable effect against Soviet forces in Afghanistan. No party was identified as being responsible. The ICFY Working Party on Confidence Building Measures, one of the six working parties we established, convened a number of meetings immediately to try to prevent a recurrence, but we soon found that the quality of the representation from the parties was not high for they kept their best-informed people on the ground, fighting. For these and other reasons the ICFY proposed the formation of the Mixed Military Working Group in Sarajevo, bringing together the UN and the three parties' military leaders, to replace the activity of the Confidence Building Working Group.

After the downing of the Italian plane all humanitarian flights into Sarajevo were immediately cancelled by UNHCR. This meant that the race against winter, already underway, suffered a major setback. UNHCR were saying that only 100 tonnes of flour and 90 tonnes of rice remained in its Sarajevo warehouses. UNHCR then had only 50 trucks and required 500.

The impending crisis in having insufficient food to feed hundreds of thousands of people in Bosnia-Herzegovina was the dominating issue that confronted us over the weeks ahead in Geneva. The promised UN intervention force was still awaited and winter was approaching. As we grappled with the food problem we were hit by another humanitarian crisis that first weekend, setting a pattern of seven-day working that was to become the rule rather than the exception. On Saturday and Sunday we as Co-Chairmen were locked in meetings with Sadako Ogata, the High Commissioner for Refugees, who had accepted our invitation to be the Chairman of the ICFY Working Group on Humanitarian Issues, and Thierry Germond of the International Red Cross. Both asked us to agree that UNPROFOR troops should go from Croatia to Bosnia and escort prisoners to safety from the Manjaca camp. The Bosnian Serb guards were being withdrawn, which meant that the camp was open and defenceless in a locality where the Serb civilians were more hostile to the inmates than their captors. There were 3,700 detainees at risk, some of them ill and requiring to be moved out fast. The ICRC also said that the Croats and Muslims must be persuaded to release Serb prisoners. The issue of principle facing us was the question whether the UN should escort people out of Bosnia-Herzegovina, thereby making itself party to ethnic cleansing. The case for doing so was that we faced a higher humanitarian need, namely to save lives. This was the first of many times that we as Co-Chairmen had to confront this horrific dilemma. We decided that the humanitarian principle of saving lives had to take priority and asked UNPROFOR to help. Fortunately, since a widening of UNPROFOR's mandate to enable it to provide protective support for relief convoys was already being discussed in New York, it was relatively easy to agree to add escorting detainees to the brief, but we had to persuade the military to act in advance of the change and to act outside the borders of Croatia.

The deployment of UNPROFOR in Croatia had been authorized by the Security Council in Resolution 743 of 21 February 1992,[13] after conditions on the ground had stabilized sufficiently to give confidence that a peacekeeping operation could succeed; a process which had been assisted by the deployment of UN Military Liaison Officers in Croatia and Serbia under UN Security Council Resolution (UNSCR) 727 of 8 January,[14] following the signing by Croatian and Serbian military authorities on 2 January of the cessation of hostilities that had been negotiated by Cyrus Vance. This peacekeeping force of initially some 15,000 men was deployed in four areas: two of mixed population and two where Serbs were greatly in the majority. The four United Nations Protected Areas (UNPAs) in Croatia, Areas East, West, North and South, were to be demilitarized under the plan, so that the inhabitants would be free from fear of attack by the Croatian army and Serb militias. This allowed the JNA to withdraw from

Map 2 Croatia, showing UN Protected Areas,
and Bosnia-Herzegovina, spring 1992

the Krajina in Croatia, which they did in the main through Bosnia-Herzegovina, in the process augmenting the Bosnian Serbs' capacity to fight by leaving behind arms and men. This reinforcement of what was by then the independent state of Bosnia-Herzegovina was one of the justifications for the UN imposing economic sanctions against the Federal Republic of Yugoslavia (FRY), namely Serbia and Montenegro, in UNSCR 757 of 20 May 1992.[15]

The deployment of UNPROFOR in Croatia under a three-star Indian General, Satish Nambiar, began on 13 March 1992 and was initially successful. Sadly, UNPROFOR never really succeeded in reducing the power and influence of the Serb militia, particularly in UNPA East, where the Croats before the war had been numerous. Croatian displaced people or refugees never had the opportunity to return to the homes they had left during or after the fighting in 1991. The Serb militia in UNPA East, which included former JNA members, numbered some 16,000 armed men, some of them with heavy weapons. The Croatian Serb authorities claimed that they were police, but their continued presence was a clear breach of the Vance Plan which the Security Council tolerated for too long and was one of the factors behind President Tudjman's repeated threat to end the UN mandate when it came up for its six-monthly renewal.

In Geneva I began to examine the maps of the military front lines of the warring parties.[16] They were soon to become all too familiar as we pored over them week by week, month by month and year by year. They were already familiar to Vance from his work over the previous ten months, and to his deputy Herb Okun, whose encyclopaedic knowledge of the territory and ability to speak Russian gave him valuable insights. His years as deputy to the US Ambassador to the UN had moreover given him, and through him gave the ICFY, a depth of knowledge on how to approach the New York UN Secretariat. These skills were matched by my deputy, Peter Hall, previously the UK Ambassador in Belgrade. An able speaker of Serbo-Croat, he had been part of Lord Carrington's negotiating team and knew the former Yugoslavia literally inside out. We all recognized that it was not sensible to look at the war in Bosnia-Herzegovina in isolation and that we had to assess the Croatian Serb forces in the East, West, North and South UNPAs in Croatia as well. Indeed, there was a constant possibility that they would formally unite militarily and politically, making the border between the two countries even more irrelevant. As it was, they moved across it freely as if they were still in the former Yugoslavia, and UN Security Council Resolutions were to them a complete irrelevance.

On 9 September I arrived for my first visit to the former Yugoslavia with Cy Vance, starting in Zagreb. We were met at the airport by General Nambiar, with a copy of a letter which he had just sent to President Izetbegovic about the most recent horror from Sarajevo. 'It is with a deep sense of outrage that I have to inform you that at approximately 1930 hours on 8 September 1992 troops under your command attacked an unarmed UNPROFOR logistical convoy at the entrance to the airport. This unprovoked attack in broad daylight, on an unmistakably UN humanitarian convoy, caused the death of two French soldiers, injury to three more, and the destruction or damage of four UN vehicles.' General Nambiar was a fine man, cool and courteous in all his dealings, but he was very angry when we talked to him about this premeditated ambush. A UN press release was also issued in the toughest terms.[17] For me the incident was peculiarly devastating. Up until then I had, perhaps naïvely, seen the Bosnian Muslims as the decent, aggrieved party. Now I was having to accommodate the fact that, while behaving less badly than the Croats and nowhere near as badly as the Serbs, they too were capable of killing in cold blood UN troops in blue berets, the very people who had been sent to help feed and house their people. Now I began to understand why in the minds of UN officials the responsibility for shooting down the Italian plane could be Muslim as well as Croat.

What was the motivation for these and other provocative actions? Presumably, under the orders of someone in political authority, though not necessarily Izetbegovic, the Bosnian Muslims were trying to plant the responsibility for their actions on to the Bosnian Serbs, thereby portraying the Serbs as even worse than they were in the eyes of world opinion. This behaviour they supposedly could justify if it brought the Americans and NATO into the war on the Muslim side. It was the end justifying the means. Within a week of taking the position of Co-Chairman I had come to realize, and to say publicly, that there were no innocents among the political and military leaders in all three parties in Bosnia-Herzegovina. That is not to say that the leaders were all the same, and it is mere escapism to pretend that there is no difference between the parties. There is and there remains a quantum difference between the horrors perpetrated by Bosnian Serb leaders and acts committed or authorized by the Bosnian Croat or Bosnian Muslim leaders.

In Zagreb President Tudjman told us about the Iranian cargo aircraft, a Boeing 747, that had landed on 4 September with a declaration that it was carrying relief supplies but was found also to hold significant quantities of various types of armaments. Tudjman's motivation in telling us was mixed, for this was not the first or by any means the last Iranian plane to land in Croatia with arms. Already the Croatian government had become skilled at evading the arms embargo which had been applied to them ever since 25 September 1991 by UNSCR 713.[18] They extracted a heavy price for being an arms conduit to Bosnia-Herzegovina, either in terms of money from the Bosnian government or by demanding 50 per cent or more of the arms for themselves; sometimes both. The landlocked Bosnian government forces, mainly Muslim, were dependent on the Croats. Yet when people talked of lifting the arms embargo for the Bosnian Muslim forces, they neglected to say that this could only happen with Zagreb's agreement, and that would mean lifting it for the Croats too. A selective lifting for the Bosnian Muslims was at that stage in the war totally impossible. Moreover, West European governments and the US tolerated and indeed in some cases condoned the Croatian government bringing arms and materials in, by road through Hungary and Slovenia and by plane and sea in the early stages of the conflict. Nor did they do anything to stop the Croatians then transferring arms on into Bosnia-Herzegovina, for there were no UN or other monitors on the border with Western Herzegovina or Posavina. These rarely acknowledged facts put the discussions surrounding the arms embargo in a better perspective. There was no effective restriction on Croatia building up effective armed forces, and it was Croatia who then controlled the quantity and quality of the arms that moved into Bosnia-Herzegovina to increase the effectiveness of the Bosnian Muslim forces.

Yet despite these ways around the arms embargo, the UN Security Resolution that imposed it will go down in history as one of the most controversial of all those passed by the UN. But it was not seen as controversial when it was first suggested, and the motion was carried in September 1991 with virtually no dissent and with the US government in the lead. Why? In part because Yugoslavia was a major exporter of arms. Arms and ammunition factories existed all over the country and continued production during the war, even in Muslim-held Sarajevo, Zenica and Gorazde. The initial effect of the embargo in 1991 was to hurt the Croatian forces, who had far fewer arms, tanks, armoured vehicles and planes than the opposing Yugoslav forces. Even so, UNSCR 713 has come to be seen by many as an example of religious discrimination and of the West's anti-Muslim bias; yet for the first six months of its operation it acted against the predominantly Roman Catholic Croats. Nor did the key members of the Security Council see fit even to consider lifting the ban when they recognized Croatia and Slovenia prior to recognizing Bosnia-Herzegovina. In the case of Croatia the arguments for keeping the ban were quite straightforward and seen to be fair, namely that the UN forces were on the ground supposedly keeping the peace and for the UN officially to arm one side in the conflict while having its forces operating within both Croatian- and Serb-controlled territory was to put those personnel and equipment at even greater risk and call into question their impartiality. There was, however, a significant difference between the EC-led recognition of Croatia and that of Bosnia-Herzegovina. When the former was recognized by most countries there was a negotiated ceasefire in place between the combatants in the Serb–Croat civil war of 1991; when the latter was recognized in 1992 by most countries it proved to be the start of a new war between the newly recognized government of Bosnia-Herzegovina and the Serbs, whether the Serbs lived in Bosnia, Croatia or Serbia and Montenegro.

The recognition of Bosnia-Herzegovina was the trigger that many had predicted it would be to the formal outbreak of a war that was already simmering in the background before recognition. The critical mistake made by the EC as well as the US was to continue down the path towards recognizing Bosnia-Herzegovina in the spring of 1992 when every single sign indicated that it would be like pouring petrol on a smouldering fire. Once they realized their mistake, to compound it by lifting the embargo and breaking cooperation with Russia inside the Security Council in 1992 was judged rightly as being far too inflammatory an action to take. There has been a tendency to blame the UN Secretary-General and Cyrus Vance for not coming to the Security Council with demands for a UN preventive force for Bosnia-Herzegovina early in 1992 – forgetting the difficulty the Security Council was already facing in finding sufficient troops and deploying them quickly enough to maintain the 2 January ceasefire in Croatia.[ix]

In July 1992 NATO and WEU ministers decided to mount naval operations in international waters in the Adriatic to monitor compliance with both the arms embargo and the newly applied economic sanctions on the

FRY (Serbia and Montenegro). This naval monitoring exercise was, however, initially conducted with no powers to enforce either the embargo or sanctions. Shipping in the Adriatic was questioned about destinations and cargoes, and suspect vessels were notified to parent governments and followed up in the UN, but stop and search was not permitted. In part this limitation arose out of the WEU involvement and the wish of the Federal Republic of Germany to participate in this whereas they could not, under their laws, participate in out-of-area NATO enforcement action. This absurdly weak action sent a signal to the Croatian government that NATO did not mind if they broke the arms embargo and, more importantly, indicated to the FRY that the oil embargo would not be rigidly enforced either. For the Bosnian Serbs it was yet another sign that no one, least of all NATO, was going to intervene to prevent ethnic cleansing.

The humanitarian airlift to Sarajevo began on 2 July 1992, mandated by UNSCR 761 of 29 June[19] and UNSCR 764 of 13 July,[20] which authorized full implementation of the concept endorsed in UNSCR 758 of 18 June.[21] This was shortly after the brave impromptu visit by President Mitterrand, who flew in at some personal risk to demonstrate that Sarajevo airport could be used, but also to damp down calls for intervention at home. Transport aircraft from a number of countries have been dedicated to that operation ever since, flying initially out of Zagreb and controlled by a small team within UNHCR in Geneva, its operations being later moved to airfields in Italy and Germany.

On 10 September it was impossible for us to fly into Sarajevo since all flights were banned because of the loss of the Italian plane. Vance and I therefore decided to drive in from Split, leaving early in the morning. After a tortuous six-hour drive over roads that were literally being carved out of the hillside by UN engineers, and travelling with General Philippe Morillon, the French Commander of UN forces in Bosnia-Herzegovina, we found a city that had been without water for eleven days and had had all its electricity cut off. Philippe Morillon was a considerable character, great fun to be with, normally informal and relaxed, but on this occasion he was sombre, truly grieving at the loss of the French soldiers. We met with President Izetbegovic in the Presidency building, to the accompaniment of shell and mortar fire which, the cynics told us, was part of the normal accompaniment to such visits. In this case they were implying it was all laid on for us by government forces: thus another of my preconceptions of innocence fell by the wayside. We encountered much the same firepower on display when we crossed the airfield to meet with Dr Karadzic at Lukavica, this time presumably laid on by the Serbs. Karadzic told us that all their heavy weapons were now concentrated in eleven positions around Sarajevo and in five positions around another four towns. The UN commanders were adamant that he was 'lying through his teeth' – and indeed, we had driven

past some tanks and artillery pieces en route to the meeting. It was one
more example of things not being what they seemed.

Because of the delay in reaching Sarajevo we had to leave with General
Morillon that same afternoon. Ours was the first plane to take off since the
Italian aircraft was downed, and we flew out with the French soldiers who
had been injured in the attack. I sat in the back of the pilot's cockpit and
the tension could be sensed in the atmosphere as men intently watched their
radar screens. When I asked Philippe Morillon what we could do if they
picked up an incoming missile, he just gave a Gallic shrug: the answer was
we had no defences, not even the capacity to put out diversionary material
like aluminium chaff to attract any approaching missile. I felt too ashamed
to show any apprehension, given the cool way in which Cy Vance and the
others behaved.

From Zagreb we flew in a Russian Yak plane chartered by the UN on to
Belgrade. The next day I met President Cosic for the first time. Prime
Minister Panic was with him, in his usual ebullient form and wanting to
control the meeting. He nearly succeeded, but we sensed Cosic wanted to
be involved and with our encouragement he began to speak up, with good
sense and dignity. The communiqué issued after the meeting,[22] condemning
ethnic cleansing and reporting on the whole visit, is described in my first
COREU to the European Foreign Ministers.[23] But what cannot easily be
captured was the personal rapport we both started to establish with Cosic.
Steadily over the next few months the nationalistic posturing dropped away
and he showed some of the qualities that have made and will in future make
the Serbs a substantial people. Then seventy-two years old, he was Serbia's
most famous living novelist, most of his works being a romantic retelling of
Serbia's long history. In dwelling on the hardships and the subjugations of
the Serbs he subtly reminds his readers that nationalism is a great calling
for which sacrifices are an essential debt which each Serb owes to the nation
and from which none should shrink. There is no invoking of ethnic
cleansing or anything so crude as racism, rather a proud affirmation of
national responsibility, and it was this aspect of his personality we tried to
foster.

A significant development during our visit was the agreement we reached
with all three Bosnian parties to resume talks in Geneva, without preconditions, on the future constitutional arrangements for Bosnia-Herzegovina.
They were scheduled to start on Friday 18 September. Yet no sooner were
we back in Geneva than we received a letter from President Izetbegovic
dated 13 September saying that the Presidency were no longer ready to take
part in the discussions because the aggression against his country continued.
Cy was more angry than I had ever seen him and drafted a forthright letter
in reply, saying we were shocked, could not accept the validity of his
reasons and could not believe that a man of honour would back away from

an agreement solemnly made. Izetbegovic then wrote to say he had received our reply and that in any case their Foreign Minister, Haris Silajdzic, would come to Geneva, while negotiations would depend on further developments. That cycle of 'will he attend or won't he?' was to repeat itself all too frequently. With some justice Izetbegovic bridled at having to negotiate while fighting continued with Bosnian Serb leaders whom he saw as the enemy and the aggressor. We had great difficulty in reconfiguring the pattern which had been established prior to the war of discussing the future among three parties. For the Muslims, to have what they called the Serb aggressors at the negotiating table in the same way as their own delegation representing an internationally recognized government was offensive. We understood this feeling, and at that stage we did not press them to sit in the same room. We were content to hold proximity talks. In late June 1992 the US government had argued for effectively 'taking sides' in favour of the legitimate government of Bosnia-Herzegovina and of those representatives of Bosnia's Muslims, Serbs and Croats who favoured a viable multi-ethnic Bosnia-Herzegovina and opposed the violent strategy and tactics of what they called the 'terrorist wing' of Karadzic's Serbian Democratic Party of Bosnia. It was ostracization and the US position was supported by the Germans in a paper to their European partners. But it was unrealistic, given that Serbia and Montenegro were not prepared to negotiate on behalf of the Bosnian Serbs. Having the three Bosnian parties present at the London Conference that August also meant that the international community was accepting that all three were indispensable to any settlement.

In all our Conference papers and meetings, however, we were scrupulous in treating Izetbegovic as President and his ministers as members of the government of an independent state, while being aware that they constituted one of the three parties to a dispute which had to have a negotiated solution. As tension between Croats and Muslims grew within the Bosnian government, it became increasingly difficult to uphold and justify this politically correct position. We could not ignore the reality that Izetbegovic was in control of only about 11 per cent of the country, while the Bosnian Croats controlled slightly more territory due to the whole-hearted support they received from the Croatian government and the presence in considerable numbers of Croatian government forces. The collective Presidency in Bosnia-Herzegovina, elected in 1990, consisted of seven people, but by 1992 was exercising less and less of the collective power given to it under the constitution. Its cohesion was not helped by the fact that Fikret Abdic, the Muslim leader in Bihac, who had polled more votes than Alija Izetbegovic in the Presidency elections, never came from Bihac to Sarajevo for meetings of the Presidency. The Serbs who had been appointed to fill the multi-ethnic vacuum left by the departure of the elected Bosnian Serb members, Nikola Koljevic and Biljana Plavsic, were never, in

extremely difficult circumstances, able to represent a significant section of
the Bosnian Serb population, while the Croat leader Mate Boban pulled out
one of the elected Croat members of the Presidency and filled the vacancy
with his party nominee. When the Croat Mile Akmadzic was appointed
Prime Minister of Bosnia-Herzegovina he made a real effort to revive the
collective leadership of the Presidency. He went back to live in Sarajevo and
used his previous experience as pre-war secretary to the Presidency to try to
restore the authority of the Muslim–Croat coalition that had won the referendum on independence which the Serbs boycotted. But by the end of 1992
it was becoming clear to all that he would fail and that power had gone to
a small group of Muslim Ministers appointed by President Izetbegovic and
their nominee as Vice-President, Ejup Ganic. The collective Presidency as a
democratic body with meaningful representation from the three constituent
nations was by the autumn of 1993 no longer a reality. The real decisions
were made elsewhere. We were in effect dealing with a Muslim government
for a predominantly Muslim population.

Dr Karadzic, despite having opposed my appointment, went out of his
way to be welcoming. His English is excellent and he can be a gracious host.
At times I fell into the trap of underestimating Karadzic. His theatrical
appearances, flamboyant statements and record as a gambler gave the
impression of his being a political lightweight. He is, however, not as confident as his tall, commanding stature suggests: his bitten-down fingernails
are witness to an anxiety underneath. Having worked in hospitals abroad,
he is a far more cosmopolitan figure than most Bosnian Serbs. He claims
never to have been a true Communist and, emphasizing his churchgoing and
commitment to a market economy, he began increasingly to distance and
distinguish himself from President Milosevic, encouraging the press during
1994 to depict him as the heir to the Mihailovic tradition. Karadzic was also
better than any other Serb except Milosevic at negotiating, usually keeping
cool, knowing when to give ground to protect a vital interest and on
occasions producing imaginative solutions. But he lacked Milosevic's
boldness and self-confidence. He was very careful not to alienate his own
constituency. He never allowed any difference to emerge between himself
and Krajisnik, and often asked for solutions to be imposed on him,
frequently claiming he would be killed by his own people if he agreed to
some difficult compromise. His stance was to hold on to what he had in
terms of territory and play for time. When his split with General Ratko
Mladic developed in 1995 he blamed the army for losing ground.

The other Bosnian Serb leader of considerable significance was Momcilo
Krajisnik, the leader of the Bosnian Serb Assembly, who, as the war ground
on, became in effect joint leader of the Bosnian Serbs. Krajisnik claims to
be a devout Orthodox Christian; he is rich, and is accused by Mladic of
being a corrupt businessman. He speaks no English but talks quietly, and

the Bosnian Muslim leaders trust him far more than they do Karadzic. He has a singlemindedness and a rigidity which are both infuriating and admirable. He owns two houses in Sarajevo and its outskirts, which made him an impossible negotiator when we came to the city itself, refusing to give up any territory and adamant that the Serbs must have a slice of Sarajevo of a size and content that no Muslim leader could ever accept.[24]

In Belgrade I met Slobodan Milosevic, the President of Serbia, for the first time. Both Prime Minister Panic and President Cosic had tried to persuade us not to see him, but Cy Vance was, rightly, firmly of the view that though his star was waning we must keep up a relationship with him. He was the man with whom Cy had negotiated the crucial ceasefire in Croatia at the end of 1991, and he suspected that Milosevic was unlikely to remain on the sidelines for long. It was clear when we met that Milosevic had a deep respect for Cyrus, as he always called him. I talked little in these early meetings, measuring up Milosevic and trying slowly to build a relationship with him, knowing it would be a long time, if ever, before I could command the same authority with him as Cy did.

With President Cosic, however, I had as good a relationship as Cy from the start. It was encouraging that Cosic appeared to have distanced himself from Milosevic and was ready to play an active role as President of the FRY and to give more support to Milan Panic. We encouraged him then and subsequently as the legitimate counterweight to Panic's flamboyance. We thought he might be ready to build a sufficient electoral power base to challenge Milosevic in the elections for the Serbian Presidency, and indeed for a short time in November it looked as if Cosic might even beat Milosevic.

One of our initial tasks was to persuade the FRY army (JA) to leave the peninsula of Prevlaka, which was part of Croatia as recognized by the international community and from where they guarded the narrow entrance to the bay of Kotor (see Map 1).[25] This meant not only meeting with General Zivota Panic, who was as fat as Prime Minister Milan Panic was lean, but also going to the Serb military headquarters in Belgrade to talk with other key generals. For all of the military Prevlaka was a key strategic need, and it was little short of a miracle that we eventually reached a settlement whereby the JA withdrew allowing the UN to take their place. We could never have done this without first winning the confidence of Cosic and then, on the basis of that relationship, building a fruitful dialogue between Cosic and Tudjman. In the detailed records of our meetings over the next few months one can trace how these all-important human contacts were built up and how, slowly, these two old Serb and Croat nationalists began to respond to each other and realize that their two countries had to resolve their differences and live together.[26] Vance and I never shifted from the view that peace in the former Yugoslavia depended, above all else, on a Belgrade–Zagreb rapprochement. It was in many ways infuriating to watch and listen as the world's press and television concentrated only on Sarajevo and the war in Bosnia-Herzegovina. That was always going to be the yardstick on which the ICFY was judged, but the significance and importance of the ICFY's major contribution to peace in bringing the two key peoples, Croatians and Serbians, together was, with a few notable exceptions, ignored by journalists. One such exception was Misha Glenny, whose book *The Fall of Yugoslavia* is the most outstanding account of the Serb–Croat war and required reading for any serious student.

After my three-day visit to the region I flew back to London from Zagreb to go to Brocket Hall, where Douglas Hurd was holding an informal weekend meeting of EC Foreign Ministers. Debbie came with me and we stayed overnight on the Saturday, which was a pleasant and quick way of meeting all the Foreign Ministers. The twelve ministers were in effect my employers since I was answerable to the Foreign Affairs Council and in particular to the Presidency. EC foreign policy was made outside the Treaty of Rome at that stage, since the Maastricht Treaty had yet to be ratified, and I was not working within the formal Common Foreign and Security Policy (CFSP) framework but under the previous arrangement called European Political Cooperation.

Back in Geneva on 14 September we heard of four separate attacks launched that morning by the Bosnian Serb air force from Banja Luka. For me this was confirmation of the need for a no-fly zone over Bosnia-Herzegovina. I could not justify to myself, let alone to anyone else, continuing the arms embargo on the Bosnian government forces while they were being attacked from the air in this way. There was an obligation on us to compensate for the Bosnian Serb supremacy in arms by neutralizing wherever possible certain categories of weapons. We had tried to do this over heavy weapons, with very little success: it was already clear that the Karadzic–Hogg agreement was dead in the water, with the Serbs declaring only a derisory number of weapons and the UN only too happy to be relieved of a commitment which they had insufficient troops to implement without jeopardizing their convoy escorting role. We now had to redress the total imbalance in air power or face renewed and more credible demands for lifting the arms embargo.

The Bush administration had been showing some interest in banning all flights over Bosnia-Herzegovina except those authorized by the UN. The question was how to ensure that a ban was complied with and, though demands by the Security Council to stop flying sounded good, it was far preferable to negotiate an agreement, under threat of imposition. The FRY had already agreed to accept UN monitors on their airfields, but General Panic had refused ECMM monitors. There was however some anxiety in London and Paris about whether enforcement from the air could pose risks to UN personnel on the ground, as well as for any aircrew involved. Also, it was feared it might have an escalatory effect on the existing level of conflict. I was convinced that what we needed was a declaration from President Bush that the US air force would shoot down any plane violating Bosnian airspace.

UNSCR 770[27] had authorized the use of all necessary measures to facilitate, in coordination with the UN, the delivery of relief by reputable humanitarian organizations and agencies. On 14 September the Security Council passed Resolution 776,[28] carrying the concept further and representing a major extension of UNPROFOR's mandate. This enabled UNPROFOR throughout Bosnia-Herzegovina to provide the type of protective support for UNHCR convoys which they had hitherto provided around Sarajevo. Even so, it was judged that the convoys had first to pre-negotiate a safe passage which could be a tiresome business, with the Bosnian Serb leaders agreeing to allow convoys through while acquiescing in delaying tactics at lower levels. Some commentators all along wanted a more aggressive stance and often, as a substitute for criticizing their own governments for inaction, they became hostile critics of the UN. But what is the UN? Many who point the finger at the UN are deliberately avoiding the fact that while the Security Council decides the mandate, its interpretation is influenced by the troop-contributing countries, for example, in determining that the convoys would proceed on the basis of cooperation and would not fight their way through. Providing a light military escort of the sort requested by UNHCR might deter the types of deliberate attack that had been taking place all too frequently, but could not fight a convoy through.

On 15 September I circulated a COREU and briefed EC permanent representatives in Geneva.[29] I warned that while I expected significant progress from our visit to Belgrade, 'a full settlement between the Bosnian parties would take years.' Agreement on monitoring the borders of Bosnia-Herzegovina was proving to be very difficult and we encountered for the first time the totally insufficient numbers of UN personnel available for all the many tasks. In a note to David Hannay in New York I suggested that 'another possibility worth exploring could be to create a new cadre of monitors/observers which would operate under the authority of the Conference Co-Chairmen.' I tried this idea out again in May 1993, after the Bosnian Serb rejection of the Vance–Owen Peace Plan, but it was not until September 1994, after the Bosnian Serb rejection of the Contact Group map, that we established the ICFY Mission in Belgrade. This had the task of monitoring the FRY government's own ban on all goods, except humanitarian supplies, crossing the border towards areas controlled by the Bosnian Serbs.

On 29 September Izetbegovic was in Geneva and we wanted to bring him and Tudjman into a relationship with Cosic. When Izetbegovic had been in prison, Cosic had intervened on his behalf and when we did get them to meet together in Geneva under our auspices, Izetbegovic in a charming way acknowledged this and thanked him.

On 30 September President Cosic and President Tudjman signed a joint declaration in Geneva which built on our visit to Belgrade. The big break-through was the agreement that the Yugoslav army would leave Prevlaka on 20 October and security in the area would be resolved by demilitariza-tion and the deployment of UN monitors. This was then buttressed by the passing of SCR 779.[30] In addition we achieved in the declaration what could have been an important warning, stating that 'the two Presidents declare their total condemnation of all practices related to "ethnic cleansing", and commit themselves to helping reverse that which has already happened. They also declare that all statements or commitments made under duress, particularly those relating to land and property, are wholly null and void.' All over Bosnia and in Croatia people were being coerced into signing away their property and rights of residence, and we hoped this declaration would have a positive effect; but it was totally ignored.

Ethnic cleansing is an evil which the world must develop the will to counter. Cy and I were still influenced by our visit to Banja Luka on 25 September. We had flown down to Zagreb and driven through UNPA West to Banja Luka urgently in response to pleas from Red Cross and UNHCR officers on the ground who were becoming ever more alarmed at the deteri-orating situation for the local Croat and Muslim population. We knew that mere condemnation would not suffice and just hoped that our physical presence might serve as a warning. Dr Karadzic insisted on being present and met us at the Sava river UN crossing-point in the western UNPA, from where we drove past the Serb military airfield into Banja Luka. The city itself was much as I remembered it as a student, but the menacing mood that hung over our visit is hard to describe. A few weeks later on a visit to Kosovo I felt something similar. We met the mayor of Banja Luka and an extremely unpleasant General Ninkovic commanding the Bosnian Serb air force, who was adamant in rejecting a no-fly zone. We saw a number of brave Muslim leaders in a hotel but they were understandably frightened, having taken the risk of retribution for even coming to see us. A few days afterwards one of them was put in prison, though we later managed to have him released. He then disappeared and both he and his family later emigrated to the US, aided by Serb friends.

We had one meeting which gave us a measure of hope, with the Roman Catholic Bishop, the Muslim Mufti and the Orthodox Bishop of Banja Luka, all three of whom were unanimous in saying that totally unaccept-able pressure was being put on both Muslims and Croats in villages around Banja Luka, particularly Prijedor. On whether ethnic cleansing was being applied in Banja Luka itself there was less unanimity, but none of the three denied that undue pressure was present. We made our intense displeasure abundantly clear to Karadzic and it probably had some effect for this was a time when the authority of the Conference was at its height. Only after the US had allowed him to overturn the VOPP, in May 1993, would Karadzic dismiss our complaints about ethnic cleansing without blanching, knowing he could get away with it. In September 1992 he was making excuses that Pale did not have sufficient authority to stop ethnic cleansing, a claim we both told him was totally bogus. The uncontrollable Serbian elements blatantly doing what they wanted in the spring and early summer were by then capable of being controlled. What happened was that the Bosnian Serbs grew better at conducting campaigns of ethnic cleansing more clandestinely and therefore without arousing so much international anger, and the world grew more complacent.

At a meeting in Zagreb next day at UNPROFOR HQ we heard from an experienced UNHCR field worker of how he had come to the confrontation line between Banja Luka and Travnik and, from a small hill, had seen buses from Prijedor draw up off the road, a mile or more away, and watched as young and old were herded out and made to walk across 'no man's land' towards the waiting UNHCR vehicles. As they walked, weighed down by bags containing the few possessions that they had been able to gather up, the Serbs started to fire small arms over their heads and a few fell wounded or dying. Then, as they moved out of range, shell fire started and he watched as they struggled on stumbling and running as shells landed around them. Some were hit. He felt unable to do anything but stand transfixed by the horror of it all, suddenly realizing that tears were streaming down his face. As he spoke there was not a dry eye in the room; military men and politicians alike were all at a loss for words. We shuffled on to other business, but I doubt that anyone who heard him will ever forget it.

If there had been any doubt in my mind as to the need for urgency it vanished that day. The pace of the Conference, already that of a seven-day week, quickened as we all worked night and day to formulate our proposals. I wrote an account of all this to Douglas Hurd, as President of the Council of Foreign Ministers, asking for the deployment of UK forces for UNPROFOR to be accelerated and for some risks to be taken in resuming the humanitarian airlift to Sarajevo. I received an immediate and sympathetic reply. Our problem was that detainees in the camps were not being offered visas elsewhere in the world and the Croats were getting worried about accepting them from Bosnia with nowhere to move them on to. Even so, 1,600 former detainees were being evacuated from Trnopolje to Karlovac in Croatia.

We were by now acutely aware of the reluctance of Defence Ministers in all NATO capitals except Ankara to take on new commitments, and I knew that there was no support for suggestions that our troops should have their mandate extended beyond that of escorting convoys, for example to a role in stopping ethnic cleansing or being deployed at Prevlaka. At that stage our priority was to get the promised UN troops in to help with the humanitarian convoys as quickly as possible, for the winter stores needed to be built up.

The pressure for the declaration of a no-fly zone (NFZ) was growing, not unreasonably, all through September. There was still anxiety about the idea in some European capitals and we gathered from newspaper reports that General Colin Powell, the Chairman of the Joint Chiefs of Defense Staff in the US, was opposed. Douglas Hurd saw Vance and me in Geneva. We discussed an NFZ and he agreed that a Security Council Resolution to press the Bosnian Serbs to accept monitors on their airfield was needed. I noted at the time that Douglas had said that he personally felt the US would have to act if planes continued to fly and monitors were not accepted in open defiance of such a Resolution.

I was very keen on the NFZ, though I remembered how firmly President Mitterrand had ruled out any use of air power in the former Yugoslavia when I saw him. Even Cy Vance had his doubts about the practicability of such a measure, but he was content to let me go on pressurizing for a Resolution, and UNSCR 781 was passed on 9 October. Another reason why I wanted an NFZ was that I was worried that we could have Iranian aircraft landing at Tuzla which would so anger the Serbs that it would put all humanitarian efforts at risk, whether relief flights into Sarajevo or convoys throughout the country.

Our visit to Moscow on 10 October, where we met the Foreign Minister, Andrei Kozyrev, and Vitaly Churkin, was worthwhile. The Russian Foreign Ministry's knowledge of the former Yugoslavia, particularly that of their expert adviser, Alexei Nikiforov, was at that stage unmatched by any other country. They felt I was too sanguine over the chances of the Serbs moving on their two sacred cows – Kosovo and the Krajina – and also that if Cosic and Panic recognised Croatia they would be disowned in Belgrade and branded as national traitors. In truth, Vance was much more cautious than I over the Krajina and probably over autonomy for Kosovo as well, mainly because he knew the area better and, having spent months negotiating with Milosevic, knew the limits to his flexibility. Our jointly agreed tactic was to push Cosic and Panic towards Tudjman while trying to persuade Milosevic not to block their agreements, in effect letting Cosic take any political flak for decisions which Milosevic knew he would have to take responsibility for if he replaced Cosic.

On the basis of extensive travelling by their diplomats inside the FRY the Russians had concluded that while at first sanctions had drawn Serbs together in a determination to hold out against foreign bullying, the consensus had now begun to crack. In the northern areas and in the cities throughout the country there was clear evidence of a shift in opinion towards the policies of Panic, though not necessarily towards support for

Panic himself, as those most likely to rehabilitate the country. This feeling was particularly strong among the intelligentsia and the young. The main exception to this picture was southern Serbia, where support for Milosevic was strong and where the proximity of the 'Albanian threat' fuelled nationalist sentiment. Apparently, Cosic told the Russians in Belgrade on 13 October that Milosevic had now dropped his mask of reasonableness and must be fought openly to the last, and it appeared that Cosic was now genuinely concerned about the survival of Serbia. The Russians were even then trying to persuade the Sanctions Committee of the case for allowing Serbia to import natural gas for humanitarian reasons but also as a carrot for Belgrade's cooperation. They eventually succeeded in February 1995.

Vance and I agreed with the Russian analysis on Cosic and Panic and we began to pursue the strategy of persuading Cosic to challenge Milosevic for the Serbian Presidency in the elections likely before the end of the year. It was essential to persuade Panic to drop his own ambitions but to provide the energy and ideas behind Cosic. It is arguable that had Cosic not developed a recurrence of prostate trouble those close to him would have persuaded him to stand. Given the eventual result which Panic achieved, I believe that Cosic could have beaten Milosevic. After his removal from office by Milosevic, Cosic reverted somewhat to his earlier nationalistic stance, keeping links to Pale and opposing the pragmatism Milosevic showed in the summer of 1994 when he argued that the Contact Group plan could be the basis for a settlement. Milosevic later privately and self-mockingly referred to his performance in 1992 as being an unfortunate period when he made many mistakes. Perhaps it was the surprising success of Cosic and Panic which made him reassess his position. During October and November, we in ICFY were able to deal with two separate centres of power in Belgrade, and in doing so hopefully made Milosevic aware that he might not be the sole arbiter of what was going to happen in Croatia, Bosnia-Herzegovina and the FRY.

On 13 October I met with Karadzic in Geneva, after President Bush had said he would enforce a no-fly zone, and virtually pinned him to the wall. At long last I had a stick to our diplomacy. Herb Okun, wearing his American hat, described in vivid terms the consequences if flights continued, and Karadzic folded. He seemed attracted to the offer that all Bosnian Serb combat aircraft could fly to UN monitored airfields in the FRY, from where they could take part in strictly limited training flights; but, ominously as it turned out, his air force officers preferred to keep their aircraft in Banja Luka. In Belgrade on 14 October Cosic gave an interview for *Politika* in which he said that if he were in Milosevic's shoes he would resign, and in the Assembly he spoke out against corruption and the paramilitaries who were criminalizing life, warning of disorder spreading and morals declining. The day before, Milan Panic visited the Albanian leader Ibrahim Rugova in

Pristina and started what proved to be a fruitless attempt to persuade the Albanians in Kosovo not to boycott the forthcoming elections but to stand and in doing so weaken Milosevic's chances. It was clear that Cosic and Panic had decided that they could not recognize Croatia before the election and they would not go beyond the Vance Plan agreed by Milosevic, Tudjman and General Kadijevic and ratified by the Presidency of the FRY before eventually being accepted by the Krajina Serbs. They were also becoming concerned that their shift of position towards the Security Council was receiving no response and Milosevic's people were talking about 'Peanuts for Panic'. For the first but not for the last time in ICFY we felt the rigidity of a Security Council that either could not see the merit of or could not deliver the diplomatic carrot which could be as valuable as the stick of sanctions.

The winter snows were meanwhile fast approaching and Mrs Ogata, drawing on UNHCR experience on the ground, was warning that 'we are poised on the edge of a humanitarian nightmare. Almost three million people – refugees, displaced persons and people trapped in besieged cities and regions – are now directly affected by the conflict in Bosnia-Herzegovina, and dependent on external aid. The numbers continue to rise daily in an horrendous spiral.'

Cy Vance reported to the Security Council on 14 October that negotiations to end the conflict in Bosnia had been taking place on a continuous basis in Geneva since 18 September. Martti Ahtisaari, who chaired the Working Group on Bosnia-Herzegovina, had so far held with great skill some twenty-five sessions with representatives of the three warring communities. The goals were an overall cessation of hostilities, the demilitarization of Sarajevo and the devising of a constitution that would respond to the aspirations of the three constituent nations and would provide strong guarantees and enforcement mechanisms for human and minority rights.

I did not attend the European Council meeting in Birmingham on 16 October because I had my own little humanitarian crisis. I had been suffering from progressively worse sciatica with pains down my leg as I sat for hour after hour in the negotiations, but foolishly ignored all the clear neurological signs that this was serious and continued with meetings until I found my foot catching on the pavement and realized there was a muscle weakness that was giving me foot drop. This was a dangerous sign that the nerve was becoming permanently damaged, and I was told by a Swiss physician and then by a Swiss neurosurgeon that same day in Geneva that I needed an immediate operation to remove a disc. I should either fly straight back to London or come into the public hospital on Monday. I decided to stay in Geneva that weekend, in the flat I had taken in the old part of the city on the Place du Bourg de Four above a restaurant called Mortimers. Debbie flew over and I went into hospital and straight into the operating theatre on Monday morning. I was up walking that evening, left hospital the following afternoon and spent all the next day, Wednesday, sitting at my desk in the Palais des Nations. The surgeon had used microsurgical techniques to remove a lumbar disc, avoiding any weakening of the vertebral column, and by thus keeping the skeletal system totally intact enabled me to avoid the weeks and months of convalescence that previously used to follow such an operation.

On 25 October the HVO imposed its authority on Mostar in a way which challenged the continuation of the referendum coalition of Muslims and Croats. The Croatian military and political leadership claimed Mostar as the capital of 'Herzeg-Bosna' and said the HVO was the sole military authority. Stjepan Kljujic, a Bosnian Croat elected member of the Presidency who was due to be the next President when Izetbegovic's term of office expired again in December 1992, having in 1991 been unilaterally extended from a one-year rotating term, was keen on a multi-ethnic Bosnia. But he now lost control of the ruling HDZ party to Mate Boban, who said: 'I do not recognize the army of the republic of Bosnia-Herzegovina as representing the peoples of this country. It is a purely Muslim militia.' In taking this stance, Boban brought closer the Croat–Muslim war which led to the virtual destruction of Mostar. From this moment on we felt in all ICFY activity a marked change in Muslim–Croat relations: whereas before there had been suspicion and tension, now there was open hostility. Those who later claimed that the Vance–Owen Peace Plan unleashed ethnic cleansing and a civil war between the Croats and Muslims are quite wrong. The referendum coalition had been breaking apart throughout 1992. The Croats in the central Bosnian town of Prozor had by the end of October embarked on an ethnic cleansing campaign to rid the town of Muslims. Croat soldiers belonging to the extreme right-wing HOS militia were looting stores and burning houses. Having seen film footage from the scene I condemned the Bosnian Croat action in Prozor on Channel Four's 7 p.m. news programme on British television, and raised just a hint of imposing sanctions.[31] The protests of injured Croatian innocence were immediate. Mate Boban in particular, when I saw him next, became most indignant. But I had come forearmed: I actually gave him the Channel Four video film and asked him to watch it, and told him that if he had any comments Channel Four had agreed to film his response, giving it equal time and prominence. No Croatian answer came. The Western world kept quiet on events in Prozor and continued the double standard that surfaced during the Croat–Serb civil war, thereby losing some moral authority with the Serbs when condemning their admittedly far more extensive ethnic cleansing.

In Sarajevo it became ever clearer that there were in fact two sieges of the city: one by the Bosnian Serb army, with shells, sniper fire and blockades, and the other by the Bosnian government army, with internal blockades and red tape bureaucracy which kept their own people from leaving. In a radio broadcast the army – not the government – said that able bodied men aged 18–65 years and women aged 18–60 years were forbidden to leave because they were needed for the city's defence; but their main reason was different. In the propaganda war the Serbian siege aroused the sympathy of the world, and for this they needed the elderly and the children to stay. It was their most emotive propaganda weapon for bringing the Americans in to fight the war, and they never wanted it to be weakened.

The French and British troop contributions to the UN humanitarian intervention were by now coming in in reasonable numbers but to understandable concern for their safety. French and British press comment was focusing on whether they had the right to shoot to kill if fired on, which in fact they did have. At the 18 October North Atlantic Council (NAC) Manfred Woerner, the NATO Secretary-General, reported that Hungary and Austria had given political approval to establishing an airborne early warning system (AWACS) orbit and to the necessary overflights so that violations of Bosnian air space could from now on be reported to UNPROFOR by NATO. Since my negotiations with Karadzic on 13 October it looked as if the Bosnian Serb planes would not fly from Banja Luka, though some left clandestinely for the airfield controlled by the Croatian Serbs at Udbina. But while the monitoring by NATO was worthwhile, there was still no readiness by NATO governments to enforce an NFZ with regular combat patrols, something which started only in 1993.

On 29 October Cyrus Vance and I flew down to Pristina in Kosovo, which the Serbs consider the cradle of their civilization, on what was one of the more extraordinary visits that I have ever been involved in. Prime Minister Panic was to accompany us, which was nothing if not brave; some would say foolhardy. In November he said to Simone Veil in the European Parliament: 'the less I know about the history of the Balkans the better I feel.' Rather stuffily in retrospect, we declined to fly in his plane, but on arrival we were obliged to go into the small office at the airport and meet with the local Serb officials. We had already indicated that we had no wish to do this, but Panic explained it was vital we did, both as a courtesy and to maintain his own authority. Approximately 3,000 Serbs carrying photographs of Milosevic and Seselj, the rabidly nationalist leader of the Radical Party, paraded with banners telling Panic to 'go back to California'. Speakers at the rally from Seselj's party spoke against Panic's meddling with the vital interests of the Serbian nation and a letter to us as Co-Chairmen called for the banning of foreign delegations from Kosovo as they provoked unrest. We separated from Panic, who was going to talk to the Serb local authority representatives, and went to see the Albanian nationalist leader Ibrahim Rugova. As we approached Pristina in the car a deep sense of gloom descended on me. Everything looked depressingly drab, the worst of

Communist architecture, and there was no sense of a proud history, no ancient monuments being visible, just dirt, grime and a foreboding of doom. Rugova was in a 'shanty town' office and to walk in you had to jump across large puddles of water. Inside, however, the welcome was warm and we eventually agreed that he would come with us to meet Panic in the official City Hall building; but he was firmly against meeting the representatives of the local Serb authorities. We did not press him at that stage. When we arrived we saw Panic, who was adamant that we should meet the Serbs with or without Rugova. So, leaving Rugova in an ante-room, we went into a meeting which can only be described as bedlam to find Panic berating the local Serbs with gusto and clearly enjoying himself.

Panic was a 63-year-old Californian who spoke English with a Serb accent and Serbo-Croat with an American accent. He had defected from Yugoslavia in 1955 during an international bicycle race when he had been a successful racer. He always claimed that 'I bicycled to freedom' and arrived in the US with two suitcases and $20, from which he soon became a millionaire. His present company was worth half a billion dollars. He later described the talks as 'rough but constructive'. We felt for a moment that we were making headway in persuading them to negotiate over the return of the Albanian schoolchildren who were being taught in their homes to their primary schools. But even that was too much for the local Serbs to concede to Panic, who would then have exploited his success against Milosevic, something they were not prepared to countenance. As we flew away I was appalled by what we had seen and felt there was no immediate prospect of even minimal autonomy being granted to the Albanians, let alone a reversion to the very considerable degree of autonomy which had operated under Tito.

UN trusteeship for Bosnia-Herzegovina was much in vogue in the newspapers. In fact, Cy Vance and I had had our first discussion on this option when we had met for lunch in New York on 6 August. Both of us were attracted to the concept then, and we discussed the issue on a number of occasions. Cy had passed me a copy of a memo written on the subject by Lloyd Cutler, a distinguished Washington lawyer whom I had met when he was working for the Carter administration. On 22 October I set out in a handwritten note for Cy why it was no longer feasible, mainly because of a lack of UN resources, both human and financial.[32]

There is no gainsaying that at this key moment in the formulation of a peace plan for Bosnia-Herzegovina we were all reluctantly but realistically facing the fact that we would never have substantial UN forces for implementation. Doubling the 7,000 humanitarian intervention force was the most we thought we could rely on from the Security Council, and a UN force of 15,000 was what Generals Nambiar and Morillon took as their target figure in working on their plans for implementing our peace plan with the demilitarization of Sarajevo, the withdrawal of heavy weapons and the withdrawal of armed forces to agreed peace settlement lines.

On 4 October we had received from Martti Ahtisaari an important paper on constitutional options, setting out the pros and cons of each.[33] For Vance and me, the five options essentially were:

1 a centralized state;
2 a centralized federal state with significant functions carried out by between four and ten regions;
3 a loose federal state of three ethnic units, not geographically continuous;
4 a loose confederation of three ethnically determined republics with significant independence, possibly even in the security field;
5 a Muslim state, with Serbs becoming part of the FRY and Croats becoming part of Croatia.

We chose option 2 as the basis for what became known as the Vance–Owen Peace Plan – the VOPP – because, as the working paper argued, it seemed the best compromise among the widely differing positions of the three parties and promised the most stable governmental form for the whole of Bosnia-Herzegovina, since much of the predicted intercommunal friction could be kept from the central government by giving the provinces competence over the most divisive issues, e.g. police, education, health and culture, while depriving them of the right to be a state within a state. Instead, however, of adopting the description of this structure as 'a centralized federal state', which was almost a contradiction in terms with 'federal' meaning many different things to different people, we called it a 'decentralized state'.

We thought hard about option 3, which was essentially that negotiated by Ambassador Cutileiro, as part of Lord Carrington's team, in the spring of 1992;[34] but even though President Izetbegovic had first accepted it on 18 March he had later changed his mind,[35] and we felt this rejection was too recent to give a plan on these lines any chance of acceptance in the international community, let alone by Izetbegovic. Much depended on the number of cantons: the Serbs wanted one large canton for themselves; others wanted many cantons, which would be difficult and more costly to govern than provinces. The US government had not liked the canton proposal then, and in the light of the London Conference anything which smacked of partition would not have been easily accepted. The core belief of the Steering Committee governments was for keeping Bosnia and Herzegovina together as one country and ensuring that the Serbs did not profit from their military actions. An important consideration in choosing provinces was that this concept had already been discussed by the parties. On 21 October President Izetbegovic gave an important press conference in Geneva after our discussions with him, at which he endorsed our chosen option in principle.

While we were designing a provincial map based on opstinas (see pp. 64–5) the real map reflecting the fighting on the ground was still changing. The fall of Jajce to the Serbs was a big blow to the Bosnian government forces, but it proved to be the last major Serb land gain. Thereafter, until the fall of Srebrenica and Zepa to the Serbs in July 1995, the confrontation line never changed in major strategic respects except for a few weeks in 1994 when the Bosnian 5th Corps broke out of the Bihac pocket. The biggest change occurred in September 1995 when Jajce fell to the Croats.

On 27 October the second meeting of the Steering Committee of the ICFY took place and in a restricted session Martti Ahtisaari presented a constitutional paper.[36] We had made a direct link between the cessation of hostilities and finding a constitutional settlement since we did not believe the parties would really stop shooting without at least an outline agreement. In view of later attitudes it was interesting that Warren Zimmerman, the senior representative of the US, stated that it was an impressive document and contained all of the relevant principles, and wanted to make representations straight away in support of our constitutional idea. We counselled delay, at least until we had presented it to the parties the following day. We said that the Co-Chairmen would be seeking endorsement of these proposals in two days' time in Belgrade and straight afterwards in Zagreb. In the main the Steering Committee was very supportive and governments' representatives' anxieties focused on the transitional period.

The Bosnian government was initially enthusiastic, to the extent that the Foreign Minister Haris Silajdzic pulled Herb Okun aside and asked that our constitutional proposals be 'imposed' on all parties. In presenting our constitutional proposals to the Bosnian Serbs, we felt the key would be to demonstrate that we had taken the process of decentralization as far as we could without creating states within a state. At a joint session of the Serbian, Krajina and Bosnian Serb Assemblies at Prijedor the following weekend, Karadzic described the ICFY proposals for the constitution as a basis for future negotiations. But he rejected the proposed division into ten provinces and instead proposed a division into five – one united Serbian area stretching from Banja Luka to Bijeljina to Trebinje, three Muslim cantons with their centres at Tuzla, Zenica and Cazin, and one for the Croats around Mostar. He opposed any form of Bosnian confederation or central control of military, foreign and monetary policy, but this was wholly predictable. The ICFY position at this time was that a minimum of seven units was essential in order to have a sufficient mix of provinces so that the provincial map did not embody disguised partition, and so that the multi-ethnic nature of the country would be preserved.

November started with Prime Minister Panic subject to a vote of no confidence. The Serbian Socialist Party (under Milosevic) and the Serbian

	% Muslim	% Serb	% Croat	% Yugoslav and Oyher
Sarajevo	49	28	7	16
Centar	51	21	7	22
Hadzici	64	26	3	7
Ilidza	43	37	10	10
Ilijas	42	45	7	6
Novi Grad	51	28	6	15
Novo Sarajevo	36	35	9	20
Pale	27	69	0	3
Stari Grad	78	10	2	9
Trnovo	69	30	0	1
Vogosca	51	36	4	9
Banovici	72	17	2	9
Banja Luka	15	55	15	16
Bihac	67	18	8	8
Bijelijina	31	59	0	9
Bileca	15	80	0	5
Bos. Dubica	20	69	2	9
Bos Gradiska	26	60	6	8
Bos. Krupa	74	24	0	2
Bos. Brod	12	34	41	13
Bos. Novi	34	60	1	5
Bos. Petrovac	21	75	0	3
Bos. Samac	7	41	45	7
Bos Grahovo	0	95	3	2
Bratunac	64	34	0	2
Brcko	44	21	25	9
Breza	76	12	6	7
Bugojno	42	19	34	5
Busovada	45	3	48	4
Cazin	98	1	0	1
Cajnice	45	53	0	2
Capljina	28	14	54	5
Celinac	8	89	0	3
Citluk	0	0	99	0
Derventa	13	41	39	8
Duboj	40	39	13	8
Donji Vakuf	55	39	3	3
Foca	52	45	0	3
Fojnica	49	0	41	9
Gacko	35	62	0	2
Glamoc	18	79	1	1
Gorazde	70	26	0	3
Gornji Vakuf	56	0	43	1
Grancanica	72	23	0	5
Gradacac	60	20	15	5
Grude	0	0	99	0
Han Pijesak	40	58	0	2
Jablanica	72	4	18	6
Jajce	39	19	35	7
Kakanj	55	9	30	2
Kalesija	80	18	0	2
Kalinovik	37	61	0	2
Kiseljak	41	3	52	4
Kladanj	73	24	0	3
Kijuc	48	50	0	2
Konjic	55	15	26	4
Kotar Varos	30	38	29	3
Kresevo	23	0	71	6
Kupres	7	51	39	3
Laktasi	2	82	9	8
Listica	0	0	99	0
Livno	15	10	72	3
Lopare	38	56	4	3
Lukavac	67	22	4	8
Ljubinje	8	90	1	1
Ljubiski	6	0	93	1
Maglaj	45	31	19	5
Modrica	29	35	27	8
Mostar	35	19	34	12
Mrkonjic Grad	12	77	8	3
Neum	5	5	88	3
Nevesinje	23	74	1	1

	% Muslim	% Serb	% Croat	% Yugoslav and Oyher
Odzak	20	20	54	6
Olovo	75	19	4	2
Orasje	7	15	75	3
Posusje	0	0	99	0
Prijedor	44	42	6	8
Prnjavor	15	72	4	9
Prozor	37	0	62	1
Pucarevo	38	13	40	9
Rogatica	60	38	0	1
Rudo	27	71	0	2
Sanski Most	47	42	7	4
Skendar Vakuf	6	68	25	1
Sokolac	30	69	0	1
Srbac	4	89	0	6
Srebrenica	73	25	0	2
Srebrenik	75	13	7	5
Stolac	45	21	32	2
Sekovici	3	94	0	2
Sipovo	19	79	0	1
Teslic	21	55	16	7
Tesanj	72	6	18	3
Titov Drvar	0	97	0	2
Tomislavgrad	11	2	87	0
Travnik	45	11	37	7
Trebinje	18	69	4	9
Tuzla	48	15	16	21
Ugijevik	41	56	0	3
Vares	30	16	41	13
Velika Kladusa	92	4	1	3
Visoka	75	16	4	5
Visegrad	63	33	0	4
Vitez	41	5	46	8
Vlasenica	55	42	0	2
Zavidovici	60	20	13	6
Zenica	55	16	16	13
Zvornik	59	38	0	3
Zepce	47	10	40	3
Zivince	81	6	7	6

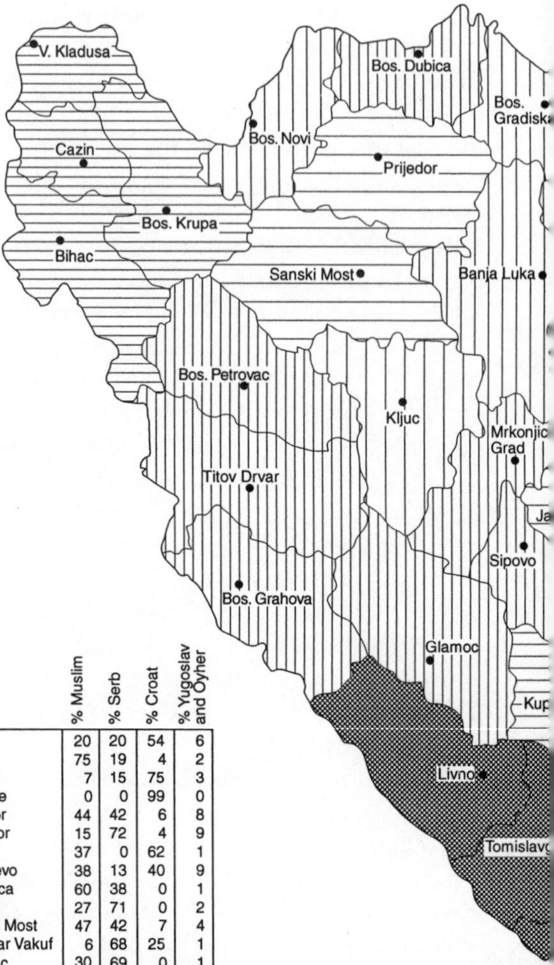

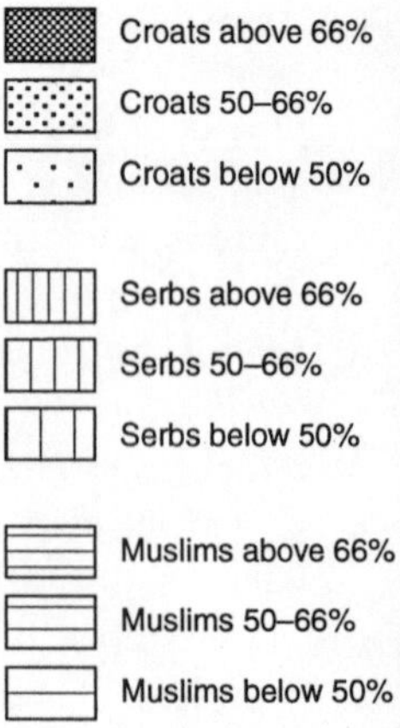

Map legend:

- Croats above 66%
- Croats 50–66%
- Croats below 50%
- Serbs above 66%
- Serbs 50–66%
- Serbs below 50%
- Muslims above 66%
- Muslims 50–66%
- Muslims below 50%

Map labels: V. Kladusa, Bos. Dubica, Bos. Gradiska, Cazin, Bos. Novi, Prijedor, Bos. Krupa, Bihac, Sanski Most, Banja Luka, Bos. Petrovac, Kljuc, Mrkonjic Grad, Titov Drvar, Ja..., Sipovo, Bos. Grahova, Glamoc, Kup..., Livno, Tomislav...

Map 3 Bosnia-Herzegovina by opstina (district)

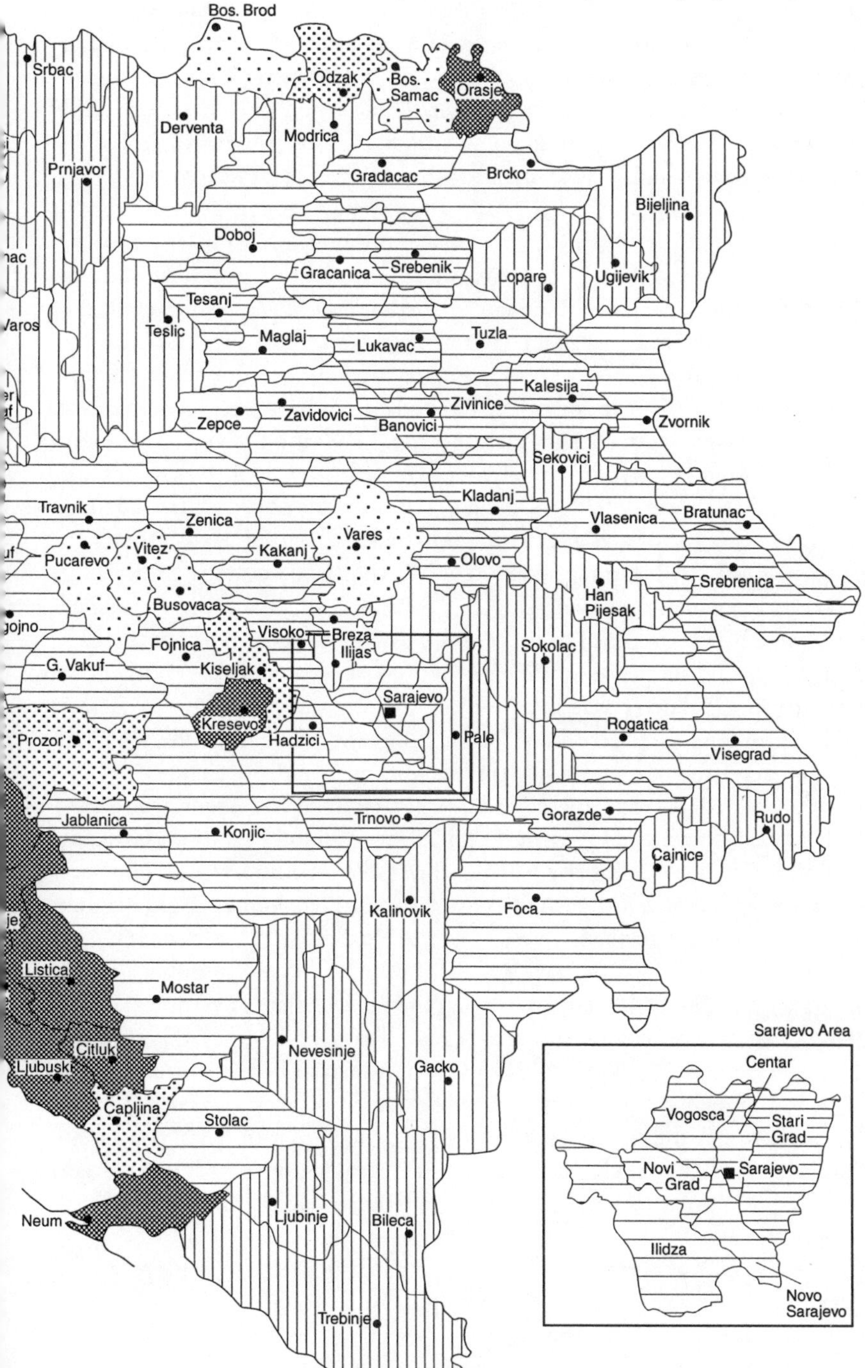

Radical Party (under Seselj), then in close collaboration with Milosevic, were totally against Panic for undermining the continuity of Yugoslavia by publicly calling for foreign involvement in Yugoslavia's internal politics and opening up the sensitive question of territorial integrity by allowing foreign mediation in Kosovo. As Prime Minister, Panic could only be removed if there was a majority censuring him in both Houses. In the Chamber of Citizens his critics had a clear majority but in the Chamber of Republics, where the Montenegrins had half the seats, Panic looked as if he might survive, with Cosic also using his influence in the Prime Minister's favour.

The policy of providing 'safe areas' was inadvertently given a substantial boost at this time when the President of the International Committee of the Red Cross (ICRC), Mr Cornelio Sommaruga, talked to the heads of the permanent missions in Geneva and launched the ICRC recommendation for the immediate setting-up of agreed 'protected zones' to accommodate vulnerable groups within Bosnia-Herzegovina. In addition to the one million people in Bosnia-Herzegovina who badly needed supplies, the ICRC calculated that there were 100,000 Muslims living in the north of the country who were being terrorized and whose only wish was to be transferred to a safe area. Additionally, there were the 4,000 vulnerable citizens gathered at the Trnopolje camp near Banja Luka. Given that no third country seemed ready, even on a provisional basis, to grant asylum to these Bosnian refugees we did face an immense challenge; but, as Vance and I explained to Sommaruga, the danger was that his well-intentioned proposal, which was based on obtaining the consent of the Bosnian Serbs and the Bosnian Muslims' agreement to effective demilitarization, would be changed by the Security Council so that there was neither consent nor demilitarization, which is exactly what happened. The ICFY was doing everything possible to build up its moral authority to halt ethnic cleansing and we thought that to make it apparent that Muslims pushed out of their homes could go into safe areas would be to flash a green light to the Serbs that ethnic cleansing could go ahead. UNHCR agreed with us, but felt inhibited in publicly criticizing governments who were advocating the policy. Also, governments who did not like the 'safe area' concept were all too hesitant to take on the arguments publicly. So it fell to us as Co-Chairmen to bear the brunt of the emotive arguments and to counter· the despairing, if understandable, advocacy of 'safe areas' which seemed to provide a platform for concerned protest. The policy was championed by the Austrian government and, rather like lifting the arms embargo, it had a superficial appeal that soon gained many adherents.

The flaws in the plan were clearly apparent to those who were prepared to ask and answer the tough questions. First and foremost, who was going to provide sufficient UN troops to man the 'safe areas'? Who was ready to insist that the Bosnian Muslims withdrew their troops? What happened if the Serbs attacked a 'safe area' with ground forces, as later happened over Gorazde? Instead of being a facilitator of humanitarian assistance deploying on the boundary of a safe area, the UN would be forced by such an attack into the position of defending, withdrawing or being overrun. To defend the perimeter was coming too close to a combatant role for most troop-contributing governments, and we knew the mandate for the humanitarian forces had been carefully designed to avoid this very situation. The creation of a safe area in Iraq had been done after the Kurds had fled, and it was marked by a line on a flat plain enforceable by allied air forces. In Bosnia we had to create 'safe areas' of towns in valleys surrounded by mountains, on many of which Serb forces already sat with heavy weapons, ready and able to cut off water and electricity, block road access and shoot down circling planes. The UN military argued passionately against the pretence of 'safe' areas, which they knew the Bosnian Serb commander Ratko Mladic had no intention of honouring if they were not demilitarized.[37]

The daunting challenge for the ICFY in November 1992 was whether, armed only with moral authority and weak economic sanctions, and with no credible threat of selective counterforce, we could roll back the Serb confrontation lines and create a new map. We took it as our mandate that we would have to ensure that the three constituent peoples lived within the internationally recognized boundaries of Bosnia-Herzegovina. Our task was to devise a structure whereby Serbs could retain control of those aspects of daily life that preserved and safeguarded their national identity. We could not, however, accept a state within a state and therefore had to avoid as far as we could a geographical continuity of Serb provinces such that Serbs could effectively control territory from Belgrade to Bijeljina in the north-east of Bosnia-Herzegovina, then the territory below the Sava river along a corridor to Banja Luka and thence to Knin inside Croatia. I knew from my first encounter with Mladic that such a territorial link was an absolute security need for him and something for which he was ready to continue to fight with the support of all Serb military leaders, wherever they came from. An essential calculation for the ICFY as we came to finalize our map would be to judge the strength of the Bosnian Serb army in relation to politicians in Belgrade, Pale and Knin. In retrospect, we underestimated General Mladic's influence.

In Belgrade in early November the Serbian police raided the Federal Interior Ministry building, which President Cosic of the FRY denounced as an act of violence which threatened the country's constitutional order. No explanation has ever been offered as to what the Serbian police were after in this sinister foray, but many assumed that they were desperate to remove any incriminating files from the 1991–2 period relating to possible war crimes. The Security Council was at the time debating the work of the commission of experts established under UNSCR 780 (1992),[38] and a high press profile was being given to war crimes with the request that the experts should actively pursue grave breaches of the Geneva Conventions and other violations. Cy Vance had also been pressing General Panic whenever we met in Belgrade about the Vukovar mass grave. Vance was convinced that he had been stopped from visiting the hospital in Vukovar back in 1991 by the Serbs because Croat patients were being taken from hospital wards, murdered and put into a mass grave in the countryside, and that the JNA were implicated. People who carried responsibility for starting and prosecuting the war, first in Croatia and then in Bosnia-Herzegovina, had every reason to fear that Prime Minister Panic might impulsively order that the files should be opened for investigation. It is easy to forget how polarized Belgrade had become between Milosevic as President of Serbia and Cosic as President of the FRY, each one at that stage determined that the other should resign. Another rumour going around Belgrade was that Milosevic's police were after files implicating Cosic. There was little doubt that paramilitary groups close to the government, in particular those led by a young thug called Arkan and the nationalist Seselj, had committed war crimes. On 9 November the Belgrade Municipal Court ordered the Serbian police and officials to evacuate the federal building, but they ignored the demand and the files were removed or destroyed.

Another essential before fixing the map was to try to carry Turkey with our policy and we felt it important, therefore, to visit Prime Minister Demirel. Vance and I met with him in Ankara on 4 November and found him persuasive when he told us of the real frustration throughout the Islamic world about Western 'idleness' and 'inactivity' over Bosnia-Herzegovina. He put the case for lifting the arms embargo and also criticized the ineffectiveness of sanctions; his call for a tightening-up was instantly passed on by Vance, who advised Boutros Ghali that this was something the Security Council should be 'prodded on'. But there was also a strand of practical realism from a man we both knew as a practitioner of the art of the possible. We did not convince him, but felt we had not alienated him.

In New York on 12 November Vance and I spoke to President Gligorov about a preventive deployment of UN troops in Macedonia. The British EC Presidency, whom I informed about our conversation, wanted us as Co-Chairmen to push the issue with Boutros Ghali rather than let the EC do this. We wrote a letter dated 18 September,[39] and I think it was an important factor in persuading the UN Secretary-General to write to the Security Council.[40]

On Friday 13 November I spoke to the Security Council,[41] saying that the Serb front line 'has to be rolled back and there is no way in which the international community can accept General Mladic's philosophy that "might is right and what they have they hold"'. I also drew attention to 'the gaping holes in the current oil embargo whether on the Danube, the

Romanian, Bulgarian or Macedonian border or on the Montenegrin coast on the Adriatic where oil is coming in by tankers'. Our concern had been triggered by finding on our most recent visit that Belgrade was suddenly awash with oil. Where long car queues had wound around the block for petrol we now found petrol stations dispensing petrol with no queues and the price had fallen dramatically. There was no hope for a peace settlement in Bosnia-Herzegovina unless Belgrade put pressure on the Bosnian Serbs to deal, and Belgrade in this relaxed atmosphere would have no incentive to push Pale. It was widely thought that Milosevic had released army fuel reserves in order to create a better atmosphere before the December elections, and free flour and sugar were made available to employees in state enterprises.

In New York Cy Vance and Herb Okun had a meeting in Cy's flat with Anthony Lake after Clinton's defeat of Bush in the presidential election. Lake had been in the State Department as a Head of the Policy Planning Staff under Cy and was now due to become the new National Security Adviser. Apparently the issue he raised repeatedly with them was the moral case for lifting the arms embargo, but Cy and Herb never gave me any impression that we were likely to have the difficulties ahead with the new administration that we were soon to encounter. Later in December, when they went down to Washington to talk to President Bush and called in at the Democrats' Transitional Office and spoke to Samuel Berger and Leon Fuerth, they found them not only going on about the arms embargo but also querying whether we were accepting too much ethnic cleansing. I did not know at the time that at Washington dinner parties aspiring candidates for the new Clinton administration were apparently criticizing Cy Vance on Yugoslavia as being ready to negotiate until the last man remained alive. In retrospect, our antennae in Geneva should have been more focused on Washington and on picking up the signs of a build-up in negative perceptions of the Geneva-based ICFY.

We left New York having witnessed the passage of UNSCR 787, which prohibited the transshipment of oil just in time to restore some credibility to the position on sanctions against the FRY, and also restored some leverage to us as Co-Chairmen. On 18 November I was sufficiently worried about Mladic's military attitude destabilizing the constitutional talks to send a personal telegram to Douglas Hurd in his capacity as President of the Council of Foreign Ministers to ask for enforcement of the no-fly zone under Chapter VII of the UN Charter.[42] This telegram revealed my private thoughts, which I could not always express publicly. I wanted 'no-fly' enforcement as a sign to the Serbs that we meant business, but as France, Britain and most other EC countries were against this, I could not say so in public, where I had to voice the EC consensus. Also, as a negotiator, I had to be sparing in my references to military pressure on the Serbs if I did not have EC support. The Serbs for their part still felt that I was more anti-Serb than Vance and far readier to bomb them into submission.

While back in Geneva the Bosnian Serbs presented a 'Proposal on Arrangement of Bosnia-Herzegovina',[43] Vance and I visited the four UNPAs in Croatia between 19 and 20 November. It was becoming clear that the Vance Plan was not being implemented and we needed to find out if anything could be done to recover lost momentum. We visited the Maslenica Bridge, which had been destroyed in the war and had to be reopened to allow Croat traffic and tourist cars and buses to flow down the main road on the Dalmatian coast. We also stood on top of the Peruca Dam, rather gingerly since it was thought to have large quantities of dynamite placed in its power plant which, if triggered by the Serbs, would blow up the dam and flood the area. Both of these issues had been endlessly discussed in Belgrade, Zagreb and Geneva and it was useful to see the problems on the ground.

In Knin we had a dreadful meeting with the Croatian Serbs, who refused to countenance anything but secession and pretended they were an independent government with their own Foreign Minister. I was adamant that we would make it clear that we considered we were in Croatia, a fact the UN tended to walk around with semantic blurring. My definition provoked a rant about how this was an independent Serb republic. I was called by one Serb leader on their local radio a rogue and a Serb-hater, whereas Vance was described as 'tolerant'. Driving into the Northern UNPA that same evening it was noticeable that very few houses had any electric light, and the battle-scarred villages we drove through appeared deserted.

The Croatian government was understandably determined from the start to avoid a repeat of what had happened in Cyprus, with the UN presence entrenching the de facto partition of the island, and so they never abided by the ceasefire. That fundamental and unavoidable tension kept an incipient Serb–Croat war simmering in the background, always dangerous and providing the fuel for an increasing disillusionment of the Croatian people and government with the UN, seen as being responsible for the status quo. As memories of how awful the war had been faded, so more Croats began to be readier to risk another war, particularly as the Croatian forces were becoming ever better equipped. By late 1992 the arms embargo was barely touching Croatia, and though the FRY sent details of arms coming in to the Security Council nothing was done to halt the supplies. Soon the Croatian army was being equipped with planes, tanks and heavy artillery, most of it coming in from surrounding European countries having been bought in what was East Germany. As this was happening in full view of the Serbs it was not hard to see why they resisted demilitarization and refused to demobilize. The Croatian Serbs were the consolidators and the Croatian government the destabilizers. The Croatian government needed to convince the Croatian Serbs that they had nothing to fear in living under their rule if there was to be peace, but they believed this would only encourage the Serb leaders to remain independent. It was a Catch-22 situation. Tudjman's style was diplomacy by histrionics, but nevertheless, from the Croat point of view, it was effective. The Croatian government-controlled press constantly identified UN peacekeepers as failing to allow Croats to return to their homes, and at times came close to depicting them as the enemies of the state, an attitude reflected in the vulgar signs flashed at passing white UN vehicles on the roads.

By the time we helicoptered into the Eastern UNPA I was beginning to despair as to how we could settle these conflicting aims. This mood was further deepened when I discovered that, far from Croats returning to their homes, Serbs in increasing numbers were arriving from other parts of former Yugoslavia, particularly Bosnia-Herzegovina, and were being relocated in Sector East. This was ethnic accretion, understandably seen by the Croats as an attempt to change the demographics of the area by creating a permanent Serbian majority where before the 1991 war there had been a Croatian majority. The large influx of Serb refugees was also leading to Serb-on-Serb violence with gang activity, extortion and protection rackets. All this was happening under the nose of the UN civilian police, who saw their role passively, as was explained to us 'to observe and report on the activities of local police and authorities and to cultivate good relationships with all residents'. Given the circumstances in Croatia at that time, and particularly after the war in Bosnia-Herzegovina started, which changed the priority that the UN could give to the Vance Plan, it was impossible to see how the UN could become anything other than the butt of everyone in Croatia, unloved and unappreciated. Unable to bring refugees back until the Serb militia were disarmed, the UN lacked the resolve, and arguably also the power, to disarm the Serbs forcibly. Deadlock continued over the next two and a half years, until in January 1995 President Tudjman deliberately tried to bring all his people's dissatisfactions to a head by unilaterally declaring that the UN mandate would end on 31 March 1995. Our visit was a sad occasion for Cy Vance, but he took the criticism of his plan from the UN people we met in the Eastern UNPA on the chin with no attempt to cover up its deficiencies, which were laid before us with painful clarity at our briefings.[44] The alternative, however, was war.

A key country in the region was Greece. When Prime Minister Mitsotakis met Vance and myself on 23 November in Geneva he said that he was ready to visit Belgrade and meet Milosevic if we and the British Prime Minister thought it useful. Panic had raised this question at a meeting with us on 25 November and he and his advisers expressed strong opposition on the grounds that such a visit would only strengthen Milosevic's position. Panic felt Greece was Milosevic's only friend in the EC, and that Milosevic would use his control of the media to portray the visit to his advantage. I advised London, as the Presidency, that on balance such a visit would not be useful since I suspected that Mitsotakis' visit would give the appearance of his being an envoy from the EC, with the personal endorsement of the British Prime Minister as President of the EC, whereas if he did go I thought it would be better for him to do so on his own initiative. But it was important that Greece, which supported our constitutional proposals, should exert influence on all the political factions in Belgrade and I urged Mitsotakis to do so. Later, over the VOPP, he was consistently helpful. A tall, commanding figure from Crete, his shrewdness and influence on Milosevic were certainly beneficial.

On 25 November Martti Ahtisaari sent invitations to President Izetbegovic, Dr Karadzic and Mr Boban to attend a meeting in Geneva starting on 7 December at which the Co-Chairmen would be present and which was expected to last for two days. He sent a map of Bosnia-Herzegovina with only the local government opstinas marked, and invited them all to put forward their ideas on the delimitation of provinces.

That same day I went to see the Spanish Prime Minister, Felipe Gonzales, and Foreign Minister, Javier Solana, in Madrid. The Spanish army was deployed in and around Mostar and was having a difficult task as Muslim–Croat relations deteriorated. I urged extreme caution on the issue of 'safe areas' and Gonzales strongly agreed that there was a risk of the worst possible decision being taken with the best of intentions. I asked whether a situation around the Spanish deployment area in Mostar could develop similar to that with French and British troops in Bihac and Vitez, who had been able to give refugees a sense of security; we might use the form of words 'relief centres'. The Spanish promised to do what they could.

Then President Tudjman invited Cy and Gay Vance, Debbie and me to come to the island of Brioni for a social weekend. It had been Tito's favourite place to stay and I hoped we would have time to discuss some of the more challenging concepts that I had in mind about how to break out of the rigid box which the world had made for both Croats and Serbs at the time of recognition. Could we break the deadlock by means of a comprehensive settlement? This was a delicate area for me, since the EC countries had rejected this in July 1991 and some were very sensitive at any hint of border changes. But my job was to think the unthinkable and to challenge conventional attitudes.[45]

My ambitions for confederal links and border adjustments became more modest as I walked around the beautiful island of Brioni with Tudjman and his Defence Minister Susak. Without giving much away, they made their underlying views pretty clear: they saw Knin as a crucial communication link and they would not give control of it to the Serbs under any circumstances. Even autonomy for the Krajina was highly suspect, and confederal linkage

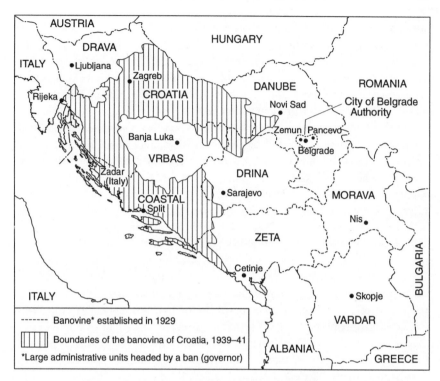

Map 4 Cvetkovic–Macek map, 1939

was going far too far. They were not prepared to reveal their hand on the Eastern UNPA. The most they were ready to talk about and actively consider was minor adjustments; and they were not ready to consider any boundary changes in advance of an overall peace settlement. I knew at this early stage that Tudjman had accepted recognition of Bosnia-Herzegovina within its internationally agreed boundaries as a necessary price for recognition of Croatia, but had never hidden his belief that Bosnia-Herzegovina was not sustainable, and the Cvetkovic–Macek map was more than a glint in his eye.

On Brioni, picking fruit, tasting wine, walking and boating, I got to know Franjo Tudjman. He was born in 1922 in Veliko Trziste in Croatia. He joined the Partisans in 1941, yet he is never very keen to talk about this period of his life. Having fought the Fascist Pavelic and his Ustashas, he now depends on much of Pavelic's indigenous support. It was deeply provocative, even allowing for its historic links, to the Serbs in Croatia for his government to choose to adopt the same symbol that Pavelic used, the red-and-white chequerboard, for the flag of an independent Croatia. But for Tudjman I suspect his Second World War years when he fought Pavelic represent the indiscretion of youth. Far from using his Partisan past to bind up the wounds between Croats and Serbs living in Croatia, he prefers to speak with pride of having been arrested and sentenced by Tito's regime to two years' imprisonment in the early 1970s, to play up his part in the 'Croatian Spring' unrest and his imprisonment for 'hostile propaganda' in 1981. His political development probably started while he was a senior figure in JNA intelligence, watching over the very Croatians living in exile who later became some of his most fervent supporters. He left the JNA with the rank of major general in 1960. As a civilian he worked as Director of the Institute for the History of the Workers Movement in Zagreb and served on the Executive Committee of the Matica Hrvatska, the Croatian cultural society, where the Croatian intelligentsia had gathered until it was suppressed by Tito. In 1967 he published a 'Declaration on Croatian Literary Language' and then resigned from all his quasi-government posts and was expelled from the League of Communists of Yugoslavia. He was stripped of his military rank in 1981. Tudjman's nationalism is worn openly on his sleeve. His soldiers know that he is ready himself to fight for Croatia. Under his Presidency Croatia has not developed the maturity of a true democracy – there are, for example, very strong government controls on the press and television – but there is no doubt that Tudjman is the genuine choice of his people to be their leader. He became Chairman of the Croatian Democratic Union (HDZ) in early 1990. In April 1990 he was appointed President by their Parliament, the Sabor, and he was directly elected President in the 1992 elections.

Tudjman's wartime leadership will be judged well by his fellow countrymen. In 1991 he held out against the Serbs and, with one-third of his country as he saw it occupied, accepted the Vance ceasefire agreement of January 1992 only as a way of gaining a pause to build up Croatia's military strength and to hit back against the Serbs. He goes through the rituals of diplomacy, pays lip service to the value of negotiations, but would strike militarily as and when he thought he could get away with it. Up to October 1995 he has chosen cleverly. Ever since he launched his January 1993 attack on the Croatian Serbs I have never believed a word he has said to me on military matters, and I think one reason why we got on was that he was perfectly aware that I ignored all of his promises to the EU, the US and the UN not to use force. There was therefore no feeling between us of resentment at being let down when he did attack across agreed ceasefire lines. Unlike Milosevic, who is a total pragmatist, Tudjman is an opportunist in the cause of Croatia. He is in many senses a Partisan general, waiting, acting, deceiving, harrying, feinting and kicking whenever there is an opening. He has one purpose in life – to control all the territory that he believes historically belongs to Croatia – and to that end he will use any means. He will do it with a smile, a quizzical look, or a fit of rage, indications of the seething activity that drives him on. Intensely competitive on the tennis court or around the negotiating table, he is a very skilled operator and I often admired his military and diplomatic interventions for their timing, even when they ruined or set back our own plans. Croatia from 1995 will be the most ethnically pure of the former Yugoslav states and after this Tudjman will be content for it to join the EU.

After the Brioni weekend Vance and I flew to Jeddah for the summit meeting of the Organization of the Islamic Conference.[46] The Saudis treated us with immense courtesy and we were allowed to speak and put our case for a negotiated settlement and advise against lifting the arms embargo. I also had a meeting with the Iranian Foreign Minister Ali-Akhbar Velayati, who had been a paediatrician. We got on reasonably well and though he refused to see Cy Vance, Cy and I felt we should try to involve Iran on the ICFY Steering Committee; but within the EC I could not assemble a consensus for them to be invited.

The British Presidency had for some weeks been trying to persuade the Greeks and the Macedonians to resolve their deep differences over calling the new state the Republic of Macedonia. To the Greeks, with the northern part of their country called Macedonia,[47] it was offensive to have an independent state called Macedonia on their borders, particularly one that many Greeks felt made ill-disguised claims to Greek territory. It was the decision to use the Vergina Star on the Macedonian flag and put on their stamps a Greek castle on the sea at Thessalonika which showed a more than theoretical claim to Greek territory. Taking all this with some contentious wording within the constitution which referred back to this historic claim, it was not surprising that nationalist politicians in Greece were able to whip up a national outcry at what was happening. When Vance and I had visited Athens in September we had found Prime Minister Mitsotakis wrestling with a major political problem which some other EC governments dismissed too lightly. For me as the EC Co-Chairman it was a very delicate matter, and I was content at that stage to let the British Presidency take the lead and to wait for the report they had commissioned from their Ambassador O'Neil. When we met President Gligorov I realized that this was going to be a hard issue to resolve; behind an external reasonableness he hid an inner resolve and inflexibility on this issue, because for him too this was an essential national interest. My job was to do everything possible to keep the Twelve together and I had no interest or wish to isolate the Greeks. I have an abiding political belief that the European Community cannot survive if it stifles the legitimate upholding of a national interest, and that its future design should not attempt to prevent the expression of a genuine national interest; this is why I consider it a folly to introduce any form of qualified majority voting into the conduct of foreign policy. There was no question that the Greek people, by then encouraged by their politicians, felt genuinely that Skopje was making an irredentist claim on Greek territory. Even if that claim owed more to past history than present intentions, it had become an issue of such importance that the Greek government's policy had to be accepted as a legitimate national interest within the scope of the Luxembourg Compromise that General de Gaulle had imposed on the then five other members of the European Community in 1966.

On 29 November, the Security Council was considering whether to put observers on the new international boundaries of Bosnia-Herzegovina and was unable to find even the resources to deploy the minimum of 6,000 personnel.[48]

Over Kosovo the world wanted the Kosovar Albanians to talk to the FRY government about autonomy, but that as yet has never been undertaken because they were only ready to consider secession. In the Balkans, intransigence is believed to be the only stance to pay off. A special Kosovo Working Group, chaired with considerable dedication by Ambassador Ahrens, with my deputy Peter Hall and Cy Vance's deputy Herb Okun also participating, met on six occasions between 30 September and early December 1992 during a time when Prime Minister Panic and some others in the FRY government were ready to consider serious arrangements for autonomy. Even so, the Albanian delegation found immense difficulty in forgoing their claim for immediate independence, for there are few gradualists in the Albanian leadership. Their leader, Rugova, was himself softly spoken and apparently reasonable but at no time did he ever give me the impression that he would settle for autonomy. Prime Minister Panic was desperate for the Albanians to put up candidates for the election at the end of December, for otherwise the Kosovo seats would go by default to hardline Serb nationalists like Seselj. Yet despite having this political leverage the Kosovo Albanians continued to boycott all Serb elections on principle, even though they were bound to win no matter what unfair electoral practice was adopted. The reason is that they are no longer even interested in a move from Belgrade to return Kosovo to something like the autonomy enjoyed under Tito. They are ready to wait until they can join up with Albania. The CSCE Mission in Pristina was ordered out by Milosevic and the Working Group's activities came to a virtual standstill. The Kosovo issue from then on was raised by us as the Co-Chairmen directly and frequently with Milosevic, but his promises of progress were never fulfilled. Milosevic had opposed establishing the Kosovo Working Group at the London Conference on the basis that this was a Serbian internal matter, and he was always hostile to any hint at internationalization of the issue. He never went as far as to deny ICFY's right to be involved in Kosovo, but he was distinctly unenthusiastic about any initiative. Our difficulty in achieving any progress was that the Kosovar Albanians' self-identification as a secessionist movement fed Serbian fears. While we could never interest the Albanians in any solution based on autonomy we had no defence or comeback when the Serbs said all they wanted was independence. Eventually the Serbs will change the boundaries of Kosovo, keeping some of the mines and monasteries, and let Pristina link up with Albania. In 1995 the Serbs from Krajina would not even in their dire circumstances go to Kosovo, for they knew the area had become Albanian.

When I first met General Mladic after the fall of Jajce I sought to persuade him not to take Travnik, for this would have had disastrous humanitarian consequences. Thereafter, whenever we met, he referred to his promise not to do so – initially as emblematic of his keeping his word, and later on as a manifestation of one of his biggest mistakes, for he said he had come to believe he had underestimated the strategic significance of Travnik to the Serbs. Despite his protestations to the contrary, all that I know of General Mladic convinces me that he would have taken Travnik had he thought it was in the Serb interest to do so. General Mladic, having emerged as the dominant military figure in the region, signalled his authority by openly declaring that might made right when he addressed a joint session of the Bosnian Serb and Croatian Serb Assemblies in Prijedor, itself the hub of ethnic cleansing and the administrative centre for a network of Serb detention camps including Omarska and Trnopolje. According to Mladic, 'the existence of the Serb Republic may be disputed in the world, but the existence of its army is indisputable. The Serb Republic exists because we have our territory, our people, our authority and all the attributes of a state. Whether they want to recognize it or not is their affair. The army is a fact.' He was not just thumbing his nose at the international community but signalling loud and clear that for him Greater Serbia had been achieved; roll it back if you dare was his challenge, and he never believed that the international community would dare. General Mladic is the authentic voice of the young Serb JNA colonels who had fought to protect, as they saw it, their fellow Serbs, first in Croatia and now in Bosnia. His pride in his new Bosnian Serb army was manifested in bringing back the characteristic hats of the Serb officers who owed their loyalty to the monarch. Mladic was in personal conversation racist in his remarks but scathing about any implication that his officers would ever condone the rape of Muslim women by his men, laughing cruelly that they would have to be sex maniacs to rape so many women. Neither Mladic nor any of his officers considered that there was an international boundary between Knin and Banja Luka. To Mladic, Serb forces were entitled to move as freely in the former Yugoslavia as they did before 1991. Indeed, for Mladic, and for many of his kind in the military, for most purposes Yugoslavia still existed. 'Safe areas' were all right as a place to 'dump' Muslims, but if they became the focus of Muslim military activity they just became another target, as he was to show over Srebrenica.

As to NATO, I sensed at my first meeting with Mladic, and never shifted my view thereafter, that he relished the thought of engaging with NATO, but on his terms. The possibility of air strikes was always included within his calculations. In one sense he wanted a real fight, believing that picking off the Muslims was beneath the dignity of the Serbs. He had that fight in August–September 1995, and withstood a fortnight of precision bombing before he took out their heavy weapons around Sarajevo.

In early December we had to make a decision as to whether Vance and I should overtly intervene in the Serbian elections. An internal ICFY note on the elections laid out the facts well enough,[49] and this was accompanied by pressure from US supporters of Panic for us to declare in his favour. Ever since I accepted an invitation from the then Norwegian Labour Prime Minister to visit Norway in 1973 to encourage young voters to vote 'Yes' in their referendum on joining the EC I have been convinced that outsiders telling people how to vote is strongly resented. Vance and I were also both still firmly of the view that only Cosic could beat Milosevic, and felt that when he had decided not to challenge any chance of Milosevic being beaten had been lost. On 15 December we had issued a public declaration which had been carefully designed to sound supportive of Panic – as we were – but to avoid attracting allegations of interference and being drawn too far into the election.[50] It seemed to both Vance and me wiser to keep our lines of communication open to all, including Milosevic, and eschew any further involvement in the elections. Indeed, I counselled the EC against even sending monitors for what would never be fair elections. Milosevic controlled the most watched television station, and his line predominated in the press.

A major new development was the involvement of NATO. On 4 December I flew from Geneva to Brussels to speak to an informal gathering of NATO Ambassadors. For me this was an important meeting as it was the first time I could speak frankly, knowing my views would not reach the newspapers but would go to capitals and in particular Washington. I took the opportunity to give a stark warning of the risk of explosion in Kosovo and signal my continued faith in the possibility of a negotiated settlement after the Serbian election.[51] Cy was dubious about involving NATO too closely with the UN, arguing that the cultures of the two organizations were very different. He feared that NATO and the UN were an oil-and-water mix; and so at times it seemed. The strains and stresses that emerged within UN–NATO relations during the next three years were very considerable. But against that, what was the alternative? Allow the Bosnian Serb air force to start strafing Bosnian Muslim forces and military targets from the air again, or, far worse, to bomb and rocket civilian hospitals, schools and churches? Vance and I decided to write a joint letter to Boutros Ghali to encourage him to approach NATO.[52]

On 10 December the delegation of the government of Bosnia-Herzegovina presented to the ICFY a paper entitled 'Brief Explanations of the Proposal of Thirteen Regions in Bosnia-Herzegovina' which outlined their proposals and emphasized keeping the country together and diluting Serb majority areas, which was from their point of view a sensible approach.[53]

The London Conference on the former Yugoslavia had invited Cyrus Vance and myself to recommend how the international community should deal with people who might have committed war crimes in the various wars that had engulfed the former Yugoslavia since 1991. Predominantly these constituted alleged crimes by Serbs against Muslims and Croats, but also included alleged crimes by Croats against Serbs and Muslims, as well as alleged crimes by Muslims against Croats and Serbs. While conscious as negotiators of the value of pardons and amnesties, we felt the nature of these crimes demanded the establishment of a court or tribunal. We would have preferred to establish, under the UN Charter, an International Criminal Court, to which cases could be referred from any part of the world, and we informed the Foreign Ministers of this in December 1992 when they attended an ICFY meeting in Geneva. Sadly, we later concluded that there was not sufficient support within the UN for such a court. We therefore recommended establishing an ad hoc tribunal specifically to deal with crimes committed in the territory of the former Yugoslavia. We believed it essential that any tribunal should be free-standing, independent and not connected in any way with the ICFY, thereby consciously divorcing its decisions from the peacemaking or peacekeeping process.

The recommendation that it should be established under the authority of Chapter VII of the UN Charter was made because this route would be faster than establishment by a treaty, which would have to be ratified by every country where accused persons might be found; and we felt the tribunal would be able to draw on the enforcement power of the Security Council to bring people to justice and comply with a warrant of arrest, in effect to extradite. Any political judgements as to the duration of the tribunal's jurisdiction would be taken by the Security Council. In this way we hoped the issue would not be subject to bargaining between the leaders of the countries involved in the war, some of whom might themselves be issued with arrest warrants to bring them to trial.

It is important to stress that the Serbian nation is not on trial. It is individuals who must be held responsible, whether Serb, Croat or Muslim, whether prominent figures or local decision-makers; and, as happened over the Nuremberg and Tokyo Tribunals, justice should proceed: individuals should be investigated and brought to trial, with arrest warrant procedures enforced by the Security Council if need be, suspects judged and, if found guilty, sentenced.[54]

Genocide is a crime against the whole of humanity. The UN Convention on Genocide defines genocide as certain 'acts committed with intent to destroy in whole or in part a national, ethnical, racial or religious group, as such'. It is a highly specific crime to eliminate a definable group from this planet. Genocide was committed against the Serbs by the Croat Ustashas in the Second World War. In the 1990s the specific problem is to distinguish between genocide and ethnic cleansing. I know of no accurate figures on the number of fatalities there have been in the war in Bosnia-Herzegovina. News organizations and specialists, after three years of war, talk of 200,000–250,000. The Bosnian government in April 1995 lowered its previous estimate to just over 145,000, about 3 per cent of the pre-war population. But George Kenney, who resigned from the State Department in 1992 to protest at the failure of US policy to do more for the Muslims, puts the figure between 25,000 and 60,000.[x] He argues that

> *Bosnia is not the Holocaust or Rwanda; it's Lebanon. A relatively large number of white people have been killed in a gruesome fashion in the first European blow-up since World War II. In response the United Nations has set up the first international war crimes trials since Nuremberg. But that does not mean the Bosnian Serbs' often brutal treatment of the Bosnian Muslims is a unique genocide.*

In fact the Greek civil war of 1945–8 was the first European blow-up but that is often seen as a follow-on from the Second World War.

These matters will be determined in large part by the International Criminal Tribunal for the Former Yugoslavia (Yugoslav War Crimes Tribunal or YWCT), established by the Security Council, with the power to prosecute persons accused of grave breaches of the Geneva Conventions of 1949, violations of the laws or customs of war, genocide and crimes against humanity. UN Resolution 827,[55] which set up the YWCT, saw it as being able 'to contribute to the restoration and maintenance of peace'. To do this it must help to deter future crimes and its deterrent function cannot be divorced from providing punishment and retribution.

None of the parties involved in the negotiations in Bosnia-Herzegovina has so far sought to raise the question of negotiating for an amnesty or pardon to impede the work of the YWCT. I do not myself believe that it would be right to grant any such request if they do. A key question the YWCT will have to address relates to 'ethnic cleansing': how will it be defined and classified? Some fear that any settlement which does not reverse all the ethnic cleansing that has taken place will in some ill-defined way ratify ethnic cleansing. I see no way in which any ratification, formal or informal, will happen. All draft peace settlements and countless bilateral and trilateral statements signed by the parties have included a condemnation of ethnic cleansing and a declaration that any documentation related to the leaving of a house, a business or land which was signed under duress is null and void. It will be very important for the future of international humanitarian law to have this whole issue of ethnic cleansing clarified and to make clear that it is a crime for which its perpetrators can be charged and punished. This is particularly relevant to the Balkans, where after the Turkish leader Kemal Ataturk defeated the Greek army in 1922 a massive population exchange followed whereby '400,000 Turks from Greek Thrace marched into Turkey, and 1,250,000 Greeks from Asia Minor went into exile in Greece – homeless, ill clothed and starving – increasing the population of Greece by 20 per cent'.[xi]

It will be for the Security Council, in relation to the YWCT, to resolve the age-old dilemma between reconciliation and retribution. It may decide that justice in this particular part of the world at some future time should not remain an absolute and agree to introduce an amnesty. I cannot see the Security Council terminating the activity of the YWCT merely because of a peace settlement. The Tribunal must now proceed to the trial and sentencing stage. The Tribunal should not give up just because some of the suspects are unlikely to be forced to leave their country and stand trial. Governments change, public opinion changes, and the 'pariah status' of not being able to travel abroad is in itself some punishment.

On 16 December we had a Ministerial Steering Committee meeting in Geneva. Vance and I chaired the meeting and gave reports, and virtually all countries were represented by their Foreign Ministers.[56] I stressed four points: first, the need for the establishment of an International Criminal Court through a Resolution by the Security Council; second, the need for a Chapter VII determination to enforce an NFZ mandated by the Security Council; third, the need for the toughening of existing sanctions; fourth, the case for a Security Council Resolution on Kosovo. Vance and I also spelt out our sense of urgency and timetable for meeting early in the New Year with all three parties and our determination to bring Izetbegovic, Karadzic and Boban around the same table for the first time. We had achieved such a negotiation with the Mixed Military Working Group, but now we were determined to prompt the politicians to debate among themselves. The US Secretary of State, Lawrence Eagleburger, came and gave the meeting world headline coverage with his naming of possible prominent war criminals, including Milosevic, Karadzic and Mladic. He also raised the need to re-examine the arms embargo. His was the speech of a man who was going out of office with a bang and not a whimper. I sat next to him at lunch afterwards, and I felt he was agonized but also nonplussed at what to do over the former Yugoslavia, a country in which he had served as US Ambassador and which he knew very well. He said to me words to the effect of 'look, I don't know whether you and Vance are right but I sure as hell don't know any better way forward, so I will support you.' It was a comforting if somewhat backhanded vote of confidence, but in keeping with his rather more intellectually honest approach than is usual among those who reach the top of the political ladder.

Lieutenant-General Nambiar and Major-General Morillon both attended the Steering Committee and made an effective presentation of the realities on the ground to ministers, and next morning we flew down to Zagreb with them. At 11 a.m. we met with President Tudjman, President Izetbegovic and Mr Boban to nail down some of the detailed boundaries of the provinces we were going to propose. In all the comment on the VOPP it tends to be forgotten that the boundaries of Mostar and Travnik in particular, as well as Posavina, Zenica and Tuzla provinces, were all agreed in advance between the Muslims and Croats at that meeting. One of Izetbegovic's key points was to convince Boban that he had to give up his aim of creating a Republic of Herzeg-Bosna. Vance and I believed that in any future election the Croats would not have a guaranteed majority in the Travnik province, but it was not in our interest to draw too much attention to this. In the last census before the war, held in 1991, it had a Croat majority, but given the influx of Muslim refugees since the spring of 1992 and the exodus of Croats it was very unlikely ever again to have a clear Croat majority. In order to give the Muslims confidence we later reached an agreement that the interim governor in Travnik province would be a Muslim, although that agreement barely lasted a few weeks before Boban denied that he had made any such deal – this in spite of the fact that the negotiations had been conducted, rather unusually, in Serbo-Croat since Boban spoke no English, with Peter Hall, who spoke the language perfectly, chairing the meeting.

Vance then flew back via London to America to see President Bush, and I left in a UN convoy to drive to Velika Kladusa to stay with the French battalion. The French government was becoming very frustrated with the operation in the Bihac pocket and wanted to move their troops to Sarajevo, which they eventually did. That night I met for the first time the leader of the Bihac Muslims, Fikret Abdic. Though later often described as a businessman and rebel Muslim leader, he was in fact a member of the collective Presidency which was the governing body of Bosnia-Herzegovina; popular as a secular Muslim, he had polled the largest number of votes. The snag was that Abdic preferred to stay during the war in the Bihac region. He talked rapidly and spoke no English; he was forthright, confident and different from the Sarajevan Muslims. He was in favour of negotiating and compromising with Croats and Serbs to achieve a settlement, and scathing about those Muslims who wanted to block any such settlement. In many ways it was easier for him to adopt this approach than Izetbegovic, for he had a regional constituency who for centuries had traded with Croats and Serbs in and around Bihac. During the Second World War Bihac Muslims had trodden an ambivalent path between the Partisans, the Croatian Ustashas and the German and Italian invaders. At this stage Abdic was semi-detached from the Sarajevo government and had no time for Izetbegovic's attitudes, believing that he was perpetuating the war, and made this unequivocally clear. I urged him to attend Presidency meetings in Sarajevo more often and to use his influence there.

Having stayed overnight in the barracks, we drove back to Zagreb across the confrontation lines and then flew to Sarajevo on the Friday morning. I had wanted to spend some time in the city, to try to get to know the key figures and to feel what it was like to live under constant shelling in a state of siege. In those days I got a taste of the atmosphere. No tap water or flushing lavatories. No lights in the streets at night. Shots ringing out and intermittent explosions. Trees all disappearing for firewood. Football pitches converted to graveyards. The grotesqueness of modern buildings with holes right through them somehow seemed more disturbing than the older buildings being knocked about. Each morning before most people were out of bed I would walk the city streets as an almost childish act of defiance against the Serb snipers looking down on me from the surrounding hills. On the first day I wore a blue helmet and flak jacket, but felt so foolish that I gave up wearing them, believing there was a slighter risk of being shot at in normal clothes. One morning I bumped into the local head of UNHCR, a young Englishman, Jeremy Brade, outside Morillon's house and he asked if he could show me the city in his UNHCR Land Rover. I went everywhere in the inner city with him, going to places I had last seen as a student. It was also refreshing to see him and Larry Hollingworth, a bearded UNHCR worker often on television talking concerned common-sense, dining in the UN officers' mess with Morillon as part of the team. One important visit I made with Jeremy, completely impromptu, was to the Kosevo hospital early one morning, where I was shown the cold operating theatre and a modern intensive care unit yet with no electricity to operate the sophisticated machinery. Two large shell holes in the wall of the recovery room were a reminder of the constant danger under which the staff worked. The contrast of having all the most modern complicated electronic monitoring equipment yet having no heat and few medicines was a stark reminder of the vulnerability of modern life to war. It left a deep impression and I felt driven over the next few days at least to negotiate the delivery of an oil supply to heat the hospital for Christmas. Each day Philippe Morillon and I shuttled to and fro between the Bosnian Serbs on the Serbian side of the airport at Lukavica and the Bosnian Presidency.

During private late-night meetings I also managed to probe some distance behind the front that Ejup Ganic presents to the world. He is the most complex person in the Bosnian government. He was born in the Sandzak in 1946. In November 1990 he was elected to the Presidency in the vacancy for a 'Yugoslav' and was made Vice-President of Bosnia-Herzegovina in 1992. Though technically representing a minority, he soon became identified as a member of the Muslim Party of Democratic Action, the SDA, and became its Vice-President in 1994. He has one central policy objective, namely to involve the US army as a combatant in the Bosnian fight to defeat the Serbs. As he sees it, to achieve this aim – of which he makes no secret – he is entitled to use whatever means are necessary. To him the end justifies those means. He orchestrates Bosnian government propaganda, operating at every level in the US – at the White House, on Capitol Hill and on the television screens in American homes. He has worked for Union Carbide in America and has had six textbooks on engineering published there, and he knows America and its people very well. There is a doggedness about his character that shows itself in his readiness to spend much time in Sarajevo and take the risks of its citizens; but the focus of his attention and his travels is on the US. He knows that you have to spend money to be heard in America and is ready therefore to employ media consultants and use all the modern techniques of communication. He believes the Serbs listen to no one but respond to power. His message to America is simple – 'we are the victims' – and like all good propagandists he does not shrink from repeating the message over and over again. He authorizes publicity to depict Muslims as victims. He fears Sarajevo going off the headlines, for that will mean less pressure on US politicians to intervene. It is a very credible but ruthless strategy from the Muslim point of view and its continuing influence is too often underrated, for Ganic's message is relayed on by Sacirbey and Silajdzic, both skilled in television and radio. Unfortunately in 1995 he had a bad car accident near Mostar and has had to have a long spell recuperating.

On Saturday morning I met General Mladic for the second time and this was when he first reminded me he had not taken Travnik. That same evening together with the young leader of the Bosnian forces, General Halilovic, I visited the 1st Motor-Rifle Brigade in Sarajevo and took Graham Messervy-Whiting, my military adviser, with me. A young photographer from Agence France-Presse acted as interpreter when I answered searching questions from the men. To my surprise there was no publicity. I was woken that night as I slept on a canvas portable bed in General Morillon's HQ by a particularly loud noise. We discovered next day it was the heavy-calibre end-of-trajectory ricochet from an unusual direct fire heavy weapon which gave small explosions with no shrapnel and which turned out to be an anti-aircraft gun now directed at buildings. It was a very personal reminder of the real horror that the citizens of Sarajevo face with such immense fortitude and self-discipline. Over Vukovar the Serb army appeared to learn the lesson that capturing urban areas in modern warfare extracts a terrible price, something the Russians forgot when they fought for Grozny. So instead, the Serbs rediscovered the medieval siege, putting citizens under barrage and psychological pressure but not launching a frontal attack. The Bosnian Serbs did their cause immense harm by their tactics over Sarajevo and would have been wiser to have pushed for UN administration from the outset. Their problem was the personal affinity with Sarajevo felt by their three political leaders Karadzic, Krajisnik and Koljevic.

Through intensive personal contacts with the most senior political and military leadership of all parties in Sarajevo during the next four days Morillon and I attempted to break the vicious circle which up until then had prevented progress on the demilitarization of Sarajevo contributing to a genuine cessation of hostilities throughout Bosnia-Herzegovina. No party had been willing to make real concessions, fearing that others could take advantage of them; but at the same time each party had insisted that the others make the first concession.[57]

I left Sarajevo for Zagreb and Geneva hopeful but worried, for I had detected that the strongest resistance to our agreement was coming not from the Bosnian Serbs but from Ejup Ganic. Demilitarization in Sarajevo would remove the most powerful weapon in his propaganda armoury for involving the US. A quiet Sarajevo was, he almost admitted, not in his interests, and he preferred a continuation of the siege. Also, in fairness, he genuinely feared that demilitarization could lead to a freezing of the confrontation line dividing the city. Philippe Morillon shared all my concerns. He had been amazingly tolerant in allowing me to intrude into his area of responsibility in our joint negotiations. We had travelled everywhere together, as the itinerary shows, in a spirit of shared endeavour. He had panache and courage; but even so, as I left him we had the hardest problem still to resolve, namely convincing the Muslim leaders that our plan was in their interest.

Sadly Ganic appeared to block a settlement. Oil went to the Kosevo hospital for a few days to cover the immediate Christmas period, but then was diverted for military use. The military talks became bogged down in minor differences and momentum was lost. The breakdown left the Serbs disillusioned and the moment for a negotiating breakthrough temporarily disappeared. Professor Nikola Koljevic, one of the Bosnian Serb leaders, who in peacetime had taught Shakespeare at Sarajevo University, believes that if I had stayed over that Christmas in Sarajevo, we could have constructed a demilitarization agreement. It haunts me to this day that perhaps he was right.

On the election in Serbia our predictions proved correct and on 20 December, with a 69 per cent turnout, despite an excellent campaign by Prime Minister Panic given where he was coming from, Milosevic gained 56 per cent of the votes and Panic 34 per cent. Some calculated that Panic lost votes from Eagleburger's intervention, calling Milosevic a war criminal, but this was not enough to have changed the result.

Exhausted after non-stop activity and travel, Christmas at home was a time for thinking and recharging batteries. Now all hinged on the VOPP negotiations due to start early in January and whether or not the parties would at long last negotiate together around the same table.

After the Ministerial Steering Committee meeting it was clear that the US government line was becoming much stronger. Lawrence Eagleburger gave me personally two impressive US talking-point papers. The tougher underlying message was music to my ears. Washington was concerned that 'Milosevic and his proxies' believed that neither Europe nor the US would take any action no matter what he did, and was particularly concerned that Milosevic might think that the US were hobbled by the Presidential transition and the EC consumed by internal problems. They wanted to draw some clear lines, give the Serbs reason to respect those lines and exact a cost if they crossed them. They were also worried that the Muslim world had lost confidence in the West over Bosnia and could go their own way, particularly if we failed to prevent a bloodbath over Kosovo. In Bosnia the US was ready to react with air power if any UN personnel were threatened or attacked and, if needed, to ensure that the humanitarian relief effort succeeded. The Americans intended to warn Milosevic that further NFZ violations would result in an enforcement Resolution and this would be imposed decisively. The US was sensitive to the concerns of countries with troops in Bosnia and was prepared to offer an assurance about UNPROFOR's contingents. This was a well-judged message with clear and achievable political and military objectives. At that time Eagleburger, Scowcroft and Bush, albeit diminished by Clinton's election victory, were nonetheless operating effectively on policy issues that really mattered, and albeit rather late in the day had come to give the former Yugoslavia the priority the US had been unwilling to accord it when James Baker was Secretary of State.

President Mitterrand appeared to shift his position in response to US attitudes, and some ten days later Yugoslavia was the main subject during his traditional televised New Year's Eve message. He spoke of nationalism based on racist or religious concepts and ancient hatreds in Eastern Europe, and described the war in former Yugoslavia as pitiless and ethnic cleansing as atrocious. Mitterrand said that arbitration, conciliation and dialogue had all been tried, with France at the origin of most proposals. He added that with nearly 5,000 soldiers on the ground, and having had nine fatalities among their own troops, no country was doing as much and he could only give his consent to further action if the UN took responsibility for it. Hoping that the current Geneva negotiations would succeed quickly, he was counting on the UN Security Council to authorize enforcement of the Bosnia no-fly zone and the clearing of routes to permit entry to the camps and to towns and cities such as Sarajevo. Mitterrand continued that the Security Council was also responsible for taking steps to prevent the conflict spreading to Kosovo, Sandzak and Macedonia. The few dozen observers already in place were not sufficient and more were required. This was the furthest that Mitterrand had gone in public in advocating French involvement in military intervention in former Yugoslavia, and the headline of the newspaper *Libération* of 1 January summed it up as 'Mitterrand Moves Towards War' ('Dans la Logique de Guerre'). However, the continuing relative caution of the French position, in the face of mounting public calls for action, was better conveyed in *Le Monde*'s comment on 2 January that 'we are far from the "Logique de Guerre" two years ago [referring to Kuwait]. The West, and not least France, will not re-take by military force the two-thirds of Bosnian territory captured and cleansed by the Serbs.'

On French television on 1 January, Jacques Delors, the President of the EC Commission, in a rare intervention on foreign policy, said that if the Geneva negotiations failed a UN Security Council Resolution would be required 'to make war, even if in a limited form'. He denounced Milosevic and his friends for their 'monstrous ideology' of ethnic cleansing and for their aim of creating a Greater Serbia, and he regretted that the Twelve had lacked vision and had not grasped the likely heavy consequences of the Yugoslav conflict.

All of this only emphasized the need for speed in pushing ahead at the start of the New Year with our peace plan. We had insisted all along that the aim of our constitutional proposals was to stop and reverse ethnic cleansing, and the proposed constitutional arrangements contained a range of very tough provisions designed to ensure the highest level of internationally recognized human and minority rights. These constitutional proposals had been on the table for some time and, though challenged by the Bosnian Serbs, we had stood firm. Our proposals included the establishment of a Human Rights Court, the majority of whose members would be appointed by the Council of Europe; an International Commission of Human Rights for Bosnia-Herzegovina; and the appointment of ombudsmen with special responsibility to reverse ethnic cleansing. Provision was also made to ensure ethnic balance in governmental decision-making bodies and to prevent discrimination in the various central and provincial civil, police and other services.[xii] Vance and I remained as determined as we had been in August to start a process of reversing ethnic cleansing and certainly not to consolidate it.

After three and a half months of kaleidoscopic activity and hectic travel, working eighteen to twenty hours a day, seven days a week, I was far more knowledgeable on the Balkans and far more sceptical about the personalities and the peoples that made up the former Yugoslavia. The problems were even more daunting than I had imagined and the urgency for a peace settlement within Bosnia-Herzegovina even greater than Cy Vance had impressed upon me in August in New York. For every week and month that went by without a settlement, ethnic cleansing was going to be harder to

3

The Vance–Owen Peace Plan (VOPP)

ON SATURDAY 2 JANUARY 1993 at 11.00 a.m. the first plenary session of the Bosnian parties convened by the ICFY took place. The meeting was attended by five delegations, headed for the Bosnian Croats by Mr Boban, for the Bosnian government by President Izetbegovic and for the Bosnian Serbs by Dr Karadzic, as well as by President Tudjman for Croatia and President Cosic for the FRY. They were all sitting around the same table for the first time since the London Conference in August, and used the opening session to let off steam.[58]

Cy Vance explained that the work would continue in two working groups: one chaired by Martti Ahtisaari, which would deal with constitutional issues, including the proposed provincial map for the administrative boundaries within Bosnia-Herzegovina, and the other presided over by the UNPROFOR Commander, General Nambiar, on military issues.

In my statement, carefully prepared with Cy Vance, I introduced our own peace plan, a three-part package comprising ten constitutional principles, a detailed cessation of hostilities agreement and a map. The main points of the plan were as follows:

The Vance–Owen Peace Plan

I. Constitutional Principles

- Defines Bosnia and Herzegovina as a decentralized state, with guaranteed freedom of movement throughout.
- Gives substantial autonomy to the provinces while denying them any international legal character.
- Provides for democratically elected national and local government and a mechanism for resolving disputes between them.
- Stresses strong, internationally monitored human rights provisions.

II. Military Paper

Requires:
– cessation of hostilities within seventy-two hours;
– withdrawal of heavy weapons from Sarajevo in five days and from remaining areas in fifteen days;
– demilitarization of Sarajevo, and eventually the whole country;
– separation of forces followed by a return of forces to designated provinces within forty-five days.

III. The Map

– Delineates a ten-province structure reconstituting Bosnia-Herzegovina.

Annex: Working Paper on Interim Arrangements

– Nine-member interim central government (three members from each party) to take decisions by consensus.
– Multi-ethnic provincial governments to be set up to reflect all groups fairly, based on the pre-war census.
– Reversal of ethnic cleansing to get under way immediately.
– International Access Authority to be established to guarantee freedom of movement.
– National authorities to be created to restore power, banking services, telecommunications and civil aviation.

We were careful not to label any provinces Serb, Croat or Muslim, contrary to the impression given by some newspapers and commentators,[i] putting only numbers and place names on the map (see p. 92). Separation of the armed forces throughout Bosnia-Herzegovina would have to be negotiated in the light of the boundaries of the new provinces. It was envisaged that there would be no military forces in Sarajevo province. Bosnian Serb forces would withdraw to provinces 2 (Banja Luka), 4 (Bijeljina) and 6 (East Herzegovina). Bosnian Croat forces could be deployed in province 3 (Posavina), and the remaining forces would, we hoped, reach agreement as to their deployment in provinces 1, 5, 8, 9 and 10. We knew this would present difficulties in some provinces between the Croat and Muslim forces. Yet, since under the VOPP's constitutional principles the whole of Bosnia-Herzegovina was to be progressively demilitarized, we hoped that the Croats and Muslims might accept that these provinces would temporarily have both sides' forces deployed within them. We knew, of course, that some of the boundaries of provinces would inevitably be treated as front lines, with roadblocks and other manifestations of confrontation, but we hoped that as confidence in the cessation of hostilities grew the barriers would soon come down. Confidence-building measures would have to be developed along with the corralling, UN supervision and eventual dismantling of much of the heavy weaponry.

The territorial implications of the proposals gave a stark message of withdrawal to the Bosnian Serbs, which explained their opposition. Even when the map was attacked as giving the Muslims too little we were reluctant to reveal how much land the Serbs had to withdraw from – nearly 40 per cent of their then land holdings. But in order to convince those critics who were accusing us of rewarding ethnic cleansing after we had made changes on 8 February (see p. 93) we later presented a map showing in black the territory which the Serbs had to give up (see p. 133). As we feared, it had a very bad effect on Bosnian Serb opinion for it clearly showed that provinces with a clear Serb majority would represent 43 per cent of the total land area of Bosnia-Herzegovina, whereas their military action had by then given them control of some 70 per cent of the territory. If the Bosnian Serbs were to accept our map or be forced to withdraw they would be retreating from about 38.6 per cent of the territory of Bosnia-Herzegovina they held. I used to challenge any critic to recall episodes in history when armies that had not been defeated had given up anything like as much territory. The most obvious example was Israel when it gave up Sinai as part of the Camp David Agreement of 1978; but that was a desert. A perceptive criticism, but one that was rarely voiced, was that we were demanding too much withdrawal from the Bosnian Serbs given that we had no means of forcing them to withdraw, and that we should have allowed the provinces in which they were likely to be in a majority to be contiguous. Yet had we done this the criticism which we were to encounter from the Clinton administration would have been much fiercer.

At the close of the meeting on 4 January the Bosnian Croats accepted our three-part package in full: the constitutional principles, the cessation of hostilities agreement and the map. For the Bosnian Serbs, Karadzic said the map was 'acceptable as a basis for starting negotiations'. He rejected constitutional principles 1 and 2 which precluded a state within a state and generally kept all the cessation of hostilities options open. It was obvious that the Bosnian Serbs would never accept the map unless and until they were totally isolated. Meanwhile, we were contemplating asking Cosic if he would consider it appropriate to include Milosevic in his delegation next time. We thought that after the election result Milosevic would be readier to put pressure on Karadzic – and more effective in doing so – than Cosic, and so later it proved.

The key to immediate progress lay with President Izetbegovic. He accepted the ten constitutional principles and also at that time the detailed proposals for a cessation of hostilities, but said the map was 'not acceptable'. Izetbegovic also commented that the two Co-Chairmen's efforts were

Map 5 Vance–Owen Peace Plan, 2 January 1993

not unprincipled. We understood his reservations, which concerned five specific areas.[59] Of course, in an ideal world a case could be made for many of his wishes; but in the mess that was then Bosnia-Herzegovina his objections, if maintained, represented a totally non-negotiable position. What was more serious was that he probably knew that if he persisted he would destroy the VOPP, as some argued he had destroyed the Carrington–Cutileiro proposals, though these were never fully defined. We had to convince those governments that could influence Izetbegovic, particularly the US, that his objections were unsustainable and that he should accept the package 'warts and all'. We then intended to turn the world's frustration and anger on to the Bosnian Serbs and pressurize them to accept the package, which meant giving up their claim for a state within a state. We invited all the parties to return to Geneva on Sunday 10 January for another round of negotiations.

I then wrote directly to President Mitterrand, who I thought could help most with Izetbegovic, and briefed all the EC heads of mission in Geneva.

Map 6 Revised Vance–Owen Peace Plan, 8 February 1993, New York

If we could persuade Izetbegovic to sign up alongside the Croats, the Bosnian Serbs might also sign rather than be isolated; otherwise we would move to the UN in New York. The Russian mission to the UN in New York then circulated on their own initiative a draft presidential statement calling on the parties to reach without delay an agreement on the Vance–Owen Peace Plan. This received strong support from all present, except the US mission to the UN, who queried the words 'without delay' and wondered whether Washington would want to imply endorsement of the plan. They also questioned how the Islamic countries would react to pressure of this sort on the Bosnian Muslims. The advice from the UN in New York was that Cy Vance should try to convince the doubters in Washington.

Meanwhile President Izetbegovic on 7 January was saying to the press in Geneva that our map ratified and legitimized the fruits of 'ethnic cleansing' and effectively prevented the return of refugees. He added, in a sharp contrast of tone to the friendly way in which the proceedings had been

handled, that at many times during the negotiations he had felt like Eduard
Benes, the President of Czechoslovakia at the time of Munich in 1938, and
he talked of a 'new fascism'. This may have been thought to be good propaganda, but it was not true and soured the atmosphere within the
Conference. When Vance and I tackled Izetbegovic personally he backed off
immediately, but the damage was done and from then on any quite legitimate pressure on the Bosnian Muslims to compromise was all too often
depicted as unfair bullying. Anthony Lewis, in the *New York Times* in a
column entitled 'Beware of Munich', even wrote: 'Cyrus Vance is one of the
great American public servants of recent decades, a man of courage and
unwavering honor. But I and some others are puzzled by where he is going
in the search for a negotiated end to the war in Bosnia.' Vance's image had
been hurt by a mix-up over Izetbegovic's visit to Washington. It was alleged
that he had asked Eagleburger not to see Izetbegovic, whereas in reality he
had rung up to ask that nothing be done to delay or stop Izetbegovic being
back in Geneva for the recommencement of the negotiations. Larry
Eagleburger and Brent Scowcroft agreed to see Izetbegovic in Washington
on 8 January and both would, we were told, support the Vance–Owen
process and urge Izetbegovic to negotiate seriously and to return to Geneva
for the meeting on 10 January rather than go direct to an OIC meeting in
Dakar. The US would disabuse him of any notion he might have that the
Americans would commit forces to come to his rescue. In the event
Izetbegovic did turn up in Geneva but the Bosnian Serb delegation was
delayed in Belgrade by fog, so we agreed he would go to Dakar and Silajdzic
would stay in Geneva.

In New York the US came forward with new wording, suggesting
'taking note of the peace plan proposed by the Co-Chairmen' and claiming
as justification that Eagleburger did not want to endorse ethnic cleansing.
Since Eagleburger had never made this criticism to us, some of the
Washington representatives of EC governments were asked to find out
what was the true position. The French told me that their ambassador had
commented that in Security Council language 'taking note' was tantamount
to 'rejecting'. Eventually an agreed formulation was adopted, but for Vance
and me the message was unmistakable – some in the US State Department
were encouraging Izetbegovic to seek changes in the map which we knew
were not negotiable and in all probability they too knew were not
negotiable. For some time in Geneva, Vance and Okun had been
complaining of US misrepresentation both of our intentions and of the
details of the plan in reporting back to the State Department. We needed
to go direct to the White House, so I talked to Stephen Wall in No. 10
Downing Street and he offered to speak to Brent Scowcroft to see if he
could convince him. Scowcroft was not persuaded by all our arguments on
the map but he did admit that he did not believe that Izetbegovic would

get a better deal and said he would tell him so in very firm terms and that he should accept what was on offer. My explanation of Scowcroft's position cheered up Vance enormously, for he was angry at the drip of criticism coming from across the Atlantic.

The State Department quite separately admitted that they had been nervous about the draft statement because it was a Russian initiative, and they were suspicious of Russian motives; but they also thought the negotiations in Geneva were evolving and they did not want to endorse specific proposals which might soon change. We were assured that neither Eagleburger nor the US administration thought Vance or I was in the business of endorsing ethnic cleansing.

Key decision-makers in the US administration had now said categorically that they had no problem with the Vance–Owen proposals and that if they did, they would have told us; if the US mission in New York had implied otherwise, they were talking out of turn. That said, the State Department did not believe that the administration should say that the Vance–Owen map was the only solution, and a statement of support would imply just that. The Bush administration did not want to get drawn into the negotiations or into passing judgement on proposals which were on the table. Their message was that the negotiating process should continue and that all parties should remain committed to it.

It was a difficult time for the outgoing Bush administration, because it had to reflect in part the views of the incoming Clinton administration. It was legitimate for Bush to do this for Clinton and it is part of the tradition that in the transition nothing is done to compromise the future President's room for action.

I had previously sent a telegram to Douglas Hurd explaining my anxieties about the US position on the VOPP, hoping that Sir Robin Renwick, our ambassador in Washington, would intervene.[60] I said:

As to whether the Resolution on the no fly zone should be passed by the Security Council before the Geneva Conference reconvenes on Sunday, 10 January all depends on what the real US attitude is to our peace package. Probably the best pressure on Belgrade would be if representation was made to Cosic privately, direct from President Bush, rather than passing the no fly Resolution. Such representation should be before President Cosic holds his planned meeting with all the parties inside the FRY and representatives from the Bosnian Serbs and the Serbs in Krajina on Saturday. What I would like President Bush's message to say would be that he had held back the no fly Resolution deliberately to avoid provoking a Serbian backlash and a feeling that they were negotiating under duress but that they should be under no illusion that if the Bosnian Serbs withheld agreement from a comprehensive package that the Bosnian Croats had also accepted then the United States would have to consider measures going beyond the enforcement of the no fly ban. Instead they would have to deal with the substantive question of how to enforce a cessation of hostilities and a comprehensive settlement. If it becomes clear that such a clear firm stand is unobtainable from the US and that they would feel resentful if we were to block the no fly Resolution I would go ahead with the no fly Resolution on Friday and risk some Serbian resentment.

I ended the telegram saying it was 'crunch time in Geneva and not time for faffing around'.

With the Bush administration being generally supportive of the VOPP in Washington and in New York, in Geneva we were watching apprehensively for signs of what we could expect from the Clinton administration. In an interview for the *New York Times* from Little Rock on 13 January the President-elect had said he supported the peace talks now taking place in Geneva. But we knew that some of his advisers had said privately in recent days that the Conference was a sham that only confirmed Serbia's takeover of certain areas of Bosnia-Herzegovina. Clinton also said that if Geneva did not lead to an end to ethnic cleansing then he would be prepared to be more assertive than the Bush administration, and he did not want to rule out something short of the introduction of a large ground force that would change the dynamics.

On the eve of the next round of negotiations the author of a *Sunday Times* article wrote:

When the two wise men of the West walk into the marble hall of the Palais des Nations in Geneva today to meet the irascible warlords of feuding Bosnia, they will be pushing a plan similar to Solomon's proposal to split a baby in half to test which alleged mother loved it more. Two of the would-be mothers, Serbia and Croatia, would be happy to get their severed chunk, but the third, representing the Muslim community headed by Alija Izetbegovic, the nominal President, claims to want the baby whole and alive or not at all.

A florid but neat summary of the dilemma we faced. We had not been helped by the killing two days before of the Deputy Prime Minister of Bosnia-Herzegovina, who had been ordered out of an UNPROFOR vehicle at a checkpoint in Sarajevo and shot by a member of the Bosnian Serb armed forces while in the vehicle. It was a devastating blow to the authority of the UN and I found it impossible to defend the way the UN soldiers had allowed the tragic episode to unfold. Because of this episode we suggested delaying Karadzic's arrival in Geneva, and then fog held him up; when he did arrive in Geneva he was on the defensive, though still determined to hold out against the constitutional principles.

It was Milosevic who suggested over lunch the face-saving formula of merging the first two constitutional principles of the Co-Chairmen's draft, without any substantive change. In the evening in the Hotel des Bergues the Serb facade of unity cracked and Vance and I witnessed late at night Cosic, Milosevic and the Montenegrin President, Bulatovic, turning on the Bosnian Serb leaders, who included General Mladic, demanding that they negotiate seriously. Splitting the Serbs was something we had to achieve, not for its own sake but because otherwise the Bosnian Serbs would remain totally intransigent, and that became the pattern for the future. First we had to convince Belgrade. Without pressure from Serbia and Montenegro the Bosnian Serbs would never give an inch, for they were not pragmatists, like Milosevic, but ideologues, Serb nationalists who did not want a single Muslim to live on the territory they claimed for themselves, and preferably no Croats either. Many were aggressively anti-Communist, practising Orthodox Christians, and intent on demonstrating their democratic credentials, hence their determination to refer all decisions to their so-called Parliament or Assembly. Too many commentators do not recognize that many Muslims live in Serbia and Montenegro, not just the Albanians in Kosovo, but also in the Sandzak and elsewhere, and that Muslims and other nationalities trade and live in their big cities, particularly Belgrade. This is a big difference between Belgrade and Pale, for the Bosnian Serb leaders wanted their 'Republika Srpska' to be an independent state without any links to the Muslim parts of Bosnia-Herzegovina, in effect a Muslim-free area. After Milosevic had made it clear that Belgrade would not go on supporting the Bosnian Serb army and had ensured that General Mladic understood this, a tired, incoherent and somewhat broken Karadzic next day caved in at the eleventh hour. Karadzic explained to the press that he had proposed eight principles, the Co-Chairmen ten principles and they had settled for nine principles. But even so, he did not sign, insisting on taking even this issue back to Pale for the endorsement of his Assembly. This small breakthrough did however sustain the Conference, for we had now achieved, on the three documents before the Conference, six of the nine signatures we needed. The Croats had signed the constitutional principles, the map and the cessation of hostilities agreement. The Muslims had signed the constitutional principles and the cessation of hostilities. The Serbs had signed the cessation of hostilities. Another important aspect of this session was that Tudjman, Cosic and Milosevic had all been able to talk together and we hoped some progress had been made on mutual recognition and on cooperation in the Krajina.

The inauguration of President Clinton was due on 20 January. A week earlier I had received a reassuring message from Washington that Tony

Lake, who was going to be the new National Security Adviser, had given an explicit commitment that the new administration would support the VOPP and that the Bosnians should be urged to accept. But still we heard in Geneva contrary views from people in Washington who were either going to be in or were close to the Clinton administration. The administration wanted to go ahead with enforcing the no-fly zone which I had already privately advocated. At that time it was the UN Secretary-General who wanted to delay enforcement, which meant that that had to be Vance's position too; and since he and I were determined never to be divided in public I went along with that line to the press. Also the Russians were becoming anxious and this was causing concern for the UN, in the first place about NATO involvement and also in respect of the stress being put on the trials of war criminals by the US. On the latter issue the US were pushing at a door which Vance and I had already opened before Christmas in our advice to the Ministerial Steering Committee to establish an International Criminal Court under Chapter VII of the UN Charter. On 13 January at a meeting in Paris of EC Foreign Ministers I urged the EC to pursue in the Security Council the establishment of a tribunal specific to Yugoslavia, and this became official EC policy. France had set up a working group of high-level specialists to examine the options and agreed to feed the results into the Danish Presidency. It was also decided at that meeting to maintain the pressure of sanctions on Serbia and consider measures for total isolation.

With President Mitterrand in Paris on 14 January I raised a sensitive option which we were considering which involved aiming for a strategic settlement giving the Serbs a land corridor through province 3 (Posavina), where the Croats had had a majority before the war, in exchange for the Croats effectively gaining control of their border by linking province 1 (Bihac) to province 10 (Mostar) at Livno. For the Muslims who would not like giving the Serbs a northern corridor the compensation would be a slightly larger Bihac province involving land near Prijedor. I was also hoping to engage the French President on the question of international boundary changes, because France had already expressed the view that there could be more flexibility. I needed at least one powerful EC country to back me up if there were any criticisms in the Council of Foreign Ministers or elsewhere of my even contemplating such changes. In addition, I hoped that by involving Mitterrand I could tie Roland Dumas, the French Foreign Minister, step by step to the ICFY process. Vance and I then put these ideas to both Tudjman and Izetbegovic in their capitals. We found that Tudjman would accept a 20 km wide corridor through Posavina in exchange for a similar corridor between Livno and Bihac. But Izetbegovic flatly rejected it. The guaranteed 'throughways' were as much as he could accept as a northern corridor. I wrote to Mitterrand again to report this reaction and gave as my view that Izetbegovic was unlikely to withdraw his demand for Brcko on the river Sava, which in fairness had had a Muslim majority prior to the war. If the Muslims were to gain access to the Sava river and have most if not all of Brcko, we needed the Croatian government to give up a small section of its territory above the Sava for a Serb corridor and to have in exchange the same number of hectares of land back from Bosnia-Herzegovina above Dubrovnik. But the Croats would not consider this unless they controlled the border between Bosnian Serb territory and the Croatian Serb area around Knin.

We visited Sarajevo on 20 January in an attempt to help reach a compromise between the Bosnian Muslims and Bosnian Croats in the light of recent serious fighting between the two. We made it clear that we wanted the discussions to go beyond this particular fight and cover all other aspects of the Muslim–Croat relationship – how to prevent such incidents in the future, command and control of the armed forces, the appointment of provincial governors, the establishment of an interim government. The truth was that the collective Presidency had broken down, something which was amply demonstrated at the meeting. It was clear from Akmadzic's stance that the Bosnian Croats were no longer going to subscribe to the idea that decisions taken alone by Izetbegovic or with his inner clique were the decisions of the Government of Bosnia-Herzegovina or its Presidency.[61]

In Geneva on Saturday 23 January we started the third plenary session with all the parties present. It was a difficult meeting. Sometimes a plenary session is necessary for the participants to let off steam and make statements which they can then give to their own newspapers,[62] after which they can accept a more informal and detailed negotiating framework. This was particularly necessary in this instance since President Tudjman had just unleashed a military attack on the Croatian Serbs in an effort to gain control of the Maslenica bridge on the Dalmatian coast. His was an understandable frustration, but it was a dangerous and disruptive time to launch an attack totally breaking Vance's 1992 ceasefire agreement.

Karadzic stressed that the main concern of his delegation was the security of the Serbian people, regardless of the area in which they lived. He mentioned that on 16 January we had been sent the Bosnian Serb delegation's written objections to our map,[63] in which they claimed that 650,000–700,000 Serbs would remain in provinces likely to be controlled by Croats and Muslims. They wanted a referendum on our proposals. In reply to Karadzic I made it clear that this was impossible in a time of war. The constitution of Bosnia-Herzegovina would make it possible to change boundaries between provinces; what we needed now, in addition to the three-part package on the table, was agreement on a paper on interim government.

On Sunday 24 January Vance and I talked to Cosic about Croatia. During our conversation, in which he was being as helpful as possible, he took a telephone call from General Panic demanding that the Yugoslav air force should be allowed to protect the Serbs in the Krajina. Whether this was a phoney call in order to show how much pressure he was under I was unable to judge, but we thought it genuine at the time. Cosic told General Panic he was not prepared to authorize such action and claimed to us that he was in control of the army. But there were worrying reports that some Yugoslav units had crossed the Drina river; we told him this would be unacceptable and that there was absolutely no way that the international community could accept the involvement of the Yugoslav army in this crisis, either in Croatia or in Bosnia-Herzegovina. Cosic stressed that public opinion in the Federal Republic was very concerned and that the UN Security Council reaction to the Croatian government's clear breach of the ceasefire was insufficient. We told him that he should publicly state that there would be no involvement by the FRY and demand action instead in the UN. It was fortunate that he was in Geneva, and these meetings undeniably helped to defuse a crisis that had been deliberately triggered by Tudjman to avoid everyone concentrating on Bosnia-Herzegovina.

On Thursday 28 January the London *Times* had a major article under the headline 'Forces for Peace'. 'The Vance–Owen Plan', it stated, 'can only succeed with military backing.' Calling our talks the 'sole best hope of peace', it castigated an America united with its allies 'by little more than hand-wringing, bowel searching and second-guessing'. It called for an ultimatum measured in days, not weeks, to the former Yugoslav republic, to accept the Vance–Owen Peace Plan, which it found 'on close examination is much more detailed and coherent than its critics wish to believe. It contains detailed protocols for military disengagement with firm timetables, worked out partly by the Serb, Croat and Muslim commanders. They cover everything from lifting the siege on Sarajevo to controlling heavy weapons.' In short, it was a welcome call for a settlement to be imposed, even if more detailed discussion might have to take place on constitutional and other questions.

Meanwhile in the US the VOPP was coming under further ill-informed attack. *Time* magazine printed a big piece with the sub-headline 'Milosevic should be pleased. The West's plan will reward his aggression by giving him almost everything he wants.' Disgracefully, the accompanying map bore so little relation to ours that it was unrecognizable. I tried to counter these stories and there was a question-and-answer piece in *Newsweek* under the heading 'We've reached the crunch',[ii] but the formidable disinformation machine that was operating in the US swamped our small press office in Geneva and we began on public relations grounds alone to think we would do better if we were physically in New York.

Zbigniew Brzezinski, appearing still to nurse a grudge from his clashes with Vance in the Carter administration, leapt into the fray with alacrity in the *Washington Post*. He called us 'negotiators whose basic concept of dealing with thugs is to talk endlessly while assuring the aggressors that their use of force will not be matched by a counterforce. Not surprisingly, the result has been that mass murders have been propitiated and "ethnic cleansing", not to speak of mass rapes, tolerated.' Vance hit back, calling the charges 'hogwash' and saying: 'If we refuse to talk, on so-called moral grounds, to all parties to a conflict, how could we ever settle any problem?' He was reported as saying in clipped tones, hammering the table with the tip of his pen in a rare moment of indignation and anger: 'Frankly, I am getting fed up with this mindless criticism that doesn't face up to a central fact. In Bosnia there is no viable alternative to a negotiated settlement. There could well be war criminals among the people we are dealing with, but I'll leave that to the courts to decide. David and I have been working round the clock to stop the slaughter of innocent civilians and keep alive the humanitarian effort. It's nonsense to say we are appeasers for talking to the people who can make a difference in our pursuit of a lasting settlement.'

But there was worse to come. On 21 January the new Secretary of State Warren Christopher, through his spokesman Richard Boucher, said that although the Clinton administration supported the negotiations, Mr Christopher 'expressed doubts about whether it can realistically be achieved, whether they can, in fact, find an agreement'. Then, to rub salt into the wound, Mr Boucher declined to say whether the Clinton administration believed the Vance–Owen plan ratified ethnic cleansing. No wonder that the *New York Times* reporter said that Mr Christopher's remarks had put the administration 'in the awkward position of publicly supporting a negotiating process, while criticising – and perhaps undermining – the particular plan that is on the table'. I saw this report in the *International Herald Tribune* on the morning of 22 January in Geneva and immediately showed it to Cy Vance. He tried to downplay it by saying that the spokesman, Boucher, was a holdover from the Bush administration, but I pointed out that this meant that he would be doubly careful to ensure he was accurately reflecting Warren Christopher's views. It seemed to us to be an amazing turnaround, given Tony Lake's reassurance of only a week before and also Warren Christopher's telephone conversation with Cy Vance only a few days earlier. The newspapers began to be full of stories about divisions of opinion within the administration over the VOPP, and Vance and I were in no doubt that we faced a monumental crisis.

Madeleine Albright, President Clinton's nominee for Ambassador to the UN, told the Senate Foreign Relations Committee on 22 January: 'I have watched with some amazement that the Europeans have not taken action. I believe that we must . . . press our European allies on this.' The US were provoking a crisis not just for us, as negotiators, but for the UN and, above all, for the twelve member states of the European Community for the VOPP had been supported by them at every stage over the nearly five months of negotiations. European ministers had not been bystanders but intimately involved and consulted on the detail. The VOPP had also won the support of the Russian Federation, with Kozyrev being closely involved, and most of the other countries on the Steering Committee of the ICFY also had, in various ways, an influence on the plan. Were they all now expected to turn turtle because a new administration had taken office in the United States? But these were minor considerations compared to the effect of the US position on Bosnian President Izetbegovic, Vice-President Ganic and Foreign Minister Silajdzic. There was now not a chance of their accepting the map unless the US position could be dramatically shifted. The renewed talk in the administration of lifting the arms embargo was also bound to under-mine our negotiations. In addition, the US position was a blow to the Croatian government, who had accepted the VOPP, and to the Bosnian Croats, who were officially part of the Bosnia-Herzegovina government. The Bosnian Serbs, so recently on the rack, must have been laughing their heads off in Pale.

Vance and I decided to stand our ground and give no quarter to our US critics. We were confident that we had the support of the EC and Russia, so we decided to go to New York and put the fate of the VOPP in the hands of the fifteen members of the Security Council. It was a high-risk strategy but if we wanted to keep the VOPP alive there was no alternative. A few European diplomatic voices could be heard from Washington arguing that the administration needed time and they could be won around, but against that was the firm belief of many Americans whom Vance and I knew in Washington that delay meant death for the VOPP. We were hearing that key members of the administration were already privately saying that the VOPP would be dead in a week, smothered in diplomatic verbiage and in press criticism, for the *Washington Post*'s editorial pages were not being helpful to us either, although they were not as mindlessly negative as those of the *New York Times*. In both cases the editorial pages come under a different editorial control from the main newspaper.

I was invited by John Major to attend a seminar on Yugoslavia at No. 10 on 22 January and after a little thought felt it did not compromise my EC status to accept. I welcomed the opportunity for an exchange of views, particularly with Robin Renwick flying in from Washington, on what was really happening in the Clinton administration, and with key British military figures serving in the UN flying in from Split. I sent in a memorandum of my own because I wanted to put the case on the table for using selective air power to impose a specific peace settlement and to have it discussed.[64] It was odd to be back around the Cabinet table, and the mixed representa-tion of the meeting reminded me of 1977 when Jim Callaghan had convened a meeting with service chiefs to draw up rules of engagement for the naval ships and submarine we were despatching to the Falkland Islands.

Malcolm Rifkind, the Defence Secretary, intelligent and sharp, was totally opposed to any imposition of a settlement and managed rather effectively to lampoon my proposal for using air power. I did not engage in a debate with him as I was not part of the UK collective decision-making body assembled around the table, but it was confirmation – not that I needed it – that there was no support in the UK government for any more military intervention than the humanitarian support which was currently being undertaken by UNPROFOR.

John Major's handling of the meeting interested me. His style was more reminiscent of Jim Callaghan than of Harold Wilson, encouraging everyone to speak and marshalling the crucial questions well, at the end painstakingly summing up our conclusions in a way which made the Cabinet Secretary's task rather redundant. Over all the time that I was Co-Chairman of the ICFY, he gave me personally every support. He would do everything possible to help alleviate the humanitarian situation, resisting Treasury strictures and finding both more money and extra men; he was always in favour of UNPROFOR staying on to help, and keen to reinforce in 1995. But he would not be edged over into a combatant role under any circumstances. He was on guard against an apparently innocent decision whose military implications had not been sufficiently thought through and which had the potential for creeping the UK commitment forward into uncharted territory.

Douglas Hurd's emphasis was slightly different. He became less certain of the value of UNPROFOR as the years went by and began increasingly to share Juppé's and my view in 1995 that without a settlement UNPROFOR should not go through a fourth winter. His attitude to the use of force was inextricably linked to whether the US would participate with troops on the ground. Despite being a strong believer in the European Union, he fretted as the strains developed in the Atlantic relationship and did everything he could to alleviate these, keeping in constant touch with Warren Christopher. No one could have tried harder to bridge the differences. He agonized in a thoughtful and concerned way about the turn of events in Bosnia-Herzegovina, and though I did not agree with him on all issues I always had a courteous and serious hearing for my suggestions.

Over the next few months with other governments I used to try to argue the case for imposing a settlement, but it never won support. All countries preferred to shield themselves behind the ideal of a negotiated settlement agreed to by all the parties, failing in that posture to acknowledge that this gave a veto power to any one of the parties, which of course they exercised, not just the Bosnian Serbs but also the Bosnian Muslims. Henry Kissinger, writing in the *New York Post* on 23 February, put his finger on the issue arguing that 'if a Bosnian settlement is to be just it will have to be imposed,' and dismissing as an illusion Warren Christopher's condition that the parties would 'voluntarily embrace' anything meaningfully. But he wanted any US participation in enforcement confined to aerial measures, since this 'will reduce the danger of American forces becoming hostages'. He did not add, but of course it was implicit, that there were already forces on the ground who ran a real risk of becoming hostages. That was the perpetual military dilemma which was rarely faced up to in either the Pentagon or the White House: if widespread air strikes were to be used it was essential that UNPROFOR be removed first, at the very least from vulnerable areas where they could be shot at or captured.

The third plenary session of the Conference had made surprising progress after the initial anger over the Croatian government's military action had abated. We brought Izetbegovic and Karadzic together, after talking to them separately, and made real progress on a draft paper on the structure of an interim government. In essence, we were suggesting nominating provincial governors, with representatives of the three constituent nations having limited central government powers acting by consensus on a central coordinating body. They agreed on a small central area of Sarajevo which would be governed by consensus rule. They agreed on proposed adjustments to opstina or local council boundaries within the province of Sarajevo. They agreed that in those areas of Bosnia-Herzegovina where existing opstina boundaries had not been changed their existing authority would be retained. Meanwhile Silajdzic and Boban were reaching agreement on the provincial pattern of government, though Silajdzic was pouring cold water on compromises designed to reach a full agreement. I sent a COREU out on 29 January explaining what we intended to do next day,[65] saying that we were not certain as to whether President Izetbegovic or Dr Karadzic would sign up on Saturday. Each was eyeing the other to see who might move first. Neither wanted to be seen to be the first to break up the Conference or to refuse to sign. We intended reporting back after Saturday's meeting to the Security Council to seek endorsement of our comprehensive settlement plan. But we wanted maximum pressure to be applied on anyone who did not sign.

Next day in Geneva, after more than a dozen lengthy bilateral and tri-lateral meetings, at the final plenary session Cy Vance said these had reinforced our view that the map submitted by us was just and equitable, based on the fundamental premise that Bosnia-Herzegovina would remain a sovereign, independent, multi-ethnic state.[66] The map did not accept the results of ethnic cleansing but was on the contrary designed to reverse them, and it struck a fair balance in the allocation of land, natural and industrial resources. In my speech I said that we were taking the dispute in effect to the world's parliament and we hoped they would all come to New York and put their case to the members of the Security Council.[67] All three parties signed the constitutional principles; the Bosnian Croats and, somewhat to our surprise, the Bosnian Serbs signed the agreement on the cessation of hostilities. Izetbegovic, having previously agreed, now said his reservations on heavy weapons precluded him from signing. On the map Karadzic got far closer to signing than we had anticipated, and I am convinced he would have signed if Izetbegovic had signed.

Washington professed to be surprised when we announced we were going to New York. The intention of moving the actual peace talks was particularly controversial for the US administration because it meant admitting to America some of the Bosnian Serb leaders, like Karadzic, whom Eagleburger had named as possible war criminals. Also, they had intended to distance themselves from the ICFY when, during Warren Christopher's confirmation hearings, he had made it clear that he would not rely solely on the negotiators in Geneva and instead would keep an independent position. The problem we had was to get the new US decision-makers to read our plan and absorb its detail, particularly the fact that the Mixed Military Working Group had met frequently and reached agreement among all the warring military commanders. For the first time in the former Yugoslavia we had a detailed plan for a cessation of hostilities.

Both Vance and I thought Karadzic had been told by Milosevic to settle. Evidence to support this was visible in Karadzic's presenting the talks as 'a great success' and briefing positively about going to New York. Karadzic said he could agree to most of the map but wanted areas under dispute to be put to a plebiscite which we had earlier ruled out. Many of those close to the Conference, diplomats and journalists alike, felt like us that if Izetbegovic had agreed to sign the map that day Karadzic would have done so too. We were certainly closer to an agreement than any of us could have imagined a week earlier. Why did Izetbegovic not sign? In essence because he sensed that Karadzic might sign if he did and he felt encouraged by US attitudes to hold out for a better deal.

I had sent a personal telegram to Robin Renwick in Washington which spelt out the issues and my frustration with the Clinton administration very frankly:[68]

> We have this Administration briefing the press in a way that could not but stiffen those Muslims who want to continue the war. We have Sacirbey openly telling everyone that the US Administration has said that they should not feel any need to sign the map. We know that Tudjman had formal representations from the US against the Croats putting any pressure on the Muslims to sign up for our package.

The telegram also referred to the most flagrant and best-documented episode of Muslim army units provoking the Serbs to fire on their fellow

Muslims. An UNMO team near Kosevo hospital in Sarajevo had witnessed a Bosnian government mortar crew set up in the grounds of the hospital and fire over the hospital into a Serb area. They had quickly packed up and gone, only for the UNMOs to see a television crew arrive and then record the retaliatory Serb shelling of the hospital. It was the very hospital that I had visited the month before and which had so shocked me with its shell holes in the recovery room. I asked General Morillon why the UN had not gone public on the issue; he wanted the truth out but said 'we've got to live here.' It was uncomfortable for the UN in Sarajevo, but if they had been bolder on the few *agent provocateur* incidents they could have been more forthright on the many Serb outrages and avoided appearing to equate the two sides. The Selous Scouts of the Rhodesian government used to incrim- inate ZANU and ZAPU forces in the 1970s, so I was aware that this type of action tended to occur in civil wars. But I found this particular Muslim provocation, involving the very hospital about the shelling of which I had personally protested strongly to General Mladic a few weeks before, especially troubling. Even at that time there was a feeling among some in UNPROFOR that albeit only a small element in the continuous sniping in the central part of Muslim held Sarajevo, was being undertaken by Muslim units firing on their own people. Those suspicions were never confirmed until August 1995 when a French UN team pinpointed some of the sniping to a building which they knew was controlled by the Bosnian government forces.[iii]

I flew to Brussels on the Sunday to brief the Danish Presidency before the Council of Ministers meeting the next day, Monday 1 February, which I had to miss in order to fly to New York to meet Warren Christopher. I hoped the Council would issue a supportive statement about the VOPP, and they did so in very clear terms.[69] I also talked through the situation with Douglas Hurd at Brussels airport, explaining how I hoped we could let the Americans take the credit for any Security Council Resolutions expressing support for the VOPP, thereby responding to President Clinton's wish to be seen to be doing something.

Our meeting with Warren Christopher in the US mission to the UN in New York in the early evening of 1 February was disillusioning, not so much for what was said but for what was unsaid and for what was appar- ently unknown. I had last met Christopher over a breakfast meeting at Carlton Gardens, the Foreign Secretary's residence, in 1978 when he came to tell us that President Carter had decided not to go ahead with the neutron bomb.[iv] Cy Vance was still suffering from a flu-like illness, but he marshalled the arguments for our plan, which covered seventy pages of typescript, with considerable skill. Yet, as the questioning went on it became painfully apparent that the Secretary of State knew very little about the detail of our plan. Particularly surprising, in view of the administration's public criticism, was that he had not been briefed on all the human rights provisions and safeguards that we had built in with the express purpose of reversing ethnic cleansing. For Cy Vance, who knew from personal experience the pressures that weigh on any new Secretary of State, it was a severe disappointment, for Warren Christopher appeared as if he had not had time to read even a short factual information sheet on what was the essence of our plan. I was baffled as to how Christopher could come so badly briefed to meet his old boss, Cy, who was under virulent public attack over a plan his critics claimed favoured ethnic cleansing. This very criticism was one on which Christopher himself had been dismayingly equivocal, and yet on our actual proposals he had clearly not even paid Vance the courtesy of having done his homework, thereby showing that he had made no real attempt to understand what it was that Cy was being criticized for. Herb Okun was very surprised by this aspect. Not that the atmosphere of the meeting was unpleasant; quite the contrary, but he was embarrassed that his old department could have so badly informed the new Secretary of State. Being charitable, perhaps the problem was Christopher's continued involvement throughout the transition period in Little Rock, Arkansas, at Clinton's request, in the selection of administration members. Whereas in the past, incoming Secretaries of State used the months of the transitional period to become well briefed and versed in all aspects of the current foreign policy agenda, Christopher had had, through no fault of his, no such opportunity. We thought during the meeting that we had enlightened him and cleared up some of his misapprehensions about the plan, and that the dialogue would continue. Christopher had told us: 'This meeting has been illuminating to me . . . We hope the process can be kept going, and we will look for ways to help it . . . I want to work with you, to move forward together . . . I will say we had a good meeting. It explained a lot I hadn't heard before. It was a candid discussion of hard issues. You've impressed us with the urgency. We hope the parties will continue to negotiate. There is a strong case that this plan, while not perfect, is the best available.'

We left with Vance saying very little to the television cameras on the sidewalk, as we had agreed, and all went back to my room in the UN Plaza Hotel for a drink. Then I switched on CNN and we watched Warren Christopher a few hundred yards down the street speak to the same television cameras. Again it was not what he said but his manner and the omissions which conveyed a clear message. No one hearing what he had said could question the *New York Times* headline next day, 'US Declines to Back Peace Plan as the Balkan Talks Shift to UN', nor the reporting that Warren Christopher was 'setting the stage for a possible confrontation between the mediators and the Clinton Administration'. The report also had a senior UN official saying that at a lunch given by the Secretary-General, Boutros Boutros Ghali, Christopher had 'expressed his "ambivalence" about the Vance–Owen plan. Mr Christopher added that he had problems "with the map included in the plan"'. The account that we had of that lunch meeting was even more disappointing than our own meeting.

I had read this *New York Times* report before publication over dinner in the Stanhope Hotel that same Monday night when it was brought over by their New York office to Johnny Apple, the chief of the *New York Times* Washington Bureau. I knew then what the nation would wake up to next morning. The new administration had already made up their mind and were intent on killing off the VOPP. This view was confirmed by Johnny who felt that behind the scenes, while giving the appearance to the European governments of still being open-minded and of considering carefully the plan, the administration had already abandoned it. Johnny told me what was really being said on a non-attributable basis in Washington, namely that Cy Vance was an 'old-style Democrat' and just what Clinton's 'new Democrats' wanted to put behind them. Clinton himself and the people in the White House closest to him, unlike Christopher, Tony Lake and Les Aspin, barely knew Cy Vance. They were from the South and West, were not influenced by the East Coast foreign affairs establishment and were determined not to be labelled a Carter Mark II administration. Johnny told me that he had seen this clash developing and on the day after Clinton's inauguration he had personally decided to give more prominence in the paper to what was said on 21 January by Boucher, the State Department's press spokesman. He warned me that the Vice-President, Al Gore, felt very strongly that the Muslims had to be helped and he confirmed that Boucher was a professional and would never have spoken as he had for a new administration without being absolutely sure of his ground. So we discussed, as friends, what I should do and in the process I became frank and too indiscreet.

Turning around a new President, we agreed, was going to be a formidable task, for every US President takes office with a groundswell of goodwill from political opponents as well as political friends. Americans vest in their new President a respect for the office akin to the feeling most Europeans give to their monarchs. Also, the moral strand of US foreign policy exemplified by Woodrow Wilson lent itself to support for the Bosnian Muslims who were widely, and not unreasonably, seen as the victims. One strategy was to play a waiting game and hope that slowly the administration would come around to the Europeans' position of support for the VOPP. But as we talked this and other options through, I think we both came to the same conclusion – it was full frontal assault or failure, for I could not expect to keep the present level of support from the European countries if they sensed that Vance and I were not in American parlance 'hanging in there'. This would particularly apply to the French, who were in turn crucial in holding the Germans to the VOPP. If Paris saw me adopting the usual British posture of bending the knee to US objections then Mitterrand would go off on his own with a purely French initiative.

Also, it would be a sign of European Community weakness were the EC to back off its considered judgement of what could bring peace to Bosnia-Herzegovina because, as it seemed from Europe, a new US administration was unwilling even to consult on a campaigning position adopted in the summer of 1992. There had been a transformation of the air strike option since the autumn 1992 decision to mount a UN humanitarian intervention, but the administration's failure to recognize the change in circumstances that occurred between July and September 1992 was to bedevil the US–EU dialogue over Bosnia-Herzegovina. I decided that night that I had not been appointed as the EC negotiator to behave like an ambassador. Mine had been a political appointment, and I would go for the jugular vein of US policy, namely their refusal to put troops on the ground in Bosnia. I would simply urge the Clinton administration to do so in every interview, with the implicit message that only then would they have the right to veto or subvert the VOPP. In the process I was bound to make myself unpopular in Washington, but I did not want another international job after this one and I had no need to ensure their patronage.

Next morning I saw that the *New York Times* interpretation was shared by the *Chicago Tribune*. Their headline read: 'US Balks at Backing Peace Plan for Bosnia'. I was reported as saying we wanted the US to endorse our proposals and, from my interview on CNN, 'It's all very well for the United States to criticize from the sidelines. Why don't they come in? It would give the peace settlement a bigger chance.' Vance and I gave a joint press conference that Tuesday in an attempt to put our case and when Vance was asked whether he was appeasing Serbian aggression he replied, 'This is hogwash. It makes me pretty damned angry.' Privately his language was even stronger and amazed those of us who knew him, for even under intense provocation he is normally the most restrained person. A few days before in Geneva we had discussed how to handle the media and Cy Vance had made it quite clear that he wanted me to put our case powerfully and rebut forcefully the charge that we were ratifying ethnic cleansing. I fully understood that it was impossible for him to criticize Warren Christopher publicly, given the history of their relationship, and that Americans would expect Vance to give his former deputy, within days of taking office, proper respect and a fair wind. Fred Eckhard, our joint press spokesman, who was doing a brilliant job for us both, recalls my warning Vance that 'some blood will be spilt on the carpet' and Cy shrugging his shoulders and saying, 'so be it.' Few ever realize how passionate a man underneath his constrained exterior Vance really is. We both felt throughout a deep sense of outrage at the behaviour of many Serbs and it hurt to be accused of favouring ethnic cleansing. We knew that in the final analysis only peace would stop ethnic cleansing and that every month of war that went by only served to set ethnic divisions harder in concrete and make them near impossible to reverse.

As I had predicted, blood was spilt the next day. The *New York Times* of 3 February carried prominently on the front page a story from R. W. Apple Jr, headlined 'Mediator is Upset at US Reluctance over Bosnia Talks – Says Muslims Await Move – "Only Act in Town" Owen Says After He and Vance Fail to Persuade Christopher'. In the text, which was a mixture of what I had said at the press conference and to Johnny himself over dinner, I was described as complaining that the Clinton administration's reluctance to back the effort threatened to 'scuttle chances of ending the war':

> *Against all the odds, even against my own expectations, we have more or less got a settlement but we have a problem. We can't get the Muslims on board. And that's largely the fault of the Americans, because the Muslims won't budge while they think Washington may come into it on their side any day now. What do they want down there, a war that goes on and on? This isn't just the best act in town, it's the only act in town. It's the best settlement you can get, and it's a bitter irony to see the Clinton people block it.*

I had talked too freely. Having arrived in New York in the morning on Concorde, I had had dinner with Johnny, at his invitation, that same evening when I had let my frustration bubble over about Warren Christopher, saying that he 'didn't really take in what I was saying' and recalling that President Clinton had promised bolder action in Bosnia in his election campaign, 'and because they've had to pull back on so much already, they're afraid to do so on this too; eventually they'll get it and help us.' This went too far when seen in newsprint. For a fleeting moment – which was entirely my fault – I had forgotten that Johnny was not just a friend but one of the best journalists in America. There was no misunderstanding between us: his notebook was open in front of me and he was taking notes throughout dinner. I should not have risked making such comments and I regretted it deeply. I suspect this, more than the substance of the VOPP, permanently damaged my relationship with Warren Christopher.

Yet one cannot have it both ways. To fight for the VOPP was always going to be traumatic. The US is the most powerful country in the world and is used to having its way in foreign policy. The diplomatic world is normally characterized by those whose priority is to avoid confrontation, for whom splitting the difference is second nature and for whom ensuring that policy remains within the middle of the pack is an art form. It was, therefore, all the more surprising that the EC countries who had so far all stayed loyal to the VOPP continued to do so. Klaus Kinkel was coming to Washington in a few days' time, and when he did he supported the plan; but he ran into criticism from within the ranks of his coalition partners the CDU and CSU for doing so. The German press and public wanted more positive action to help the Muslims and were pressing for the lifting of the arms embargo. It was my responsibility to keep the EC together, but I was now attempting to do so on a high-risk policy, with no country in Europe really wanting to damage relations with the new US administration. I knew that I risked being disowned by the EC, but felt there was no alternative if we were to achieve a decent peace settlement.

On 4 February I had dinner with Jane and Morley Safer, old friends from their days in London. They had invited Mike Wallace, Morley's fellow presenter on *Sixty Minutes*, a major television programme, and two others prominent in the US media. They were all adamant that the Clinton administration reacted to pressure: if we did not hit back very visibly and challenge the administration on the issue we could be sure our plan would be dumped. So I agreed to take the argument on to television, appearing on a wide range of programmes – even finding myself on the *Phil Donahue Show*, a popular programme having little to do with current affairs. On the morning of his live show, after reading in a newspaper that he was planning to talk about rape in Bosnia, with an audience discussion, I cancelled my appearance – only to be rung up by Phil Donahue trying to persuade me to go on. Eventually I did, but as my price I had a full twenty minutes to explain our plan, with a map on the screen, before there was any discussion of rapes.

In fact rape and the treatment of women in Bosnia-Herzegovina was already rightly becoming an issue of immense concern. The European Council in Edinburgh in December 1992 had established a working group which reported on the situation.[70] The UN General Assembly passed two Resolutions, both entitled 'Rape and abuse of women in the area of armed conflict in the former Yugoslavia'.[v] Rape was included as an important innovation in the category of crimes against humanity in the statute of the YWCT.[71] Soldiers raping women is a frequent accompaniment of victory in war, and it happened on all sides, but the Serbs were responsible for by far the most cases and this has led people to link rape to the charge of genocide. There were also cases of male rape. Women and children were not, however, murdered as often as men of fighting age. It will not be easy in the fog of war and amid charge and counter-charge to draw clear lines in this and other areas that are before the Tribunal, but it is very important for the future and for humanitarian law that they try.

I have little doubt that had we not fought our corner the VOPP would have been dead in the water by the middle of February and we would have never reached the stage of having it approved in Athens by all of the parties

three months later. On the McNeil–Lehrer current affairs television show a
Democrat Congressman, Frank McCloskey from Indiana, who had earlier
referred to our 'appeasement strategy', launched into an emotive string of
soundbites to which I finally retorted: 'Congressman, that is not a policy,
that is a rant.' This exchange encapsulated the essence of the problem.
Vance and I certainly had the same deep emotional feelings as our critics,
and so did European intellectuals and politicians, but emotion is not of itself
a policy. The UN Security Council, with a nasty, brutal war on its hands,
had for months confined itself to rhetoric in its many Resolutions. Now, in
fairness, many countries in the Security Council knew that there was an
urgent need for solutions. There was no sign, however, that the Clinton
administration had done any new thinking during the transition period
between one President and another. They promised to come up with an
alternative policy over the next few weeks, but in the meantime seemed
intent on killing off a detailed plan backed by all their allies and close to
being agreed by the parties. It was by any standard of international diplomacy outrageous conduct.

The headline of the *New York Times* of 4 February read 'US Will Not
Push Muslims to Accept Bosnia Peace Plan – Readies its own Proposal –
Vance–Owen Approach Flawed, Washington Says, but Few Options are
Apparent'. The *Los Angeles Times* had an editorial the same day headlined
'The Secretary Ducks a Rather Clever Trap' – 'Christopher says, rightly,
"no thank you" to Lord Owen'. It went on to argue that 'Owen's attempt
to turn his and Vance's failure into Clinton's failure is just outrageous
enough to suggest a paradoxical intent. That is, if his demand for a US
military rescue of the plan is rejected, Washington might seem, like the
European Community, to have finally acquiesced in Serb aggression. Or so
the ruse would go.' The newspaper advocated a separate bilateral initiative
with Russia, but ignored the fact that the Russians had been closely
involved by us in the formulation of the VOPP and were broadly content
with its provisions. The *Christian Science Monitor* in an editorial on 5
February entitled 'Lord Owen's Diplomatic Arm-Twist', wrote, 'If such
guilt and pressure tactics seem familiar, it may be because they are the same
ones Vance and Owen used on the wretched Muslims in Geneva – telling
them that unless they give up their rights and accept defeat, the world will
hold them responsible.'

But it was not all criticism. Under an ironic headline in the *New York
Times*, 'The Crime of Vance and Owen', A. M. Rosenthal wrote:

> *When everybody is screaming nobody is listening. Rarely have so many
> American commentators, editorial writers and think tankers screamed
> so loud and bitterly at any Western diplomats as they are doing . . .
> villains, Vance, Owen villains . . . The truth is that the Vance–Owen*

plan is trying to create Bosnia, not to destroy it – a fact that the screamers cannot hear over themselves . . . The Clinton Administration is doing something more dangerous for a great power than screaming – mumbling. The mumblemouths say Washington does not oppose the plan but will not ask the parties to accept it – death through lockjaw . . . If Vance–Owen is rejected, the war will go on, Bosnia will probably disappear in Serbian–Croatian partition . . . More likely somebody will get a bright idea – that's enough killing, let's tell these people they have to live together in a decentralised state in which they share power. And somebody else will wonder it out loud – say whatever happened to those fellows, you know the quiet American and the other one, the kind of crabby Englishman?

My brief foray into US domestic politics was nearly over – apart from a blast at the East Coast liberals at a Foreign Affairs Council lunch meeting in New York for not defending Cy Vance enough. I knew it was time now to let the internal debate we had triggered take its course, and go back to quiet diplomacy. The European Community countries had made it clear that they stood by the VOPP. We now had to rely on that innate decency which characterizes most American attitudes, albeit sometimes overlaid by a vulgarity and loudness that do not truly reflect the inner voice of a fine democracy. I felt confident even in the midst of all this controversy that there was no new or different policy for the Clinton administration to discover and that this truth would now come to the surface far sooner than would have otherwise been the case. The key question was whether this would happen in time for the VOPP to be rescued and put back on the negotiating table. President Ozal of Turkey came to Washington and advocated force as the only thing the Serbs would ever understand, which did not help; the Prime Minister of Canada, Brian Mulroney, visited Washington and emphasized that a lot of constructive work had been done on the VOPP and that any inadequacies in it could be fixed with some amendments and greater American involvement, which did help. Not for the first or last time, the Canadian voice in the crisis of former Yugoslavia was that of common sense stemming from a readiness to share the UN military burden and a depth of understanding of what the UN could and should be able to achieve.

The *New York Times* continued to be the most influential of our critics and attacked me personally in an editorial, headlined 'Lord Owen's Googly', for my 'cheeky, almost condescending lecture'. They defined a googly, a disguised leg-break in cricket, as getting a novice in baseball to swing at a trick pitch. That was followed later by an explosive encounter with their editorial board that masterminded their Bosnian policy. One of their critical columnists, Anthony Lewis, was kind enough to travel to New

York from Boston for a chat after we had talked on the telephone; but his next column, while putting my argument fairly, ended: 'In any event, Lord Owen should not believe that President Bill Clinton will put pressure on the victims, the Muslims, to accept the plan.' The Europeans, however, remained very steady, helped by President Mitterrand voicing strong support and promising that, even if the VOPP were rejected by the Security Council, France would remain attached to the principles that inspired it: a single Bosnian state, flexible and autonomous internal structures and a consensus between the three communities for matters of common interest.

Over the weekend of 6–7 February, following the diplomatic absence of President Izetbegovic, the Bosnian government's Foreign Minister, Haris Silajdzic, had come to New York for talks with Dr Karadzic and Mr Boban. Karadzic was protesting because he had been confined by the New York police to a small area of ten blocks close to the UN and also because as a consequence he could not attend the Orthodox church on Sunday. I always felt, perhaps unfairly, that Karadzic paraded his churchgoing for political purposes, with the aim of solidifying his support among the Mihailovic tradition within Serb nationalism, which was well represented among the American Serbs. The UN also had trouble with Prime Minister Akmadzic, who claimed the right to speak to the Security Council since, though a Croat, he was senior to Foreign Minister Silajdzic in the Bosnia-Herzegovina government. This only exposed how much of a sham the post-referendum coalition had become, with the Croats within the coalition now openly differing from the Muslims on every issue. The UN Secretary-General saw Akmadzic; the Security Council decided that he could see the Council President but not speak to the Council.

Silajdzic, however, refused to meet the other parties, which had always been his preferred line in Geneva. Instead, he tabled a paper of preconditions covering heavy weapons and agreement on a full constitution; when told that would take three months, he indicated that was an acceptable timetable, as his objections were related more to the implementation of the plan than to its fundamentals. Boban had been quite helpful in suggesting adaptations to the map in the north and west, particularly in the areas of Prijedor and Brcko, both of importance to Izetbegovic, but he was not ready to give ground in the south. For Karadzic, the problems with the map remained the same, mainly that it did not give the Serbs contiguous territory, so that Bosnian Serbs could not cross from one province to another without passing through what he called 'enemy territory'.

On Monday 8 February I briefed EC ambassadors in New York. I said it was vital that the EC should stand its ground and warned that there was a risk that the US would put forward non-negotiable changes in the map. We were in no hurry for a Security Council Resolution, and that afternoon Vance and I talked to the ambassadors of the five permanent members for we were keen to brief the new US ambassador, Madeleine Albright. We told them that Silajdzic had shown interest in NATO implementing the no-fly zone as part of the peacekeeping plan, obtaining credible – unlike in Croatia – heavy weapons control from the UN, free access to all areas in Bosnia-Herzegovina for UNPROFOR and other UN agencies, establishment of an international commission on human rights for Bosnia-Herzegovina by a Security Council Resolution and also the establishment of a war crimes tribunal. The Russians reported that there was now friction between Belgrade and Karadzic. The British wanted us to press on on the basis of a revised map we had suggested, but to stop speaking about imposing solutions and instead talk about friendly persuasion. These ideas were welcomed by the Americans. Afterwards we briefed the Security Council members; it was very interesting to watch their faces as we dealt with many of their concerns and it became clear that we now had majority support. As we left together to talk to the press Cy turned to me and said that meeting had shown we were right to leave Geneva and come to New York, where we could not be sidelined and where we could deal directly with all the key countries. We had initiated an influential process of working directly with the Security Council and thereby forcing the US to set their policy in that forum.

Meanwhile, UNHCR deliveries to Bosnia-Herzegovina were only averaging half the weekly target of 8,000 tonnes, and that week had fallen to 3,500 tonnes. The airlift had been suspended after an attack on a plane carrying humanitarian supplies, though it had since been resumed. The attack on the Mostar convoy on 2 February, with nine shells on the same target, showed serious intent and had put the Mostar road out of use; convoys were now using secondary roads from Split. Bihac remained isolated with no assistance getting through because of a Serb blockade. Also in central Bosnia 7,000 people had been forced to leave besieged areas and seek refuge in Tuzla and about 4,500, mainly Muslims, had been expelled by the Serbs from Trebinje and had sought refuge in Montenegro, where they had been well received. Indeed, a rare encouraging feature of the whole tragedy was that refugees in Montenegro and Serbia were well looked after, mainly in people's own homes under UNHCR supervision, throughout the war. Also, despite the Muslim–Croat war of 1993–4 the Croatian government went on receiving refugees and supported the UNHCR camps. UNHCR had placed experienced rape counsellors in Sarajevo, Mostar and Zenica and was undertaking a joint mission with UNICEF to help abandoned babies.

As yet it had been a mild winter and humanitarian supplies, albeit in insufficient quantities, had nevertheless got through. However, we had alarming reports on the humanitarian situation from the military in the field, which served to stimulate Vance and me to greater activity.[72] In New

York among many of the diplomats we found there was never the same sense of urgency over the humanitarian crisis that was evident in Geneva, perhaps because the UNHCR HQ and ICRC were not there, or simply because of the width of the Atlantic and the focus of the Security Council on military matters.

In Washington on 10 February Christopher announced the new policy of the US administration.[73] It had been extensively leaked in advance, and the London *Times* on 9 February had a story headlined 'American Bluster Marks Qualified Approval for Peace Plan'. 'It is becoming plain', the article remarked, 'that the Clinton Administration cannot have a policy in the Balkans without committing ground troops.' Since they had no intention of committing troops, we hoped they would develop a more supportive and coherent policy. Warren Christopher's statement was far better than either Vance or I had hoped for in relation to the VOPP. Cy felt comfortable with it and told me that it totally justified us putting them under so much public pressure. The *New York Times* headline the next day was for once a joy to read – 'US Backs Bosnian Peace Plan' – and the paper said that the administration had abandoned the tough campaign talk and embraced an international peace process. The administration appointed an envoy to participate in our negotiations and promised that if a viable agreement containing enforcement provisions was reached, the United States would be prepared to join with the United Nations, NATO and others in implementing and enforcing it, including possible US military action. That promise was to haunt the Clinton administration, for it was immediately seized on by the Europeans and it became the source of much of the friction that developed across the Atlantic, particularly when it became clear that it was a commitment entered into by the administration only reluctantly and that it was questionable whether it would ever be fulfilled.

We had, by going public, prevented the administration from consigning our plan quietly to an American garbage can. Now we were ameliorative and issued a low-key statement through our press spokesman welcoming the appointment of the US envoy, Ambassador Reginald Bartholomew. Interestingly, perhaps in a Freudian slip, Warren Christopher had twice called Bartholomew 'Owen' at the press conference announcing the envoy's appointment.

The Russian President, Boris Yeltsin, neatly countered the US announcement by asking that his own envoy, Vitaly Churkin, who was already close to the negotiations, be given observer status too. Neither the US or Russia at this stage wanted their envoys to be negotiators at the table but we were delighted to have them in any guise. Both Vance and I knew that when confronted by the realities they were both wise enough to give good advice to their governments, and this could only help us. In New York

Ambassador Bartholomew, after attending his first meeting with us, said to the press: 'I made it very clear that our interest is in helping the process. We are not here to supplant the process. We don't want to turn this into an American process.'

For me the one depressing feature of Warren Christopher's 10 February speech was his refusal to countenance ever imposing a solution. I could not accept that policy. I had fought against it before his speech and I continued to fight against it, for it was to emasculate our diplomacy and send a signal to the Bosnian Serbs in Pale that we had no bottom line to the negotiating process.

Meanwhile, President Izetbegovic had written to us to say that 'the revisions you have made to the proposed map of Bosnia-Herzegovina can be understood as a certain correction, but yet are not sufficient.' What was important was that we had revised our map as a result of the discussions in New York with all three parties and before the US had announced its policy and appointed its envoy. This meant that the Serbs could not depict the changes as having been dictated by the Americans. The significant change in our map was that the UN 'throughway' road which provided the guaranteed northern corridor for the Serbs now went through not just the Posavina province, which had had a Croat majority before the war, but also through the Muslim majority province of Tuzla, since we had extended that province to Brcko. Posavina province was by 1993 full of Serb refugees and Izetbegovic feared it might become a pawn in a Serb–Croat carve-up, even to the extent of the Serbs being allowed to remain in the majority at Posavina in exchange for more land in Western Herzegovina. Also, the extra land we had provided for the Bihac province around Prijedor meant that we could be more certain that some of the worst ethnic cleansing would be reversed. But Vance and I were in no doubt that we had stretched the elastic very tight and that these changes, while making it easier for the Americans to support the VOPP and constituting the key factor in bringing the Muslims to accept the plan, were also significantly stiffening Serb resistance to the VOPP. I believe that linking up Tuzla with Brcko, although ethnically totally justified in that every village as well as the town had had a Muslim majority before 1992, meant that General Mladic strategically became an implacable opponent of our plan. He was always going to resist anything other than a territorial northern corridor of about 8–10 km wide. Yet had we not made this adjustment we would have lost the VOPP in New York in early February.

The British position throughout my open battle with the US administration had been totally supportive, largely due to John Major, but also to consistent backing from Sir David Hannay, our representative at the UN in New York. His nerve and backbone had been decisive in countering the wobbles from our Embassy in Washington who had wanted to be onside with the new administration. As the flak began to fly, the Foreign Office in London, under the then Political Director Len Appleyard, also held steady. Douglas Hurd, after a little understandable anxiety, reflected in a telephone conversation we had, rallied to my support when I admitted the Johnny Apple interview had come out badly and had been my mistake. The British press were split between those who wanted me to stand up to the US and those who preferred the traditional diplomatic posture of at least publicly pretending to be in total accord. The EC Presidency had by now passed from Britain to Denmark and the Danish Foreign Ministers, first Uffe Elleman-Jensen and then Niels Helveg Petersen, both very committed Europeans, were firm throughout in their belief that we had an agreed EC policy and that we should uphold it, even if that meant upsetting the Americans. On 16 February Helveg Petersen, speaking for the EC Presidency in Washington, said that the EC had arrived at a clear position of support for the VOPP and that he could see no reason to trim.

At one time reports out of Washington tried to imply that my personal position with Cy Vance was under strain at this period and that Cy would soon bow out, but that story did not run since Vance made it utterly clear to everyone, from Warren Christopher downwards, that he stood by me and what I was saying. All this time, too, Boutros Boutros Ghali was firm in standing by us both, helped by his long-standing friendship with Cy Vance. Our negotiating team, though now divided between Geneva and New York, was totally united and there were none of the self-serving leaks about unnamed individuals having their own personal reservations that can be so debilitating and which the parties would have exploited.

On 18 February Haris Silajdzic, as Foreign Minister of the Bosnia-Herzegovina government, gave his testimony at a hearing of the European Affairs Sub-Committee of the Senate Foreign Relations Committee,[vi] chaired by Senator Biden who presented his own peace plan. Prime Minister Akmadzic also wanted to speak, but was not heard, and then disowned Silajdzic's testimony in a letter to Senator Biden and to the UN Secretary-General.[74] Martti Ahtisaari, Paul Szasz and Fred Eckhard went down to Washington to brief Congress on the ICFY and the VOPP.

The public relations propaganda war was by this stage a feature of the war in Bosnia-Herzegovina. Documents filed with the US Justice Department showed that Croatia was paying Ruder Finn Global Public Affairs, a Washington-based PR firm, $10,000 a month plus expenses to present 'a positive Croatian image' to members of Congress, administration officials and the news media. For their part, the Bosnian government were paying for services which included 'writing and placing op-ed articles, guest columns and letters to the editor'. According to the *Atlanta Journal/Constitution* of 28 February 1993, between June and December 1992 Ruder Finn on behalf of the Bosnian government

set up more than 30 interviews with major US news organizations and
distributed 13 news releases, 37 fax updates, 17 official letters and eight
official statements . . . arranged meetings between Bosnian officials and
Vice-Presidential candidate Al Gore, acting Secretary of State Lawrence
Eagleburger and 10 influential Senators, including majority Leader
George Mitchell and minority Leader Robert Dole. It made 48 phone
calls to members of the House, 20 calls to members of the Senate and
more than 80 calls to newspaper columnists, television anchors and
other journalists.

We in ICFY had no resources capable of matching any of this. This experience gives me some sympathy with those countries who feel the need to
maintain a very large embassy staff in Washington. The Israelis were the
first to understand the significance of lobbying Congress on international
affairs. Some governments even employ public relations companies to help
put their own case. Perhaps we are entering a new era where no UN
sanctions package will be complete without a ban on employing public
relations firms.

In Geneva, Cy Vance and I had tended to avoid public comment on many
of the issues while negotiations were in progress, but we had become
concerned at our own inability to relay the facts as we saw them across the
Atlantic. The ICFY with Fred Eckhard as our spokesman was as open as
possible with the press, but often even he could not comment during negotiations, whatever the provocation, and this gave the Bosnian Muslims an
opening which they used effectively. The most trenchant comment after a
year in Sarajevo came from General Sir Michael Rose in a talk to the Royal
United Services Institute on 30 March 1995.[vii] He said: 'It is of course quite
understandable that a Government struggling for survival should have a
propaganda machine. It is not understandable that the international media
should become part of that machine. Mischievous distortion of reality can
only undermine the work of those who are pursuing the path towards
peace.' Reuters, Agence France-Presse and the BBC kept a fair balance, but
much of the reporting out of Bosnia took place with shells landing around
the cameramen, and was bound to be emotive. It is no use politicians and
diplomats bewailing the so-called CNN effect. It is here to stay and in that
it means millions of people know more about the world we live in politicians and diplomats will have to learn the skills to counter instant emotions
and to present facts and complexities with better skill than those who
distort or slant information.

The deterioration in the humanitarian situation inside Bosnia-Herzegovina
forced Mrs Ogata to announce from Nairobi that UNHCR was suspending
its operations in Bosnia-Herzegovina until the political leaders on all sides
honoured their commitments to allow convoys of urgently needed food and

medicine to pass through without obstructing or stealing the supplies. I had great sympathy for her predicament. General Philippe Morillon, surprised by the sudden announcement, said he took his orders from the UN Secretary-General, and Boutros Boutros Ghali was very annoyed to hear the news without any warning. Technically the Secretary-General is not in charge of UNHCR and it was within Mrs Ogata's power to take the decision, but it was quickly reversed. She felt she had consulted Cy Vance, who for his part thought he had advised her to clear her lines first with the Secretary-General. It was not long before Vance and I were being blamed for masterminding the decision in order to pressurize the Muslims, but this was quite wrong. Mrs Ogata worked closely with ICFY but she is a self-sufficient, principled and determined woman who guards her independence of action and that of the UNHCR with commendable vigour.

The US debate over lifting the arms embargo was a strangely ill-informed one, with the Croatian role in controlling all arms supplies to the Bosnian government, and the fact that they exercised virtually a total ban on heavy weapons going to the Muslims, in case they were turned on the Croats instead of the Serbs, never featuring. The image of Bosnian Muslims with no arms was not diminished even when President Izetbegovic openly acknowledged on Sarajevo television that the Bosnian government had smuggled arms in through secret channels: 'We managed to get hold of 30,000 rifles and machine guns, 20 million bullets, 37,000 mines, 46,000 anti-armour rockets, 20,000 hand grenades, 90,000 military uniforms and 120,000 pairs of boots.' Izetbegovic presumably felt he could not afford to allow the impression of being the victim to develop into that of an army devoid of any weaponry and therefore bound to lose and not worth helping. In that same interview he said that the VOPP, following inevitable modifications, could be accepted as the basis for a peace settlement, since it secured the preservation of the Bosnian state. It was as if he had now recognized that the US government would not rescue the Bosnian Muslims by intervening militarily and that it was time to come back to the VOPP, after distancing himself and his government from it for nearly two damaging months. Yet it was to take us another month of persuasive diplomacy[75] eventually to obtain President Izetbegovic's signature on all four of the peace plan's documents, the fourth being the complex and sensitive arrangements for an interim government to take power during the transitional period.

In Bosnia, General Morillon had met Karadzic, who had claimed that his troops had discovered a mass grave of fifty Serb bodies, allegedly killed by Muslims, south of Zvornik. We had just had the report of a preliminary site exploration of the mass graves of Croats supposed to have been killed by Serbs outside Vukovar, and there was another alleged mass grave in the UN protected areas of Serbs supposedly killed by the Croats. For months past

Vance and I had been trying to have the bodies in the Eastern UNPA exhumed and a forensic pathology investigation undertaken. As time passed, the excuses varied – the ground was frozen, or muddy, or the temperature too hot – but conditions, it seemed, were never suitable. The harsh facts were that governments were reluctant to take the responsibility for mounting these investigations and, with UNPROFOR lacking resources and direction, it was left too much to the UN's own investigative Commission.

It had become very apparent to Vance and me that the strong position of the ICFY in the protection of human rights was being ignored. Since it was an area in which we had both been actively involved for many years we were determined to put this right, so we started to work on an annex to the next of our regular reports to the UN Security Council which would give an account of all that we were doing and proposed doing.[76] We were also close to winning support in the Council of Europe on a standing mechanism which would facilitate the establishment of a human rights court for countries like Bosnia-Herzegovina, which I had suggested when I had gone with Paul Szasz to talk to the Assembly in Strasbourg on 8 October. This was incorporated as part of the interim arrangements. It was a transitional human rights mechanism drawing on the competence and experience of the central organs of the European Convention on Human Rights, which I hoped would promote the process of accession to full membership of the Council of Europe.[viii]

Towards the end of February it was still not clear where the US administration was heading. Discussion of the American military operation to parachute food and medicine into remote areas of Bosnia led to few European offers of help. Christopher explained that Clinton wanted to move towards a settlement building on the VOPP that was just, workable and durable and preserved Bosnia as a state. Implementation, he said, did not necessarily mean deployment of US ground forces and he made it clear he did not see an enforceable agreement just around the corner. The former Secretary of State Lawrence Eagleburger, when asked on CNN on 23 February what he thought the Clinton administration's policy was and what it should be in regard to the Vance–Owen plan, said: 'To the degree I can figure it out, and I don't mean that critically, I think basically they support the plan but they want amendments to it. I think it is clear that they feel that the Vance–Owen plan has given too much to the Serbs and they would like to see that reduced. I understand that concern. I don't happen to believe that it is going to be possible – and I hope I am wrong – to convince the Serbs to take the plan if, in fact, it cuts back on the proposals that Vance and Owen made.' It is salutary to remember that the VOPP gave the Serbs only 43 per cent of territory in a unified state, whereas by 1994–5 the Clinton administration as part of the Contact Group of nations were offering the Serbs 49 per cent in a state partitioned into two entities.

President Izetbegovic had arrived in Washington on 27 February and accepted an invitation to meet Vance and me in New York on Monday evening. Karadzic had arrived on Saturday 28 February, fortunately after, not before, the bomb in the World Trade Center had gone off amid initial rumours that a fifteen-minute warning had been given by Serbs. In fact it turned out to be the work of an extremist Muslim group based in the US. At our meeting with Izetbegovic it was clear that despite our arguing that time did not play for him, but for the Serbs, he was still not ready to accept our map.

I reported to the EC by COREU telegram on a frustrating day of bilateral negotiations.[77] Next day the UNHCR report made a devastating contrast to the complacency of the politicians, describing the situation on the ground in eastern Bosnia as 'total domination of war logic over humanitarian concerns'. While the UNHCR's cancellation of the convoys had impacted internationally, the situation on the ground had reached an 'unspeakable state'. This situation we tried to highlight in a press statement drawing attention to the heavy fighting around Srebrenica, where the Serbs were continuing to impede access. The Serbs' linkage of humanitarian access to political and military conditions was deplorable; but even as one's tongue formed words of condemnation one knew the international community would accept and even tolerate it. This was the daily discomfort that we lived with – my weapon was words and beyond them there was no prospect of international power being exercised. Here we were in New York talking to the Security Council at the apex of international power, and yet these humanitarian horrors might have been happening on another planet for all the deterrent response they elicited. My powerlessness was uncomfortable for me, but for the UNHCR worker in Sarajevo or Srebrenica the situation was a living nightmare.

The slow soft shuffle of the Clinton administration towards supporting our peace plan was under way but nothing was going to happen quickly, particularly while the Muslim politicians from Sarajevo were not evincing the need for speed. I suppose because of my medical training I could never accept this disconnection between war and peace: for me, the more serious the symptoms the greater the need for early treatment. As negotiators, we had to be optimistic and buoyant in order to create and foster an atmosphere of hope. A negotiator in a time of war has this constant problem of how to build and sustain momentum when the parties to a negotiation, particularly their politicians not directly involved on the battle-field, often have a vested interest in appearing pessimistic and downbeat and want to give the impression that their negotiations are getting nowhere in order to justify and give heart to those condemned to fight on the home front and in the battle lines. Negotiating during a war can only be compared with negotiating during a strike, but at least in a strike those whose services are being disrupted raise their voices in favour of resolving the dispute. In a war the civilians facing hardship cannot easily demand peace without being accused of undermining the morale of the fighters at the front. The saddest feature of the war in Bosnia-Herzegovina was that the voice of its people was but rarely heard. We tried to raise the profile of the multi-ethnic civic groups, decent people wanting to live together as before the war, but their voice, while championed by a few abroad, was drowned out by the propaganda of war. We knew the urge for peace was there but it manifested itself only in little things, like the tears in the eyes of the mainly female interpreters brought out from Sarajevo as they realized that we had reached deadlock, or in their pleading to us to carry on negotiating into the night – even when they personally were obviously tired out, for interpreting can be hard work. Sometimes, when there was a real interchange and the negotiation moved beyond set speeches, we could sense the relief and hope in the interpreters. This small number of ordinary people, sometimes mothers with children, were far more important than they probably realized in keeping up our flagging spirits and in making us sit for so many long hours searching for a settlement. By contrast the Bosnian politicians, whether Serb, Muslim or Croat, were almost without exception impossibly negative. Izetbegovic would not meet with Karadzic, who was being totally unyielding over the map, and this put Karadzic in an even fouler mood. The humiliation of still being restricted wherever he went in New York, and having the threat of a civil law action being served on him at any time for alleged war crimes, was taking its toll. The Serbs preferred the less confrontational atmosphere of Geneva.

I flew back to Europe for an EC Foreign Ministers' meeting on 8 March in Brussels. The member states were constructive in their comments and positive about standing firm on the VOPP; many echoed the view that keeping Russia onside was essential. I felt proud of the EC. It could not have been easy for many of those Foreign Ministers personally to go out so far on a limb against US policy. But the EC had stuck together under considerable pressure and given me every backing with virtually no second-guessing or running around behind my back to undercut me in Washington. The Dutch were the least committed to the VOPP, followed by the Germans, while the other countries were very solid.

On 9 March it was announced from Paris that Vance and I had asked President Mitterrand to invite President Milosevic to Paris for talks with the Co-Chairmen, which while 'under the auspices of France is a working session between negotiators.' We wanted to persuade Milosevic to put pressure on Karadzic, and we believed Mitterrand could personally be of crucial importance in achieving this, so on 5 March we had asked the French Ambassador to the UN, Mérimée, to see if he could arrange it. In Le Monde there was a forthright recognition that Milosevic held the key to any solution, for he could 'launch his troops against Croatia, trigger rebellions in Krajina,

Slavonia or Bosnia, back ethnic cleansing or suddenly pose as "champion of peace" when political talks are on the verge of breakdown'. In the US there was, as yet, no readiness to concede the importance of Milosevic.

We met at the Elysée Palace on 11 March in the late afternoon. President Mitterrand had a preliminary *tête-à-tête* with Milosevic. During the five hours of meetings that followed, the greater part of which President Mitterrand attended, he was in top form: he was well briefed and his interventions were timely and frequently delivered with great emotion, notably when he spoke of Serbia's historical ties with France and when drawing from his own personal experiences. More than once Mitterrand referred to his time as a prisoner of war, when he had been greatly impressed by the resilience of Serb prisoners under conditions much worse than his own. For him, Serbia's current disappearance from the European scene, and the vacuum it left, conjured up the same feelings he had experienced on hearing of the fall of Belgrade in 1941. He allowed Vance and me to take the lead for much of the time and reinforced our arguments where appropriate to great effect. Looking to us for guidance in his response, and making clear his full support for our proposals, he described the plan at one stage as a baby more beautiful than its parents believed. I was greatly struck by the verve and stamina he showed, in marked contrast to his performance when I had last met him in December.

Mitterrand used all forms of persuasion and argument when dealing with Milosevic. France, he said, was one of Serbia's historical friends, and did not want to see Serbia isolated or unfairly punished; but Milosevic had to face the realities of the current situation and the international climate. If the war continued there would be little even Serbia's oldest friends and allies could do to prevent its further isolation. Even Russia was unlikely to step out of line if the international community called for tighter sanctions. It was imperative to get an agreement in the coming days. Milosevic was faced with a historic choice. No one was claiming he could twist the Bosnian Serbs around his little finger, but they looked to him as their 'big brother': he had real authority. Either 'the war continues, the tragedy gets worse, sanctions get tougher', or it is halted, enabling Serbia to rebuild its economy and play its rightful role in Europe. Coming on the heels of President Mitterrand's visit to Washington and immediately before his visit to Moscow, the meeting was all the more timely.

We explained that the plan we had developed was a fair one, and had the firm support of the European Community and many traditional friends of the Serbs such as Russia. It offered protection for Serbian national identity and culture, and was not biased against the Serbs. In recent weeks we could easily have gained Izetbegovic's signature by further adjusting the map at the expense of the Serbs, but had stoutly refused the pressure to do so. During the afternoon session Milosevic appeared to be little moved by these arguments, referring to the injustice of the treatment meted out to Serbia compared with that of Croatia and the Muslims in Bosnia-Herzegovina. Serbia was being persecuted for something over which it had no control. He too wanted peace and would do what he could to help, but there were limits to his influence. While he had been able to bring influence to bear in respect of the constitutional principles and the military agreement, he could not influence the Bosnian Serbs on the map. This was a question for the three Bosnian parties to resolve among themselves. He suggested that there should be an immediate ceasefire, and that the military agreement should be implemented, leaving the question of the map to be resolved later. We stressed that agreement on the map was an integral part of the package, as it delineated the provinces into which troops would withdraw under the military agreement. Agreement would establish provisional provincial boundaries; a boundary commission would be established to settle the final lines. The map should not be regarded as the be all and end all of any settlement.

Vance and I felt after the afternoon session that if Milosevic was going to risk his neck over Bosnia-Herzegovina, he would want something significant for it. That view was reinforced by Milosevic's parting comment of the afternoon to me after Mitterrand's powerful peroration: 'Why did he not raise the lifting of sanctions?' Ever the pragmatist, the emotion had not seemingly moved him at all. What he wanted was a bargain and to be treated equally. Sanctions were to him a slight on the Serbian nation as well as an economic millstone. He was ready to deal over economic sanctions then, and he showed even greater readiness a month later in Belgrade.

When Mitterrand rejoined the meeting in the evening, he had clearly thought long and hard about the importance Milosevic attached to economic arguments, and in particular the question of lifting sanctions. He had obviously decided that if progress was to be made with Milosevic, this bullet had to be bitten, and he set out France's position in dramatic and unambiguous terms. If the map was accepted, 'then sanctions must and should be lifted as soon as technically feasible.' He admitted that this stance would no doubt be opposed in some quarters, but he would put his full weight behind getting others such as Chancellor Kohl to support it. France would 'fight and win the battle to lift sanctions'. He left Milosevic in no doubt about what was on offer, but also made it clear that there was a real danger of losing this opportunity. The time for taking a decision was very short: in three weeks he would have lost his majority in the French National Assembly, and his power would be only some 60 per cent of what it was now. Thereafter it would be much more difficult for him to deliver.

I detected a marked change in Milosevic's attitude as he realized the opportunities Mitterrand was offering if there were a peaceful settlement.

He returned to the question of the map in specific terms, and with greater interest, suggesting possible trade-offs of land on a hectare-for-hectare basis. When he learnt that Karadzic had singularly failed to engage in such negotiations he appeared genuinely surprised, and undertook to ask Karadzic to go to New York on 14 March for talks on the map and this time to negotiate seriously. We rose from dinner well content with what Mitterrand had achieved. Now we had to tighten sanctions but give a little time before they came into effect to act as an incentive for Milosevic to deliver.

What of Slobodan Milosevic the man? I had now studied him with great attention and considerable fascination for six months. Milosevic was born in August 1941, the son of a Serbian Orthodox clergyman of Montenegrin origin. His parents separated when he was young and both later committed suicide. A crucial figure in his life is Mirjana Markovic, his wife, for they are extremely close personally and politically. He joined the League of Communists in 1959 and graduated from Belgrade University's Law Faculty in 1964. He was involved in ideological and political activities with the League of Communists, was economic adviser to the mayor of Belgrade and worked in the Information Department of Belgrade city government, where he learnt his media skills, which are formidable. Above all he understands the power of television. He was director general of the enterprise 'Tehnogas' from 1970 to 1978 and then president of a Belgrade bank from 1978 to 1982, a period during which he travelled to America and elsewhere, acquiring fluent English along the way. Thereafter he returned to full-time officialdom in the League of Communists: head of the party organization in Belgrade in 1984–6, he was party chief for the entire republic from 1986 to 1989.

Milosevic first became identified in the minds of the general public with Serbian grievances with his criticism of the amount of money the central government demanded of them in comparison with the other republics. This public profile was suddenly raised in April 1987 when Milosevic twice visited the Serbian community in Kosovo, who were complaining about their plight as a minority and about being beaten up by the local Albanian police. On his second visit Milosevic became uncharacteristically emotional, proclaiming: 'No one will be allowed to beat you! No one will be allowed to beat you!' He then, with manipulative skill, set about getting Serbian politicians thought to be soft on the Albanian question voted out of their positions. Riding the wave of nationalism, he overturned the provincial Communist leadership and insisted that Belgrade must be able to exercise effective control over Serbia's two autonomous provinces of Kosovo and Vojvodina. As a popular hero, 'Slobo', he began to draw large audiences and in November 1988 he addressed a Belgrade rally of around a million people. By this time he was speaking for most Serbs, and he had a knack of poking fun affectionately at Tito. 'Even before his death the system didn't function, Tito functioned. After his death nothing has functioned and nobody has been able to reach agreement on anything.' He understood that Tito had spawned mechanisms for inertia and then filled the vacuum with his own initiatives.

On the question of what powers should be held by central government and what by regional or national grouping, Milosevic has clear views: he is a centralist. But we, coming from outside Serbia, had to recognize that there is a wide diversity of views on devolution even among democratic politicians in our own countries. For example, many British MPs believe a legislative parliament for Scotland would only whet the appetite for secession, while others think that it would reduce the appeal of the Scottish nationalists and enhance the unity of the United Kingdom. In the US some hate any federal powers, wanting power to stay with the states. Tito's autonomy package for Kosovo was more far-reaching than most other examples of devolution in the world, and it will be hard for Milosevic ever to agree to return that degree of power from the centre. He might prefer eventually to relinquish part of Kosovo to Albania.

There is a ruthlessness and a pursuit of power for its own sake about Milosevic that underpins the pragmatism that otherwise seems so neatly to characterize Milosevic's political personality. He has no affection for the trappings of power: he lives modestly and does not seek for the present to be the President of the FRY – indeed, he seems to like sending someone else to do the boring job of representing the FRY officially. He is content to manipulate people and events. In his study upstairs in the Serbian Presidency in the heart of Belgrade his desk was piled high with paper, but the appearance downstairs in the reception rooms was of controlled calm. A considerate host, he always appeared to have plenty of time: meetings were long and were usually accompanied at his insistence by lunch or dinner. At the Elysée he was not in the least overawed by his surroundings. If he noticed any slight in the absence of any French minister at the airport, it was brushed aside as only showing bad manners, or as he liked to say 'an absence of style'. The private man is not a racist, nor is he paranoid about the rest of the world. Only once over the years did he make an aside which offended me on racial grounds, and he checked himself as he said it. Proud of Serbia, he gives vent to a paranoia about the international community in public almost as an obligatory jibe, but even so not to an excessive degree. Milosevic carries his nationalism lightly and it does not intrude in an offensive manner in conversations with foreigners. He has used nationalism for the purpose of gaining and holding power but his economic attitudes are those of a man fully conscious of international realities. He knows America well and will talk knowledgeably about Democrat and Republican politics and the changing importance of the New Hampshire primary. When in Athens in 1995, I flew back to Belgrade in a Yugoslav plane which had just flown in the FRY Ambassador to Greece, Milan Milutinovic, who became

Foreign Minister in August 1995, and the former chairman of the US Democratic Party in New Hampshire, Chris Spiro, who had just seen Milosevic. In a chat in the airport he claimed that at a recent meeting with President Clinton he had told him that the last thing they wanted was for Bosnia to become a campaign issue in New Hampshire, and urged a peace before campaigning started in the autumn of 1995. I hoped that this domestic need would concentrate Clinton's mind so as to cut a deal over the heads of his foreign policy advisers, and this is what appeared to happen in August 1995 when he sent his National Security Adviser around Europe with a package that at last had political realism within it.

Milosevic was not a European social democrat in December 1989 and he made no bones about why: 'I really see no reason why any society, if it is not thoroughly tyrannical, should prevent a diversity of political views and organizations . . . However, if this so called political pluralism is used as another term to supplant Yugoslavia and socialism then we in Serbia are against it.' He showed his ruthless side when he manipulated federal authorization for JNA tanks to be used on 9 March 1991 nominally to crush street demonstrations in Belgrade but in reality in a failed attempt to have martial law declared. He never hesitates to ensure, when he wants to, that his view monopolizes the media. On the other hand, he has been content to forgo the non-stop personal publicity that usually accompanies autocratic power. It is a clever way of exercising control. His appeal to many people in Serbia initially was not rooted solely in ethnic nationalism: in 1991 he was also popular because he stood against the absurd bureaucracy of Tito's time. Milosevic's leadership was seen to be competent and not corrupt. He chaired a group of experts, the 'Commission for Questions of Social Reform', which proposed market-oriented reforms and the stimulation and streamlining of the self-management system; but its recommendation was not the elimination of state functions, rather changes in their 'mentality and style'. The goal was a mixed economy with social ownership and public production, not the continental social market model. Nevertheless it was sufficiently different and coherent in comparison to Tito's failed economic model that it attracted support from the younger technocrats. When faced by criticism Milosevic can bridle and quickly deride alternative viewpoints, but he can also be changing his attitude as he talks. For someone who built a reputation campaigning against bureaucracy he has created an immense one, not of pens behind desks but in the large and well-armed militia which now rules over Serbia. It is strong enough to keep opposition political parties in their place, strong enough to act as a counterforce to a greatly depleted army and well placed to destroy the mafia that now flourishes on the corruption that surrounds sanctions.

One aspect of Milosevic's character is his readiness to regard individuals as disposable: to use them and then discard them. Just as he had risen within the Communist Party on the back of his friendship with Ivan Stambolic and then brushed him aside, so he still brooks no opposition. Perhaps when the wars in Croatia and Bosnia-Herzegovina are over Milosevic will allow some relaxation of police powers, some genuine dissent, even move towards social democracy. But history is against such a benign transformation. If he is to avoid a malign fate, he needs to remember, and recite to himself each day when shaving, Lord Acton's famous dictum: 'Power tends to corrupt, and absolute power corrupts absolutely.'

On almost every occasion that we met I would at some stage raise Kosovo, and when I did I knew I was striking a jarring note. Over Kosovo the polite mask sometimes broke and we would be into an ugly confrontation. It was as if he knew this was the area of his most indefensible behaviour on which he was personally vulnerable, and he would sometimes turn snarling on me or anyone who raised it. I suspect none of those close to him ever did confront him. Yet once we had confronted each other he would soon return to a courteous dialogue, almost as if he welcomed someone standing up to him. It was on Kosovo that Milosevic had risen to power and in the process had spoken for almost all Serbs, who genuinely believed Tito had sacrificed their interests for the sake of keeping the Albanians quiet. It was in part over Kosovo that Milosevic broke up the Carrington plan for autonomy because it mirrored that for the Krajina; yet Milosevic will know that Kosovo could be his undoing after the fall of the Krajina in 1995. I have often likened him to someone who has jumped on to the tiger of nationalism and is finding it difficult to get off again without the tiger eating him. In Paris he saw an opportunity for getting off at least that portion of the tiger's anatomy marked Bosnia-Herzegovina, and in fairness he stayed true to that strand of policy from then onwards.

In early March 1993 our strategy was in place. We felt confident that Izetbegovic would soon sign up for all four papers in the VOPP, putting his signature to the interim government paper as well as the map. Karadzic would, we felt, accept the interim government paper with some adjustments but on the map was going to remain very difficult. To put maximum pressure on the Serbs we needed a Security Council Resolution toughening sanctions and covering FRY economic assets passed with an implementation date set around the middle of April.

Another aspect of winning support for the VOPP was to have in position a credible implementation force. The Europeans, including the French, believed that our original proposal for a purely UN implementation force was now insufficient and were adamant that the US had to be involved. But the US had their bottom line defined with some exactness by the Chairman of the Joint Chiefs of Staff, General Colin Powell. In his autobiography Powell describes how the early meetings of the administration on Bosnia were full of 'belligerent rhetoric' and how the 'debate exploded at one session when Madeleine Albright, our ambassador to the UN, asked me in frustration "What's the point of having this superb military that you're always talking about if we can't use it?" I thought I would have an aneurysm!'[ix] Powell then explained to her that tough political goals had to be established first. For him it had to be a NATO operation under UN authority with adequate command and control arrangements, and he would not countenance the French sidelining NATO's Supreme Allied Commander (SACEUR) – then General Shalikashvili – nor his HQ, SHAPE. SACEUR had authority over the American Admiral, then Mike Boorda as CINCSOUTH, Naples, and the involvement of SHAPE was in Powell's view essential for the success of the operation. Most Europeans felt they had to meet these criteria, for Clinton was in no position to override Powell's advice after the debacle over removing the ban on homosexuals serving in the army. The French were the apparent obstacle but many believed, as I did, that their military chief Admiral Lanxade would know when to settle differences with the Americans.

Never far from our minds was the deteriorating humanitarian situation. Sir Donald Acheson, whom I knew and thoroughly respected, was the WHO special representative, having just retired as the Chief Medical Officer in the Department of Health for England and Wales, and was keeping me in regular touch, often by telephone, with what was happening on the ground. On 16 March he sent me a copy of his fourteenth and final report in his period in office, after having travelled widely in Bosnia in an attempt to make a general assessment of the health of the people for his successor. His most striking conclusion was that although the degree of suffering varied, the nature of the misery was similar everywhere: insufficient food, both in quantity and quality; interrupted electricity supplies; compromised water supplies; inadequate collection of rubbish; large numbers of refugees and displaced persons with varying degrees of malnutrition; and often a high prevalence of lice and scabies – all in the midst of economic collapse. In Sarajevo, in addition to these problems, there was destruction of the utilities and serious damage to the sewage system. He concluded that, having survived the winter, the people of Bosnia, many of whom had reduced resistance to infection due to malnutrition, now faced the equally threatening problems of warm weather with its attendant hazards of illnesses due to microbial and rodent multiplication. It was impossible for me to forget my medical training and to ignore the existence of this physical misery, quite apart from the shelling and shooting. I knew by now that serious outside military intervention was completely out of the question and that the US, despite sometimes giving an impression that it was under consideration, were really grandstanding with an even greater reluctance than hitherto to committing forces on the ground. It was therefore imperative that we implemented the VOPP and pressurized for peace.

The Serbian stranglehold around the Srebrenica enclave was now becoming critical. One report said succinctly: 'There is no food and people are stealing and begging from each other. Situation is bad.' Pneumonia plus malnutrition was killing twenty to thirty people every day, and there were 100–200 extremely ill patients as well as some 300 less seriously ill but who required evacuation. The population had swollen far beyond the capacity of the town's water supplies, which were functioning only intermittently, and its sewage capacity. There were some sixty cases of tuberculosis. At this time General Philippe Morillon, wanting to do something about Srebrenica, had travelled courageously by road into the town and found himself stuck there, in effect a hostage, having been refused permission to leave by the Muslim soldiers within the enclave. With his typical aplomb Philippe publicly identified with the suffering Muslim people and said, standing on a UN vehicle, that he would stay until the surrounding Serbs agreed to aid convoys entering the enclave and to have the wounded evacuated. My attitude to this *démarche* was that of Pierre Bosquet on the Charge of the Light Brigade at Balaklava: 'C'est magnifique, mais ce n'est pas la guerre.' I soon became personally involved because Morillon's deputy, then a British brigadier, rang hoping I could persuade the Serbs to give permission for UN relief helicopters to fly in via Tuzla. I had the radio transcripts of the messages faxed to me, which started: 'C'est le Général qui parle.' Morillon's urgency in pressing for helicopters to be flown in was understandable, but he had no up-to-date intelligence information on the risks involved. The Serbs were saying that because one Bosnian government white-painted helicopter had flown into and out of Tuzla any white UN helicopter might be fired on by their troops thinking it was a Muslim helicopter. At one point the brigadier in Sarajevo was in a very difficult position with Morillon wanting the helicopters to fly while he held in his hand information that the Serbs were getting ready to shell Tuzla airport. I told him that he should treat the opinion of his general, who was by now hopelessly out of touch, as on a par with that of a platoon commander. The brigadier did stop the UN helicopters, and at the very moment when they would have been flying into Tuzla a Serb artillery barrage was unleashed which could have downed many of them. Eventually General Morillon, with courage and panache, negotiated the demilitarization of Srebrenica with the local Serb and Muslim commanders, and the crisis was averted for the time. This episode revived in people's minds the 'safe areas' concept as a way of at least doing something. Yet by the time the local demilitarization agreement came to be scrutinized by the Muslim political leaders in Sarajevo it became clear that they were totally opposed to any demilitarization, and the Srebrenica Muslim commander never properly complied with the agreement.

The whole Srebrenica episode showed General Mladic at his most intransigent and did not augur well for implementation of the VOPP. At that time the French claimed the US was seeing implementation under the NATO Treaty as a straight Article V operation. In fact this was nonsense, as Article V involves repelling an attack on NATO territory. The real French anxiety was that it meant involving NATO's integrated military structure and employing the whole NATO command chain from SACEUR downwards, which they had always hitherto tried to confine to Article V and avoid for Article IV or other military action. General Wahlgren, who had taken over from General Nambiar as Commander of UNPROFOR, was meanwhile conducting talks with a NATO team. He was Swedish, a sage, calm figure with a lot of UN experience – and he needed all of it to assuage the legitimate concerns of both NATO and the UN about any joint operation.

On 12 March I was back in New York and on 16 March Karadzic and the FRY Foreign Minister Jovanovic arrived, as Milosevic had promised in Paris. We were not sure whether Izetbegovic would be coming the next day, but he was at least out of Sarajevo and in Zagreb. Vance and I met with the ambassadors from the permanent five members of the Security Council. The general feeling was that Izetbegovic might now accept the map but that Karadzic's signature was going to be far more difficult to achieve. What was needed was a mixture of sticks and carrots. The Russians wanted the emphasis of any new sanctions to fall on the Bosnian Serbs and mentioned the idea of monitors along the borders. Vance pointed out that Milosevic would not accept this if it also involved sanctions against the Knin Serbs, and we discussed the problem of traffic transiting from Serbia through Bosnia. I said that I felt enforcement of the NFZ was now inevitable and the Russians felt this would be acceptable in the context of Karadzic's failing to sign a settlement. We all agreed to go ahead with the Resolution toughening sanctions.

The Srebrenica situation was deteriorating, and I was rung up in the early hours of the morning of 19 March in New York by the French Prime Minister, Bérégovoy, in the midst of their election campaign demanding that I take action. His protest was for the newspapers, but I wrote back to him that morning to tell him the facts about Morillon's activity, which I am sure he already knew. In Geneva, meanwhile, Ambassadors Okun and Ahrens were again trying to negotiate an agreement in Croatia over the implementation of UNSCR 802 and they came to New York to report on their difficulties. From 16 to 25 March we were locked in negotiations with the Bosnian parties, made more difficult by the Bosnian Serbs' conduct around Srebrenica and in eastern Bosnia in general, where they were blocking all convoys and generally behaving in a way which made the Bosnia-Herzegovina government threaten to refuse to negotiate with them. We started with bilaterals between the Bosnian Serbs and Croats and only saw President Izetbegovic on 18 March in his hotel, where discussion focused on

Map 7 Areas of Serb withdrawal under Vance–Owen Peace Plan

the form of an interim government with discussion on 19 March on what ministries an interim central government would need. The Bosnian Serb position was that they could not see the need for an interim President to be head of state, or for a Presidency, or indeed for any form of central government: all they wanted was a central coordinating body. Their position had hardened since the Geneva round of negotiations in January.

On 24 March, after a five-hour session, the Bosnian government and Bosnian Croat sides reached agreement on the interim arrangements after Boban had threatened Izetbegovic with the dissolution of their then military alliance. On 25 March, in a bizarre ceremony in the basement of the UN building, we waited for four hours with Boban, and with Karadzic who was not going to sign, for President Izetbegovic to come in from his hotel. Karadzic was psychoanalysing what he described as Izetbegovic's habitual indecision in Freudian terms as anal fixation. The Bosnian government and the Bosnian Croats eventually signed both the interim arrangements and the provincial map. President Izetbegovic made his signature conditional on a statement, put out as Annex V to the Report of the Secretary-General,[78] which rendered his signature invalid if the Serbs, described as the aggressor side, did not sign within a reasonable time-frame, or if the international community did not undertake effective measures of implementation and if the aggression continued. The Secretary-General wrote to the Security Council: 'The moment has arrived for the international community to come to grips with the process that has been conducted by the Co-Chairmen and with the results obtained. After seven months of the most intensive negotiations, ten of the required twelve signatures have been obtained. Only one side – the Bosnian Serbs – now lags behind in signature of the provincial map and the agreement on interim arrangements.' In a ringing endorsement he called for Security Council approval of the whole peace package and, after final agreement, for rapid and robust implementation.

It had taken us two difficult months to obtain the Bosnian government's agreement to the VOPP package and the delay had been very damaging. We now had the hardest task of all still left: to get the Bosnian Serbs to sign. I knew that only Milosevic could deliver the Bosnian Serbs and that he was vulnerable in one area: financial sanctions. The Security Council had to squeeze assets. This time the US were correct, and the UK Treasury position was obtuse. We had to tighten every area of sanctions, for there was much economic intelligence showing that Milosevic was becoming really worried about the Serbian economy.[79]

The Pentagon was estimating that an implementation force of 50,000–70,000 was needed in Bosnia and General Powell was arguing seriously for going in with even larger forces initially to get the situation under control, with a view to winding down after six months. I was now openly calling for the Security Council to back its words with actions and bring a range of pressures to bear on the Bosnian Serbs. Ambassador Bartholomew, who had been helpful in nursing the Bosnia-Herzegovina government over the final hurdle, was now looking for every means of pressure to be exerted on the Serbs. Vitaly Churkin had tried with Karadzic, but had not made much headway. Jovanovic had been of no use whatsoever. I argued that sanctions should be tough on the FRY and that we should enforce the NFZ and try again to put UNMOs on the Bosnia-Herzegovina borders. There was a cockiness about the Bosnian Serb leaders that had to be knocked out of them. General Morillon had gone to see Milosevic in the hope that he might make Mladic see sense and order a ceasefire around Srebrenica, but to little effect. There then followed an intensive period of diplomatic activity from 26 March to 16 April 1993.[80]

On 16 April I spoke on the telephone to President Milosevic about my anxiety that, despite repeated assurances from Dr Karadzic that he had no intention of taking Srebrenica, the Bosnian Serb army was now proceeding to do just that. The pocket was greatly reduced in size. I had rarely heard

Milosevic so exasperated, but also so worried: he feared that if the Bosnian Serb troops entered Srebrenica there would be a bloodbath because of the tremendous bad blood that existed between the two armies. The Bosnian Serbs held the young Muslim commander in Srebrenica, Naser Oric, responsible for a massacre near Bratunac in December 1992 in which many Serb civilians had been killed. Milosevic believed it would be a great mistake for the Bosnian Serbs to take Srebrenica and promised to tell Karadzic so. He did not think we would be able to get Canadian troops into Srebrenica for some time but thought we might be able to negotiate UN monitors. I agreed to meet Milosevic in Belgrade for lunch on Wednesday 21 April. Churkin, who was in Belgrade, was also arguing against taking Srebrenica and was getting into some useful exchanges about the map. He believed that if some changes, in his view more symbolic than substantive, could be accommodated the Serbs would sign the interim agreement with no more than cosmetic changes.

In Belgrade my February interview in *Foreign Affairs*,[81] which I had undertaken before the New York negotiations, but in which I had predicted that the Serbs would not sign, was being interpreted as indicating that the move to New York was deliberately manufactured to secure a Muslim signature on the map, isolate the Serbs and thus justify the introduction of tougher sanctions.

The Security Council fatefully decided to demand that Srebrenica and its surroundings be treated as a safe area to be free from armed attack, while neither demilitarizing nor demarcating the boundaries of the area. It also, more helpfully, decided to bring forward the draft Resolution on sanctions. John Major, along with other leaders, had written to Boris Yeltsin to say that the Srebrenica situation demanded that they act without delay in the UN over sanctions and that Kozyrev's earlier agreement with Douglas Hurd in Tokyo to delay the Resolution could no longer apply. Cy Vance came back from holiday for the Security Council debate but I decided to stay in London. I sent a cable to the British Embassy in Moscow asking them to tell the Russians we had no intention of meeting with Karadzic soon unless he came up with some serious proposals. It read: 'The Co-Chairmen intend to take a very firm line with Karadzic. He must get used to the idea that the negotiations cannot continue to be dragged out. It is not a never-ending process. They do not want to offer him the chance to use negotiations as a cover while he continues his utterly despicable conduct *vis-à-vis* Srebrenica.' They could tell Churkin in confidence that I had asked Milosevic to arrange for me to meet with General Mladic and that I thought there was room for flexibility on the deployment of UN troops along the northern corridor. 'It is unlikely to be possible to have just Russian troops. It could perhaps be Russians backed up by Canadians, Americans or other serious troops. As regards the suggested map changes, if these were all that Karadzic was after they would offer the basis for serious talks, but all the indications are that they are the tip of an iceberg.'

John Major rang me at home prior to his speaking to President Clinton and we talked about how to put maximum pressure on the Serbs to halt their attack on Srebrenica and about UNSCR 819,[82] which made Srebrenica the first UN protected 'safe area'. We also discussed the planned financial sanctions, and how to tighten up on breaches of sanctions by land, sea and river, a point which I had been pushing for some time.

The UN financial sanctions Resolution had gone through in New York late that Saturday night and I heard about it driving into the BBC studios for a David Frost interview on breakfast television on Sunday 18 April. The French had been adamant that there had to be a vote that day, whereas the US and UK had been ready to give Moscow another day. The UN Commanders, Wahlgren and Morillon, having just negotiated a ceasefire agreement, were afraid that if sanctions were adopted that night the Serbs would cease to cooperate. The Russian Ambassador consulted Moscow and eventually got Yeltsin's agreement to abstain on the vote; so UNSCR 820 [83] was then adopted just before midnight on Saturday, with thirteen votes in favour and Russia and China abstaining. In the Frost interview I talked of interdiction of the Bosnian Serb supply lines by air until they agreed the VOPP.[84] My military adviser, Brigadier Messervy-Whiting, had sent me a well-thought-through options paper concluding that interdiction warranted further study inside NATO.[85] But I could never get any major government interested in developing a sound military counter-force strategy of a sort that might have carried the Russians and really made General Mladic pause.

In Washington, where there was considerable anger at what was happening in Srebrenica, there was some sympathy for my call for air intervention to cut Bosnian Serb supply lines, though also a recognition of UK and French concerns that this could lead to retaliation against UN forces. Some were arguing that if air strikes were not agreed then lifting the arms embargo was the only way forward. They were forgetting that whereas Belgrade might see well-judged interdiction as not necessitating their further involvement, 'lift and strike' would be far more likely to bring about their overt intervention. Washington never understood that splitting the Serbs was a delicate matter requiring some finesse, in part because some of them were obsessed with 'getting Milosevic' rather than using his influence for our purposes.

The Serbs now had nine days before financial sanctions would take effect, and this meant that during my visit to Belgrade I was going to be able to put them under the maximum pressure. I went on BBC radio and deliberately toughened my stance another few notches. 'At the moment the Serbs are still taking territory and they are not being checked. So it's up to the governments of the world − are they going to be rolled over by the

Serbs? I would counsel governments against ruling out military pressure. In a war situation to rule out military pressure is very dangerous.' The EC Foreign Ministers, although they publicly acknowledged that the behaviour of the Bosnian Serbs around Srebrenica obliged them to do something, and although they left open the option of air strikes, were all hesitant to take up my suggestion to threaten to interdict the Bosnian Serb supply lines from the air.[86]

We were now looking to turn sanctions into a blockade. In the Adriatic from 26 April we were empowered to prohibit all commercial and maritime traffic from entering the territorial waters of the FRY. On the Danube there were plans for a WEU monitoring flotilla and for more effective coordination between the riparian states to close existing loopholes. There could now be a closure of all land freight crossing points, with only limited exceptions, and there would be more sanctions assistance missions to help the customs authorities of the neighbouring states. Also, action could now be taken against all of the FRY financial assets. If complied with, this was going to be a formidable package and would, I hoped, give Milosevic pause for thought.

In a first reaction to UNSCR 820, Karadzic said in an interview for Radio Belgrade that the Bosnian Serbs would, as they had warned Lord Owen, leave the ICFY talks, although whether they did so before or after 26 April would be decided by the Bosnian Serb Assembly, which was to meet on 23 or 24 April. Karadzic reserved special criticism for me, saying my 'willingness to envisage military intervention against the Bosnian Serbs had confirmed his partiality and disqualified him as an intermediary'.

After the emergency session on 18 April Jovanovic expanded on the FRY government statement in an interview for Belgrade television. He claimed that the logic of the UN's ultimatum approach was effectively to exclude the possibility of continuing the peace process. He said that he undertook to continue, through forthcoming contacts with visiting Russian parliamentarians and with me, to try to preserve the prospects for peace from the damaging effects of the Resolution: but I would need to come to Belgrade with something more 'attractive' than mere cosmetic changes to the map. The world could not hope for a better and more willing partner in the talks than the FRY, but it should recognize that no nation could be expected to abandon a significant proportion of its people as the Resolution required. Jovanovic also criticized me in terms similar to Karadzic's for advocating consideration of the military option against the Bosnian Serbs. There then followed a week of detailed diplomacy in advance of my visit to Belgrade.[87]

On the morning of 21 April, en route to Belgrade, I met Susak, the Croatian Minister of Defence. At a time when the world was trying to put the maximum pressure on the Bosnian Serbs and the US was trying to lift the arms embargo on the Bosnian Muslims there was a significant increase in clashes between Croat and Muslim forces in central Bosnia. It was not possible to pretend that there was any longer a truly representative Bosnia-Herzegovina government armed force. We were dealing with two separate armies in most parts of Bosnia-Herzegovina and the cooperation which still existed, mainly around Tuzla, was becoming very strained. At one stage Susak cited as an example of how bad things had become in eastern Herzegovina the fact that two Croat villages had put themselves in the hands of what he called the 'Chetniks' – Serbs – rather than risk coming under Muslim control. This disarray was bound to make the Bosnian Serbs even more confident. There was no sign of any basic agreement on joint command and control procedures being reached. There was no pretence about Susak, and I found I could do serious business with him. He did not bother to pretend that Croatian government forces were not inside Bosnia-Herzegovina fighting with the Bosnian Croats. Susak was born in western Herzegovina and was fiercely anti-Communist. He was devoted to Tudjman and had raised a lot of money for him and the Croatian nationalist cause while running a highly successful chain of pizza restaurants in Canada.

Before meeting Cosic or Milosevic I had received a message from Stojanovic, Cosic's adviser, that although tough criticisms of the VOPP and me were still being put out publicly, Cosic, Milosevic and Bulatovic were all interested in putting the rhetoric aside and having serious discussions on our plan. Apparently Karadzic was in the wings, waiting to meet me, but I was determined not to be rushed into a meeting with him. I wanted to be certain that he came to any meeting only after he had had a firm steer from Milosevic.

I arrived in Belgrade to find that the FRY press agency, Tanjug, had put out an editorial in the name of its chief editor, himself a Milosevic appointee – as are the heads of all the state media – accusing me of disqualifying myself as an impartial mediator in the Yugoslav crisis. The article asked whether, in the light of my most recent statement on the need for targeted air strikes, I would not be better described as a courier who was coming to Belgrade to deliver threats and blackmail prepared in advance. The fact that I had shown no intention of holding talks with the Bosnian Serbs during my latest visit only confirmed that my aim was not to find a solution, but to increase the pressure without putting forward any new proposals. Throughout the civilized world, the editorial said, it was accepted that mediators did not threaten one of the sides in negotiations. Belgrade however remained open to people of goodwill.

Aleksa Buha, the Bosnian Serb 'Foreign Minister', had also said that the time had come for Britain and Europe to appoint a new person to lead future negotiations. He did not see what the Serbs could discuss with a man who publicly and persistently advocated the bombing of Serbs. So much for

Muslim prisoners in Serb camp at Manjaca, near Banja Luka, August 1992.

Above: Cyrus Vance and David Owen, Co-Chairmen of the ICFY Steering Committee, 1992–3. *Below:* Vance and Owen meet Greek Prime Minister Constantine Mitsotakis in Athens, September 1992.

No. 802
Friday
11 Sept. '92

80p

The front cover of *Private Eye* magazine, 11 September 1992.

Above: Talks with President Izetbegovic at Sarajevo, December 1992. On the left is General Philippe Morillon, and to his left Brigadier Graham Messervy-Whiting. *Below:* DO with General Morillon and General Ratko Mladic, Lukavica Barracks, Sarajevo, December 1992.

LORD OWEN — CO-CHAIRMEN — THORVALD STOLTENBERG

Above: Co-Chairmen Owen and Stoltenberg with Ogata Sadako, UN High Commissioner for Refugees, in Geneva, January 1993. *Below:* Skopje, April 1993: President Gligorov meets the ICFY team – left to right: Fred Eckhard, Geert Ahrens, Herbert Okun, DO, Peter Hall, David Ludlow.

Destroyed and desecrated:
Above, the Catholic church of Mary Mother of God in the suburbs of Sarajevo;
Opposite top, Orthodox church in Vukovar;
Opposite below, the mosque at Ahmici, near Vitez.

Mostar, May 1993: a Croat soldier in house-to-house fighting against the Muslims.

the myth that as negotiators we never threatened the Serbs with force. Buha went on to confirm that the Bosnian Serbs had rejected Churkin's proposal for a UN-guaranteed, Russian-patrolled corridor in northern Bosnia. The Serbs did not need 'someone else's corridor' through their own territory and had seen the efficacy of UN guarantees in the Krajina. The proposal was, in any case, only a variation on the corridor ideas contained in the Vance–Owen plan.

I began my visit to Belgrade on 21 April by meeting Cosic and Jovanovic. This was followed by a meeting and lunch with Milosevic and Jovanovic, after which I had a private meeting with Milosevic. One of my harshest messages concerned the extent of the Yugoslav army's involvement in Bosnia-Herzegovina. I gave Cosic and Milosevic details which carried conviction. Cosic was quite shaken and had possibly not known the full extent of their involvement, but Milosevic batted not an eyelid for I told him facts of which I am sure he was fully informed, probably having authorized every aspect of the military relationship.

Milosevic said the meeting with General Mladic which I had previously requested was fixed, though he informed me that Karadzic was strongly opposed to such a meeting taking place. My two-and-a-half-hour conversation with Mladic was particularly detailed, and quite unlike any conversation I had had, or probably could expect to have, with Karadzic. He started by analysing the other sides' strategic needs. The Croats needed to re-establish strategic communication to Dalmatia, then to Slavonia. Conditions were now right for direct talks between the Croats, the Krajina Serbs and the Bosnian Serbs. The Muslims had no central authority functioning throughout their state, were almost cut off from the outside world and had the problem of Sarajevo. More Bosnian Croats lived in central and northern Bosnia than in the compact 'Herzeg-Bosna' in the south, but they were dispersed in penny packets throughout these areas. The Muslims, said Mladic, were fighting to drive the Croats out but the Bosnian Serbs would not allow them to do this, and if the Muslims destroyed the power-generating facilities in the Neretva valley, the Bosnian Croats in the Mostar area would be 'finished'. The Bosnian Serbs already had a territorial corridor in Posavina, peopled by Serbs who would stay to defend it. They had managed to 'homogenize' their territory in eastern Bosnia. The Drina valley with its power stations was the Serbs' 'backbone'. Their main problems were the narrowness of the corridor in the Brcko area, though they did not want to resolve this militarily; lack of access to the Neretva valley; and Popovo Polje, where they were aiming for access to the sea. Mladic's ideal solution was for direct talks among the three sides, with Croatia and Serbia, leading to trade-offs in land and the *de facto* partitioning of Bosnia-Herzegovina.

At my private meeting with Cosic and Milosevic, we were later joined by Karadzic – but only when I had been convinced that this time he was

serious. At all the meetings I stressed the critical nature of the current situation. The increased sanctions would come into effect automatically in a few
days; the pressure was growing for military action; more and more bellicose
noises were coming from the US. A settlement had to be reached by Sunday
if sanctions were not to start on Monday and if we were not to go plunging
off the edge of a precipice. Any settlement, moreover, should look beyond
the problems of Bosnia-Herzegovina alone and try to solve broader
Serb–Croat issues. There were some of the usual noises about the unfairness of the way the Serbs were being treated, but there were no hysterics,
and the meetings were businesslike and constructive.

Milosevic made clear his opposition to the Bosnian Serbs' attempt to
negotiate a territorial link between Zvornik and Sekovici in eastern Bosnia,
which he said was stupid. He undertook to try to persuade them to drop
this demand, and he was involved in a heated discussion with Karadzic
about this when I left for the airport. The results of Milosevic's efforts on
this issue would, I believed, be an important pointer for the future. Mladic,
at my request, had undertaken to extend the demilitarization time limit and
the ceasefire around Srebrenica at least until Sunday and we arranged with
UNPROFOR for Wahlgren to ring him. We left Belgrade not completely
ruling out the chance that it would be worth trying to get the three parties
together by Sunday, but a lot depended on what happened between now
and then. Milosevic was particularly keen to arrange such a meeting and
wanted to include Croatian Serb leaders.

I then travelled to Skopje, the capital of the Former Yugoslav Republic
of Macedonia (FYROM), to see President Gligorov and then to Athens to
see Prime Minister Mitsotakis, to push forward the negotiations Vance and
I had been having in New York. On 23 April we dropped off at Skopje
airport again to brief Gligorov; then we flew on to Podgorica to see
President Bulatovic of Montenegro, who was as helpful as usual, referring
to our talks as having 'goodwill and a high degree of understanding' on
both sides.

I saw Milosevic that night and, as I had promised when Milosevic said
Karadzic would be in a more open frame of mind, I agreed to see Karadzic's
team without Milosevic next morning. Karadzic, when he arrived in
Belgrade from Novi Grad, talked about being 'ready for compromise'. This
mood was reflected in the Belgrade papers and Cosic was quoted as saying
in the Italian newspaper *Corriere della Sera* that he was 'vitally interested'
in adoption of the VOPP. Before flying to Zagreb we went through the
areas of contention with the Bosnian Serbs, but I did not sense any substantive give. After I left Karadzic talked to the press about possible conditional
acceptance of the VOPP. But Mladic was still saying that a northern
corridor through an area that was already Serb territory and in Serb hands
was not an inducement for signing the rest of the map.

Travelling through the Balkans at such a pace meant we had to have a mobile office, and my private secretary David Ludlow's skill on a portable computer, typing in cars or in the uncomfortable Russian plane used by the UN, Yak by name and Yak by nature, was much used. On this occasion we put together a long message to the EC Foreign Ministers, who were attending an informal meeting at Hindsgav Castle in Denmark. I then flew to Zagreb to meet with Presidents Tudjman and Izetbegovic. A nasty incident involving Croat Nazi extremists which had taken place at Santici near Vitez did not help the atmosphere at the meeting, which was very tough at the outset with some vicious exchanges and shouting between the two men. Both the Croat and the Muslim generals were present, and eventually we patched up the differences. Responsibility for the clashes was seen in the press as lying with the Croats, but both sides were at fault. In a telephone conversation with Douglas Hurd in Denmark before the second day of the Foreign Ministers' meeting I told him I was returning to Belgrade in not a very hopeful frame of mind and that it was unlikely that this last-minute diplomacy would result in last-minute concessions from the Bosnian Serbs.

The EC Foreign Ministers had been asked by the Americans not to pre-empt discussions which Warren Christopher hoped to have in Europe the following week, but of course they had to discuss the various options and the noises coming out of Washington were again all about air strikes and lifting the arms embargo. France, Spain and Britain all thought limited air strikes preferable to lifting the arms embargo. The German position on the arms embargo was closer to that of the US and there was pressure in the Bundestag to lift the embargo, but Germany would not move forward alone on this.

My memo to the Foreign Ministers was a long one, running to twenty-five paragraphs.[88] The last four dealt with putting pressure on the Bosnian Serbs:

There are three military possibilities suggested for pressurizing the Belgrade Serbs:

– lifting the arms embargo for the Muslims;
– interdicting by air Bosnian Serb supply lines within Bosnia-Herzegovina;
– and conducting air strikes against Bosnian Serb military targets, particularly heavy weapons.

Lifting the arms embargo is presented as giving the Muslims the chance to defend themselves against the more heavily armed and better equipped Serbs. I cannot stress enough to all of you that I believe this would be a profound mistake. I understand the political pressure to do this coming from the United States, but I cannot see how anyone reading my earlier account of Croat–Muslim tensions in Central Bosnia could believe that this option would be anything other than profoundly damaging. But I also believe that far from helping tilt the balance towards the Bosnian Muslims, the almost inevitable supplies of 1990s weapons from the former Soviet Union to the JA are more likely to tilt the balance even further towards the Serbs. It might salve people's consciences for a few weeks, but it could be a fatal step towards a wider Balkan war.

But if we do not lift the arms embargo, we have to be ready to take further action within the UN to tilt the military balance against the Serbs. We have done this since October when under President Bush's threat of enforcement I was able to negotiate with Dr Karadzic the grounding of all combat aircraft. We have taken a symbolic further step by enforcing the No-Fly Zone. It is a perfectly logical next step to ask the Security Council, if sanctions fail to dissuade the Belgrade Serbs from supplying the Bosnian Serb army, for authorization to take the necessary measures to interdict the supply lines from the air. Of course this action would not of itself defeat the Bosnian Serbs, but it would tilt the balance in favour of the two armies that have signed up for the peace plan. It would be difficult for the Russians to accept such action, but it is far more likely that they would accept this limited peace-keeping action than authorize offensive air-to-ground attacks on military targets. Any of these military actions would almost certainly lead to the withdrawal of UNPROFOR troops and affect the humanitarian effort, but with the winter over it is easier to give the highest priority to ending the war.

My own advice is to do everything to contain the fighting to Bosnia-Herzegovina: and facing down the Bosnian Serbs' direct challenge to the authority of the Security Council now is, for all its problems, a far better option than trying to halt a Serb–Croat war, or increased Serbian oppression in Kosovo.

One of the worrying aspects of the developing US policy was that the Joint Chiefs of Staff appeared to be growing less resistant to lifting the arms embargo because they saw it as easier than the alternative, which would involve the US for the first time in accepting part of the responsibility for implementing a settlement. Though they knew that lifting the arms embargo would almost certainly provoke a pre-emptive Bosnian Serb strike they hoped to forestall it by warning Belgrade that if this happened they would themselves be attacked. They thought air strikes would take place only for a limited period and would exclude them from implementation of any settlement on the ground. What these advisers wanted to avoid at all costs was putting US ground troops into Bosnia-Herzegovina, whether to implement a settlement or to impose a settlement. What the European countries wanted to avoid at all costs was becoming combatants in the war without US troops to help.

In the margins of the Izetbegovic–Tudjman meeting in Zagreb I sounded out Izetbegovic over possible territorial deals. He suggested waiting until the Russian referendum, on the grounds that if Yeltsin won it could moderate the Bosnian Serb opposition to the VOPP. He was ready to accept a Serb territorial link to Sekovici, but not via Zvornik, a possible exchange of territory between Ozren and Kljuc, and an exchange of territory in the northern corridor for the Rudo–Cajnice area.

I left for Belgrade on Sunday morning accompanied by Peter Hall and Herb Okun, as I had been throughout the trip. Herb was ably representing Cy Vance, but even so we had made arrangements to keep Cy, who was still in New York, abreast of all developments. We were well aware that it was crucial to persuade Milosevic that this was his last chance to avoid the new sanctions package. We had one message: if the Bosnian Serbs signed up for the VOPP before Monday's deadline on UNSCR 820, new sanctions would not start. At the meeting with Milosevic I was told the Bosnian Serbs were no longer pushing to link Zvornik with Sekovici, which was a significant indication of realism. Milosevic then presented me with a Bosnian Serb 'memorandum of understanding' which I could not possibly sign up to, but I was able to offer Milosevic specific detailed reassurance on the sovereign road through the northern corridor with demilitarization on both sides. I also was able to point out exactly where many of the points in the memorandum had already been accepted in our texts for signature. Following my talk with Izetbegovic, I could promise that Sekovici would be linked to Serb territory, but not via Zvornik. A crucial clarification actually agreed with Vance over the telephone was that the interim Presidency would reflect the three constituent nations and operate by consensus.

Milosevic, who had mastered all the detail in the documents, then said that with these changes he would recommend Karadzic to accept the VOPP, and summoned Karadzic and Krajisnik to the meeting. They both had to delay their departure by road to Bijeljina, where the Assembly was due to meet. I again explained our position in painstaking detail, for they had not anywhere near the same knowledge of our actual proposals as Milosevic. Eventually they left us, now seemingly ready to accept the VOPP, a decision both Cosic and Bulatovic had been strongly urging them to take. Over a late lunch Milosevic was in an expansive mood and said, stretching his arms above his head, that he felt comfortable with the decision. He knew there would be a lot of criticism, but the plan was fair and it was time for peace. He showed no signs of being in any doubt as to the outcome in the Bosnian Serb Assembly. I agreed to stay overnight in Belgrade so that in the event of acceptance we could put the formal documents to the UN early that morning, certifying agreement to the VOPP and therefore stopping the introduction of financial sanctions.

The relief that we had seemingly broken through left us all a little light-headed and, as it turned out, over-confident. I had no doubt then, and have never doubted since, that it was the prospect of financial sanctions which Milosevic most feared: the chance of avoiding any further economic misery was too attractive domestically for him to go on humouring Karadzic as he obstructed virtually any deal. As far as Milosevic was concerned, the Bosnian Serbs had protected all their vital interests and in that sense had won. That it was not Greater Serbia in terms of one country stretching from Belgrade to Banja Luka to Knin had not been vital for him since our meetings in Geneva in January. I do not believe he was particularly concerned by the talk of US military action, which continued to be rather unfocused, though it made the useful point that NATO's patience was running out; but so, fortunately, was Milosevic's with the Bosnian Serbs. From this point, 25 April 1993, onwards Milosevic formally gave up Greater Serbia and argued for a settlement on terms a majority in the Security Council could have accepted, and throughout the next two years he did not waver in seeking such a solution. The interests of Serbia and Montenegro from then on were the decisive factor, and he grew more and more disillusioned with Karadzic's lack of courage as a true Serbian leader in the process. In this respect sanctions had worked. Unfortunately, in the US the demonization of Milosevic had reached such a level that adminis-tration, Congress and media alike seemed unable to adjust to this new reality and kept talking about Milosevic being committed to a Greater Serbia.

Apparently late that evening Milosevic was alerted that all was not going well in the Bosnian Serb Assembly discussion in Bijeljina. A somewhat peremptory letter from the three Presidents Cosic, Milosevic and Bulatovic was drafted sometime after midnight when it became clear that the mood of the Assembly was moving against signature of the VOPP. Jovanovic was dispatched by helicopter to Bijeljina at around 1.30 a.m. to deliver the message to the Assembly, which he did in a closed session starting at 4.30 a.m. The text of the letter was read in full on radio news bulletins from 2.00 a.m. onwards and was published in special late editions of the morning's papers in Belgrade on 26 April.

In their letter the three Presidents urged the Assembly to accept the VOPP, as developed and amended in talks over the weekend with our team. The letter criticized 'irresponsible statements' by certain participants in the Bosnian Serb Parliament: this was 'not the moment for each of us to try to be more patriotic than the other', but for a 'well-considered, far-sighted and courageous decision'. It detailed where talks in the last few days with us in ICFY had secured a number of commitments.

The letter claimed that changes to the maps could be achieved more successfully through political negotiation and consensus, within the framework of the ICFY, the provisional Presidency and the Border Commission, than through a continuation of 'confrontation and bloodshed': the citizens of Yugoslavia, Serbia and Montenegro had shown the highest degree of solidarity with the Bosnian Serbs, perhaps even more than their resources allowed; they would continue to do so regardless of all pressures, but the Bosnian Serbs had 'no right' to inflict international sanctions on '10 million citizens of Yugoslavia' because of the remaining areas of dispute, which were much less significant than the results already achieved in negotiations. The Bosnian Serbs should take account of these factors, and 'accept the plan'; this was a question of war and peace, and Yugoslavia chose peace. It was 'an honourable peace' which guaranteed the Bosnian Serbs 'equality and freedom'. Then, shortly before 6.00 a.m. local time, the Bosnian Serb Assembly decided unanimously that it was unable to take a final decision on the VOPP, and that the question would be put to the people in a referendum. This was interpreted in the domestic and international press as a rejection of the VOPP, though no text issued from Bijeljina stated this in as many words. Karadzic said only that there had been no final decision and that this would have to be taken in a referendum in about three weeks' time, around 15–16 May. The Assembly had earlier issued a declaration calling on all Serbs to 'respond to the call to join the struggle for the salvation of Serbs, to defend their land and character' and to 'stand unbendingly in the defence of our homeland, join ranks and carry the struggle through to its end'.

In conversation at the airport that morning before I flew to Geneva, Stojanovic, Cosic's adviser, said he assessed the mood in Serbia, following the weekend's discussions and the vote, as finely balanced between a strong wish to see sanctions lifted and normality return, and a characteristic Serbian fatalism coupled with a sense that Serbs still needed to stand together, despite their different interests. He added that he considered that Milosevic had taken a 'bold step' in urging acceptance of the VOPP in its latest form, given that this would bring him into confrontation with nationalist extremists such as Seselj in Serbia as well as with the Bosnian Serbs.

Once back in Geneva I flew on to see Klaus Kinkel in Bonn, where one subject of our conversation was his wish to convene another London-style conference – an idea on which I knew opinion in the EC was divided. I then flew to Copenhagen that evening to brief the Foreign Minister of Denmark, holder of the Presidency, and he decided to consult other countries over whether to have such a conference. He also briefed me on the Foreign Ministers' informal meeting. I had in the meantime sent out from Bonn a COREU telegram in which I raised the question of deploying UN monitors on the Serbian–Montenegrin frontier with Bosnia-Herzegovina and returned to the arguments for considering air interdiction of supply lines within the confines of all UNSCRs on sanctions, which I hoped might not invoke a Russian veto.[89]

President Yeltsin, having won his referendum on 26 April, became quite outspoken, saying Russia would not protect those who opposed the world community, and Kozyrev and Churkin were enthusiastic about the three Presidents' letter, feeling the problem had now become sharply focused. They felt, as I did, that if this initiative had come a few days earlier we would have had an acceptance from the Bijeljina Assembly. In retrospect this was a tragic error and I kicked myself for not going to Belgrade two days earlier, as soon as the UNSCR had been passed.

On 27 April Warren Christopher, giving testimony before a Senate Appropriations Committee, laid out four strict tests for the use of force: the goal must be stated clearly; there must be a strong likelihood of success; there must be 'an exit strategy'; and the action must win substantial public support. It was clear that none of these conditions was likely to be met in the early stages of implementation. I began to understand that Christopher's insistence in his statement of 10 February on not imposing a settlement, which I had thought was to protect himself against having to impose a settlement on the Bosnian Muslims, was really applicable to all sides. He was not ready to impose even when, as now, it was the Serbs who were holding out against a settlement. By sticking strictly to the line of no imposition he had made it very unlikely that there would be any US involvement with implementation; by adding these four additional factors at his testimony he was making it virtually impossible. It looked an odd preparation for his proposed trip to Europe to discuss a new US policy initiative. President Clinton then told twenty Congressional politicians, whom he met to determine the degree of support on Capitol Hill, that he had yet to define the initiative. To add to the conflicting messages, Admiral David Jeremiah, Vice-Chairman of the Joint Chiefs of Staff, told reporters that air strikes in Bosnia could lead to a difficult, drawn-out commitment that would include civilian deaths and damage to civilian areas. If the assumption is, he said, that bombing 'will be a painless action, it will not be, because there will clearly be collateral military damage . . . you cannot allow somebody to go forward and assume you're going to get in and out with a "quickie".' Field Marshal Sir Richard Vincent, chairman of NATO's military committee, emphasized the enormous commitment of resources and time needed to move tens of thousands of troops to Bosnia. 'You cannot defy the law of military logistics,' he said; armies with inadequate logistic support end up with 'retreats from Moscow such as occurred in 1812'. The London *Times* in an editorial rebuke next day denounced his speech as 'A gift to the Serbs. NATO Commanders should leave politics to politicians.'

I saw Prime Minister Balladur in Paris on 27 April before flying to New York on the 28th to continue discussion on FYROM. Balladur was intelligent, but, as Admiral Lanxade had warned me when we met skiing with mutual French friends in Meribel, he was very precise and cautious over involving French troops further in Yugoslavia. In contrast to Alain Juppé's modern, relaxed style, in conversation his every gesture was carefully calculated and constrained. There would certainly be less flamboyance about French policy from now on and instead a careful calculation of interest.

When I was in Athens on 22 April I had asked Mitsotakis if he would host a meeting of the parties in Athens; he had accepted and raised the issue with Milosevic. Karadzic had said he was ready to come soon after the Bijeljina meeting. Amid all the talk of convening a London conference I was far more attracted to a working session of ICFY in the region, with Mitsotakis adding his weight to the pressure on the Bosnian Serbs. Cosic on 28 April called for a further international meeting, but with far too many countries for a serious negotiation. What we needed was an arm-twisting session. Meanwhile I was becoming very interested in the political realignment that was taking place in Serbia. Draskovic now supported the VOPP and if Kostunica could be persuaded to express his support there would be a strong pro-VOPP majority in Serbia.[90]

On 28 April Vance and I met in New York with the Greeks and then the Macedonians and put to them a draft treaty. This draft did not refer to a name to replace FYROM, which would be added later, but sought to commit the Macedonians to change the preamble and Articles 3 and 49 of their constitution, and to commit to amend certain discriminating laws and procedures. They agreed to take it away and cogitate. I was sent a note in New York from General Wilson, our link in ICFY with UNPROFOR, indicating that General Wahlgren was ready to deploy monitors on the FRY border with Serbia and Montenegro and that it would require only 800 troops as he would be prepared to consider a more symbolic monitoring presence at perhaps 10–15 major crossing points. This deployment would be dependent on President Cosic's agreement, which I did not expect to be forthcoming because in his recent offer he had linked FRY border monitoring to Croatian border monitoring, something the UN Security Council was unlikely to introduce. Meanwhile Boutros Boutros Ghali and Manfred Woerner met to discuss NATO–UN cooperation.

In London on 29 April a young man tragically set himself alight in Parliament Square as a protest against the war in Bosnia-Herzegovina. The same day in the House of Commons the Prime Minister said air strikes were not ruled out, while officials were reported as saying limited air strikes might succeed in pressurizing the Serbs to accept the VOPP. The former Conservative Prime Minister Sir Edward Heath called on me to resign because it was no use having a peace negotiator who was advocating war. 'The people in this country don't want us to go to war. They don't want planes bringing back dead bodies . . . Why should there be any risk that we are going to be pushed into military action by a President of the United States?' Another former Prime Minister, Baroness Thatcher, hitherto an uncritical supporter of Croatia and an advocate of bombing the Serbs, wisely cancelled her visit to Zagreb to receive an honorary degree in protest against the killings by Croats in central Bosnia. Douglas Hurd warned: 'We must not allow the Atlantic Alliance to fracture over Bosnia-Herzegovina.'

In New York on the same day we announced that all three parties, as well as the Presidents of Croatia, the FRY, Serbia and Montenegro, had agreed to meet in Athens on Saturday 2 May. Boutros Ghali decided to delay the moment that Cy Vance would step down as Co-Chairman until Sunday 3 May and Thorvald Stoltenberg, whose appointment as Vance's successor had been announced on 2 April, was to attend as Co-Chairman designate. Warren Christopher excused himself from a White House meeting on Bosnia to tell reporters that the Athens meeting would not change their plans at all, confirming that President Clinton would make his much-trumpeted policy decision at the end of the week. Both Churkin and Bartholomew accepted our invitation to come to Athens. On Saturday it was announced in Washington that Christopher would fly to Britain for a meeting with John Major and Douglas Hurd at the Foreign Secretary's country residence, Chevening, on Sunday evening and would then go to France, Russia, Germany and Brussels for talks with NATO and the European Community on Thursday 6 May. President Clinton had apparently agreed on a number of military steps for stronger action in Bosnia-Herzegovina but the administration would not elaborate further.

In Athens on a fine Saturday afternoon in a hotel complex by the sea the participants began to arrive. I said that 'peace was within our grasp' and that we hoped to sign all the parties up to the VOPP. Prime Minister Mitsotakis opened the evening session with an appeal for boldness and courage; Cy Vance then spoke, saying that what was urgently needed to bring the plan into force was for Dr Karadzic to sign the provisional provincial map and the agreement on interim arrangements. I then introduced a carefully worded document which was designed to win over Dr Karadzic but also, just as importantly, to avoid objections from President Izetbegovic, and this was given to all parties to scrutinize.[91] I hoped that it would now be possible for the Bosnian Serb delegation to agree to sign the two outstanding documents. Vance then quickly closed the formal conference down for the night, and the real work began. Churkin, Mitsotakis and Milosevic argued with Karadzic into the small hours of the night and started again early next morning. Cy Vance and I were consulted from time to time while we and Ambassador Bartholomew dealt with the various anxieties of President Izetbegovic's delegation. With Churkin we worked on a statement which Vance would read out next morning. A key sentence related to UN forces in the northern corridor and read: 'It is our view that the force should include highly professional contingents from North America, Western Europe and the Russian Federation.' Mid-morning Vance and I were invited by Mitsotakis into his room in the hotel to be told Karadzic would sign subject to a caveat about having to get the agreement of the Assembly of the Republika Srpska at a meeting which was eventually fixed for 8 May. Milosevic was so convinced that Karadzic might change his mind between the room and the plenary meeting place that he wanted us to sign the two documents then and there, but we agreed only to witness his caveat statement there and insisted on him signing openly in front of Izetbegovic, Tudjman and Boban. We then all as quickly as possible assembled in plenary session. Vance made his statement, followed by an apprehensive hush as the two documents were signed by Karadzic. I immediately brought the proceedings to an end without any further discussion. Karadzic was in a state of high emotion, clearly having been bullied all night into submission, but what was more worrying in retrospect was the attitude of Krajisnik, who when I met him in the hotel lift was shaking his head, clearly very unhappy. I was reminded of how in Geneva time after time when it came to the crunch Karadzic tried to evade carrying sole responsibility. I knew that he was not a brave leader in dealing with arguments among his colleagues, but a man who spent his time looking over his shoulder, and I should have spent more time with Krajisnik. It was a mistake I did not make again, devoting a lot of time thereafter to Krajisnik. Yet Mitsotakis had agreed to go to Pale with Milosevic to help Karadzic persuade his Assembly, and most of us felt that this would be sufficient.

I went on various countries' television shows and the bright sun and the lifting of the strain of four months' intensive negotiations since we had begun to win acceptance of the VOPP in Geneva at the start of the New Year encouraged me to lower my guard and talk of a 'bright day' for the Balkans – for so it seemed. Implementation, we knew, would be difficult, but I really felt we had won the peace that Sunday. As I said goodbye to catch my afternoon flight back to London I looked back and there, sitting in swimming trunks by the hotel pool, was Cy Vance on his last day as Co-Chairman, looking like a man with a load off his shoulders. I thought what a wonderful retirement present it was for him and so richly deserved. I knew I would miss him greatly in the months ahead, for it had been a joy to work together, while Athens appeared to be an excellent starting point for Thorvald Stoltenberg. Flying over the Acropolis I could barely believe it, but it seemed this bloody Bosnian war was over at last.

4

The Ditching of the VOPP

O N SUNDAY 2 MAY, while we were prematurely celebrating in Athens, Warren Christopher took off from Washington for Britain, where the *Sunday Telegraph*'s headline over a big article said: 'Bosnia: Will it be Clinton's Vietnam?' The article went on: 'The American military is deeply apprehensive about becoming involved in a war under a President it has distrusted from the start.' It noted that on Wednesday the Chief of the Air Force, General Merrill McPeak, had raised eyebrows in Washington testifying before the Senate that it was perfectly feasible to destroy the Serb guns shelling civilians in Bosnia, and claimed that the Pentagon chief was currying favour with President Clinton in a bid to succeed General Powell. Contrasting this advice with that of Admiral Jeremiah, the Vice-Chairman of the Joint Chiefs, it further claimed that in a tactical concession the Joint Chiefs had yielded somewhat on the issue of lifting the embargo as 'the path of least resistance, and it may have the advantage of obviating, to some degree, the need to deploy US ground troops'.

In Athens I had acknowledged that the threat of new military action by the US 'helped concentrate people's minds' but I said too that it was the tightening of economic sanctions that had finally persuaded President Milosevic a week earlier. I called for a prompt Security Council Resolution to authorize the deployment of a large UN force. When asked whether Milosevic had abandoned his designs for a Greater Serbia I replied: 'I don't know. You would have to be a mind-reader to be able to answer that one.'

In the *Guardian* the next day a sceptical Martin Woolacott said: 'We do not yet know how much Lord Owen has given away, but that he has given something is certain . . . Lord Owen's relief at having, as it seems, finally clinched a deal is understandable. But that does not mean it is, as he puts it, a "happy day".' We had in fact given nothing more than was in the Conference papers — nor could we with the Bosnian Muslims and the US suspiciously watching every comma – but he was right in saying that it proved to be not a happy day. One of the reasons for this lay not in Athens but in what was going on that evening between the US and UK. At the meeting in the Foreign Secretary's country residence, Chevening, Christopher was joined by Ambassador Bartholomew, who flew in from Athens and who had told me before leaving that he had warned Milosevic that the best way of showing his commitment to the peace plan was to stop all military supplies to the Bosnian Serbs. I had also underlined that message in my last words with Milosevic. We all knew that a signature on paper meant nothing to these people. Karadzic would twist and turn and would have to be pressurized to settle. 'Pressure' was the word I now tended to use because I knew 'imposition' was a word that Christopher could not live with. Our own ICFY spokesman, Fred Eckhard, had said in Athens that getting the signatures was the 'easy part'; I had slightly bridled at this, but it was nevertheless the truth. The problem facing Warren Christopher was that after much agonizing President Clinton had decided on a policy of 'lift and strike', which Christopher was meant to champion, but from the moment his plane touched down in Britain he faced a different problem, namely that the new post-Athens situation demanded immediate pressure on the Serbs to keep to the Athens agreement. The very last thing that was needed was advocacy of a policy bound to split NATO members.

On 4 May the Russian Foreign Minister Andrei Kozyrev said he was ready to see monitors being placed on the Serbian border with Bosnia but was anxious about the EC opposing the participation of the FRY in the World Health Organization. This was another sign of an inability to adapt quickly on the part of the EC Foreign Ministers, who had decided at their meeting in Denmark to remove the FRY from international bodies as the lesser alternative to total isolation. This policy was now being implemented when, after Athens, they should have changed gear and have been more welcoming to the FRY, indicating that they appreciated what had been done in Athens, while saying clearly what else we expected from them. The reality was that Milosevic still aroused strong feelings in the EC; people had neither forgotten nor forgiven him his role in starting the war in 1991. The idea that he was now in favour of peace was too difficult for some to swallow. Differences in perceptions of Milosevic's intentions also lay behind a continuing tension in the diplomatic cooperation between Russia, the EC and the US.

In the UK there was no readiness to move militarily to implementation of the VOPP until the character of the peace was clearer, and for the US to be involved meant sorting out the key outstanding issue relating to who was in control of the implementation force: NATO and SACEUR, the UN, or both. A *Daily Telegraph* editorial headlined 'Washington's Line Smacks of Gesture' said: 'The highest objectives of British policy are to avoid an open breach with Washington, and to escape a reckless and indefinite entanglement in Bosnia.' Meanwhile in the *New York Times*, A. M. Rosenthal, in a piece entitled 'Tell Vance and Owen You're Sorry', wrote:

Apology is due to these two honourable men from all the columnists, editorial writers, politicians and academics who vilified them while they fought for a political basis for peace. I have been in rooms where journalists treated them as prisoners in the dock. In print they were accused of being Chamberlains, of creating a new Munich, of selling out freedom and human rights by outlining a political settlement. Americans, private and journalistic, sent hate mail and spiced dinner table nastiness.

He then analysed the last few months and ended on a handsome note, saying that since we were unlikely to get our apology here was one of his own: 'In one column I referred to Lord Owen as a rather crabby Englishman. He corrected me, Welshman, he said, Welshman.'

In France, Alain Juppé warned on the Sunday: 'There is a division of tasks that I don't think is acceptable – that of some flying in planes and dropping bombs, and others, the Europeans, especially the French, on the ground.' France and the US were still at odds over SACEUR's role in any implementation of a settlement after Christopher's visit to Paris. On Wednesday 5 May I visited Manfred Woerner in NATO and spoke for the second time to the NATO Ambassadors. I found out that the French were sending in a team to NATO the next day in an attempt to resolve the differences over command and control. I had one hour with Manfred Woerner, followed by an hour with NATO permanent representatives, and a subsequent working session with the Chairman of the Military Committee and SACEUR's Chief of Staff.[92] In order to tighten up coordination between the Co-Chairmen and both NATO and the UN I arranged for my own military adviser, Brigadier Messervy-Whiting, to remain at NATO HQ for the next couple of weeks or so and Stoltenberg's military adviser from UNPROFOR, an Australian, Brigadier John Wilson, to go to UN headquarters in New York for the same purpose, which was greatly welcomed.

That same day Christopher met with President Yeltsin and Kozyrev in Moscow. The day before, visiting US Senators led by Nunn and Lugar had been told by the Russian military that the conditions in the Yugoslav theatre made air strikes both dangerous and useless, but Yeltsin avoided commenting on what would happen if the Bosnian Serbs did not sign up and instead wanted only to commit to supply Soviet forces to help with implementation.

At noon that day, while I was in NATO and the US and Russians were talking in Moscow, the Bosnian Serb Assembly began its meeting in Pale on the signature of the Vance–Owen Peace Plan. The session was addressed by Karadzic, Plavsic, Cosic, Milosevic, Bulatovic and Mitsotakis; Karadzic sat on the fence and Mrs Plavsic opposed signature. Karadzic told delegates that the Bosnian Serbs' minimum requirement had been security. The

Vance–Owen plan gave them this, by guaranteeing that only UNPROFOR troops could enter Serb majority areas outside Serb provinces. He also stressed once again that the maps were provisional and all decisions in the transitional government would be taken by consensus. The war had to finish. It was difficult to give up hard-won territory at the instant it had been gained, but even 43 per cent of territory under Serb control was more than had been enjoyed for two centuries. The options now were the Vance–Owen plan or an attack by NATO forces. But it was noticeable that Karadzic received only polite applause from the seventy-five deputies.

The hardliner Mrs Plavsic spoke against relinquishing territory and said sardonically: 'The distinguished guests have today bowed to our flag, we must not trample on this flag.' The Bosnian Serb Minister of Information, Miroslav Toholj, said: 'Military intervention will never happen . . . Americans are only bluffing.' But the real problem was Krajisnik, the President of the Assembly, who ended the debate before a vote had been taken and went into a session of only Bosnian Serbs.

Around midnight, Buha, the Bosnian Serb 'Foreign Minister', released a text of a document drafted by a Commission of the Parliament, listing nine conditions for the Parliament's acceptance of the plan which amounted to a barely disguised rejection.[93]

The debate then went back into closed session, during which Milosevic, Cosic, Bulatovic and Mitsotakis all addressed the Assembly for a second time, reportedly in more forthright tones than earlier in the day, calling for unconditional signature. Milosevic described the nine conditions as 'children's games', and said that they made him 'very angry'. During the subsequent debate it appears that the nine conditions were whittled down to three or four: lifting of sanctions, suspension of the no-fly zone, Serb possession of Posavina and other corridors, and deployment of UN observers on front lines. It was then decided to drop the conditioned signature approach and opt for a referendum.

Shortly before 5.00 a.m. local time on the morning of 6 May, after a sixteen-hour session, the Bosnian Serb Assembly in Pale voted 51 to 2, with 12 abstentions, against ratification of the Vance–Owen plan and for the holding of the referendum, previously agreed, on 15–16 May. Speaking to the press afterwards, Karadzic and Krajisnik stated categorically that the Assembly had not rejected the plan, but would put the decision to the people. Immediately after the vote Karadzic, pliable as ever, told the press that acceptance or rejection of the plan would have been equally tragic, though he saw no reason for military intervention. The Bosnian Serbs would not take one more metre of territory. They were, however, in a mood to sacrifice themselves, which is a most dangerous state for any nation to be in. In response to a direct question he said that he did not plan to resign, since the Vance–Owen plan had not been rejected.

Milosevic left the session through a side door, without speaking to the press. Cosic accused the Bosnian Serb Assembly of taking the 'worst and most fatal' decision: political sense had been defeated; the country and the people now faced great uncertainty and there was no knowing what the coming days and nights would bring.

Milosevic rang me that morning in London, having driven back to Belgrade. He had been up all night and was angry, fed up and tired. He was vitriolic about Krajisnik for delaying the vote when he was afraid it would have been won and said that Mladic had intervened in the small hours against acceptance of the plan to considerable effect. We agreed to meet when we had both had time to reassess the situation, but he said he would take measures to make the Bosnian Serbs aware of their responsibilities, which I took to mean some form of sanctions. I learnt that Cosic too was 'tired and angry' and had apparently described the deputies, privately, as a band of ignorant peasants, military fanatics and war profiteers. He very much doubted whether many of them had even read the Vance–Owen plan. He had also been horrified by some of the scenes of devastation he had driven through on his way to Pale. As far as Cosic was concerned, Karadzic had been a disaster. Instead of coming out firmly for the plan, he had been more interested in sitting on the fence and preserving his political skin. Cosic considered Krajisnik to have been the villain of the piece, closely followed by Mladic. Krajisnik had deliberately made the voting public so as to shame the undecided. He had arranged for television to show the initial speeches of the visitors, but had not allowed the cameras to broadcast their much tougher second speeches. The three Presidents now intended to release the texts of the latter. There was also evidence of bribery. Mladic had pointed out the dangers of military intervention, but had then come down firmly against ratification. He swung the meeting by showing a detailed map of Serb-held areas and towns which would be 'lost' under the plan. Mladic had done this despite a meeting the previous day with the Yugoslav army hierarchy near the Bosnian border, at which he had supposedly been warned that supplies and other help would be stopped if the plan was not ratified. I had doubts as to whether Mladic was in fact given a serious warning. The JA at this stage was not fully under Milosevic's control; it still recognized Cosic's presidential role and contained many senior officers who openly supported Mladic. The April shift in Milosevic's position to acceptance of the VOPP was still contentious with the military in the FRY. They did not like our proposal for a throughway instead of a territorial corridor any more than Mladic did. Though General Panic had not been an impressive head of the JA, no one had emerged as a strong alternative, and I believed that Mladic had judged correctly that he had considerable support within the JA – also because Seselj had done well in the elections. This was a factor weakening Milosevic's authority with the military.

General Ratko Mladic was arguably, for a moment, the most powerful Serb. He was born on 12 March 1943 in Bosnia at Bozinovici, near Kalinovik, some 50 km south of Sarajevo, and both his parents had fought with the Partisans. His father was killed by Croatian Ustasha fighters in a raid on Bradina, the home of the Ustasha leader, Ante Pavelic, when Mladic was only two years old. Much has been written about how this experience made him nurse a grievance and gave him a permanent hatred of the Croats, but I found no evidence that he was particularly anti-Croat. He joined the League of Communists in 1965 after attending the Military Academy, and in the 1991 census chose as his nationality to be classified as a Yugoslav. In Pale he was quite close to Mrs Plavsic, but he eschewed too close a public identification with any politician. Whenever in discussion with me there had been an opportunity to adopt a party political position he had been careful to step back, usually with a wry smile and a remark about 'being a simple general and not a politician'. The one thing he is not is a simple general. He has had a brilliant military career and emerged from the Command Staff Academy in 1978 as an officer marked for the highest commands. Given the traditions of the JNA at that time he would not have progressed as a battalion and brigade commander so quickly if there had been any hint of his being a rabid Serb nationalist. When the Serb–Croat war started in June 1991 he was Chief of Staff of the 9th Army Corps based in Knin. Like many other corps it was disintegrating as officers and men started identifying themselves as Croat or Slovene and began to leave the JNA, either to join up with their national forces or to quit military service and in some cases leave the country. Those, mainly Serbs, who remained with the JNA did not have it all their own way and many were humiliatingly blockaded into their barracks by surrounding Croatian forces – one reason why the JNA responded so massively in places like Vukovar. By that stage a classic civil war had developed, with the army splitting up and brother officers breaking friendships and leaving to fight each other. The atmosphere at this time is well caught in Misha Glenny's *Fall of Yugoslavia*.[i] Mladic was widely judged to have fought with considerable skill around Knin; but he also developed a reputation as a braggart. Whether he has committed war crimes will be for the War Crimes Tribunal to decide. If the Tribunal does find that there is a case to answer it will have to be a very different and powerful government in Belgrade to respond to an arrest warrant from the Tribunal and deliver Mladic up for trial, for he will be protected by the JA. Indeed, so confident is he of that protection that I doubt he is much influenced by the existence of the Tribunal.

In May 1992 Milosevic was personally responsible for promoting Mladic above many more senior people to command Serb forces in Bosnia-Herzegovina. He was appointed a Lieutenant-Colonel General in August 1992 and a Colonel General in June 1994. On a number of occasions he has made quite absurd claims, such as that he would bomb London, which have had to be disowned by his political masters. But these bravado statements are calculated to boost the morale of his peasant soldiers, who see him as a hero. He often visits the front line, and in September 1994 near Bihac was injured and nearly caught by Bosnian government forces. On these visits he sleeps, eats, drinks and talks with his men in their dugouts. Yet the same man can conduct a serious debate in Geneva or Belgrade on the strategies of Clausewitz and the lessons of the 1991 Iraq war. He is well informed on all NATO weapons systems and studies their capacities with great attention. Public bully, private calculator – these are but elements in his complex make up. He is purported to have watched in May 1992 as the house in which he had lived with his brother was burnt down, an experience which helped to harden his Serb identity. His remarks about Muslims are often racist, about Croats and Muslims contemptuous. Our conversations were dignified, with none of the bombast he unleashed on others, but I found little evidence of a softer inner side to his character, though I do believe the story that he is devoted to his wife and son. After his 23-year-old medical student daughter's suicide I commiserated with him in terms of my own son's childhood leukaemia, which was fortunately cured. For a brief spell we were fathers first and foremost; but within minutes we were back to a wary confrontation and mock jocularity. He never lowered his guard in the many hours of conversation I had with him. He wanted a Serbia extending in one continuous territorial swathe to include Trebinje, Pale, Bijeljina, Banja Luka and Knin, with Montenegro and possibly Macedonia. If it was called Yugoslavia so be it, but I suspect he would have preferred it to be called Serbia. He attends the Orthodox Church ceremonies that have become a feature in Pale, but I suspect out of duty rather than conviction.

He never appeared afraid of NATO air strikes or US threats to lift the arms embargo. Probably he would have welcomed both as getting the politicians off his back and allowing him to wage war with the gloves off. He assesses the UN capabilities and the consequences of any defiance and then decides when to back off and when to confront. The prospect of continuing the fighting into the twenty-first century is one he views with total equanimity. He has not yet been tempted by any of Milosevic's offers to hold higher rank within the JA. When he defied Milosevic over the VOPP in Pale in the early hours of the morning on 6 May, and as Milosevic stormed out, defeated, to drive back to Belgrade, Mladic used a football analogy, saying with a grin: 'It's fantastic, just like during Real Madrid's best days' – a remark well judged to appeal to his countrymen, who remain football crazy.

Some observers explain the Pale Assembly decision in terms of a power struggle within the Bosnian Serb leadership between the civilians and the military, with the latter keen to be on top, in part for fear that skeletons in their cupboard, such as massacres and war crimes, would be uncovered by the UN if they accepted the peace plan. We will probably never know what effect the publicity over the Tribunal had on the peace process and on the minds of the key leaders, at this moment and at other times. I am afraid my explanation is simpler: I think at Pale the Bosnian Serbs calculated they could 'cock a snook' at Belgrade and the world and get away with it, and unfortunately they were right.

In Belgrade we were given information that the Serbian leadership's dominant concern would now be to persuade the international community not to channel its military efforts into punitive military strikes and other measures, such as lifting the arms embargo, which would make it impossible for them to continue to support the VOPP. Senior advisers to the leadership were however prepared to consider favourably military imposition of the VOPP, and I summarized their suggestions as follows:

1 The rules of engagement of a UN implementation force should be not to shoot first, but to respond with force when attacked. The act of firing on the UN force should be declared by the FRY as a crime against humanity, for which the military leaders of the troops involved, such as Mladic, would henceforth be held personally responsible and brought to account by the FRY.

2 The FRY leadership, on the basis of such a threat, would gain acceptance in the FRY and then in Bosnia for the concept of an implementation force as an occupying force rather than as a hostile attacking aggressor force: moreover, as had been the case with Tito's 'Trieste' position, the Serb population in Bosnia could be persuaded that neither they nor the army should ever fire on the troops of countries who had been their allies in two World Wars. Therefore the predominant nationalities in the UN force would have to be British, French, American and Russian.

3 The UN should issue an ultimatum as soon as they were ready, giving the Serbian forces surrounding the Muslim enclaves in eastern Bosnia a period of, say, three days during which they should withdraw their troops to a perimeter line and their heavy weapons to a position 30 km behind that, after which the UN would move in to establish demilitarized zones. A similar 'ultimatum' approach should be used to 'occupy' the areas outside designated Croatian and Muslim provinces currently under Serbian control.

4 Yugoslav Army liaison officers should be attached to UN forces in Serb populated areas. This would ostensibly be on the basis of offering guarantees to the local population, but they would equally serve as a 'protective shield' for the UN. Similarly, JA liaison officers should be attached to UN humanitarian aid convoys to provide them

with an additional 'protective shield' during the initial period of VOPP implementation.

5 The Geneva negotiations should not give up their search for additional guarantees that could be offered to the Bosnian Serbs. The feeling that the UN could no longer be relied on, following January's attack by the Croatian government on the Croatian Serbs in the Krajina, had been mentioned by many speakers at Pale as evidence that VOPP guarantees were insufficient. There was also a feeling that even an adequate military force could be withdrawn at short notice for UN budgetary reasons.

The VOPP should have been imposed along these lines and President Clinton should have approached President Yeltsin for a joint initiative. Such an initiative might well have been able to involve the JA military in the planning for imposition on Bosnian Serb territory. Some of the ideas we were given were impracticable and unlikely to have been accepted by Milosevic or Cosic, but there was no doubt in my mind that Belgrade did expect and wanted the Security Council to take tough action against the Bosnian Serb leaders in Pale and that there would have been no real objection from Belgrade if we had imposed the VOPP. Indeed, I believe Milosevic expected us to do so. Instead, the US were still hooked on 'lift and strike', a policy which the Russians and their main European allies rejected and which bore no immediate relation to a settlement but on the contrary would, at least initially, ignite the war. It was a reminder of how fateful and mistaken had been Warren Christopher's 10 February undertaking never to impose a settlement.

According to President Clinton, the Bosnian Serb rejection had given added impetus to Warren Christopher's round of consultations, which would be intensified. He said: 'America has made its position clear and is ready to do its part, but Europe must be willing to act with us. We must go forward together.' General Powell had told Congressional leaders that it would be difficult to take effective aerial action to silence Serb artillery, or to cut Serb supply lines to Bosnia, but it could undoubtedly be done, although it would not be cost-free and there would be US casualties.

In Brussels on 6 May Warren Christopher met with the Troika, consisting of the Danish as current holders of the EC Presidency, the Belgians as the next holders of the Presidency and the UK as the immediately previous holders. The Danish Presidency, who briefed me immediately after the meeting, were surprised to find Christopher not talking about how to pressurize the Bosnian Serbs to implement the VOPP, but instead being only too eager to drop the plan. Although Christopher agreed with Helveg Petersen when the latter said that the Pale decision had not diminished the importance of Milosevic's commitment since Athens to the VOPP, he added that while Milosevic's attitude was promising it was not a panacea and that we had now arrived in the 'failed VOPP' scenario. A new approach was needed and additional measures must be considered, and he talked of four policy options as he had done elsewhere in his consultations:

1 Increased sanctions: Christopher felt these would not work fast enough.
2 An enforced ceasefire: this would be affirming the status quo, rewarding aggression and ethnic cleansing, but might be something we had to consider.
3 Air strikes: these would involve collateral damage of an unacceptable kind and would not work alone. Targets would be concealed, the conflict would escalate and massive ground deployment would become necessary.
4 Lifting the arms embargo: any Serbian offensive surge would be met by short-term air strikes to stop the Serbs taking advantage during the early period. A new UNSCR and measures to enhance the safety of UNPROFOR would be required.

The US administration favoured the fourth option of lifting the arms embargo, with improved monitoring in Kosovo and strengthening of the tripwire force in Macedonia. The EC Troika, by contrast, were all unconvinced that the VOPP had failed: it had suffered a setback, but it should not be abandoned. The Commission represented by van den Broek also said we should stick with the VOPP, urge Milosevic to interdict supplies to Bosnia and use air power to protect the safe areas. Christopher then said he did not in fact think the VOPP had failed completely: it contained many features which could be useful again; but it risked becoming a distraction at the moment. Milosevic was not a magic bullet. He had only won two votes at Pale. His price would be a relaxation of sanctions but this was too much to pay. Milosevic should not become the focus of our policy. Christopher was adamant that air power would not protect the safe areas, for which very large ground forces would be needed. He added that General Powell took a strong line on this. There could be no question of putting US troops at risk or of needing to be rescued from the Serbs, as was happening to the Canadians in Srebrenica.

Another sign that the Americans were not ready to go ahead with trying to implement the VOPP was given in New York that evening in a consultation on a draft French Resolution. The French, introducing their draft, which endorsed the VOPP and asked for border monitors, said it was designed to respond to a new situation and to confirm that the VOPP was not dead. But the US delegation, in a rather instructive statement, noted that Secretary Christopher was discussing 'other measures' in Europe. They also questioned whether it would be the right signal to send to say that the Security Council was planning for implementation of the peace plan when, in fact, some delegations were thinking about a different track. Prior to that discussion the Security Council passed the Non-Aligned Security Council Resolution 824,[94] which decided against the weight of professional advice that Sarajevo, Tuzla, Zepa, Gorazde, Bihac and their surroundings would be treated as 'safe areas'. The Security Council had determined on 16 April with UNSCR 819 that Srebrenica should be a 'safe area'. The Security Council acted under Chapter VII in both resolutions, but in the context of UNSCR 815,[95] which referred to the security of UN personnel and was not taken as being an enforcement measure.

On 7 May it became clear that the US even had reservations on the intro-duction of FRY border monitors. They felt it would have little effect and minimal credibility with public opinion. It would also expose UN personnel and perhaps, more importantly for the US, would close off some of the military options which they wanted to keep open. But at no stage was the US ready to say what 'lift and strike' was intended to achieve. Victory for the Bosnia-Herzegovina government forces? When the Croat part of the government was starting a serious fight with its supposed partners, the Muslims, in that government? Some countries, for example Germany, were already asking the US if the arms were to help the Muslims fight the Croats. Would NATO forces strike Croat forces as well as Serb forces? If it was to achieve a negotiated settlement, what was the basis for that negotiation? If it was not the VOPP, since the US was arguing that this was unenforceable and was openly expressing doubts about the VOPP map, what settlement did the US propose? Could we really expect the Bosnian Muslims to start a meaningful negotiation from scratch in the midst of lift and strike which would give them the hope of outright victory? Perhaps it was the US inten-tion to concentrate on developing a new map. But hitherto the US had wanted the VOPP map to be more generous to the Muslims. We did not then know that in a few weeks' time in Washington the US would be saying that a map should be more generous to the Serbs. On all these vital aspects the US policy-makers were silent during their European consultations. Instead, they advocated 'lift and strike' with UNPROFOR *in situ*, although differently configured, but with UNHCR convoys stopping. They did not know how long air strikes would have to continue while humanitarian supplies ran short. There was no obvious sign of any thought having been given to what might be an acceptable peace settlement. It was no wonder that US policy started to be derided as 'lift and pray'. It was inconceivable that even America's closest European allies would say 'yes' to Warren Christopher in his consultation, because there was no thought-out package to say 'yes' to.

In the meantime, while Europe pondered this US initiative, according to Elizabeth Drew's well-informed account[ii] President Clinton, having just read

Balkan Ghosts by Robert Kaplan[iii] and an op ed article by Arthur Schlesinger, a wise historian, in the *Wall Street Journal*,[iv] was having second thoughts about 'lift and strike'. Her account has Les Aspin, then Defense Secretary, returning to the Pentagon after his talk with Clinton in the White House and ringing Peter Tarnoff at the State Department and Tony Lake, the National Security Adviser, to say, 'Guys, he's going south on this policy. His heart isn't in it.' Warren Christopher, still in Europe, was immediately told about this shift in the President's position. Soon after he returned to Washington it became clear that 'lift and strike' was dead, killed appropriately by the very person who would have had to carry the responsibility for it – the US President. I do not criticize President Clinton as strongly as some because I had travelled the same route months earlier and ruled out 'lift and strike' as being an impossible strategy unless it was to impose a specific settlement and accompanied by at least partial withdrawal of UN forces and personnel. Clinton had been involved in electioneering virtually since the wars in Yugoslavia started; travelling on the stump non-stop, it was understandable that he did not know all aspects of Balkan history. It was not a weakness to rethink his Bosnian strategy, nor should he be disparaged for reading and listening.

The fact that the President had developed cold feet mid-consultation seemed to stimulate many people connected with the administration to try to put the blame on the Europeans. The tactic of scapegoating, at which the Clinton administration was becoming a past master, was once more swinging into operation. A new policy had begun to emerge under the rubric of 'containment': damp down the conflict, take Bosnia off the front pages, send some troops to join the UN effort in Macedonia to quieten the 'do something' lobby and above all avoid getting any US troops on the ground in Bosnia-Herzegovina; also ensure that the VOPP was killed off at the same time as 'lift and strike'.

By 8 May the US was saying that concerted international action was needed but its exact form had yet to be decided. The Americans were now ready to look at border monitoring, despite having said only a day before that they were against it. They were dismissing safe areas as an unreal exercise, despite having voted for the UNSCR which established them only two days before. For someone like myself trying to mobilize maximum pressure on the Serbs to implement the VOPP, every day was a nightmare. US policy was impossible to decipher. It all depended on who was talking, and then on whether it was a private or public conversation. The administration were blaming the Europeans, particularly the UK for their briefing after Warren Christopher's Chevening meeting. They were trying to give the impression that all options were still open as, understandably, they were shielding their President over his change of mind on 'lift and strike'. Now we know from Elizabeth Drew's account that President Clinton could not state his policy, after 5 May, because the administration did not have one: damage limitation was all that could be undertaken. But in Europe at the time we were not aware that this fundamental shift in US policy had taken place. It was all very confused, with diplomats thinking that our arguments had influenced US policy when in fact the President had changed his own mind. A vigorous discussion took place in the Foreign Affairs Council on 10 May.[96] There was total support for the VOPP but not for imposing it by force.

I then flew to New York to continue my negotiations with Cyrus Vance on the vexed question of the Former Yugoslav Republic of Macedonia. In New York, after much discussion, we gave the Macedonians and the Greeks a draft treaty on 14 May and simultaneously sent the Secretary-General a report for the Security Council.[97] The proposed treaty covered many subjects of importance to one party or the other. Among its central provisions was one in which the Macedonians gave a formal interpretation of several provisions of their constitution – in lieu of amending that instrument, which would have required a two-thirds majority in the Parliament, which the government could not muster. The draft treaty's main feature was that it balanced a number of 'confidence building measures' desired primarily by Greece, and painful to FYROM, against a number of provisions establishing normal friendly and neighbourly relations which the Greeks considered premature. At Boutros Ghali's suggestion we chose, after much thought, the name 'Republic of Nova Makedonija', to be used for all domestic and international purposes, relying on the technique the Ivory Coast had used when some years ago it insisted that the French form of its name be used in all languages. However, soon after this both parties, for opposite reasons, rejected that name and the proposed treaty.

In the US I found bubbling resentment that the Europeans had rejected the US position on former Yugoslavia. Even Congress did not yet know that it was their President who had rejected his own position. Above all, there was the usual US wish to be seen to be leading from the front while not facing the hard fact that it is difficult to do this when one's troops are deliberately left behind. US attitudes to European unity have been essentially ambivalent for decades. Ever since President Kennedy gave support to the Common Market and the idea of European unity, American foreign policy has been based on encouraging EC unity, but with the unstated proviso that it supports US policy. The moment European unity manifested itself as being critical of US policy the US had a tendency to revert to bilateral consultation to head off a united European position. That divide and rule policy had served them pretty well in NATO and other fora. The ICFY was seen by some in Washington as an undesirable innovation in that it was a formalized mechanism for achieving an EC policy and tying that in to the UN, leaving the US to either cooperate or be challenged. Also, when Russia chose to cooperate this increased Russian rapport with the EC at the expense of the US.[98] A revealing moment in Warren Christopher's European visit occurred at NATO HQ. Manfred Woerner, who had been calling for tough military action for a year, met Christopher expecting a display of American leadership and saying he was ready to convene an immediate meeting of the permanent representatives to lay out and endorse the 'lift and strike' policy and to push them into urgent agreement. Christopher was said to have been startled and said he preferred to hold bilateral meetings first, almost as if he was afraid for the US to take the lead on this issue.

When Warren Christopher was questioned by a Senate Committee on his supposed failure to convince his European allies, Senator Biden said, 'What you've encountered, it seems to me, was a discouraging mosaic of indifference, timidity, self-delusion and hypocrisy . . . I can't even begin to express my anger for a European policy that's now asking us to participate in what amounts to a codification of a Serbian victory.' Even the *Wall Street Journal*, a critic of Clinton's policy, offered him sympathy over European attitudes.

I went on American television to say 'we've got to be very careful against having Europeans thinking of the Americans as cowboys and Americans thinking of Europeans as wimps,' and I argued that there was no 'risk-free war' in the skies above Bosnia-Herzegovina. The American journalist George Will was also warning that the real 'Vietnam syndrome' was 'the belief of civilians that they can cleverly administer violence and other coercion in precise and manipulative doses. Vietnam, remember, was a professors' war, long on theories and nuances.' I too had to be wary of falling into this trap in my continued advocacy of interdiction air strikes on the Bosnian side of the FRY border to impose UN sanctions against the Bosnian Serbs. Such strikes would have had to be very carefully targeted to avoid civilian casualties. I was calculating among other things that, faced by such a Security Council decision, Milosevic would agree to having serious border monitors introduced so as to avoid being sucked into the war. He was still objecting to having UN monitors on the borders to police the sanctions he himself had announced, not, I suspected, as was claimed, because of the impact on sovereign Serb territory but because it would affect his ability to control the transit traffic to the Croatian Serbs. This was one more demonstration of how difficult it was to deal with Bosnia-Herzegovina separately from Croatia. I calculated that Milosevic would need to be pushed hard to accept border monitors, given the criticism from within Serbia as well as from the Bosnian and Croatian Serbs. But I was never able to mobilize the key Security Council countries to put real pressure on Milosevic on this issue.[99]

The French press reported a conversation on 13 May between Juppé and French journalists on the French proposal for 'safe areas' in Bosnia-

Herzegovina. Juppé revealed that France had given the US, UK and Russia a non-paper – which in diplomatic terms means that formally it does not exist – elaborating on French thinking. This they hoped would serve as a basis for a new UNSCR which would enforce UNSCR 824 and spell out the military and other modalities of the operation. Juppé underlined that there was no question of reconquering territory occupied by the Serbs, nor of providing complete armed protection around the designated safe areas, since that would require a massive UN presence of 50,000–60,000 troops on the ground. But 10,000–12,000 would suffice to cover – 'sanctuarize' – the areas. This would be done on the light Srebrenica model, which would imply reinforcement of UNPROFOR by a further two battalions. These troops should come from countries other than the UK and France, and include the Americans and Russians in particular. Juppé admitted that the Americans were not enthusiastic, but was quite right in saying that a US and Russian presence would have a different effect on the Bosnian Serbs, making them think twice about attacking the 'safe areas'. Juppé reaffirmed that the overall objective remained Bosnian Serb signature of the VOPP. Once that happened, he said, the US should commit ground forces to VOPP implementation. The command and control problem, he said, had been resolved – a four-star French general as deputy to a US commander, with a British HQ in Bosnia – but Juppé avoided mention of the NATO command structures. He warned that since the VOPP, as drafted, implied larger-scale Serb withdrawal from conquered areas it would be a long time, perhaps five years, before it could be fully implemented, and there was no guarantee that it would be.

Juppé repeated that no options were excluded. In the worst case, the UN would withdraw, the arms embargo would be lifted and there would be air strikes. But that would be a counsel of despair and Juppé had underlined before the National Assembly on 12 May that this was not the way to go.

The Americans were saying that they would not stand in the way of establishing 'safe areas' but they were concerned that these areas could become giant refugee camps, effectively ratifying ethnic cleansing. They would not contribute US troops, and their military thought more troops were needed than the French were proposing.

Meanwhile, observations of the FRY border crossings by a military observer indicated that the restrictions imposed by the Serbian and Montenegrin authorities on cross-border traffic from FRY to Bosnia-Herzegovina were real, and therefore removed a great deal of the burden which would apply to a full-scale monitoring exercise. In such a situation a relatively small number of monitors, at least at this initial stage, would, some thought, be adequate to observe the small amount of traffic being allowed across the border, mainly private vehicles. It was suggested that a team of three at each of the sixteen crossings would be able to provide effective

24-hour coverage. But not only were we unable to get Milosevic and Cosic to accept such monitors, there was no real pressure to go ahead and mount the necessary diplomatic pressure to ensure that they were deployed.

Stoltenberg and I, who had met as Co-Chairmen on 7 May, then flew to Moscow on 15 May to discuss the next steps, particularly how to pressurize Milosevic on border monitors and to pursue our ideas for progressive implementation of the VOPP. But as we were doing this the US was starting to set the stage for the killing off of the VOPP and, in marked contrast to the last three months of US criticisms based on the VOPP not being sufficiently generous to the Muslims, there began to be hints of the view now being taken that the VOPP was too hard on the Serbs. They were contemplating whether in practice Serb-dominated eastern Bosnia could be handed back to the Muslims. They felt that a considerable movement of people would be required to match up populations with the Vance–Owen map and that this would not be enforceable. It was obvious that the US problem with the map was that they did not want any US implementation force to have to confront Bosnian Serb forces who were not ready to withdraw. This lay behind their anxiety, obvious at Athens, that significant confirmatory action on the ground from the Bosnian Serbs of their acceptance of the plan before implementation was a precondition for the US going ahead with implementation.

Over lunch in Moscow on 16 May Kozyrev said he totally agreed with our phrase 'progressive implementation', and proceeded to use it extensively in the press conference that followed. He accepted that the Russian Federation should provide border monitors for the Serbian–Montenegrin border, but said he would have to clear this with President Yeltsin. He also agreed with our view that the Croatian–Bosnia-Herzegovina border should be monitored as well and noted that Tudjman had accepted this in discussion with Churkin; Tudjman had also asked for monitors on the Croatian–Serbian border, which Kozyrev thought was reasonable. Churkin reported that Milosevic, in a telephone conversation on Saturday, had still been anxious that outside monitors on the borders would create problems for him internally, giving a lever to his Serbian critics. We reminded Kozyrev that the FRY already had UN monitors on their airfields, and that Cosic was in principle keener on the idea than Milosevic, provided Croatia was also involved. We raised the possibility of 2,000 Russian troops as a contribution to implementing the safe areas Resolution, and asked for their very quick deployment. Kozyrev promised to discuss this with Yeltsin, and gave the press afterwards the strong impression that Russia would contribute both monitors and peacekeepers.

Kozyrev stated his intention to table a framework Resolution for Security Council decision at a ministerial-level meeting on Friday 21 May. He was likely to fly to Belgrade to see Milosevic and Cosic, and was attracted by our suggestion of meeting Izetbegovic and Tudjman in Split in the early morning of 18 May. He then intended to fly to Rome and talk to European Foreign Ministers in the margins of the WEU meeting on 19 May, after which he would go to Washington to speak to Christopher. He was well aware that the US was far from convinced of the value of a debate in the Security Council, and I suggested that if he framed his Resolution around progressive implementation it might be more acceptable.

On 18 May Stoltenberg and I met with Tudjman and Izetbegovic at Medjugorje to try to stop the fighting that was raging in central Bosnia between the Croats and Muslims. Mostar, where we had planned to meet, was too unsafe even to visit because of the fighting. That day the European Union, in a Political Cooperation press release, had reiterated that they would 'continue to lend their full support to the Vance–Owen plan' and promised 'to bring heavy pressure to bear on Serbia/Montenegro and the Bosnian Serbs, with no option being excluded'. To demonstrate that commitment at great personal inconvenience, given that it was referendum day in his own country, Helveg Petersen had come to the meeting, flying in from Denmark to Zagreb, then on to Split and by helicopter to Medjugorje. Progressive implementation was accepted and on that basis we hoped to be able to use UNPROFOR to monitor the ceasefire more extensively and help us start an agreed provincial government in those provinces where there were few Serbs and in which the Serbs had no interest, and whose borders, though not yet finalized, had nevertheless been agreed between the Croat and Muslim leaders in December 1992 before the VOPP map was presented.

The heads of the British, French and Spanish delegations of the European Community Monitoring Mission (ECMM) had undertaken a fact-finding mission from 3 to 9 May 1993, and they gave us their report before the meeting. It was an excellent, clear document which made depressing reading. While the world was focusing solely on Serb–Muslim hostilities, the report gave an alarming picture of increasing conflict between Croats and Muslims, which at the current rate of escalation seemed set to erupt into yet more bloody fighting.[100] In the view of the delegation heads the difference between what the Serbs and the Croats, respectively, were doing to the Muslims was one only of scale. Indeed, in the event the actions of these two sides against the Muslims were complementary. However, although there may well have been contacts between the Serbs and the Croats, the ECMM found no evidence that they were actually working together. In fact, their interests would appear to clash, both parties aiming to expel Muslims from territory to which they laid claim. Either way, the Muslims were squeezed. What had hitherto been tension between Croats and Muslims had now escalated into direct conflict. The situation in Mostar suggested that it was reaching crisis proportions.

The Danish Presidency had sent a very strong letter to President Tudjman threatening EC sanctions, but Klaus Kinkel had visited Zagreb and, while talking toughly, had nevertheless left the Croats with the impression that there would be no real sanctions. After our meeting in Medjugorje Tudjman did try to limit Boban's activities, realizing that Bosnian Croat behaviour was damaging the image of the Croatian government in the eyes of the world. Even so, the Bosnian Croats, though not as strong as the Bosnian Muslims, were not prepared to stop fighting, and Zagreb was not prepared to see them beaten by the Muslims. The third war in the disintegration of Yugoslavia was now under way, a savage Muslim–Croat civil war which raged for a year before the Croat–Muslim Federation was established in 1994 under the Washington Accords.

Meanwhile the new US policy of 'containment' for Bosnia-Herzegovina was spelt out by Warren Christopher on 18 May before the House Foreign Affairs Committee, a testimony he concluded by saying, 'At heart, this is a European problem.' Critics of the VOPP still had nothing positive to put in its place except the so-called 'safe areas' policy, so often discussed and just as frequently – after hearing the arguments for and against – rejected. This time France was advocating a 'safe areas' Resolution and Russia wanted a Security Council debate, which the US was blocking. There were the makings of a deal around perhaps the phased, as distinct from progressive, implementation of the VOPP and that is what we and, I believe, Kozyrev thought was going to develop.

On 19 May Stoltenberg and I were in Naples for a presentation of the VOPP by the NATO's Southern Commander, Admiral Boorda, and SACEUR, General Shalikashvili, came for lunch. It was a relaxed and for me fascinating occasion. The VOPP had been carefully analysed and translated into military parlance – so much so that at times I was hard pressed to recognize it, but all the essentials were there and the hard edges of implementation, particularly putting UNPROFOR into the Serb areas where there had been ethnic cleansing, with the intention of facilitating the return of people who had been forced to leave, had been faced up to and well provided for in terms of UN numbers. I rang Churkin in Rome and all seemed to be well after Kozyrev's meeting with Tudjman and Izetbegovic in Split and meetings in the margins of the WEU session. Churkin was talking the language of progressive implementation as they flew off to Washington, while Stoltenberg and I set off for the Ukraine to see if we could persuade the government in Kiev to contribute more troops to UNPROFOR, and to Belarus to see if they too would start contributing forces to the UN.

It was clear that the Russian proposal for a ministerial Security Council meeting over the implementation of the VOPP was likely to be postponed as a result of the American refusal to attend. Back in London on 21 May I found in my pile of telegrams from the Foreign Office one from Washington about a new diplomatic initiative involving the US, France, the UK and Russia. I had just finished reading it when my assistant, Maggie Smart, was rung up to say that it had been sent to me in error – which meant that, for the first time I was aware of since I had been appointed Co-Chairman, I was being deliberately kept in the dark by the British on a substantive question. In fairness to the British government, I served the European Community, and in this case the British and French governments were embarking on a diplomatic initiative in an attempt to heal the Atlantic rift, knowing this was contrary to EC policy. Douglas Hurd and Alain Juppé were entitled to try to do this, and to involve me would have presented me with conflicting loyalties – particularly since the Presidency was held by the Danes, for if I had known this was going on I would have had to warn the Danish Presidency.

It was obvious from the telegram that Washington, London and Paris had been in communication for four to five days on the substance as well as on the form of the initiative. Christopher and Kozyrev had now agreed a text, after negotiating for most of 20 May, and this was being passed to the French. The two of them had apparently agreed to say nothing to the press about the statement and the US had asked the British to hold it very close. Nevertheless, CNN had already got wind of its existence and some of the details. Douglas Hurd had flown out to the US by Concorde to arrive in time for meetings that morning, and Alain Juppé was coming to Washington for a meeting on the following Saturday. Assuming that neither had difficulties with the draft an announcement was planned for that day, 22 May.

The problem with this tidy arrangement was that the whole story was in Friday's edition of the *New York Times* under the headline: 'US and Russia Agree on Strategy Accepting Serbian Gains for Now'. Douglas Hurd rang me from the US to explain, unaware that I had the actual text of the US–Russian draft in front of me. There was a certain negative humour to the whole conversation. I was hearing the death knell of the VOPP wrapped up in diplomatic language. Douglas kept stressing how he was trying to get adjustments made towards acknowledging the VOPP while I kept coming back to the *New York Times* story, pointing out that his intentions had been completely overtaken by events. The whole package was bound to be seen for what it was – depressingly from the European Community viewpoint, jubilantly from Pale, despairingly from Sarajevo and cynically from Belgrade. We were back with the basic incoherence of the 10 February US position. Nothing should be imposed, and yet without the threat of imposition why should the Bosnian Serbs withdraw? To be credible, implementation had to have an element of imposition or there would be no Serb withdrawal from the really sensitive territory which their forces currently occupied. It was bizarre and, for me personally, exasperating that the US, who had been against the VOPP map for favouring ethnic cleansing, was now advocating a map that allowed the Serbs to keep more territory. Nor could I see any evidence that they were facing up to the inevitable consequence, namely the

partition, not the unification, of Bosnia-Herzegovina. Allowing the Serbs
more territory might enable any peace plan to be monitored – not implemented – by a smaller UN force, but it also meant partition, and the death
of most of the London Principles. I was determined to make the European
politicians face this reality if they chose to go along with the Americans.
Ditching the VOPP meant ditching almost all the European countries' statements about reversing ethnic cleansing. Their track record suggested that the
US and European Foreign Ministers would try to do all this by stealth,
denying that there had been any change. In the US, scapegoating was a
hallmark of the new administration's style, and we could expect this shift to
be carried out at the expense of the Europeans. I still hoped that the EC,
particularly with the Germans as late converts to the VOPP, might see that
holding firmly on to our plan was the right course, not only morally but also
politically. But to be credible in doing this the EC would have to be able to
mobilize a European defence commitment to implement the plan without
the US.

I kept stressing to Douglas Hurd on the telephone that since it was the
State Department who had given authority to the political story in the *New
York Times*, he and Juppé had to dissociate themselves from the story or
the VOPP was dead.[v] Datelined Washington, May 20, the story read:

> The United States and Russia agreed today to forge a common strategy
> with other European nations that accepts, at least for the moment, the
> territorial gains made by the Serbs in Bosnia.
>
> The goal would no longer be to roll back any of the gains achieved by
> the Bosnian Serbs in 14 months of fighting, but rather, in the words of a
> senior Administration official, 'to contain and stabilize the situation and
> to put the brakes on the killing.'
>
> When asked whether this approach appeared to reward the 'ethnic
> cleansing' campaign by the Bosnian Serbs, the official replied, 'First
> things first'.

Vance–Owen Plan Put Off

> The new strategy, which was discussed by Secretary of State Warren
> Christopher and Foreign Minister Andrei V. Kozyrev of Russia at the
> State Department today, would essentially set aside for now the over-
> arching goal of the Vance–Owen peace plan, which would require the
> Bosnian Serbs to withdraw from about half of the territory they hold.

I gathered from Douglas that the problem facing the French, British and
Russians in Washington for the drafting of an agreed text was the deep
American pessimism, verging on hostility, towards the Vance–Owen peace
plan. He confirmed that the US argument had changed completely in recent

days: whereas they had originally argued that the VOPP was too generous to the Serbs, they were now saying it was unrealistic to expect the Serbs to give up so much territory.

Alain Juppé, when first confronted by the US text, saw immediately that it was a loose assembly of ideas which skirted around the key question of the VOPP. I had been working ever more closely with the French government since Milosevic's visit to Paris. I was aware that the Quai d'Orsay wanted a better relationship with America, particularly under Alain Juppé who, though a very convinced European, had no truck with anti-Americanism for its own sake. I already sensed that Juppé could emerge as one of the most formidable post-war French Foreign Ministers. Quick-witted and decisive, he was not one to nurse a grudge if we differed, as we did from time to time, on policy. I had little doubt that he would become a major figure in domestic French politics and, for that very reason, was bound like Douglas Hurd to take a wider view of French–American and European–American relations.

Nor could I ignore these vital wider questions of US–European relations. It was doing none of us any good to have these differences on the former Yugoslavia: the friction was affecting NATO, GATT and other very important aspects of mutual concern. Even so, it was galling for other EC nations to have these crucial issues pre-empted; yet sometimes the need for quiet decisive action and secrecy will necessitate a smaller group of EC countries taking their responsibilities on national shoulders. I did not envy Juppé and Hurd the task facing them. Some changes were made to the document but they were largely cosmetic, for in truth Warren Christopher had presented them with a *fait accompli*, having already got Andrei Kozyrev to agree the text. Later Kozyrev was to claim publicly on British Channel Four television that he too had been 'bounced'. The decision to bring in Javier Solana, the Spanish Foreign Minister, because Spain was a member of the Security Council – a decision taken with Kozyrev's full support – was a wise one because it gave Juppé and Hurd some cover in relation to the other European Foreign Ministers. Everyone in the Foreign Affairs Council liked Solana and involving Spain gave the whole initiative far more of an EC flavour. Kozyrev told me afterwards that he had been amazed to read the story in Friday's New York Times, and had had no idea the previous day that the text could be used as the basis for such an anti-VOPP stance in the press. He had, he said, stressed to President Clinton the importance of the VOPP, in that it had been created by the international community, who had successfully pressed Milosevic to accept it, all reasonable parties on the ground had signed up to it and only Karadzic was holding out. In a London Times story by Nick Gowing, headlined 'Deceit Devours Diplomacy in Bosnia Last Rites', which appeared in August, Kozyrev publicly explained that the Russian position had been misrepresented in the New York Times story of 21 May and that he never agreed to accept Serbian gains. He said, 'This is a totally inaccurate quotation of what I said and thought. From the beginning I was insisting on a Serbian roll back.' Kozyrev also 'conceded that he might have been "bounced" by the leak into appearing to back an American effort to kill the Vance–Owen plan'.[101]

In fairness to Kozyrev, it should be said that Warren Christopher had baited the trap with great cunning. The Russians had always believed that Vance and I had been too tough on the Serbs in terms of territory, and in particular that they should have territorial continuity and a land corridor in the north. It was inconceivable that the Russians would reject an offer from the Americans of more land for the Serbs. Also, they valued at that time the opportunity to be accepted as a fully fledged partner in a 'Big Four' initiative to resolve the Yugoslav problem. The text which eventually emerged did contain references to the 'Vance–Owen peace process' but the 'plan' was not mentioned – a significant omission. The other ministers did resist the American attempt to abolish the ICFY and substitute a purely governmental mechanism, but though there was no commitment in the statement to the continued operation of these countries as a formal group, most expected that informal coordination would result in a structure capable of ending the Atlantic rift. Indeed, on the basis that this might be achieved and given the deteriorating situation at the time, I suspect that had I been British Foreign Secretary, I would have been sorely tempted to sign up that Saturday in Washington to the so-called Joint Action Programme on Bosnia.[102] Disillusioned though I was, therefore, I felt I could not in all decency publicly single out Douglas Hurd for criticism. He had been courteous, considerate and open in all his dealings with me. He had wider British interests to defend, whereas I had to protect the EC position.

Although I went through the motions of keeping open the European Community position on the VOPP and the WEU option for the next few days I knew that the plan had now been effectively ditched by the Americans and could never be got back on the road. The only way to revive it would have been for the Europeans to say that they would implement the VOPP through the WEU and hive off from NATO the command and control structures to do so; then to rally sufficient troop numbers from non-EU countries like Russia, the Ukraine, Poland, the Czech Republic and Slovakia to give the implementation force credibility. The truth was that there was not the political or military will in Europe without France and Britain to do this and in my heart I knew it.

As to the Joint Action Programme (JAP), it was destined to fail. The US military, who were more clear-headed than their political leaders, did not pretend that the immediate objective of the JAP, while introducing 'safe areas', was to stop the killing, for to do that effectively there needed to be a clear reinforcement plan that had not even been worked out for the safe areas. The UN had done work on increased force numbers, but many of us felt it needed rules of engagement and command and control procedures for peace enforcement, not peacekeeping, if the areas were to be kept safe. The US were adamant about not committing their own troops and their military saw great difficulty in the so-called 'oil slick' approach of trying to use force to gradually enlarge the 'safe areas'. One redeeming feature of the JAP was the commitment to establish the Yugoslav War Crimes Tribunal; but that apart, it was in effect an inaction programme.

The press had no illusions as to what had happened in Washington. Taking their cue from the *New York Times* story of Friday 21 May, all press and television comment throughout Europe and America saw the JAP as an endorsement of the Serbs' territorial conquests. Alain Juppé was quoted in *Le Monde* as saying defensively, 'Contrary to what is written here and there, the JAP is a confirmation of the Vance–Owen process.' Izetbegovic, in a statement from Sarajevo on 23 May, derisively rejected the JAP. Referring to what the 'great four' had to say, he claimed that the programme would allow the Serbs to retain territory taken by force, prevent displaced populations from returning to their homes, and turn safe areas into reservations. It was therefore absolutely unacceptable. Signature of the VOPP had been the Bosnian government's final word. It was the minimum they could accept and they would not waste their time any longer in futile negotiations. Izetbegovic called upon all those citizens who loved Bosnia to unite and defend, with all permissible means, its integrity and freedom. I agreed with every word and I felt very sorry for the predicament in which Izetbegovic now found himself. The US had totally let him down.

What I feared was that the Bosnian armed forces would now turn on the Croat forces as an easier target than the Serbs and try to gain the territory they needed from that source. Towards the end of May I had initiated negotiations between the Bosnian Muslims and Bosnian Croats, nominally still in the same government, for a set of decrees that the government of Bosnia-Herzegovina might issue so as to begin instituting the VOPP on a bilateral Muslim–Croat basis. These largely concerned human rights issues, but also included the establishment of a Military Committee and of the provinces and their governance. But soon all our hopes of tying the Muslims and Croats together with progressive implementation were doomed, and it would be many months before we could even attempt to bring Croats and Muslims together again, for the Croats had read the signs that opposition to the VOPP paid off and were carving out their own areas, like the Serbs. As for Milosevic, I knew it would not be easy to persuade or pressurize him to separate himself from the Bosnian Serb leaders again, and without splitting Belgrade from Pale the Bosnian Serbs would continue to block any sensible settlement.

In Belgrade Cosic's aides were describing Milosevic as being in one of his periodic phases of deep depression and indecision. Milosevic knew that he had to do something about Seselj soon, but was not sure what. He had built Seselj up; now he needed to knock him down. Milosevic was also beginning to have doubts about his own mythical ability to deliver and to feel that he had overreached himself, giving Karadzic and the Radicals in Serbia the opening they wanted to accuse him of caving in to American posturing and failing to stand up for the interests of fellow Serbs. Milosevic was also worried about the support of Bosnian Serb and Krajina 'cadres' in the Yugoslav army, and particularly the Serbian militia, on whom he had traditionally depended as his ultimate prop. It was a telling sign that he had recently replaced the special unit of Krajina-recruited militia in charge of his personal protection.

The leader of the SPO (Serbian Renewal Movement), Draskovic, had given a depressing account of his own position to diplomats in Belgrade following what he described as the American 'climb-down'. He similarly accused the Americans of having taken the worst possible course, by both backing down on military intervention and refusing to back our plan. Those in the opposition who had supported the VOPP were now vulnerable and isolated. In his view Seselj and Karadzic had won, and Milosevic would soon start blowing with the nationalist wind again. The whole Belgrade leadership was now thoroughly tangled up in nationalist knots, largely of its own creation, but with even less room for manoeuvre now that the Americans had deprived them of the argument that, for the sake of the Serbian nation as a whole, they had little alternative but to support the VOPP.

I was only glad that Cy Vance had been able to leave Athens on such a high note and did not have to face the personal anguish which now engulfed me: should I resign or battle on? I had said nothing over the weekend and when I flew in to Geneva all I would say was: 'I am facing a new situation following the Washington meeting and I want to talk to a number of my colleagues in Europe. My role as a negotiator stems from the European Community and I want to talk to them.' Thorvald Stoltenberg called the Joint Action Programme a 'very real basis for progressive implementation of the Vance–Owen plan'. I wished I could agree with him but I held my tongue. On reflection it is the only time that I can recollect when we ever disagreed on a major issue, and for Thorvald the next few days must have been very trying. I was clearly on the point of resigning, while he was very keen I should stay. Yet I was well aware that Thorvald had only been in the job a few weeks and, just as Cy had carried me for my first months in post with his knowledge and experience of the key players, so Thorvald needed my help for at least a few more months.

I was no stranger to resigning on policy questions. I had given up being a Labour frontbench spokesman on defence in 1972 because of Harold Wilson's about-turn over membership of the European Community. I had resigned from the Shadow Cabinet when Michael Foot was elected Labour leader in November 1980 because of his opposition to the EC and his belief in unilateral nuclear disarmament. I had resigned from the Labour Party in February 1981 after Labour's Special Conference had rejected one member, one vote to elect its leader. I had also resigned as leader of the SDP after the members' ballot decision to negotiate to join up with the Liberal Party. Each of these four resignations had a purpose behind it; each was part of a strategy for challenging and changing policies with which I profoundly disagreed. But a resignation over the VOPP would not bring it back to life or change US policy (if one could dignify it with such a name). Also, my differences were with the US administration, not the European Community, who had given Vance and me their full backing for many months. This was borne out in a cable I saw from New York reporting how delighted someone in the US mission to the UN was that the press out of Geneva were predicting that I would soon resign. If anything that comment inclined me to think that perhaps I should stay and live with the partition that was inevitably now going to be part of any peace settlement, in order to rescue as much as I could from the VOPP.

A crucial factor in my eventual decision was Douglas Hurd's insistence on sending his deputy, Douglas Hogg, out to spend two and a half hours with me over lunch in Geneva on 26 May. He was accompanied by Jeremy Greenstock, the Foreign Office official with whom I had dealt most frequently and for whom I had considerable respect. I said a few harsh things about the Washington agreement, the Americans' behaviour and the British government's position but it was never a bad-tempered exchange and we went thoroughly and frankly over the way ahead, Douglas Hogg doing me the courtesy afterwards of sending me a record of what he reported to the Foreign Secretary and the Prime Minister.

I began by describing the growing resentment of the Washington Joint Action Programme among EC partners. The Danish Presidency, the Germans, Dutch and Italians, and the President of the Commission, Jacques Delors, were all opposed to what had been done. Alain Juppé was now beginning to regret signing up for it. The UK had handled things badly and now had in the JAP a flawed policy. On the central justification for acting in this way, I doubted that it would improve British–American relations given the tensions that would arise from the contradictions in this new policy. The Americans had all along wanted to kill the VOPP, and had come to regret the commitment to implement it given by Christopher in February. They had unscrupulously argued first that it was anti-Muslim and then that the Serbs needed more territory. The latter line had been designed to win over Kozyrev, who came to Washington desperate for a foreign policy success. But Britain, I argued, need not have signed up, for the danger of a lifting of the arms embargo had largely passed: there were not enough votes in the Security Council for it. Douglas Hogg wanted me to admit that the VOPP was dead; I conceded that it could only be carried forward by a Europe ready to take on the full burden of military implementation, without the US, but with the eastern Europeans. Under progressive implementation we would have to threaten the Croatians with economic sanctions to drive them into a proper partnership with the Muslims. UN European troops could then start with the demilitarization of Sarajevo, which I thought the Serbs would accept, and then spread out through the provinces not allocated to the Serbs. Larger numbers of UN personnel would be needed on the ground and we would need the Russians, Ukrainians and Belarussians there. At some point we would have to face down the Serbs and demand withdrawal. Belgrade still needed to escape sanctions and when a certain point was reached, we might be able to lift the arms embargo on the Muslims to help them defend their provincial boundaries, but only when a Croat/Muslim partnership had been re-established.

My other option, if as I expected there was no European will to shoulder the military burden without the US, was to reopen the question of national borders in the former Yugoslavia, implicitly admitting that recognition of Bosnia was a mistake. We should confirm the boundaries of Slovenia and Macedonia, and then do a deal between Bosnia, Croatia and Serbia. Only through such a wider negotiation could enough territory be won for a viable Muslim state. I believed that with international support we could square the Croatians and the Serbs, and though some Muslims would not like it we could give them a viable state. I used for the first time the expression 'from the Sava to the sea'. I told them that I intended to go to Zagreb, Sarajevo and Belgrade between 2 and 6 June to see Tudjman, Izetbegovic and, if possible, Milosevic. I wanted to feel my way forward on the possibilities for the second option and, if I got a reasonable response, I intended to present the two options to EC Foreign Ministers on 8 June, where I envisaged a long session with ministers only or restricted to 'one plus one'. I called the redrawing borders option 'the solution which dare not speak its name'. I knew it could only come from Stoltenberg and me and that any hint of British support or collusion over the next two weeks would alienate EC partners.

Douglas Hogg expressed cautious interest, commenting that Douglas Hurd and he both felt that we now needed to move away from the VOPP towards a new strategy. He asked whether I would need new international backing for what I was proposing, and I thought a London Conference-style meeting, involving the parties at some point, was inevitable. I regarded myself as answerable to the EC alone and was disinclined to look for American support at this stage. In logic the US, having backed off from implementation, should *de facto* accept partition, be ready to let the Europeans carry the political and military burden and stop moralizing. But I had my doubts whether this would happen.

As for my own future, I told Douglas Hogg to tell the Prime Minister, through his wife who was John Major's chief policy adviser, as well as to tell Douglas Hurd, that I was not about to cut and run. But I did talk about going at the summer break or perhaps in September, and that was what I expected to do.

With some reluctance, having been bounced into it after initially agreeing to see the Presidency alone, I then briefed the EC heads of mission in Geneva that same afternoon. I said that my words to the press, that the Co-Chairmen now found themselves in a completely new situation, had been an understatement. I had said virtually nothing to the press since the JAP was announced, and intended to keep it that way and did not propose to comment in detail at this briefing. The meeting of EC Foreign Ministers on 8 June would be the right time to elaborate. All concerned should use the intervening period for calm reflection while the dust settled. I stressed that many in Europe still did not understand the significance of the *New York Times* story of 21 May which had let the cat out of the bag and highlighted the new US willingness to let the Bosnian Serbs hold what territory they had grabbed. This story had set the tone for the Washington meeting and the bad press that followed it.

The latest developments had left Milosevic and Cosic badly bruised. They might still support sanctions between the FRY and the Bosnian Serbs, but these were likely to become increasingly leaky. Tudjman had likewise reacted badly to being left supporting the VOPP while its key sponsors had dropped it. Trying to preserve some sort of peace between the Croats and Muslims was now even more important, but would be even more complicated. The Croats had taken some steps to follow up the agreement reached at Mostar on partial implementation of the VOPP but Izetbegovic had taken no action and I thought that he would now back away from the agreement. Moreover, if the Croats saw that the Serbs were making headway with a Republika Srpska then they would see no reason not to press for their own Herzeg-Bosna Republic.

The German Ambassador then strongly criticized the JAP, saying it was aimed more at bridging differences between western governments than at bringing peace to Bosnia. Germany would repeat these points at the ministerial meeting on 8 June. The French Ambassador emphasized that the JAP was a programme and not a plan. It was emphatically not a substitute for the VOPP, but rather a series of measures to be taken immediately as part of a wider process. It was easy for those governments without troops on the ground to criticize whatever proposals were put forward. He asked me to comment on how the 'safe areas' might be protected and whether the concept should be extended to non-Muslim areas such as Mostar. He also asked whether the London Conference or its Steering Committee should be reconvened.

My misgivings about the original Security Council Resolution establishing a safe area in Srebrenica and my overall reservations had, I said, grown. UNPROFOR alone could not provide the necessary protection or aerial cover and there were few signs of extra UN troops. The 'safe areas' could well turn into Muslim garrisons from which they would launch attacks which would not go unanswered, and Serbian counter-attacks would then pose serious problems for UNPROFOR within the supposed safe area.

On future ICFY work I praised Stoltenberg's appointment to coordinate all work on the former Yugoslavia as Special Representative of the UN Secretary-General and said much of ICFY activity would now be centred on Zagreb. The Confidence Building Working Group had no role and would probably be wound up. The Group on Succession Issues, though running into Serbian obstructions, and the Working Group on Minorities would be retained.

The British Ambassador, Martin Morland, was an old friend and I had talked freely to him, but even so I was rather surprised to find he had cabled London to say that I had told him the previous evening that Vance was advising me to quit but that I felt to down tools now might look like pique. I had deliberately kept Cy Vance's advice very private, but his judgement was troubling me and I found it hard to determine what was the best course of action.

Then that night I had dinner with Javier Solana in the Spanish Embassy. He had flown in on his way back from Turkey especially so that we could talk together personally on my predicament and he left later that night for Madrid. We had known each other since I had invited Felipe Gonzales to London for a semi-official visit in 1979 when he was in opposition and I was in government. It was a generous gesture to stop off in Geneva, and his entreaty to stay and hammer out a new policy with him and others on the Foreign Affairs Council was very hard to resist, for unlike Peter Carrington I had no complaints about European support. I suspect that this was the moment that I really decided to stay. But I left my options open for one further meeting. I wanted to know what President Izetbegovic wanted me to do. So, when I saw him in Sarajevo on 4 June I asked him in front of Thorvald Stoltenberg whether I should stay: he made it crystal clear that he wanted me to do so and that it would be damaging to the Bosnian government's interests if I left. That was the clinching argument, which helped counter the humiliation of my meeting in Pale with Dr Karadzic, who was revelling in my discomfort, savouring every moment of his victory in holding on to more Serb land and seeing off the VOPP.

It was on 4 June, too, that UNSCR 836 on 'safe areas' was passed,[103] which referred to Chapter VII without any qualification for the first time, and the Council embarked on the path of enforcement with no intention of backing it with the necessary resources: the most irresponsible decision taken during my time as Co-Chairman and taken by four of the permanent members as part of their JAP.

Milosevic's first counter-move was to combine with Seselj to remove Cosic from the post of FRY President, to which he had in effect appointed

him over a year ago, and to round on SPO leader Vuk Draskovic and
Danica Draskovic with a sentence of sixty days' imprisonment for an
alleged breach of the peace. Cosic hit back at Milosevic's 'despotic self-
will'.[104] I felt very sad. I had grown fond of Cosic, who had allowed the
responsibility of office to temper many of his more nationalistic views,
demonstrated a readiness to listen to international opinion and won respect
around the negotiating table from Izetbegovic and Tudjman.

On 3 June President Mitterrand and Chancellor Kohl met at Beaune to
patch up their differences over the Washington summit which the German
Defence Minister, Volker Ruehe, also attended; he had previously called the
JAP 'morally catastrophic'. Klaus Kinkel had been more restrained in public,
but in private he had been irritated by the process whereby Germany had
been excluded as much as by the product. Chancellor Kohl tried to point up
the words in the JAP which talked of the refusal to accept Serb gains won
by force. During a debate in the Dutch Parliament, whose members had not
hitherto been noticeable for their support of the VOPP, there was much criticism of the JAP. Speakers said it represented a low point in the diplomacy
of the last few months and a slap in the face for European Political
Cooperation in the foreign policy field; and their Foreign Minister Kooijmans
said that the way three EC partners had behaved was not the way countries
in the Community should treat one another. In Canada, Foreign Minister
Barbara McDougall was unhappy and unclear about what seemed to have
happened to the VOPP in Washington. But it was slowly sinking in to the
Europeans that the London Principles had been ditched in Washington along
with the VOPP and that roll-back on anything like the scale that Vance and
I had fought for was now impossible. The moral authority of the EC and the
UN, and therefore the ICFY, had been dealt a terrible blow, and in part that
was an American objective. In Paris and in London the fall-out was to be an
even greater wariness of being sucked further into Bosnia militarily.

On 8 June at the Foreign Affairs Council meeting in Luxembourg I read
from an unpublished text,[105] which I had never done before, since I had to
weigh every word with care.

*On the morning of Friday 21 May I learnt that the New York Times was
carrying a prominent story with the headline 'US and Russia agree on
strategy accepting Serbian gains for now'. The article which clearly
followed a briefing from the US State Department went on to say that
the 'new strategy . . . would essentially set aside for now the overarching
goal of the Vance–Owen peace plan, which would require the Bosnian
Serbs to withdraw from about half of the territory that they hold'.
Actually we envisaged withdrawal from 39 per cent and a period of two
years before elections with human rights monitors could take place and
while ethnic cleansing started to be reversed.*

This article appeared before our British, French and Spanish colleagues had even landed in the United States, let alone begun discussing amendments to the US–Soviet text. I pay tribute to the fact that they were able to make substantive revisions to that text to reflect European Community concerns and policy. But the damage that newspaper article had already done meant that the text was largely ignored and the impression which was left has been deeply damaging. I have said nothing publicly, other than to say we face a new situation, for over a fortnight.

It is ironic that the new US administration which for four months from January onwards had been castigating the Vance–Owen plan for favouring the Serbs, for rewarding aggression and for accepting ethnic cleansing, had now gone through a 180 degree turn and was telling Dr Karadzic loud and clear that the pressure from every other country in the world, including the FRY, to withdraw was being relaxed. This meeting, hopefully in private, cannot ignore the political fall-out of this major change in US policy, whatever we may decide to say in public. I hope we will be careful in public not to exacerbate feelings across the Atlantic which can only help those who want to stay on their present territorial gains in Bosnia and Croatia and profit from ethnic cleansing.

Firstly, I think we need to analyse why the US changed its policy. In part, I believe they had come to realize that their initial criticism of the Vance–Owen plan was misconceived, but the main reason why they have done this about-face, I am convinced, is that they wanted to get out of the commitment that Warren Christopher made in February to help with implementation of the peace plan. It is no use bewailing what has happened – we have to adjust and adapt to present realities.

Given that NATO is continuing to plan for implementation of the Vance–Owen peace plan, I believe it is to our advantage in handling the Americans to openly acknowledge that far from there being 25,000 US troops we are likely to have no US ground troops for implementation. The most we might hope for are troops on the ground to help with communications. I suggest Admiral Boorda, who has done excellent work in his NATO Naples Headquarters over implementation, should be joined now by the French General who would be his deputy for implementation. I suggest too that the Russians should also be invited to send a senior military officer to Naples. We should do all we can from now on to involve Eastern as well as Western European forces, with contributions from Muslim and other countries outside Europe. We need US air support for 'safe area' defence. We will need also their maritime support, equipment and logistical back-up for implementation. We will also need a substantial UN civilian police force for implementation. Without such overall support for implementation we cannot hope to have fair elections within two years or start to reverse ethnic cleansing, and the War Crimes Tribunal will be a sick joke. We should aim over the next few weeks to determine whether there is still the political will, or the military resources, or the necessary financial support for credible implementation. If not, the Community should have the courage to say so, and not pretend that the Vance–Owen plan is still on the agenda as a figleaf to cover our impotence.

Secondly, the 'safe area' policy urgently needs a rapid injection of high-quality troops to be deployed in Bosnia. It is essential that the Russians contribute at least 1,000 men. At present they are showing every sign of ducking their responsibility. I am afraid that if the Russians back off implementing Resolution 836 and there are no new combat troops committed by Community countries then we may well not get the hoped-for extra Swedish and Norwegian contribution. It is a simple fact that existing UNPROFOR force levels in Bosnia cannot cope with the safe area policy, as they are already considerably overstretched. It is certain that the Bosnian government forces will continue to launch attacks from the designated 'safe areas', and UNPROFOR will be required to tread a very delicate and dangerous line if they are not to be dragged into a combatant role.

Thirdly, Milosevic must not be allowed to escape his commitment to the Vance–Owen peace plan. Tightening sanctions will concentrate his mind but there is an understandable likelihood that he will relax his pressure on the Bosnian Serbs. We will know more about his attitude after Thorvald Stoltenberg and I meet him tomorrow. His problem and ours is that Karadzic and Mladic are like cats licking the cream; they believe Republika Srpska is a fait accompli. An additional problem is that Republika Krajina, after their referendum, is going to link up, having as the capital of the new Republic of Serbs in Bosnia and Krajina, Banja Luka. General Mladic will then formally control not just the Bosnian Serb army but the Croatian Serb forces as well. He will be returning to the Knin where he built his reputation before Milosevic appointed him to command the JNA in Bosnia-Herzegovina. Unless they feel they have a guaranteed corridor to Serbia they will push down to the Dalmatian coast. They may well do this anyhow, and I do not think the Croats will be strong enough to stop them given their poor performance when trying to gain control over the Maslenica bridge.

Fourthly, Tudjman must not be allowed to escape his responsibility for encouraging the concept of Herzeg-Bosna. Mostar was an ugly episode of ethnic cleansing with the definite involvement, authorized by Tudjman, of his army. Though we are trying to broker a Muslim–Croat rapprochement with another meeting of the Coordination Body following Medjugorje in Geneva this weekend, the mutual distrust and the difficulty of controlling extremist elements on both sides are immense. As a Community we need to design a package of political and economic measures to pressurize Tudjman to abandon his support for a confederal solution, which is essentially in his eyes a desire to match Republika Srpska with Herzeg-Bosna to become effectively part of Croatia. Tudjman needs to be told what is in the pipeline by Monday 14 June and asked to see the Troika before the Copenhagen European Council meeting to sign a political declaration. Partition within the box of the present boundaries of Bosnia-Herzegovina will mean too small a Muslim state. It will be to create a Palestine within Europe, a certain recipe for continued fighting, terrorism and discontent.

The mandate for UNPROFOR in Croatia is also up for renewal at the end of this month, and we need to consider carefully our attitude to a three-month renewal. The Force Commander wants an extra two battalions to supervise a ceasefire which we have yet to negotiate. The main case for renewing the mandate is that if the UN withdraws it makes a Serbian–Croatian clash in the Eastern Sector very much more likely. The case for a refusal to renew is to confront Tudjman and Milosevic with the need to negotiate an overall settlement, which while the UN prop remains both refuse to do.

Against this uncertain background, I believe you would be wise to reaffirm the present Community strategy while quickly undertaking a fundamental reassessment before you meet again at the European Council meeting in Copenhagen. By then a number of these issues may have become clearer. By then almost certainly Thorvald Stoltenberg and I will have been able to arrange a trilateral meeting with Milosevic, Tudjman and Izetbegovic. They all want to meet. At that meeting we will confront all three with some home truths and encourage them to take a broader and deeper look at their problems than they have done hitherto.

The discussion that followed was a mixture of unreality in trying to pretend the VOPP was still alive, suppressed anger at the adoption of the JAP and resigned acceptance that we were in a mess and needed some time to sort it out. Nevertheless there was an impressive closing of ranks and ministers left me with a strong feeling of sympathetic support. An EC declaration issued next day was defiant in its support for the VOPP, but in truth sounded a little desperate.[106]

I briefed the press in terms which the US did not like, given that Christopher was going to meet the FAC the next day, but I felt it necessary to spell out a few home truths because I could see that the blame for not reversing ethnic cleansing and achieving greater Serb roll-back in the next plan was already being laid at the door of the Europeans. In the diplomatic cover-up over the JAP the US were starting to escape from their own role in ditching the VOPP. The Foreign Ministers knew that as my price for staying on as Co-Chairman I expected to be supported as before if I stood up against the US on their behalf when the US was acting in ways which the EC felt worked against a peace settlement. It was one thing for the EC to acquiesce in the *fait accompli* of the JAP; it was quite another to become an accomplice to US policies. The old Cold War days of European defer-ence and automatic solidarity with US decisions overriding even genuine differences were over.

Most Foreign Ministers were reported as offering fresh public words of support for the Vance–Owen Peace Plan as a long-term goal, but privately officials conceded that there was no political will to go beyond the defence of 'safe areas' for now. I was quoted as saying the failure to roll back aggression could mean that Serbian and Croatian expansion would consign Bosnia's Muslims to an enclave that would remain a debilitating sore, 'like creating a Palestine in the middle of Europe'. And of US reluctance to send troops to Bosnia I said, 'It is weakening and debilitating if the United States, as the most powerful country in NATO, will not contribute ground forces, but it is not the end of the world.' As it appeared there would be no US soldiers in 'an up-front military role', NATO planners would have to ask whether the gap could be filled by other nations; I was reported as mentioning Russia, Belarus and Ukraine as countries that might furnish peacekeeping forces and saying that reservations about using troops from countries from the region around the former Yugoslavia should be reviewed.

The London *Times* headline was 'Owen Sees "Careful Jigsaw" of Bosnia Peace Come Apart'. On BBC radio I said: 'Sadly, the perception of the Washington summit of the five [nations] . . . was that we were accepting the Serbian gains. That message – that you could sit on the territory that you have acquired by force – encouraged the Croats in Mostar to start taking territory and pushing Muslims out and has produced a counter-reaction of Muslims against Croats.' I had raised the question that diplo-mats suffering Bosnia-fatigue would prefer to avoid. Setting up temporary Muslim enclaves was no strategy. Either the UN balanced the interests of Serbs, Muslims and Croats inside Bosnia, or the outside powers should admit that they would leave the map to be drawn up by the warlords. A peace plan can only survive, I was reported to have added, if soldiers are sent to enforce it.

In the US Peter Tarnoff, an intelligent, knowledgeable man, had tried to rationalize Christopher's mission to Europe by pointing out the limits of US policy. This had, however, provoked an emotional counter-action, with his views being disowned by Tony Lake and Warren Christopher because they smacked of an abdication of US leadership. But Tarnoff was reflecting the confusion of thought in the State Department; whereas on 15 February what was happening in Bosnia was defined as a vital US interest, now in June Warren Christopher had repeatedly said it was not a vital interest.

What seemed, in part, to be behind US thinking over the VOPP was a resentment at the structure of the ICFY. The incoming US administration had been surprised that, for instance, Eagleburger had been prepared to come to the ministerial meeting of the ICFY and sit in a room under the chairmanship of Cy Vance and myself. Warren Christopher was never ready to accept that format, nor did he appear to like the political authority which the Conference had built up, and he revealed his desire for the US to take power back from the ICFY in Congressional hearings before taking office. In addition, it was always difficult to determine how large an element of US attitudes to the VOPP stemmed from Christopher's personal relations with Vance. Superficially correct and controlled as their relationship was, it was obvious that there was always a tension between them that, I suspected, had its origins in the time that Christopher had been Vance's deputy, notably in the circumstances surrounding Vance's resignation in 1980 over his opposition to President Carter's support for the military plan to spring the Americans taken hostages in their Embassy in Tehran. Despite this episode, Vance nevertheless recommended to Carter that Christopher should be his successor, but Carter appointed Senator Muskie instead. Whatever the truth of the relationship in the past, I had little doubt that Christopher did not find it pleasant to have Vance so visible in such a prominent foreign policy role for his first few months as Secretary of State. As soon as Vance left the Co-Chairmanship of the ICFY in Athens, Christopher tried to abolish the Conference and took the opportunity to dump the VOPP.

In ditching the VOPP, the Clinton administration were abandoning their attempt to claim the moral high ground of keeping Bosnia-Herzegovina together as a unified state. They had decided that the price for putting US troops on the ground in order to reverse ethnic cleansing was too high. They were not ready even to stand up to the Bosnian Serb leaders with the backing of the FRY, the Serbian and Montenegrin Presidents, the Greek Prime Minister, the EC governments and Russia, but preferred to back down and offer Karadzic and Mladic the opportunity to remain on more territory than envisaged on the VOPP map. The consequences were to be dire, for the authority of the US as well as for the cause of a just peace and the rule of international law. It is rare for history to show within a few years the folly of governments' decisions, but by August 1995 it was painfully apparent how damaging the US decision to ditch the VOPP in May 1993 had been. The Bosnian Muslims had now been ethnically cleansed from Zepa and Srebrenica and the Croatian Serbs from the Krajina. There was no longer any talk, or hope, of reversing ethnic cleansing.

5

A Union of Three Republics

THORVALD STOLTENBERG AND I left Brussels on 8 June
knowing that the EC ministers' meeting with Warren Christopher
and the subsequent NATO meeting were bound to be unsatisfactory,
since some thought the VOPP was still alive, others thought that it was
dying and a few knew that it was actually dead. For once it was a relief to
fly back to the Balkans.

In Belgrade on 9 June we had to decide how to cope with the crisis over
Vuk Draskovic. It was a disgrace that the leader of the main opposition
party could be beaten with impunity by the police force while gangsters
were given virtual immunity to run illegal paramilitary armies. Milosevic
had to be made well aware of our anger and decent Serbs given practical
proof of ICFY's concern. I had received a letter from a group of distinguished Serbian doctors who were looking after Draskovic, including an
eminent neurologist dealing with the head injuries inflicted on him by
President Milosevic's militia. A flamboyant intervention would win world
headlines but achieve nothing, because Milosevic was incensed that one of
his policemen had been killed in the incident and would be immovable.
Only Serb criticism might make him reconsider, for he still wanted to win
back the Serb intellectuals who had once supported him. Thorvald
Stoltenberg and I talked it over and we agreed that the best approach was
for me to visit the clinic alone, without any press coverage, as a medical
doctor and neurologist, then talk to Milosevic over dinner that night. I
escaped the press around the hotel, but unfortunately was picked up en
route by a television crew; arriving at the hospital before them, I insisted
that they should not come into the clinic. All the doctors were seriously
worried that Draskovic's refusal to eat was affecting the chances of his
making a full recovery. I listened carefully to their arguments and took
away an appeal for clemency, having decided it would weaken my chance
of persuading Milosevic to free him if I visited Draskovic at his hospital
bed. I drove straight to the Serbian Presidency and raised the matter with

Milosevic over a pre-dinner drink after the formal part of our meeting. He knew exactly where I had been, commenting on my attempt to avoid the press. He was initially very dismissive about Madame Mitterrand's recent representations in Belgrade, saying this was a criminal and not a political issue. Then we were joined by Dr Karadzic who was genuinely helpful. When I said that the men who had written to me were distinguished Serbian doctors, Karadzic asked to look at the list and then urged Milosevic to take these people, who were all good Serbs and not political figures, seriously. Milosevic was still dismissive of Draskovic's motives and sceptical about his true medical condition, but promised to think about it and soon thereafter Draskovic was released from the clinic. I am ready to give some credit on this occasion to Dr Karadzic.

Radovan Karadzic was born on 19 June 1944 in the village of Pemica on Mt Durmitor, Montenegro. He lived in Sarajevo from the age of fifteen and enrolled at the Medical Secondary School, later graduating from the Medical Faculty in the city, and specializing in psychiatry. He completed parts of his education in the US. His main activity had been in the state hospital in Sarajevo. Before the war he was a reasonably well known psychiatrist. He spent eleven months in investigative detention in 1987 and was discharged as innocent – a fairly unusual finding in the Yugoslav republic of Bosnia-Herzegovina – since it was never proved that he had built his summerhouse in Pale with embezzled money. Krajisnik was also jailed and charged for involvement in the same case, and this is where their relationship was forged in an atmosphere of adversity.

In 1968 Karadzic made an emotional Serb nationalist speech from the roof of the Faculty of Philosophy in Sarajevo, after which he claimed he was put under constant surveillance by the Yugoslav secret police. In 1989 he was chosen as president of the Serbian Democratic Party (SDS) – as he tells people, because nobody else wished to take on the job. At the founding congress of the SDS, Izetbegovic was guest of honour and received the longest applause. In the summer of 1990 Karadzic and Izetbegovic went to a memorial meeting for Serb and Muslim Second World War victims on a bridge over the Drina river in Foca, and both said that 'blood must never flow down the Drina river ever again.' At the time, Karadzic was reported as saying, 'our Muslims are much closer to us [Bosnian Serbs], than many Christian peoples in Europe'. I watched as, hour by hour, that relationship deteriorated. At times one saw a flicker of the old relationship and Karadzic would call Izetbegovic 'Alija', but Izetbegovic never referred to the other man in my hearing as 'Radovan'. They talked together eventually without our presence, but it was a guarded and at times hostile relationship.

Karadzic's especial skill, and it is a considerable one, is to deflect and defuse a hostile question with an innocent facial expression and apparent concern in his voice. When asked, 'Why are you shelling Sarajevo?', he replies, 'We're not, it's the Muslims. We're not attacking, just protecting our homes in and around Sarajevo.' He claims, 'Muslims were never our enemies. Only the Ustashas are our natural enemies. Serbs and Muslims have never clashed, and history proves this, unless a third party was involved.' Again and again I have heard him claiming, 'Serbs and Croats were never enemies before 1918, when they entered a joint state. Serbs and Croats will never be enemies once they separate their states.' He once said, 'Serbs cannot live together with Muslims and Croats. I told Owen not to dump us into the same sack like cats and dogs.'

Perhaps because we have both trained as physicians I have found it hard to believe that he could be a practitioner of ethnic cleansing and espouse such an odious philosophy, so totally at odds with the Hippocratic Oath. I initially hoped that there was more respect within the inner man for human life and dignity, but I was doomed to disillusion. He is a poet and has written four books, but despite my own love of poetry, I never talked of poetry to him. I suppose it says something that I have never wanted to talk about medicine with him either, even when we were discussing inconsequential matters. We had to socialize over meals while we negotiated but I never wanted a relationship with him of any degree of intimacy.

The substance of our meeting with Milosevic in Belgrade that evening was the search for a comprehensive settlement, for which we were casting our eyes beyond the strict confines of the borders of Bosnia-Herzegovina, and since this was so controversial I was grateful for the press concentrating only on Draskovic. Douglas Hurd was being helpful in quietly reinforcing the hints that I had left with EC Foreign Ministers, through conversations with Solana and Kozyrev, of a new approach going wider than Bosnia. I had stressed that the ideas were tentative and that I would need to come back for a specific mandate after having taken soundings; what I had in mind was neither partition of Bosnia-Herzegovina nor a large-scale redrawing of former Yugoslav republic boundaries, rather a series of limited trade-offs, involving in particular the northern corridor and the Dubrovnik area.[107] We left for Tirana the following morning to see the Albanian President Berisha, then flew to Podgorica to see President Bulatovic and then back to spend the night in Belgrade before meeting with Milosevic again on Friday morning.

The *Washington Post* of 10 June carried a story headlined in next day's British *Guardian*, 'Bosnia Partition Foreseen by US Intelligence Analyst'. The analyst was bluntly deriding US support for the so-called Joint Action Programme, saying the safe havens would become 'refugee camps' and 'you basically wind up moving populations'. The analyst predicted partition, with two large separate Muslim provinces and a chunk of Bosnia going to the Croats and the largest Serb part to Serbia. Such an outcome would have represented total defeat for the London Conference principles and was something Stoltenberg and I were not authorized even to consider at that stage. We knew we had to move on from the VOPP, but the question was how. I agreed with Fred Eckhard that, despite knowing that the VOPP was dead, he should on behalf of ICFY as a last gesture of respect defend it in a letter to the *Guardian* against one of its most persistent and deeply prejudiced critics who was frequently having his letters published in that paper.[108]

On 14 June we visited Bonn to meet Foreign Minister Kinkel, and after a short lunch together he escorted us to a meeting with Chancellor Kohl. Kinkel had been quite shocked at our suggestion that the VOPP would have to be changed. He was particularly concerned about the effect on public opinion this would have. I explained that the plan had been not just severely damaged but holed below the water in Washington. Kohl took a much more realistic approach, and immediately accepted the need to change the plan. But he added that whatever changes had to be made to the map, the end result could not be a small Muslim enclave in the middle of Bosnia-Herzegovina. They were both very supportive of the need to send a very strong and clear message to Tudjman not to launch any more attacks against the Krajina Serbs, and to be cooperative on Bosnia. Kohl said he would not hesitate to warn Tudjman and Kinkel flew from the Human Rights Conference in Vienna on 15 June expressly to meet the Croatian President on his arrival in Geneva before Tudjman saw us that evening. Chancellor Kohl warned that the countries of the former Yugoslavia were going to be looking for funds after the war for their reconstruction and since Germany had already paid out vast sums of money for the GDR, Eastern Europe and the ex-USSR, it was not going to pay up automatically again. The Germans would use their money to extend democracy.

I had last had a proper talk with Chancellor Kohl in the summer of 1986, when I was leader of the SDP. Now, after his handling of the unification of his country, he was the most powerful leader in Europe. He had seemingly grown in intellectual as well as political stature, for his analysis of the implications of the disintegration of Yugoslavia was of a high order, laced with a surprising amount of relevant European history. He had not lost his earthiness, but there was a new Bismarckian quality to his approach that I found impressive. There was no obvious anti-Serbian German bias, fear of which had long haunted leaders in Belgrade. Kohl, having a broader base of support than Kinkel's FDP, seemed less vulnerable to the vocal claims of the many Croatians living in Germany and more objective about Tudjman's behaviour. But that is not how most Serbs see Kohl. In October 1991 General Kadijevic, Yugoslavia's Minister of Defence, claimed that 'Germany is about to attack our country for a third time this century.' Milosevic told *Pravda* in February 1993 that the dissolution of Yugoslavia was 'in the German–Catholic alliance's interest' and that as soon as Germany became united they began to punish the Second World War victors. 'Yugoslavia was the first casualty of the policy of revanchism.' Yet on other occasions I found Milosevic to be more realistic about Germany, pointing to the queues of German businessmen in Belgrade waiting for sanctions to be lifted. My task, representing the European Community, was to try to persuade the Serbs to break out of their historic hatred of Germany, and equally to ensure that EC policy reflected accurately the new post-Cold War democratic consensus that saw Serbia as just as much a part of the wider Europe as Bulgaria, Romania, Macedonia and Albania.

The German media had been hostile to the VOPP, but by this stage, albeit too late, had reluctantly come to accept it. They were now sensitive to any possible partition, particularly of Sarajevo. Their initial stridently anti-Serb, pro-Muslim stance had been somewhat toned down as the complexities and the difficulties of finding a solution became increasingly apparent. But in the German government the voices of the Foreign and Defence Ministries were at times sharply at variance over former Yugoslavia, most markedly over the extent to which it was constitutionally possible for the German armed forces to become involved. There are two pillars of German foreign policy: the first is to stay close to the French in Europe and the second, within NATO, is to stay close to the US. On Yugoslavia these policies came into conflict and it was fascinating to watch Bonn wrestle with the contradictions. The Germans were shocked not to have been involved by Washington in the 22 May meeting and were resentful of the way in which the EU support for the VOPP had been overturned without consultation by the French, British and Spanish. While Klaus Kinkel was determined to heal the wounds left by Hans-Dietrich Genscher's bulldozer tactics in the EC over the recognition of Croatia, Germany as a whole continued to be driven by a belief that self-determination was an absolute, not a qualified, right. In their hearts the Germans were always in favour of lifting the arms embargo for the Croats and by extension for the Muslims. This meant that when the Clinton administration came in, the German position was to favour the US line and diverge somewhat from that of the French and British. Nevertheless, the differences were always manageable, helped by the basic decency of Klaus Kinkel to colleagues on the Foreign Affairs Council and by the fact that both he and Kohl are true believers in European unity and are therefore prepared sometimes to sacrifice German views for a wider European cohesion. But over Croatia, the German position was ruthlessly pursued. The Germans turned more than a blind eye to arms sales to Croatia and countenanced a large Croatian army presence in Bosnia-Herzegovina throughout the war, while castigating the far less flagrant breaches of the FRY army, and they were never prepared to allow any real economic sanctions to be taken against Croatia.

Stoltenberg and I were determined that we would not make the first move away from the VOPP. That had to come from the parties. On 11 June

Map 8 Serb proposal for Union of Three Republics, June 1993

in Belgrade, Milosevic showed us a first very tentative draft of a new map, which I managed to pocket, giving the Muslims only less than 24 per cent of the territory of Bosnia-Herzegovina. On 13 June the first full meeting of the Presidency of Bosnia-Herzegovina since independence took place and the process of constructing a complex deal began.[109]

Over 15–16 June we met with Milosevic, Tudjman, Bulatovic and Izetbegovic, Karadzic and Boban. These meetings laid the foundations for three plans, all basically of the same family: the Union of Three Republics that was finalized on HMS *Invincible*; the EU Action Plan; and the Contact Group Plan. All these plans gave the Serbs their own contiguous area for a republic within a Union of Bosnia-Herzegovina. It was a delicate time and Stoltenberg and I were treading on eggshells. I still had EC authority only to explore new ideas, with no formal agreement as yet to move off the VOPP. The reporting COREU telegram I sent conveys the atmosphere and content of the meeting.[110]

Most EC governments were now ready to switch off life support for the

VOPP, which had been brain-dead since the American press briefing in Washington on 21 May. We agreed with Tudjman, Milosevic and Izetbegovic that the talks would continue and no maps would be published or leaked. Tudjman kept everything very general when he briefed the press, saying they all had maps in their brains and pockets. Izetbegovic had left the meeting of the three Presidents in a good atmosphere with smiles all round; we, as Co-Chairmen, had agreed he should not negotiate on the map at this stage and promised to fight his corner for him and enlarge the Muslim area from the Sava to the sea. In what I thought was a clever diversionary tactic, however, Izetbegovic told the press on leaving the villa that he would take no further part in negotiations because of what was happening in Gorazde. This prompted 'Izetbegovic walks out' stories which were resented by his fellow Presidents. Milosevic, when questioned on whether this was a new plan replacing the VOPP, said 'we are speaking about an evolution which we have been expecting', and spoke of a 'really huge advance'. But however much the change was downplayed we were now dealing with a three-part division. I was determined that what emerged should not be called the Owen–Stoltenberg map, a label which all the parties for different reasons were only too keen to slap on to it: this was neither our map nor our plan and it was important that it should be seen to have come from the Serbs and the Croats. Our task was to see if it could evolve in a way that would make it acceptable to President Izetbegovic. We went before the Geneva press corps after the parties had had their say and most of them had left Geneva. We were brutally honest; without ever pronouncing the last rites I conceded the VOPP was dead, saying: 'Time moves on and sadly as it does so the situation deteriorates. We have seen the provincial map torn up in front of our very eyes by all three sides in the last few months.' Explaining that on the VOPP there was no use my standing on vanity I said, 'We've got to stand up to the bloody realities of the situation.' The London *Times* headline was 'Muslims Bridle as Serbs and Croats Gloat over Old Maps'.

The State Department announced that Reggie Bartholomew was to be the new US Ambassador to Italy and was to be replaced as Special Envoy by Charles Redman. Given all the promises Bartholomew had made to Izetbegovic about how Serb advances would be rolled back in order to induce him to sign up for the VOPP, it was a wise move, though we would miss him. He had been a tough-talking hard hitter, but keen to fix up a deal on the VOPP. Now, with their new policy, described loosely as 'containment', the Americans needed a different, quieter voice to take Bosnia off the headlines.

With Stoltenberg, as much because of his Scandinavian connections as because of his UN role, I flew to Copenhagen to see the EC Presidency and meet with Helveg Petersen and the Danish Prime Minister, Rasmussen. After the meeting I wrote to Helveg Petersen.[111]

The US reaction to our new ideas was more forthcoming than I had expected. President Clinton actually used the word I was trying to avoid – partition – and said they could accept partition as long as it was freely and willingly accepted by the parties themselves. The State Department took a stronger line, evincing reluctance to be put in the position of having to pressurize the Bosnian Muslims to sign up. Meeting Jackovitch, the US Ambassador to Bosnia, by chance in Geneva, I briefed him. He surprised me when he said that Ganic and Silajdzic could live with the new proposals and that even the map, while needing improvement, was not too bad. Stoltenberg offered to go to the US to brief the State Department but they stalled, saying we should first go ahead with the meetings planned for 23 June in Geneva.

The Atlantic rift at that moment was between the US and Germany, with Kohl and Kinkel furious at Christopher's public criticism of Germany's behaviour over recognition of Croatia and Slovenia. The Germans could not see what the US had to gain from criticizing them, unless it was to distract attention from growing domestic criticism of the ineffectiveness of US policy on the crisis in former Yugoslavia. *Die Welt* described Christopher's words as the 'strongest public criticism of German policy from a US Secretary of State in recent decades'. In Ljubljana, Kinkel said the Europeans might have to accept 'albeit with gritted teeth' that the VOPP was dead. Hans van den Broek, the EU's External Affairs Commissioner, said that 'the Vance–Owen plan is as dead as a doornail and everybody knows it' and, while deploring partition, asked: 'If you do not see any possibility of helping these people out, how can you morally deny them the right of letting them arm themselves?' The Düsseldorf-based *Westdeutsche Zeitung* wrote: 'Those who kill, banish and rape have won the day.' I did not take it amiss when Cy Vance spoke out against the new direction, for he and I had rejected the partition option in favour of ten provinces with no ethnic contiguity. Cy's words as quoted were: 'We always said, there can be no partition. It's wrong. It's the equivalent of endorsing ethnic cleansing,' and so it was; I never tried to pretend that anything based on division was a mere extension of the VOPP, which had been based on integration. It was a heart-rending time for me.

I amazed the Geneva press in frankly making it clear in answers to questions that the VOPP was a far better and more principled peace settlement than anything that I would be able to negotiate from now on. I said that henceforth I did not expect to be able to claim that what we achieved was an 'honourable settlement'. Nor did I hesitate to lay responsibility clearly at the door of the Clinton administration who, while talking much about morality, had ditched the one plan which could claim to have a moral basis and offered the prospect of actually reversing some ethnic cleansing.

We met with the twelve Foreign Ministers and Commissioner van den

Broek on the evening of 22 June, before the European Council meeting in Copenhagen. It was one of the most thorough meetings we ever had, with the issues pre-eminent – not, as was so often the case, spending too much time drafting statements for the press.[112] Helveg Petersen, for the Presidency, said that he had spoken to Christopher and Kozyrev in the past few days. Kozyrev had said that all our efforts had failed and that we needed to look for new solutions based on protection of fundamental human rights, a ceasefire, withdrawal of troops and the guaranteed territorial integrity of Bosnia-Herzegovina. The safe areas concept remained relevant but Kozyrev did not foresee any Russian UN troop deployment. Sanctions should also be maintained, but there should be clear carrots available for the Serbs. Christopher was unwilling to pressurize the Muslims to act on the Serb–Croat plan and felt they should have time to evaluate it. The US wanted to maintain close coordination with the EC, though Christopher considered the Vance–Owen Peace Plan dead. Helveg Petersen had promised to report to Christopher and Kozyrev on safe areas after the meeting.

I described the background to the talks in Geneva between Izetbegovic, Tudjman and Milosevic and quoted from notes by General Morillon and a report by Stoltenberg to show that the situation on the ground had deteriorated badly since I last spoke to the Foreign Ministers. I then showed them on a big map the three republics suggested by the Serbs and Croats, divided into five areas: two Croat, two Muslim and one contiguous Serb territory. I concentrated on the central Muslim majority area which I stressed had to be extended so that we could genuinely claim that it went from the Sava river in the north to the Adriatic Sea in the south. I wanted the Foreign Ministers to ask themselves whether they could accept a return to the three-part confederation idea which had first been proposed in the Carrington-Cutileiro cantonal plan fifteen months ago before the war started. Alain Juppé for France welcomed my report but, uncharacteristically for him, tried to have it all ways, saying there was no reason to claim that the Vance–Owen plan was dead. The Dutch Foreign Minister, Kooijmans, said he felt like Alice in Wonderland. Having reaffirmed support for the Vance–Owen plan ten days ago, the Council was now declaring it dead on the basis of a Serb–Croat proposal. Then Helveg Petersen, in summing up, said that Foreign Ministers would report to their heads of government that full confidence had been expressed in the Co-Chairmen. He added that Izetbegovic had asked to address the European Council in order to explain Muslim views on the Serb–Croat plan and that Lord Owen had argued that the Troika should urge Izetbegovic to go to Geneva to resume the talks and to consult the rest of the Bosnian Presidency. After some discussion, it was agreed that the Troika should see Izetbegovic on 21 June.

In Geneva on 23 June nine constitutional principles emerged from a five-hour discussion with Presidents Bulatovic, Milosevic and Tudjman.[113] We described these as Serb–Croat proposals, and though the three Presidents did not wish the principles to be ascribed to them they were supportive, and instrumental in their design. Karadzic and Boban seemed genuinely committed and we undertook to put their proposal to the seven members of the Presidency of Bosnia-Herzegovina who were present – three Croats, three Serbs and one Muslim. We encouraged these seven not to take a collective view on the nine principles then and there, as we felt they should be discussed first with Izetbegovic and Ganic, who had not come to Geneva; and we warned that complex negotiations lay ahead.[114]

I asked my new deputy, the French Ambassador Jean-Pierre Masset, to visit Sarajevo and give Izetbegovic a private letter, for he had asked on the telephone for my personal views as he faced the critical decision on whether to open negotiations with Karadzic and Boban. Ambassador Masset conveyed my letter to him personally, answered questions and brought back a report to me. I had in my letter of 1 July included a detailed annex on many issues which were at the time still very private.[115] I told him that I would personally have far preferred to be able still to write to him about the Vance–Owen Peace Plan, but that it had tragically been killed off by some people and governments who were now loudly protesting their total support for it. I still thought the VOPP would have been best for his country. I reminded him that, when I had last visited Sarajevo, he had urged me to remain as a Co-Chairman, perhaps sensing rightly that I was very close to resigning. I had thought about what he said then and had decided that I should stay and try to rescue as much as possible from the wreckage of the VOPP. Of course, I could not guarantee to achieve all of the objectives that I spelt out in the annex, but I thought it would help him to know what I was thinking and how we were approaching the vexed problem of establishing a new peace plan that offered some hope to his beleaguered country. I advised him to start negotiations as soon as he judged opinion in his country could accept his doing so. I hoped he knew that, over the months we had worked together, I had grown to respect greatly his stance in the most difficult of circumstances. I felt therefore that I owed him an explanation of the sort of clarifications that we were trying to achieve. The annex reveals that Izetbegovic was given a very frank appraisal of the likely shape of a Union of Three Republics well before he took his decision to negotiate on the new plan and, what is more important, that Thorvald Stoltenberg and I then delivered on all its aspects in the final HMS *Invincible* package. So there was never any truth in the propaganda that we bullied or misled Izetbegovic down this path.

On 7 July Izetbegovic sent his reply. He was worried that the stronger and louder elements in his public opinion were not ready to face the unfortunate fact that partition had taken place on the ground, and were against ethnic partition. Yet he himself had grasped the reality that the face of

Bosnia had changed. He felt we needed more private discussion before he could agree to negotiate with all three parties around the same table. This was to be expected, and I had some idea now as to what was crucially important to him. The Bosnian Croat town of Neum, along Bosnia-Herzegovina's few kilometres of historic coastline, was going to be troublesome. Izetbegovic recognized that our experts' assessment that it would make a bad harbour was correct, but it clearly had great symbolic importance in Sarajevo.

What would obviously be helpful prior to any negotiations was a generalized ceasefire. Yet this posed a real problem. As seen from Izetbegovic's vantage point in Sarajevo, to negotiate while being shelled was to act under duress. Yet the Serbs in Pale believed that unless they put pressure on the Muslim leaders by shelling they would never compromise at the negotiating table. Progress over negotiations hovered perpetually between these two positions. My sympathies were wholly with Izetbegovic, but the need for negotiations was great. Even if no progress was made during negotiations, the fighting reduced in intensity and the humanitarian convoys passed. We got used to the opening session of negotiations following a regular pattern of protest and counter-protest, with Thorvald Stoltenberg having to go away and check allegations with UNPROFOR commanders. Quite often alleged attacks had not taken place. On other occasions, if they had, we could only start negotiations when the people responsible, usually but not invariably the Serbs, agreed to intervene and to ring up their commanders to tell them to stop – even then, sometimes they did, at other times they blithely continued. It was frustrating and time-consuming, but somehow we managed to keep negotiations going.

The most important result from our two meetings on 9 July, respectively in Belgrade and Zagreb, was that Milosevic and Tudjman were now committed to reaching 30 per cent of territory for a Muslim majority republic. Over lunch with me, Tudjman seemed grudgingly to accept that if the Croats wanted Novi Travnik, Vitez and Busovaca then the arithmetic alone dictated that they would have to give Stolac to the Muslims. A map for a predominantly Muslim republic from the Sava to the sea was now becoming closer to reality and the original Tudjman–Milosevic minimalist proposal of only 23 per cent was firmly set aside. Izetbegovic was now closer to being offered something serious and I was nearer to having what I had promised to deliver to the EC Foreign Ministers. The Belgrade media were positive, with Milosevic talking of the negotiations being 'on the verge of a final solution'. Izetbegovic was saying from Sarajevo that he could accept a confederal solution for Bosnia, although it was 'exceptionally difficult', for it effectively meant the ethnic division of Bosnia, but this was a 'delicate decision' which had to be taken collectively, not by him as an individual.

On the evening of Friday 9 July I was rung up by Elaine Sciolino, the Washington reporter for the *New York Times*, who had written the demise of the VOPP story. She read out a State Department telegram that she had in her possession reputing to report a discussion with Mrs Ogata and a General Jones in which Mrs Ogata said that the Co-Chairmen would contact the Bosnian Presidency with the threat to recommend that the UN withdraw from Bosnia-Herzegovina if they refused to negotiate. I sensed that unless I convinced her, the story to be published the following day would be headlined something like 'peace negotiators blackmail Bosnian Muslims'. I warned Marrack Goulding at the UN, after having told Sciolino that there was no truth in the story about my threatening the Bosnian Muslims. First, it was not part of my responsibility as EC negotiator to recommend UN action. This was a matter for Stoltenberg, as Special Representative of the Secretary-General, and I was certain he neither had spoken nor intended to speak in these terms to Izetbegovic; later, I confirmed this. Secondly, far from it being UNPROFOR who were keen to withdraw, as her story implied, it was UNHCR who had been saying for some time that they could not continue. It was we as peace negotiators who had persuaded UNHCR to stay through the summer at least and, although the situation on the ground was deteriorating, there had been no formal request from UNHCR to withdraw. Thirdly, the new French force commander, General Cot, was touring his command and would certainly not have had the time to make a security assessment or come up with the complicated plan needed for withdrawal. I said that we, as Co-Chairmen, had been at pains to let the Bosnian Muslims take their time and make a free choice on the new approach being put forward by Tudjman and Milosevic. If they refused and the humanitarian and security situation further deteriorated, then and only then would the specialized assessments come up to Stoltenberg and he would have to consider his recommendation to the UN Secretary-General.

It appeared from a telephone conversation which Stoltenberg had with Mrs Ogata that she probably had spoken far more frankly about her view than was wise, but she was horrified that a State Department telegram could be leaked in this way. She was now sadder but wiser. To complicate matters the Pakistani UN Ambassador was alleged to have told the Security Council that Ambassador Sacirbey had stated that Mr Stoltenberg and Mrs Ogata had personally told President Izetbegovic that unless he agreed to the partition of Bosnia-Herzegovina into three countries, the United Nations and UNHCR would pull out of his country. These endless rumours, half-truths and general buck-passing made up one of the most unattractive aspects of the whole job. It was particularly objectionable that people in the State Department were trying to put the Co-Chairmen in the line of fire over the inevitable shift of policy following the US role in the demise of the VOPP.

On 12 July Izetbegovic wrote to us as ICFY Co-Chairmen, the UN Secretary-General, the President of the European Union, and Warren Christopher, saying that he was ready to attend the next round of talks on Bosnia in Geneva but that 'it is at the same time indispensable that attacks aimed at gaining new territory should cease and that food, water and energy supplies should not be used for blackmailing and waging war against Sarajevo and other towns'. The Bosnian government also circulated a press release giving some details of the constitutional proposals discussed by the Presidency in Zagreb on 11 July, namely that an agreement should be based on a federal arrangement with equality for all citizens and equal rights for all three constituent nations. The federal units could not be divided exclusively along ethnic lines. Much of this was unrealistic but they were right to stress that only the state, rather than its constituent parts, would have international status.

In effect, behind all the public relations propaganda being put out by all sides, we now had agreement from the three parties to the principle of a Union of Three Republics with the predominantly Muslim Republic having a minimum of 30 per cent of territory and the Croats arguing they should have more than 20 per cent. We were embarking on negotiations based on an agreed new framework. The transition from the VOPP had taken about eight weeks – too short a time for some governments, who were still trying to pretend to their public opinion that they were clinging to all the London principles within the new framework.

On 14 July Thorvald Stoltenberg briefed Security Council members in informal consultations and spoke to the press, explaining that the VOPP remained our point of reference but that the breakdown in cooperation between the Croats and Muslims had removed one of the essential ingredients for its progressive implementation. Fighting on the ground having intensified, it had become clear that resources required for implementing the VOPP would not be forthcoming. Under those circumstances, the choice was stark: either there would be talks on a new basis leading to a durable settlement, or fighting would continue. Stoltenberg emphasized that all three sides had told the Co-Chairmen that they were in favour of negotiations around the new framework and he noted that during the Co-Chairmen's meeting with the Bosnian Presidency on 10 July it had become clear that eight members of the Presidency were in favour of holding the talks. Since all three parties had now come up with proposals for discussion, the Co-Chairmen had sought to promote talks, to act as an intermediary for proposals, but without taking any position themselves on these proposals. It was a deft presentation. Stoltenberg went on to say that there were enough indications from all three sides to suggest that if they were to sit down to discuss their differences, it would be possible to arrive at a durable settlement. The present situation could not last much longer. Winter was approaching, humanitarian operations were being deliberately obstructed on all sides, and it was hard to see how in the absence of further resources the humanitarian effort could continue. He asked Council members to support Mrs Ogata's appeal for additional resources and to promote the speedy reinforcement of UNPROFOR in the safe areas. The alternative to negotiations, Stoltenberg said, would be a prolonged war which would lead to more suffering, and reduce the chances for a negotiated peace in the future. This did not mean that there should be peace at any price: but it was time for the parties to see if it was possible to achieve an agreement for a lasting peace.

Stoltenberg had wanted to visit Washington to brief the administration, as a result of a prior invitation, but the US had said that they had no new thoughts to offer and it was clear that the Administration were content with containment and did not want any involvement prior to the new negotiations starting in Geneva on 19 July. In the European Parliament, where debates on Yugoslavia were an unedifying mixture of cant and humbug, I was being strongly criticized as if it were I who had ditched the VOPP. I was beginning to feel I should have left with the VOPP; and Thorvald admitted to me over dinner on his return from the United States that it looked as if we had been set up as the scapegoats for partition, with no one in America ready to admit that it was they who had argued that more land should be given to the Bosnian Serbs.

The Belgian government now held the Presidency of the EC and I was working closely with their Foreign Minister, Willy Claes. Now was the time for a political strategy in relation to the negotiations, with the military strategy taking second place, and I was very concerned about the pressures still mounting for wide use of air strikes against the Serbs. NATO was arguing with the UN Secretary-General over the interpretation of UNSCR 770, and a divorce between NATO and the UN just at that moment, when we were potentially moving into an important partnership, was the last thing we needed. It was a difficult balancing act to keep military pressure behind the political process, not in front of it, but this was what we did our best to achieve.

Once again, as over 'lift and strike', US opinion would not face up to the reality that wider air strikes threatened the UN humanitarian mission since they were strung out all over the country in small groups, vulnerable to being seized as hostages and capable of being blocked in position for weeks on end or just turned around with the convoys. The Pentagon knew these realities but for some reason could not get the message through to Vice-President Gore or Ambassador Madeleine Albright, both of whom appeared to think these issues could be resolved by bombing the Serbs irrespective of where we were in negotiations or where the UN was on the ground. The State Department seemed to be paralysed by its own divisions while the

White House wanted to practise realpolitik and simultaneously preach moralism. Yet we were going to need the United States to pressurize Izetbegovic to accept the map when we had squeezed the last hectare from the Serb–Croat proposals in Brcko, eastern Bosnia, the Bihac pocket and central Bosnia. It was also absolutely essential to get the Serbs to rethink their approach to Sarajevo, which still held the key to an overall solution.

In the final paragraphs of the section on Sarajevo in our report as Co-Chairmen to the Security Council[116] we paved the way for Sarajevo to become a UN city. We did not spell out in the report how this would be done, though we could see little alternative to outright UN administration. It looked as if only in the aftermath of a settlement would we be able to break down the virtual Berlin Wall that now divided the city. The world outside Yugoslavia did not want to recognize that many Serbs had long lived in Sarajevo and that there were areas in the city where Serbs had been in a majority before the war started. We knew Boutros Ghali was very sensitive, particularly at that moment, about his responsibility being eroded and felt that the UN was grossly overstretched. Taking on the administration of Sarajevo would be a pretty thankless task, so we wanted the UN to be given the opportunity to make it their idea, and their initiative. Some months before, when Boutros was in Geneva in December, Vance and I had raised the idea of Sarajevo being an 'open city,' and Boutros had used the phrase when visiting Sarajevo.

Once again there was a legitimate difference between Muslim and Serb interests. The Muslims could not accept the present confrontation line: therefore it was in their interest to destabilize it by provoking incidents and planning breaches. The Serb interest, by contrast, was in maintaining the status quo. At that time the prevailing view of the UN military commanders as expressed to Stoltenberg and me was that UNPROFOR's worst problems were with the Muslims, that the Muslims were responsible for most of the ceasefire violations and that they represented the main threat to the 'safe areas' because they conducted military operations under UN cover. But the Muslims were bound to provoke, at least in so far as they could without causing UNHCR to abandon the humanitarian effort. This UN view appeared to some journalists to be indicative of an anti-Muslim bias, while in fact it was the military mind seeking order in the midst of chaos. It was important for us as negotiators not to reflect UNPROFOR's frustrations, even though Muslim military activity undoubtedly did have an adverse impact on our negotiations, as did the activities of Croatian government forces in Croatia. I was very conscious of the Muslims' problem and tried to see the issue from their viewpoint, but I also continued to think that an early peace was in the interests of the Bosnian Muslims. Delay had already forced partition on to the negotiating agenda, and as ethnic cleansing took root with the passage of time its reversal became ever harder to imagine.

The main flaw to the concept of 'safe areas' from the perspective of the UN military was that the UN Security Council were allowing the Muslims to evade any demilitarization provision. This made the whole concept unsafe. The Serbs appeared not to want to physically take any of the so-called safe areas, even though they could have done so: urban fighting is very costly in terms of devastation and loss of life, as the Serbs had discovered when taking Vukovar from its Croatian defenders in 1991. We were trying to persuade the Bosnian Serbs to accept a predominantly Muslim republic with a contiguous area in East Bosnia covering the three safe areas, Srebrenica, Zepa and Gorazde. We believed that Mladic might be brought to accept that, but the difficulty was in linking Gorazde geographically to the Muslims in Sarajevo without cutting Serbs in East Herzegovina off from Serbs in Pale and Sarajevo.

As to peacekeeping in the former Yugoslavia generally, the military felt the UN had failed initially to understand the difficulties of operating in a former Communist country with a tradition of state-controlled media. Izetbegovic, Tudjman and Milosevic all simply manipulated public opinion by using their control over television and much of the written press, a control which made it very difficult to get the UN message of impartiality through. Moreover, Communist command and control practices meant that each commander in the former Yugoslav army down to a low level was a dictator in his area of responsibility who could have one of his soldiers taken out and shot whenever he commanded. These extremes of delegation explained why permits for convoys were continually blocked at a low level. The UN military were full of praise for UNHCR but bitter in their denunciation of some of the NGOs who to them were a pestilential nuisance, resisting all attempts at coordination and then complaining that they were not being properly protected. Again the military's priority was order, and they failed to see that the attraction of voluntary organizations is their ability to be unconventional, daring and in the process difficult.

These senior UN officers were practical military men dealing with an appallingly difficult problem on the ground, inevitably seeing their role as preserving order and drawing on classic peacekeeping models from previous UN experience. What they had difficulty in appreciating was that order was exactly what the Bosnian Muslims, for perfectly understandable reasons, were against. Disorder and destabilization were essential parts of the Bosnian Muslim strategy. They had to prevent Serb front lines being established as permanent divisions in people's minds. Also, they saw nothing wrong in being protected in safe areas by the UN and at the same time attacking out of the safe areas. I assumed the Muslim commanders' thinking was that if the UN Security Council passed inconsistent Resolutions that was not their problem. They would seek to get away with anything they could that was in their interests. Essentially the UN and Bosnian Muslim commanders were bound to grate on each other's nerves and it was a sad affair to listen as the various generals in Sarajevo – the Canadian Mackenzie, the Frenchman Morillon, the Belgian Briquemont, then the British Generals Rose and initially Smith – came under personal criticism in Sarajevo and in America for being pro-Serb as they struggled to implement both a humanitarian and a peacekeeping mandate which demanded impartiality. On many of the contentious political questions the UN Security Council was tending under US pressure not even to pretend to be totally impartial. Politicians, ambassadors and military advisers wanted the UN commanders to reflect their committed political views on the ground. It is, however, one thing to pass a Resolution in New York as a result of days of bargaining and compromise, and quite another actually to implement it. For example, a Security Council injunction to 'control' heavy weapons meant in reality on the ground for UN military commanders constrained by their inadequate military capability 'monitor', or, when very hard pressed for people, 'observe'. The more the military concentrated on their original humanitarian mandate the easier it was to explain their role, and they found that the safe area addition to their mandate compromised their impartiality, making their humanitarian task more difficult.

President Tudjman and President Milosevic came to Geneva on 17 July and while the public reason for the meeting, at Milosevic's insistence, was to discuss a solution in Bosnia, the talks were also intended to deal with Serb–Croat relations, in particular connected with the reopening of the Maslenica bridge. When Stoltenberg spoke to Izetbegovic, who was in a good mood, on 15 July to invite him as well, he told Stoltenberg that though he was ready to negotiate he could not come to Geneva until water and gas supplies had been restored to Sarajevo, but that 'when we get to the table, I don't think it will take a long time since you have done such good preparatory work.'

We met with the Croatian and Serbian Presidents in the Alabama rooms of the Hotel de Ville in Geneva, as much as anything to demonstrate by a change of venue from the Palais des Nations that this was a bilateral meeting. Much of the time they talked between themselves and afterwards issued a joint statement denying that they were about to partition Bosnia and welcoming a solution to the problem of the Maslenica bridge.[117] This bridge was one of our constant preoccupations, for the Croatians had a vital need to keep the Dalmatian coast road under their control and not to allow it to be cut by the Serbs at Maslenica. The other endlessly debated question was how to open the Zagreb–Belgrade highway. Milosevic supported Tudjman's need for both of these key routes to be opened, but could not persuade the Krajina Serb leaders.

I met Klaus Kinkel in the margins of the Foreign Affairs Council in Brussels on 19 July and told him that I wanted to clarify his position *vis-à-*

vis Croatia lest there develop a misunderstanding between us. I welcomed the pressure that Germany had brought to bear on Croatia and reiterated my view that the threat of sanctions tended to be more effective than their actual imposition, but I felt more pressure had to be exerted over the situation around Mostar. He agreed that reports of further ethnic cleansing there were particularly worrying and said he had made the German position very clear to Foreign Minister Granic when he had met him the previous week, telling him that if Croatia did not behave as the EC expected it to, it would face sanctions and, moreover, Germany would lift its protective hand. The four areas on which a specific warning was issued were Maslenica (the Croatians were not to take any unilateral actions, a warning further reinforced in a letter sent on 16 July); Mostar (ethnic cleansing had to stop); Bosnia (the Serbs and Croats could not carve up the country at the expense of the Muslims); and convoys (there was to be no interruption of the humanitarian effort). The Croatian response had been generally positive but Kinkel agreed Mostar was the biggest problem. He asked whether there was now a case for sanctions. He had felt hitherto it was better to keep the pressure on through the threat of sanctions. The Croats were clearly worried by the pressure they had come under but, up until now, not sufficiently to clamp down on some of their extreme elements. Kinkel saw a danger of pushing them out of the European fold altogether and provoking a very negative response. It was a good meeting and I felt happy that we were both working on the same lines.

At the Foreign Affairs Council everyone seemed content for Stoltenberg and me to continue to develop the details of a Union of Three Republics. The Council was however anxious whether 30 per cent for Izetbegovic was acceptable, and the Italian Foreign Minister admitted frankly: 'Public opinion stops me putting pressure on the Bosnian Muslims; perhaps Lord Owen can but we cannot.' I already realized that the figure could certainly not be less than 30 per cent and preferably should be more, and indeed I could see that the EC governments were not going to apply much pressure unless it was more.

One of the difficult questions for the Union was the wish of many Muslims for a single currency within the Union. I arranged to go and see experts in the Bank of England in an attempt to depoliticize the issue. On their suggestion we assembled a few European experts who came to Geneva and advised the Bosnian government experts on the matter. I felt that unless there was a single decision-maker as Governor it was not in their interest to involve the Serbs or Croats. The predominantly Muslim Republic was likely to have better access to funds than the other two republics and their territory had some of the best industrial assets and infrastructure. Tying themselves into the same currency as the Serbs would weaken their currency. The technical advice was clearly against three national decision centres and came down firmly in favour of one currency matched by one central bank. As the Serbs insisted on a consensus of three decision-makers for a single currency it looked impractical and the reality was faced that the Serbs would take the Belgrade dinar and the Croats the Zagreb kunar.

On 20 July we sent a letter inviting all the parties to come to Geneva on 23 July. Izetbegovic, when I spoke to him, said no, and suggested postponing for three days. Karadzic suggested waiting until the autumn. At times I felt like a travel agent, endlessly fixing up and then postponing meetings.

The negotiations in July and August in Geneva were destined to be very complicated. On 27 July Karadzic came with a proposed map giving the predominantly Muslim republic 28.4 per cent and the predominantly Croat republic 17.3 per cent of Bosnia-Herzegovina. The next day Boban came with 26.7 per cent and 21.3 per cent respectively. Both knew that at the end of the day, with Tudjman and Milosevic signed up for 30 per cent, that was what it would have to be. But for weeks we struggled to deliver this crucial percentage on what was a Serb–Croat map, and not an Owen–Stoltenberg map as the press wrongly called it. This, we were determined, was to be a bottom-up negotiation for however long it took, and we would just cajole and pressurize all the parties until we reached the percentage figures that all could agree on.

I was reluctant to brief EC ambassadors in detail in Geneva as I had done on a virtually daily basis in New York and since then in Geneva, because they were arousing jealousies among the other ambassadors in the expanded ICFY Steering Committee. There was also the risk of leaks on the map in Geneva, which could ignite passions and lobbying from towns or villages, presently Serb-controlled, that might have to be given up. Thorvald Stoltenberg used to brief the Secretary-General in New York by UN coded cables and I used a special restricted COREU telegram that went only to EU capitals and was marked for Foreign Ministers. Churkin attended most sessions to keep Moscow informed, and Bartholomew, and then Redman, did the same for Washington. This sequence of COREU cables, which I often wrote late at night together with David Ludlow, my private secretary, is interesting to read if one wishes to absorb the detail,[118] but the essential aspects of the negotiations are easily summarized. We decided to first build on the agreed principles and tie down a constitution for a Union of Three Republics.[119] In the VOPP we had postponed those negotiations until after the ceasefire; now we needed a less complex constitution since the powers of the overall Bosnia-Herzegovina government would be much less and governed by consensus. We eventually reached agreement on a constitution with Izetbegovic, Karadzic and Boban. Abdic, who came to most sessions with Izetbegovic, showed himself to be an excellent negotiator, flexible but never deserting Izetbegovic's position in front of us. The most sensitive aspect was that Izetbegovic wanted and got a constitution which preserved continuity and legitimacy and retained a single internationally recognized state. Elections for the Union Parliament were to be supervised by the UN and EC. There was to be a Presidency, Council of Ministers, Supreme Court, Constitutional Court and Court of Human Rights. On the map, Muslim industry in Tuzla needed access to the Sava river port facilities in Brcko while not cutting the Serbs' northern corridor from Bijeljina to Banja Luka. We also needed to ensure that Muslim industry in Zenica and Sarajevo would have access by road and rail through Mostar to the sea. It was not sufficient for the Muslims just to have guaranteed access to the Croatian port of Ploce, through which most of Bosnia-Herzegovina's heavy import and export goods passed prior to 1992. Izetbegovic wanted to have other options. We designed a maritime exit, using the navigable part of the Neretva river up into Bosnia-Herzegovina territory and ensuring that they had a port for barges on the southernmost tip of the predominantly Muslim republic.[120] By 31 July there was agreement that Stolac should go to the Muslims, so that including the three eastern Bosnian enclaves of Srebrenica, Zepa and Gorazde, on the overall map the territory of the majority Muslim republic would constitute 30 per cent. But this was not sufficient. In addition Izetbegovic felt they needed to have a part of the port of Neum, a tourist resort in which rich Sarajevans had built holiday homes. This need was far more psychological than strategic, but it meant the Muslim republic having a bridge crossing the main Dalmatian road connecting Dalmatia to the rest of Croatia.[121] For Tudjman this was literally a bridge too far.

Fortunately, by the time we reached this most delicate issue we had helicoptered down to the area with the engineers and on return had grilled them on their findings. Therefore we at times knew more than some of the parties' own negotiators about Ploce, Neum and the Neretva estuary and river. The German and French barge experts who had flown down to make an independent assessment were fortunately able to prove that the large commercial barges of continental Europe could pass under a crucial bridge with just a few inches to spare. At times during these negotiations I felt that I was a construction engineer, an inland waterways expert and a port customs and commercial officer, so detailed and complex did the proposals we put to the parties become. Without our input the parties easily reverted to generalized abuse; with concrete plans before them they would for the most part respond sensibly. Holiday plans were all upset and I managed only one weekend in Portugal and another in Italy with my family all that summer.

Overshadowing the negotiations was the emergence of Bosnian Serb forces on Mt Igman above Sarajevo, which led to delays in the negotiations and to calls for air strikes to remove them. A full-scale debate about whether or not there could be NATO air strikes while UNPROFOR was still on the ground was arranged on 2 August for the NATO Council holding a special meeting in Brussels. I wrote on behalf of the ICFY to NATO's Secretary-General Manfred Woerner,[122] asking for Ambassador Masset to brief the NAC, which he did before the US presented their case. One consequence was a further deterioration in US–ICFY relations. I also cabled the EC Foreign Ministers about the detail of our negotiations and then went on to warn about the NAC meeting at ambassadorial level next day at NATO HQ.

As you know, I support the principle of air strikes being used in accordance with UNSCR 836, and after the attacks on the French and the Spanish forces, it was sensible to have some public warning about our determination to respond and protect our forces. It is, however, very clear that the US has a very different concept of air strikes in mind. They seem to believe that Sarajevo is under imminent threat and that widespread air strikes is the way to stop this.

It is true, of course, that the Serbs can take Sarajevo, and could have done so at any time over the last 18 months. It is a political decision not to do so, and I see no evidence that they have changed their mind. Mladic's current operations to the south of Sarajevo seem to me to be designed primarily to pressurize the Bosnian army forces on Mount Igman, not to threaten Sarajevo directly.

The present suggestion from the US, and which I understand will be presented by Ambassador Bartholomew, excludes lifting the arms embargo, but unless we were prepared to reinforce on the ground, logic would dictate that following widespread air strikes, the UNHCR would have to be pulled out, UNPROFOR at the very least would have to give up convoy escorting and pull in their horns, and the lifting of the arms embargo would follow, as would many nations wanting to withdraw their forces.

For these and many other reasons, I believe it is essential that we make a success of these negotiations. Talk of wide use of air strikes at the present juncture is unhelpful and I would have preferred to have been negotiating without constant speculation in the press about this. Perhaps surprisingly, to date it has not affected the tone of the negotiations either way. To be blunt, the Serbs tend to treat such threats with a certain levity, perhaps because they have lived with such threats, and they think they know what they are going to do if attacked from the air.

My biggest fear is not how the Serbs are reacting, but that such talk will encourage Ganic and others who want to continue with the war that the Americans are about to intervene. Ganic certainly is attempting to derail the negotiations and is hoping for air strikes. We may even now be seeing a slowing in the tempo of the negotiations because of the NAC meeting. Izetbegovic is talking openly about needing 4–5 days more for negotiations. Silajdzic and others here have been most unhelpful and have been trying to undermine Izetbegovic's negotiating position, but so far to no avail.

The fact that the NAC is meeting on Monday could, however, be turned to the advantage of the negotiations if there was a detailed discussion of implementation of an agreed settlement. It would also be extremely helpful if the prior press line concentrated on this aspect rather than just air strikes. The mixed military working group is meeting in Sarajevo today and I will see that you get a report on this. The UN is also actively working on implementation. If the message came out of Brussels that NATO was working on the implementation on the basis of three republics, and that in some ways this was an easier task than implementing the VOPP with its 10 provinces, and that the US was ready to commit forces to the implementation, it would be very helpful. Silajdzic attaches a lot of importance to guaranteed implementation.

In Geneva on the morning of the NAC meeting there was a buzz in the corridors that Izetbegovic was withdrawing from the talks discussing Sarajevo. Eventually, late in the evening, he came to say that he would stay in Geneva but would not participate until the Serb offensive on Mt Igman ended, though he would talk to the Croats. After eleven and a half hours of deliberations Manfred Woerner issued a long press statement that night.[123] It said very little new, one of the reasons being that Canada had used all its unrivalled expertise of UN operations to circulate a letter which ensured that some fundamental questions would have to be answered before Canada would be ready to agree to NATO action. This had the advantage of not being an Atlantic rift but a US–Canada division of opinion and was therefore easier to manage within NATO. I blessed the fact that I had been keeping Ottawa fully informed of ICFY views. The Canadians had made representations to Stoltenberg and me about not being as up to date on our thinking as other troop-contributing countries and for convenience and speed we had decided to ask the UK to put Canada on my cable circuit. The US heard about this and were miffed, in spite of the fact that I had been sharing all this information with them. The US special envoys had unlimited access to ICFY material but the US government preferred to act for the most part as if ICFY did not exist. The US, in a nutshell, wanted to move from agreed close air support for the UN to wider air attacks, not to help impose a negotiated settlement but with a specific military aim, namely to force the Serbs off the Igman mountain near Sarajevo. The US also did not want the UN to retain control of decisions under the dual key, and this provoked an anxious debate within NATO. The wording of the NAC communiqué presented by Woerner talked about 'appropriate command and control decision making arrangements', which was in fact a fudge for no decisions having been taken.

At this time in Geneva I was sometimes seeing French reports through Ambassador Masset, as well as UK and UN reports of the same meetings. It was fascinating to note that what was highlighted in one could be downplayed in another. But, more importantly, it kept me well informed on the changes in US attitudes, even though neither Stoltenberg nor I was briefed other than occasionally by Bartholomew or, later, his successor Charles Redman. It was obvious that there were differences inside the US administration. These divisions became public when the Bosnian desk officer, Marshall Freeman Harris, resigned one year after his predecessor George Kenney had resigned, saying, 'I can no longer serve in a Department of State that accepts the forceful dismemberment of a European state and that will not act against genocide and the Serbian officials who perpetrate it.'

Early in August we had sent to New York an account of the negotiations up to 30 July.[124] The main focus in the Security Council was on Article 1 of the constitutional agreement, which the Bosnia-Herzegovina government claimed raised questions about their continued membership of the UN. Paul Szasz was quite confident that there was no problem about this. Szasz was our totally trustworthy ICFY lawyer; possessed of a fine mind, he had been deputy head of the UN Legal Department for many years, and his integrity was widely respected. Though we tried hard, it took some time to pacify the false alarm that had been generated. We were in the midst of a propaganda war and its main theme at that time was that the Co-Chairmen were forcing Izetbegovic to negotiate and compromise away his principles. A sub-theme, slightly contradictory, was the old jibe that we were Chamberlain-like figures. It all became quite nasty and the British government insisted I have a bomb-proof car from Beirut and personal security because of a death threat that had emerged from a ceremony akin to a *fatwa* held in a Muslim refugee camp in Croatia. We were having Muslim-led demonstrations outside the UN building and there were threats to ICFY staff on the telephone. The Swiss police were very helpful, but it was unpleasant and I thought I had given up having personal security protection when I ceased to be Foreign Secretary and then party leader.

On 4 August we called Milosevic and Tudjman to Geneva in an attempt to unblock the talks. Milosevic told us that the only way to persuade Mladic to accept UN troops replacing his forces on Mt Igman and thereby to free up the talks and get Izetbegovic to attend, was to send Karadzic and Krajisnik back to Pale to talk to him directly. Telephone conversations with

Mladic in his view were ineffective. He asked us to take personal responsibility for adjourning the talks, which we did in the hope that their return would bring a change of heart in the Bosnian Serb army.

The UN senior military were telling Stoltenberg that the Serb presence on Mt Igman was not a strategic threat and that to divert UN peacekeepers on to Igman was, in the UN's view, a waste of scarce resources. Stoltenberg had to demand that it be done for the sake of the Geneva negotiations, but the UN military were most reluctant and felt the Serbs gained by the diversion of French UN soldiers to police Mt Igman, which relieved the Serb military for other more harmful tasks against the Muslims. There was a surreal quality to it all. The world's press and the US government were pressing for punitive air strikes on the basis that it was militarily vital to clear Mt Igman, and French and British senior UN officers actually on the ground in Sarajevo were taking a totally different strategic attitude.

In Germany the Bundestag and the German press were criticizing the Geneva process. The German Foreign Ministry was, they admitted, under pressure to encourage Izetbegovic to stall, but they were very reluctant to add to what they referred to as the myth that their actions had started the war a second myth, namely that they were responsible for stalling the peace. They were also not unreasonably having difficulty in squaring the Union of Three Republics as just, equitable and in line with the London Conference principles. I blessed the fact that I had refused to go along with the pretence surrounding the ditching of the VOPP and insisted publicly on people facing the turnaround on US policy implicit in letting the Bosnian Serbs retain more of the land their army currently occupied.

The Germans had interesting reasons for resisting the application of sanctions against Croatia. The less important reason was a notion of justice in that, unlike Serbia, Croatia had suffered direct damage from the war. Its territory had been attacked and occupied; its communications were cut; and it had a large number of refugees on its territory. Imposing sanctions on Serbia was a way of demonstrating that war had a cost; the Croatians already knew that. The major reason for Germany opposing sanctions, however, was their fear that the Croatians would respond by closing all the refugee camps in their country and that a large number of these refugees would inevitably turn up in Germany. Keeping the refugees in Croatia and out of Germany, which had already taken in 400,000, had become for the Germans a national interest which they began to protect staunchly. Nor was this unreasonable, given that Germany had taken in far more refugees than the rest of the EC combined, and was still taking in more.

Izetbegovic was now talking seriously and in detail about the Serb–Croat proposal for a union of three republics. I believed it would be possible to get an agreement acceptable to Izetbegovic on all issues – except Sarajevo. It was difficult to see Izetbegovic, or indeed anyone else, accepting the Serbs' idea of their keeping a territorial 'bill-hook' around Sarajevo, crossing the two main road and rail access routes. Some progress, however, was being made over Mt Igman. It was obvious that Milosevic's influence among the Bosnian Serbs had waned, and though his intervention had been helpful Mladic was increasingly difficult to control. Krajisnik had become more important, too, and he was a tough, rigid operator. He and Karadzic worked well together but both had become a bit cocky and needed sobering down. All the talk of air strikes I hoped might have an effect in Pale, but it seemed pretty minimal from our ringside seat. Most of the time the Bosnian Serb leaders were blissfully unaware of NATO decisions, EC policy or Security Council declarations and I knew that they hardly read the letters of protest that poured in, even those from heads of government.

Douglas Hurd rang me in Geneva on 5 August, worried by the prospect of our adjourning and saying it was important to avoid a breakdown in the next few days. We felt there would be a risk of just such a breakdown if we tried to bring the parties together before the weekend, as proposed by the Americans: Izetbegovic, who was playing for time, would not be willing to negotiate seriously on Friday. However, I agreed that the talks must be kept going, with some prospect of useful meetings after the weekend, so on 6 August we adjourned the conference and briefed the Steering Committee.[125]

I was more concerned than I admitted to the Steering Committee about Izetbegovic's reported comments about wanting to drop the provision for the demilitarization of Bosnia-Herzegovina – a proposal that the parties had indicated they preferred over the original ICFY proposal for some kind of joint command structure for their separate armed forces. For if it was true that Izetbegovic was now saying that he would not demilitarize the Muslim majority republic, a view he had not expressed to us as Co-Chairmen but which some journalists were saying he had stated publicly, then a Union of Three Republics would look very different, with three separate armies, and would be hard to present as one country. It also showed that Izetbegovic was now moving towards a separate Muslim republic and that realistic talk of keeping Bosnia-Herzegovina together was over. An independent Muslim state was not a solution to which I in principle objected, and I had never believed that a Muslim state in Europe was intrinsically unacceptable; but I was very sure that such a solution was not within the terms of reference of the London Conference, which was one reason why Vance and I had rejected this option the previous October. The US Ambassador to Bosnia said that the first he had heard of this abandonment of demilitarization was at the Steering Committee briefing; he undertook to follow it up with Izetbegovic when he saw him later that evening. After this it dropped away from discussion until November. I was surprised by the ease with which the constitutional agreement was later stretched, in the EU Action Plan (see Chapter 6), to embrace three republics each with their own army without making more countries denounce the whole arrangement as *de facto* partition.

In the *Washington Post*, amid all the CNN and other media excitement that bombs might be about to fall, one journalist, Charles Krauthammer, questioned the strategy. In an article headlined, 'Does Clinton See Where He's Headed?' he wrote about the Americans riding in at the last moment threatening to bomb the Serbs.

> *Having so successfully bombed North Vietnam into reason and moderation and good faith, we shall do so again with Serbia. This time the calibration will be perfect . . . It seems beyond the ken of Mr Clinton's social engineers to understand that if you tilt the scales of a delicate negotiation against one party you are perhaps tilting it toward another, and that this other is perfectly capable of prolonging the war.*

On 8 August the Germans distributed a COREU raising some of their doubts about the negotiations in Geneva and the Netherlands said they were in full agreement. I replied in another COREU on 10 August.[126] But these were mild reservations compared with the criticism that now began to be heaped upon Stoltenberg and myself. It was as if the guilt of the Western world was focusing in on us. The *Washington Post* reporter Peter Maass wrote a story under the headline 'Embattled Bosnian Muslims Ask Mediator – Which Side Are You On?' Since we were spending most of our time trying to push the Serbs and Croats into offering more territory so that the Muslims could accept what was on offer, we were charged with being Serb–Croat spokesmen. It was a classic case of 'shooting the negotiators', but it was sad that the US government in particular was all too ready to shield behind criticism of us and to forget that it had been they, not us, who had said that the Serbs should have more territory and they, not us, who had abandoned the VOPP, the only plan ever put forward that ruled out partition. At least President Izetbegovic was not yet saying I should be dismissed, commenting wryly that if Lord Owen did not exist, the United Nations and the European Union would find another Lord Owen. He said: 'We cannot blame the international community's passiveness on only one man. There would be no changes by changing one man. We need to change the policy.'

But a more damaging charge was made by Jim Hoagland in the *Washington Post*, and because it was reprinted in the *Herald Tribune* I decided for once to rebut publicly his totally false allegation: that we were advocating the partition of Sarajevo, when in fact for weeks we had been trying to persuade the UN Secretary-General to accept the onerous responsibility of taking the whole city and its environs under UN administration. What made this allegation indefensible was that it was written three or four days after we had publicly reported that this was our intention to the Security Council.[127] The German press were also even more hostile than usual, and to cap it all on 11 August Izetbegovic challenged our report to the UN Secretary-General of 6 August.[128] Fortunately Thorvald Stoltenberg remained calm and dignified throughout these attacks and our partnership became ever more solid in the process. We could laugh together and get angry together, and it was a great relief to share the burden.

On 17 August in the Security Council Madeleine Albright, who was the Council President that month, launched into an attack on UNPROFOR commanders, naming General Francis Briquemont, Brigadier Vere Hayes and their press spokesman. Ambassador Albright's complaints about their comments on the usefulness of air strikes were then leaked to the press. There was no doubt that Hayes' remark, 'What does Clinton think he is doing?', was out of order. But with a large press corps in Sarajevo it was difficult for the UN to avoid comment. The truth as to the effect of the open debate and disagreements on air strikes was hard to discern. On balance, I felt it was marginally helpful, for all the false alarms and problems it caused us. But that was the case only as long as air strikes did not actually take place. If they had, the vulnerability of the UN's position on the ground would have been embarrassingly revealed. The increasing US pressure, led by the Joint Chiefs of Staff, to have a strictly NATO-run implementation operation following a settlement in Bosnia-Herzegovina, was leading to a military operation which was not in blue helmets, not under Security Council control and not financed by the UN. I personally saw advantages to this in terms of a coherent command and control, but it was hard to see the Russians acquiescing in being pushed aside, and if they objected then it would be hard to have the continued legitimacy of UN Resolutions. Also, even a Union of Three Republics needed a civilian component for implementation, though not as many as would have been needed for the VOPP. NATO had no such infrastructure and though the WEU might help it would have been hard to create all the UN civilian infrastructure and support that we tended to take for granted. This all pointed to the need for a cooperative relationship between NATO and the UN, with the involvement of Russian troops and that of other European countries, rather than a purely NATO operation.

In Geneva on 20 August I briefed EC missions and circulated the documents for a Bosnia settlement to which the leaders of the three parties had agreed in principle. The leaders were going to consult their 'parliaments' and give their final response to the Co-Chairmen at a meeting in Geneva on 31 August. As Co-Chairmen we had warned against trying to make further significant changes to the agreements. We believed that, except for eastern Bosnia, the outcome met all the criteria set by the EC Foreign Affairs Council in June. Including their part of Sarajevo, which accounted for 2 per cent, the Muslims would get 30 per cent of the total territory of Bosnia-Herzegovina. All the constitutional principles of the Vance–Owen plan, for what they were now worth, with some additional points such as commitments against armies simply being turned into police forces, had been built into the agreements in the form of a complete constitutional instrument. Muslim access to the Sava and Adriatic was guaranteed. Mostar was to be placed under an EC administrator for up to two years along the same lines as UN administration of Sarajevo. Tudjman had been implacably opposed to UN control of Mostar, so I had suggested that the EC should take it on and Tudjman had accepted this across the negotiating table; fortunately the EC later backed me. It was agreed that part of the city would operate as the capital of the Croat majority republic. On eastern Bosnia we were disappointed that we could not negotiate a territorial link between the Muslim areas of Zepa and Gorazde, but this the Serbs fiercely resisted. The best we could achieve was a road link to be maintained and policed by the Muslims. Central Bosnia was the most difficult part of the negotiations: here Boban was finally persuaded to give up Croatian claims to 1 per cent of territory which then went to the Muslims. Tension in the area remained high, however, and we feared that further fierce fighting could erupt, particularly around Gornji Vakuf.

Overall I warned the EC that the final outcome was still on a knife-edge. We thought Izetbegovic would give a fair wind to the agreement, and other members of the Bosnian Presidency had reacted fairly positively when we briefed them. The areas from which the Serbs were to withdraw on the proposed map amounted to 16.7 per cent of the whole country and 23.9 per cent of Serb-held territory – significantly less than in the VOPP.

The package then faced the same US prevarication which had accompanied the VOPP. Their special envoy, Redman, who knew all the twists and turns of the negotiations and seemed personally sympathetic, was working within a remit which appeared to consist of never being wrong-footed into ending up in opposition to the Bosnia-Herzegovina government. The US were adamant that, although they were not prepared to pronounce on the details, they would say to the Bosnia-Herzegovina government that the package warranted very serious consideration and that it was the best chance for the moment. The Non-Aligned Movement had a UNSCR at an advanced stage before the Security Council which threatened to establish new principles for a settlement. So it became necessary for Stoltenberg to travel to New York to put the case for the package which was, we had to stress yet again, not an Owen–Stoltenberg package but one agreed by the parties, negotiated over a tense and difficult month in Geneva. A Serb negotiator quoted by the *Financial Times* as saying, 'The Turks [a derogatory term for Bosnian Muslims] are going to be like walnuts in a Serb/Croat nutcracker' did not help. Izetbegovic said on 22 August in Zenica that he would probably recommend his Assembly to reject the plan. The US, in negotiating over the UNSCR text, agreed to 'note [the package] with appreciation' but not to 'welcome' it. The Germans, much to the fury of the French, decided to remain silent on the package because of their reservations that it was not in conformity with the London Conference principles since it accepted that territory taken by force would remain in Serb hands. With Stoltenberg I saw Klaus Kinkel in Frankfurt and the Dutch Foreign Minister, Peter Kooijmans, in The Hague on 25 August, to clarify some issues and attempt to induce them to be more supportive, but in both countries public opinion, as over the VOPP, was hostile, and EC unity was fraying at the edges.

After thirty-six hours in which the Serbs and Muslims seemed to be vying with one another to avoid being the first to come out totally in favour or totally against the package, the Bosnian Serbs in their Assembly voted 55 to 14 in favour. The Muslim-majority Bosnian Parliament however voted unanimously only in favour of continuing the negotiations. Izetbegovic said his main problem was with the map: he wanted Foca, Bratunac, Visegrad, Prijedor, Kozarac and Sanski Most – all Muslim towns before the war, and all in provinces likely to elect a Muslim majority under the VOPP. He also wanted access to the sea at Neum. The Bosnian Croat Parliament approved the package with only one vote against.

The EC Commissioner for External Affairs, van den Broek, then accused the Co-Chairmen publicly of a 'strategy of capitulation' and 'legitimized aggression' and said: 'As far as I am concerned Owen and Stoltenberg could well have asked for a tougher mandate when it came to making a credible threat to use force.' It was strange conduct from a basically very decent man, but he had for some months shown signs of being traumatized by his own painful experiences during the Dutch Presidency in the second half of 1991. It was as if he regretted not being able to mobilize opinion for military intervention at the time of the shelling of Vukovar and Dubrovnik, and was keen to be seen at all times as a hawk. He therefore kept trying to put forward a military option without any consistent or coherent strategy for implementing it or sustaining it. As a consequence I fear he was barely listened to by the other Foreign Ministers in the Council when he argued his rather maverick positions, which seemed to have no firm support in the Commission.

It looked as if we might have difficult meetings with the parties in Geneva on 31 August and 1 September, for Tudjman was refusing categorically to give up Neum; and so it proved.[129] In New York Izetbegovic was telling the Security Council that they should ask Stoltenberg for an explanation why territories which had been ethnically cleansed would remain under Serbian or Croatian control. He said that this in practice represented the surrender of law to force, and how could anyone expect the persecuted and the persecutor to agree on a solution? Once again, I had sympathy for his argument, for every single piece of territory he was asking for had been placed in a Muslim-majority province under the VOPP. In terms of justice, I had already made my views clear: now, months later, the governments who had ditched the VOPP were keeping quiet. I stress this not to complain, because in many respects going out in front and acting as a lightning conductor for public criticism is the role of and justification for international negotiators, but it was becoming ever more obvious to me that the ICFY process was not of itself enough. We needed more input from governments and particularly we needed to unify the EC, for the US and the Bosnian Muslims were exploiting the German and Dutch differences with the EC strategy.

In a joint appearance with Clinton before the press on 9 August, Izetbegovic underlined the importance which he attached to the US helping to implement any agreement, which was useful to the administration in dealing with Congressional critics of the Geneva package. Izetbegovic also told the press that Clinton had supported all his requirements for changes to the map. This was apparently not true, and the *New York Times* inter-pretation was 'Clinton Rebuffs Bosnia Leader in Plea for Help'. If this report was accurate, this was a helpful intervention and confirmed my feeling that, left to his own devices, Clinton's inclinations were often more realistic and relevant than the administration's formal policy which emerged out of seemingly endless debates among a group called the 'Principals Committee', which consisted usually of Anthony Lake, Warren Christopher, the Secretary of Defense, the Chairman of the Joint Chiefs of Staff, the CIA Director and Madeleine Albright, as well as Lake's deputy Samuel Berger and Vice-President Gore's representative on the NSC staff, Leon Fuerth. When President Clinton attended, then so did Gore and the White House Chief of Staff.[i]

I sent a detailed five-page background note to EC Foreign Ministers before their weekend meeting at Alden Bissen in Belgium, which I attended. It argued that we should not immediately reconvene the negotiations but wait until there was a clear sign that Izetbegovic's position had shifted much closer to accepting the package, and that we should in the meantime look for face-saving formulas. I also asked the Foreign Ministers to look again at some sanctions relief for Milosevic. I then went on to mention the unspoken option which fell outside the terms of reference of the London Conference, namely a separate Muslim state. Izetbegovic was attracted by this option but afraid of a backlash from some of his supporters; the running on this issue had to come from the Muslims and we ought to do nothing to encourage it. In my view the EC had three choices:

1 Wait patiently while encouraging Izetbegovic to sign the present package, warts and all, which was my recommendation.

2 Develop a new package with the inducement of early withdrawal of sanctions and the threat of real military measures which I did not believe we had the collective will to devise or deliver.

3 In effect sign off – withdraw Europe's military contribution to UNPROFOR, whereby the humanitarian effort would take a heavy penalty, let the US carry a Resolution to lift the embargo and let the battlefield be the arbiter.

The Foreign Ministers agreed that while the package on offer was not good, there was a bloody war going on and it might at least stop that, so most appeared ready to push ahead on that basis, but with the caveat that the Muslims had to have access to the sea. In addition, the Ministers agreed to administer Mostar, a pretty thankless task which I had landed them with.

A declaration on a Serb–Muslim cessation of hostilities, modelled on the Croat–Muslim declaration signed by President Tudjman and President Izetbegovic on a cessation of hostilities between the Bosnian Croat HVO and the BiH army on 14 September, was discussed in Montenegro for three hours on 15 September by myself, Stoltenberg, Krajisnik and Buha.[130] We then flew them to Geneva, after a long wait at the airport for FRY air clearance, which we felt might have been deliberately engineered to remind us of the inconvenience of sanctions. In Geneva we had a further two and a half hours of discussion that evening with Izetbegovic and Silajdzic in the presence of Krajisnik and Buha. The key question was whether implementation would create a climate to allow territorial adjustments over the two-year period or whether holding out for territorial adjustments prior to implementation was the best way forward. Izetbegovic was seriously questioning which was the best approach. At one stage he asked Krajisnik if he would find it easier to give more territory if he knew that he could secede and have a totally independent republic. Krajisnik said 'no': the Bosnian Serbs could not concede more territory at this moment, even under these circumstances, and the present package for the time being was as far as they could go. Krajisnik however asked for a referendum in the Bosnian Serb republic on this issue in two years' time. We pointed out that the present constitution allowed for secession only if all three republics agreed. It was then that Izetbegovic said that if they were satisfied on territory by then the Bosnian Muslims might not object to secession. This combination of a constitutional mechanism and a political incentive did for the first time give the Serbs a reason for coming forward during the UN administration of Sarajevo with territorial adjustments that would meet at least some of the Muslims' territorial claims. We felt it was a wise move on Izetbegovic's part and would lead to the Muslims having Sarajevo.

The Muslim–Serb declaration that was signed by Izetbegovic and Krajisnik allowed for the three republics in the union to hold referenda after two years on whether their citizens wished to remain in the union or leave the union, on the condition that there was an agreement on territorial division between the republics. Silajdzic only wanted to sign it in isolation, whereas Krajisnik wanted to sign it as an annex to the overall package. Krajisnik had made it very clear that the present package was coming under increasing attack from Bosnian Serbs and was in grave danger of unravelling. But Silajdzic began to have cold feet in the meeting since he did not want a purely Muslim state, and it came as no surprise that he found an excuse not to be there the next morning for the signing of the bilateral agreement,[131] which included in paragraph 5 the provision for a referendum on secession after two years. The Croats, who were not a party to this agreement, were apprehensive that it might establish a precedent for the Krajina; the US and some other countries were anxious that it might lead to a divided Bosnia-Herzegovina within two years and, though in theory ready to go along with it if agreed by all three parties, seemed to be encouraging the Croats to object.

It was interesting that Haris Silajdzic had in effect opposed what could have turned the key to a separate Muslim state, for he of all the Muslim leaders had the closest formal links to Islam: he had been counsellor to the Reis-Ul-Ulema, the head of the Muslim faith in Yugoslavia. Born in 1945 in Sarajevo, he graduated in 1971 in Benghazi at the Faculty of Arabic and Islamic studies and has published a number of articles on Islamic themes. He spent a year studying in Washington for his doctoral thesis on US–Albanian relations and shares with Ganic a good insight into American attitudes. I believe that for all the intensity of his manner and the way he can be disruptive and difficult in negotiations, alternately cold and passionate, he is a democrat. He showed this when he was appointed Prime Minister and started to clamp down on the Muslim mafia that was starting to hold sway in Sarajevo. It needed courage to take on these well-armed thugs and he did not shrug their challenge off but faced them down. Lives were lost in that struggle, and it would have been hard to engage in it if there had not been a commitment to a democratic civil life at his core. Those whom I respected in the UN who dealt closely with him in Sarajevo thought he was genuinely trying to counter some of the undemocratic practices that had grown up during the war. In private Silajdzic is a quiet and thoughtful man who agonized over the choices involved in settling for peace. He developed a close relationship with Granic, the Croatian Foreign Minister, and seemed to get on well with the US envoy Redman. His influence on Izetbegovic appeared to wane in 1994 and he seemed to resent Sacirbey's influence. He signed the Washington Accords and in many senses was their architect on the Muslim side. Privately he was more realistic than Ganic about the likelihood of the Clinton administration actually delivering military support. Perhaps I deluded myself when at times I detected a wish in Silajdzic to be more flexible at the negotiating table than prudent self-interest or ambition allowed. We were destined to be at loggerheads in public over the reasonableness or unreasonableness of the Bosnian Muslim negotiating side, but I never lost respect for this somewhat melancholic man, or for the acuity of his mind and his public support for a multi-ethnic Bosnia.

As Co-Chairmen we felt sufficiently encouraged after this Geneva meeting to embark on a round of intensive discussions in the hope of clinching a comprehensive agreement. In Belgrade late on 17 September we pressed the Bosnian Serbs through Milosevic to make territorial concessions, particularly in eastern Bosnia. On 18 September we visited Neum in Bosnia and flew over Ploce in Croatia in a helicopter to see for ourselves the outlets to the sea being considered for the land-locked putative Muslim majority republic. On 19 September we saw Tudjman and again urged flexibility. We had by this time met with and received the report from the French and German experts, which was given to the parties on the helicopter flying out to HMS *Invincible*. It ruled out on practical grounds the development of Neum or the nearby peninsula of Kosa as a major port for the Muslim-majority republic; instead it recommended concentration on Ploce, with guaranteed access down the Neretva river from a new inland port belonging to the Muslim-majority republic at Visici/Capljina.

On 20 September the Royal Navy acted as host for all three parties plus Tudjman, Milosevic and Bulatovic on HMS *Invincible*, steaming in international waters in the Adriatic. Sadly, David Ludlow was ill and could not come with us; Jeremy Brade and Graham Messervy-Whiting helped fill the gap, but David's knowledge, humour and skill were sorely missed. For me, helicoptering on to the ship was an unforgettable experience, for its design had been one of the most controversial issues of my time as Under-Secretary for the Royal Navy between 1968 and 1970.

The Royal Navy was its usual quiet, efficient self and the arrangements for our meeting in the officers' wardroom were excellent. During eight hours of continuous session, while HMS *Invincible* moved quietly through the water, the talks produced a new agreement on access to the sea for the Bosnian Muslims,[132] made possible because President Tudjman was ready to stretch his country's position to the limit. On the map, the Bosnian Serbs offered only about 0.3 per cent extra land in eastern Bosnia on the river Drina, from just above Gorazde to 8 km or so below Visegrad. There was some initial hesitation and doubt, but after a talk with President Milosevic, President Izetbegovic and Silajdzic both negotiated as if they wanted agreement. A meeting of the Bosnian Assembly was to be held in Sarajevo on Monday 27 September; Milosevic was hopeful it would endorse the revised proposals and that Izetbegovic might give more of a lead this time than before.

President Tudjman, very depressed that Izetbegovic would not sign up then and there on HMS *Invincible*, returned from the meeting to Split that

Map 9 Union of Three Republics, August 1993

night in a bitter mood, expressing his disappointment at the result of all the exhausting negotiations and remarking that the only thing that impressed him was the aircraft carrier itself. Izetbegovic flew back from Split to Zagreb in a UN plane with Stoltenberg and myself as well as Silajdzic. They were relaxed and in good form, with Izetbegovic reminiscing about his time in prison under Tito. They both said they would try to get a 'yes' vote from their Assembly and it appeared they were genuinely attracted by the improvements negotiated.

If the Assembly rejected this modified package I feared that the negotiating process might collapse, for the Serbs would withdraw what they considered were for them concessions and the situation on the ground could crumble quickly. We hoped that while there had been no movement on Muslim demands in western Bosnia, the recent bilateral Croat–Muslim and Serb–Muslim agreements allowed for further territorial adjustments. The latter, providing for a referendum on possible secession only after territorial issues had been settled, was the main defence in Sarajevo against those who

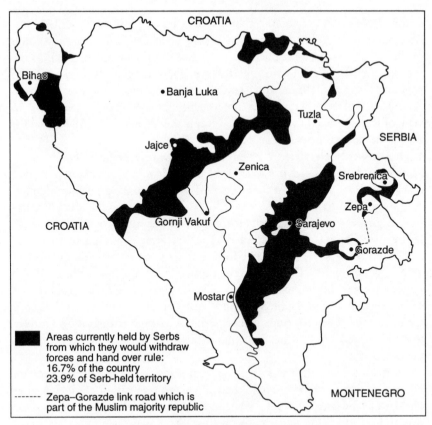

Map 10 Areas of Serb withdrawal under
Union of Three Republics map, August 1993

wanted to press for Izetbegovic's demand for 4 per cent more territory. I remained nervous, however, for we knew that some Americans had been encouraging the Muslims to hold out for that 4 per cent. I hoped that further strategic assurances would now come from the international community, particularly the Americans, which would be helpful in stiffening Izetbegovic before the Bosnian Assembly meeting and might just clinch a deal.

As Co-Chairmen we were due to attend a meeting of the North Atlantic Council in Brussels on 22 September to discuss the implementation of a settlement. On command and control considerable common ground had developed within NATO on the division of responsibility between the UN and NATO. It seemed now to be accepted that Stoltenberg, as the UN Secretary-General's Special Representative, should coordinate all UN efforts in theatre and identify political/strategic objectives for the NATO theatre commander, US Admiral Mike Boorda, who would be responsible for carrying out all military operations. The main unresolved area was the role

of the NATO chain of command above Boorda, in particular SACEUR. The
Americans were going to insist on involving SACEUR as a precondition
to their participation. I thought this would be difficult but not impossible
for the French. Washington and Paris might arrange a bilateral split of
command responsibilities with General Jean Cot, who was already envisaged as Boorda's deputy, to be involved in any consultations, not least in
view of the envisaged role of the ACE Rapid Reaction Corps (ARRC) which
was to be headed by a British general.

Our hopes were dashed when I read in the *Herald Tribune* on 22
September that Izetbegovic had said the day before, on arriving in Sarajevo,
that 'I personally am not inclined toward' the proposal, a position diamet-
rically opposed to the one he had adopted on the plane less than twenty-
four hours earlier. The *Economist* described the turnaround as 'vintage
Izetbegovic'. Now our only hope was a very firm commitment to implementation from NATO and some form of guarantee that Silajdzic could use
with any waverers. Unfortunately, the main discussion within NATO
became focused on an 'exit strategy'. The headline in the *New York Times*
of 24 September read 'Nunn Says He Wants Exit Strategy Before US Troops
Go to Bosnia'. Even so, Ambassador Redman told me after visiting Sarajevo
that his impression was that Izetbegovic saw no alternative to accepting the
present package.

As it turned out, it was Izetbegovic's meeting with the Bosnian military
on 26 September which proved crucial. We had sent him a clarifying letter
on Mostar and NATO's role,[133] but the military leaders apparently wanted
to continue to fight, particularly against the Croats. Certainly President
Clinton's speech to the UN, listing stiff terms for sending US troops to
Bosnia, did not help, and by 29 September the newspapers were all carrying
reports of the Bosnian Parliament being divided over the peace plan.
The all-Muslim Congress first in effect rejected the package by calling for
conditional acceptance provided all territories taken by force were returned,
and this was confirmed by the Bosnian Parliament.

I had a long telephone conversation on 30 September with Redman, who
had been present in Sarajevo for the meeting of the Muslim Congress and
the Parliament. I also spoke with Churkin, who was very depressed. Our
own reporting showed that Izetbegovic had appeared to be in the pro-peace
camp, but had never championed it; his performance was low-key and
detached at all times. Ganic's position was very hardline. It had been strik-
ingly noticeable that he continued to talk about the need for land on the
sea and was not satisfied with the proposed solution of Ploce and a port on
the Neretva. He probably would have held out against the plan even if the
Serbs had given up more territory in eastern Bosnia. Silajdzic was apparently trying to reach a deal with the Croats, having spent two weeks in
Zagreb talking with Foreign Minister Mate Granic to get the proposed

Muslim–Croat working groups off the ground, being aware that at one stage the SDA leaders had come very close to declaring a Muslim state. Apparently Muhamed Filipovic, a Muslim opposition leader not in the SDA and a former professor, later ambassador in London, who had frequently attended the Geneva talks as part of Izetbegovic's delegation, had drafted the critical declaration for the Parliament. He had been very emotional in his speech and highly critical of the West, and was reported to have said that time was on the side of the Muslims and the Bosnian Serbs would be forced to make further concessions by Belgrade as the sanctions bit deeper.

The Muslims had clearly chosen to continue with the war, believing that sanctions would soften up the Serbs and, on the advice of their military commanders, that they could defeat the Croats in central Bosnia. They knew that the concessions they were demanding from the Serbs went far beyond fine-tuning. They were looking for serious amounts of territory which at present were non-negotiable. The street assessment in Sarajevo was that the politicians' decision to continue the war was not far out of step with the views of the people, who while saying they wanted peace quickly qualified it by adding that the Serbs must give up more territory.

The intentions of the Serbs and the Croats were not yet clear. Both were holding their own assemblies, at Banja Luka and Neum respectively. Both had their own agendas and reasons for wanting to see the war ended soon, but both were fed up with the Bosnian Muslims and not ready for new negotiations. Almost the only good news was that Milosevic had at last taken on Seselj. In recent army sackings Milosevic removed not only General Panic but many of Seselj's men as well. Milosevic's call for all decent sectors of Serbian society to come together to defend the Republic against Seselj's brand of ultranationalism looked like a signal to those in the democratic opposition, such as Micunovic's Democrats and the smaller centre parties, that the way was now clear for them to consider joining some form of coalition with the SPS. Draskovic's SPO, however, refused to get involved in Milosevic's and Seselj's 'family affair'.

Now Abdic, sensing Izetbegovic was vulnerable to criticism from those who wanted peace, particularly the Bihac Muslim community, began to force the pace over local autonomy in that region. It looked as if there could develop a military confrontation between himself and those loyal to him in Velika Kladusa, and General Dudatovic, the able Commander of the Bosnian 5th Corps with barracks in Cazin and Bihac. Izetbegovic said of Abdic on Sarajevo television: 'Muslims have finally succeeded in becoming state-building and constitutional people. Abdic is trying to pull us for at least fifty years back just to become a head of the state. He is cleaving us to tribes, he is trying to feudalize us, he is giving our territories to Serbs and Croats.' The two men had worked surprisingly effectively together at the end of July and early August in Geneva over the *Invincible* package; now the Izetbegovic–Abdic relationship was sulphurous. We had urged Abdic to stay in the collective Presidency and warned him that his influence would go if he broke away, that he would be depicted by the world's press as a pawn of the Serbs while within the Presidency his influence was legitimate and benefited from his realism. Tragically, he was tempted by Milosevic and Tudjman to break out on his own.

In the wake of Sarajevo's rejection everything was starting to look scratchy and indecisive. My major concern was that Karadzic would go back on the most difficult changes in the map that he had made under the pressure of the negotiating process – indeed, he had already told me before the Sarajevo rejection that he had come under so much criticism from the military over the Brcko flyover arrangement in the *Invincible* package that this would be withdrawn if the Muslims did not endorse the package. Stoltenberg and I then wrote to all the parties in an attempt to hold on to those aspects that had been agreed and tried to encourage Izetbegovic to continue to negotiate.[134]

I also wrote to Willy Claes, giving voice to some rather heretical political thoughts about a Geneva Conference mirroring the 1992 London Conference which Boutros Ghali and the Belgian Prime Minister, Jean-Luc Dehaene, might chair, copying the letter to other key countries.[135] Such a conference would, however, have been unlikely to succeed and the idea was in the event superseded by the launch of the EU Action Plan. I knew that I had to get more land for the majority Muslim republic if EU governments were to give the plan their wholehearted support. Thirty per cent was just not enough for them in terms of justice as well as in handling their own domestic public opinion.

On 3 October 1993 the Americans lost eighteen soldiers in a tragic accident in Somalia while they were under direct American command – not, as many thought, under UN command. Nevertheless, the UN was blamed and the US forces came out in stages, a miserable finale to what had proved in the end to be an ill-fated humanitarian intervention. The US were judged to have crossed from humanitarian relief to developing a governing structure, and then chasing a particular warlord at the expense of their impartiality; thereafter, that was referred to as 'crossing the Mogadishu line' in UN humanitarian operations. The whole episode had a profound effect on US political attitudes to the UN and to intervention in Bosnia-Herzegovina.

6

The EU Action Plan

D URING OCTOBER 1993 the mood in Europe moved steadily towards building on the HMS *Invincible* package, fearing a continuation of the war. On 1 October I had written to US envoy Redman,[136] for discussion in Washington, as well as in European capitals, on the ethical dimension of prolonging the war, the need to keep alive the prospect of peace if the humanitarian supplies were to get through during the winter, and with thoughts on a comprehensive settlement. There had followed some detailed discussions with the parties.[137]

An extensive consultative exercise was then conducted where countries had been challenged on some of the basic diplomatic assumptions prevalent since 1991, culminating in the FAC meeting on 26 October. In the process some had discovered strengths in the *Invincible* package that they had not appreciated before. In particular, the Netherlands and Germany were now ready to give full backing to a Union of Three Republics and regretfully accept that it was necessary to forgo many of the London principles. There was also a readiness to link recognition of Croatia by the FRY with sanctions relief. This pleased the Germans although they were still very cautious, because then they were not yet ready for a full comprehensive settlement and wanted to concentrate on Bosnia. On 14 October, Milosevic had persuaded Karadzic to put the *Invincible* package back on the table and resume negotiations.

On 1 November I sent to Redman for discussion in Washington a revised paper which I had given to the Foreign Ministers and which represented the best consensus within the Twelve that I could find on our global approach.[138] The Belgian Presidency and we as Co-Chairmen had failed to engage the US fully in our consultative exercise but at least they were kept informed, which was crucial given the coordinated attempt by the US administration on 17 October in separate interviews with the *Washington Post* to shift the blame for their Bosnian policy back to Europe. *The Times* of 18 October, under the headline 'Clinton Attacks UK and France over

Bosnia War', read: 'With his Secretary of State remarking witheringly that Europe was "no longer the dominant area of the world" President Clinton yesterday brought simmering US–European tensions into the open by launching a stinging attack on Britain and France for their refusal to lift the Bosnian arms embargo.' Clinton went as far as to say 'John Major told me he wasn't sure he could sustain his government if he approved the plan.' To which Downing Street replied truthfully that the whole British Cabinet was against lifting the embargo. But a lot more was also said by known if, unnamed, senior figures in London. One comment printed by the *Independent* on 19 October summed up the mood about President Clinton: 'People had had few illusions about him as a statesman as it was. But if they had any at all left they don't now. He's like a little child, saying "I'm not guilty".' What might have fed US anger was a report in the *Wall Street Journal* of 15 October that Warren Christopher had privately asked Douglas Hurd whether the US could avoid sending peacekeepers, and which was thought to have stemmed from their meeting at Dumbarton Oaks and been leaked by the British. It was a sad commentary on the so-called Joint Action Programme of 22 May, undertaken unenthusiastically by Hurd and Juppé to heal Atlantic rifts over Bosnia, that five months later the divisions and animosities were, if anything, greater. Meanwhile, we had lost the VOPP and still did not have the Americans on board for the Union of Three Republics.

A special European Council meeting on 30 October issued a declaration on the situation in the former Yugoslavia which called for 'the use of all appropriate means to support the convoying of humanitarian aid' and for 'reinforcing UNPROFOR so that more troops [would be] available to protect the aid routes'. In addition, the Council requested me to communicate their humanitarian demands 'with urgency and insistence to the leaders of all three parties who are responsible for passing on the necessary orders to local leadership', and ended by inviting the FAC 'to adopt detailed provisions for joint action on the basis of the above, while maintaining close coordination with the United Nations'.

On 5 November I submitted to Foreign Ministers of what had now become officially the European Union (EU) a long paper, entitled 'Joint Action on the Former Yugoslavia',[139] in which I posed twenty-eight specific questions to focus discussion. The nine most urgent I had starred, hoping that decisions on these could be taken soon. In this instance the ICFY was servicing the Foreign Affairs Council, giving them both the detailed background information and pointing up a way ahead. Such a function is normally fulfilled by the Council's own permanent secretariat, but on so complex an issue as the former Yugoslavia a specially focused effort, in this case from the ICFY, served a particularly useful function. Neither the rotating Presidency nor the Commissioner for External Affairs would have had the time to keep constantly moving between the parties to take initiatives and to follow through negotiating leads. The Yugoslavian situation lent itself to the appointment of a politician as a negotiator with a small team answerable directly to EU Foreign Ministers. The effectiveness of the ICFY as a mechanism for future EU–UN diplomacy is, I hope, revealed in the depth and range of the diplomacy, not just in Bosnia but also in Croatia and FYROM, which was not always apparent at the time; and also in how the EU Action Plan was developed from the EC's involvement in the former Yugoslavia from 1991 onwards, through the shaping of the *Invincible* package in the summer of 1993 in Geneva and as the EC Foreign Ministers and their officials became parties to the negotiating process and then actually negotiators over the EU Action Plan, which led on to the Contact Group Plan and the US-led negotiations in 1995.

At a North Atlantic Council meeting on 3 November Canada and the US voiced concern over the European Council declaration on the former Yugoslavia, and the lack of consultation. The European initiative had implications for Canadian forces on the ground in the former Yugoslavia, and media reports of discussions by European leaders had been followed with interest and some concern. Canada wished to be in the loop and consulted, for which NATO seemed the obvious forum. Particular questions arose on the reference to the 'use of all appropriate means'. Was it intended to consult the UN and UNPROFOR? Would military means be used to remove any blockades on relief routes, or would negotiations be attempted first? The US associated themselves with the Canadian intervention and acknowledged that the situation in Bosnia needed to be addressed with the utmost gravity and urgency. But it was necessary to consider NATO engagement with other institutions, and new procedures might need to be elaborated. Manfred Woerner said that the Canadian concerns pointed to the need for close consultation going beyond an exchange of information, and since NATO was acknowledged by all concerned as the principal forum for consultations on security and defence matters, the NAC was the appropriate body for consultations on matters such as this.

What these protests showed was that EU action on security questions, particularly if the UN were involved, could not ignore NATO, and that this would be the case even if we had an effective WEU in operation, which we did not then have. I was to become even more convinced over the next few months that NATO should be the main forum for Bosnian discussions because it involved not only Canada and the US but also Turkey, which was important for our credibility with the Islamic nations. Yet France was never comfortable with using NATO and a scratchy standoff between the EU and NATO continued until the explosion in the market place in Sarajevo in February 1994, when the French suddenly began to call for NATO action. This was a shortlived honeymoon, however, and French suspicions resurfaced as American insensitivity to the views of the troop-contributing countries increased. The input from the European Community Monitoring Mission (ECMM), whose reports were sometimes excellent, helped to give those EU countries with no or few UN troops on the ground a degree of detailed information which they would otherwise never have had. But inevitably there was overlap between ECMM activity and that of the UN monitors and UN Civil Affairs Staff. Probably we would not have chosen to establish the ECMM as a link between the EC and the UN if the ICFY had been in existence in 1991, but once it was established it was easier to keep the monitors in place, and certainly they helped the EU administer Mostar and added to the strength and experience of the ICFY mission in Belgrade.

In Annex C attached to my report of 5 November to the Foreign Ministers, Geert Ahrens reported on the negotiations, conducted with his fellow ICFY ambassador Knut Vollebaek, between the Croatian Serbs and the Croatian government in Beitostolen, Norway. Initially, Bonn and Paris had been keen to launch a joint initiative and were invited by the ICFY to act as hosts, but both had declined unless a successful outcome could be guaranteed, a not infrequent inhibition on governments' involvement. Nevertheless, both were represented at the meeting. For some time in the ICFY we had been attracted by the idea of secret talks over Bosnia and Croatia, but we had never been able to obtain the degree of cooperation necessary among the parties to keep anything secret. Even with all possible precautions taken by the Norwegian government there were prior leaks of this meeting, and during the meeting the Croatian Serbs went on television and revealed their whereabouts, so thereafter our enthusiasm for secret meetings somewhat waned.

The meeting in Norway was divided into two parallel sessions. One dealt with military aspects, including the all-important ceasefire which we maintained was the only sound basis on which to work; the other group covered economic and political issues. In the early stages we were encouraged by the apparently constructive approach of the two sides in each of the working groups. Unfortunately, the atmosphere suddenly turned sour. The reasons for this were not entirely clear, though the arrival of Tudjman's letter setting out his peace proposals, most of which was a regurgitation of provisions already in the constitution and existing law, was a factor. But the Croatian Serbs had had an earlier sight of the proposals in Belgrade and a public announcement of the letter could not have come as a total surprise to their negotiators in Norway. This suggests that they used the letter as a pretext for breaking off the talks. There were divisions within the two camps which were also to blame. Whether Tudjman's letter had been deliberately aimed, as some believed, at scuppering the talks, we will probably never know. A Croatian parliamentary delegation was visiting the Council of Europe at the time of the letter's release and its contents were doubtless intended in part to have a positive impact in Strasbourg. But its effect on the Norwegian meeting would not have been difficult to predict by Tudjman's government. The Croatian government had been severely shaken by the Bosnian Muslims defeating the Bosnian Croats in Bosnia-Herzegovina and taking Vares. They were also stung by international criticism and allegations over the alleged Stupni Do massacre, where Croats killed Muslims, and the killing of Serbs in the Medak by Croatian government forces. The UN had documented in considerable detail serious violations of human rights in the Medak, which was very damaging. When Zagreb came under pressure domestically they usually launched a diplomatic initiative or military action, sometimes both. In this case Tudjman's letter was probably a deliberate diversion.

It was hard to assess Milosevic's role in these negotiations. There was no doubt that, with an eye on sanctions being lifted, he wanted to see a durable ceasefire come into force. But, like Tudjman, he thrived or survived on shifting alliances, not wanting to or finding it impossible to exert his influence on all the key Serbian players simultaneously. The hardline Krajina Serbs believed foolishly that time was on their side, and while Milosevic was pushing the Bosnian Serbs into further negotiations he professed to believe he could not afford another inter-Serb row.

One positive outcome of this failed meeting was that the French and Germans, having come together to try to resolve differences over Croatia, found some essential common ground on the lifting of sanctions on the FRY over Bosnia. The European Union Action Plan stemmed from a letter sent by Klaus Kinkel and Alain Juppé on 7 November to the then President of the Foreign Affairs Council, Willy Claes.[140] It was a development I both wanted and needed. Their letter did not contain much that was new in policy terms, but what was new was the full political involvement of their two governments. Up until then, as Co-Chairman, I had always been out in front taking initiatives on behalf of the EU which, in fairness, were then usually supported. But what we in ICFY lacked was the authority in terms of a detailed plan backed by governments. In effect, the German–French letter was demanding 3 per cent more territory for a Muslim-majority republic within Bosnia-Herzegovina so that it covered a third of the country, and also what they called a modus vivendi between the FRY and Croatia on the Krajina. In return the FRY was offered specific relief from sanctions. It also meant that Germany was accepting the *Invincible* package of a Union of Three Republics, on which they had hitherto been equivocal to the point of encouraging the US to stand their distance and Izetbegovic to ask for more land. The letter was soon public. It was carefully phrased in terms of buttressing ICFY and not eroding our position, while complementing our activity. There was nothing which ran counter to any aspect of the *Invincible* package or our negotiations on Croatia, so we were enthusiastic supporters.

At the Foreign Affairs Council meeting the President, Willy Claes, asked the Presidency Political Director to give an account of the prior discussion among Political Directors on the Joint Action documents circulated by me and the letter of 7 November to the Presidency from Juppé and Kinkel. The Political Directors had reached general agreement that the European Union should reiterate that the provisional agreements reached on board HMS *Invincible* remained a basis for a political settlement in Bosnia and should urge all the parties to return to the negotiating table. Particular effort had now to be made to secure further territorial concessions for the Muslims, and the European Union should repeat its readiness to participate actively in the implementation of a settlement. The Union should continue to pursue the possibility of a global conference in the medium term once the immediate issues in ex-Yugoslavia had been resolved. The Union would consider relaxation of sanctions in the framework of the implementation of a Bosnia settlement and a modus vivendi for the UNPAs in Croatia. The Union attached importance to the delivery of aid, but its implementation was not unconditional; the parties had to accept their responsibilities. A meeting to secure this would be held in Geneva. The Union would consider the possibility of observing the elections in Serbia on 19 December if that might contribute to resolving the problems in former Yugoslavia.

Kinkel said that he and Juppé had felt that a further effort was needed to bring the various efforts on aid and a political settlement together. Political Directors should consider how the ideas in my paper and the Kinkel/Juppé letter could be put into practice. Juppé agreed. It was time for the European Union to act. In the medium term, it would be right to consider a global conference to discuss a range of issues, including reconstruction and demilitarization. But in the short term, it was right to push the parties to reach a settlement on Bosnia alone. We had to support the Muslim claim for extra territory and offer guarantees for a settlement. However, the Muslims had to understand that military options would now lead only to a dead end and would alienate the European Union. Pressure on the Serbs over territory had to be balanced by a commitment to progressive lifting of sanctions. Both carrots and sticks were needed with the Croats, including the threat of sanctions.

The Italian Foreign Minister Andreatta said there was a valuable window of opportunity with the Serb elections and fears of the coming winter perhaps helping to bring more flexibility. But rapid decisions were needed. Andreatta suggested that Foreign Ministers meet in extraordinary session in the margins of the WEU Council meeting on 22 November.

Douglas Hurd agreed to the need for an extra meeting. The discussions ministers were having, on the basis of papers insufficiently digested, showed the difficulty of agreeing decisions and actions on a European basis. It was sensible for the Political Committee to examine the two documents, but ministers then needed to take decisions themselves. The UK had no difficulties with the general lines of the Kinkel/Juppé letter, but the issues raised needed to be turned into concrete proposals. There were things that could be done in the very short term. The Commission should tell the governments what more the EU task force could accomplish, under its existing remit, to keep roads open. The ECMM might use its experience to help monitor, with local forces, the safety of bridges. It was right to seek enlarged troop contributions to UNPROFOR by member states. The UK could not contribute further, but third countries might if they were encouraged and perhaps helped with equipment. A further, less rushed but decision-orientated session was needed so that the Council could take steps forward on both political and aid issues before Christmas.

Kinkel intervened again, agreeing to a further Foreign Ministers' meeting but stressing that it would only be productive if it were conducted on the basis of a very tight paper which led to clear instructions from the Council. After a brief consultation, it was agreed that Foreign Ministers should meet in Luxembourg on 22 November to discuss options prepared by the Common Foreign and Security Policy machinery.

The US were sceptical, even hostile, towards the Franco-German initiative and the EU activity generally. In particular they were wary about the linkage between the lifting of sanctions on the FRY and the peace settlement. On Sarajevo, the US noted that Krajisnik had made no serious proposals at his meeting with Izetbegovic. It was not clear what 3–4 per cent additional territory the Bosnians really wanted or would accept, and the US would not coerce the Muslims to accept just what the Serbs offered.

I had a useful meeting with the Croatian Defence Minister, Susak, in my office in London on 11 November: he was focusing on building up Croat military strength and links with the US. After a meeting the following day with Milosevic and the Bosnian Serbs I sent a detailed report to the Political Directors of the Twelve to help them in their deliberations.[141] The biggest obstacle to peace now lay in the intensive Muslim–Croat fighting which everyone expected to go on throughout the winter and which we felt might well scupper all negotiations, even if the Serbs and Muslims could make progress. In many respects the bitterness between Bosnian Croats and Bosnian Muslims was more intense than either's relationship with the Serbs, something which the US were beginning both to understand and to want to alleviate. For the UK it was a bit galling to see the Franco-German initiative prosper, but underneath Franco-British agreement was solid, embracing their military as well as the diplomats. Also, Douglas Hurd had a broad enough view to see that the prize of pulling the Germans on board was considerable and that this was a task for which the French were well suited.

On 13 November we wrote to Izetbegovic to explain how we saw progress and suggested meeting in Geneva, but he replied that he was in

Sarajevo after twelve days' travelling abroad and suggested we meet with Silajdzic instead. So in Geneva on 18 November we had separate meetings with Silajdzic, Karadzic and Boban. I also had a joint meeting with Karadzic and Silajdzic, after they both had spent around four hours together with Krajisnik. Silajdzic and Boban, however, refused our offer to hold a joint meeting – not surprisingly, since they personally disliked each other and Bosnian Muslim–Bosnian Croat relations were deteriorating by the day.

Late in the evening with Karadzic and Mladic we pursued UNPROFOR concerns. Mrs Ogata had also come to see me to stress that the European Union was falling behind in its considerable financial commitments to the humanitarian effort. I reported all of these meetings to EU Foreign Ministers.[142] I also warned them that it would certainly make any EU Action Plan look pretty hollow if the press picked up from UNHCR that we were not delivering on our financial promises, particularly since the overall UNHCR shortfall now stood at US$62 million for the implementation of its operation until the end of 1993.

One interesting aspect of these meetings was that we raised the issue of war crimes with Karadzic for the first time. I emphasized to Karadzic that despite his publicized agreement with Abdic that war criminals would be tried by local courts, there could be no amnesty for war criminals, and local trials would not prevent cases being brought before the international Tribunal. He said no Serbs would be sent out of the country to be put on trial. I then warned EU ministers that we were clearly going to have difficulty over arrest warrants and suggested they might wish to say something about that in the Action Plan, though it would fall mainly to the Security Council, under Chapter VII, to act.

On 8 November, in an International Health Lecture at the Royal College of Surgeons in Dublin,[143] I warned that interfering with the dynamics of war can all too easily perpetuate hostilities. If you feed the warriors, that might be a price worth paying if peace is near, if negotiations are serious; but if new offensives are about to be launched, what price humanitarian aid? Privately, I was warning that tying ourselves into meeting all the territorial demands made by the Muslim leaders in Sarajevo would result in an undeliverable package. There were also dangers in locking ourselves into detailed discussions of where the extra percentage was to come from. It would be difficult enough to extract 33.3 per cent even by keeping open the possibility of some part of this coming from the Croats. Ideally the parties should talk less about percentages and instead do a deal over the whole of Sarajevo, which for the Muslims was far more important economically and politically. The UK, in particular, continued to believe that the US would contribute to an implementation force. But the emphasis was shifting towards self-policing and achieving a strategic balance, hence the feeling it would be easier with the three republics having their own armies, so that such a large UN implementation force as we had previously envisaged would not now be required – in effect making a virtue of the reality, namely that a US contribution would not be forthcoming. If the Croats defended their republic and the Serbs theirs, we could have a UN monitoring and observer force in the Muslim republic, located on the boundaries. For this to be credible, the UN force could be small but it had to be efficient, with EU countries well represented and the NATO no-fly zone maintained in force. The virtue of the 'three republics' solution was that it looked the most stable in the long term.

The EU Political Committee met on 16 November to take detailed planning for the Action Plan further. I had fed in ideas on Sarajevo via a COREU the day before.[144] Considerable progress was made at the meeting, with the UK now working closely with the Germans and the French. All this time I was coordinating with the Belgian Presidency, who kept me very well informed. We were feeding ICFY ideas into the French and German Foreign Ministries, and I was pushing my own ideas into the UK decision-making process, with Douglas Hurd and the then UK Political Director, Len Appleyard, giving them every consideration. It was a creative period in diplomatic activity; also, one that should give heart to those who believe that the EU countries can develop a Common Foreign and Security Policy by consensus without formal voting mechanisms or being dependent on a European Commission input.

Stoltenberg briefed Security Council members in informal consultations on 18 November and later briefed the press. He noted the degree to which all matters affecting Bosnia had been driven off the front pages of the world's newspapers by other events and how Bosnia was losing out in the competition not only for attention, but also for humanitarian resources. So far the UN had successfully averted a humanitarian crisis. Apart from central Bosnia, there was less fighting now than at any time over the last nineteen months. The conflict in Croatia had flared up on several occasions and then died down. Preventive deployment in Macedonia was working. Some elements of previous draft peace settlements, on human rights, transport, communications, access to the sea, were now taken as read by all the parties. Everyone also agreed on the need for cooperation on transborder issues in the former Yugoslavia once a political settlement had been reached.

Washington was holding itself aloof from the ICFY; Stoltenberg tried once more to gain access but was unable to get a hearing with Christopher. The US were also appearing very restless about the amount of detail that the EU Action Plan looked like including on progressive lifting of sanctions and were communicating this back to the Belgian EU Presidency, and directly in Bonn, Paris and London. The Dutch government was also arguing for only a suspension rather than a lifting of sanctions, and was sceptical about whether the Bosnian Muslims had the political will and cohesion to reach a settlement even if they had an additional 3–4 per cent of territory.

We pointed out that the Bosnian Muslim leaders' lack of cohesion meant they had lost a number of chances of halting the war. First they had turned down the Carrington–Cutileiro package; then they had spent months questioning whether to accept the VOPP, weakening it in the process; and now they had rejected the *Invincible* package at the last minute. All of this pointed to the need for outside governmental persuasion if any EU Action Plan was to be accepted. The American response was merely to reiterate that they could not pressurize the Muslims, who were the victims. What most European political leaders hoped was that if we could extract significantly more territory from the Serbs, EU pressure on the Muslim leaders would work – but only provided the US stayed on the sidelines rather than as in the past encourage the Muslims to hold out for better terms. There were few illusions that despite every effort to consult the US, the EU still had big differences with the Clinton administration. What we were to discover was that the US could neither advocate a settlement nor abdicate from a settlement. They could not forgo the appearance of exerting power, but they were not ready or seemingly able to accept the compromises and the responsibility that go with the exercise of power.

The Foreign Affairs Council in Luxembourg on 22 November was an impressive meeting, taking specific decisions in good order. The first piece of business was for the Humanitarian Action Plan to be adopted. On the political process there was a long discussion.[145] It was agreed that the Foreign Ministers of the Twelve, along with myself and Stoltenberg, should meet the parties and the Presidents in Geneva on 29 November and that Redman and Churkin should be invited to attend as observers. Then, after a presentation of the EU position, the Co-Chairmen of the ICFY would be asked to pursue detailed negotiations.

On the humanitarian situation Willy Claes asked Generals Cot and Briquemont to describe the position on the ground. General Cot said that convoys could not secure access by force. A prior solid agreement by the military and political hierarchies of each party to the conflict actively to help aid get through was required. The parties themselves recognized that force would be needed against uncontrolled elements on all sides. Cot said that the Croats were the main obstacle at the moment: they had destroyed two bridges over the Neretva river and were still blocking the Route Diamond from Split to Vitez via Gornji Vakuf. There was total collusion between Zagreb and the Bosnian Croats.

In response to questions, Cot said that he had no misgivings about using close air support to help secure access for aid. The NATO mechanism was already in place. But air support was not a panacea. Bridges would still need to be repaired and convoys negotiated through. General Briquemont said that the UN was facing a humanitarian disaster in Bosnia. Any solemn declaration by the parties would be worthless if military leaders were not fully associated with it. Briquemont hoped that aid deliveries would not be stopped as a result of each UN death. Of the possible routes, that from Metkovic to Sarajevo via Mostar which went through Croatian-controlled territory was by far the most important. Mountain roads were liable to blockage during the winter. Even if Tuzla airport did reopen, he said, it could never replace overland convoy capacity.

At a preliminary coordinating session in Geneva on the morning of 29 November, before meeting the representatives from the former Yugoslavia, the twelve Foreign Ministers agreed that the EU should not enter into detail on a programme for suspension of sanctions with the parties, and that prior to that expert talks with the Americans were urgently needed to reach an agreed position. While the American and Russian envoys should be invited to the afternoon bilaterals with the parties, representatives of members of the ICFY Steering Committee would attend the plenary sessions only. Willy Claes noted that the Serb military commander, Mladic, had refused to come to Geneva to attend a follow-up meeting with Mrs Ogata and General Cot and General Briquemont on humanitarian access.

The meeting then opened with a statement agreed in advance between the Foreign Ministers, read out by Willy Claes. This called for immediate negotiations towards a Bosnia settlement and a modus vivendi in the UNPAs in Croatia. The EU expected the Serbian side to make further territorial concessions of the same magnitude as the Bosnian government demands on the eve of the HMS *Invincible* meeting on 20 September. The Bosnian government was called upon to confirm that such territorial demands still constituted the basis of a peace settlement. The Croatians were expected to maintain their previous concessions on access to the sea and port facilities and to demonstrate a constructive attitude in the negotiations.

If the Serbs concluded a Bosnia agreement, accepted a modus vivendi in the UNPAs and cooperated in implementation then the EU would work towards gradual and conditional suspension of sanctions as implementation proceeded, with the ultimate aim of lifting sanctions when the UN Security Council had confirmed Serb implementation. The EU and the international community would help with effective implementation and reconstruction. The EU would increase its cooperation and economic assistance with Croatia if it accepted the modus vivendi. On the other hand, Croatian recourse to military action would inevitably lead to negative reactions from the international community.

Stoltenberg then read out a message from the UN Secretary-General which called on the parties to examine every possibility of reaching agreement on the small percentage of territory over which agreement was still outstanding. Speaking personally, Stoltenberg added that the passage of time could lead to events which could be detrimental to the peace process. The impasse should be broken now.

Mrs Ogata reported that since the commitment of the parties to unimpeded humanitarian deliveries at her meeting in Geneva on 18 November over 3,000 metric tonnes of food and winterization materials had been supplied by road. A new route had been opened and a limited amount of some materials previously blocked had been allowed through. A convoy with building materials would leave for Srebrenica on 1 December; this would be an important test. Overall, the conclusion was that the parties' latest commitments had so far brought no significant improvement. A peace settlement was urgently needed if a humanitarian catastrophe was to be avoided. The parties were then invited to speak, in alphabetical order.[146]

The detailed EU position was presented to the parties in a plenary session and in bilaterals. Izetbegovic called for the return of occupied territories, Muslim sovereignty over Neum, and stationing of US/NATO forces only on territory of the Bosnian Muslim-majority republic in implementation of a settlement. Tudjman accepted the appeal for a modus vivendi in the UNPAs if a date were set for the implementation of the Vance Plan. In a hardline statement, Milosevic sought immediate suspension of sanctions and concentration on Serb–Muslim talks on Sarajevo and Croat–Muslim talks on access to the sea.

Izetbegovic confirmed that Muslim territorial demands had not changed since the *Invincible* talks but insisted on sovereignty over Neum. Tudjman refused to concede sovereignty over Neum. Milosevic again criticized sanctions and rejected international involvement over Kosovo. Karadzic ruled out reopening Tuzla airport. A new humanitarian aid agreement was signed by military leaders. I confirmed that the negotiations with the parties would resume over the next forty-eight hours and Willy Claes ended the meeting by suggesting a further meeting in December to review progress.

Stoltenberg and I began negotiations immediately to see if we could get a map for a Muslim-majority republic with 33.3 per cent of Bosnia-Herzegovina. I passed on to EU Foreign Ministers by COREU a nightly account of what had happened from 29 November to 2 December as the parties went backwards and forwards.[147] It was agreed all three parties would meet again on 12 December.

On 2 December the EU and US experts had an unproductive meeting on sanctions in which it became obvious that the US would not formulate ideas in detail until the shape of an agreed settlement was clear and implementation at hand. They were particularly critical of the frontloading of sanctions relief which Germany argued was essential if the package was to have any credibility in Serbia. I reported back to the FAC over lunch on 6 December and stressed the Muslim request for NATO security guarantees. On 9 December Stoltenberg and I visited Belgrade and had a meeting with

Milosevic,[148] followed by a private meeting with Karadzic and his team and Sarinic, President Tudjman's security adviser, who was accompanied by Akmadzic whom we flew into a JA military airfield in a UN plane. It looked as if the Bosnian Croat leader Boban was being nudged aside, which we felt would help ease relations with the Muslims. At that meeting we made some real progress on the map, with the Croats being ready to accept the Neretva river as far south as Tasovcici as the dividing line between the Muslim- and Croat-majority republics and with Mostar still to be administered by the EU. But Silajdzic sent a depressing message which arrived during the meeting saying that the Muslims wanted Neum and were no longer interested in having an outlet to the sea at Prevlaka as put forward by the Croats. Also, Izetbegovic could no longer come to the proposed meeting in Thessalonika on 12 December. We therefore cancelled that meeting in favour of one at Geneva on the morning of 21 December; but it was a bad sign and we took it to mean that the Bosnian Muslims wanted to go on fighting the Bosnian Croats and as yet felt under no pressure to negotiate. We later invited them all to go on from Geneva to Brussels so that the parties could again meet with the Foreign Ministers, in the hope that this would engender a better mood. We had by this time given up on being able to negotiate over Sarajevo and were resigned to having to have UN administration and postponing this most difficult of all issues.

The Foreign Ministers discussed Yugoslavia in a separate session in the margins of the European Council and over dinner in Brussels on 10 December. I reported on our Belgrade meeting, saying that the EU initiative of 29 November remained on course despite difficulties. The humanitarian aid position had improved, with convoys able to deliver food, winterization materials and fuel. Political negotiations were continuing, though Izetbegovic's rejection of Tudjman's offer of access to the sea via Prevlaka had been a setback. On territory, the package being discussed was coming closer to the 33.3 per cent required for the Muslims, which would amount to 31.3 per cent of the rest of Bosnia plus two-thirds of Sarajevo which was another 2 per cent overall. Silajdzic now said he was unwilling to discuss Sarajevo and temporary UN administration of Sarajevo and continued EU administration of Mostar might be necessary. On sanctions, having seen that there was more oil than ever in Serbia, most of it coming via Macedonia, I asked why more could not be done to give Gligorov a financial incentive to clamp down on this flagrant abuse, saying it was not making our task any easier if the FRY felt that sanctions were no longer biting. I argued that the key to Muslim acceptance of a package might be to extend NATO air cover during the implementation process. This process could in part take place within existing provisions, for example the NFZ, but ministers might consider agreeing wording in NATO to give 'support for the territorial integrity of Bosnia in the early years'. That would be a tremendous help to the Bosnian Muslims, and yet the only ground troops necessary would be from the UN implementation force.

The EU Foreign Ministers repeatedly pressed me to specify territorial concessions within an overall 33.3 per cent now which the EU might support as reasonable to give the Muslims a viable republic. It was clear that the ministers wanted to be able to brief the press that they had pressed me to take a tougher line, which they duly did. In a way this helped us negotiate with the Serbs, since one of the advantages of having the EU actively involved was that they had to show they had more clout than we as Co-Chairmen and that we were only negotiating on their behalf. But no one addressed the growing reluctance of the Bosnian Muslims to settle and to stop fighting. It was a tougher conversation than I normally had with the ministers, but as a politician I could not object because their reputations were now on the line; they were rightly becoming worried that the EU initiative was losing momentum. I tried to explain that the negotiating positions of the parties were more complicated than just achieving the 33.3 per cent figure now close to being put on the table. The parties were still bargaining with each other. I felt that the Serbs would make their final territorial offer when the parties met on 21 December. It was sensible that the EU had never said that the Muslims could dictate exactly where their 33.3 per cent of territory should be. When Kooijmans said it would be unacceptable if ethnic cleansing was rewarded, I refrained from reminding him that even the Dutch had accepted that the EU Action Plan was not compatible with London Conference principles. I realized that he was under domestic pressure and, since I liked him personally, I did not want to over-react. Having the Dutch taking a moralistic line was not a bad thing anyhow, for it indicated what was likely to be the US position, and there was no sign that the US were encouraging the Muslim leaders to settle. Kooijmans then visited Sarajevo on 14 December, and the Bosnia-Herzegovina government told him they were not looking for Article 5 guarantees from NATO but for a highly visible implementation force with credible air support. This was useful clarification.

Douglas Hurd suggested helpfully that pressure was best applied over a series of four or five key points rather than over a set map. These might include 33.3 per cent of territory, access to the sea at Prevlaka and more territory in central Bosnia. Kinkel echoed these three points and added a modus vivendi in the Krajina and temporary international administrations in Sarajevo (UN-led) and Mostar (EU-led). He added that those member states with influence over certain parties should press them to negotiate. Greece and France, with Churkin present, might tackle the Serbs. Germany and the Netherlands might press the Croats.

As the search for more territory for the Muslims gathered momentum the Croatian government once again, and without any attempt to pretend that

CROATIA

1
Bihac

2
• Banja Luka

Brcko

Tuzla

SERBIA

3

Jajce •

Zenica

Srebrenica

CROATIA

Gornji Vakuf •

Zepa •

4

Sarajevo

SARAJEVO
DISTRICT

5

• Gorazde

EU Action Plan for Bosnian
Muslim majority republic
comprising over one-third
of territory of Bosnia and
Herzegovina

Mostar •

Area 1	4.2%
Area 2	65.4%
Area 3	24.6%
Area 4	1.4%
Area 5	1.3%
Sarajevo district	3.1%

Total for Muslim majority republic, including
Sarajevo District on a 2–1 basis, = 33.56%

MONTENEGRO

Map 11 EU Action Plan, December 1993–February 1994

they did not set policy for the Bosnian Croats, stated to all the EU ambassadors in Zagreb that there had to be 17.5 per cent for any predominantly Croatian republic and in no circumstances could Vitez and Busovaca be given up. They also reverted to their traditional stance that the offer of access to the sea at Molunat near Prevlaka for the Serbs must be part of a general settlement including the UNPAs. Their formal position was set out in a letter to us from President Tudjman on 20 December.[149] Another important aspect was that they could not accept the Bosnian Serb republic withdrawing from the Union just because of an agreement with the Muslim republic. The letter said that all three republics had to agree. As much as anything else, this was a move by the Croats to protect their interests in Neum, since we and the Muslims insisted that if Bosnia were to be split up they would have to be given sovereignty over this Croat area so that the Muslim state would have access to the sea.

As Co-Chairmen we decided to put our own suggestions to the Serbs and the Croats, with four options for achieving the 33.3 per cent figure: by refusing to state our preference among the four we hoped they might take up some parts from each of the options and put them together in their own package. We presented these ideas on 17 December in another Serb–Croat meeting in Belgrade and reported back to Foreign Ministers.[150] It was clear that only negotiations with Tudjman and Milosevic present could bring a breakthrough from the parties and we tentatively arranged to meet in Brussels on the Monday evening or Tuesday morning before the parties met again with the whole FAC. We did think that in Croatia we could have a Christmas ceasefire signed and approach the needed modus vivendi.

On 20 December there was a preparatory meeting of Political Directors at which, on the basis of a German text, a series of requests to all the parties was made which, despite a plea from the UK that the Co-Chairmen should be consulted on the detail, was sent out to the parties without our knowing its content.[151] If we had seen it we would have warned against two particularly bald statements, one asking the Serbs on Sarajevo 'to renounce partition of the city' and the other asking the Croats to 'renounce partition of Mostar'. Only people who had not been involved in the delicate negotiations which had led to Tudjman accepting my suggestion for EU administration of Mostar and the Serbs despite constant to-ing and fro-ing accepting UN administration of Sarajevo would have plumped such provocative words down on the table. The Belgian Presidency, who had said they would consult the Co-Chairmen, were, I was later told, dissuaded from doing so by German officials because they feared I would query this particular aspect and because Kinkel had already given the paper to Andrei Kozyrev at the weekend.

On the night of 21 December Tudjman met Izetbegovic for an hour in Geneva and next morning we as Co-Chairmen met with Tudjman and Sarinic and then with Milosevic. Then Tudjman, Sarinic and Milosevic met by themselves for nearly two hours. This was followed by a large Serb–Croat meeting which went on with occasional intermissions for six hours, at times with heated arguments between Tudjman and Milosevic. Shortly before Tudjman had to leave for Brussels, a joint agreement was reached on a map claimed to provide over 33.3 per cent for the Muslim republic. We checked the exact figures by computer that evening and found the total was 33.5 per cent.

The Serbs and Croats had agreed to leave aside their own boundaries, for example in Posavina and above Dubrovnik, for further discussion, but the Serbs committed themselves to finding 17.5 per cent for the majority Croatian republic. This was the moment when the 49 per cent–51 per cent division of Bosnia-Herzegovina between the Serbs on the one hand and the Croats and Muslims on the other came about, the result of months of hectare-by-hectare negotiations. Both the Serbs and the Croats were prepared to continue with the Union of Three Republics, but now damagingly

they both rejected putting Sarajevo and Mostar under UN and EU administration. We hoped they might change their positions on this, but the
phrasing of the EU questionnaire on partition had heightened their anxiety.
The Croats were determined that at least West Mostar should be part of
the Croatian republic. The Bosnian Serbs were not prepared to give up, at
least at this stage, their concept of two cities in and around Sarajevo, even
though Milosevic always dismissed it as a fantasy.

When we brought Karadzic, Krajisnik and Milosevic together with
Izetbegovic and Silajdzic, the Muslims criticized the map on all the aspects
about which the Co-Chairmen had warned the Serbs and Croats. We urged
the Serbs and Muslims to negotiate again on all these points, and this
started in a low-key way which we hoped would continue that evening.

Meanwhile we sent a cable out from Geneva to the ministers coming to
the meeting next morning summarizing all this negotiating activity; and I
suggested that EU ministers, having heard both sides of the argument, might
want to focus on Brcko, Sarajevo and Mostar. It looked certain that
Milosevic would be very determined that sanctions must be suspended on
signature. Already it was obvious that there would have to be more negotiations after our Geneva meeting: the gap was still deep, if not as wide as
before. At least the parties were arguing on a map which had 33.3 per cent
as the baseline for a Muslim republic, the major EU demand on which they
had asked us, as Co-Chairmen, to deliver. The omens, however, for
reaching agreement in Brussels were not good and we flew in with our small
ICFY team from Geneva early next morning fearing that the Muslims were
in no mood to settle and preferred to continue to fight against the Croats
in central Bosnia.

The EU Foreign Ministers held their day of talks in Brussels with the
former Yugoslav parties following the same format that had been used in
Geneva on 29 November. At an initial EU coordinating meeting Stoltenberg
and I argued that the EU should not foreclose the possibility of the parties
agreeing a coherent division of Sarajevo and Mostar. Klaus Kinkel and
Kooijmans, however, said we should stick to the EU preference for
undivided cities, with, I am afraid, little idea of how damaging this new
definition was, particularly in relation to Sarajevo where hitherto UN
administration had been the mechanism for resolving this question over two
years. To attempt to resolve it over a few hours was courting disaster.

At the first plenary session Willy Claes for the Presidency read out a
prepared statement and I described the position after our 21 December Geneva
talks. The Muslims were to have 33.5 per cent of the territory, and the Croats
17.5 per cent. There would be a mixed technical and political group on Brcko
which would draw on European expert help to solve access problems. On
Sarajevo and Mostar, the Muslims would accept territorial delineation if satisfied with Serb concessions, otherwise they would go for temporary UN and

EU administration respectively. There remained differences over territory and size of corridors in eastern Bosnia. The Muslims wanted access to the sea at Neum, not at Prevlaka. The gap between the parties was bridgeable and I hoped for intensive negotiations to reach agreement by Christmas. We then arranged bilateral meetings with the three parties.

At an EU stocktaking meeting Kinkel said he had pressed the Muslims over lunch but without result. They had become much more self-confident. Douglas Hogg, who was attending for Douglas Hurd, commented that his visit to central Bosnia over the last two days had inclined him to the view that the Muslims believed they could make more military progress. We should leave detailed negotiations to the Co-Chairmen. For Denmark, Helveg Petersen agreed they should not become involved in detail. He was appalled by the parties' lack of will to reach a settlement. Van den Broek believed we should stick to UN and EU administration of Sarajevo and Mostar.

Then Churkin, who as the Russian observer was not expected to speak, asked to have the floor and when this was granted suggested that sanctions should be suspended if the negotiations were blocked by a non-Serb party. Willy Claes, fuming at Churkin for what he considered was a break with the EU line, then tried to sum up, called for a Christmas ceasefire and said allocating a third of the land to the Muslims and 17.5 per cent to the Croats was uncontested. He suggested that temporary UN administration of Sarajevo would be the only solution. Karadzic disagreed. On access to the sea, Claes said that the *Invincible* formula was preferred by the EU. Tudjman commented that a condominium was probably not acceptable but he would explore it. Izetbegovic said this was a serious option. Milosevic agreed with Claes that the Muslims should have access to the Sava river, but Karadzic said the Serbs were entitled to withdraw the concessions on this made on *Invincible* as no solution had ensued.

On Mostar, Boban said that EU administration would only be logical if also extended to Zenica and Tuzla, where the Croat populations were larger than Muslim numbers in Mostar. Izetbegovic said EU administration was an absolute necessity. Tudjman said he would try to persuade the Bosnian Croats. Boban said that he would go along with this but only under protest. On the Krajina, Milosevic agreed with Claes that progress had been made. Serbia was not a partner in these talks. On Tuzla airport, Claes insisted that the monitoring regime used for the Sarajevo airlift could be applied to counter fears of arms smuggling.

Then Juppé rounded angrily on Karadzic for refusing a settlement by rejecting UN administration for Sarajevo. He also demanded an answer on Tuzla airport. Karadzic replied that weapons were being smuggled to Muslims in Sarajevo via Tuzla airport. He would only agree to a reopening of Tuzla airport when a peace agreement was signed. Juppé said he was outraged by Karadzic's remarks. Karadzic retorted that 12 million Serbs were hostage to EU policy. Claes accused Karadzic of falsifying history and lashed out at Churkin's suggestion for relaxing sanctions which was, he considered, unsuitable for an observer. After all this sound and fury it was agreed the Co-Chairmen would carry on negotiations and everyone left the room somewhat shaken and amazed that experienced politicians like Juppé and Claes should have appeared to have lost control of themselves in front of the parties. Milosevic said to me quietly as we were leaving the room that he would never attend another session like that. The US special envoy Redman told some delegations that they should not underestimate the Muslim strength of feeling on Neum and the German delegation commented gloomily that the US were supporting the Muslim position on that point.

It was left to the Co-Chairmen to bring the pieces together. Tudjman had already left to fly back to Zagreb and our first task was to stop Milosevic from flying home as well. He reluctantly agreed to stay late that night and, while insisting that he would have to be in Belgrade early next morning, he agreed to meet with Izetbegovic. At that meeting, against all the odds, significant progress was made. It seemed to be a matter of 1 per cent separating the parties and Izetbegovic said that if Karadzic would come up overnight with 0.5 per cent in eastern Bosnia and 0.5 per cent in western Bosnia we would have an agreement. If Milosevic had stayed that night he might have bullied Karadzic to deliver; but next day, true to form, Karadzic and Krajisnik came up with a miserly 0.25–0.3 per cent in eastern Bosnia and nothing in western Bosnia.

When I said goodbye to Milosevic over dinner in Belgrade on 5 June 1995, we were reminiscing and he identified this as a point where things might have turned out differently. He said it had been one of his biggest mistakes to have left late that night. I believe that history may show that this was a moment when Izetbegovic should have settled. His army had done well against the Croats. Tudjman was under maximum pressure from the EU and a three-way partition, with each republic having its own army, was the most stable solution the Muslims were ever likely to get. They would have emerged stronger militarily and economically than either the Bosnian Croats or the Bosnian Serbs who would be dependent on, and controlled by, Zagreb and Belgrade respectively. They would have had Zepa, Srebrenica and Gorazde linked to Sarajevo. The small independent Muslim state that would probably have emerged would have been guaranteed its independence because of the collective guilt of the international community. Thereafter, from 1994 to 1995 the Croat position strengthened at the Muslims' expense, particularly around Bihac, the Muslims lost territory in eastern Bosnia to the Serbs in 1995 and a Croat–Muslim Federation link to Bihac meant the Croats gaining territory at the Muslims' expense.

We continued negotiations next day and I sent a full COREU reporting to the Ministers,[152] but the EU Action Plan was stalled. Though we agreed to meet on 15 January, I doubt that any one of us had a realistic hope of a result. The fact that a Muslim offensive was actually launched that day against Vitez, and Tudjman in Zagreb nearly withdrew his delegation in Brussels, summed it all up. The Muslims were intent on fighting the Croats, and the Bosnian Serbs were not prepared to give any more territory beyond that envisaged in their map. The ICFY team left for Christmas with their families and I suspect I was not the only one who asked how much longer I could ask my family to put up with my time and energy being spent swimming hard to keep my head up in this Balkan sewer.

Revived by the Christmas and New Year break, Stoltenberg and I embarked on another attempt to salvage the negotiations and arranged to meet Krajisnik privately for several hours on the afternoon of 3 January at the residence of Daniel Boyer in Paris. Daniel was born in Yugoslavia, survived Dachau concentration camp as a young boy and became an American citizen. A Serb, he is now a successful publisher who, whether in Geneva or Paris, was always ready to host private meetings with Yugoslavs. He did so between Muslims and Serbs in Geneva in December 1993 and proved to be very useful and discreet in arranging private contacts for Vance, myself, Stoltenberg and also some governments. The talks on this occasion were detailed and focused on why we thought it was so important to have a two-year period of UN administration of Sarajevo. We called our policy 'Sarajevo first' and it was in effect another attempt, as in December 1992, to put this issue of demilitarizing Sarajevo before everything else on the basis that if this could be solved much else would follow. The obstacle we knew was Krajisnik who believed Sarajevo belonged as much to the Serbs as to the Muslims. He had lived in and around Sarajevo all his life and with two houses, both in areas which I felt the Serbs should give up, he was intransigent. In Paris we hoped to cajole him to a more reasonable position and Karadzic raised no objections.

Krajisnik claimed that the Bosnian Serbs would only accept UN administration in Sarajevo if their republic were allowed immediate independence, with any areas of Sarajevo agreed after negotiation to be part of the Serb-majority republic joining it later. Krajisnik accepted that this was not likely to produce as good a deal for the Serbs, but he was more interested in early independence. He returned to the idea that the Muslims should give up part of eastern Bosnia for this. According to him, the recent Assembly meeting had been strongly against widening the linkage in eastern Bosnia between Zepa and Gorazde, saying the original proposals should stand.

This more private and intimate meeting softened Krajisnik's persistent hard line on Sarajevo. We met again on 5 January in Belgrade, where Stoltenberg and I also met Karadzic and Koljevic.[153] We succeeded in getting the Bosnian Serbs to accept UN administration again for the whole of Sarajevo district. The Paris meeting helped, but acceptance was hedged around with a caveat about independence for the republic. We then flew to Budapest and found the Hungarian Foreign Minister far keener on a settlement than before, saying that 'an unjust peace is better than national annihilation' and that they were now going to warm up their relations with Milosevic. The Hungarians were getting increasingly worried about the harm sanctions against the FRY were doing to their economy.

We then flew to Bonn, where I expected some tough talking on Croatia. I had commented publicly on television about the extensive presence of the Croatian army in Bosnia, and while I had said sanctions were unlikely the US Ambassador to Croatia had helpfully said Croatia risked sanctions if it continued to give military support to the Bosnian Croats. The Germans arranged what they called a brainstorming session before and during dinner with Klaus Kinkel and asked that it should be an off-the-record occasion. Stoltenberg and I then met Juppé on the morning of 7 January in Paris. We agreed that a crucial point had been reached, with the Muslims now on the offensive, launching an assault on Grbavica, a Serb suburb of Sarajevo, on the Serbs' Christmas day and also on Croat positions in central Bosnia. French public opinion was apparently changing, and if the fighting continued the pressure to withdraw troops and leave the parties to fight it out would grow. Juppé's view was that the parties now had to be faced with a stark choice: either reach a settlement or see the UN pull out. Mitterrand seemed to want to stay. Juppé and Balladur were cautious but contemplated leaving, while the Defence Minister Leotard's mood was changing back and forth. Juppé wanted the NATO summit to come out with a strong political message, but was worried that the UK would want the weakest language possible. He hoped that the UK and Germany would support the French line and I promised to contact Douglas Hurd and John Major, which I did.[154] Juppé wanted three main points included in the statement: first, that a negotiated settlement could be reached on the EU Action Plan; second, that NATO was ready to help the UN implement a settlement: and third, that NATO would commit itself to implement the relevant UNSCRs and in particular ensure that the 'safe areas' were respected.

As promised, the Bosnian Serbs delivered a further map. Its figures were checked by an independent company in Geneva, and this came out at 33.6 per cent for the Bosnian Muslims, with Sarajevo district on a 2:1 Muslim–Serb allocation, and a corridor to Neum modelled on the Muslim map. The extra 0.3 per cent we thought would be valuable in discussions over further adjustments. The Bosnian Serbs had given more territory, close to 0.5 per cent in eastern Bosnia, but only 0.2–0.3 per cent in western Bosnia below Bihac in an area of no interest to the Muslims, but of some interest to Croatia.

We had asked the Germans to host a Croat–Muslim meeting which they arranged at Petersberg, a modernized hotel complex on a hill above Bonn with a wonderful view of the river. Again we had to postpone the talks due to take place on Saturday 8 January because Izetbegovic was refusing to fly out of Sarajevo. There had been Serb shelling, itself a reaction to three Muslim assaults on Grbavica. Fortunately Tudjman had not left Zagreb and it was agreed to reschedule the talks for 9 January. Stoltenberg arranged that the UN would fly in from Zagreb and that Izetbegovic would fly out on the UN plane which was scheduled to arrive in Sarajevo early on Sunday morning.

In the very early hours of Sunday morning the Bosnian Ministry of the Interior contacted the UN in Sarajevo and informed them that they had evidence of a threat against the UN plane. Stoltenberg then managed to arrange, after hours of telephone diplomacy, for the UN to re-route their plane; but within twenty minutes of take-off a mortar bomb landed in the middle of the runway in Sarajevo, and the plane had to return to Zagreb. UN preliminary analysis of the crater on the runway, which was quickly filled in, appeared to be of not much help in determining whether this was a Muslim or a Serb mortar round. Around this time the UN had clear evidence that Muslim forces would from time to time shell the airport to stop the relief flights and refocus world attention on the siege of Sarajevo. As the Deputy Commander in Chief US European Command from 1992 to 1995 describes it,[i]

> *The press and some governments, including that of the United States, usually attribute all such fire to the Serbs, but no seasoned observer in Sarajevo doubts for a moment that Muslim forces have found it in their interest to shell friendly targets. In this case, the shelling usually closes the airport for a time, driving up the price of black-market goods that enter the city via routes controlled by Bosnian army commanders and government officials. Similarly, during the winter of 1993–94, the municipal government helped deny water to the city's population. An American foundation had implemented an innovative scheme to pump water into the city's empty lines, only to be denied permission by the government for health reasons. The denial had less to do with water purity than with the opposition of some Sarajevo officials who were reselling UN fuel donated to help distribute water. And, of course, the sight of Sarajevans lining up at water distribution points, sometimes under mortar and sniper fire, was a poignant image.*

Of course, it was the Serbs who had shelled Sarajevo almost daily for sixteen months, and they were clearly responsible for the vast majority of incidents.

After extensive negotiations involving Stoltenberg in Bonn, the UN and Izetbegovic in Sarajevo, Ambassador Masset at the Quai d'Orsay and the German diplomat Michael Steiner in the Auswärtiges Amt, it was eventually agreed that Izetbegovic would come. But it was only after a French plane had been circling over Sarajevo for some time and the UN APCs had stood waiting outside the Presidency with their engines running that Izetbegovic accepted the security guarantees of Stoltenberg and the UN risk assessment rather than the anxieties of his own personal security advisers. The UN plane took off for Split, from where Izetbegovic flew to Bonn on a German aircraft to arrive at 17.00. Tudjman then agreed to come as well.

I had warned the EU by COREU that the Muslims were likely to ask that Neum be put under EU administration for a temporary period and I asked for authority to explore this option and to accept it if President Tudjman could live with it. We felt Tudjman might want to define the area to be less than Neum opstina. The Muslims were ready to have the Split–Dubrovnik road described as a sovereign road for the Republic of Croatia. Stoltenberg agreed with me that there were advantages in this area being administered by the EU, as there could then be some trade-off between Croat and Muslim sensitivities in Neum and Mostar. Also, by postponing the issue in this way we might allow passions to cool and wiser heads to prevail.

Coinciding with the NATO summit in Brussels, the Petersberg two-day meeting made no real progress and, what was worse, personal relations between Izetbegovic and Tudjman deteriorated even further. The Croats had presented the Muslims with a fully-drafted Treaty of Cooperation which was an extension of the joint Croat–Muslim declaration of 14 September 1993.[155] The Muslim side argued that it would be better to solve issues in dispute before agreeing a Treaty. They proposed a demilitarized central zone in Bosnia. The Croats responded negatively. While the Croats, who were losing ground in the Muslim–Croat war, clearly had a strong interest in a breakthrough and a renewal in Muslim–Croat cooperation, the Muslims, who were gaining, were unwilling to enter into definite commitments and sought always to keep their options open, including continuing fighting. Conversations in the margins confirmed that this was their intention. The Muslims were enjoying a renewed confidence in their fighting ability and seemed determined to concentrate attacks on the Croats leaving the Serbs until they had gained what they needed in central Bosnia. The German view, which I shared, was that an agreement could have been made at Petersberg but the Muslims had come with the intention of not making any progress. Despite its lack of concrete progress, the Petersberg meeting laid the foundation for the emergence of the Muslim–Croat Federation in the Washington Accords three months later.

Over dinner at the end of the meeting, which Izetbegovic attended only under considerable pressure from us and the Germans, I had my last intimate talk with the Bosnian President. He likened the Muslim situation to Britain in 1940 and said he felt his role was to never give up. I had to admire his new, quiet resolve to fight almost regardless of the consequences, something which I had never heard Izetbegovic express before. He was confident of taking more land from the Croatian army. When I asked why he did not let Muslim children and their mothers leave Sarajevo he retorted that the British would never have let them leave London during the Blitz and seemed genuinely surprised when I told him how Churchill's government arranged for children not only to leave London but to go as far afield as Canada.

The NATO summit made a number of statements which threatened stronger military action but some of the more divisive NATO-inspired demands on the UN were shelved. I sent out a COREU[156] with an assessment from the UN viewpoint of the situation at Srebrenica and Tuzla airport which had been discussed at the meeting and which I had passed to John Major while he was actually at the meeting; I gathered he had shown it to President Clinton.

On 11 January the *Washington Post* reported that severe tensions had arisen between the Secretary-General Boutros Boutros Ghali and the top commander of UN forces in the Balkans, General Jean Cot of France, who, it reported, had repeatedly ignored or challenged the authority of his civilian superiors at UN headquarters. Thorvald Stoltenberg had just given up being, as well as Co-Chairman, the UN Secretary-General's Special Representative, in part because of problems he had faced with General Cot, a 59-year-old five-star French general who had been commanding the 27,000 UN forces in Bosnia and Croatia since July. Stoltenberg's replacement in the UN role was Yasushi Akashi, the UN diplomat who had been responsible for the successful UN operation in Cambodia, and I soon established an excellent working relationship with him. Always cool-headed, he could operate with an air of detachment amid charge and counter-charge from the Americans about his partiality or cravenness that perhaps only someone who did not stem from Europe could have achieved. In fact he was impartial and tough.

NATO leaders issued a new threat to use air power to support UN forces delivering humanitarian aid in Bosnia and implied the UN had stopped it being executed. According to various UN Security Council Resolutions, the final go-ahead for the use of air power had to be given by Boutros Ghali on the advice of UN officials in Bosnia, including Cot. But Boutros Ghali said, speaking from Paris, 'I have received no request for the use of air power' from UN officials in Bosnia; 'the day I receive such a request, and if I have the support of UN officials who believe it is urgent to use air power, I will be the first to back its use.' The problem, as so often, was rooted in terminology, for NATO discussion usually referred to air strikes without qualification, whereas over Srebrenica and Tuzla what was actually envisaged was close air support in defence of UN personnel carrying out their humanitarian mandate. What the UN feared were the consequences of generalized air strikes on Serb military targets, not close air support specifically related to weapons systems that were used to attack UN personnel. The Russians had accepted close air support as being a necessary arm of peacekeeping and while UNPROFOR issued an open memo to try to clear up these misunderstandings,[157] it was bound to fail, for some in the US administration did actually want generalized air strikes and were deliberately refusing to make a distinction. They wanted air power to be less circumscribed and for NATO not to be constrained by the dual key limitation on which most UN countries insisted. Apparently Boutros Ghali had despatched a cable to Cot prompted by the general saying in an interview with Le Monde the previous week that he had repeatedly asked Boutros Ghali to delegate to him the authority to call in air strikes and that the Secretary-General refused. The cable, described by diplomats as by far the strongest reprimand ever sent to a UN commander, was reported as saying that his actions were 'inappropriate' and 'incompatible' with his position. Cot was also reported as having told Yasushi Akashi that he would lobby governments with troops in Bosnia to press Boutros Ghali to change his mind and appeared to be attempting to open a channel of communications directly to the Security Council, circumventing the Secretary-General, to press his case. The odd part of the row was that Cot had been an outspoken opponent of the wider use of air power in Bosnia and was still only advocating circumscribed close air support. Thereafter, it was only a matter of time before Cot was replaced. Another French general, de Lapresle, took over; he established an excellent working relationship with everyone in the UN and soon the atmosphere in the UN HQ at Zagreb was transformed. What was clearly emerging, however, was a new level of frustration in governments and within the UN over the callous Bosnian Serb shelling of Sarajevo which I totally shared. At the NATO summit a psychological threshold appeared to have been crossed, making it very likely that the next major shelling incident would be met by air power, even at the risk of escalation.

Boutros Ghali accepted that since the NATO meeting he did not have to report further to the Security Council on Srebrenica and Tuzla in such a way as to require a further Council decision on air support, and his mind was not closed to delegating the power to authorize use of close air support, in these two operations to his Special Representative, Akashi. The Americans felt that the use of air power, whether in the form of close air support or air strikes by NATO, was now necessary and had been authorized by the relevant Security Council Resolutions. The Russians felt that NATO's readiness to carry out air strikes against the Serbs was illogical in present circumstances as the Muslims were the real instigators of the present spiral of tension in Bosnia-Herzegovina and the Muslims had been encouraged to provoke the Serbs because of NATO threats. Russia was, however, ready to engage seriously in a search for solutions in Tuzla and Srebrenica. The Russians argued that a decision by the Secretary-General to use NATO air power should be taken by the Secretary-General only 'in consultation with the members of the Security Council'. Their argument was based on the words 'under the authority of the Security Council' in paragraph 10 of Security Council Resolution 836 taken together with the statement in the report of the Secretary-General approved by UNSCR 844 that the Secretary-General's first decision to initiate the use of air resources would be taken 'in consultation with the members of the Council'. In most NATO countries' view, the consultation referred to in the report took place in August 1993. The words 'under the authority of the Security Council' in SCR 836 did not imply that the Security Council had to be consulted at each and every stage, and the modalities of the implementation of UNSCR 836 had been set out in the Secretary-General's report. Even if, for one reason or another, the Secretary-General did decide to 'consult' the members of the Council, it was up to him to decide how to do this, and it was in the nature of such consultation that it did not give a right to those consulted to have their views accepted. This debate among the permanent members of the Security Council was not resolved but it was important that the issues had been aired well in advance of the decision to act in February.

I was now operating under the Greek Presidency and so on 17 January in Athens Stoltenberg and I met Karolos Papoulias, the Greek Foreign Minister, who spoke German but no English. I found him knowledgeable about the Balkans and, coming from the Greek border near Albania, he had a subtle approach to Bosnia which reflected a sensitivity to Muslim attitudes and in part stemmed from his long-standing interest in developing relations with Yasser Arafat. He later developed a link with the Iranian Foreign Minister on Balkan questions. It was not an easy time to take over the Presidency. Greece was in a minority of one over the Macedonia question and their recent imposition of economic sanctions against the Former Yugoslav Republic of Macedonia (FYROM), which was its UN and EU name, and blocking of CSCE membership, still angered other member states. My task was to minimize the problems and I found that although the Greeks disagreed from time to time with the EU position they never tried to block EU action or statements unless they felt it was crucial to their dispute over FYROM, which was for them a vital interest.

At the regular weekly UNHCR briefing of donors on 19 January in Geneva UNHCR made a point of spelling out their attitude towards the opening of Tuzla airport, which had surprisingly now become NATO's main focus following the summit. Mrs Ogata had told me that while the

opening of the airport would be 'useful' if it could be achieved by negotiation she was against any use of force. She also showed some understanding
of Karadzic's point about possible misuse of the airport by planes flying in
the radar shadow of UNHCR flights, about which there were now well
documented UN suspicions. She had pressed Karadzic instead at a meeting
on 19 January to help get more road convoys through. He had said he
would work on this and she appeared to think that he would make an effort
to deliver. One reason why little was getting through to Tuzla was that it
was at the end of a convoy route which first supplied Zenica, and goods
were frequently lifted off by unauthorized actions. UNHCR was therefore
in favour of changing tack and working on sending more convoys from
Belgrade, so that Tuzla would be at the beginning of the supply line.

UNHCR said that since the Sarajevo airlift had resumed flights on 12
January, two planes, one German and one Latvian chartered flight, had
been hit by small arms fire. Both were now out of service, the latter permanently, as the charter company refused to continue. By contrast, the mainly
US air drops were going well, with up to sixteen drops delivering 100–115
metric tonnes a night. What no one could assess was whether the Serbs
reacted to air-lifts by clamping down on convoys or whether the air-lifts
were vital to overcome the lack of convoys.

The security situation for UNHCR aid workers was deteriorating, particularly as it was now clear that aid workers were definite targets. In Banja
Luka on 17 January a bomb had been planted under an ICRC vehicle,
destroying it and seriously damaging the ICRC residence. Only an average
of 800 metric tonnes of aid per day was reaching its destination, less than
half the requirement. There was no widespread starvation yet, but there was
serious malnourishment in Maglaj which was solely dependent on air drops
as convoys had not reached this enclave of 16,000 people for five months.
All in all it was a very depressing picture and augured badly for the
remaining winter months.

All three parties, Presidents Tudjman, Milosevic and Bulatovic, met in
Geneva on 18–19 January for two full days of talks with and without us as
Co-Chairmen being present. Most of the time was spent in trying to close
the gaps on the map, using the latest Serb proposal of 33.56 per cent for a
Muslim-majority republic as a basis. It was clear that the Bosnian Serbs
were not prepared to give up any further territory, particularly in western
and eastern Bosnia, and equally clear that the Muslims were not prepared
to sign up unless there was substantial movement on the areas they were
still demanding. There were also significant differences between the Croats
and Muslims over central Bosnia, though just before Tudjman left he and
Izetbegovic were reported to have decided that Vitez would remain in the
Croat-majority republic and the arms factory would be shared, something
we had suggested at Petersberg. Granic and Silajdzic were apparently also

going to meet soon to discuss other disputed areas. This was almost
certainly a Muslim response to the growing evidence of a Serb–Croat
alliance and I told Redman after the meeting that I hoped he and the US
would exploit this and revive the Petersberg confederation proposal, for it
was clear to us all that we had to stop the Croat–Muslim war. Tudjman
left Geneva after meeting Milosevic, claiming jubilantly on television in
Zagreb of their agreement, 'This is recognition of Croatia', only for that to
be firmly denied from Belgrade. What they had agreed was to establish
permanent offices in each other's capitals, a significant advance. We had
deliberately absented ourselves from their signing ceremony because we
feared it would be seen as the start of a Serb–Croat anti-Muslim alliance.
We wanted the improvement in Zagreb–Belgrade relations, but not with
ICFY appearing to further polarize the conflict.

Faced with deadlock over the map, we attempted to develop a mechanism for dealing with both the Croat and the Muslim disputed territories,
which would be integrated with the existing proposals for the boundary
commission. We proposed that an arbitration commission be established
and a mechanism whereby disputes, if the parties still failed to reach agreement, could be put to the UN Security Council. With some reluctance this
was accepted by the Serbs and Croats. The Security Council provision was
essential if the map was to be changed despite one party disagreeing. The
Muslims had earlier indicated acceptance but, once the Serbs surprisingly
said yes, argued that this mechanism did not offer them enough, particularly since the armed forces currently holding the disputed areas would not
be leaving, and they proposed instead independent administration. We felt
it would be impractical to put all these disputed areas under a UN or EU
special administrative regime, and in any case the Serbs had made it clear
that this would not be acceptable to them. This volte-face in the Muslim
negotiating position indicated to us that the Muslim side neither had nor
wanted the authority to reach a final settlement at this round of negotiations. It was also clear that they were embarked on a course of bypassing
us as Co-Chairmen, diminishing our authority and relying on their influence
in the US administration as well as in Germany. The Germans were now
beginning to decouple themselves from the EU Action Plan, attaching more
importance to relations with Washington than with Paris over Bosnia, and
also to concentrate on Croatia.

In order to keep at least a flicker of life in the EU Action Plan we
suggested that the parties should try to implement some confidence-building
measures such as hotlines and placement of liaison officers in general
headquarters. All three agreed to the hotlines, but Izetbegovic wanted to
consult his military on the liaison officer proposal, saying it might be hard
to find volunteers. The Bosnian Croats and the Bosnian Serbs planned to go
ahead with exchanging liaison officers between Pale and Mostar. The Croats

offered to lease to the Muslims a coastal resort on the Croatian Peljesac peninsula which was opposite Ploce in the Adriatic and would have to be reached by boat, with the Croats offering a 7 km by 1 km strip of coastline. It seems that Izetbegovic and Tudjman did agree on sea access to this strip of land just before Tudjman left, but as always the devil would be in the detail. Tudjman's offer would have possibly been acceptable in the context of the Union; we felt that if there were no Union, Tudjman would have to review his offer of a lease and upgrade it to a sovereign land offer if he was to get the town of Neum as the territory of the Croatian majority republic.

All three parties agreed to meet again on 10 February, without Tudjman and Milosevic, to discuss progress. Izetbegovic, however, warned that he might not come and would instead send Silajdzic in his place with full delegated powers. I said goodbye to Izetbegovic with affection but with both of us knowing that we were not likely to meet again in the same relationship as existed between us for the last one and a half years. The ICFY process has to be impartial, but for President Izetbegovic the Americans offered sympathetic support and I could not claim that his interests might not now be best served by linking his fortunes to that of the most powerful country in the world. My personal opinion was that he was making a mistake and that he and the Muslims would regret taking this path of sole reliance on the US, who were already becoming pro-Croat.

At a press conference following the meeting I was asked whether now was the time to be considering convening a new London Conference and I replied that following the experiences of EU ministers with the parties in Brussels in December such a prospect was unlikely to be looked upon by them or by any of the parties with much relish. I felt it would be unwise for EU ministers to expose themselves again without much more evidence of a shift in position from the Muslims or enthusiasm from the Americans on the EU Action Plan. The one important new feature was that the US were now ready to engage themselves in the negotiating process and Ambassador Redman told me that he had instructions to explore how Croat–Muslim relations might be improved, as – quite rightly – Washington was becoming ever more horrified at how this internecine struggle was helping the Serbs to consolidate their position. The EU was also helpfully ready to look at administering Mostar in advance of a settlement.[158]

To sour the atmosphere even more and to demonstrate their frustration at the unsuccessful efforts to halt the war in Bosnia, the European Parliament called for my dismissal as the European Union's mediator to the Yugoslav peace process in a vote of 160 to 90, with 13 abstentions. The fact that only half the European Union's 518-member Assembly had voted, and that all the British MEPs, Labour as well as Conservative, had voted against, was important to me, but I could have done without this as it gave some specious support to the propaganda campaign that we as

Co-Chairmen were too pro-Serb. Our problem was that most of the burden of negotiating more territory from the Serbs for the Muslims fell on us. We were therefore often seen with the Serbs and were by that very process becoming identified with what was their map. Indeed, despite all our disclaimers the press still often labelled it the Owen–Stoltenberg map. There was scant coverage of the Parliament's decision in the German press, which would not have been the case six months earlier, and I thought it was indicative of the feeling that this was not a seriously taken decision, indeed bordered on the flippant. It was also helpful when both Kinkel and Kooijmans, the two Foreign Ministers who had had the greatest reservations about my views in the past, strongly and publicly defended me. Once again I had no cause for complaint about the way the EU Foreign Ministers behaved to me personally, and much to be grateful for. It seemed they had learnt their lesson from the way they had treated Lord Carrington in 1991 and recognized that loyalty to their negotiator was crucial.

At the end of the month Chancellor Kohl was due to go to Washington, and most in Europe felt that he was in the best position to convey to President Clinton EU fears and frustrations over his attitude to Bosnia. The French had just tried, with Alain Juppé meeting Warren Christopher in Paris, but this had unleashed a war of words in the US and French press. The State Department had said that Juppé had used 'a strange moral calculus' and their spokesman said, 'it is hard to understand his logic'; to which the French had replied, 'if we are talking on a moral level the choice today is between merely watching the fighting or doing everything possible to stop it.'

The German analysis of the American position was that military intervention was not an option as the Americans were not ready to go down this track, and the Germans felt that air strikes alone would simply prolong the war. The US were still semi-detached from the peace negotiations, hiding behind the wise-sounding word 'containment'. But 'containment' in practice began to look increasingly like merely stopping the war in Bosnia-Herzegovina from spreading to other parts of the former Yugoslavia, while accepting the prolongation of the war so that the Bosnian Muslim army could become stronger, particularly if joined by Croatian forces. One of the many adverse consequences of this policy was that it meant letting the ethnic cleansing continue by default and watching while ethnic partition deepened. Even if the Muslims fought on indefinitely and made some territorial gains they could not, in most military experts' view, actually win control of all the territory of Bosnia-Herzegovina. Lifting the arms embargo and leaving the warring factions to fight also opened the door to third-party involvement which is what everyone feared, particularly if it involved the Iranians attempting to fly in troops as well as arms, risking being shot down.

As to the arms embargo, we were all looking the other way. Muslim money bought arms, and these were smuggled into Bosnia through the channels of the sophisticated international arms trade. Some thought the US were covertly involved in speeding up this process. French military officers claimed to have evidence that the US was using its air drops to supply some arms and equipment to the Bosnian army but no action other than the regular UNHCR inspections could stop it, for they were US planes flying from US bases. The Muslim problem was that the Croats were now stopping all arms getting through because of their own Muslim–Croat war. As for the Serbs, they too were getting more sophisticated radar and missiles on the Russian black market with the help of the Russian military. All of this was just about tolerable provided governments did not overtly break the arms embargo, for then we would have members of the Security Council supplying different sides in the war and risk a collapse in Security Council cooperation.

What everyone wanted was for the US to become fully engaged in the actual negotiations and to start sullying their hands with the sordid compromises necessary for any peacemaking let alone mapmaking. There had now been four lost peace initiatives: the Carrington–Cutileiro plan before the war started; the VOPP; the *Invincible* package; and now the EU Action Plan. Most Europeans, I judged, felt any further effort while the US remained on the sidelines was doomed, for it allowed the Muslims to escape the necessity of compromise inherent in any negotiation. Since the US would not appoint a high-level political negotiator I felt it was best for the US to give Redman, who knew the ins and outs of the map, greater authority so as to negotiate for them, not just observe. The ICFY was ready to give him every assistance possible. The US position that it was immoral to put pressure on the Bosnian Muslims would, I felt, stand up only until President Clinton felt a real political need to rid himself of the electoral liability of Bosnia. I was afraid that this might not happen until nearer the 1996 presidential election campaign, when the Republican Party might try to do to President Clinton over Bosnia what Clinton had quite successfully done to President Bush. This interpretation of US domestic politics was reinforced when at the end of January the US Senate approved by 89 to 9 an amendment to the State Department Authorization Bill which urged President Clinton to lift the arms embargo.

The only activity the ICFY could sensibly undertake was to refine our suggestions for an arbitration commission, which I explained in a COREU stimulated by a suggestion from the Dutch Foreign Minister.[159] Also, we had to do our best to safeguard the main elements of the EU Action Plan. This looked as if it was going to be unpicked when, in front of Islamic governments, the US Ambassador to the UN, Madeleine Albright, spoke in terms of an aim of 40 per cent of Bosnia-Herzegovina for the Bosnian Muslims. I

wrote to Douglas Hurd to see if this rumour could be countered immediately,[160] because if it became US policy it would finally kill off the EU
Action Plan and leave a yawning political vacuum. Apparently the figure of
40 per cent had arisen in a brainstorming meeting held by Ambassador
Albright on 1 February and was not to be taken as a policy suggestion. The
US claimed they did not wish to reject any elements of the peace plan
already accepted by all three parties and they regarded the one-third figure
for the Bosnian Muslims as falling into this category. The flexibility the
Americans sought from the negotiating process over the EU Action Plan
referred only to those elements of the plan not yet agreed by all the parties.
This was an important clarification and it laid the foundation for the
Contact Group map. Essentially, the 33.5 per cent we had extracted in the
Serb map for the predominantly Muslim republic and the 17.5 per cent
offered but never drawn on a map by the Serbs for the predominantly
Croatian republic stayed, and these figures were added up to form the 51
per cent for the Muslim–Croat Federation.

We held a meeting of the ICFY Steering Committee in Geneva on
2 February,[161] which served as a wider forum for countries to accept the
depressing truth that while the three parties remained determined to fight
on, there was little to be done.

Could the EU Action Plan have succeeded? This was the first time that
EU Foreign Ministers had themselves negotiated as a group on a major
issue. Given all the obvious difficulties of coordinating twelve governments,
the preparation for and the handling of the negotiations had been well done.
The Bosnian Muslims had on offer by December 1993 a viable republic
within Bosnia-Herzegovina which they could defend with their own troops
and which, if they wished, after a satisfactory negotiation over Sarajevo
following on from the UN administration, could have been the basis for an
independent state of Bosnia. The European Union was never opposed to a
separate Muslim state if that came about by popular consent. The one
essential element missing was US support when it was needed in the middle
of December, particularly in offering a NATO guarantee for the boundaries
of the Muslim republic. A more self-confident EU would have sent a firm
message to the Americans: 'Unless you support this plan fully and make this
clear to the Bosnian government, all EU member states who are contributing
to UNPROFOR will serve notice to the UN that they will pull out their
contingents in the early spring of 1994.' The EU, instead, attached tremendous importance to involving the US and not going it alone, and the
US knew it. A further attempt to involve the US administration was
now inevitable, although all the indications were that it would not be
easy to develop with them either a coherent policy or one which would be
implemented, let alone imposed.

7

The Contact Group

I WAS AT HOME IN WILTSHIRE when I heard from the Press Association that at 12.37 that afternoon, Saturday 5 February 1994, a mortar bomb had exploded in the open-air market in the centre of Sarajevo near the Presidency building, killing 49 people and wounding over 200 others. I immediately contacted UNPROFOR headquarters in Zagreb and was warned that the death toll might rise. It eventually reached 69.

UNPROFOR had confirmed that the explosion in the middle of a large crowd of civilians who were shopping in the market on a Saturday afternoon, was caused by a single 120 mm mortar bomb fired from north-east of the market. However, UNPROFOR military experts, after analysing the explosion crater, had not so far been able to determine with certainty exactly where the mortar had been launched from. Yasushi Akashi, Special Representative of the Secretary-General, expressed his outrage and that of the whole international community at this unspeakable act of barbarity, and said he would travel to Sarajevo the next day with the UNPROFOR Commander, General Jean Cot.

I spoke to Thorvald Stoltenberg in Rome and agreed what we as Co-Chairmen of the ICFY would say to the press. After expressing our horror at the massacre, we said that at a meeting with Dr Karadzic in Pale that very morning our representative, General Bo Pellnas, had received an assurance from the Bosnian Serbs that they were ready to negotiate on UN administration and demilitarization of Sarajevo district as defined in the peace plan under discussion in Geneva, and to do so urgently in advance of a final settlement in Bosnia-Herzegovina. The concept had first been put to the Bosnian Serbs in Geneva on 19 January. We would now follow up this important development, which was about to be discussed in the confidence-building talks actually taking place at Sarajevo airport when news of a shell having landed in the market-place in Sarajevo came in. In the light of that day's tragedy, we decided to fly to Belgrade the next day to meet

Dr Karadzic in order to demand the urgent implementation of a separate political and military peace agreement involving Sarajevo district as the first step to an overall peace settlement. So as not to clash with Akashi's meeting we planned to meet in the evening of Sunday 6 February, at Zvornik on the border.

On the Saturday I also spoke to Douglas Hurd, who was due to speak with Warren Christopher and Alain Juppé, and thanked him for the RAF making available a plane to fly me to Rome next morning to pick up Thorvald Stoltenberg and then on to Belgrade. It was clear that there would be activity in the Security Council and the North Atlantic Council, and Douglas hoped to be able to agree a positive line of action soon but felt that nothing they were contemplating conflicted with our strategy; rather, they complemented each other. I drove up to appear on the Sunday BBC breakfast-time programme with David Frost and then on to the RAF air base at Northolt in London.

As I read telegrams and newspapers on the plane about discussions in New York it became apparent that Alain Juppé wanted more than just air strikes and was hoping for a major initiative to end the siege of Sarajevo. UNPROFOR were clear that the day before the market-place bomb the Bosnian Serbs had been responsible for action in Dobrinja, a Sarajevo suburb, which had killed ten people, and were ready to use this to justify a UN request for NATO action even if the responsibility for the market-place bomb was less clear. I only discovered later that while the Americans wanted heavy weapons removed in Sarajevo they were even then wary of committing to demilitarization of the city as they felt it might mean putting them in conflict with the Muslim leadership. We, on that Sunday, felt our main task was to convince Karadzic that he should negotiate constructively with the UN to exclude heavy weapons from Sarajevo and see it as part of the wider demilitarization agreement that he had told General Pellnas on Saturday morning he was ready to accept. We knew that with the Serbs it was always easiest to develop a line of policy already agreed, and we had been talking to them about our 'Sarajevo first' initiative for a month since seeing Krajisnik privately in Paris. We met Karadzic overlooking the Drina in Zvornik, we having travelled by car from Belgrade, he from Pale. We convinced him that he should continue the discussions he had already had that day with Akashi and General Rose about excluding heavy weapons as part of a general demilitarization. We issued a press statement and I reported by COREU to Foreign Ministers.[162] For the Serbs, to negotiate about heavy weapons only was against their interest, for while they had the vast bulk of such weapons they felt they needed these to offset the preponderance of Bosnian government infantry, who for their part needed Serb heavy weapons to be removed. The Bosnian Serbs were also very angry about the constant use of the word 'ultimatum' because it was the emotive word used by the Germans before the bombing of Belgrade in 1941. Karadzic was vehement in denying that his forces had fired a mortar bomb into the market-place and claimed that it had been done by the Muslims. Having now been exposed for eighteen months to the three parties' claims and counter-claims I was capable of believing that any of them could have been responsible.

Thorvald and I flew back from Belgrade into Brussels on Monday morning for the meeting of the FAC. In the car driving into the Charlemagne building I was given a summary of press and government attitudes from around the world as I had not seen or heard much reporting for nearly twenty-four hours. The French media were focusing massively on the carnage in Sarajevo. The Serbs were being blamed, and the feeling was that enough was enough and that action must now be taken. The ultimatum proposed by France, giving the Serbs a few days to remove their heavy weapons, was widely supported. There was some criticism of the US for its alleged unwillingness to join in imposing a peace settlement on the belligerents. But there was no evidence of much planning beyond the ultimatum. The effect of air strikes on humanitarian aid or the safety of UNPROFOR troops was not discussed.

A long and lively discussion began as soon as we arrived at the Charlemagne building. The Greek Foreign Minister, Karolos Papoulias, for the Presidency, introduced the discussion by saying that we should stand by the principles of the EU peace plan and try to find ways of breathing new life into it. He then gave the floor to me. Unusually for me, I had prepared speaking notes on the plane and I spoke from these.[163] In retrospect, I did not focus enough on Juppé's ultimatum, which some ministers considered was the only issue to discuss. I had come straight from talking with the Serbs and had not been able to watch the television coverage on Sunday and Monday morning. I circulated a shorter version of my six points to the meeting. I urged them to stick to the EU Action Plan and to try for a 'Sarajevo first' policy with UN administration and demilitarization. I warned that if we did not make the distinction between close air support and punitive air strikes we would lose the Russians. I further argued that EU administration of Mostar should take place as soon as possible and in advance of a settlement.

Alain Juppé spoke immediately after me with passion and clarity. He agreed that we should stick to the EU plan. But the siege in Sarajevo had to be lifted. An ultimatum, preferably giving the Serbs a few days to withdraw from a 30 km exclusion zone around Sarajevo, was needed. This would involve risks for UNPROFOR, but these had to be taken. The Spanish Foreign Minister Javier Solana said our aim should be to reach a modus vivendi in Sarajevo. The military side was important, but we should concentrate on the possibility of progress on Sarajevo through the peace process. For Denmark, Helveg Petersen hoped that tackling Sarajevo first was practical. We needed to look carefully at the pros and cons of using air strikes. Andreatta said Italy could go along with the idea of an ultimatum and accepted that any air strikes should target Serbian command and control systems. We also needed to tackle the involvement of Croatian government troops in Bosnia.

Douglas Hurd said that on Sarajevo an ultimatum might be the right answer. Before we could decide, however, we needed to address such questions as: Were the military assets available adequate? Were the risks reasonable? What effect would military action have on UNHCR's activities and the humanitarian effort? These were matters for NATO to assess and therefore it was right that NATO should take the decisions, though the role of Rose, Cot and Akashi would be crucial. He added that it was well worth pursuing my idea of a separate peace agreement for Sarajevo.

For the Netherlands, Peter Kooijmans strongly supported Juppé, as did Belgium's Willy Claes. Claes also said that it was right to ask for answers to the sort of questions raised by Douglas Hurd, but ultimately the need to defend civilized values must prevail. It was for politicians, therefore, not soldiers to take the final decisions. Claes could not accept any easing of sanctions against Serbia. Jacques Poos for Luxembourg drew attention to recent comments by General Briquemont and US Defense Secretary William Perry on the dangers of resorting to air strikes, and he asked that my six points be included in the FAC's conclusions.

Klaus Kinkel said he could do nothing because of Germany's constitutional position. But the spotlight was on the EU. They could not leave the Council and face the press without having taken clear decisions. He proposed a long press statement, including the possibility of presenting the Serbs with a one-week ultimatum. He believed we should examine with the Russians the shape of air action and its consequences. The Portuguese Minister, Barroso, said that the EU was not trying to satisfy public opinion, but to help achieve peace. It would be important to sort out the details of possible US involvement. It would be wrong for the EU to try to decide on a military ultimatum – that was for the NAC. Van den Broek for the Commission supported Juppé. US involvement was essential. We needed to work out with the Americans and the Muslims what our bottom line was.

Juppé intervened again to say that he was not responding to public opinion, but to the need to preserve the values of civilization. It was impossible to be certain of the consequences of air strikes, but the experts had had six months to consider this. He was against reproducing my six points in the conclusions. He favoured a recast FAC statement in which the EU would agree to argue within NATO for an ultimatum to be issued to the Serbs. I replied that in talking of 'lifting the siege' Juppé was technically incorrect and had oversimplified the situation. Those parts of Sarajevo which the Serbs controlled, like Grbavica, would not give up heavy weapons unless they had negotiated safeguards involving UN forces against being overrun by superior numbers of Muslim infantry. The road blocks, the small arms sniping, the confrontation line would only be lifted by detailed negotiations; excluding heavy weapons was valuable, but it would not of itself lift the siege. Also, 30 km was too wide an exclusion zone and was an old Muslim proposal from the demilitarization talks of December 1992; and more time was needed, at least seven days rather than three, to get the heavy weapons out. The time fixed for any deadline ought to be set by the UN and only implemented by NATO. NATO might lose some planes and unless the West was prepared for large-scale ground intervention we did not require a crystal ball to see what could happen. Vukovar was a clear precedent. Stoltenberg asked what would happen after the first air strikes in Sarajevo to UN personnel and to the humanitarian aid programme. He added that only eight towns were now at issue between the Bosnians and the Serbs on the maps. It was difficult to see this as sufficient justification for continuing a civil war.

The Greek Presidency concluded that we should continue to maintain and promote the EU plan. We should cooperate closely with the US and, if possible, the Russians. Papoulias said he knew that France had wanted to reach agreement today on an ultimatum, but he hoped that his proposed conclusion that these matters should be discussed in NATO was acceptable. Juppé said that he could accept this as a minimum, but with sadness. He hoped that the NAC would show more backbone than the FAC. Helveg Petersen asked that something be added to the conclusions condemning Croatian regular forces being in Bosnia, but Kinkel was not keen and suggested that a reference be made instead to the need for progress over opening Tuzla airport. Neither of these suggestions was in the end taken up. Juppé had moved the debate closer to the ultimatum, but I had won two more crucial days' negotiating time for the UN, which General Rose then used to great effect. My argument was not against enforcement action but I was horrified to see the EU Council being pushed into making military decisions because France wanted action taken immediately and wanted the EU rather than NATO to be the public forum for the decision. Ministers were acting in a very dangerous area, for Sarajevo was a fuse that could ignite much more. I was very worried that the Russians were not being involved sufficiently and the emphasis on NATO to the exclusion of the UN would heighten the Russian sense of indignation at being treated as a second-class power.

Alain Juppé had shown the steely purpose of a good leader, and though he had not won outright he had shifted the Council decisively towards action. He complained to his staff afterwards that Lord Owen 'shot my fox', but he never appeared to hold a grudge. He briefed the French press to the effect that I had been against any action. I was left admiring his drive but felt he had not absorbed all the dangers. But at least he as a Frenchman was prepared to take risks with French UN soldiers' lives, since it was they who were concentrated in Sarajevo. His views therefore demanded respect, for he was accepting real responsibility. Juppé explained fully his interpretation of the French position in a question-and-answer interview for *Le Nouvel Observateur*.[i]

A private meeting took place among NATO ambassadors in Brussels that Monday. I was glad to see that all the questions Stoltenberg and I had raised about the consequences of air strikes, for the citizens of Sarajevo in terms of fiercer shelling, for the peace process, for humanitarian aid and for the safety of UN personnel, were raised by the Canadian representative, but most others seemed even more gung-ho than their ministers. Manfred Woerner was known to be dying of cancer, but with typical courage was ready to come out of hospital and chair the NAC meeting which was fixed for Wednesday 9 February. Also, General Rose's meeting with the parties on excluding heavy weapons in Sarajevo on Monday made significant progress and it looked as if we might get what the UN desperately wanted – a negotiated agreement before the NAC met.

On Tuesday 8 February I wrote to Douglas Hurd querying the US objection to demilitarization and arguing for an exclusion zone smaller than the 30 km radius advocated by the French and accompanied by confidence-building measures.[164] The Bosnian government delegation which was due to negotiate did not however turn up at Sarajevo airport for the negotiating session that morning. General Rose was reportedly furious and went to the Bosnian Presidency to persuade President Izetbegovic and his military chief, General Delic, to attend. Those around General Rose have never made any secret of the fact that at that meeting he told the Bosnian Muslim leaders that he had just received technical information which pointed to the mortar bomb having come not from Serb-controlled areas but from a Muslim-controlled area. If this information were made available there would be a very different outcome in the NATO meeting, and if Izetbegovic tried to stall the UN negotiations in order to wait for the NATO meeting he, Rose, would feel obliged to release the preliminary evidence of the UN investigation. If the government negotiating team were not at Sarajevo airport on Wednesday 9 February then he would call a press conference. General Rose himself has been more circumspect about what happened at his meeting, but I know that he had sent on Tuesday a report that said the mortar shell might have been launched by the Bosnian army side and that they were continuing their investigation. In addition, a senior ballistics expert in Zagreb had studied a map of likely trajectory patterns produced by UN investigators in Sarajevo and believed the angle at which the mortar had hit the roof of the market stall indicated that the firing point was more likely to be 1,100–2,000 metres from the impact than 2,000–3,000 metres, and that this would tend to indicate that the mortar had been fired from a Bosnian army position. When this highly charged information reached the UN in New York on Tuesday everything was done to clamp down on the number of people who saw it so as to reduce the chance of a press leak. The trouble with that response was that among the UN in Sarajevo the information was more widely known and there was every chance that it would reach the Russians as well as the Bosnian Serbs. In the Serbs' mood of extreme paranoia and resentment at being held responsible for something they still maintained they had not done, a cover-up by the UN would have been highly damaging. Yet the basic problem of the siege of Sarajevo still demanded that we try to stop the shelling, and the fact that the Muslims might have fired on their own people to provoke NATO to come in and fight on their side, one of their long-standing objectives, did not alter the need for preventive action.

Thorvald Stoltenberg and I also had advance information that the Yugoslav press agency, Tanjug, was about to issue a story datelined Sarajevo 8 February saying that the Serbs expected the UN ballistic experts to confirm the content of leaked UNPROFOR documents about the shell which caused the tragedy in Sarajevo's open market. Tanjug claimed:[165]

The spot from where it was fired is some 1–1.5 km inside the territory under Muslim control, measured from the demarcation line with the RS army positions. This fact was confirmed tonight for Tanjug by highly reliable and confidential sources within UNPROFOR HQs who wished to remain anonymous, and it was also stated in the report by UNPROFOR's Commission of Experts that conducted an investigation. The report was sent this morning to the UN HQ in New York.

I later sent this passage, in quotes, in a COREU dated 12 February. Unfortunately the Greek Presidency transmitted the COREU without the quotes, so at a later stage when we had our first leak of my COREU telegrams it was construed that the passage in my telegram, without quotes, was my opinion rather than Tanjug's. But at that precise moment on Tuesday evening in Geneva we had to determine ICFY's stance. We had been tipped off that Karadzic would state on Thursday morning that he could only negotiate if we would agree to a commission of inquiry, with representatives nominated by the Muslim and Serb parties, to investigate the mortar incident. We knew that the UN in New York were going to be very anxious about conceding to any such demand and might attempt to stifle the report which they had had from UNPROFOR, on the basis that it was not an official commission of inquiry, just experts in the field. We knew that if the Bosnian Serbs got a negative response over establishing an inquiry the Geneva talks would collapse. Our dilemma was acute, for if the slightest hint that the Muslims were thought to be responsible came out of the ICFY in Geneva, the Bosnian Muslims would not attend. NATO, having just taken its decision, would also be in disarray if the public perception of the Serbs being responsible for the market-place bomb were suddenly shattered. What was needed was a little news management of the sort that international organizations are not very good at; above all, the UN in New York had to come under pressure from the press to establish the facts, and I arranged quietly that this was done. I did not feel it was right for me to do anything more than this. I was in receipt of privileged information from the UN. I could not allow a cover-up, but equally it was not for me to break the story. I knew, however, that if the press was hammering at the UN's door the Secretary-General would be advised to accede to our request, which we intended to convey to him the next day, to grant Karadzic an inquiry.

What was vitally important was that General Rose's straight talking to President Izetbegovic had a powerful impact on the Muslim leadership and they authorized their military to turn up on Wednesday at Sarajevo airport. In the late afternoon – fortunately well before the NATO declaration was agreed late that night – the UN had an all-party agreement to a Sarajevo exclusion zone that did not mention NATO air strikes or a NATO ultimatum. In this way the Bosnian Serbs' face was somewhat saved. But to the world's media the UN agreement was of little consequence. They gave every appearance of longing for a ringside seat at an air-launched firework show.

Manfred Woerner told the NAC at the start of their meeting that this was a decisive moment for NATO: the eyes of the world were upon them, and the only way to answer the challenge was by acting, and acting that day. The question that haunted the whole discussion was how far outside the exclusion zone NATO wanted to go in hitting Serb electronic warfare and surface-to-air missile sites. Eventually, after ten hours of discussion, a Council decision text was agreed.[166] It was compatible with the UN-negotiated agreement and gave the Bosnian Serbs ten days to withdraw, or regroup and place under UNPROFOR control, all heavy weapons, including tanks, artillery pieces, mortars, multiple rocket launchers, missiles and anti-aircraft weapons, and the Bosnian government the same period to put their heavy weapons too under UNPROFOR control; it defined the exclusion zone as 20 km from the centre of Sarajevo, excluding an area within 2 km of the Bosnian Serb working capital, Pale. It prudently made no specific mention of the market-place bombing incident, something which surprisingly was never commented on by the press but was an indication that some within NATO had already been tipped off about the need for the decision to be a free-standing one, not linked to any particular incident. As far as the text related to us negotiators, the EU Action Plan had been commended and the US had dropped their objection to demilitarization with the wording 'commends the current effort of UN negotiators towards securing the demilitarization of Sarajevo'.

The decision was one of the few operational decisions NATO has ever had to take and it took them into a new non-Article 5 role and mission. Woerner's mistake in his press conference, which I watched on television from my hotel in Geneva, was to overplay NATO at the expense of the UN, so that the fact that it had been taken in response to a request from the UN Secretary-General was lost sight of. Later, when problems arose with the UN dual key, the public saw UN impartiality as NATO weakness, which did considerable damage to its record as the most successful of all multi-national organizations. NATO's real interest was to make it clear from the start that this was not a NATO operation but a NATO action on behalf of the UN, subject to all the limitations of UN operations.

On Wednesday 9 February in Geneva our dialogue with the neighbouring states went off pleasantly enough, but it lacked substance and I felt it was not likely to develop any momentum of its own. I reported on our talks to the EU in a COREU,[167] and also attached a report on the history of our 'Sarajevo first' approach.

Predictably, before the Conference session started on 10 February the Bosnian Serbs said they would not negotiate until an inquiry was established, and wanted the inquiry to include both Serb and Muslim representatives. This was resisted by Silajdzic, who was attending the meeting in Geneva instead of Izetbegovic. Eventually it was agreed, following contact with the UN in New York and with Akashi in Zagreb, that both parties could appoint liaison officers who would follow the work of an official UNPROFOR investigation rather than participate in it. Finally, late on Thursday afternoon, discussions on substantive questions finally got under way.[168] We explained in bilateral meetings what we wanted in our Sarajevo 'first approach' and agreed to meet in plenary session the next day. We had useful discussions with the Croats. Mate Boban had stepped down and the Bosnian Croats had a new commander, General Ante Roso, which helped maintain a good atmosphere even after the Croatian government Foreign Minister, Granic, who got on well with Silajdzic, had returned to Zagreb. Karadzic reluctantly recommitted himself to a Union of Three Republics and to a two-year transitional period of UN administration of Sarajevo, after which he still hoped for a referendum on independence. Silajdzic was unwilling to discuss with the Croatians any boundary line between their two republics in central Bosnia, and we got our first hint of what became the Federation with the Croatian representative in the Bosnian government delegation producing a cantonal map which would have the effect of bringing the two republics together. Silajdzic became particularly incensed discussing central Bosnia, saying that delineating boundaries meant drawing lines with blood, and returned to the idea of a unified state which the Bosnian Croats rejected.

During this time there were slightly contradictory signals about Russian attitudes. I was being briefed by Churkin and Redman in Geneva and also from London. It appeared that after numerous delays, some technical and some because Yeltsin genuinely had flu, Clinton finally managed to speak to Yeltsin by telephone on 11 February. Clinton apparently explained the rationale behind the NATO decision and asked for Russian support, saying that NATO was being even-handed between the Serbs and the Muslims and that the US would use their influence with the Muslims to try to bring about a negotiated settlement. Clinton also apparently stressed that he had tried to talk to Yeltsin before the NATO decision, but this had proved impossible.

Yeltsin was claimed to have said that he did not think there was any disagreement over the decision NATO had taken and he did not want any misunderstandings over this to become exaggerated. Russia shared the same objectives, namely to end the bombardment of Sarajevo, and to promote a political settlement. But he felt there was a need for a new mandate from the UN to authorize UNPROFOR to take control of the weapons around Sarajevo. This might take the form of a new UNSCR. Apparently Clinton said that he did not think a new UNSCR was necessary.

Churkin, however, was taking a tougher line than the Americans claimed Yeltsin had taken and he said Kozyrev was too, which I had confirmed to me by the British. In essence, the Churkin interpretation of the Russian view was that they still wanted cooperation with the West but they had to be consulted properly in advance. Window-dressing consultation was not enough and did not deceive them. The Russians were pressing the case for a Security Council on 11 February, to result in a new Security Council Resolution which could be presented to Russian public opinion as the most important event of the week, taking precedence over the Sarajevo UN agreement and the NATO deadline. It would also demonstrate a unified position among the four permanent members of the Security Council actively involved in the former Yugoslavia. A Security Council Resolution was, they claimed, not only desirable domestically but also necessary as UNPROFOR had no mandate to monitor artillery, nor was the 20 km radius around Sarajevo defined in a Security Council Resolution. A new, innovative mandate needed to be adopted. The UN Secretary-General's key role in calling for air strikes or air support also needed to be reiterated.

The NATO countries, however, had no wish to open up every aspect of NATO's decision in New York. They claimed the NATO approach was a change of method, not a change of policy, and was firmly rooted in existing UN Security Council Resolutions. The British and French were also worried about others in the Security Council, not just Russia. The previous year they had had a real difficulty over the arms embargo and it was still not clear that they would now succeed in seeing off pressure from the Islamic countries and the Americans to have the embargo lifted. I was hearing from Churkin a more alarmist, even pleading, note than was coming from either Yeltsin or Kozyrev, and from my recent visit I sensed Churkin's reading of the Russian military was accurate, for he had good contacts. But when I talked to Redman he told me he was receiving a much more nuanced message from Churkin. I judged Churkin was not yet sure which way Yeltsin would go and was deliberately sending mixed signals, a worrying situation as the deadline approached with still no real movement from the Bosnian Serbs. It was starting to look as if the Bosnian Serbs were playing poker with dynamite. Meanwhile negotiations continued in Geneva and in national capitals.[169]

On Tuesday 15 February in Moscow Major and Hurd received a veritable blast from President Yeltsin about NATO air strikes, first publicly at their initial meeting in the Kremlin and subsequently even more toughly in private conversations over the next two days. It was as if Yeltsin had somewhat belatedly realized that air strikes were likely, that his public opinion would not accept his acquiescence in their happening, and that this could be the moment when the Russian rapprochement with Europe and the Americans hit the buffers of nationalist opinion in Russia. It was never the issue itself that was the sticking point so much as the humiliation of being pushed to the sidelines. Yeltsin's sense of national pride was hit, and the bruise was beginning to swell. On Monday 14 February the UN had asked if Russian troops stationed in Sector East UNPA in Croatia could be moved to Sarajevo to help police the UN-brokered military agreement. The Russians refused.

I had planned before the market-place bomb to write to the Greek Presidency after this round of Geneva talks and say I now wished to step down. Frustrated at the ever-present gap between rhetoric and reality on the Security Council, I felt that at least the US were now becoming engaged in the diplomatic search for a peace and that someone from the EU with better relations with them would be able to influence them.

My worry now was whether after the market-place bomb I could stand down when we were still in the middle of the ultimatum period, for I did not want to weaken the cohesion of the EU which was under some strain. If I went now it would look like a resignation; but it might look even more so if I went a few weeks after the ultimatum expired.

I returned to my home in Wiltshire for the weekend and decided to draft both a letter to the Greek President saying I would step down and a final COREU to the Foreign Ministers, and then consult Douglas Hurd. I did not want to appear to be resigning publicly in the wake of the bombing that I

thought was now very likely after the Bosnian Serbs had not complied with
NATO's deadline of the following weekend. But I felt I could just squeeze
notification to the Greek Presidency of my decision to go in now before the
deadline which might need to be announced publicly later. I tried to contact
Douglas Hurd on the Saturday but only spoke to him on the Sunday
evening, when I read out to him my proposed letter. He seemed surprised
and worried that I had released or was about to release it publicly, then
relieved when he realized that I was genuinely consulting him and had
neither sent the letter nor was demanding it be public at that stage. I owed
both Major and Hurd genuine consultations and not a bounce. I felt more
than a little guilty at leaving at that juncture anyhow. Hurd wanted to
consult the Prime Minister and, since he was going to Moscow, asked if we
could meet and discuss my stepping down on his return. I felt this would
bring sending my letter too close to the deadline and thus risked its being
misconstrued as a resignation over any air strikes. Douglas Hurd rang back
on Monday 14 February, but from Moscow, despite messages that he would
ring me from his car en route to the plane. Talking from Moscow was a
major inhibition, but he made it clear that the Prime Minister was unhappy
for me to go so soon. It was a clever way of handling me, playing for time
and hoping that I would at least stay on for a few more months. I had no
option other than to stay, and I sent out a revised COREU the next day.[170]
It argued that before starting widespread bombing the NAC should tie the
Americans down over their negotiating position and their attitude to the EU
Action Plan, for the outcome I dreaded most was having air strikes in a
political vacuum. We needed to be able to point to a viable peace settlement, otherwise we could be bombing to defeat the Serbs rather than to
help bring about a negotiated settlement. The COREU ended by saying: 'I
am not passing the buck when I say I am convinced that the European
responsibility for a peace settlement in Bosnia-Herzegovina, as distinct from
the former Yugoslavia, must now pass from the ICFY and the EU input
should be through NATO and the Security Council, while leaving ICFY to
continue its important work in other areas such as the Krajina talks,
Kosovo, minorities and succession issues.' The Washington Post that day
had run a story out of Sarajevo saying that General Rose was aiming to
'monitor' rather than 'control' heavy weapons as it became clear that more
weapons would have to be regrouped within the zone. With less than a
week to go until the deadline the Serbs had turned over only thirty-three
heavy weapons from their arsenal of hundreds, whereas the Muslims with
a much smaller number of heavy weapons had handed in ten. But this disappointing return was matched by a marked fall in the incoming shelling and
during the last week there had been only one fatality.

The US were pushing to have a clear understanding in advance as to the
arrangements for the use of air power after expiry of the deadline. Akashi,

Presidents Tudjman and Milosevic study the EU Action Plan, Geneva, December 1993.

The sixteenth-century bridge at Mostar: before and after.

Above: Yasushi Akashi at the bombed marketplace in Sarajevo, February 1994.
Below: General Mladic (extreme right) ordering the shelling of Gorazde, 23 April 1994.

Above: On HMS *Invincible*, 20 September 1993: the Co-Chairmen meet the parties and Presidents. *Below:* Geneva, August 1993: the Co-Chairmen discuss the Union of Three Republics – round table clockwise from bottom left: Akmadzic, Krajisnik, Karadzic, DO, interpreter, Stoltenberg, Izetbegovic, Abdic, Boban.

Above: The ICFY team, September 1993: left to right, Geert Ahrens, Jean-Pierre Masset, DO, Thorvald Stoltenberg, Bertie Ramcharan, Martti Ahtisaari, Jean Durieux, Vincente Berasategui. *Below:* At the Vatican, 15 October 1993.

Above: Splitting the Serbs: President Milosevic distancing himself from Karadzic, Krajisnik and Buha. *Below:* Maps past midnight.

Above: Ejup Ganic with General Sir Michael Rose, Sarajevo, 1994.
Below: The Co-Chairmen with Hrvoe Sarinic, head of President Tudjman's office, Zagreb, December 1994.

Serb refugees from the Krajina are shelled by Croats, August 1995.

Cot, Boorda and Rose had met again recently and since the previous August well-understood military procedures for the control of air power had been worked out and put in place. This was effectively a dual-key procedure. Only in circumstances where the UNPROFOR and NATO commanders were unable to agree would it be necessary to revert for guidance to political authorities. Boorda had proposed to Akashi that, should there be a disagreement, he and Akashi should meet to discuss an agreed line to take.

UNPROFOR was considering what should happen if on D-Day + 10 some 98 per cent of the weapons had been removed or put under UN control but 2 per cent remained. The US felt that no doubt must be left in the minds of the Serbs that all weapons must be withdrawn or UN-controlled by D + 10; they did not wish to hear on day 9 or 10 arguments about the vulnerability of UNHCR or UN troops on the ground. It was the US view that if the UN were to have credibility there must be 100 per cent compliance. 'Placed under control' meant weapons being secured, not any lesser state such as monitoring. It was important that this should be defined ahead of time.

On Wednesday 16 February, two days after saying no, the Russians went back to the UN and accepted moving their troops from the UNPA East in Croatia to Sarajevo, saying they would move them in through Serbia as quickly as possible, some coming immediately during the night. On Thursday, General Mladic was confronted by fellow officers in the Yugoslav army and told that with Russian troops coming into the most sensitive areas for the Serbs he had to order his heavy weapons out of the exclusion zone or regroup them, and this time they insisted he did as he was told. The Bosnian Serbs started to move their weapons that afternoon with snow falling on the mountain slopes. The Russian initiative seemed to have been taken without informing the US and without the knowledge of Major and Hurd in Moscow. The Russians had not hidden their intense irritation at the NATO decision, from which they felt excluded. They warned that Mladic would be delighted if NATO air strikes took place, since it would unite all Serbs and give him the freedom he did not currently have. This was also our reading of Mladic in the ICFY.

The Russian initiative, announced on Thursday 17 February, gave them a spectacular coup. Most Europeans were fulsome in their welcome for the Russian UN troops coming into Sarajevo. In Washington the reaction was more reserved. They appeared to fear that the presence of Russian UN troops in the Serb areas like Grbavica would inhibit air strikes and were most reluctant to involve the Russian formally with NATO decision-making. There were still people in Washington hoping that air strikes could be launched against truant Serb artillery.

On 20 February Akashi announced that he was satisfied that effective compliance had been achieved with the requirement to remove or place under UNPROFOR control all heavy weapons within the zone and that it was not necessary at this stage for him to request the use of NATO air power. Some said this was a vindication of the threat of air strikes and a sign that the Bosnian Serbs would crumble under threat. I felt that it was the Russians who had taken the threat of NATO air strikes seriously and that it was their decision to move their troops to Sarajevo which had forced Mladic to act over his heavy weapons. We had gone very close, in my judgement, to stretching the elastic in the Russian–Western relationship to breaking point. The crisis was yet another warning to push on faster and achieve a permanent peace settlement and to involve both the Russians and the Americans in so doing.

The United States then began to involve itself in the search for a negotiated settlement. The Americans successfully sponsored negotiations between the Bosnian Muslims – now called 'Bosniacs', an old appellation recently revived – and the Bosnian Croats, in which the government of the Republic of Croatia also joined. The first results of these negotiations were a 'Framework Agreement for the Federation' and an 'Outline of a Preliminary Agreement on the Principles and Foundations for the Establishment of a Confederation Between the Republic of Croatia and the Federation'.[171] President Tudjman, in a special broadcast to the Croatian nation on 3 March to present these agreements, described them as of historic and far-reaching significance and the best way of defending the national interest in present international circumstances, saying that Croatia now had the support of the international community, including that of some countries which had once been against Croatian independence. Wisely, Tudjman made a particular point of emphasizing that a Croat–Muslim federation was not directed against the Bosnian Serbs, nor was it a preparation for the renewal of hostilities. Croatia would continue to seek a peaceful political solution on outstanding issues and the normalization of Croatian–Serbian relations on the basis of mutual recognition of sovereignty and territorial integrity.

In Belgrade Milosevic, after seeing Redman, said that a Muslim–Croat agreement was not a matter for the Serbs so long as their interests were not affected. Nor did the Bosnian Serbs over-react, as might have been expected, because they saw that the Americans, by recognizing that the Croats and the Muslims could have a confederation with Croatia, had made it hard to deprive the Serbs of the same right to choose.

On 13 March in Vienna a final agreement on the Constitution of the Federation of Bosnia and Herzegovina was reached.[172] A signing ceremony at Blair House, presided over by President Clinton, was fixed and Thorvald and I were invited to attend, as was the EU Troika. In London on 14 March at a press conference, I said: 'Brokering the Muslim–Croat arrangement, particularly dealing with the need to bring its armed forces together, was much better done by, in this case, the United States with some help from Germany,' adding: 'It would have been very, very difficult indeed for us to have done it, without compromising our impartiality.'

In Washington on 18 March 1994 President Clinton presided over the signing ceremony of the 'Preliminary Agreement Concerning the Establishment of a Confederation Between the Federation of Bosnia and Herzegovina and the Republic of Croatia'. The ceremony was also attended by Tudjman, Izetbegovic, the EU Troika, the Turkish, Austrian and Canadian Foreign Ministers, and myself and Stoltenberg. Vitaly Churkin was present, as was the main architect of the Federation, Chuck Redman.

I met President Clinton before the signing of the ceremony for a short private talk almost by chance. He was in the centre of the reception room in Blair House, talking to Croat and Muslim political leaders, and I was holding back on the fringe of the room when he broke away and came up, having never met me before, with hand outstretched, saying, 'I am so sorry Cy Vance couldn't come today.' It was an opening bound to win my heart and we chatted away animatedly for a few minutes, during which I reminded him that both of us were saying the same thing about the use of air power in July 1992. He smiled, saying, 'it's a lot harder in government.' He is a much larger man when you meet him than you expect from television. He has the gift of empathy and a relaxed manner. Even in that short time I thought what a pity it was that he gave so little of his time to foreign affairs and how much better it would have been if he had made more of the political judgements himself earlier, instead of leaving so much of the conduct of foreign policy on the Balkans to the so-called 'Principals'.

In his speech President Clinton wisely did not overdramatize the importance of the Agreement, describing it as a first step in the right direction.[173] But there was a general air of bemusement about what this step really signified. Above all, was this Federation a natural or an artificial creation? Up until now many of us watching and listening to these particular political leaders had formed the impression that there was an even greater incompatibility between Croats and Muslims than between Serbs and Muslims. But this tension was inspired by Croats from Western Herzegovina, and not so apparent among Zagreb Croats and those who lived around Bihac. So there was some ground for hoping that the Federation might have real potential. I felt that much would depend on the personal relationship existing between the two Foreign Ministers, Granic and Silajdzic.

When he met the EU Troika, President Tudjman was less committed to the Agreement than in his public speech. He implied that the US would now back him to the hilt in squeezing a deal out of the Krajina Serbs. In the EU there was some anxiety about how far the Americans had gone in promising not to alter the sanctions regime imposed on the FRY because of the war in

Bosnia-Herzegovina until there was a settlement in Croatia as well.

When I talked to President Izetbegovic he showed little enthusiasm for the whole proceedings, particularly when authenticating with President Tudjman the text on the Confederation between the Federation and Croatia, which looks a doubtful starter. He wanted Turkish UN troops on the ground and had told the Americans he would accept the Greeks if that was a necessary condition. As to the ICFY, our conversation confirmed my January impression that his primary relationship was now with the US. I wondered whether he had not put himself so far within the Croatian embrace that the Bosnian Muslims would either suffocate or restart their war with the Croats. Much would depend on what influence the Americans brought to bear on Tudjman.

In a Washington background briefing for the press Redman said the constitution would not be put up for formal approval until it was clear whether the Serbs wanted to participate in the Federation, but he agreed that all the signs were against Serb involvement. And indeed, on 22 March the Serbs duly demanded delineation of the borders of Republika Srpska with the Croat–Muslim Federation and recognition as an independent state.

On television in Washington on 22 March Redman was very generous, saying:

> *Almost everything that we have done has been built, in large measure, on the work that has been done by the Conference, by Lord Owen, Mr Stoltenberg, by the European Union and the engagement of their Ministers, particularly in November and December and on into January and February, so that we had added our weight to that effort. No doubt we have brought some new elements to the table just by virtue of having another actor, and it may also be that the time is right, that the parties have sensed that this is the time to move to a negotiated solution, so we may be profiting from a more favourable environment in that sense.*
>
> *But the bottom line here is that none of this is going to get done at the end of the day unless all of us stick together, and that's why I have always stressed from the very start of our more intensive engagement that this was a real partnership with the European Union, with whom we began this diplomatic effort, and, secondly, with the Russian Federation, who have been very important players and with whom we have extensive consultation, and, of course, with the United Nations system in general and with the International Conference.*

I was reasonably sanguine, seeing the Federation as a mechanism for ending the Croat–Muslim war, avoiding the need to agree a demarcation line between these two republics and providing a forum in which the less nationalistic Croats might be able to come to the fore and reduce the influence of nationalistic Croats from Western Herzegovina. It was also helpful for keeping the US engaged that their first negotiating initiative had been crowned with success. What was now crucial was that the Americans demonstrated to the Serbs that they were not doing this simply to create an anti-Serb alliance and were not going to become, like Germany, a pro-Croat nation.

Meanwhile in Zagreb negotiations began for the start of an ICFY–American–Russian negotiating partnership, referred to as the Z4 grouping because of the involvement of four people: the US and Russian Ambassadors to Croatia and two diplomats from the ICFY, Geert Ahrens and Kai Eide. Kai was Norwegian and proved to be a tower of strength in Zagreb for the ICFY, getting on well personally with the US Ambassador Galbraith but also being ready to challenge his views.[174]

My wife Debbie and I flew with the Swiss air force to Greece for the Foreign Ministers' informal weekend meeting in Ioannina on Saturday 26 March.. Discussion on Yugoslavia in the afternoon involved a frank discussion during which all eleven other member states made it clear that the Greeks should lift their economic embargo on the Former Yugoslav Republic of Macedonia. Next day we flew to Belgrade and then by helicopter along the Danube to another of Tito's country residences to spend the day with Milosevic and his wife, Mira Markovic. I had wanted to meet her for some time and I had deliberately planned this meeting around my wife's visit to Greece. A Belgrade magazine carried pieces from her diary, which is now available in book form and published in English.[ii] She writes about nature and about her family, reminisces about the delights of Yugoslavia in the 1960s and 1970s, and also discusses politics, with occasional virulent attacks on nationalist leaders like Karadzic, Plavsic and Seselj.

Markovic is a professor at the Faculty of Natural Sciences and Mathematics of the University of Belgrade. A Marxist theorist, as is obvious from her words, she helped found the League of Communists Movement for Yugoslavia (SK-PJ) in 1990, which later became part of JUL (the Yugoslav United Left), and members of her party are increasingly in posts of influence where one might have expected to see members of Milosevic's own party. Before lunch, while walking in the grounds with President Milosevic, I said to him that I had no difficulty in saying that he was not a racist but I could not convince people he was not a nationalist. He put up some arguments as to why he was not a nationalist but he could see that neither Debbie nor I found them convincing. When we returned to the house for lunch and were joined by him and his wife, she came straight to the point, saying: 'I gather from my husband that he has failed to convince you that he is not a nationalist. I will tell you why he is not. I would never have married or stayed married to him if he was a nationalist.' Personally I do not believe that he is a nationalist, or even was one in the late 1980s, but rather that he played the nationalist card to gain and hold power. We had many hours that day of fascinating conversation and I sent a rather unconventional COREU describing them so as to give Foreign Ministers some insight into Milosevic's family background.[175]

It is somewhat bizarre that Mira Markovic had been arguing the case for reconstructing Yugoslavia ever since it fell apart while her husband is widely believed to have been the chief instigator of its break-up. She has encouraged her husband to think in terms of Yugoslavia or, as some diplomats refer to it, 'the Y-word'. She had a shadowy influence on Milosevic in the late 1980s and early 1990s but is now playing a public and decisive part in pulling her husband back from the nationalistic 'Serbia first' stance that went to his head in the late 1980s and early 1990s. Her broader view that reintegration is what Serbian nationhood should be all about will be reflected ever more strongly in his policies. In 1994 she visited and talked to Muslims in the Sandzak on behalf of her party. She is openly championing a return to a confederal relationship. The realist in her probably accepts that, after the fall of the Krajina, Croatia has gone for ever, but I suspect she still hopes that the Muslims in Bosnia-Herzegovina will hive off from the Croats in the Federation and that the Former Yugoslav Republic of Macedonia will be linked economically, and eventually politically, to Serbia and Montenegro. It is not possible to anticipate where Milosevic will lead his country without also analysing the views of his wife. Fortunately he does not take much note of her economic views and shows every sign of wanting his country to have a market economy.

We convened a meeting of the ICFY expanded Steering Committee at ambassadorial level on 30 March in Geneva to bring them up to date following my meeting with EU Foreign Ministers in Ioannina and Stoltenberg's meeting with the Security Council, and to brief them on negotiations in Croatia.[176]

The state of affairs in Gorazde began to cause concern on 4 April when Izetbegovic made several telephone calls to Washington with dire reports about the situation there. The Serbs appeared to have taken several villages in the enclave south of the Drina; artillery was being moved forward and people were fleeing. The Americans knew that General Rose was trying to get into Gorazde and hoped to get Ukrainian troops deployed there, but were very anxious lest an enclave declared by the UN to be a safe area be overrun and wanted to warn the Serbs. This gave rise to a major disagreement over the use of air strikes between the UN on the ground and the US in Washington, New York and NATO. The arguments were political, strategic and technical and continued throughout my time as Co-Chairman.[177]

On Sunday 10 April NATO air power was used against the Bosnian Serb forces attacking Gorazde. I later sent a detailed chronology of events from 10 to 16 April,[178] prepared by General Rose's staff, to EU Foreign Ministers; we also handed this over to Karadzic in an attempt to convince him that, given General Mladic's behaviour, General Rose had no alternative but to call in close air support. Stoltenberg and I met in private with Krajisnik and Koljevic in Daniel Boyer's flat in Paris on 12 April in a meeting during which we tried to keep the Serbs within some form of negotiating framework. It was odd to be so far away and yet so near to the battle going on in Gorazde. Time and time again Krajisnik came back to his belief that taking a firm stand in Gorazde would improve the chances for peace negotiations, and that the Bosnian Serbs should never have agreed to get off Mt Igman the previous August, for this had encouraged the Bosnian Muslims to reject the *Invincible* package. They were now not going to stop until they controlled the town, for they could not justify keeping troops tied down in eastern Bosnia stopping repeated Muslim attacks out of the Gorazde pocket towards the FRY border closest to Sandzak. This was a vital strategic issue for them. Krajisnik was as immovable as granite and left us with the impression that there was no difference between him and Mladic on this issue.

We then flew in the early evening in the French President's plane to Zagreb, after having encountered a student demonstration on Bosnia outside the French National Assembly at the bridge over the Seine. The traffic had suddenly been stopped by a chain hung in front of the car three ahead of ours. Students swarmed everywhere distributing leaflets demanding that more be done to help the Bosnian Muslims in Gorazde. I immediately stepped out of the car on to the pavement and quickly crossed the bridge, avoiding recognition, picked up another car from the Quai d'Orsay and drove to Villacoubly military airfield. The student protest was a vivid reminder of how indignation was mounting in Europe, with considerable justification, not just against the Serbs but also against the perceived impotence of Western governments.

Next morning we flew into Sarajevo and the contrast to my previous visits was immense. There was no background noise of shelling and we drove in a UN armoured Land Rover, not an armoured vehicle, from the airport. We did not go through any roadblocks and the streets were alive with people and vehicles. Apart from the familiar destruction of buildings it was not so different from our drive that morning through Zagreb to the airport, and even the trams were coming back on to the streets. Superficially, the exclusion zone had certainly changed the situation dramatically. Yet the Bosnian Serb army still controlled air, road and rail access to the city. Though the water and electricity services were all functioning normally and lavatories flushed, the precariousness of the city's existence was unchanged.

We met General Rose at his HQ, which was the house where I had stayed with General Morillon. It was now surrounded by many more temporary buildings in the grounds as Rose had brought all the essential elements from Kiseljak, outside Sarajevo, into the city, ending the divided command and control. Both Churkin and Redman were present and we discussed quite dispassionately the case for further close air support. Serb hostage-taking was starting to be a major anxiety but the situation appeared very much under Rose's control. It was my first meeting with him and since I have known a number of people who have served in the SAS the steely informality behind the boyish good looks and the blue eyes, the sometimes breathless, clipped speech and almost simplistic presentation caused me little surprise. But I sensed that Thorvald Stoltenberg found the impression troubling. Though Stoltenberg himself is a typical relaxed Scandinavian he had been surprised that Rose had not been at the airport to meet him. As we drove to Pale after seeing Izetbegovic, he queried whether Rose had the sensitivity to handle all the complex political factors that had to be weighed and I tried to reassure him.

We had dinner in Pale in an old factory with Karadzic and his team and tried to convince them that the impartiality of the UN had not ended merely because of the use of air power. Their mood was fatalistic, expecting further bombs as soon as we left. Pale was blacked out and we stayed in a ski lodge with no electricity before driving down next morning to Sarajevo, where at Rose's HQ we met with Redman and for a brief moment with Churkin, who then left for Pale. As we talked a British major came into the room to say that Tuzla, another safe area, had just been shelled by the Serbs and that they would need permission to call in air support. Instantly General Rose became a different person: the words stopped tumbling out, his questions were precise and detailed, his manner coldly objective and measured. He immediately ran through a range of options, including whether he could use the guns on the Danish Leopard tanks to reply, instead of air power. I felt not just in myself but, more importantly, from Thorvald Stoltenberg sitting beside me a wave of reassurance as we witnessed a transformation from scoutmaster to general. From that moment neither of us had any doubts that the UN forces in Bosnia were lucky to have a very exceptional person leading them, and as his handling of that crisis developed in front of us we felt totally confident that he understood both the power and the limitations of his UN role.

I have no doubt that General Rose and the overall French Force Commander, de Lapresle, were the key people in making it possible for the UN to remain in Bosnia-Herzegovina and feed the population for a third winter. They had that special courage which has the confidence not to need to prove itself. So when even their own British and French political leaders were demanding a more 'robust', 'muscular' UN response, under US pressure to do something stronger, they did not feel obliged to demonstrate their virility. They withstood with cool disdain denigration and disinformation from politicians who should have known better than to criticize field commanders publicly, and from laptop bombardiers, whose journalistic professionalism should have kept them from asking field commanders to put the lives of the people under their command unnecessarily at risk. Throughout, with Akashi, they maintained the only bedrock on which the operation could survive, UN impartiality.

The US initiative over the Croat–Muslim Federation through March and the Russian and US involvement with the two ICFY Ambassadors Ahrens and Eide in brokering a ceasefire between the Croatian government and the Croatian Serbs in Zagreb were both signs that purely EU–UN cooperation was insufficient and that the US and Russia wanted and needed to be fully involved.[179] This view was strengthened after the fighting over Gorazde, when Redman and Churkin in addition to Stoltenberg and myself had been involved in negotiating in Pale, Sarajevo and Belgrade.

Over the Croat–Muslim negotiations in Bosnia-Herzegovina, Redman had already briefed the EU Ad Hoc Group on the former Yugoslavia in Brussels on 15 March and had instituted useful meetings for keeping the French, German and British governments up to date at expert level. The US wanted EU involvement but they were not prepared to get into the business of involving all twelve governments and the Troika mechanism was not very attractive for them. Anything from Europe made little sense if it excluded the British and French, who were necessary for coordinating action in the Security Council within the established procedure of consulting in depth the US and Russia – China, the fifth permanent member, being only intermittently involved, in effect when they wanted to be. Also, at that time, the EU Troika involved the Greek Presidency, a government which was totally out of sympathy with US policy over the Balkans and had abstained within NATO over the exclusion zone decision.

I told Douglas Hurd in a telephone conversation on 14 April that we in the ICFY were ready to go along with the British suggestion to bring in Redman and Churkin as ICFY Co-Chairmen, but I suspected this would have little attraction for the Americans and it soon proved to be a non-starter.

On our flight from Belgrade on the morning of 15 April Stoltenberg and I, Ambassador Masset and Bertie Ramcharan, who was now the Director of the ICFY Secretariat and is wise, hard-working and sensitive to UN feelings, had a frank discussion on how the US suggestion for proximity talks on a territorial settlement in Bosnia could be handled. We all wanted US and Russian involvement and were ready to bend over backwards to help the process along. With Stoltenberg I went very frankly over the arguments why there had to be government representatives of France and the UK to do the fundamental negotiation on the map with the Americans, and why the Germans could not be excluded. In view of the problems the EU faced in relation to US attitudes to Greece, I did not see how we could use the Troika. Since the end of the Second World War, it had been necessary to coordinate negotiating positions quickly in relation to the Soviet Union when they were the occupying powers in Berlin with the full involvement of their Foreign Ministers. In my view, the hardest task was going to be to keep Vice-President Gore, Christopher, Lake and Albright on board for a collective position and we needed a small confidential framework which could also involve the Russians.

Stoltenberg's anxieties related to how he could protect Boutros Ghali's position and the UN Security Council. He could not accept that they should be sidelined and in New York they were already somewhat sensitive on this score. We both agreed, nevertheless, that we could not see how the UN could be involved as a decision-maker in what was essentially going to be inter-governmental negotiation. Indeed, I recognized that I as EU Co-Chairman could not be formally involved either. I would be kept informed through the British network and, through Masset, the French network and could feed in Stoltenberg's views along with my own. Stoltenberg said the UN would find it easiest if the Co-Chairmen were to ask three experienced diplomats to represent the ICFY in the proximity talks with Redman and Churkin, and Stoltenberg would raise no objection to the ICFY appointing three people effectively nominated by France, Germany and the UK. I said I would prefer this too and I would consult; but I made no promises, for this delicate problem would have to be sorted out between capitals within the EU.

Ambassador Masset was due to leave the ICFY fairly soon and I had agreed with Alain Juppé that he would propose a successor. It would obviously help if the French nominated for the Contact Group either Masset or his successor. As far as German representation was concerned, Michael Steiner had already, at our invitation, been associated closely with the ICFY, attending our negotiating sessions with both the Croats and the Muslims in December and January; he was bright and would be an excellent addition, but it was of course up to Klaus Kinkel whom he nominated. Similarly, for the British representation it was up to Douglas Hurd. Stoltenberg said he would be ready to justify this arrangement on the basis that France and the UK were permanent members of the Security Council, and Steiner had been closely associated with the Conference's work. I thought it would be helpful if David Ludlow, my private secretary, who was the most knowledgeable on the maps, attended Contact Group meetings to provide liaison with the Co-Chairmen. Also, when constitutional questions relating to Republika Srpska's relations with the Federation arose, Paul Szasz should be present, which would provide a UN input, and he would be seen as Stoltenberg's representative.

When the EU Foreign Ministers met in Luxembourg on 18 April I stressed that EU governmental involvement with the US, Russia and the UN was of great importance, explained that the Americans were not content to work within the ICFY framework and suggested we needed new coordinating mechanisms. I was advised not to spell out specifically what I had in mind, but I felt that I had identified the problem sufficiently to act in the light of the ministerial discussions. Since we were sitting under the Greek Presidency I deliberately did not question the Troika, but I had briefed their Political Director before the meeting in quite explicit terms. In the margins of the meeting I talked the problem through with the British Political Director, Pauline Neville Jones, who had been sent a full report of my conversations with Stoltenberg on the plane which had also been passed on through Masset to the French. The French Political Director was emphatic that we had to act, and the Germans, who would be next in the Presidency, were cautious but ready for me to move. But since it was all so sensitive in relation to the structures of a Common Foreign and Security Policy (CFSP) for the EU, they all felt that only I could take the initiative. The other EU countries were bound to be suspicious and feel excluded, and I was unhappy to have to act in what I knew would for some appear a divisive way, for I had conscientiously tried to involve the Twelve in all aspects of the ICFY negotiations. Yet given the institutional inertia and, paradoxically, passion surrounding future CFSP negotiations, only a *fait accompli* could win reluctant acquiescence. I had worked with Pauline Neville Jones back in 1976 when I was a Minister of State dealing with EC questions and had always found her a delight, clear-headed with an innovative mind. Now she promised that I would not be shut out as a result of forming the Contact Group from even the most sensitive cable traffic as had happened in May 1993. So without enthusiasm I said I would take the decision and with it any flak that might come my way.

Next day I issued a COREU,[180] in effect establishing the Contact Group and creating what may become an important precedent for the EU as it expands from fifteen to twenty and more countries. I had been influenced by the effectiveness of the Contact Group mechanism which we used in 1977 over Namibia when the US, UK, France, Germany and Canada, then all on the Security Council, came together.[iii] The close negotiating relationship we five ministers established – Vance, Genscher, de Guiringaud, Jamieson and myself – proved invaluable in overcoming serious differences among our five countries over applying economic sanctions against the South African government's apartheid policy, developing policies towards Namibia and the then illegal government of Rhodesia. That Contact Group's activity had had a large UN element and we would coordinate in capitals as well as in New York before Security Council meetings. We had also negotiated face to face as five ministers with the then South African Prime Minister, P. W.

Botha, and their Foreign Minister, Pik Botha, and shown we could maintain our unity around a negotiating table.

The atmosphere in Moscow on 20 April when Stoltenberg and I visited was surprisingly realistic.[181] Kozyrev seemed to have taken over more day-to-day control of policy, with Churkin somewhat chastened by the effect on certain members of the Duma of some of his very hostile, though fully deserved, comments about the Bosnian Serbs. It was significant that on 20 April the Russian Security Council, under Yeltsin's chairmanship, failed to echo Churkin's exasperation with the Serbs after they had duped him over Gorazde. For Yeltsin, as before, it was crucial that in Moscow nobody thought that Russia's views were being ignored by the West.

The first meeting of the Contact Group officials was fixed to take place in London on 26 April.[182] Thereafter they met in different capitals whenever convenient. The Contact Group would report in a fairly bland way to the EU from time to time which I would pass on from the ICFY through a COREU. The first such report was made after meeting President Izetbegovic on 28 April in Sarajevo. Stoltenberg also kept the UN Secretary-General informed.

On 10 May in Brussels the Political Directors of the EU discussed for two and a half hours the legitimacy of my decision to appoint three experts to participate in the Contact Group. An exchange of COREUs had shown the seriousness of this issue for the Netherlands and some other countries. The Maastricht Treaty made no explicit provision for ad hoc arrangements like this, only for the Presidency or the Troika. Spain questioned whether the 18 April FAC had given me a mandate. It was however noted with satisfaction that the Troika would be represented at the Contact Group ministerial meetings. Germany said I had been mandated to intensify contacts with the US and Russia The French said I had fulfilled my mandate by appointing members of my staff, a somewhat disingenuous argument.

On 11 May I attended with Stoltenberg at the Hotel Crillon in Paris what was really a UN internal meeting called by Boutros Ghali with Kofi Annan, the Under-Secretary for Peacekeeping from New York, Akashi, and General de Lapresle, whom I found very impressive. He warned that the humanitarian basis of their work was becoming less important and UNPROFOR was starting to slide from a humanitarian role into a combatant position. They were however 'not there yet, thank God,' and he stressed that the composition of the force did not enable it to fight. The main worry expressed at the meeting was of NATO wanting to prove its credibility in Yugoslavia.

At the first meeting of Contact Group ministers, also attended by the EU Troika with Commissioner Hans van den Broek, at Geneva on 13 May, much time was spent drafting the ministerial communiqué.[183] The concept developed of giving the Serbs a clear idea of the linkage between the suspension of sanctions and their compliance with a settlement. But tightening existing sanctions remained controversial. Kozyrev highlighted increasing domestic opposition to sanctions and claimed that Russian financial losses due to sanctions were greater than its total foreign aid receipts. In the end ministers agreed to enforce existing UNSCRs strictly but also to offer an incentive to the Serbs – namely, that good faith implementation of a peace settlement that included provisions for withdrawal to agreed territorial limits would lead to phased suspension of the sanctions imposed by the UN.

For the Contact Group to come up with its own map implied a readiness to impose a solution, but this was still anathema to the US. There were also fears about presenting a package on a take it or leave it basis. What happened if the parties did not accept? Did the international community pull out and leave the parties to fight it out? Hurd spoke particularly passionately about this, and urged caution. The lifting of the arms embargo was another contentious issue. On 12 May the US Senate had voted for both unilateral and multilateral lifting. The Russian Duma reacted to this on 13 May by voting for a resolution calling on Yeltsin to work for the lifting of sanctions. Juppé said that although he had long opposed it, the time might now be coming when there was no alternative.

Clearly there remained many more differences on the detail, but in their public statement ministers endorsed the two-track approach, including a territorial delimitation on the 51–49 per cent basis. They also called for a four-month cessation of hostilities and invited the parties to begin negotiations on an overall settlement under the aegis of the Contact Group within the following two weeks. We, as Co-Chairmen, participated only in the latter part of the meeting, after the communiqué had been virtually finalized; this was on the insistence of the US, perhaps to underline that the ICFY was not a formal decision-maker, but we had been able to feed in our views through our representatives on the Contact Group. It was a rather frustrating procedure but we decided to grin and bear it. When consulted, we stressed the need for the five governments to back up with resources the decisions for which they voted in the UN, otherwise UNPROFOR would continue to be unable to meet all the demands being placed on it. Most activity now centered on designing a Contact Group map.[184]

On 17 May Stoltenberg and I visited Belgrade to see Milosevic and the Bosnian Serbs in Zvornik and then went on to see Tudjman in Zagreb.[185] In Geneva on Thursday 2 June Churkin, somewhat surprisingly, told us that the Russians were broadly content with the working map developed by the Contact Group, including elements which I expected to be unacceptable to the Serbs, such as the Serbs relinquishing total control of Visegrad, and the Federation retaining territory on the east bank of the Drina near Gorazde beyond that currently under UN control. Churkin claimed to have shown the map to Milosevic who, while saying it was an issue for the Bosnian Serbs, did not proffer any adverse reaction. However, Milosevic was obviously not going to sell a settlement to the Bosnian Serbs again as he had done in Athens. It was left to the Contact Group ambassadors to start meeting the parties on 25 May in the French lakeside resort of Talloires, with Krajisnik nominated by Karadzic to head the Bosnian Serb delegation and Silajdzic and Zubak representing the Federation.

On Friday 3 June in Geneva I had a two-and-a-half-hour conversation with General Mladic.[186] The meeting was private, with just his chief military aide and his interpreter present. My main object was to try to ensure that Mladic saw the issues in a wider international perspective and to give him an opportunity to raise questions. He also saw General Galvin in the US Embassy that same day. In fact, most of the input from Mladic came in the form of questions. As I had found before, in these sort of talks he is quiet and unassuming and there is none of the bravado and boasting of some of his public performances. My impression was that he was calculating carefully the advantages and disadvantages of signing a map with a 49 per cent–51 per cent split. He would, I think, have preferred the cessation of hostilities under discussion with Akashi in Geneva to coincide with the signing of the map, but he did not rule out signing a cessation of hostilities agreement first. I was convinced that for the first time since I had been talking to Mladic he would listen to a serious threat to impose this settlement.

Mladic's whole stance was one of absorbing information and giving little away. He clearly now understood much more English and admitted that he had been trying to master the language with, he claimed, little success. My overall impressions were of a man who was beginning to count the cost of this war, prompted by his daughter's suicide as well as the daily toll of deaths among his own troops. When he professed that the map was a matter for the politicians I scoffed at that, and I think I did get through to him when I argued that he could not shuffle this responsibility off on to the politicians, that he owed it to his own troops to be involved and to share the responsibility for a painful and difficult withdrawal. We ended up agreeing that it often required more bravery to forge a peace than to continue to wage a war. It was important to get this message through to Mladic because he is obsessed with demonstrating his bravery, to the point of barbarity. Slitting the throat of a pig in front of the Dutch Commander in Srebrenica to prove he was the braver of the two is but one example. Mladic is not a madman, but he conducts his battles on two different levels: on one he is an intellectual, on the other a barbarian.

On 4 June, the same day the Contact Group ambassadors met the parties for a second time in Geneva, I wrote to Hurd, Juppé and Kinkel.[187] My intention was to focus on the politics of a deal over Bosnia-Herzegovina and in particular on how to convince President Clinton of the necessity not only to forge a detailed bottom-line peace proposal for Bosnia but to recognize that such a deal had to be backed with a package of disincentives and

Map 12 Contact Group map, July 1994

incentives so as to impose a settlement. It was not in my judgement sufficient to say, as one State Department official was quoted as saying, 'we
basically offer a solution, but it is up to them to decide whether to accept.'
It also seemed odd that the US would talk up air power as a response on
the battlefield but rule out air power for imposing a settlement stemming
from the negotiating table.

I told the three ministers that Redman, with General Galvin, had told
Stoltenberg and me that he felt the next two weeks were crucial. He felt
Churkin would support the map and that 'grey areas' involving the UN
would be necessary, particularly around Prijedor. Given the shortage of
UN personnel to man the ceasefire line, we all agreed that any areas of UN
administration would have to be kept to the minimum. There were some
signs that Redman was not yet ready to go firm on the map, saying he
needed more time in Washington. I urged a very early meeting of the
Contact Group at ministerial level to maintain momentum.

I put forward to the three Foreign Ministers proposals, which I had argued for publicly in the middle of May 1993, for a strategy to use air power to impose such a settlement. I hoped that this would make the map more realistic if it was designed against the knowledge that it was to be imposed. There was already a danger of the map reflecting Muslim aspirations rather than negotiable realities or an imposable bottom line. The Contact Group map would be a bitter pill for all the Bosnian parties. If it was to gain acceptance the US, EU, Russia and the UN would have to put their full weight behind it, exploit the albeit limited leverage we had to the full and offer real incentives. It seemed to me politically inconceivable that these five governments could now just leave such a map on the table. But it was more than conceivable: it was exactly what they did.

I suggested to the ministers that they let the Muslim–Croat Federation know that if they accepted the map and associated constitutional arrangements, and the Serbs did not, the arms embargo would be lifted and under UN Resolutions NATO air assets would do all they could to prevent the Serbs taking military advantage. Most, if not all, UN ground forces and UNHCR personnel would have to be withdrawn during this period. This was *leave* as well as 'lift and strike', and it contained two crucial differences from what President Clinton had suggested a year before: first, it would be air action threatened in support of a specific peace plan; and second, it would be air action which had Russian acquiescence, perhaps even Russian support. The Serbs could be told that sanctions would be suspended if they accepted the map and associated constitutional arrangements, even if the Federation refused to sign, and also that the arms embargo would not be lifted.

If the fighting continued, either the Federation or the Serbs, whichever had not signed up, could opt for peace at any time. A major advantage was that the UN would not be asking NATO to apply air strikes in a political vacuum. A potential problem for Clinton was Christopher's February 1993 statement, which ruled out imposing a settlement. The way around that would be to say that the Bosnian parties would be doing the ground fighting and taking the big risks, while NATO would be helping the UN to carry out its mandate and, while doing this, tilting the balance of fighting towards a particular settlement.

In the US administration only Clinton, in my view, had the political instincts sufficient to want to cut a deal, as he had recently shown over most-favoured-nation trade with China. There was no guarantee that the Russian position as espoused by Churkin would remain as flexible for much longer. Yeltsin's personal involvement seemed crucial and, without needing a heads of government meeting, Moscow could be a venue for the next meeting of the Contact Group at ministerial level. At such a meeting the parties could be asked to attend, having been given the map, and I believed an associated constitution was needed for consultation prior to signature.

There should be no bogus wartime referenda or negotiators going back for Assembly ratification: negotiators needed plenipotential powers.

The risk of bringing these matters to a head was of igniting the war not just in Bosnia-Herzegovina but also in Croatia. But that was now a very real danger in any case. The Bosnian Serbs were deliberately coinciding the cessation of hostilities and map negotiations. If these negotiations failed, Bosnian Serbs and Croatian Serbs were ready to merge politically and militarily. Tudjman was coming under increasing pressure not to renew the UN mandate in September, and the existing UN mandate in Bosnia-Herzegovina would be ever harder to fulfil. Calls for air strikes were likely to multiply.

No one, I argued to Hurd, Juppé and Kinkel, could be happy with any strategy which risked having to engage air power against the Bosnian Serbs and maybe the Croatian Serbs. But we were already living with that risk, and over the last few months had only just avoided punitive air strikes. My proposals were discussed twice in the Contact Group at official level. Sadly, the Contact Group did not develop a really effective negotiating position in the summer of 1994. I believed Yeltsin could have been persuaded to accept the use of air power for a peace settlement; and in the right climate Russia would accept being involved, together with NATO, in carrying out any air action.

I fear that, just as in May 1993, my plea for using air power actually to implement a peace settlement was too much for these five governments to accept. They preferred to rest on the need for all-party agreement and on ad hoc threats of air strikes reacting to circumstances, a far more unstable and dangerous strategy. As it turned out they were prepared to leave their own Contact Group map on the table for over a year without even negotiating on it. The disastrous consequences of that strategy were seen in July 1995 when, with the fall of Srebrenica and Zepa, the Bosnian Serbs in effect tore up the Contact Group map.

On Tuesday 7 June in Geneva we met with Milan Martic, the self-styled President of the Croatian Serbs, and discussed starting economic talks.[188] Meanwhile, also in Geneva, Akashi and Rose were locked in difficult talks between the Bosnian Federation and the Bosnian Serbs, the parties eventually agreeing on 8 June not to engage in offensive military operations or other provocative actions for a period of one month. This outcome was a bitter disappointment to Akashi, who believed that he had gained American support for a four-month cessation, only to see that position change in the process of negotiating, with Ganic refusing four months and the US representative in Geneva acquiescing.

On 9 June the House of Representatives voted for unilateral mandatory lifting of the arms embargo which, though it had no immediate legal effect, was another pressure on the Clinton administration. On 15 June I received an assessment of the use of air power from our own ICFY advisers which highlighted some of the problems.[189]

The Russians were claiming that they had discussed 'lift and strike' with General Rose, who had called the policy 'nonsense', and that both he and de Lapresle saw UN troops becoming hostages if such a policy were implemented. The Russians 'knew' what the Serbs would do: as soon as the lifting of the arms embargo was announced they would attack the Muslims, the Croats and UNPROFOR and immediately capture Srebrenica, Zepa and Gorazde.

In Moscow there were plans for the withdrawal of Russian troops in the event of the embargo being lifted. They claimed to be better situated than most, since they were near Sarajevo airport; but even so the Russian commanders expected significant casualties, not least because they would be caught in the crossfire. The Russian Defence Minister Grachev, who had been involved in the war in Afghanistan, believed that in Bosnia air strikes would be even less successful than they had been in Afghanistan, given the mountainous, wooded terrain.

The Americans were saying that if the Serbs refused to sign the Contact Group map the disincentive they wanted was to lift the arms embargo. Yet they knew that if the embargo were lifted the British and French UN forces would be removed and very likely the whole of UNPROFOR would follow. There was no 'lift and stay' option; but the US found it hard to accept 'leave, lift and strike', for that meant taking responsibility for the serious humanitarian consequences of any such action.

I have always believed that successful diplomacy needs muscle behind it, and throughout my tenure as Co-Chairman I was arguing for applying force selectively, sensibly but in support of a specific settlement. Sometimes the Muslims, the US and some critics in Europe would depict my stance as being opposed in principle to the case for air power, which was never the case, as the factual record makes clear. But my public and private views could not always be the same: in public the Co-Chairmen always had to be saying the same thing, and I could not be too far from the centre of gravity of EU opinion.

A series of bilateral meetings between ministers and officials, including a meeting between Christopher and Kozyrev in Brussels on 22 June, before the next Group meeting, was planned, with the military aspects high on the agenda. Stoltenberg and I met with the EU Foreign Ministers and Kozyrev at the EU summit in Corfu on 24 June and expressed our concern that the Russians had not, as the US had with the Muslims, obtained prior Serb agreement to the map. We believed that the allocation of a substantial part of Brcko and the east bank of the Drina around Gorazde and a part of Visegrad to the Federation, along with Doboj and Jajce and other sensitive changes, though accepted by the Russians, would remain a major obstacle to Serb acceptance. As a result of our specific concerns about the northern corridor, we suggested an area of demilitarization on either side of the cross-over bridges at Brcko. This was agreed and we felt it would help assuage the Serb military a little, but we remained very pessimistic about their accepting the map.

The Russians promised the Contact Group to continue to attempt to bring the Serbs round, and Yeltsin gave a personal commitment to this effect when he met Chancellor Kohl in Bonn. Nikiforov was despatched to Belgrade to meet the Bosnian Serb leadership and to update them on the Group's work. The effect of this attempt to apply pressure was limited. Much to the annoyance of Milosevic, Karadzic, in a radio broadcast on 1 July, called the map degrading and alleged that it was designed to result in Serb rejection, thus allowing the international community to blame them for continuing the war. Nevertheless, he said the Serb leadership would study it to see if there was any way to continue the process.

To balance the first Geneva meeting held in the US Embassy, the second ministerial Contact Group meeting was due to be held in the Russian mission to the UN on 5 July. The Group met, as before, on the eve of the meeting to prepare the documentation. Nikiforov arrived with the message that the Serbs were ready to accept the map as it stood, but only if it was linked to a clear proposal on the constitution. This was seen as a wrecking move and involved reversing the decision taken in Paris to leave discussion of the constitution aside. It would be impossible to reach agreement in the time available and it was felt that the Federation would not accept secession following a referendum, as Izetbegovic had signed up for with the Serbs on 16 September 1993. At that time there had to be first a mutually agreed territorial division before any referendum. Secession, it was argued, could only be contemplated if it was agreed by the parties.

Contact Group ministers met in the afternoon of 5 July and agreed the list of incentives and disincentives prepared by the Group's ambassadors. They all felt this was the easy part, and that after the parties were presented with the map next day by the ambassadors there would have to be a delay to gauge the parties' reactions. Next day there were predictable objections on the map from all sides. But Karadzic also brought up the question of the constitution, saying that everything depended on their having Republika Srpska and on a final decision on the treatment of Sarajevo.

On 18 July the EU Foreign Ministers issued a declaration urging acceptance of the plan. The Federation voted to accept. The Serb Assembly, after a much longer meeting than many had predicted, voted on 19 July to send a sealed response which would only be revealed when Karadzic met the Contact Group. The impression was generated that this was a 'yes, and . . .'. When the Contact Group met on 19 July in Geneva, Russian information was that the Serb response would be positive, although the formulation might not be totally satisfactory. This would be remedied in time for the ministerial meeting. Milosevic was pressing the Bosnian Serbs hard, as were the Russians, but more time was needed. It seems that the Russians and Milosevic had worked out a form of words which they expected Karadzic to be able to get through the Assembly. In the event Karadzic was unable, or unwilling, to do so and a revised formulation was drafted, without the input of Milosevic, and it was this which was brought to Geneva.

The Contact Group ambassadors met the Federation delegation on 20 July to receive their brief response to the Contact Group map. Silajdzic informed them that the Assembly had voted overwhelmingly for clear and unconditional acceptance of the map. Even though it was unjust, it preserved Bosnia and Herzegovina's territorial integrity and sovereignty. After delivering this short statement, the delegation left. The Bosnian Muslim strategy was clearly to present the Contact Group map to the world as a take it or leave it offer which they, the Bosnian Muslims, accepted.

The meeting with the Serbs was not so easy. Karadzic handed over a sealed pink envelope containing the response. In a typically theatrical performance, he claimed it was the sole copy, and indeed asked for a photocopy to keep himself. The Serbs continued in this light-hearted mood. When the Group accepted their request for the time of the next meeting to be shifted one hour, Krajisnik quipped that this was the first time the Group had ever acknowledged the wishes of the Serbs. The document stated that the Assembly was not in a position to decide on the map until all elements of the peace plan were clear, and further work had been done on the map. The map could serve 'in considerable measure, as a basis for further negotiations'. It was not the answer the Group was looking for, and the meeting was adjourned to allow time for consideration.

At a further meeting with the Serbs that evening the Group expressed their great disappointment and urged a change of mind. They tried to show the Serbs that some of their concerns had been met, and that changes to the map could be made in direct negotiations. Karadzic attempted to argue that the response was not negative, and that they had shown they were ready to participate in the negotiating process. But there was no evidence of the Serbs being ready to change their fundamental position that the map was unacceptable and there could be no agreement without details of the constitution. Krajisnik said the Group had miscalculated and put down a proposal which was 'not a map for peace'. Buha unhelpfully returned even to the basic question of the 49–51 per cent split. It was very hard for the Group to salvage anything from this. The Federation's response to this Serb reply was also one of disappointment, though not surprise. Silajdzic's main fear was an intensification of the fighting.

I then took the risky step – risky in terms of there being a leak of my view that we should toughen sanctions and adopt 'leave, lift and strike' –

of sending what I felt was the most important COREU in my period as Co-Chairman to EU Foreign Ministers on 22 July:

From Lord Owen

Personal for Foreign Ministers only

Subject: Bosnia

1. *The EU is now facing its first real challenge to its CFSP over the former Yugoslavia. Letting the VOPP be ditched last May was just about defensible. The Clinton administration had never been supportive to it and European/US relations were deteriorating. The Co-Chairmen's authority could be weakened, provided it was reinforced by a greater EU ministerial involvement, which started in June in the Copenhagen Summit and led on to the EU Action Plan. Nevertheless there were serious consequences of allowing the Bosnian Serbs in May 1993 to call the EU's bluff. One of those was the undermining of Milosevic's authority with the Bosnian Serbs following his overt support for the VOPP and his half-hearted gesture towards closing the border.*

2. *Now in the summer of 1994 allowing the Bosnian Serbs to call our bluff again is far more dangerous. Firstly the authority of the EU itself is on the line and secondly there is no Co-Chairmen's proposal to act as a buffer. Also the US, by continuing to advocate lift and strike, have cleverly contrived their own escape hatch. While the Russians, already in problems with their Duma, can just shrug their shoulders, saying they tried their best. The EU has, therefore, by far the most to lose from a failure of the Contact Group. Not just politically, but also militarily, for EU member states are exposed on the ground as UN peacekeepers. These peacekeepers face an increasing danger of being sucked in as combatants, since the US is clearly trying to arrange a progressive pattern of air strikes that seriously risk drawing the UN, and the EU by implication, in to a lift, stay and strike policy.*

3. *The key as always is Milosevic. He understands power and he will only pressurize the Bosnian Serbs further if the Contact Group convince him that they are serious. He must receive a sharp reminder as a result of the Ministerial Contact Group meeting that we expect him to act against the Bosnian Serbs, and that if he does not deliver, we will take further action against him. This means Milosevic being well aware of the contents of two draft UN resolutions over sanctions by the end of this month, one of which encourages him to isolate the Bosnian Serbs,*

the other of which shows him the heavy price he will pay for a failure to cooperate.

4. *There is only one threatened action which Milosevic will respect, and that is if the resolution addresses the closure of Serbia's border with Macedonia. We have the power to do it, and it will be seen as pusillanimous behaviour if we do not both threaten this and clearly mean to carry it out. The latest figures for traffic across the border show 1,018 trucks and 148 railway wagons going north in one week, and 1,173 trucks and 351 railway wagons going south. This is an intolerable situation. We know that President Gligorov's freedom to act is circumscribed by the continuing weakness of his economy. Without the black market dealing it would be in an even worse situation. He has to be granted generous financial support immediately, and the vehicle to use is Article 50 of the UN Charter, and a Security Council Resolution taken under Chapter VII, which will automatically bind all European Union states. There will also have to be a simultaneous strengthening of the UN presence in Macedonia. Any other action on sanctions, be it further attempts to free Serbian assets or demands on the neighbouring governments, will not be taken seriously either by those governments or by the rest of the world.*

5. *The second fundamental sanctions issue is to deal with Serb extraction of oil from the wells in the Djeletovci area in the eastern UNPA. UNPROFOR in UNPA East think that there are currently 12 wells operating over an area of 5–10 km. The estimated production varies from 300–400 tons per day. Accurate information is impossible to obtain as the Serbs deny all access to this area. The oil is moved by a pipeline under the Danube (which existed before the war began) for refining in Serbia either at Novi Sad or Pancevo, just outside Belgrade. The refined products are moved by road. Serbia charges for the refining and is paid in food. Karadzic openly boasts that all this oil comes back through the Republika Srpska either for their use, or for onward shipment to the RSK, and there is every reason to believe that this is the case. We cannot be sure that even if Milosevic seals the border, some oil will not get across. There is an overwhelming case for passing a Security Council Resolution that oil production in the Djeletovci area should cease and UNPROFOR should be given all necessary powers under Chapter VII to ensure that no oil passes down the pipeline. If we find that UNPROFOR does not have the military capacity to deal with this, then this is a further case for the withdrawal of UNPROFOR, so as to free us up to use air power to tilt the balance in favour of the Croatian army within the borders we have*

recognized for Croatia, and for the Bosnian government army in Bosnia and Herzegovina.

6. It is my conviction that unless we can persuade Milosevic to act against the Bosnian Serbs we have no option but to remove the UN from both Croatia and Bosnia and Herzegovina soon and to follow a lift and strike policy before the winter closes in and the weather makes air strikes less effective, and the humanitarian situation deteriorates. The longer we delay a decision to remove the UN, the more we are closing the air strike option and accepting we just have to muddle through another winter. But can we really envisage holding the present line for another nine months? I believe the risks of being sucked in on the ground in this strategy are even greater.

7. Adopting lift and strike now, as opposed to when the US first proposed it, is a very different strategy. Now we have a concrete plan to which we can hold the Muslims, and one to which the Russians as well as the US are firmly committed. Provided air strikes are limited to Bosnian Serb territory, the Russians ought to be able to tolerate them, and there is little risk that they will feel driven to put their aircraft into Serbia. If the Croat and the Muslim forces are not sufficiently strong with outside air power, then the world will have to live with a Serb-imposed solution. At least both the Croatian and Bosnian governments are in a far better position in 1994 to stand up against the Serbs than they have been at any time since the fighting began in 1991. It will have to be very clearly stated that NATO will not under any circumstances put troops in on the ground, and that the Muslims and Croats will have to live with the consequences of a strategy which they have asked for, whereby they do the ground fighting, and over which many NATO nations have military doubts as to the efficacy of air strikes. The alternative, in the absence of Milosevic cooperating, is to watch the progressive erosion of the authority of the Contact Group nations and a situation in which the Serbs assert their authority with the world never knowing whether or not the route suggested by the US could have been successful.

Afterwards I wondered whether sending a COREU like this had any effect, and whether it could produce any rethinking in capitals. The Germans were in favour of lifting the arms embargo but, like the US, reluctant about accepting, let alone advocating, the corollary that UNPROFOR should go. There was no feedback from any EU government to the challenge laid down in that COREU, and the Dutch government was strangely silent.

On 29 July the third ministerial Contact Group meeting took place in Geneva. Work was to continue on a UNSCR tightening sanctions and on planning for stronger enforcement measures. It was going to be a long-drawn-out process. I asked David Ludlow, the ICFY's representative on the Contact Group, to write a report on the Group's activities before he left in the autumn.[190]

The US administration seemed paralysed by indecision. It would not have been hard for them to mobilize Security Council support for UNPROFOR to leave. Senator Dole, who later that autumn came over to London to give a lecture, when I had a brief chat with him, was by this time ready to acknowledge that UNPROFOR would have to get out first if the arms embargo was to be lifted, and because he was so committed to NATO he accepted that NATO should help extract the UN force. The reason the US held back was presumably exactly what the Europeans already suspected, namely that US advocacy of lifting the embargo was only for public relations purposes. The US knew in their hearts that UNPROFOR would have to go before the arms embargo was lifted, and that if they did leave the tempo of the fighting would increase. The US feared that they would then be faced with cries for help from a Muslim population who were under savage attack from the Serbs and might not be helped by air strikes. The US feared that after a failure of air strikes they would then be compelled to go in on the ground to help the Bosnian Muslims. Arguments like mine, which took their own proposal for lifting the arms embargo seriously but linked it to imposing a settlement after the UN had left, were an embarrassment to them; they preferred posturing.

I believed that threats of air strikes unencumbered by a UN presence on the ground would be taken seriously by the Bosnian Serbs, particularly if the Russians acquiesced and air strikes did not involve Serbia or Montenegro. There was a risk that threats might not be enough and that 'leave, lift and strike' might have to be implemented. But even if air strikes failed I did not believe we should feel we had to become combatants, and the Bosnian Muslims would have to take that reality into account when asking for the lifting of the arms embargo.

I went back over my papers to when I had been advocating interdicting Bosnian Serb supply lines by air in May 1993 to impose the VOPP and read again the paper (see p. 136) by my then military adviser. While he had specified the arguments against using air power and said they 'are valid to a degree', he had pointed out that 'the counter views are not often given a public airing' and clearly set out the case for those who wanted air strikes:

Heavy weapons – *Many of the heavy weapons cannot be quickly and easily moved. The BSA is often using them to prosecute a medieval strategy of town siege and domination of roads from the high ground.*

Whilst the lighter artillery, mortars and air defence cannon are highly mobile, many of the heavier guns and tanks involved in the sieges, as we saw en route to and from Pale in December, are well dug into semi-permanent positions. These are mostly well known to the B-H Army, the HVO and increasingly to UNPROFOR (particularly the UNMOs) and to other agencies such as ECMM. The operational doctrine for the use of these weapons and their lines of supply are fairly inflexible and predictable. The BSA's lack of trained manpower results in some of the guns, certainly around Sarajevo, at times being unmanned, with crews being bussed from position to position to fire them. Where such weapons are static and their positions known, the terrain factor may well be of net benefit to aircraft conducting surprise attacks at low level. Even if such attacks did drive the BSA to a greater use of more mobile systems, such as mortars, this would be likely to reduce the effectiveness of their fireplans: they would lose range and would not quickly be able to redeploy trained manpower onto lighter systems.

The most critical element of such offensive air action would of course be the politically directed mission. If this were broadly to take on the BSA across the board and enforce their withdrawal to designated provinces, then substantial ground forces would indeed be needed. However, the mission could be limited to one of degrading – one would not need to destroy all guns – the BSA's ability to use fairly static heavy-weapon lines to continue to attack particular civilian targets (such as Sarajevo city centre) in flagrant contravention of the 1907 Hague Convention and subsequent instruments of international law. The ground forces' contribution, for this particular purpose, could then probably be limited to specialist intelligence, targeting and communications teams (such as those which would make up the ACE Rapid Reaction Corps' Intelligence and Targeting Group).

Attacking aircraft would of course be vulnerable to ground fire, but vulnerability can be minimized by the expert offensive air planners; use of a judicious mix of surprise, electronic warfare measures, medium-altitude attack with laser designation and single-pass attacks at low altitude.

Such operations would indeed have a major impact on all military and civilian agencies throughout former Yugoslavia, particularly in the Serb-held areas and those which they could dominate by fire but, with Spring now here, signs of donor fatigue already setting in and the BS feeling cocky, it could be argued that the days of the primacy of the 'food and blankets' mission might be numbered.

Interdiction of Bosnian Serb lines of communication (LOC) – *The Banja Luka and Titov Drvar Corps do have long and vulnerable LOC which could probably be taken on most effectively east of the Posavina corridor, in the Bijeljina opstina. In Eastern Bosnia, there are signs that*

*the BSA may be using three rail lines: the line into Bijeljina from the
north-east, the line from Zvornik towards Tuzla and possibly the line
cutting through the eastern edge of Rudo opstina. Interdiction of the
road Zvornik–Vlasenica–lian–Pijesak–Sokolac–Pale would undoubtedly affect the BSA's offensive capability in this area*

These arguments I found even more valid in August 1994 than in May
1993, for the chances of Milosevic allowing the JA to intervene were even
less, given the depth of the split between him and Karadzic. Also, the
humanitarian relief effort by 1994 had reached a point where, if the military
escorts were withdrawn, I felt that the alternative 'black market' supply
routes for the Bosnian Muslims were sufficiently robust that they would
have continued despite political or military pressure from Croatian or
Bosnian Serb leaders to stop trading across the confrontation lines. Too
much money was changing hands for these political leaders to be heeded,
and anyhow many of them were involved in the racketeering. In addition,
UNHCR was supplying the Bosnian Serbs with humanitarian aid; if they
clamped down on UNHCR aid to the Muslims, they too would be affected.
I believed governments exaggerated the humanitarian cost of withdrawing
UNPROFOR in summer 1994. Its most vital task had been in the winter of
1992–3 when chaos reigned and there were no alternative supply routes.

I knew from my talks with Mladic that he had very little wishful thinking
in his strategic analysis. He was contemptuous about the pusillanimous
behaviour of the Western democracies but he also knew that Russia was
hesitant to lock horns with the US. He hoped that Milosevic would in the
last analysis not dare leave him and the Bosnian Serb army to be defeated
on the battlefield, but he knew that he had deeply offended Milosevic over
the VOPP and I sensed that he was wary about having another personal
clash over the Contact Group plan. Mladic's intransigence was always
qualified. There was just enough flexibility to let the minimal amount of
UN food aid through. He would return UN hostages after having exposed
UN vulnerability, accept some NATO close air support if his field commanders went too far, but react very strongly to punitive NATO air strikes
because he knew they could do real damage. I felt in 1994 that he would be
able to make the Bosnian Serbs withdraw when they knew our strategic
analysis made sense. 'Leave, lift and strike' in the context of imposing a
specific peace settlement did make sense, and Mladic knew this. For all his
bluster about the UN leaving, I believe Mladic knew that UN troops were
his ultimate safeguard against NATO air power tilting the balance against
him. Sadly, 'leave, lift and strike' was not adopted in August 1994 by the
Contact Group countries. They waited until August 1995 to use air power,
by which time the soldiers had changed the Contact Group map and the
people had suffered a renewed bout of extensive ethnic cleansing.

8

Soldiering On

INEVITABLY AS A NEGOTIATOR I tended to exaggerate the dangers of inaction. A critic of my view that UNPROFOR should now, in the summer of 1994, plan to leave, in order to be able credibly to threaten to use NATO air strikes to impose a Contact Group plan and lift the embargo, could with some justice argue that I underestimated the benefits of just soldiering on into 1995. In fact, while applying sticking plaster here and there to keep the Contact Group show on the road, these five countries did stay together in the same vehicle throughout a third winter. Time was bought during which the Muslim armed forces steadily improved their professionalism and, with help from the Croats bringing in more arms, their military effectiveness increased. If time was the enemy of the Bosnian Serb army, by giving the Muslims more time the Contact Group might have hoped to wait for the day when there was a better balance of forces on the ground, which of itself would make for a better-balanced peace settlement on the basis of the Contact Group Plan. This was, I suspected, the real meaning of the word containment as applied to Bosnia by some in the Contact Group from early 1994 onwards. My fear was that unless the Contact Group map was changed through negotiations soon, the Bosnian Serbs would not accept being tied down by Muslim and Croat attacks across the existing confrontation line. They would hit back and at the very least take the so-called 'safe areas' in eastern Bosnia, Srebrenica and Zepa, as they constantly warned they would. I also feared that war would break out again in Croatia, for Tudjman's impatience was palpable.

In the summer of 1994 attempts to draft UNSCRs on easing and tight-ening sanctions had run into further problems, with the Russians and Americans once again at odds. The UN Secretary-General issued a letter saying he would recommend that UNPROFOR hand over to a multinational task force run by the Contact Group representatives. This caused something of a panic, for real responsibility was the last thing the Contact Group countries wanted, and the UN provided a useful scapegoat. The US, let alone the UK and France, had never accepted that this situation was comparable to the Iraq–Kuwait war, necessitating a multinational task force, and they had every wish to continue under UN cover. The UNSG's letter just got lost in the New York diplomatic toing and froing. But his concern for the effect on the UN of the Contact Group's incoherence registered. The situation was not helped when the Russians tabled a completely unacceptable draft on easing sanctions at a meeting of experts in New York. It now appeared impossible that drafts would be agreed before the Contact Group ministerial meeting and tensions increased all round.

The Bosnian Serbs once again closed roads into and out of Sarajevo, allegedly to end smuggling, and Serb snipers shot and killed a British soldier escorting a convoy. Warren Christopher, speaking in Congress on 28 July, called for a tightening of the exclusion zones around Sarajevo and Gorazde and described the Serb response to the Group's proposals as tantamount to rejection. The arms embargo issue resurfaced and since the Security Council did not accept multilateral lift, the US administration was committed to consulting Congress on unilateral lift.

The Contact Group held its preparatory meeting for the ministerial in Geneva on 28 July. The mood was pessimistic, but it was agreed to remain firm on the strategy previously adopted. There was further discussion on measures for increasing the pressure on the Bosnian Serbs to accept the map. The possibility of offering Milosevic some form of sanctions relief if he closed the borders with the Bosnian Serbs, which I was very keen on, remained on the table. The outcome of the Bosnian Serb Assembly meeting, when it came, offered no comfort. It demanded further changes to the map, and the right to unite with neighbouring states. There was no basis on which the Contact Group ministers could interpret the Serb response as anything but a rejection. This news sparked the Group into further debate about ways of getting Milosevic to seal his borders. The strategy the Group favoured was to present a draft UNSCR on sanctions tightening, while making it clear to Milosevic that if he took action to seal his borders between the announcement and the Resolution's adoption, he would be rewarded. Churkin argued that Milosevic would require a significant incentive, for sealing the borders would have major political repercussions for him in Serbia. David Ludlow argued on our behalf in the Contact Group that the proposed Resolution on sanctions tightening should not appear to be directed specifically against Serbia and Montenegro while there was any chance of a positive reaction from Milosevic, but should appear to be targeted at the Bosnian Serbs. Others argued that it would be impossible to impose sanctions in such a direct way.

On possible military measures, both the UK and France refused to commit themselves until NATO planning had been completed. Stricter enforcement of exclusion zones was likely to provoke major Serb retaliation, and the consequence of this would be the withdrawal of UNPROFOR. It was argued that a weak communiqué from the ministerial meeting would let loose a clamour for unilateral lifting of the arms embargo in the US. Ministers could not just go on saying what they would not do; they had to say what they were prepared to do. The Group seemed on the verge of losing its unity.

President Milosevic, having assembled the Serb leaders in Belgrade and spent many hours on the evening of 25 July and into the morning of 26 July attempting to bring Karadzic round to acceptance of the map, reported that he was not at all convinced his attempts would produce results and he remained opposed to the idea of sealing the FRY borders in an effort to step up the pressure. Churkin, who with Russian Defence Minister Pavel Grachev had met Milosevic, felt the Serb President was supportive of the Group's efforts, but with Karadzic they were disappointed. They were in no doubt – nor were we in the ICFY – that Milosevic's political influence over the Bosnian Serbs had waned dramatically. This erosion in his authority was the direct consequence of Washington's ditching of the VOPP, which had boosted Karadzic at the expense of Milosevic.

At the third Geneva ministerial Contact Group meeting on 30 July ministers were once more forced to compromise in their public conclusions in order to keep the Group together. Work was to continue on a UNSCR tightening sanctions and on planning for stronger enforcement measures. They did agree, after Stoltenberg and I intervened, that a private approach should be made to Milosevic to persuade him to seal the borders and thus live up to his claims that he wanted to bring pressure to bear on the Bosnian Serbs, but they did not agree to put any incentive into their sanctions package and all the long-standing US concerns about working with Milosevic were evident. Ministers left Geneva resigned to waiting for the outcome of a drawn-out process. But they left behind a document with wording that was to bedevil the start of any negotiations. They insisted that for the Bosnian Serbs 'acceptance of the Contact Group proposals is the essential first step' and it was this word 'acceptance' over which the Contact Group then argued with Karadzic for nearly a year until the fall of Srebrenica and Zepa changed their map by force of arms instead of through negotiations.

The Bosnian Serbs, well aware of the fact that the five governments were not going to use their full military capabilities to force them off the territory they occupied, stayed firm. Faced with this reality, the Contact Group officials, and we, played for time. Ministers felt that to wash their hands of the negotiations would result in even more criticism than they faced for indecisiveness. The only action they could agree to was to keep the Contact Group ambassadors in perpetual motion.

On 31 July in Sarajevo, answering questions from the press, Izetbegovic said that he did not feel deceived by the Contact Group communiqué, but wanted them now to stick to their agreed plan. He did not exclude the possibility that those concerned might yet generate the necessary pressure on the Serbs. Nor did he rule out further negotiations if, but only if, the Serbs changed their position. There were many things which needed to be made more precise. Despite recent improvements to the army's equipment, Bosnia would face a long war in the absence of the lifting of the arms embargo. Seeking peace was preferable. But Serb aggression continued. Izetbegovic had informed the UN Secretary-General and UNPROFOR HQ in Zagreb on the recent build-up of heavy weapons around Sarajevo and Gorazde and now expected effective action to defend all safe areas and to implement more fully the exclusion zones. Silajdzic complained at the absence of a commitment to protecting Bosnia's borders, which he regarded as the key to peace in the whole region, and at the way in which the communiqué put aggressor and victim on an equal footing through use of expressions such as 'the two sides'. He objected to the description of the Bosnian state delegation, which he claimed also spoke for many Serbs and others, as a 'Bosniac/Croat delegation'.

In Belgrade the 31 July edition of *Politika*, the main pro-government daily, carried on its front page the text of a statement given by Milosevic supporting the Contact Group proposals which was far tougher than I had expected and meant that once again, as over the VOPP, we had split Belgrade from Pale.

> *The overriding interest of the Serbian nation is peace, and no one has the right to reject that . . . The goal of freedom and justice for the Serbian nation is achieved. Now is the time for concessions. The Contact Group proposals – which legalize the Bosnian Serb Republic and give it half of Bosnia and Herzegovina – is not anti-Serbian . . . Accepting the plan does not mean an end to territorial exchanges. All sides have an interest in further swaps . . . The Bosnian Serb Republic could never have been formed without the help of FRY. The very least that the Yugoslavs can expect from the Bosnian Serbs is that they save them from further sanctions. There are no moral grounds whatsoever to justify additional sacrifices from the FRY and the entire Serbian people.*

Milosevic concluded: 'At this time it takes more courage and moral strength to choose peace than to choose war. In the interest of all citizens of FRY, RSK and the Bosnian Serb Republic, peace must be the choice. That means accepting the Contact Group proposals and allowing the peace process to continue.'

In taking this step, Milosevic had exposed his flank to Seselj and other nationalist critics, who immediately launched strident accusations of a sell-out. Despite his humiliation when the VOPP was rejected, in giving this unequivocal and public support for a peace plan he had put his prestige firmly on the line for a second time. On 4 August 1994 the following measures were ordered by the government of the FRY, to come into effect the same day: 'To break off political and economic relations with the Republika Srpska. To prohibit the stay of the members of the leadership of the Republika Srpska (Parliament, Presidency and Government) in the territory of the Federal Republic of Yugoslavia. As of today the border of the Federal Republic of Yugoslavia is closed for all transport towards the Republika Srpska, except food, clothing and medicine.'

Stoltenberg was asked by Boutros Ghali to undertake direct contact with the leadership in Belgrade and Pale.[191] I was in America on holiday, which helped since the Contact Group were standing firm on their plan and refusing to talk, and were reluctant for me as the EU representative to be seen by Sarajevo as weakening their stance by opening negotiations.

During the summer, now that our ICFY role had been reduced, in my view inevitably, by the involvement of governments, I had pondered on my future. Also, I was fed up with the Contact Group countries for refusing to impose a settlement. My working relationship with Thorvald Stoltenberg was however a delight and he was very keen I should stay. I came to the conclusion that I would stay only if the Germans, who had just assumed the EU Presidency, wanted me to do so, for I was challenging a number of their policies. I decided therefore to take up the long-standing offer of a non-executive directorship on the Board of Coats Viyella plc, an international textile company, to operate from London as well as Geneva and to prepare for life after the Balkans. I wrote to Kinkel and then went to see him, saying that if the Germans felt that being a Co-Chairman precluded my taking such a part-time appointment I would leave and there need be no ill-feeling between us. Somewhat to my surprise the Germans were keen for me to stay and saw no objection to my accepting this limited time commitment in private business. I announced it all in a low-key way and once the British press discovered I had asked for my ICFY salary to be reduced by the same amount I would now get from Coats Viyella, they lost all interest in the obvious story that I was profiting from war. Anyhow, many of them knew that I had taken no salary for the first few months, hoping the job would be over in the six months Cy Vance had originally estimated.

Stoltenberg and I were very worried that, as in May 1993 over the Vance–Owen Peace Plan, when Milosevic applied border sanctions against the Bosnian Serbs and met with no encouragement from the international community, we were in danger of losing his commitment again. So we flew down to see Milosevic for dinner in Tito's hunting lodge just outside Belgrade on Sunday 4 September. Kozyrev had returned from his visit to Belgrade saying that according to all information at their disposal the

embargo was being strictly enforced and the FRY government had now
requested UNHCR and ICRC to send personnel to the border to check that
only humanitarian aid was going through to the Bosnian Serbs. We had
heard from Mrs Ogata that she did not see how UNHCR could accept the
invitation to monitor sanctions by the FRY (Serbia and Montenegro) against
one of the parties, namely the Bosnian Serbs, with whom UNHCR was
dealing over humanitarian aid on a day-to-day basis and on whose cooperation the whole operation was very dependent. We knew ICRC had already
written to the FRY that it was impossible for them to undertake this responsibility. Thorvald and I, after careful thought, decided to offer that ICFY
would establish a sanctions mission. We too saw problems if as negotiators
we were identified by the Bosnian Serbs with sanctions against them, but
we felt it was a risk we had to run because of the overriding importance
for the peace process of binding Milosevic to his declared acceptance of the
Contact Group Plan as a starting point for negotiations. Splitting the Serbs
was far more important than holding out for a totally sealed border, which
was never going to happen. Milosevic accepted that we, as Co-Chairmen,
were seen in Serbia as impartial and not under the control of the US, so
that an ICFY mission was a sellable alternative, and he then set about
finding ways to win support for it publicly. We explained that the Mission
would be civilian, not military, and drawn from Contact Group countries
and other mutually acceptable countries. We would try to avoid using the
term 'monitor' and after much discussion settled for the simple, unprovoca-
tive title of 'ICFY Mission': no uniforms, no insignia. Bo Pellnas, who was
travelling with us and was no longer the general in charge of the UNMOs
but a civilian on our staff, would be our choice as the Mission coordinator.
The Mission's terms of reference would be the declaration made by the FRY
government on 4 August. The Mission would be dependent on the cooperation of the FRY authorities and if we did not receive that support in full
measure from the police and customs authorities we, as Co-Chairmen,
would withdraw the Mission immediately.

We all knew as we drew up the parameters for the Mission that we were
skating on very thin ice: Milosevic, because he was trying to avoid this
being seen as international monitoring; we because we did not wish the
Mission so to infuriate the Bosnian Serbs that they ceased to respect our
impartiality and refused to work with the ICFY. Apart from the principles
that would have to guide the Mission, the problems of implementation were
considerable. We had to start from scratch with no existing organization
and little precedent. To raise the money for the operation we had to
minimize costs and we decided that each country would be responsible for
salaries and travel, with the exception that the Swiss offered to fly the
Mission in to Belgrade on the first occasion as their contribution. The
Mission would not be financed from our normal ICFY budget and we also

had to persuade governments to provide or encourage their NGOs to provide people with the relevant skills as soon as possible.

In Podgorica, the capital of Montenegro, we saw President Bulatovic. He was very keen that pressure should be put on the Bosnian Serbs, despite having just been personally threatened by them over the border closure. I had always found Bulatovic helpful and decent. He had been brave to rebel against the Milosevic line in 1991, when he accepted the first part of the Hague proposal which undercut Serbia's claim to be the successor state to Yugoslavia and paved the way for Montenegrin independence. But when Montenegrins voted overwhelmingly in their referendum to stay with Serbia in Yugoslavia, Bulatovic had no option but to work first with Cosic and then with Milosevic. There was no obvious rancour left to sour their relationship, however, and the two worked well together.

From Podgorica we then drove along the coast road and, stopping off at Prevlaka en route, had looked at the fishing village of Molunat, where at the right time the Croats, we hoped, would offer the Bosnian Serbs access to the sea. As we walked around the small UN area at Prevlaka on the west side of the mouth of the sea estuary I was amazed that Vance and I had been able to persuade President Cosic to agree that the Yugoslav army should pull out in November 1992: for the tip of the peninsula totally commanded the entrance to what was now the main port for the FRY navy. Of course weapons could be fired into the entrance from outside the UN area by Croatian government forces very easily, but the psychological effect of having Croatian forces on the tip of Prevlaka was bound to be very upsetting for the Serbs who had, apart from Prevlaka, withdrawn from the Dubrovnik area in the spring of 1992 as part of the Vance Plan signed that January.

As soon as we reached Dubrovnik Thorvald Stoltenberg began to ring around to rally support for the ICFY Mission, drawing on the Scandinavian NGOs who are ready to deploy at a few days' notice to trouble spots around the world. By next morning Thorvald had succeeded in obtaining pledges from all four of the Scandinavian Foreign Ministers of sixty people to come out to the Mission within ten days and start-up funding of over $400,000. It looked as if the Mission would now succeed, within twenty-four hours of discussing it with Milosevic. In the heady atmosphere of having won the acceptance of the Contact Group and achieved a break-through, we had no idea of the problems the Mission would pose for us and ICFY, in particular the hostility with which it would be viewed by some sections of the US administration, to the extent that in operating the Mission our own integrity would be challenged continuously at levels right up to and including the Secretary of State, Warren Christopher.[192]

We sent a message to the Contact Group who were meeting in Berlin next day because we wanted it to reach Christopher and Kozyrev directly,

not at the discretion of the EU members. From our memorandum it is clear
that the US were given all the crucial information about the deal we had
done with Milosevic. They were informed how Pellnas would report to us
and we to the UN Security Council and the EU Presidency, and of the
importance of opening the Zagreb–Belgrade highway for stopping oil trans-
shipments through Bosnia-Herzegovina to the Croatian Serbs in the Knin.
The message that came back was that the Contact Group was content.

On 8 September I attended a meeting of French diplomats in the Quai
d'Orsay over breakfast. I explained that the US Ambassador, Galbraith, in
Zagreb was now wisely pushing for the sort of comprehensive package for
settling all aspects of the Croatian problem that the ICFY had been
preparing for some months. He had said the Americans were keen to bring
Croatian and Bosnian settlements together. To this end, we agreed after
consulting the Germans that Ahrens, Eide and Szasz from ICFY and
Galbraith and the Russian Ambassador would work intensively over the
next three to four days in Zagreb to produce a constitutional settlement for
Croatia. This already existed in draft in Geneva and provided for
maximalist autonomy for the Krajina, a phased Serb handover, first of
Western Slavonia to Croatian governance and then of Eastern Slavonia after
UN administration of the Eastern UNPA.

In the autumn of 1994 there was once again mounting concern about the
continued ethnic cleansing by the Bosnian Serbs, particularly around
Bijeljina, which Akashi had taken up directly with Karadzic in August. At
that time Karadzic had attributed the problem to criminals and had undertaken to replace the Chief of Police. This was done, but the UNHCR office
in Tuzla nevertheless continued to report the arrival of large numbers of
Muslim refugees who had been forced to leave the Bijeljina area – 106 on
18 August, 187 on 24 August, 430 on 29 August, 566 on 2 September and
780 on 4 September. Akashi issued a tough press statement on 6 September
and spoke to Karadzic on the telephone, when he was told that Karadzic
had taken measures to identify, arrest and prosecute those responsible.
Nevertheless the process of ethnic cleansing in the Bijeljina area indefensibly
continued and Karadzic was clearly responsible for this.

Ever since I had clashed with Karadzic in Banja Luka over ethnic
cleansing in September 1992 there was a degree of personal antagonism in
our relationship which I had to keep under control in order that it did not
hinder my task as a negotiator. Meetings with him were often difficult but
I managed to discipline my underlying disdain for him. Whereas Boban, the
leader of the Bosnian Croats for the first eighteen months of the ICFY's
existence, was to my mind a racist in much the same overt way as Mladic
in language and actions, Karadzic in the early days was more wheedling and
careful to avoid racist remarks, even quite quick to condemn racist actions.
His excuses for ethnic cleansing were always practical, relating to the effects

of the war or the conduct of a particular individual, be he a police chief or a mayor; he would always promise action, and sometimes would volunteer follow-up information when we next met. It appeared that UNHCR and ICRC had similar experiences. Of course, it was a clever tactic to keep us feeling that our representations were having some impact, some influence in moderating the worst effects of this evil practice. Also, in the negotiating room Karadzic never raised any objections to our championing human rights safeguards, and from the start over the Vance–Owen plan acquiesced without objection in the jurisdiction in Serb areas of a human rights court with some outside international judges, in human rights monitors operating in Serb areas and in the appointment of human rights ombudsmen. All this, however, was a facade to cover up a deep-seated commitment to Serbs not living alongside Muslims and to conducting an ethnic cleansing programme with a barefaced dishonour of even greater magnitude than his continued inability to respect or even to know the truth.

I had watched Karadzic become coarsened by war and ever more extreme in his championing of Serb nationalism. Racist remarks began to appear in his speech, particularly with whisky inside him. Simultaneously, he began to project an increasingly devout image and attend publicly more and more Orthodox Church ceremonies. Karadzic also adopted a harsher, more uncompromising attitude, not just to the peace negotiations but also to the taking of hostages. Initially, civilians held by the Bosnian Serbs were always carefully alleged to have undertaken specific criminal offences, but gradually that facade dropped too until in 1995 we found ourselves haggling over French pharmacists taken as hostages with not even a transparent accusation of criminal conduct to justify their being held in prison. This process of coarsening I believe gathered pace through the end of 1994 and early 1995 as the isolation of Pale increased. Karadzic also became obsessed with his struggle with Milosevic. When Stoltenberg and I started to see the Bosnian Serb leaders infrequently, we had to take the first few hours of our meetings to bring them down to earth, to remind them of the real world. This even began to apply to Karadzic, who was in many ways the most sophisticated and worldly of them all.

It is not for me to determine whether Radovan Karadzic is a war criminal. That is for the due process of the Yugoslav War Crimes Tribunal. All I can say is when I heard that Judge Richard Goldstone as Chief Prosecutor had issued an arrest order for his trial, I felt not one tinge of sympathy, looked for not one shred of justification for his conduct, and when I stepped down from being Co-Chairman in June 1995 I was glad that I would not have to negotiate with him under such an order or indeed ever have to meet him again.

It will be for the Tribunal to determine what did or did not happen in Bosnia-Herzegovina in 1992, who really was in control of the Arkan and

Seselj irregulars, who controlled all elements of the Bosnian Serb army and the local militia or police and who could have stopped the rapes, the torture and killing of many Muslims in the detention camps. I am satisfied that in and around Bijeljina in 1994 and 1995 the writ of the Bosnian Serbs' political leaders and their so-called President, Radovan Karadzic, did run, and had he chosen to intervene many more Muslims could have stayed and lived in their homes in that area and not fled to Tuzla. The same applies to Banja Luka. In both places there were few security fears and no possibility that the Muslim population could constitute a threat. Leaving to one side the findings of the War Crimes Tribunal, the medical profession in Belgrade in my judgement should never again let Dr Karadzic practise medicine in their country.

After an initial hesitation in April 1993 I was in little doubt that Milosevic's breach with Karadzic had by August 1994 developed many of the ingredients of a grudge match. They both wanted to be king of the Serbs. Karadzic was trying to be the successful war leader, a non-Communist and a devout Orthodox Christian in the Mihailovic tradition. Milosevic wanted to be the leader who, having fought for and won all the essential Serb interests during the break-up of Yugoslavia, was now bringing peace and prosperity. I saw no reason for us to be involved in their feud, which was why I was opposed to the US and German line of not talking to the Bosnian Serbs, for I could envisage circumstances where their interests might prove to be closer to ours than Milosevic's. This happened for example over Croatia in the spring of 1995, when the Bosnian Serbs did not attack the Croatian government forces in Western Slavonia who were attacking the Croatian Serbs. President Tudjman perceptively kept up a private dialogue with the Bosnian Serb leadership throughout the time they were not talking to President Milosevic.

An informal meeting of EU Foreign Ministers was held on 10–11 September at Usedom in Germany, and at the Sunday lunch we had a discussion on Bosnia.[193] There was general endorsement of the Contact Group's work and a welcome emphasis on the need to seal the FRY border with the Bosnian Serbs. Concern was expressed at developments in Bihac and Sarajevo and the need felt for the UN and NATO to do more to ensure protection of the UN safe areas. There was firm opposition to lifting the arms embargo, but a general recognition that it might be unavoidable as a last resort. But the ministers skated around the core question of imposing a settlement, and not one of them raised my July COREU asking for the use of force.

On 20 September I flew into Washington to attend a dinner at the British Embassy for Cy Vance, who was being given an honorary knighthood by our Ambassador. It was a happy occasion, with all Cy's family present and many of those who had served under him in the State Department. Warren

Christopher came, which was itself a generous gesture, particularly since Cy's speech was full of praise for British policy in Yugoslavia, which could only be taken as criticism of US policy. Many old friends of mine were present too, some of whom were again serving in the State Department and expressed sympathy for our difficulties with American policy. My paper on a global solution had been stiffly acknowledged in a letter from Peter Tarnoff before I arrived. I talked to Richard Holbrooke, whom I knew from passing contacts over the years and who was now involved as Assistant Secretary of State with responsibility for former Yugoslavia, having been promoted from his post as Ambassador to Bonn, where he was replaced by Chuck Redman. Involved in South-East Asia under President Carter, he later joined Lehman Brothers investment bankers. Worldly but intellectual, he was already milking Misha Glenny for information. I believed Holbrooke would inject a dose of much-needed realism into Washington's policy and I welcomed his appointment. I left the next day, glad that I had decided not to take up a long-standing invitation to speak at the Washington Press Club, which would have only further complicated my relations with the administration. It was for European governments now to take Washington on when there were policy disagreements; with the Contact Group in place it was no longer something which the ICFY had to undertake.

The problem for the Americans was that the global solution I advocated meant putting Milosevic and Tudjman together, which was a combination they disliked and which their Croat–Muslim Federation diplomacy had been designed to avoid. It was to be another nine months before American diplomacy would seriously engage with Milosevic, and even then they would shy away and disown the deal in May 1995 which had been negotiated by their special envoy Robert Frasure, one of their most experienced diplomats, directly with Milosevic. I believed we would not see a settlement in the Balkans influenced by the international Community until the US resolved their ambivalent attitude towards Milosevic.

The Z4 plan offered a framework for peace in Croatia on which both parties, given goodwill, should have been able to build a settlement. But there was no goodwill, so first we needed to make progress on economic cooperation.[194] In particular, we had to try to open up the Zagreb–Belgrade highway and turn on water and electricity supplies to and from the Krajina, for these factors were creating problems that were needlessly souring local Croat–Serb relations. On the political dialogue, neither President Tudjman's government, which wanted full reintegration, nor the Croatian Serbs, who demanded secession, were ready to compromise. It was a 'winner takes all' stand-off, which Tudjman won.

When I saw Kozyrev at the British Prime Minister's country house, Chequers, at a dinner for President Yeltsin on Saturday 24 September, he was still very fed up with US policy. He felt the sanctions relief for

Milosevic was derisory and that it was absurd for the Americans to demand 100 per cent closure of the Serb–Montenegrin border with Bosnia-Herzegovina, a long and in many parts mountainous border over which some smuggling would always continue. He was however greatly relieved that the US administration had persuaded Izetbegovic to say that he wanted to defer lifting the arms embargo for six months.

Apart from Croatia and Bosnia-Herzegovina, the Kosovo dispute was simmering, ready to boil over at any moment. On Wednesday 2 November Stoltenberg and I met for two and a half hours in Geneva with Ibrahim Rugova and his advisers to discuss the situation in Kosovo.[195] This meeting followed on from an earlier meeting Stoltenberg had had with Rugova in Oslo and from frequent discussions we as Co-Chairmen had had with President Milosevic on how to handle the Kosovo issues. There had been a considerable amount of ICFY activity on Kosovo in the past, but it had gone largely unreported. Rugova was as firmly wedded to secession as when I first met him in 1992. Autonomy had no appeal.

On Tuesday 15 November at the UN Camp Pleso, alongside Zagreb airport, we met with the Croatian government and the Croatian Serbs, whose delegations were led respectively by Hrvoe Sarinic and Borislav Mikelic, and the American and Russian Ambassadors to Croatia, and made significant progress. Next day, after a very helpful intervention with President Tudjman the night before from the US Ambassador, Peter Galbraith, we met with Tudjman and then sent the text of an agreement on water, electricity, oil, the highway and railway to the two sides. The Croatian Serbs were unhappy with some aspects of the agreement which I reported to the EU later, sending them the agreement and the letters but saying we were now close to settling on a major economic agreement.[196]

On 17 November the Contact Group met briefly in London: it was a disappointing meeting which produced only slight results. They reaffirmed their existing policy of not negotiating with the Bosnian Serbs until they had accepted the Contact Group map but failed to agree on a sanctions package.

At this time the Special Rapporteur on Human Rights in the former Yugoslavia, Mazowiecki, who had been Prime Minister of Poland, said in another of his regular reports that the Bosnian Serbs' current wave of ethnic cleansing was the longest since the summer of 1992. So here we were, two years on from the creation of the ICFY, witnessing the worst bout of ethnic cleansing and only able to watch as the Contact Group map started to show every sign of going the same way as the VOPP, the *Invincible* plan and the EU Action Plan. Once again one party, in this case the Serbs, safe in the knowledge that no one would impose a settlement, was able to block a settlement. But the ethnic cleansing was not just happening in Bosnia, where Banja Luka and Bijeljina were suffering particularly; it was also being perpetrated in Croatia. Mazowiecki described harassment of Serbs in Zenica by

Muslims and complaints by Croats and Serbs of harassment in Bugojno; how the Bosnian Croatian authorities in Mostar were displacing Muslims and how the Federation had interfered with humanitarian aid in Travnik. In Croatia he expressed concern about serious human rights violations and patterns of discriminatory treatment against minority groups. In the FRY, where he had no cooperation, the continuing violence of the police caused great concern, as did discrimination at the workplace and in mobilization. In Kosovo he detected a deterioration with an increase in the number of violent house searches, raids and arbitrary arrests. As with the Special Prosecutor, his role was totally independent of ours in ICFY and I think this was correct, assuring him and us of an independent position with the parties.

Douglas Hurd, knowing of my grave concern about the political vacuum which was developing, told me towards the end of November that he wanted to restart direct talks with the parties and that he would convey this message to Warren Christopher, and hope for an early ministerial Contact Group meeting which was then fixed for early December in Brussels. John Major was also pushing for the Contact Group to regain the initiative.

The whole Bihac episode showed up yet again the folly of the Security Council 'safe area' policy. For the US there had been an additional and painful lesson, of which their military did not need convincing but which their politicians were still trying to evade: namely, air strikes cannot save a 'safe area' if the UN's troops are stationed in the urban parts of the area. So, true to form, the US administration looked for a scapegoat and found it in General Rose. Madeleine Albright was reported as being very angry about an alleged statement by Rose to the effect that the Bosnian government should throw away the Contact Group map and accept a new negotiating framework. If made, it was an unwise remark; but the US were making impossible demands on UNPROFOR and, as if to deflect criticism of their withdrawal from the WEU/NATO maritime force enforcing the arms embargo in the Adriatic, were trying to 'up the ante' on Europe generally. The French intervened to stop NATO flying two reconnaissance aircraft and thirty-seven combat aircraft together over Bosnian air space because they feared that it would look like a raid on Serb radar and that the flights were designed as much to tempt the Serbs to switch on their radar so that NATO could strike at them in self-defence as to serve any UNPROFOR purpose. Notwithstanding this reasonable French fear, with the daily activation of many more SAM 2s and 6s by the Serbs NATO did need many more planes for jamming and air defence suppression. The problem was that flights were no longer seen as being reconnaissance by the Serbs but as hostile. For me, Bihac, where five armies fought each other over a 'safe area', proved that we should have imposed a settlement before the third winter. Even though the UN escaped being dragged in as

a combatant that was only because of the hard-headed realism of Generals
de Lapresle and Rose. General Rose paid a heavy price for first Gorazde
and then Bihac in terms of his acceptability to the Bosnian government and
to the US. He was charged by the Bosnian Prime Minister with having the
blood of thousands of Muslims in Bihac on his hands in an emotive statement to the television cameras in Rose's presence in the Presidency
building in Sarajevo, which was played on prime time right across
America. Only later, when the true facts came out and the much smaller
number of people who lost their lives in Bihac was known, was Silajdzic
challenged to withdraw his allegations. The BBC *Panorama* interview in
which Silajdzic refused to do so is one of the most riveting television
broadcasts and demonstrated that instant television has its drawbacks as
well as advantages for those, like Silajdzic, who exploit it so effectively.
Rose's dignity or humiliation, however one saw it, under the initial public
attack at the time was shown in a very different light as Silajdzic shifted,
twisted and turned when the facts were known.[197] I only wished that the
same treatment could have been meted out to Serb leaders like Karadzic
or Croat and Muslim leaders whose explanations and claims have all too
easily been accepted as the instant wisdom of the hour when they were
totally false.

One of my concerns was that after Bihac, Karadzic's position, and that
of the leading Serb politicians challenging Milosevic, had been strengthened.
Every political party leader in Belgrade, including Draskovic, had
condemned the NATO air strikes. Milosevic did not however switch away
from supporting the Contact Group Plan although the Group could not
hold out a real prospect of sanctions relief. In the US there were still people
who believed that Milosevic and Karadzic were in cahoots together and that
all this apparent division between them was a ploy. I asked myself this
question time and time again over all of this period. I wondered whether
the ICFY Mission was also part of a deception. But a conspiracy of such
complexity simply did not add up with all the anecdotal and other evidence
we had to the contrary.

In Germany, the Serbs retaking the positions in Bihac they had earlier
lost rekindled old suspicions of French and British motives. The conservative and pro-Croat *Frankfurter Allgemeine Zeitung* took the view that what
they described as these countries' pro-Serb views were founded on a wish
to have good relations with a state which would provide a regional balance
to the pro-German Croatia.

The problem with clever conspiracy theories is that they overlook
domestic political forces which are usually far more pressing and relevant.
Germany's pro-Croat policy was heavily influenced by Croats who voted in
Germany and who had hitherto preferentially voted for Genscher's Liberal
Party (FDP). The British government's attitudes to what its troops serving

with the UN could do were strongly influenced by Parliament and public opinion, where there was never anything remotely approaching a majority for becoming a combatant in a civil war. The French Conservative government's policy reflected anxiety about being embroiled on the ground with an eye to their presidential elections due in the spring of 1995. Mitterrand's own wartime experience as a prisoner in Germany, where he learnt respect for Serbia's history and staying power, ensured that he remained sceptical of military involvement. On 30 November Juppé went as far as to claim that NATO had lost its credibility in Bihac. The US meanwhile were content to go on blaming the UN. It was all becoming ugly. Bihac represented the nadir in UN–NATO and US–EU relations.

On 4 December Juppé and Hurd visited the region together and went to Belgrade, Sarajevo, Pale and Zagreb. The importance of their trip was in what it said for the *entente cordiale*, and though it revealed little that was new it gave both men direct contact with the parties and the feel for the issues that can be gained only from face-to-face contact. Flying in each other's planes, speaking each other's language to each other's press, it was an impressive performance. I knew it helped convince Milosevic in much the same way as his visit to Paris to see Mitterrand convinced him that some Contact Group countries were serious players and that sanctions relief was not just a mirage but still on the agenda, despite US reluctance and German apprehension.

The US were beginning to wonder how they would handle the renewal of sanctions relief on Serbia and Montenegro after the first 100 days, which would fall due on 15 January. Senator Dole and Congressman Gingrich had gone public on their strategy of the UN leaving, a unilateral lift of the arms embargo, and a robust strategic bombing campaign against the Bosnian Serbs – different from Clinton's old policy in one vital respect: having accepted that the UN had to leave, the Republicans were prepared for US troops to be made available to help with any UN departure. But by now the Clinton Administration and Warren Christopher were publicly calling Dole's policy a war strategy. General Shalikashvili had, helpfully for the administration, said publicly that it would not work, and it was clear where his and their anxiety lay. If the bombing did not help the Muslims and the Serbs began to look triumphant they did not see how they could avoid responsibility and resist calls to put US ground troops in. For the first time the US were showing flexibility and the wish to open negotiations with Karadzic. Anthony Lake, in a speech on 30 November, said they disliked a Confederation in Bosnia-Herzegovina but would not stand in the way, and they also began to try out different forms of words with Karadzic to overcome the previous insistence that he should 'accept' the Contact Group Plan.

Just at this delicate moment Thorvald Stoltenberg and I feared we might not be able to implement the economic agreement with the Croatian Serbs because of the possibility that a Non-Aligned Resolution in the Security Council might be passed banning all flexibility on oil going to the Croatian Serbs. On 2 December I wrote to Douglas Hurd saying that we were encouraging the Russians to use the veto as the Resolution would stop us using oil trans-shipments through Bosnia as a lever on the Croatian Serbs and saying that my new private secretary on the Contact Group would raise the issue yet again in the Contact Group. In fact Kozyrev ordered the Russian representative to use their veto in New York hours after the Contact Group ministerial meeting in Brussels: the first veto the new Russia had cast, and a wise one too. Just before that meeting we discovered that Redman had been sent from Bonn, where he was now Ambassador, to Sarajevo and was about to break the Contact Group ban on meeting Karadzic in Pale. Stoltenberg mentioned this casually in his introduction which amazed the Europeans and outraged the Germans. Juppé asked me in front of Warren Christopher at the meeting what I thought of this, which put me on the spot, since I had long believed that isolating Karadzic was foolish: I decided to break ranks, saying I thought it was inevitable and right, which caused a slight intaking of breath and more from the French, British and Germans. In my defence, I was being asked for my best advice; I had been ready to criticize the Americans when they were wrong frequently enough, so now, when Holbrooke was trying to open the door to negotiations, it seemed disingenuous not to welcome his initiative.

The German position over Bosnia in the Contact Group shifted in December 1994 from the closeness of the Kinkel/Juppé letter the year before back towards support for the US position. In part this was because they were worried about the deterioration in German–US and European–US relations and they did not want the Contact Group to break down; in part it was because of the tilt of US policy towards Croatia. I understood and respected that judgement. Just as the British and French had moved over the VOPP to the US side in May 1993 for wider reasons, now Germany was doing the same. This meant Germany leaving France and Britain to fight their corner, and it also meant that I had to adjust the centre of gravity of my position as EU negotiator to reflect this new reality within the EU. In respect of Croatia it meant that Tudjman was to be granted ever more licence. It was wise geostrategic politics by the Germans, given their pro-Croatian position, but it showed up the shallowness of German demands for qualified majority voting in EU foreign policy. As in December 1991 over recognition of Croatia, so now in December 1994 Germany was exercising its right to have and to hold its own foreign policy on an area of vital interest. For the German position was not by any stretch of the imagi-nation then representative of mainstream EU thinking; Denmark and Sweden were very critical of the Croatian human rights record. It was however a perfectly reasonable exercise of German choice from which I believe the EU and NATO overall benefited, even though it made our lives more difficult in working for negotiated settlements. The Bismarck tradition of independent thought was still alive in Bonn and I for one, far from being suspicious of it, believed it to be a natural and inevitable part of a confident new democratic and unified Germany.

Stoltenberg and I went back to Belgrade and Zagreb on 6–7 December to try and keep up the momentum for implementation of the economic agreement,[198] and we hoped to open the highway on 14 December. Meanwhile Bo Pellnas, the ICFY Mission Coordinator in Belgrade, was feeling ever more frustrated: yet another US non-paper alleging border violations was in circulation and still the US did not give him the information and intelligence to plug any real gaps. Pellnas was worried about being short-handed over Christmas and though personally doing a magnificent job he was understandably fed up and decided to retire. A very conscientious man who liked the US, he could simply not understand why the Mission was being perpetually undermined.

The former FRY president Cosic wrote to us on 8 December to urge us to lift the political isolation of Karadzic: 'Pale is the place where to decide about the peace, not Belgrade.' Yet now that the US were coming closer to adopting a policy of realpolitik over Bosnia, with Holbrooke's arrival in the State Department, so Stoltenberg and I felt we had to leave the negotiations with the Bosnian Serbs to the Contact Group and not barge in and go to Pale ourselves. We kept that opinion under constant review, however, and were chafing at the diplomatic delay. Milosevic was still not able to influence Pale, and we felt he had to be readier to take on his own senior JA officers who were playing with Mladic behind his back. When discussing the problems with Milosevic one could almost see him calculating whether to woo Mladic or ditch him.

By now Abdic was back in control of his traditional fiefdom around Velika Kladusa. The Bosnian 5th Corps' hitherto successful commander, General Atif Dudakovic, was however overcoming his setback, recognizing that he had overstretched his forces and invited the Serbs to counter-attack. Dudakovic had served with Mladic in the JNA, attacking the Croats in Knin, so he was both distrusted by the Croats and grudgingly admired by Mladic. The 5th Corps were still a force to be reckoned with in the Bihac pocket; never allowing themselves to be totally defeated, in August 1995 they obtained their reward when they helped the Croats to lift the siege on Bihac.

On 14 December, in a CNN interview, Karadzic offered a six-point peace plan and, in an obviously prearranged statement, former US President Jimmy Carter announced he would travel to Pale. Stoltenberg and I took a positive attitude to this, for we believed that anything that could bring diplomatic movement was welcome. It was apparent, too, that just as over

Haiti the White House were far closer to this initiative than was being admitted by the far more cautious State Department. Carter's stress on an immediate pre-Christmas ceasefire was wise, for Akashi had been doing much spadework and this was an achievable objective. Izetbegovic however needed a lot of convincing. Milosevic, who saw that Karadzic had scored a point by involving Carter, cleverly invited the former US President to visit Belgrade and was upbeat about Carter's chances when we saw him on 16 December. Carter travelled to Sarajevo on Monday 19 December despite US Ambassador Galbraith arguing that in the absence of prior acceptance of the Contact Group Plan by Karadzic Carter's trip would not be helpful. Carter claimed to have been told that the US view was that the Contact Group language 'on the basis of' did not mean a prior acceptance of the plan, which might ease some of the Bosnian Serbs' fears.

Jimmy Carter's trip to Sarajevo and Pale encountered many difficulties but he managed to confirm the ceasefire, which raised the profile of his trip in public relations terms, even though Akashi would almost certainly have achieved this. On the opening of negotiations Carter had unfortunately only been able to extract two different forms of words, one acceptable to Izetbegovic, the other to Karadzic, and the stalemate was sadly set to continue for months ahead. In the process Carter alienated the Bosnian Muslims: Izetbegovic called his visit 'counter-productive, because it favours not only Karadzic but the Bosnian Serbs as well'. They thereafter refused to deal with Jimmy Carter. For my part I was full of admiration for a man who was prepared to take on such a difficult journey and at least try his hand. I had always seen much to praise in Jimmy Carter's personal contribution to Camp David. In his role as a former President he seemed to have won more respect both worldwide and in the US than during his actual tenure as President. Stoltenberg had kept in close touch with the Carter Center and had given them every encouragement to become involved. The Contact Group, visiting Belgrade in December, felt Carter's mission had set back the prospect of winning over a majority in the Pale Assembly to their form of words, but they left Milosevic with a more explicit position paper to use with any wavering Bosnian Serbs.

In Belgrade Mikelic told us that he would now not sign the economic agreement, so we immediately cut off all oil supplies transiting Bosnia from Serbia to Croatia. This caught the Croatian Serb leaders by surprise and infuriated them. We had however long believed that we would have to use our leverage on oil trans-shipments at the right time and our fight with the US to keep this option open was now going to be tested. On 20 December I wrote to Douglas Hurd to explain the situation on oil supplies to the Krajina and to ask the Contact Group to provide the maximum freedom of manoeuvre during the next fourteen days. I concluded: 'If it is possible to conduct a delicate operation in a cesspit, this is what we are doing. We can accept the smear campaign about our activity from the US, despite the fact that the Contact Group has been kept informed of most of these facts, and the US have their means of knowing all the facts.' We went back to Belgrade on 23 December to negotiate with a much chastened Mikelic, and saw Milosevic, who never complained about the pressure we were putting Mikelic under, though he was grateful that we had deliberately not consulted him. I sent both a COREU and a more explicit memorandum[199] about what we were doing to Sir David Hannay, our Ambassador in New York, and the French Ambassador Mérimée in case the issue suddenly blew up over the Christmas holidays.

All over Christmas and the New Year the telephone was busy between us and Mikelic in Belgrade. We continued to squeeze him over oil trans-shipments, and when he eventually agreed to open the highway and we had confirmation that it was actually open, we authorized oil supplies to go to the Western UNPA but not to the Southern or Northern UNPAs. This was a classic case, albeit in miniature, of why diplomacy needs the leverage of sticks and carrots to succeed. Even so, the Dutch objected in a COREU that we were breaching UNSCR 820 para. 12. But by this time the highway was open and oil could pass to the Croatian Serbs direct from Croatia and with the agreement of the Croatian government. Tudjman knew what we were doing and approved throughout, despite public protests from lower down in his government.

I approached 1995 with trepidation. There was no Contact Group peace-making to match UN peacekeeping. UNPROFOR's authority was running out. UNHCR had been able to restart the airlift in Sarajevo and convoys were starting to get through with the approaching ceasefire; fortunately, the winter so far had again been a mild one, but a cold spell would be devastating. On the Contact Group map I thought it most unwise for the Bosnian Muslims not to have started to discuss swapping Zepa and Srebrenica for land around Sarajevo. But only the US had any influence on President Izetbegovic, Ganic and Sacirbey, and they seemed reluctant to exercise it.

The New Year started auspiciously enough, with the four-month cessation of hostilities holding. Its potentially most important feature was a separation of forces along the confrontation lines, with UN troops to be interposed between the warring factions in certain areas. Boutros Boutros Ghali then raised the question with the Contact Group of having a single negotiator, suggesting that one man might be more effective than a college. He proposed Stoltenberg because he did not belong to a Contact Group country. I had considerable sympathy with this suggestion, for we had all become frustrated by the cumbersome structure of the Contact Group. But we had to remind ourselves that the Contact Group had emerged because of the need to involve the Americans at every stage in the negotiations. A single person who had the confidence of all five nations would be hard to

find. I certainly would not have the support of the US and the suggestion
of Stoltenberg was turned down by other Contact Group countries. It
appeared that, having become so heavily involved, no capital relished giving
up its opportunity to influence the process at all stages. My preference was
to have a French politician acceptable to the French EU Presidency, which
had begun in January, and that this person be appointed to replace me,
having a double-hatted function as Co-Chairman of the Conference and also
being designated to negotiate on behalf of the Contact Group. I discussed
the issue very frankly with Douglas Hurd on Sunday 15 January and then
went to Paris to talk to my deputy, Jacques Alain de Sédouy. I was now
determined to set in motion an irreversible mechanism so as to ensure I
would be a free man by no later than the middle of June. I had seriously
contemplated stepping down in May 1993, February 1994 and September
1994, and it was now necessary for family and future career reasons to make
final arrangements.

I wrote to John Major and told him that I had left behind in Paris a letter
for President Mitterrand,[200] the operative paragraphs of which read as
follows:

> I write to you as current President of the European Council to say that I
> would like to step down from my post at a time convenient to the French
> Presidency. In order to preserve your freedom for manoeuvre over my
> replacement I have told no one else of my decision other than John
> Major and Douglas Hurd.
>
> If the Contact Group Ministers wish to appoint a politician as a
> single negotiator for Bosnia-Herzegovina to work in coordination with
> the Contact Group of Ambassadors then I believe that would be the
> right time for the European Union to appoint someone to replace me.
> If, on the other hand, you decide to appoint a diplomat as a single
> negotiator and wish me to stay in my post for a few more months I
> would be ready to do so. Whatever timing is chosen I hope that it will
> be possible to make the announcement no later than the June European
> Council.

As I explained to Alain Juppé at the end of January in Paris, we had a
six-week window of opportunity in which we might be able to pressurize
the parties into a settlement, not just in Bosnia-Herzegovina but in Croatia
as well. Without pressure from the five Foreign Ministers, with France in
the lead role, the war in Bosnia would start afresh and there would be
fighting in Croatia by the spring. I saw no alternative to keeping the
Contact Group ambassadors in orbit, negotiating as best they could;
perhaps letting the Zagreb 4 ambassadors test the water on the plan for
Croatia, with Stoltenberg and me continuing to promote a Zagreb–Belgrade

Map 13 Possibilities for adopting Contact Group map,
Lord Owen to Alain Juppé, 10 February 1995

rapprochement. But all of this would fail if it was not backed by secret diplomacy led from Paris to assemble a package which France would put on its own authority to the four other governments in the Contact Group immediately prior to a formal meeting with all the key players in the region. Most of the facts were known; what was missing was a global approach in which no one gained all that they wanted but everyone signed up simultaneously for peace. I wrote to John Major saying that France, holding the EU Presidency, was best placed to bring these issues to a head and as a Contact Group government had the chance of holding the US to such a package. I would wait for a decision from the French government as to how they wanted to play things but my personal preference would be to go sooner rather than later; and I would be grateful if knowledge of the letter could be kept very restricted while the French decided how they wanted to handle the situation.

John Major replied on 3 February, saying: 'By any standards you have had your shoulder at this wheel for as long as anyone could have a right to expect. But I hope that if the Presidency do not propose another senior negotiator in the next few weeks, you will agree to stay on, at least for a while. By June the position may be clear.'

Silajdzic was warning that the Bosnians would resume hostilities in May if no peace settlement was forthcoming and wanted to see a policy of 'lift and stay', claiming that the UN did not need to go before the embargo was lifted. He was full of criticism of the UK and me personally for allowing oil to transit Bosnia, and even went so far as claiming that Britain was fomenting discord in Tuzla. The Bosnian Muslims were also concerned that Jimmy Carter was now quietly advocating the lifting of all sanctions against the FRY, immediate changes to the map and equal treatment of Sarajevo and Pale. There was little doubt that Karadzic's bid to present himself as a modern Mihailovic had succeeded as far as the former US President was concerned, and the third birthday celebrations of Republika Srpska in Pale were euphoric. The White House, however, was discouraging Carter from returning to Sarajevo and the Contact Group were against further meetings with Karadzic – until he first accepted the map. They feared that if they opened up their map to discussion they would lose it and be back to zero, but they failed to recognize that they could also lose it by the Serbs taking Muslim-controlled territory.

In Zagreb on 10 January Tudjman told the Contact Group ambassadors plus China, Italy and the Holy See that the Croatian government had thoroughly considered its options in the light of what they claimed as the failure by UNPROFOR to implement its mandate. They appeared to want to ignore the opening of the Zagreb–Belgrade highway on 22 December for daytime traffic and two weeks later for twenty-four hours a day, seven days a week. On implementing the economic agreement, they claimed that the Croatian Serbs were procrastinating and said they were not ready to allow Milosevic to dictate the pace of events, Croatia resolved not to agree to extend UNPROFOR's mandate after 31 March. It was vintage Tudjman and one had to admire his sheer nerve. There was no reason for UNPROFOR to withdraw its HQ from Zagreb, Tudjman added, a recognition of the sizeable revenue that this brought in, and he was ready to allow the UN to make a phased departure over one to three months.

With total predictability the Croatian Serbs used this provocative Croatian government decision over the UN mandate as the reason for not signing the Joint Commercial Oil Company Agreement which we had been painstakingly assembling over the previous six weeks. They also refused even to accept the Z4 plan from the four ambassadors who had travelled to hand it to them in Knin, and thereafter they generally withheld all cooperation. The Croatian government had carefully calculated their options. They had decided that Martic and Babic were still refusing to live within Croatia and so they judged it was in their interests to confront them rather than stay with the hated status quo. Though it created immense problems for Stoltenberg and myself I had to accept that Tudjman's basic judgment was probably correct in that Martic in marked contrast to Mikelic, was still totally recalcitrant on any meaningful dialogue. The dangers should have been obvious to the Serbs. Tudjman had baited a trap and a few months later Martic walked into it. The Croatian Serb leadership in Knin would never face up to the fact that Tudjman had used the last three years provided by the Vance Plan to create a modern and well-equipped army. Tudjman was clearly poised to take the Western UNPA, the most vulnerable of the protected areas, into Croatia and was looking for an excuse to do so. Meanwhile on 12 January Tudjman wrote officially to the UN Secretary-General to 'inform you that the UNPROFOR mandate is hereby terminated effective 31 March 1995 in accordance with Resolution 949 (1994)'.

Having lost confidence in the Contact Group's ability to move things forward, I was trying to encourage the French government, as the EU Presidency, closely allied with the British, to take an initiative with Milosevic over recognition of Bosnia-Herzegovina and if possible Croatia,[201] and to bring both Tudjman and Milosevic to Paris. So I began to send Juppé direct messages, as President of the Council, rather than rely only on COREUs. After my meetings with Presidents Milosevic and Tudjman I saw Juppé in Paris on 30 January.[202] Then, in Zvornik on 1 February, Stoltenberg and I, with French support, saw Karadzic and Krajisnik for the first time since July 1994. We reported back to French officials on 2 February in Paris. This irritated Holbrooke, who demanded we should not see them for a follow-up, as he now wanted again to stop all contact.

I wrote to Juppé on 8 February warning about a mood change in Belgrade and how we needed 'to convince Milosevic that economic sanctions is not a tunnel with no end'.[203] I also challenged the Contact Group's decision that land deals going beyond the boundaries of Bosnia-Herzegovina were not within their remit. I then wrote to him again on 10 February with four map options which kept to the 51 per cent–49 per cent division, but joined up Livno to Bihac, as happened six months later.[204]

Stoltenberg and I were trying, as it turned out to no avail, to start negotiations on the Contact Group map before the Bosnian Muslims broke the ceasefire and the Bosnian Serbs decided to make changes by force of arms, as we were quite certain they would do some time in the summer. Every time I spoke to Karadzic or people in close contact with him they were talking of launching new offensives and saying that while they would prefer to negotiate land swaps, if everyone continued to ostracize them they would attack. Unfortunately we were unable to obtain a hearing for our message. It was four months before the Bosnian Serbs seized Srebrenica and Zepa and the Contact Group map was unilaterally changed. At any time during those months it would have been possible to negotiate swaps whereby these enclaves would have been given up in return for land which the Muslims wanted around Sarajevo. The US and Germany on the Contact Group were afraid to negotiate and the Bosnian Muslim leaders, as so often in the past, unwilling to compromise. I remain of the view that it was grossly irresponsible not to have conducted negotiations in the spring of 1995 and to have brought the parties around the table, as we had done in virtually continuous session until the Contact Group had been formed.

Stoltenberg and I visited Zagreb and Belgrade again on 13–15 February, and on 16 February we had lunch with Kozyrev in Moscow.[205] He was in an interrogative mood and had not yet decided on whether to urge Milosevic to accept the sanctions package put up by the European members of the Contact Group. Nor was Alexandr Zotov, who had replaced Churkin, at all sure he would go to Belgrade, though he did eventually decide to go. The Russians felt that the helicopter controversy, where the UNMOs watching the Serb radar screen at Belgrade airport had picked up tracks of what might have been helicopters flying from Bosnia to Serbia, was designed to discredit Milosevic. Investigation by experts from Contact Group countries was inconclusive. For my own part I had little doubt that the tracks were those of helicopters which had flown into Bosnia undetected, flying low at very slow speeds of around 60 m.p.h. which made them appear as lorries from airborne radar and satellite and, by travelling in the deep valleys, were able to avoid being seen or heard by ICFY Mission personnel on the ground. Then on the return flight they were flying high to avoid using much petrol and believed they would not have been detected on radar.

On 17 February I again wrote to Juppé, warning that Croatian public opinion was being daily stiffened against the UN continuing and that Milosevic could not recognize Croatia unless the mandate in some form was renewed.[206] I suggested trying to agree a reconfiguration of UNPROFOR within Croatia and specifically that the Croatian Serbs should give up the Western UNPA and we should start UN administration in the Eastern UNPA. It was ambitious, but far preferable to Tudjman taking the Western sector, which is what happened weeks later. On 2 March Stoltenberg and I issued an upbeat statement on the economic agreement: more than 160,000 vehicles had now used the highway, the oil pipeline blocked in UNPA Sector North had been put into operation, railway repairs were under way and though the oil agreement had not been signed the Croatian government was supplying oil and Sarinic and Mikelic were in constant touch.[207]

The Contact Group were now starting to focus on persuading Milosevic to recognize Bosnia-Herzegovina, which was easier for him than Croatia where there was still a danger of war. The Americans, out of distrust of Milosevic, and the Russians, out of frustration at America, were tending to distance themselves from the dialogue and the lead was being taken by the European three, particularly the British and French, for the Germans were worried about delinking Bosnia from Croatia and putting its recognition further back in time. Also, German public opinion and the Bundestag were very antagonistic to Milosevic, so any deal involving him and the Bosnian Muslims at the expense of the Croats was not going to be a popular mix, as Kinkel knew very well. The Americans were concentrating on persuading Tudjman to renew the UN mandate, while in Bosnia the Bosnian government forces were gearing up for a spring offensive. But Izetbegovic had committed himself to renewing the cessation of hostilities agreement if there had been prior recognition by the FRY, and many of us hoped that at that time there might be an opportunity to start negotiating on the map and swapping territory. But it was all becoming very fraught inside the Contact Group.

On 23 March we met Mikelic and Milosevic in Belgrade.[208] Stoltenberg had been charged with pursuing the new UN mandate negotiations and for the first time we began to sense that Mikelic and the President of the Croatian Serb Assembly were ready to commence political talks. That afternoon we drove to Zvornik to see Karadzic and Krajisnik. The cessation of hostilities agreement had virtually broken down and Karadzic was on his way to Tuzla, where the Serbs had suffered some losses. We discussed how to overcome the deadlock over the word 'accept' and we hit on the idea of the Bosnian Serbs negotiating while still under FRY sanctions, for Milosevic would lift his sanctions if they agreed to use the word 'accept'. In return the Bosnian Serbs would use all the existing wording about negotiating on the basis of the Contact Group plan, and a 'starting point', but not use the word 'accept'. We gave the exchange of letters to Bob Frasure, with whom I had a drink in the US Embassy in Belgrade, but though he promised to give it a fair wind I did not feel it was likely to get anywhere in Washington. We also reported to Juppé.

On 27 March 1995 I saw Douglas Hurd and warned him that if the Bosnian Muslims continued to attack it would only be a matter of time before the Serbs launched a massive counter-offensive. The outcome of that offensive might determine whether a settlement would remain a 49 per cent–51 per cent Serb–Federation split. I also believed the UN would have to withdraw before the winter if there were no negotiated settlement in the autumn, as the UN's authority was eroding by the day.

Events were spiralling out of control. On 18 April Stoltenberg and I met Milosevic in Belgrade and as a result recommended to the French that they should push ahead very fast with an Izetbegovic–Milosevic meeting in Paris.

We then drove along the highway to Zagreb and saw the long queue of Serbian lorries that had been stopped without any warning by members of the Sanctions Assistance Mission who had now come on the border of the Eastern UNPA. Tension was rising; we tried to persuade the head of the Mission in Zagreb to defuse the situation, but it was a difficult issue for them and the Sanctions Committee in New York, for there was little flexibility built into the sanctions regime.

On 20 April Ganic and Sacirbey met with the Contact Group in Vienna and confirmed that they would extend the cessation of hostilities if the FRY clearly recognized Bosnia-Herzegovina and effectively sealed its border, or if Karadzic accepted the Contact Group plan. Otherwise they said they would go on fighting.

On 24 April it was announced in the Hague that the Yugoslav War Crimes Tribunal was to begin investigative proceedings against Karadzic, Mladic and Mico Stanisic, the former head of the Bosnian Serb police.

On the evening of 28 April a physical fight developed between a Croat and a Serb at a petrol station on the Zagreb–Belgrade highway and the Serb was stabbed and killed. Later a man claiming to be the brother of the murdered man fired three rifle shots at Croatian cars, damaging their tyres. The highway was closed by the Croatian Serbs that night, but some vehicles still on it were fired on and a Croat driving along was killed, causing a following minibus to swerve out of control and flip over, killing two and injuring three of the passengers. On 29 April the Serb authorities detained four Croatian civilians, and though the highway was due to open later that day it did not do so. The Croats had been handed their opportunity.

On 1 May Croatian government forces launched an attack on UNPA West, focusing on the highway from the West and the East and on severing the links to Bosnia-Herzegovina across the Sava bridge. The Croatians used tanks, mortar and infantry. Three Jordanian UN troops were seriously injured as a result of tank fire. Croatian air force MiGs were used, dropping bombs very close to UN positions on the Sava river. Okucani fell to the Croats on 2 May.

The UN Security Council made the noises of criticism but was not ready to apply sanctions on the Croats. The Serb leader Martic went wild and ordered a missile attack on Zagreb. It looked as if the situation might get out of control, but the speed of the Croatian government's attack and the complete collapse of the Croatian Serbs' army meant that by the time a ceasefire had been agreed with the UN the battle was over. The Croats had won. The mystery was the lack of response from the Bosnian Serbs in nearby Banja Luka; they were, in Sherlock Holmes's terms, 'the dog that did not bark in the night'. I believe that Tudjman had bought the Bosnian Serbs off with oil supplies to offset those which they were no longer getting from Milosevic. This also showed up all Karadzic's talk of Pale and Knin coming together as being humbug. I then remembered Tudjman's delight some months before when he had told me about Karadzic's private map proposal to his government which gave significant parts of the Krajina to the Croats. Milosevic, who blamed Martic for closing the highway and provoking the Croats, was powerless to do anything more than show by troop movements that he would protect the Eastern UNPA. The victor was Tudjman; the loser, the Krajina Serb leader Martic. The UN was caught in the middle. The US and Germany had long since abandoned any pretence of impartiality and were now overtly supporting the Croatian government. The EU was left on the sidelines.

There was no more economic or political progress to be made in talks between the Croatian Serbs and the Croatian government, not just in May but for some months ahead. The Knin leaders typically fought between themselves as to who was responsible for the debacle and their defeat. Paradoxically, the Croatian government could now renew the mandate for UNPROFOR since Tudjman in victory had no difficulty with public opinion in reversing engines and appearing to go along with international opinion for a four-month UN mandate renewal until the end of September. The UN Resolution virtually had to be accepted by the now weakened Croatian Serbs, and no one objected to their calling the UN force in the three remaining UN sectors by the French acronym for UN Confidence Restoring Operation, since they objected to UNCRO, as a face-saver.

Martic, who had used his control over the militia to close the Zagreb–Belgrade highway, in part because of the blocked lorries at Lipovac, in part because of the incident in the road, managed to hang on with Babic's support. Babic, having changed sides yet again, deserted Mikelic. Milosevic, utterly fed up with Martic, having lost his loyal supporter Mikelic and with him the best and only chance of negotiating a settlement for Croatia, seemed totally frustrated. A new general for the RSK forces, Mile Mrksic, who had only just finished serving as the Chief of Staff to the Head of the JA, was appointed, which demonstrated just how close the military links still were between the Knin and Belgrade. When I talked to Milosevic I sensed he was now set on giving Martic enough rope to hang himself. He began to mention that even if the Croats took Knin, fighting would go on in the hills and the forests, as if he accepted that losing the Krajina was becoming inevitable.

Meanwhile on 1 May the cessation of hostilities agreement in Bosnia-Herzegovina had ended, making a fragile situation even more precarious. Serious fighting was now predicted by UNPROFOR for June. Sarajevo airport was closed and the only way in was through Serb checkpoints, or over Mt Igman and then across the airport, or being taken by the Muslims through their tunnel under the airport. The obvious way to renewal of the agreement was to make progress on the Contact Group negotiations with

Milosevic over recognition and the sanctions package, but the Americans were still not prepared to be flexible over sanctions.

In FYROM, where Ambassador Ahrens had just visited Skopje for the third round of renewed trilateral talks between the government and the three Albanian parties, the trial in Tetovo of Professor Sulejmani, the Rector of the newly proclaimed Albanian University, was heightening tension. The Albanians had raised in the talks the issue of the use of their language in Parliament, to which the Minister of Justice had replied that this was a matter of 'massive sensitivity', and we in ICFY were trying to explore the logistics of having simultaneous translation of oral statements. In Kosovo many of the pupils involved in the 'illegal' Albanian language secondary and elementary school classes had been readmitted into the official school system. In ICFY we believed that a flare-up was now more likely in Tetovo than in Kosovo.

So now every part of the former Yugoslavia was again in a state of tension and the five-nation Contact Group seemed quite unable to bring their act together. The French were warning that a new government after the presidential elections, which Chirac looked likely to win, would withdraw from UNPROFOR if their two conditions – renewal of the cessation of hostilities agreement and strengthening of UNPROFOR in terms of its assets and its rules of engagement – were not met.

I minuted Paris and London on my ideas for revising the Mixed Military Working Group to negotiate on the map, using this forum to let Mladic's authority override the Pale politicians.[209] I had tried this out on Milosevic, who seemed keen. At the recent Bosnian Serb Assembly at Sanski Most, Mladic had, according to someone who was present, invited all racketeers and war profiteers to leave the room. Karadzic foolishly asked who he had in mind; one of the three people named by Mladic was Krajisnik, who then asked on what authority Mladic made this allegation, to which Mladic replied that if he, Krajisnik, did not leave the room he would have his bodyguards remove him. When Karadzic had protested Mladic had said to him in public, 'Without me, you are dead.' This was Ruritanian farce, but to me it was also a sign of a serious breakdown in relations in Pale. Yet others still saw it as an elaborate Serbian hoax in order to convince sceptical Americans that the Karadzic/Milosevic/Mladic splits were genuine.

The one glimmer of light was the US member of the Contact Group, Ambassador Robert Frasure. A born negotiator, laconic, full of *bons mots*, he was building an empathetic relationship with Milosevic. Frasure had served with Ray Seitz, US Ambassador in London, and Ray, an old friend of mine, spoke warmly about him, as did a number of my African friends. The key problem in the negotiations with Milosevic was how, if sanctions against the FRY were suspended or lifted in return for recognition of Bosnia-Herzegovina and renewed pressure on Pale for a settlement, they could be reimposed if Milosevic defaulted. The US did not believe the Russians would vote for reimposition of sanctions in those circumstances. Milosevic, on the other hand, did not accept any lift or suspension which the US could override to reimpose sanctions at their own discretion. He needed a significant period, he hoped for a full year, before the threat of reimposition could become operative.

On 7 May Silajdzic summoned all ambassadors in Sarajevo to a meeting in the early evening in front of television cameras to draw attention to the shelling of Butmir that afternoon, where the latest figures showed nine dead and over forty injured. This was not an isolated incident, he claimed, but a deliberate terrorist act to kill, showing that genocide in Bosnia continued. The cameras left and the ambassadors were then told that the passive attitude of the UN Security Council and UNPROFOR had allowed the Serbs to start using heavy weapons again killing and injuring civilians. In the last eight months of 1994 240 people had been killed in Sarajevo. In April 1995 twenty-six were killed. On 1 May fourteen were killed. They had given General Smith the precise coordinates of all Serb heavy weapons emplacements, most of which were fixed and many not in populated areas. They asked for air strikes. This was all later repeated to the press by Silajdzic, flanked at his request by the French and British ambassadors. Much of the Bosnian Muslims' understandable anger arose from the fact that the shells had fallen on people waiting to cross through the foot tunnel under the airport into Sarajevo, and the Serbs had deliberately targeted this concentration of people.

The Bosnian request for air strikes went up the UN chain of command on 8 May and, no doubt because it was such a difficult choice, it reached Boutros Ghali in Moscow. He, after carefully consulting Stoltenberg, said no, because what had been requested was not close air support but wider air strikes. His decision was one with which I fully agreed. The US predictably protested at the decision but, fatefully and perhaps because the British General Rupert Smith had asked for the political authority on this occasion, Douglas Hurd disagreed and wrote to Boutros Ghali challenging the decision. The French did not raise any objection to Boutros's decision, but when he received Hurd's letter on Friday 12 May in Paris, Boutros discussed it with Alain Juppé and with Thorvald Stoltenberg. He was clearly very perturbed, for while it was one thing for a UN Secretary-General to hold out against the US, to hold out against the view of the US and Britain in future was going to be very difficult. The Security Council is any Secretary-General's real power base. A Secretary-General can separate himself from the centre of gravity of opinion among the permanent members from time to time, but if there is a persistent gap between them, the authority of the Secretary-General dissipates. Boutros Ghali was now determined that the basic contradiction in policy, where UNPROFOR attempts to be impartial while the Security Council abandons impartiality, had to be faced.

Very worried, I wrote to Douglas Hurd on Saturday 13 May and faxed the letter to him immediately so that he knew my views before he met Juppé. I said that air strikes, as distinct from close air support, meant escalation of the war and UNPROFOR having to either fight or withdraw. My essential message was that the recent differences of opinion over air raids had meant that Akashi and probably Boutros Ghali, would not now resist should they get another request from General Smith, and I hoped that he and Juppé would agree that there should be no question of going beyond close air support until the Security Council had at least the opportunity of making a rational choice and facing the consequence in terms of risk to the lives of UNPROFOR and the virtual certainty of substantial numbers of UN hostages being taken by the Serbs in deeply humiliating circumstances.

Meanwhile in Belgrade Frasure, with apparently the full support of Holbrooke, was embarking on a series of dialogues with Milosevic. British and French officials who had pioneered the initiative had expected to do this, but Douglas Hurd judged it was better to put the US in the driving seat. Milosevic was quite happy with our suggestion that the OSCE should take over the ICFY Mission, and we hoped that this would allow the OSCE also to come back into Kosovo and that it would free the ICFY from a thankless task. The US sanctions team, which had easy access to Vice-President Gore, were however still resisting any negotiable sanctions package, so Frasure was going to have a difficult task.

On 16 May the Secretary-General briefed the Security Council about the deteriorating situation facing the UN, saying that to date 162 peacekeepers had been killed and 1,420 injured and that in his view there were four options: the status quo; a more robust approach; withdrawal of UNPROFOR; or redeployment and reduction of UNPROFOR troops. In reality redeployment was code for coming out of Zepa, Srebrenica and probably Gorazde. The US responded immediately to say they were against any redeployment which meant abandoning the Eastern enclaves, and they wanted NATO air power to be used instead. The Secretary-General pointed out that this was a point of view not shared by any of his advisers, whether civilian or military.

On 18 May Frasure, after long and detailed negotiations, reached a deal ad referendum to Washington and the Contact Group. The negotiations were discussed with Stoltenberg and me by Milosevic, who felt that a breakthrough had been made. Over the next few days the deal fell apart because the US would not accept reimposition being dependent on the UN Secretary-General. In effect, the US had insisted on being able to reimpose sanctions themselves, which was a position that Milosevic was never likely to accept.

To cover their tracks the US publicly blamed Milosevic; this he took uncom-plainingly, and did not in public reveal the details of the package.

To Stoltenberg and me, the collapse of the Frasure–Milosevic talks was a disaster and we feared the consequences for Croatia as well as Bosnia-Herzegovina. We did not have to wait long. On 24 May there had been some 2,700 firing incidents around Bosnia and General Rupert Smith had issued an ultimatum about the return of four heavy weapons seized by the Bosnian Serbs. On 25 May NATO aircraft launched air strikes against two Serb ammunition dumps near Pale. The Bosnian Muslims, who had also had heavy weapons in the Sarajevo exclusion zone, were told to remove them by 26 May. In the lull before the storm, the new French Foreign Minister, Hervé de Charette, fixed a Contact Group ministerial meeting in the Hague in the margins of the NATO meeting the evening after the Foreign Affairs Council meeting earlier that day in Brussels. I was asked to attend both. By now we had CNN almost continuously showing UNMO hostages, one shackled to a stake, another to railings on a bridge, in and around Pale. The US wanted further air strikes. The Serbs shelled a café area in Tuzla, killing seventy-five people. On 26 May NATO air strikes took place again, followed by wholesale hostage-taking by the Bosnian Serbs. In retrospect, Akashi believed that this second round of air strikes tipped the Bosnian Serbs over the brink into seeing the UN as the enemy. That same day I saw the British member of the Contact Group and his successor, and told them that I was determined to leave on the timetable I had set out to President Mitterrand.

On Sunday 28 May John Major convened the Overseas Policy and Defence Committee of the Cabinet with the Chief of Defence Staff in atten-dance and considered the capture of thirty British soldiers in Gorazde earlier that day. They wisely decided to send two artillery batteries and an armoured engineer squadron to Bosnia as soon as possible, and in consul-tation with UNPROFOR to prepare 24 Air Mobile Brigade to deploy to Bosnia. That evening I flew to Brussels and saw Juppé's remarks on French television that the air strikes had been badly prepared. The truth was that it was impossible to withdraw the UN quickly, for example, an UNMO in Pale or UN troops at a heavy weapons collection point, for the Serbs would not allow them to leave unless their replacements were already in position. No one else had publicly criticized the air strike decision but with 375 UN personnel now taken hostage there was both anxiety and apprehension about how we found ourselves in this mess.

Next morning before the FAC I met Douglas Hurd, who had breakfasted with the new French Foreign Minister, Hervé de Charette. I told Douglas I supported the UK decision to reinforce UNPROFOR but there now had to be serious negotiating and a quick settlement with Milosevic on mutual recognition; also, there would have to be some contact with Karadzic, for we could not rely on Milosevic being able, with Mladic, to topple Karadzic. Douglas said he and de Charette wanted to revert to the idea of a single negotiator for the Contact Group and they were thinking of Carl Bildt. I said that, as before in January when we had discussed it, I thought it was a good idea but that the person chosen should also be the EU Co-Chairman of the Conference; I did not believe the job should be split. Anyhow, I intended to go in June as I had said I would in my letter to Mitterrand. Douglas said he would tell de Charette and we two should talk. I warned him about any dramatic SAS action over British hostages, though obviously I hoped they were on hand if the hostages' lives came to be at risk. I believed the hostages would be in great danger of having their throats slit if any such attack went wrong, whereas I was very confident that in a few weeks, as over Gorazde, we would be able to pressurize the Serbs to release all UN hostages.

The Foreign Affairs Council was due to discuss the former Yugoslavia over lunch, so I went back to my room and talked to my wife, who was adamant that I should pre-empt any leaks and write to Chirac immediately, reiterating the terms of my letter to Mitterrand. This I did before lunch.[210] At lunch there was no hint of any Contact Group negotiator being appointed and so I said nothing about my letter to Chirac but repeated much of what I had said to Douglas Hurd about the need for negotiations. The Council's mood was subdued. The only area of controversy emerged when I said it was unwise in their statement to mention the need to protect the safe areas when it was obvious that UNPROFOR was already unable to defend all six safe areas and that this was pre-empting a discussion to be held in the Security Council.

One minister said there was confusion among the great powers: the French talked of withdrawal, the British reinforced, the Americans and Germans seemed all over the place. There was a considerable danger unless the members of the Contact Group spoke as one. A vain hope, I thought to myself, already looking forward to my impending departure.

I left by car for the Hague to meet with Stoltenberg prior to the ministerial Contact Group meeting. The usual communiqué had been prepared beforehand, but this time without Russian participation, though it was all fairly bland. At the meeting, which the French invited us both to attend throughout, the Russians suggested a few amendments, one in particular changing the wording from the Bosnians Serbs having to 'accept' the Contact Group Plan to their having to 'adopt' the plan. I had spoken firmly in favour of starting these talks soon as well as restarting the Milosevic dialogue, and so when the French put 'adopt' in the new draft I held my breath. But Germany and the US objected, so no change was made. It was incredible that even after the debacle of the air strikes, with 375 hostages having been taken, some ministers seemed to be blissfully unaware that the Contact Group map was now likely to go the way of the VOPP, the *Invincible* map and the EU

Action Plan. In particular, the safe areas of Srebrenica and Zepa were now very vulnerable to Serb attack. When Kozyrev, to demonstrate that Russia should have been involved in the drafting of the communiqué, began after midnight to quibble about detail I left for a night's sleep, wondering whether the Contact Group could continue unless the Americans negotiated with more realism directly with Milosevic.

I mentioned to Douglas Hurd that I thought I would make my maiden speech in the House of Lords debate on Wednesday. It had been agreed between us that the French would delay my statement about my stepping down for about a week, and apparently Carl Bildt was going to be formally approached by the French after some more soundings with EU politicians that were due to take place in the margins of the NATO meeting.

Just as I was about to be called to speak in the Lords on Wednesday 31 May I had a message passed to me on the cross benches from my personal assistant, Maggie Smart, to say that Alain Juppé had announced in the French National Assembly that I had decided to end my responsibilities as Co-Chairman of the ICFY Steering Committee. So I had to make a last-minute addition about stepping down. My speech mentioned that the summer months could still provide a window of opportunity; otherwise the UN would have to leave before the winter.[211] Next day I received generous letters acknowledging my decision from President Chirac and from Boutros Boutros Ghali.

I visited Zagreb with Thorvald Stoltenberg for a farewell lunch with President Tudjman and dinner in Belgrade with President Milosevic on Monday 5 June. Both occasions were pleasant; we reminisced about lost opportunities and tried to be optimistic. Milosevic told us that the American F-16 pilot shot down by the Serbs on 2 June had parachuted down alive and was being tracked down. I went back to the British Chargé Ivor Roberts's house to pay my farewells. He had been a tower of strength and full of sense, with excellent access to Milosevic. Bob Frasure came round for a drink and was as relaxed as ever; I told him that the US pilot had been found and had shed some equipment and it looked as if he was unhurt but in hiding. He was rescued fit and well on 8 June by US helicopters.

I sent my final COREU in a low-key tone, deliberately avoiding any last-minute lecture on what should be done in the future.[212] I was leaving in an atmosphere of goodwill with no reason for recrimination: the Foreign Ministers had all treated me well and had given me much support over the years. I had one last duty to perform. Tudjman had asked me to find out from Milosevic why he had called off a private meeting between them in a European capital. For nearly three years, first Vance and I and then Stoltenberg and I had arranged to bring together these two men and even more frequently arranged private meetings between intermediaries. I rang Tudjman and told him Milosevic's reasons and we had a friendly chat. His last words were to the effect: 'I am right to go on trying to build on this dialogue between us and Belgrade,' and I said: 'Yes, Mr President, there is no other way for peace in your region.'

Carl Bildt was appointed by the EU heads of government at an informal dinner in Paris on Friday 9 June and confirmed at the Foreign Affairs Council in Luxembourg on Monday. I was no longer Co-Chairman; but I went to the Steering Committee in Geneva on the Tuesday to say goodbye and attended an excellent farewell party with the ICFY staff who had done so much for me personally. It had been a long and eventful journey, my almost three-year Balkan odyssey, and I could only hope that no negotiator would ever again have to experience anything like the frustration, torment and tragedy that had unfolded during this period of Balkan history.

Even Karadzic now understood that keeping the hostages was becoming counter-productive in view of the world-wide condemnation. But, as so often in the past, it still required very heavy pressure on him from Milosevic, and a trade-off of military equipment with Mladic, as well as an intervention from Papoulias, the Greek Foreign Minister, to secure their release. By 18 June every single one of the hostages had been returned.

For a moment under President Chirac it appeared France wanted the new reinforcements to operate outside the UN, but it was soon clear that they were going to take the form of a rapid reaction force operating within a UN mandate and not be an intervention force. General Rupert Smith might have been tempted to conclude that the fiasco and the humiliation for the UN following the NATO air strikes on Pale was a price worth paying to get these reinforcements in, for they undoubtedly restored some credibility to UNPROFOR and gave it a useful new artillery capacity. But there was also a serious downside, for the actual announcements about reinforcement helped trigger the Bosnian Serb army decision to take Srebrenica and Zepa before these new forces were effectively deployed. I doubt Milosevic could have prevented Mladic from taking these eastern enclaves even if he had tried to. He had frustratingly seen his agreement with Frasure on recognition of Bosnia-Herzegovina in exchange for a suspension of sanctions turned down in Washington. Milosevic now, like Tudjman, may well have thought it best to have the map changed by force of arms, having seen the divisions in the Contact Group and the chance of a negotiated territorial trade-off recede.

On 7 July an observation post of the Dutch contingent in Srebrenica came under attack from Bosnian Serb tanks. The Dutch commander requested close air support. This was allegedly refused by General Smith in Sarajevo on the grounds that the attack did not yet justify it, and that close air support would interfere with negotiations. The next day the Dutch withdrew from the observation post but were fired at by Bosnian government troops, who killed one Dutch soldier. Another observation post was overrun by the

Bosnian Serbs, who took hostage the Dutch soldiers manning it. In total, fifty-five Dutch soldiers were taken hostage during the Bosnian Serb assault on Srebrenica. On 9 July the Dutch put up a blocking position on the southern road into the town. The Muslim soldiers had not put up any serious resistance against the Bosnian Serb advance. Their commander had left Srebrenica some days before the final assault, and, according to the Dutch government, on 10 July most Muslim men of fighting age, totalling 15,000, of whom some 3,000–4,000 carried arms, were thought to have slipped out of the enclave. But it now looks as if some of them never managed to escape and were massacred. That evening the Dutch commander put in another request for close air support, which was also refused, this time because of bad visibility. On 11 July the Serbs launched a frontal attack on Srebrenica. After several more requests from the Dutch commander on the ground, two successful air strikes by Dutch and American F-16s on Serb tanks were launched in the afternoon, but UNPROFOR Commander General Janvier and the Dutch government were concerned about the safety of the Dutch hostages and called off further strikes. The Dutch soldiers withdrew to Potocari, accompanied by thousands of panic-stricken Muslim refugees. Those men of fighting age who had remained were separated by the Serbs from their families, and the older men, women and children were put on buses to Tuzla. Some 40,000 Muslims were ethnically cleansed. On 21 July the Dutch soldiers were allowed to leave the enclave.

The War Crimes Tribunal will investigate whether after the fall of Srebrenica an appalling massacre of male Muslims took place – the very thing which many of us had feared would happen in the spring of 1993. I had actually discussed this with Milosevic, who was himself very concerned that the bad blood that existed between the Serbs around Bratunac and the Muslims in Srebrenica would lead to some horror. It will also be for the War Crimes Tribunal to determine the truth over the allegations about the role of General Mladic. The whole tragic episode of the fall of Srebrenica has many lessons attached to it for us all. The Dutch soldiers had been placed in an impossibly difficult position. For the Dutch government it was a moment of truth, because for years Dutch ministers had lectured their European colleagues about the use of force in the former Yugoslavia and had sought to adopt a tough moralistic stance; now their public wanted to know more about what had happened. The problems of and the limitations on the use of force, whether by NATO in the air or the UN on the ground, were painfully exposed before the eyes of the world in Srebrenica.

Zepa, where there was a small contingent of Ukrainian soldiers, was then surrounded by the Bosnian Serbs and subsequently shelled. The Ukrainian soldiers at one point found themselves effectively held hostage inside Zepa by the Muslim forces, who took their weapons and threatened to kill them if NATO did not launch air strikes against the Serbs, while the

Serbs threatened to shell the Ukrainians if air strikes did take place. A withdrawal of UNPROFOR and Muslim civilians to Tuzla was later negotiated, while most Muslim soldiers went into hiding in the hills surrounding Zepa. The enclave was taken by the Serbs on 25 July. The Contact Group map had been shredded, while the five governments that had put their name to it felt unable to do anything. The so-called rapid reaction force was never configured in such a way as to be able to save Srebrenica and Zepa if the Bosnian Serbs decided to take these enclaves, which the UN commanders had long predicted would happen. The question now was whether Mladic intended to take Gorazde. All the signs were that the Bosnian Muslim forces inside Gorazde would put up a serious fight here, and the Bosnian Serbs knew that launching a frontal attack into a well-defended built-up area could be very costly in terms of casualties, something which the Bosnian Muslims themselves had experienced only a few weeks earlier when their attacks in the Sarajevo area had been repulsed with heavy loss of life.

On Friday 21 July in London the Foreign and Defence Ministers of the troop-contributing countries met under the chairmanship of John Major. It was decided that Gorazde would be defended by NATO air strikes and authority was vested in UNPROFOR Commander General Janvier and NATO's Admiral Leighton Smith to carry out this decision. Quietly steps were taken to withdraw British and Ukrainian UN soldiers from Gorazde, an essential prelude to any air strikes.

On 19 July 1995 the Croatian Serb army attacked the Bihac pocket in an attempt to cut it in half. There was no readiness to commit the rapid reaction force to its defence. The Bosnian 5th Corps lost ground but resisted strongly. On 22 July Presidents Tudjman and Izetbegovic met in Split and the Croatian government promised to use its forces to help Bihac. The Croatian army then attacked cleverly, first inside Bosnia-Herzegovina, moving from Livno up towards Bihac, taking Bosansko Grahovo and Glamoc from the Bosnian Serb army. On Wednesday 2 August in Belgrade the US Ambassador to Croatia, Peter Galbraith, talked to the Croatian Serb leader Babic, reflecting concern in Washington, and persuaded him to sign a five-point statement to head off an attack from the Croatian government forces.

On Thursday 3 August talks between the Croatian government and the Krajina Serbs were held in Geneva under the auspices of the ICFY Co-Chairman Thorvald Stoltenberg and agreement was reached on all the main substantive points. UN and EU diplomats hailed this as a breakthrough, but the decision to attack had already been taken in Zagreb. That same day Carl Bildt was rebuffed in Washington when he met with Vice-President Gore and was told the US could not agree to the results of his negotiation with President Milosevic, which had followed up on the negotiations undertaken by US envoy Robert Frasure.

On Friday 4 August at 5 a.m., with Knin cut off from the Bosnian Serb army, the Croatian government attacked the Krajina on a number of fronts and by 6 August the whole area, including Knin, was effectively in their hands. The entire Croatian Serb army and almost the whole Serb population, more than 150,000 people, was swept out of the Krajina. It was now the Serbs who had been ethnically cleansed and there were many people who felt that it served them right. The American Ambassador in Croatia, Peter Galbraith, argued that this was not ethnic cleansing, but in the *Washington Post* Charles Krauthammer, in an article headlined 'When Serbs Are "Cleansed," Moralists Stay Silent', challenged the muted criticism. Saying 'there is either one moral standard regarding ethnic cleansing, or none. There cannot be two,' Carl Bildt criticized the Croatian government, mentioning President Tudjman in the context of war crimes. He was declared persona non grata in Croatia and they shunned him as a negotiator, but he continued to work with Holbrooke.

Once again President Tudjman had seen an opening and seized the opportunity. By this stage, I do not believe that, even if the US had wished to stop the Croatian army, Tudjman would have held back. The Croatian Serb leader, Martic, and the military and political leaders around him had committed every mistake in the book from the moment that Tudjman had provoked them with his announcement in January that the UN mandate would not be renewed. Martic had blocked the economic agreement, he had thrown out Mikelic and in the process seriously alienated Milosevic. The Croatian Serbs in losing Western Slavonia to the Croatian government forces had exposed their weakness. To have provoked a battle in July over Bihac, without securing an agreement from the Bosnian Serbs to protect Knin, when it was clear that Tudjman was looking for an excuse to attack other parts of the Krajina, was a folly. Tudjman calculated that Karadzic and Mladic, locked in a personal battle, were too weak to intervene, and he knew that Milosevic was now resigned to the fact that he could no longer protect the Croatian Serbs from their own actions. The Croatian attack was launched so swiftly and so devastatingly it caught the world by surprise. Tudjman was now creating a new map of Croatia and Bosnia.

A human tragedy of massive proportions had unfolded in the former Yugoslavia in the space of less than a month. Bosnian Muslims had been ethnically cleansed from Zepa and Srebrenica and Croatian Serbs from the Krajina. The map of the Balkans had undergone a fundamental transformation. If it provides stability, those who believe in ethnic cleansing will claim that it justifies their policy, and the world will become an even harsher place.

The Contact Group nations, by failing to impose a settlement on the basis of the map that they had presented to the Bosnian parties a year before, had lost authority in the region, and the Bosnian Serbs and the Croatian government had felt emboldened to take aggressive action. By acquiescing in the Croatian government's seizure of Western Slavonia, the

Contact Group had in effect given the green light to the Bosnian Serbs to attack Srebrenica and Zepa, which then encouraged the Croatian Serbs to attack Bihac. It was an irony that the Croatian government was able to invoke the Bosnian Muslims' plight in Bihac to justify their attack into the Krajina, for it was now the Croats who had the upper hand in Bosnia.

Of course, in the wake of this misery and mayhem there was an opening for a comprehensive settlement, but this had been bought at a bitter price and on an agenda dictated by President Tudjman. President Clinton sent his National Security Adviser, Anthony Lake, to Europe on 10 and 11 August with realistic proposals. A mission led by Assistant Secretary of State Richard Holbrooke went one week later to Belgrade and Zagreb. Tragically, Robert Frasure, who had done most to lay the foundations for a change in the US position, was killed on 19 August when the APC in which he was travelling slipped off the Mt Igman route into Sarajevo.

The US initiative accepted many of the crucial points that the Americans had resisted putting on the negotiating table within the Contact Group for more than a year. In addition to the Croat–Muslim Federation there would be a 'Republika Srpska'. The Bosnian Serbs would have broadly the same linkage with Serbia as the Croat–Muslim Federation had with Croatia in the Washington Accords. The hard question for the negotiation would be the extent to which the Serbs and the Muslims would agree on exchanging Gorazde for parts of Sarajevo. A new map for Bosnia-Herzegovina was now starting to emerge, but the US were not very specific on this. The Serbs would keep more territory in eastern Bosnia than in the Contact Group plan and have a corridor in the north to Banja Luka. Also, Bihac would be linked to Livno, ensuring that the Federation territory was contiguous.

Not surprisingly this initiative was welcomed in the EU, though with an understandable frustration that the Americans could not have agreed to put it on the negotiating table months earlier, a sentiment shared fully by the Russians. In Belgrade, the initiative posed no problems for Milosevic, who had been arguing these points for months. Only in Pale and in Sarajevo were there elements who still preferred to fight, but even there the mood was changing. Krajisnik came to Geneva and showed more flexibility than hitherto, and Milosevic had won his power struggle with a chastened Karadzic. The Bosnian Serb Assembly, in a meeting that started on Monday 28 August and lasted until 5 a.m. the following day, appeared to have moved the Bosnian Serb negotiating position significantly and, most importantly, ratified the weekend agreement that Milosevic should negotiate on their behalf.

But on 28 August a mortar bomb was fired into Sarajevo, killing thirty-seven people and injuring many others. After twenty-four hours of investigation, the UN declared that they were satisfied beyond reasonable doubt that it had been fired by the Bosnian Serbs, by which time the last of the

Welch Fusiliers had left Gorazde for Serbia. For the first time since the autumn of 1992 UNPROFOR was no longer spread out across the whole of Bosnia-Herzegovina and vulnerable to Bosnian Serb retaliation and hostage-taking. UNPROFOR was out of Zepa, Srebrenica and Gorazde. Bihac was now safe. There were no significant UN forces in Serb controlled areas anywhere in Bosnia-Herzegovina. UNPROFOR was no longer manning heavy weapons collection points in Sarajevo. It was inevitable, therefore, that the UN and NATO would take action against the Bosnian Serbs for the mortar bomb attack, which was a flagrant breach of the heavy weapons exclusion zone in Sarajevo, and action was well within the UN mandate.

On Wednesday night in Belgrade Presidents Milosevic and Bulatovic, accompanied by the head of the Yugoslav Army, met with the Bosnian Serb leaders and hammered out an agreement, witnessed by the Patriarch of the Serb Orthodox Church, which also ratified the previous agreement that Milosevic should lead a joint Serbian team for negotiations on the US initiative, and, crucially, that Milosevic would hold the casting vote. Interestingly, the Bosnian Serb delegation included, in addition to Karadzic, Krajisnik and Koljevic, Mrs Plavsic. She is the civilian leader closest to General Mladic and, having been one of the hardliners from the time she was a member of the Presidency of Bosnia-Herzegovina, had now come to believe that a peace settlement was necessary. Meanwhile, Richard Holbrooke had seen President Izetbegovic in Paris on Monday 28 August, met with Contact Group officials on Tuesday and then seen President Milosevic on Wednesday. Milosevic the pragmatist understood why in the early hours of that morning NATO and UNPROFOR had jointly launched a combination of air strikes and artillery attacks by the rapid reaction force against Bosnian Serb military positions on Mt Igman with a view to enforcing the much abused Sarajevo heavy weapons exclusion zone. Indeed, Milosevic showed his attitude to the Bosnian Serb leadership by negotiating with Holbrooke while the NATO bombing was taking place.

President Yeltsin criticized the NATO bombing but Russia was in effect acquiescent; they wanted proper consultation. Though the Bosnian Serbs shot down a French Mirage, there was no serious attempt to attack UNPROFOR on the ground. The NATO/UN attacks continued for three days, but at much reduced levels, and by Friday the US, with Holbrooke negotiating in Belgrade, were making it clear they wanted the attacks put on hold. This was a sign that the US negotiations with Milosevic were making progress. Mladic was still refusing to comply with the exclusion zone, saying it did nothing to stop Bosnian Muslim attacks. It seemed only a matter of time before the Bosnian Muslims and the Bosnian Serbs accepted the American-brokered deal which had been effectively put together with Tudjman and Milosevic. Behind Mladic's concern about NATO's order to remove all his heavy weapons from the exclusion zone was the long-standing Serb fear that this could encourage the Muslims to attack, not to settle, since their army commanders would start to believe that they could advance with their superior numbers of soldiers. It was the old story that had haunted so many Sarajevo-based initiatives back again. What was needed was the demilitarization of Sarajevo.

It was crucial for success that the initial US package brought over to Europe in August by Anthony Lake should remain in its essentials unchanged, and that it should be accompanied by a map agreed with the Muslims before NATO air strikes became widespread. It was a time for the American position to reflect the advice given by General Charles Boyd, who had just retired, having been the US Deputy Commander in Europe for nearly three years, and whose frank appraisal of American policy had just been published in the American journal *Foreign Affairs*.[i]

> *To think with clarity about the former Yugoslavia that exists rather than the one the US Administration would prefer and then to speak with honesty about it will be very difficult given the distance this government had traveled down the road of Serb vilification and Muslim and Croat approval. But until the US government can come to grips with the essential similarities between Serb, Croat and Muslim and recognize that the fears and aspirations of all are equally important, no effective policy can possibly be drafted that would help produce an enduring peace.*

As Mladic refused to withdraw heavy weapons, NATO felt they had no alternative to continuing their air attacks in the run-up to the conference in Geneva which Richard Holbrooke had convened in order for the Contact Group to meet, under his chairmanship, with the Foreign Ministers of Bosnia-Herzegovina, Croatia and the FRY (Serbia and Montenegro). On Thursday 7 September the five Contact Group Foreign Ministers, along with the Troika and the Canadian and Dutch Foreign Ministers, met with the Organization of the Islamic Conference in Paris. On Friday 8 September the negotiations started as planned in Geneva, with Koljevic and Buha from the Bosnian Serb leadership as members of the Yugoslav delegation. The meeting was a welcome success in that the Contact Group Plan of July 1994 was accepted as the basis for the negotiations. Significantly the Americans and Germans within the Contact Group now formally accepted what had hitherto been only a private understanding in the Group, namely that there would be two entities within Bosnia-Herzegovina: Republika Srpska, with its own constitution, and the Croat–Muslim Federation, with the constitution that had been agreed in the Washington Accords of March 1994. The basic 51 per cent for the Bosnian Muslims and Bosnian Croats which the Bosnian Serbs had accepted in the EU Action Plan in December 1993 but rejected in July 1994 was agreed by the Bosnian Serb leaders within the Yugoslav delegation.

This was spelt out in three 'Agreed Basic Principles'. These stipulated that Bosnia-Herzegovina would continue its legal existence with its present borders and continuing international recognition, and would consist of two entities, the Federation of Bosnia and Herzegovina as established by the Washington Agreements, and the Republika Srpska, the territorial split between them to be based on the 51–49 per cent territorial proposal put forward by the Contact Group, while being open for adjustment by mutual agreement. Provision was made for the preservation of the present constitution of each entity, subject to amendment to accommodate the basic principles, and for the establishment of special relationships with neighbouring countries; and the two entities agreed to undertake reciprocal commitments to hold elections, adhere to international human rights standards and engage in binding arbitration to resolve disputes between them. Agreement in principle was also reached on the establishment of institutions to address these issues.

The task ahead was to agree an overall map for Bosnia-Herzegovina. Given my knowledge of Milosevic's views on the map, including his flexibility over Sarajevo, which he had reiterated constantly over the years, and the fact that he had the casting vote, I did not expect this to be too difficult, provided the Americans stuck to their view put forward in early August by Anthony Lake. I also felt confident that the constitution for a Union of Three Republics in Bosnia-Herzegovina agreed in August 1993 could be adapted to accommodate the Federation. The problems were likely to be over the determination of monetary policy and foreign policy. A consensus of the three constituent nations in Bosnia-Herzegovina would not provide clear decisions in either of these divisive fields and yet any form of majority voting meant that any combination of two nations could impose their view. While it might be tempting to believe that the Muslims and Croats would provide a natural majority, the disappointing progress in welding the two together in the Federation did not make it inevitable that this combination would survive. The Bosnian Muslims could find themselves in the minority quite easily since the Bosnian Croats and Bosnian Serbs had frequently combined together over the past few years. The other difficult question was agreement over Eastern Slavonia, the only remaining sector where the UN was present in Croatia. This would have to be resolved between President Tudjman and President Milosevic, and Thorvald Stoltenberg had wisely concentrated his authority in this crucial area from early August. UN administration had been part of the Z4 plan, but Tudjman would not want the UN to administer Eastern Slavonia, while Milosevic would want the duration of independent administration to be longer than Tudjman; also, Milosevic would want some way of consulting the people living in the area as to what degree of autonomy they wanted from Zagreb. Tudjman, after his victories on the battlefield, was not likely to accept even the slightest hint of any continuing influence from Belgrade. Yet Milosevic would be aware that without Tudjman being satisfied on these aspects, it would be hard to get the Croats to show the degree of flexibility necessary for a settlement in Bosnia-Herzegovina, particularly on the Bosnian Serb wish for a territorial corridor in the north.

As the moment for an overall settlement came close, it was inevitable that the succession issue would raise its head at the negotiating table,[213] with President Milosevic insisting on the Federal Republic of Yugoslavia being accepted as the continuation of the Socialist Federal Republic of Yugoslavia, but that was something over which Tudjman had already indicated that he would be flexible. Of course, as always in the Balkans, nothing could be certain; but I felt that with the Americans now firmly taking the lead, with Richard Holbrooke an experienced practitioner in the art of realpolitik, neither Tudjman nor Milosevic would allow this opportunity for a comprehensive settlement to pass by.

The NATO bombing of bridges around Foca, defensible in order to inhibit heavy weapons going from Sarajevo to Gorazde, nevertheless began to give the impression that the UN and NATO commanders were now taking the attacks wider than Sarajevo and the Bosnian Serb air defences. In Moscow on Friday 9 September President Yeltsin uttered comments reminiscent of those he had made in February 1994, and warned that the bombing of the Bosnian Serbs was a 'first sign' of how an expanded NATO would behave. On Saturday the Russian Duma met and was sharply critical of NATO bombing. On Sunday a meeting between the UN Commander General Janvier and General Mladic produced no agreement, and that same evening NATO launched thirteen cruise missiles on military targets near Banja Luka. On Monday in Brussels, after a meeting with NATO ambassadors, Vitaly Churkin, now Russia's ambassador in Brussels, criticized the wider air strikes; since he had been instrumental in the placing of Russian troops in Sarajevo in February 1994 he knew better than most why Mladic was not ready to remove his heavy weapons without a firm commitment by the UN and NATO to stop the Bosnian Muslim infantry from attacking within Sarajevo.

The United States, by sending Warren Christopher's deputy Strobe Talbott to Russia to talk to Kozyrev, demonstrated that it still valued Russian participation in the Contact Group, and within NATO there was more discussion on how to involve Russian troops in any implementation force.

The question now was whether the Security Council would authorize the UN Military Commander to agree to what was termed 'Option 3', which was a sharply escalated air campaign with targets that included railroads and power plants. Yet there was a need for the balanced demilitarization of Sarajevo, which would really open up the city and prevent infantry attacks.

On Monday 11 September the Russians circulated a draft Resolution to the Security Council calling for the suspension of air strikes, but gained little support for it. A more ominous sign for the future was a call from the Russian Defence Minister Grachev to his US counterpart Perry, threatening to review some international military treaties, thereby completely bypassing Foreign Minister Kozyrev, whose ministry had been singled out for criticism by President Yeltsin. In Europe, concern was growing over the deterioration in US–Russian relations, and there was a wish to develop the offer made to Churkin at his meeting with the NATO ambassadors that Russian troops should help police a peace settlement. What was needed was another initiative such as that taken by the Russians in February 1994 to address the problem of heavy weapons withdrawal, involving either more Russian troops (which was unlikely) or the deployment of part of the Rapid Reaction Force into Sarajevo.

Meanwhile in the US a more realistic assessment of what had been achieved at Holbrooke's Geneva meeting began to make itself heard. In an article in the *New York Times* headlined 'This is Not an Outcome the West Can be Proud of', Anthony Lewis wrote: 'The mystery is why Washington has brought the parties to an agreement seemingly so favourable to the Serbian leaders' ambitions. Indeed, it is more favourable than the settlement crafted by Cyrus Vance and David Owen, which might well have been achieved when the Serbs were in a much stronger position.' There was some wry satisfaction for me in his acknowledgement that our plan 'did preserve a genuinely sovereign Bosnia'. But if only he and other liberal intellectuals and editorial-writers on the *New York Times* had been as forthcoming two and a half years previously, I doubt the Clinton administration's hostile attitude to the VOPP would have been anywhere near as marked.

What was needed urgently was a revision of the Contact Group map to be put before the parties, and I hoped that map-making, too long neglected, would become the main activity of the Contact Group at its meeting planned for Thursday 14 September in Geneva. However, this meeting was understandably postponed because Holbrooke had managed to negotiate, in a meeting with Milosevic, the removal of the Bosnian Serbs' heavy weapons around Sarajevo; and then, as in July and August, dramatic changes in the map began to be made by the soldiers on the ground. Croat forces took Jajce from the Serbs on 15 September, and Bosnian government forces took Donji Vakuf. It looked to me suspiciously as if the Serbs wanted the Croats, rather than the Muslims, to take Jajce. At the negotiating table Karadzic has always shown marked reluctance to allow the whole of Jajce to come under Muslim control. Not only did the hydro-electric plants there supply Banja Luka, but Jajce was strategically situated on the road to Bihac. Thereafter, day by day, the map altered. It was hard to be sure whether what was happening was a retreat or a rout of the Bosnian Serb army. The

Serb civilian population moved out in advance of the fighting from places like Bosanski Petrovac and Drvar, fleeing towards Banja Luka and blocking the roads. The Croat and Muslim armies, advancing with their tails up, pushed the Serbs back so that by 21 September a large tract of land hitherto occupied by the Serbs since 1992 was now in the hands of the Federation, and the confrontation line ran close to Bosanski Novi, Prijedor and Sanski Most, with Kljuc controlled by the Federation. The overall distribution of land in Bosnia-Herzegovina was approaching the agreed division of 51 per cent to the Federation and 49 per cent to the Serbs, but the problem for the Bosnian Muslims was that of that 51 per cent some 26 per cent was in the hands of the Croatian forces, and there were clashes developing on the ground within the Federation. A particularly nasty fire-fight took place when the Bosnian government's 7th Corps, the so-called refugee army, was refused permission by Croatian government forces to enter Jajce, and there was also fighting in Bosanski Petrovac.

It was now obvious to the world that General Mladic and his army, who did not fold up with the first wave of NATO bombing as so many commentators had confidently predicted, and had by Tuesday 12 September been bombed for a fortnight without withdrawing their heavy weapons around Sarajevo, had nevertheless suffered severe disruption. Though the NATO–UN air strikes had been suspended on the night of 14 September, it took a little time for events on the ground to reveal how far they had tilted the balance of power. NATO had flown 3,400 air sorties, of which about 750 were attack missions against 56 ground targets with 350 aiming points: individual sheds, warehouses, radars, command bunkers, ammunition dumps, armament factories, repair facilities, as well as a few selected bridges. Though the effect of much of this was not immediate, the damage to the communication system had been felt instantly. Not only had Serb military relay systems been destroyed, their civilian telephone network had also been incapacitated. Instead of the Serbs having the capacity to redeploy rapidly and reinforce at will, it was the Croatian and Bosnian Muslim forces with indirect access to US satellite intelligence who now had the over-the-horizon capacity and the ability to react quickly.

Karadzic, when challenged that Serb forces had deliberately withdrawn, hotly denied it; but the suspicion remained that, with General Mladic undergoing hospital treatment in Belgrade, it was more than a coincidence that the soldiers' map had begun to reflect a design which Tudjman had long wanted. Also, it was a map that Milosevic could easily endorse, since it was no longer necessary, following the fall of Knin, for the Serbs to maintain access to the Krajina from Banja Luka. At one stage many commentators, mainly those based in Sarajevo, were predicting that Banja Luka would fall, and this was obviously the test case as to whether Tudjman and Milosevic were in control of what was happening. In the event, Tudjman wisely pulled his forces back,

Government-held Bihac Region
Total Population: 225,000
Serbs: negligible
Croats: 6,000
Muslims: 219,000

Serb-held Northern and Eastern Bosnia
Total Population: 1,355,000–1,415,000
Serbs: 1,330,000–1,390,000
Croats: 15,000
Muslims: 10,000

CROATIA

Bosanski Novi
Prijedor
Derventa
Orasje
Brcko
Bosanska Krupa
Bihac
Sanski Most
Banja Luka
Doboj
Posavina corridor
Bosanski Petrovac
Kljuc
Maglaj
Tuzla
SERBIA
Mrkonjic Grad
Jajce
Zepce
Zvornik
Donji Vakuf
Vitez
Srebrenica
Kupres
Zepa
CROATIA
Kiseljak
Sarajevo
Livno
Pale
Gorazde

Croat-held Western Bosnia
Total Population: 480,000
Serbs: negligible
Croats: 380,000
Muslims: 100,000
Note: Includes Orasje pocket near the Posavina corridor

Mostar

Government-held Central Bosnia, Sarajevo, and Gorazde
Total Population: 1,055,000
Serbs: 60,000
Croats: 155,000
Muslims: 840,000
Note: Includes Croat-controlled pockets

Trebinje

Map 14 The situation on 12 October 1995.
(Population estimates, which take into account refugee flows until
October 1995, are not necessarily authoritative.)

a decision helped by a strong counter-attack on Croat forces from the air by
the Bosnian Serb army. Tudjman would have noted that the Serb aeroplanes
which had flown on this bombing mission from Banja Luka were not shot
down by NATO planes in enforcement of the NFZ, nor was their airfield
subjected to NATO air strikes: a clear indication that NATO and UN
commanders did not want the military balance tilted so sharply that the
Contact Group's 51–49 per cent split was put in jeopardy. These same Galeb
fighter planes were also used against Bosnian government forces without
NATO retaliation: another sign that a more sophisticated pressure was being
applied on all parties, amounting to the imposition of a settlement.

The Bosnian government, as had been expected for some time, announced that there would not be a confederation between Bosnia-Herzegovina and the Republic of Croatia, as had been agreed in principle in the Washington Accords of 1994. The Croats did not seem keen either, so both sides were burying an idea which had never carried much conviction. In addition the Bosnian government was demanding as the price of a ceasefire that the Bosnian Serbs should demilitarize the Banja Luka region, open up Sarajevo and provide a territorial link to Gorazde.

There was concern that Sacirbey, Foreign Minister of Bosnia-Herzegovina, might not attend a planned meeting in New York, reflecting deep tensions among the Bosnian Muslim leaders. In early August Silajdzic had resigned as Foreign Minister, only to be reinstated when it became clear to Izetbegovic that public opinion disapproved of his departure. According to a journalist on the Sarajevan daily *Oslobodjenje*,[ii]

> *Izetbegovic and Silajdzic represent two very different futures for an independent Bosnia: a return to the absolute power of a single-party state under the control of a party that is out-dated, increasingly repressive and is taking over the country in the name of a factitious patriotism; or the western-looking, democratic country its troops have been fighting for. The hardliners in Izetbegovic's SDA want a population totally subordinate to the state; in return, they promise a genuinely Muslim country, however small, in which the well-off moneymen and sycophants around the ruling party can have a free hand. In the name of their 'patriotism', young men have been mobilized for the army while others have found a new prosperity thanks to the parallel economy, the 'private' businesses that feed on the misery of the population, and those who have the privilege of access to the funds brought in by a variety of foreign humanitarian organizations.*

After an American delegation visited Sarajevo, Sacirbey met with the Foreign Ministers of Croatia and the FRY in New York under the chairmanship of Richard Holbrooke and a further three principles were agreed to be added to those negotiated in Geneva.[214]

The first of these concerned the undertaking by both entities to honour the international obligations of Bosnia-Herzegovina, with the exception of a financial obligation incurred by one entity without the consent of the other; the second and third set out the acknowledged goal of holding free democratic elections in both entities as soon as social conditions should permit, with OSCE monitors adjudging when conditions were such that elections could properly be held and the governments required to hold the poll within thirty days of this point. The institutional structure to come into being after these elections was described, consisting of a parliament, presidency, cabinet and constitutional court, with safeguards for the proper representation of each constituent entity in Bosnia-Herzegovina.

After the meeting, Holbrooke returned to the region in the hope of achieving a lasting ceasefire. The Bosnian government was keen to go on fighting, but with the Croats holding off, the Serbs started to push the Bosnisn 5th Corps back around Bosanska Krupa. There were already signs that the Serb withdrawal had not been as costly as some had imagined, nor their fighting potential so reduced as some had predicted. The new confrontation line appeared to be defensible by the Bosnian Serbs. Everything hinged on the private dialogue over Eastern Slavonia which Thorvald Stoltenberg had continued to nurture skilfully. At a meeting in Erdut on 3 October Stoltenberg and the US Ambassador to Croatia, Peter Galbraith, had jointly chaired a meeting with Sarinic and local Serb leaders. Sarinic had been active on Tudjman's behalf for over a year in public and private diplomacy with the Serbs, demonstrating patience and resolve. Eleven principles were agreed,[215] covering international forces and administration of the region for a transitional period, though disagreement remained as to whether this would be eighteen months, as the Croats wanted, or five years, as the Serbs wanted. It was likely that the US and the Russian Federation would be playing the major role in implementing the agreement in Croatia, rather than the UN, which Tudjman disliked.

In Sarajevo and in New York the Americans were for the first time exerting real pressure on the Bosnian Muslims to agree to an overall settlement package. It was apparent that NATO was ready to implement such a settlement after a genuine cessation of hostilities, and was talking to the Russian Federation about the command and control procedures which would allow their troops, as well as those from other non-NATO countries, to participate. In the EU there was a growing view that with the exception of Slovenia, which should remain on a faster track in its association with the EU, all the republics of the former Yugoslavia should be treated in a similar way and there should not be discrimination against the FRY. In FYROM, despite the appalling assassination attempt against President Gligorov, the parliament agreed a few days later to change their flag and thus ensured the Vance-brokered agreement with Greece could be implemented.

Then, on 5 October, President Clinton announced that a ceasefire would come into force in Bosnia-Herzegovina on 10 October, provided that a full gas and electricity utility supply had been restored to Sarajevo. The ceasefire was to last for sixty days or until the completion of 'proximity peace talks', to be held near Washington, and a subsequent peace conference in Paris, whichever was the later. Under the ceasefire agreement all parties would provide free passage for non-military and UNPROFOR traffic, and unimpeded access between Sarajevo and Gorazde.

Richard Holbrooke deserved much credit for the breakthrough, and American political muscle and ability to fine-tune NATO's air strikes had been crucial. I could now see an end to the wars in the former Yugoslavia. I felt personally an immense sense of relief, for even though I had stepped down in June, I was never able to put what was happening in the region out of my mind. Now, with Milosevic and Tudjman firmly anchored into the diplomacy, I felt confident that all the elements of a settlement were in place. My odyssey was over.

The ceasefire was postponed by the Bosnian government, while Sanski Most fell to the Bosnian Muslims and Mrkonjic Grad to Croatian government forces who had openly recrossed the border to secure the Jajce–Bihac road. It was hard to escape the thought that this border adjustment was welcomed in Belgrade, for the Bosnian Serbs would have had to cede both towns at the negotiating table. But it produced more harrowing scenes, with thousands of refugees (Serbs and Muslims) fleeing the battle zones. On Thursday 12 October the ceasefire took effect. The new territorial division (Map 14, p. 337) corresponded to the EU Action Plan's 51–49 per cent split of December 1993; the big difference was that ethnic cleansing had by now all but partitioned Bosnia-Herzegovina into three separate ethnic entities, with strains already evident in the Croat–Muslim Federation.

Exhaustion had taken its toll of the Bosnian Serb army and NATO air strikes had sapped its confidence, at the same time giving confidence to President Izetbegovic and his army and allowing the NATO countries to sign off with more credit than they probably deserved. The cost of war for the civilians in the former Yugoslavia had been horrendous. It was a peace without honour.

While the UN had escaped the fate of Yugoslavia being its Abyssinia, no friend of the UN could deny that it had been damaged. UN troops, however, had saved many lives and in the process 204 of them had lost theirs, as had six EC monitors and three American peace negotiators. Peace exacts a price, and there will never be world order without a readiness to enforce its laws and impose its settlements. The world is still a long way from achieving Tennyson's dream, a text which US President Truman carried in his wallet all his life[iii] and which Winston Churchill called the most wonderful of modern prophecies:

For I dipt into the future; far as human eye could see.
Saw the Vision of the world, and all the wonder that would be . . .
Heard the heavens fill with shouting, and there rain'd a ghastly dew
From the nations' airy navies grappling in the central blue . . .
Till the war-drum throbb'd no longer and the battle flags were furl'd
In the Parliament of Man, the Federation of the World.

9

Lessons for the Future

ONE OF THE GREATEST of ancient historians, Thucydides, found that people go to war out of honour, fear and interest. Wars are but rarely fought solely between the forces of good and evil where there are only villains and victims. This is so even for wars across state boundaries. Where the wars are in whole or in part civil wars, as is the case in the four wars fought so far in the former Yugoslavia, we delude ourselves if we think of the issues in simplistic terms, or portray the struggle as one between 'good guys' and 'bad guys'.

The Russian Federation, for example, will for many years hence be grappling with their crisis in Chechnya. It will not be easy to negotiate a settlement and disarm the Muslim Chechen fighters while ruling out their claim to independence. The world did not like watching the disproportionate use of force during the Russian siege of Grozny and the destruction of this city of 400,000 people before the war. But the Security Council did not intervene. Russian troops are also fighting on the Tajik–Afghan border and the world barely glances at the long-standing civil war in Tajikistan which is now threatening, as the Russians see it, the independent states of Uzbekistan, Kyrgystan and Kazakhstan. And these concerns are quite apart from the Russian government's anxiety about their two big autonomous republics with large Muslim populations, Bashkortostan and Tatarstan, which are well inside the borders of the Russian Federation. All this explains why maintaining its national boundary and territory is by far and away Russia's first and overriding national interest.

Such present-day happenings make it a little easier to look back with some objectivity and understanding at what has happened to the former Yugoslavia. Intervention in the internal affairs of a UN member state is restricted under the UN Charter, and prior to the end of the Cold War there would have been no possibility of the Security Council becoming as involved as it did in what was still Yugoslavia in 1991–2. It will be some time before the Security Council even contemplates doing so again. Also, after recent experience humanitarian interventions which require a delicate interpretation of the UN Charter will be harder to mount and will be viewed with greater scepticism. First over the Kurd safe area in Iraq, then in Somalia, now in Bosnia-Herzegovina, it has been found hard to maintain the impartiality of the UN – particularly when the United States has strong political views on how the humanitarian intervention should be handled and who is the guilty party.

The North Atlantic Alliance, the EC and the CSCE tried unavailingly to keep Yugoslavia together in 1991 – even to the extent of the then US Secretary of State, James Baker, visiting Yugoslavia to warn Croatia publicly against declaring independence four days before the announcement was made. As the Serb–Croat war gathered momentum in the autumn of 1991 NATO watched the savage siege and destruction of Vukovar and did not intervene by land or air; nor, when public opinion was outraged by the shelling of the historic port of Dubrovnik, was there any intervention from the sea. The Security Council implicitly took the judgement that it was watching a civil war and a struggle for secession, and it was left to the European Community, optimistically claiming that this was the 'hour of Europe', to lead a political initiative. The UN only involved itself initially to keep the peace of a UN-brokered Croat–Serb ceasefire in Croatia in January 1992, while warning through its Secretary-General against premature recognition of any of the parts of Yugoslavia.

The French have a saying that for all the 'ifs' in the world you can put Paris in a bottle. There are many 'ifs' surrounding the former Yugoslavia, and many lessons to be learnt in the conduct of foreign policy by the EU and the UN Security Council. In retrospect, the biggest mistake, and the one that made the continuation of war inevitable, was not premature recognition but, as I have argued in Chapter 2, the rejection by EC Foreign Ministers on 29 July 1991 of the suggestion made by the Dutch Presidency in a COREU telegram sent out on 13 July. If the EC had launched a political initiative in August 1991 to address the key problem facing the parties to the dispute, namely the republics' borders, and had openly been ready to see an orderly and agreed secession of separate states in revised borders, then in conjunction with NATO a credible call could have been made for an immediate ceasefire. If in addition NATO had been ready to enforce that ceasefire as well as provide peacekeeping forces for immediate deployment following a UN Security Council Resolution authorizing all necessary measures to be taken to restore peace, the Serb–Croat war would have been stopped in its tracks. It is in the first few days and weeks of a conflict developing that conflict resolution has its greatest chance of success. In July 1991 there was such an opportunity; once missed, it took until 1995 for war exhaustion to become the determining factor.

The unwarranted insistence on ruling out changes to what had been internal administrative boundaries within a sovereign state was a fatal flaw in the attempted peacemaking in Yugoslavia. Of course there was a complex history behind the formation of Yugoslavia in 1918; but so there is for most sovereign states. Of course the world has to be aware of the dangers of drawing state borders along ethnic lines; but the world also has to recognize the dangers of ignoring ethnic and national voices. The division of Czechoslovakia went ahead against the advice of the international community. Their 'velvet divorce' succeeded, though admittedly the Czechs and Slovaks had the advantage that their internal boundary was not disputed. Nevertheless there are important lessons here for the European Union.

Another 'if only' relates to the decisions taken over the recognition of Croatia. Crucial to understanding this issue are four letters written at the end of 1991 – by Lord Carrington, Chairman of the EC Peace Conference on Yugoslavia, and Perez de Cuellar, then UN Secretary-General, to Hans van den Broek, then President of the EC Council of Foreign Ministers, and a letter in reply to the UN Secretary-General written for some unexplained reason by Hans-Dietrich Genscher, which Perez de Cuellar immediately and sternly answered.[216] Carrington wrote, 'An early recognition of Croatia would undoubtedly mean the break-up of the conference' and went on to say:

> There is also a real danger, perhaps even a probability, that Bosnia-Herzegovina would also ask for independence and recognition, which would be wholly unacceptable to the Serbs in that republic in which there are something like 100,000 JNA troops, some of whom had withdrawn there from Croatia. Milosevic has hinted that military action would take place there if Croatia and Slovenia were recognized. This might well be the spark that sets Bosnia-Herzegovina alight.

Perez de Cuellar's first letter recalled that leaders of Bosnia-Herzegovina and Macedonia had expressed strong fears that premature recognition was a 'potential time bomb' and said: 'I am deeply worried that any early, selective recognition would widen the present conflict and fuel an explosive situation especially in Bosnia-Herzegovina and also Macedonia, indeed serious consequences could ensue for the entire Balkan region.'

Genscher's letter to Perez de Cuellar, written in German, referred to public statements exacerbating tensions in Yugoslavia and to the Treaty of Paris but, as Perez de Cuellar reminded him in his reply, omitted to mention the EC Declaration issued in Rome on 8 November 1991 which stated that 'the prospect of recognition of the independence of those Republics wishing it, can only be envisaged in the framework of an overall settlement.' Given the German government's strong views it would have been legitimate for Germany within the EC to invoke an overriding national interest and to recognize unilaterally. What was surprising was that the French and British, whose Foreign Ministers Dumas and Hurd had eloquently argued against recognition, withdrew their opposition in favour of a deeply damaging EC consensus. Under the Maastricht Treaty, which had not even been ratified at that time, there was no obligation to agree, only to try to find common ground; this France and Britain certainly had already done. The EC mistake over recognizing Croatia could have been overcome if it had not been compounded by going forward regardless of the consequences with the recognition of Bosnia-Herzegovina. The US, who had opposed recognition of Croatia in December 1991, became very active in pushing for recognition of Bosnia-Herzegovina in the spring of 1992. Yet it should not have been judged inevitable, nor indeed was it logical, to push ahead and recognize Bosnia-Herzegovina, an internal republic of Yugoslavia that contained three large constituent peoples with very different views on independence. To do so without the prior presence of a UN Prevention Force was foolhardy in the extreme.

The December 1991 recognition decision by the EC is a sombre warning of how a dangerous decision, with predicted consequences, can be made in an atmosphere where maintaining unity among the member states becomes an end in itself. It is a clear demonstration of why the whole concept of qualified majority voting is flawed for an EU Common Foreign and Security Policy. Even in its now most minimal suggested form of 'fifteen minus one', qualified majority voting is designed to override the views of a single member state, even if that state considers the matter at issue to involve a vital national interest. It is a recipe not for unity but for division within the EU. The Maastricht Treaty wisely does not allow for any form of voting on a Common Foreign and Security Policy unless there is first unanimity that a matter should be the subject of joint action, and then unanimity on which decisions are to be taken by a qualified majority. For the Inter-Governmental Conference in 1996–7 to try to change this provision would be blithely to ignore the record of the EU's mistakes over the former Yugoslavia. I believe that the EU should never invoke this provision for a qualified majority vote, because by raising expectations and increasing the pressure for more widespread application it would not advance but set back progress towards the desirable objective of a Common Foreign and Security Policy based on intergovernmental consensus.

Foreign and defence policy, even more than monetary policy, is the *raison d'être* of an independent nation-state. In these areas the European Union would be wise to uphold the thinking that underlay the Luxembourg Compromise forced by General de Gaulle on the five other member states in 1966, asserting France's right to refuse to apply the qualified majority vote. In the National Assembly on 12 May 1992, prior to the French refer-endum on the Maastricht Treaty, the then French Prime Minister Pierre

Bérégovoy made the French government's position clear: 'Finally, a few words about the Luxembourg Compromise. France has never relinquished, and will not relinquish the right, in the event of a serious crisis, to protect her fundamental interests. So the states' mutual commitment to go on seeking agreement between them all, when it has been impossible to achieve unanimity and application of the majority rule would jeopardize interests one of them deems vital, still stands.'[217]

Though the purists rightly argue that the Luxembourg Compromise has never been given treaty status, it is nevertheless a guiding light for politicians who want to operate within the political framework of a European Union of nation-states. In the UK I championed British membership throughout my twenty-six years as a Member of Parliament and still do so today in the House of Lords; but always within the knowledge that nothing in the practice of the then European Community and now within the Maastricht Treaty for the European Union carries an obligation on any member state to forgo its right to uphold, even in a minority of one, its own national interest – particularly since in the field of foreign affairs and defence policy national interests on occasion genuinely divide states. Sadly, over the years, some countries abused the definition of national interest within the scope of the Treaties of Rome of 1957 and the Single European Act of 1986, invoking it for minor economic or trade matters. Some extension of majority voting in the running of the single market could be worthwhile if it were accompanied by a formal acceptance of the right of a member state to invoke its vital national interests and a reweighting of votes to take account of the demographic and economic weight of the member states.

Over the name, flag and constitution of the Former Yugoslav Republic of Macedonia from 1991 onwards the Greeks could justly claim they were acting under the Luxembourg Compromise in blocking European Community/Union policy when it went counter, as they judged, to their vital national interests. The issues involved a newly independent state that was being created on the Greek border. The key question for the European Union was whether Greek politicians would uphold their interest with wisdom, letting a consensus prevail on all but the most vital questions. In my judgement, throughout my period as Co-Chairman the Greeks trod that delicate line with skill and, given their domestic problems, the governments both of the right under Mitsotakis and of the left under Papandreou showed due consideration for the all-important unity of the European Union. Eventually, in September 1995 in an agreement brokered by Cyrus Vance, normal relations were to be established between Greece and FYROM; the Greek embargo was to be lifted and FYROM agreed to remove from its flag the sixteen-point Vergina Star, which Greece had maintained implied a claim to Greek territory. Qualified majority voting, or fifteen minus one voting, would have hindered, not helped, the working of the Foreign Affairs Council in dealing with the dispute between Greece and FYROM and indeed the overall management of the Balkan crisis. In effect, in the vote of 17 December 1991 over the recognition of Croatia informal majority voting was allowed to apply, and even many Germans have come to accept that this was not the European Community's finest hour.

There is a need for one significant reform if a sensible enhancement of a Common Foreign and Security Policy is to be achieved. That is to link the European Council of heads of government with the Council Secretariat which serves the EU Foreign Affairs Council and the WEU, the only body that can develop a defence policy for Europe.

President Chirac on 31 August 1995 suggested creating a new post of Secretary-General, tasked with representing the Union abroad and implementing the mandates given by the European Council of heads of government.[218] I believe this is an excellent proposal, but the role of such a Secretary-General must be very clearly defined. Chirac rightly states that the CFSP must preserve its intergovernmental nature and continue to be directed by the Council alone. That means the post must be called the European Council's Secretary-General and the appointment must be made solely by the European Council of heads of government; and the person who holds the post must be answerable to them, not to the Foreign Affairs Council or the European Parliament. The Secretary-General to the European Council should in all respects be, like the Secretary-General of NATO, a political figure, charged with helping to create in the European Council the same consensus which has been achieved within NATO, where there has been no voting mechanism other than unanimity throughout its existence. The key to making this an effective reform would be for the existing Secretary-General of the Foreign Affairs Council Secretariat and the existing Secretary-General of the WEU to be charged by their respective bodies with working under the authority of the Secretary-General of the European Council of heads of government and the Presidency of the European Union for those matters, and only those matters, which are before the European Council at any one time. Unless such a clear linkage and a relevant hierarchy are established, any new appointment could easily result in wasteful and tedious duplication and rivalry.

There are three linked issues relating to past Security Council decisions that need to be re-examined to see if different actions could have been taken, namely putting UN personnel on the borders of Bosnia-Herzegovina to control the movement of troops and to stop the transfer of arms, whether there should or should not have been an arms embargo, and the mandate. All through the war in Bosnia-Herzegovina the question of how to monitor its borders with Croatia and the FRY has rightly loomed large.

Decisive action and a readiness to find the UN troops at the end of 1992, when the Security Council had its best-informed discussion on controlling the borders of Bosnia-Herzegovina, would have shortened the war. However, the Security Council was not prepared to find the troops, and was able to rationalize this stance since none of the parties wanted border closure. The Bosnian Serbs and the Croatian Serbs wanted open borders so that the Southern, Northern and Western UNPAs could all communicate freely with Banja Luka and Belgrade. The Eastern UNPA already had an open border with Serbia. Neither the Croatian government nor the Bosnia-Herzegovina government were keen to have international monitoring of the borders that they controlled between themselves. The reason was the transporting into Bosnia-Herzegovina of arms that came down via the Dalmatian coast by road or were smuggled in via the Dalmatian ports; the UN, if placed on these borders, would have had to try to stop the arms getting through. The Western democracies, feeling somewhat guilty about the unfairness inherent in the arms embargo and conscious that the Serb–Montenegrin border was at this time being used to supply arms to the Bosnian and Croatian Serbs, never pressed very hard for those parts of the Bosnia-Herzegovina–Croatia border to be sealed by UNMOs or Sanctions Assistance Missions. The Security Council, for its part, was ready to hide behind an inability to find the large numbers of UN troops that would be required for border monitoring.

Only during the Croat–Muslim war that raged from spring 1993 to spring 1994 were virtually no arms supplies allowed by the Croatians to cross the border for the Bosnian Muslim armed forces. Before this civil war flared up, and again after it quietened down, the Croatian government was not only ready to supply arms but allowed a black market trade to flourish; but always within certain limits, for President Tudjman was never going to let President Izetbegovic's forces become militarily stronger than the combined Croat forces, and therefore heavy weapons and some sophisticated weaponry were not allowed to pass into Bosnia-Herzegovina. Even the Bosnian Serbs were purchasing goods and oil from the Croats through most of the war in which they were supposed to be locked in conflict, for the Croats wanted to keep the Bosnian Serbs sufficiently close to them in case they needed their military strength against the Muslims. There was therefore not just a double game but a triple game being played out on the ground. The morality of the arms embargo was being discussed as a matter of high principle, while the Bosnian Muslims pretended that they had no arms, the Croatians kept very quiet about the arms they were collecting and passing on, and both were manufacturing them.

Another reason why border monitors between Croatia and Bosnia-Herzegovina were never installed was the wish of the parties to move troops across the border. It was always difficult for UNPROFOR to verify the claims that this was happening because the Croat and Serb forces all looked the same. The Croatian army (HV) and the Bosnian Croat army (HVO) have the same weapons and interchangeable insignia on exactly the same uniforms. FRY (Serbia and Montenegro) allegations in October 1992 claimed that 60,000 Croatian government soldiers, 120 tanks and around 150 artillery of 100 mm calibre and greater were in Bosnia-Herzegovina. These and other claims by the FRY were felt by the UN to be gross exaggerations, but no one doubted that there were at all times Croatian government forces operating across the border in Western Herzegovina, central Bosnia and Posavina, with Bosnian Croat forces as an integral element, and for the whole war this was a significant presence. The issue was, however, largely ignored by the Western democracies when the Russians or the FRY raised the matter in the Security Council, for the reason that the Russians and the FRY were in no position to criticize the Croats. Although the Yugoslav People's Army had nominally withdrawn from Bosnia-Herzegovina by May 1992, they had left behind almost all Serbs born in Bosnia-Herzegovina serving in the JNA, had left materials behind and continued rotating JA troops and special militia overtly across from the FRY (Serbia and Montenegro) until August 1994. Some Serb forces operating in Croatia and Bosnia were still being paid by Belgrade, as were many pensions. Also, special arms and munitions were taken across the border to supplement the existing large reserves and manufacturing capacity whenever necessary. General Mladic was in constant communication with JA HQ in the FRY and remained close to the Croatian Serb forces, which he had officially commanded in 1991. After August 1994 military links with the FRY were more covert and the supplies of men and material much less significant;[219] but the Bosnian Serb and Croatian Serb generals never lacked crucial items of equipment. What the Croatian Serb generals lacked was men.

President Milosevic, when challenged in private, always denied these military links, unlike President Tudjman, who in private conversation never made any serious distinction between Croat forces in Western Herzegovina and in his own country. To both Presidents the Bosnia-Herzegovina border was largely theoretical and in political terms did not exist. President Milosevic, until the first split with Pale in May 1993, regarded the Serbs in all three countries as owing their allegiance to him. The Croatian Serb leader Mikelic would openly refer to Milosevic as 'my President'. So while the Security Council and the international community generally were referring to the three countries as independent entities the situation on the ground was vastly different, making extra difficulties for UNPROFOR when it came to implementing Security Council Resolutions.

Many claim that the decision not to lift the arms embargo on Bosnia-Herzegovina was wrong and indefensible. This was, as the facts I have enumerated make clear, never a clear-cut moral issue. Nor was its lifting a

question of a spineless Europe and a committed Russia confronting a principled America. So much humbug has been written and spoken about the
arms embargo that it is hard for most people outside government to be
aware of the facts. The EU and the US administration, however, have
always known the facts. They know the compromises and the conniving
over the embargo that have gone on, they know all the obfuscations and
circumventions. Not one of these governments is entitled to shroud itself in
a white veil of virginal purity. The importance of not having different
permanent members of the Security Council openly supplying different sides
to the dispute with arms, as could easily have happened in 1991 in the
absence of an embargo, is considerable – as is the fact that so far the most
modern weapons have yet to appear in large quantities in the former
Yugoslavia.

Living with the arms embargo, for all its inconsistencies and evasions, was
never an immoral position for it ensured the continuation of UNPROFOR's
humanitarian mandate for the first few years, when it saved hundreds of
thousands of lives. In practice, as I have shown, a pragmatic relaxation of
the embargo developed and there was never any purist enforcement action.
A number of governments have helped arm the Croats and, through the
Croats, the Muslims. The Russian government in comparison by and large
maintained the arms embargo against the Serbs; spare parts were in the main
obtained by direct arrangement with Russian generals on a black market by
both Serbs and Croats. Moreover, the Serbs did not need to import more
weapons and did not choose to spend their very limited reserves of hard
currency on new and sophisticated Russian weapons.

Lifting the embargo has for most of the time had more disadvantages
than advantages, something which many critics know but prefer not to
admit publicly. I believe, however, that there were two occasions in my
period as Co-Chairman when it did make sense to be ready to use air
power, as part of a strategy for achieving a well worked-out, broadly
accepted peace settlement, and on both occasions I advocated this course
within the European Union. The first was in the middle of May 1993, when
I wanted the VOPP to be imposed and was ready to see the UN pull out
and the arms embargo lifted as a consequence of NATO interdicting
Bosnian Serb supply lines in Bosnia from the air (see Chapter 3, pp. 141–2).
The second was in the summer of 1994, when I wanted to impose a
modified Contact Group plan by being ready to tilt the balance of fighting
on the ground by the use of NATO air strikes after withdrawing UN troops
(see Chapter 7, pp. 282, 289). My 'leave, lift and strike' proposals were first
raised in the Contact Group on 5 June 1994, in a preliminary discussion,
when even the American representative Redman thought my proposals were
not realistic in terms of the existing political climate. On 16 June the
Contact Group met in London with the Political Directors and there was

again no support for my proposals, with the British and Russians against; only the French thought that lifting the embargo might become inevitable, and it would have to be accompanied by air strikes to avoid letting the Serbs gain the upper hand before supplies of weapons came on-stream. I recognized then, and still do today, that there were honest arguments against what I was advocating and that I might well have been wrong. Lives would have been lost; but far fewer, I felt, than if the war was allowed to continue until it reached an exhausted stand-off.

The duplicities of the war in Bosnia-Herzegovina have never been better illustrated than by a conversation between a Muslim commander and his Serb counterpart picked up by intercept radios during the Muslim–Croat war. First they bargained over the price in Deutschmarks of Serb shells which the Muslims wanted to buy from the Serbs to fire on the Croats in Mostar. After a price was agreed and routes for the supply in lorries arranged, the Muslim commander was heard to come back and ask if the Serbs could for a little extra money fire the shells if they were given the cross-bearings. After a brief haggle on the number of extra Deutschmarks this would involve, the Serbs duly fired on the Croats, paid for by the Muslims. When Stoltenberg and I told President Milosevic about this on 12 November 1993 he was very angry and asked Karadzic in our presence whether this had happened. Karadzic confirmed that it had, but said orders had been issued that it must not happen again. Another example was when in early 1995 fuel came in from Split and Zadar through the Krajina corridor to the Bosnian Serb army, with the complicity of the Croats, at a time when Milosevic was prohibiting oil to the Bosnian Serbs. The Croats sold fuel to the Bosnian Serb army partly in return for their protection of Bosnian Croat areas against Muslim attacks, and partly to underwrite the Bosnian Serbs' assistance to the Bihac Muslim leader Abdic, who had strong links with the Croat financial community. The fuel was brought in at a price of 1.2–1.8 DM per litre and then sold on to the Bosnian Serbs at 3.2–4.0 DM per litre; occasional payments were made to local commanders to persuade them to stop fighting while the fuel trucks passed through safely. Abdic was also being supported from Belgrade.

Trade in all directions across the confrontation lines continued throughout the war, demonstrating not just the complexities but also the contradictions of civil war. The particular viciousness of civil war lies in the fact that you know the people you are killing; the absurdity of it in the fact that you know you may all too soon have to live and trade with each other again, even if by then you are living in different communities.

Only the US can chronicle any strategic thinking that lay behind the Washington Accords of March 1994 that brought about a Federation of Croats and Muslims within Bosnia-Herzegovina and also an agreement in principle for a Confederation between this new Federation and the Republic of Croatia. The best account of how that relationship developed is to be found in *The Death of Yugoslavia* by Laura Silber and Allan Little.[i] The immediate justification for the Accords was that they stopped the Croat–Muslim war, which is indubitable. Unfortunately, the Accords were increasingly perceived by the Bosnian Serbs and Croatian Serbs as an anti-Serb alliance. Yet instead of making a hard-nosed political and military assessment of the strengths of the Muslims and Croats working together, the Serb leaders in Knin and Pale still refused to be serious about negotiating. Only Milosevic saw how the Washington Accords could be turned to the advantage of the Serbs. That is why he backed the Contact Group Plan in July 1994 but insisted that there must be similar confederal links with the FRY for the Bosnian Serbs. That is why he wanted an economic cooperation agreement in Croatia, for he knew that the Serbs had to be encouraged to drop their demand for secession and to be given the confidence to live within Croatia. A high priority in 1994, if war was to be avoided in the Krajina in 1995, was to build quickly on an economic agreement in Croatia. To do this we, as Co-Chairmen, needed to offer both a carrot and a stick to the moderate Croatian Serb leader Mikelic, who wanted a negotiated settlement with the Croatian government and was the only person who could stand up to the hardliner Martic. But he, and we, needed Milosevic's help. The Contact Group also needed a carrot and stick to coax and push the Bosnian Serbs to the negotiating table and end the war in Bosnia-Herzegovina. In this too Milosevic's help was crucial.

Yet there were key people in Washington and Bonn who still saw Milosevic as the fount of all evil and really did not want to have any negotiations with him at all. Some were so antagonistic that they were ready to contemplate bombing Serbia and Montenegro. In particular, they had in their sights the air defence system in the FRY, which was integrated with the air defence system nominally controlled by the Croatian Serb army in Croatia and the Bosnian Serb army in Bosnia-Herzegovina, but in reality controlled and even staffed from Belgrade. Even Senator Sam Nunn, the most influential and sensible Senator on defence questions, had raised publicly the possibility of extending the range of air attacks to these sites if NATO planes were shot down over Bosnia-Herzegovina at the time of the imposition of the Sarajevo exclusion zone. In London and Paris the view held strongly by both political and military figures was that such action would not only destroy Russian cooperation across the board but risk prompting an insistence by the Russian military that Russian air force planes be flown into FRY airfields. This assessment was one I fully shared and it lay behind my anxiety over the handling of the Russians at the time of the Sarajevo exclusion zone in 1994.

Another strand in the US administration was one that saw Milosevic as a strategic genius always three or four moves ahead of us on the chessboard of Balkan politics and who believed that nothing connected with him was as it seemed and that he was always playing according to the Greater Serbia game plan. On this view – which was in part shared by some in the EU, particularly in the Dutch and German governments – any apparent movement towards our position, as in April 1993 over the VOPP, was a foul plot from which we should steer clear. In the eyes of people who thought like this, to establish the ICFY Mission in Belgrade in September 1994 was to be hoodwinked from the outset. It would have been too tedious to chronicle here all the petty arguments we had to have, as Co-Chairmen, with Washington and later with Bonn, to sustain the ICFY Mission. The factual record is covered in our published reports as Co-Chairmen to the UN Secretary-General. The US administration seemed to operate in separate compartments, with a sanctions team that would not face up to the importance of the ICFY Mission for their Contact Group members' negotiating strategy with Milosevic. The result was to prevent serious negotiations on the Contact Group Plan for over a year, during which the situation deteriorated sharply in both Bosnia-Herzegovina and Croatia.

Aware of most, if not all, of the military links between the three Serbian armies, I was convinced that they were in effect operating as one on the strategic level, and this is why I never felt it right for the EU, NATO or the UN to take a purist line on the implementation of the arms embargo or to spend time and effort stopping arms coming through to the Croats and Muslims in the various illegal ways that were established. In the Nelson tradition, I was content for a blind eye to be turned. Yet, just as there was no purity in my attitude to the arms embargo on the Muslims, so I did not feel unduly shocked by the assumption that Milosevic was from September 1994 onwards ensuring that key items of equipment and logistical support got through to General Mladic, if for no other reason than to keep Mladic apart from Karadzic and as a potential ally. The IFCY Mission was bound, just as the NATO and WEU naval patrols in the Adriatic and Sanctions Assistance Missions around the former Yugoslavia were bound, to enforce international law. None of us could connive at the breaking of sanctions, but we did not have to be naïve about what was actually going on. It seemed to me, and to many other political leaders in Europe, a matter of calculating what was in our interest at any one time.

After the Washington Accords the US appeared increasingly to join Germany in seeing Tudjman's government as a strategic as well as a political ally against the Serbs. This relationship made it much easier for the Croatian government to defy the UN in Croatia, and to some extent the EU, as well as to risk attacking the Serbs living in Croatia rather than continuing the admittedly frustrating negotiations with them over Western Slavonia and the Krajina. The Croatian attack into Western Slavonia in the Western UNPA in early May 1995 resulted in 15,000 Croatian Serb refugees fleeing across the border into the Banja Luka district. The Croatian government attack on the Krajina in early August 1995 created the biggest single flood of refugees – over 150,000 Croatian Serbs – in the break-up of Yugoslavia. Taking into account also the forced exodus of over 50,000 Muslims following the Bosnian Serbs' attacks on Srebrenica and Zepa in June and July, in the three and a half months from May to August 1995 the map of Croatia and Bosnia-Herzegovina was dramatically changed. The loss of life and casualties from the fighting were accompanied by appalling atrocities and ethnic cleansing by all parties on a scale that we had not seen before in such a concentrated period of time. The international community looked on helpless and divided, its diplomacy in tatters, the UN forces irrelevant. A Balkan solution had been imposed on the battlefield, tearing up the Contact Group map, destroying the Zagreb 4 plan and raising fundamental questions about the relevance of any of the various involvements from outside the region since 1991. The Security Council passed Resolutions of condemnation but they were ignored by the Croatian government army in Western Slavonia, the Bosnian Serb army in Zepa and Srebrenica and the Croatian and Bosnian government armies in the Krajina.

The fact that neither Belgrade nor Pale came to the aid of the Croatian Serbs was a sign that the direct and indirect dialogue that Tudjman had maintained with both Milosevic and Karadzic paid off for the Croats. Zagreb and Belgrade had been heading for a regional solution for some time, making deals on the ground to change the map in the former Yugoslavia to order their own relationship, with scant regard for the international community. The danger for the Bosnian Muslims is that this rearrangement will be at their expense. Though the US and Germany will do all they can to prevent this in the short term, in the longer term it may well prove to be that the Washington Accords have the effect that many feared of legitimizing a greater Croatia.

The victors in the Yugoslav wars of 1991–5 have been the Croats and President Tudjman. The losers have been the Croatian Serbs and their useless leader, Martic. Whether the Bosnian Muslims will let the Croatian ascendancy in Bosnia continue unchallenged is the big question. In the immediate circumstances they have little alternative, since Milosevic and Tudjman can prevent war continuing. But the strains within the Federation will be very considerable in the next few years, and the US and the EU will have to do much more of the type of action the EU is taking in Mostar to prevent a recrudescence of the Muslim–Croat war of 1993–4. As to Milosevic, he has beaten off Karadzic's challenge to be the King of the Serbs. He appears to have rescued the Serbs from what they see as their fate, winning battles but losing the peace. He will gain a larger Serbia, but not the Greater Serbia of the nationalists' dreams. I never considered Milosevic as being on our side when he supported the VOPP in April 1993, the

Union of Three Republics in September 1993, the EU Action Plan in December 1993 or the Contact Group Plan in July 1994. It was just a case of his interests and ours coinciding for a period. But it is hard to gainsay his judgement of 9 August 1995: 'Hundreds of thousands of people would have avoided the horrors of war if the Vance–Owen Plan had been accepted over two years ago.'[ii] Milosevic blamed the Bosnian Serb leadership, but leaders in Washington bear a heavy responsibility too for prolonging a war, with miserable consequences: as I predicted in May 1993, there is no honour left for any settlement.

The third issue to review is how the UN mandate for its forces in the former Yugoslavia changed over time, and whether these changes were wise. It is easy to forget that it was only as a humanitarian intervention force that UNPROFOR was initially mandated to go into Bosnia-Herzegovina. This was when it secured Sarajevo airport by agreement with the Bosnian Serbs. At the time of the autumn 1992 deployment to Bosnia-Herzegovina UNPROFOR's mandate still did not include any element of enforcement. This was a recognition of the fact that by then the Bosnian Serbs controlled nearly 70 per cent of Bosnia-Herzegovina, and for all the frustrations involved the UN had to operate in a way that reflected that reality. Humanitarian intervention where troops assist aid workers is not a traditional peacekeeping operation in the sense that there is no ceasefire to observe or monitor, no agreed confrontation line on which to interpose UN forces; but experience in Somalia showed that such intervention has to operate under the peacekeeping rubric of impartiality and not cross the 'Mogadishu line' unless the Security Council and the troop-contributing nations are ready to become combatants. In Bosnia-Herzegovina the need for strict impartiality on the part of the UN was even greater than in Somalia. The route for UNPROFOR and UNHCR convoys from central Bosnia to Gorazde, for example, crossed 55 miles of Bosnian Serb-held territory, crossed two mountain ranges and over forty-four bridges, and passed through narrow defiles. Quite apart from what two men and a mortar can do in such an environment, a group of women held a French convoy hostage for five weeks only a few miles from Sarajevo in 1994. Calls for 'robust' or 'muscular' action from politicians, retired generals and commentators in television studios were greeted with hollow laughs by the men on the ground.

There was no peace enforcement component to the 'safe area' concept at its inception in April 1993 relating to Srebrenica;[220] nor when the concept was extended to Sarajevo, Tuzla, Zepa, Gorazde, Bihac and their surroundings.[221] Although in both these Resolutions the Security Council acted under Chapter VII of the UN Charter, the chapter that allows the UN to take military action to restore international peace and security, it was cited in relation to the provisions of an earlier Resolution ensuring the security of UNPROFOR personnel.[222] While the Resolution of 4 June 1993 did refer to

Chapter VII without any qualification,[223] and did not oblige UNPROFOR to seek the consent of the parties, the parameters for the use of force remained those of self-defence. The Council irresponsibly chose a 'light option' of a 7,500 troop reinforcement to carry out the mandate related to the 'safe areas',[224] despite the UN in New York settling for 15,000 and knowing that their military wanted 35,000 to enforce the 'safe areas' properly. This was the worst single decision taken by the Security Council during my tenure as Co-Chairman of the ICFY. The 'safe area' mandate was a totally inconsistent one: for the areas to be safe they had to be demilitarized, then defined, and then defended by the UN. As it was, in the absence of consent and cooperation it was impossible to fulfil the mandate, and Serb attacks into and Muslim attacks out of 'safe areas' continued.

NATO air forces, having at the UN's request taken control of the skies to enforce the no-fly zone over Bosnia Herzegovina in 1993, on 8 February 1994 shot down four Bosnian Serb warplanes over central Bosnia. This action by two US F-16s was the first military strike by NATO in its history. The most successful innovation in UN enforcement measures was NATO-operated close air support. This was aimed at dealing with localized aggression against UN forces and provided for a proportionate response. The Russians accepted this as a legitimate extension of returning fire by artillery in circumstances where no suitable UN guns were available. The first close air support action was undertaken on 10 April 1994 when two US F-16s attacked Serb positions near Gorazde.

The first air strikes choosing targets not directly related to attacks that had been undertaken took place when NATO jets bombed the Bosnian Serb ammunition dump near Pale on 25 May 1995. A far better judged use of air strikes was the action taken on 30 August to enforce the Sarajevo exclusion zone. When targets were bombed as far afield as Banja Luka, relating to Serb air defences, and bridges bombed around Foca, air power was also sending a political message to the Bosnian Serbs. NATO appeared to be coming very close to imposing a negotiated settlement, similar to the kind of action that I had advocated in May 1993 and in July 1994. There was no specific map to enforce, however, since the Contact Group map had yet to be changed. It is very dangerous for air strikes to be used in a political vacuum, when there is no settlement on the table and when continued action can easily become partisan. This exemplified the delicate tightrope the UN had to walk between enforcing peace and becoming a combatant. I often stressed that the UN must not be seen as being at war with the Serbs, or at war on behalf of the Muslims and Croats. To be seen as taking sides would have put at risk cooperation with the Russian Federation and made it more likely that the split between Belgrade and Pale would close. In the event the Contact Group map was developed by the soldiers as the Croats took Jajce and the Muslims land in western Bosnia, and the 51–49 per cent split became a reality.

The active promotion of peace is an essential part of the UN Charter. Impartiality has long been recognized as one of the unique qualities the UN can bring to the resolution of conflicts. Yet impartiality does not mean inaction. UN impartiality does not mean neutrality or moral equivalence. Condemnation has to be an accompaniment to negotiation. Humanitarian intervention can buy time for a peace settlement to be reached; pressure for a peace settlement, whether from political or economic sanctions, and military peacekeeping and protection, are legitimate elements in the promotion of peace. Proportionate action when the UN is attacked is a right. Implementation can be a key ingredient of any settlement. In truth, all of these factors are the ingredients for pressurizing for, and even imposing, a settlement. I believed that interdiction from the air of supply lines to the Bosnian Serbs to enforce UN sanctions would have been a legitimate pressure for peace on a number of occasions. Suppression of Bosnian Serb air defences was a legitimate accompaniment of action to enforce the heavy weapons exclusion zone around Sarajevo. It might have been needed in February 1994. It was needed in August 1995. Correctly judged, none of these actions challenge UN impartiality or themselves turn the UN into a combatant.

The role of the negotiator is a complex one, and there can be no specific rules. Sometimes silence is golden, at other times it can be interpreted as complicity. I have not taken the easy way out of claiming that a negotiator has to remain silent in order to be fair and impartial; at various times I have spoken out against all the parties in the former Yugoslavia. The negotiator is a lightning conductor for governments. But a negotiator has to be able to move between the parties and for this reason it was helpful that there was a UN Special Rapporteur, pinning violations of human rights on the parties. It was also helpful that it was for the prosecutor of the Yugoslav War Crimes Tribunal to determine whether what was going on in the former Yugoslavia at any stage constituted genocide, who had committed war crimes, practised ethnic cleansing and perpetrated any other crimes against humanity.

For the UN military on the ground, impartiality demanded that threatening the Bosnian Serbs with air attacks for having heavy weapons in the exclusion zones meant threatening attacks on the Bosnian Muslims too if they used such weapons or sought to take military advantage. Similarly, close air support had to apply to all parties. The US commanders in NATO have not been allowed to accept this discipline of impartiality, being under orders to refer to Washington if there were any question of taking action against anyone other than the Serbs. Air drops were undertaken for UNHCR and therefore could involve only humanitarian supplies, but some UNPROFOR commanders believe that US planes also dropped military supplies to the Bosnian Muslims. Likewise, while the no-fly zone was meant to apply to all fixed-wing aircraft, this too, UNPROFOR commanders believe, was breached to allow planes unauthorized by either NATO or the UN to fly into Cazin and Tuzla. Impartiality must also apply to sanctions, although there is more room here for political judgement. The UN in Bosnia-Herzegovina stretched the boundaries of its mandate to the limit, particularly that between Chapter VI and Chapter VII UN military action. The UN tried to operate in an area of partial enforcement called by some 'Chapter VI and a half'; the attempt was legitimate, but extremely complicated to execute.

It was the American Republican Senator Vandenberg who said in 1945 on the use of force: 'through the UN wherever possible, within the Charter, always.' That is a truth which no US administration should seek to circumvent. The UN Charter and Security Council mandates must not be manipulated to achieve desirable political objectives or moral outcomes, even by the most powerful country in the world. UN officials have always had to avoid the siren voices of those member states who want short-cut solutions, and steering between Scylla and Charybdis is an essential task of any UN Secretary-General or UN field commander. They will rarely win accolades, but their independence has to be maintained; and the fact that many courageously ensured that the UN was impartial meant that the UN, though disparaged, was not destroyed in Bosnia-Herzegovina.

The UN, as opposed to the member states, cannot however be immune from criticism for not enforcing its mandate where it has been given the resources by the Security Council to do so. I believe that the UN could have done more in the spring of 1992 to disarm the Serb militias in the Eastern UNPA in Croatia. They needed better-quality troops, but there was a certain lack of resolve from the outset to create a climate in which Croatian refugees could return. The erosion of the UN's authority in Bosnia-Herzegovina was largely a reflection on the mandates and the resources they were given by the Security Council. But there were incidents when UNPROFOR looked unnecessarily powerless, the most blatant example being the shooting of the Bosnian Deputy Prime Minister, Turajlic, in a UN APC in Sarajevo. The authority of the UN is not always a question of the number of troops, or even of the standard of their equipment, but of the determination and quality of the commanders and their men. It is this combination of factors which marks the difference between a failed and a successful peacekeeping mission.

I am convinced that if President Bush had won re-election in November 1992 there would have been a settlement in Bosnia-Herzegovina in February 1993 on the basis of the Vance–Owen Peace Plan, implemented predominantly by the UN, probably without US troops but with a firm US commitment to logistical support and assistance from the air for implementation. It is often forgotten that implementation of the Vance–Owen Peace Plan in January 1993 did not involve NATO troops, but envisaged a deployment of

15,000 UN troops, later revised upwards to 25,000. It was the Clinton administration who offered US troops for implementation in February 1993 and insisted they come under NATO command. By May 1993 implementation of the VOPP would have been far more effectively done by the envisaged 60,000–70,000 force whose tasks had been fully thought through by NATO, but by then US leadership was an essential ingredient. It was a tragedy that President Clinton did not exercise that leadership and insist on implementation of the plan that summer. Instead the US used Karadzic as an excuse for not acting. The Europeans were not ready to go ahead in backing the plan without US support on the ground to implement it, and none of them showed any readiness to impose that plan with NATO air power. Again in the summer of 1994 the Contact Group nations were not ready to impose their own settlement. Though there was far less planning for its implementation than had been the case with the VOPP, the task would have been simpler under the two-way split by then envisaged for Bosnia-Herzegovina. I believe that, properly handled, the Russian Federation, which supported the VOPP and was a participant in the Contact Group, would not have blocked imposition of either plan; nor would imposition in 1993 or 1994 have provoked the FRY (Serbia and Montenegro) to intervene on the side of the Bosnian Serbs.

Relationships with the Russian Federation in the Security Council throughout the period of the break-up of former Yugoslavia have been serious and mainly friendly. The EU has had fewer problems and differences with the Russians than with the Americans. If anything, the EU and the US have exaggerated the links between Russia and the Serbs and therefore their influence and capacity to deliver. The Russian–Serbian relationship is one of declining sentiment, not one of vital interest. But it did become the symbolic measure within Russia of whether Russians were being treated as genuine partners by the US and Europe: slights were too often interpreted as being of far greater significance than was ever intended. Yeltsin therefore has to tread carefully in the domestic arena; but he himself shares this basic Russian sentiment of pride and refuses to accept a Russian loss of power. Kozyrev had to navigate a path between pragmatism and sentiment with care, and he did so with considerable skill. Whenever Russia had to choose between its vital interests, usually involving keeping on good terms with the US, and its sentimental attachments, as for example over the Contact Group map, it came down on the side of interest. Russia's most decisive action was when it put troops into Sarajevo in February 1994: that was done because Russia saw more clearly than the US the dangers ahead and the logic of war, which would have led to the bombing of Serbia. For the Russians, NATO air attacks on Serbia and Montenegro were bound to challenge their authority in a way they judged could not be accepted. Russia will never be treated as an inferior partner in any Contact Group, and whenever that prospect emerged the Russians became difficult. At times Russia came close to dropping its membership of the Contact Group and would have acted independently within the Security Council if it had felt its status was being undermined. What the diplomacy over former Yugoslavia has shown is that if the Russians are treated as proper partners they will be party to compromise and joint endeavour. I also believe that NATO must ensure that the Russians are carefully persuaded to accept joint implementation of the settlement, to the extent of contributing Russian troops and aircraft to serve and fly under command structures that would in effect be those of NATO.

For a long time the UN–NATO relationship in the former Yugoslavia was, as Cy Vance had predicted, an oil-and-water mix.[225] Joint UN–NATO action in the summer of 1995 was welcome, but tensions and suspicions remained. The question is whether the relationship could have been handled differently at an earlier stage. I believe that if Manfred Woerner, the then NATO Secretary-General, had not been searching for a new role for the organization when NATO was first asked for help by the UN, the relationship could have been smoother – but only by NATO playing down, not playing up, its role. It would have meant NATO ensuring that the UN profile was high and that all operations were seen to be fundamentally UN operations, taken at the request of the UN and under UN control, with the limitations attached to impartiality being openly acknowledged from the start. Now that the US administration and Congress have comprehensively challenged the principle of the dual-key mechanism I see fewer possibilities of joint UN–NATO operations for some years ahead. In future, NATO involvement in peacekeeping will probably occur only in the form of a multinational peacekeeping operation on the basis of Security Council Resolutions, where the UN has delegated all necessary powers to it, as was done for the multinational task force over the Iraqi invasion of Kuwait.

UN peacekeeping with regional defence associations will, however, still be needed and should in future be done by Europeans acting under the WEU. The European Union now needs to champion a structure for WEU–NATO cooperation that puts in place a framework for WEU peacekeeping that can operate without undue detriment to, and without unnecessary duplication between, the two organizations. It is also important for the WEU to build a peacekeeping relationship between itself, the Russian Federation and other non-EU European countries, so that a wider Europe can respond to any request from the UN Secretary-General under the Charter for help from a regional defence association.

NATO's proven command and control arrangements are too important to risk over arguments about 'dual key' operations. It is far better for them to remain 'unsullied' and for the US Congress to continue to have confidence that US servicemen and women can participate in NATO and take orders in the field from someone who is not always a US national. Building up the peacekeeping role of the WEU and its relations with Russia will allow NATO to focus on its original purpose: to deter aggression and to be utterly committed to fighting for the territorial integrity of every one of its member states. The US administration should rethink its sudden shift of policy at the end of 1994 which accelerated NATO's study of enlargement, causing concern in Germany and apoplexy in Russia. It trampled on Russia's sensitivities and its perceived vital interests with no commensurate return. At the very least NATO should pull back on the link between joining Partnership for Peace and becoming a member of the Alliance, described by one American analyst as threatening Russia with 'rolling encirclement'.[iii] EU membership for Poland and the Czech Republic, linked to a limited and selective early enlargement of NATO in the year 2000, remains however a geopolitical imperative.

The final area for change in the light of Yugoslav experience must above all else be the Security Council itself. Here I believe it is vital to concentrate not on which countries belong (though the case for Germany, Japan and India is overwhelming) but rather on how they make their decisions and on what they bring to the Council as members, whether permanently or for their two years on rotation.

The Security Council's decisions in the former Yugoslavia over the mounting, deploying and controlling of UN ground troops in peacekeeping operations have come under criticism because of the widely acknowledged gap between the rhetoric of their Resolutions and the realities on the ground. In the case of peace enforcement operations in Bosnia this gap became a chasm, and pointed to a fundamental problem in the way the Security Council members function.

When a country's Cabinet and Parliament commit their armed services to a military operation, they know that they will be held accountable by their citizens for the lives, safety and honour of those forces. Few decisions, therefore, are taken more seriously by national politicians than those involving the mounting, deploying and controlling of their own troops. Power and responsibility go hand in hand. No one taking part in military decisions should be able to divorce themselves from the consequences of those decisions. That linkage is not sufficiently built into the Security Council. A UN peacekeeping operation can in theory involve the armed forces of none of the member states of the Security Council. Most often, a few members of the Security Council are involved on the ground, ensuring that at least some of those contributing to the debate speak from the knowledge base of a country also contributing troops. But it is very rare for as many as nine member states, the number required to make a decision in the Council, to have troops on the ground in any particular operation. It is this divorce from responsibility which accounts for much of the mismatch in Security Council Resolutions between rhetoric and reality.

The Security Council needs an almost instantly deployable UN Brigade capable of operating within days in the period between the decision to deploy UN forces and the expiry of the time it takes to assemble a normal UN peacekeeping operation. That period, even under the UN Stand-by Arrangements System introduced in 1993 and with the quickest of national decision-making, stretches to a few weeks. Such a permanent stand-by brigade would be complementary to existing practice; when the decision was taken to use it simultaneous decisions would need to be taken to provide for its reinforcement and replacement by the Stand-by Arrangements System, and calls would have to be made on regional defence organizations.

An excellent analysis of what is needed was published by the Dutch government in January 1995 in *A UN Rapid Deployment Brigade: A Preliminary Study*. The point at which the Dutch government's proposal becomes controversial is where it says: 'The personnel of the brigade should be recruited on an individual basis, following a procedure similar to the one which currently applies to the recruitment of personnel for the UN Secretariat.' My fear is that a directly recruited UN Brigade would widen the gap in the Security Council between rhetoric and reality and increase the divorce between power and responsibility.

An individually recruited force would, if things went wrong, quickly become in the mouths of the member states the UN Secretary-General's force: immediately disavowable. We have seen in recent years how major governments escape their responsibilities as soon as something goes wrong. In Somalia, when the American-led UN operation crossed the 'Mogadishu line' between peacekeeper and combatant, responsibility was barely acknowledged by the US administration, who had run the whole operation; it became the UN's fault. The other member states on the Security Council who had passed the same Resolutions also shuffled off their responsibilities on to the UN as fast as they could. Initially, the US Congress and the US media did not accept that it was right for their government to escape responsibility in Somalia quite so easily; but soon they too began to talk as if it were all the UN's fault – as happened over Bosnia-Herzegovina. How much easier would it be for the Security Council member states to evade their responsibility if a directly recruited, instantly deployable UN Brigade ran into difficulties? Some argue that it is the UN's fate to be the world's safety-valve and scapegoat, and there is a degree of truth in that claim; but it cannot be used as a reason for avoiding reform.

Only when the Security Council members accept, as part of the obligation associated with membership of the Council, making a contribution from their own armed services to a permanent, instantly deployable UN Brigade will power and responsibility come together on the Council.[226] Some may say that it is unfair to require a small, poor country to jump such a hurdle in order to become a Security Council member; but for power to be properly exercised, the responsibilities that stem from that power must be assumed. A country not willing to fund and contribute from their own armed services a fair proportion to an instantly deployable UN Brigade would not be eligible for nomination to the Security Council. The permanent members would all be expected to contribute, in particular logistically, where a commitment for more than two years is necessary in order to operate and service heavy-lift fixed-wing aircraft, helicopters, ships and the state-of-the-art communication and other equipment that is so essential. If it were felt that the two years of Council membership were too short a period of service for troops, given the need for integrated training, it could be specified that the troop commitment should extend for one year after a country's membership has ceased, that is, to three years in all.

In this way Security Council decisions would gain an immediacy and relevance in all member countries. If their ambassadors voted, for example, for something like the creation of 'safe areas' in Bosnia-Herzegovina with a force of only 7,500, knowing that the UN military advisers had recommended 35,000, they would all have to justify the decision in the knowledge that if the force were inadequate they would be putting at risk by immediate deployment some 300–700 of their own nationals. That linkage would concentrate their minds on arriving at a proper mandate and ensure that every ambassador in the Security Council in New York, if they were receiving conflicting advice, really did clear their line with their government back home, including their Ministry of Defence and their generals. To believe there should be no such linkage is to use the arguments that many have advanced down the centuries for deploying mercenaries.

The linkage to national governments would further ensure that if the troops of the UN Brigade were taken as hostages it would be national governments, not just the UN, campaigning for their release. Further still, if troops of the UN Brigade were killed it would be their ministers at the airport to comfort the relatives and on their feet in national parliaments explaining the whys and wherefores. Conversely, if the troops were accused of bad conduct it would be for their government and the UN to defend or discipline them.

Such a reform of the conditions of Security Council membership would mark the end of sending other countries' armies, and not your own, into UN peacekeeping operations. The permanent members may be the most resistant to this reform, particularly given the current mood in the US against allowing their servicemen to participate under UN command. US Congressional resistance could be reduced by the US government contribution being met by their government employing civilian pilots and chartering planes and ships for logistical support from private companies in much the same way as the UN and the US army increasingly contract out their logistic back-up. The fact that they were not in US uniform and were not part of the troop contingent would not substantially weaken the sense of US involvement, for logistical support is not risk-free – as we saw with the pilots flying in and out of Sarajevo airport. In this way the UN Brigade would best gain access to sophisticated logistical support from the US, a resource of immense value to any rapid reaction force.

The funding of the UN Brigade could be a cost associated with Security Council membership, and national parliaments would have to delegate the power of decision in such quick-reaction operations to their government while a member of the Security Council. If a country voted against an operation in the Security Council then they would not be obliged to contribute to the Brigade, and this is a reason why it would be better to plan for a Brigade of 5,000, the upper limit of the range thought desirable.

Such a restructured Security Council membership would make different and wiser decisions on mounting, deploying and controlling UN operations. Members would all be troop contributors and on the key questions of enforcement would reflect most carefully on the dangers and limitations of any operation. The senior general commanding the UN Brigade would be able to act as adviser not just to the Secretary-General but also to the Security Council, and to attend Council meetings on a semi-permanent basis. If this system had been operating a few years ago, and if one examines the Security Council record on Bosnia-Herzegovina against such a background, it is possible to see many Resolutions where different and wiser military decisions would have been taken.

Also, a Security Council restructured in this way would have recognized economic sanctions as being a far more crucial lever for peace than was the case in the former Yugoslavia. There would have been a better appreciation within the Council of sanctions as both a stick and a carrot. They are usually applied too late and too weakly and maintained for too long. Economic sanctions were applied far too slowly on the FRY (Serbia and Montenegro) and were soon ineffective – in the main because Serbia had a virtually open border with Macedonia and Albania, both of which developed a thriving black market business, particularly in breaching oil sanctions. At various crucial times this was very damaging diplomatically as petrol became easily available in Belgrade. Financial sanctions, when applied by private banks in the latter part of the 1980s, were the one effective measure which made the apartheid regime in South Africa change its attitude. Financial sanctions should have been applied on the FRY as part of the first sanctions package in May 1992. They finally did come into action at the end of April 1993; trying to avoid them was the key factor influencing Milosevic to endorse the VOPP. Conversely, a greater readiness in the Security Council to offer Milosevic an inducement by suspending some sanctions might have been more forthcoming if all members had been accepting responsibility on the ground. In particular, if such a carrot had been offered in return for recognition of Bosnia-Herzegovina in the talks held by Ambassador Frasure in May 1995, this would have led to the reinstatement of the cessation of hostilities agreement, which of itself should have led on to direct talks on the Contact Group Plan. There can be no doubt that this would have avoided the fall of Srebrenica and Zepa and the consequential Serb redrawing of the Contact Group map, and, very probably, the Croatian attack on the Krajina as well.

Some will argue that I am placing too much emphasis on Security Council reform; but part of the reason for the Security Council's rhetoric was that its members were trying to square too many audiences outside the Council, with differing agendas and differing policy objectives. A better-informed and more responsible debate within a Security Council whose members were all troop-contributing countries would have made it harder to dissociate peacekeeping on the ground from diplomatic peacemaking in Croatia in 1991 and later in Bosnia-Herzegovina. If all the countries in the Council chamber had been taking casualties among their UN forces from 1992 onwards, there would have been a far greater commitment to the VOPP, the *Invincible* package, the EU Action Plan and the Contact Group Plan. There would have been more questioning about why the three parties to the dispute in Bosnia-Herzegovina stopped negotiating around the same table for such a long period after 12 February 1994; also, why there were no negotiations on the Contact Group map for so long after it was tabled in July 1994. It was no accident that in the Security Council France, Britain and Russia, the countries on the ground in Bosnia-Herzegovina, were readier to argue that the earlier a settlement was reached, the better that settlement would be for the Bosnian Muslims. These countries understood what Izetbegovic did not see at various moments, namely that a delayed settlement would hurt his people's interests. But it is not surprising, given that his back was against the wall, that he always kept open the option of fighting and exaggerated the likely extent of US help in his struggle with the Croats.

Two US administrations neither pressurized nor even cajoled the parties to accept, let alone threatened to impose, any one of four successive peace proposals: the Carrington–Cutileiro plan of March 1992, the VOPP in May 1993, the EU Action Plan in December 1993 and the Contact Group Plan in July 1994. In 1995, because of the failure to make any of these maps stick, progressively less Muslim territory in Bosnia-Herzegovina exists to be occupied by Muslims, for they have lost land in eastern Bosnia to the Serbs and land in central Bosnia to the Croats. In western Bosnia the Muslims have lost influence to the Croats around Bihac. There has also been a progressive increase in Muslim suffering from ethnic cleansing as the war has gone on. Delay has meant that the Muslims are unlikely to occupy the 33.5 per cent of Bosnia-Herzegovina offered by the Serbs in the EU Action Plan.

The search for a juster peace than was obtainable at the negotiating table has inflicted hardship and havoc on innocent civilians within the former Yugoslavia and exacted a heavy price from the already weak economies of the neighbouring states. It has also helped to create greater regional instability, for at no stage were those rich countries that led the UN call for sanctions ready to compensate adequately those countries or individuals, as they were empowered to do under the UN Charter. It is to be hoped that they will honour their obligations in full to reconstruction in peacetime.

The big difference between the European Union and the United States of America over the former Yugoslavia since 1991 has been over the pace of a settlement. The EU broadly believed that its own diplomacy and its support for the UN in Croatia and in Bosnia-Herzegovina were designed to buy time for negotiated settlements, and that as time went on the terms of those settlements would be ever more to the disadvantage of the Muslim citizens in Bosnia-Herzegovina. The Bosnian Muslims of the three constituent peoples suffered, and were it was felt bound to continue to suffer, by far the most the longer the war went on. In that belief the majority of the EU countries were ready to promote, and pressurize for, an early peace. The United States neither shared the Europeans' view of what the UN's peacekeeping mandate in Croatia or humanitarian mandate in Bosnia-Herzegovina was designed to do politically, nor accepted the limitation of impartiality on the UN's military involvement. In late 1994 the US gradually began to believe, with no early prospect of successful autonomy negotiations in the Krajina, that the Croatian government forces should not be inhibited from breaking ceasefire agreements and taking on the Croatian and Bosnian Serbs.

These differences of opinion would have been more manageable if the US had been ready to put its troops on the ground in Croatia and Bosnia-Herzegovina, either under NATO command or under the UN. Their refusal to do so entrenched these differences of opinion into a division of interest. That division has hurt, and will continue to impact on the North Atlantic Alliance. I suspect, however, that in reality it will do less damage than some claim since Germany found the US lining up more and more with its long-standing pro-Croatian stance.

From the spring of 1993 to the summer of 1995, in my judgement, the effect of US policy, despite its being called 'containment', was to prolong the war of the Bosnian Serbs in Bosnia-Herzegovina. Whether prolongation was recognized as being the policy, I do not know. Prolonging the war meant prolonging the Serbs' ethnic cleansing, prolonging the casualties of war. In 1993 and 1994 there were still substantial numbers of Muslims living in areas likely to be in a majority Serb republic. They were still living in and around Bijeljina and Banja Luka. As the war continued, they were cleansed from there too. Prolongation of the war also carried the risk that it could spread to Croatia; it did, and but for the diplomacy involving Milosevic it might even have involved Serbia. Against that, the US could argue with truth that prolongation allowed the Bosnian army to build up its effectiveness and the Croat–Muslim Federation to grow further together. In my assessment the balance of these arguments, as judged by events, comes out against prolongation and in favour of imposition, in 1993 and again in 1994. The price of that prolongation paid in terms of human misery over more than two years, particularly in Sarajevo, Mostar, central Bosnia and Bihac, and more recently in Zepa, Srebrenica and the Krajina, has been very high. The resulting shifts in population will have profound consequences for many years ahead: for they do not forget in the Balkans.

People of good will and serious intentions will disagree on my conclusion. The balance to be struck in international diplomacy between waiting for the ideal and settling for the achievable is never an easy one to find. Certainly I made mistakes, both of omission and of commission, during my tenure as Co-Chairman. There has, however, been no betrayal by the governments outside the former Yugoslavia. Throughout the conflict in the former Yugoslavia too many false analogies have been drawn with Europe in the 1930s and 1940s. The twelve countries of the European Community, later fifteen within the European Union, whom I attempted to serve all tried desperately hard to marry up the moral, humanitarian, political and military factors that were so often in conflict in Croatia as well as in Bosnia-Herzegovina. For the most part they acknowledged earlier mistakes and sought to remedy them.

As to the ICFY, I believe the record will show that we were the most consistent protectors of the interests of the Bosnian Muslim citizens. As for the UN, its humanitarian intervention in Bosnia-Herzegovina for the first two winters of 1992 and 1993 had to be undertaken, and it saved many lives. By the summer of 1994, however, I believe that its intervention had begun to inhibit imposition of a settlement.

What the Clinton administration seemed to want until 1994, when they first began to assert themselves positively in the Balkans, was power without responsibility. By the end of 1994 US policy, influenced by both Robert Frasure and Richard Holbrooke, began to incorporate a greater readiness to accept realities on the ground. In August 1995 US policy dramatically changed and President Clinton accepted the responsibilities of US political power in the former Yugoslavia. It was an important recognition of the fact that if the US is to assert leadership in the post-Cold War world they have to bear the military consequences of their political decisions, as they did in the Cold War period and later over the invasion of Kuwait by Iraq. The world has seen that the US was not ready to do this in the Balkans until 1995. It was open to the Clinton administration to follow the Bush administration line and leave the former Yugoslavia largely to the European Community, the UN and the Russians within ICFY and to let them get on with it, unhampered. But the Clinton administration did not find the self-confidence or self-discipline to accept this limited role, and indulged a compulsive urge to moralize from the high ground while their military stayed in the air.

The member states of the European Union and their Foreign Ministers did accept responsibility and devoted much time and effort and considerable resources in terms of both people and money on the ground, in association with the UN, to help resolve the crisis in the former Yugoslavia. But they never exercised power: in part because they believed that they did not have sufficient power to exercise without the participation of the United States, in part because the EU does not yet know how to exercise power. The central question for the European Union is whether, after its experience in the former Yugoslavia, it will determine to build and sustain in defence and international affairs the intergovernmental power structures to support a Common Foreign and Security Policy for its member states.

Notes and References

Notes to Textual Sources

Chapter 1 Mission Impossible?

i   David Owen, *Seven Ages: Poetry for a Lifetime* (London: Michael Joseph, 1992, Penguin, 1995).

ii   Rebecca West, *Black Lamb and Grey Falcon* (Edinburgh: Canongate Classics, 1993).

iii   Fitzroy Maclean, *Eastern Approaches* (London: Penguin, 1991).

iv   John Hackett, *The Third World War* (London: Barclay Books, 1980).

v   Jasper Ridley, *Tito: A Biography* (London: Constable, 1994), p. 161.

vi   Fred Singleton, *A Short History of the Yugoslav Peoples* (Cambridge: Cambridge University Press, 1989).

vii   Martin Gilbert, *Winston S. Churchill*, vol. VII: *Road to Victory 1941–45* (London: Heinemann, 1986), pp. 571–2.

viii   Ibid., p. 729.

ix   Ibid.

x   Michael Howard, letter to *The Times*, 18 June 1983.

xi   *Evening Standard*, 30 July 1992.

xii   *Daily Mail*, 31 July 1992.

xiii   *The Observer*, Sunday 2 August 1992.

xiv   Andrew Gimson, *Sunday Telegraph*, 2 August 1992.

xv   The Earl of Beaconsfield, *Hansard* (House of Lords), 18 July 1878, cols 1759–1760.

xvi   David Owen, *Time to Declare* (London: Michael Joseph, 1991), p. 444.

Chapter 2 Establishing the Conference

i   Henry Wijnaendts, *Joegoslavische Kroniek, Juli 1991–Augustus 1992* (Amsterdam: RAP, 1993).

ii   Slavoljub Djukic, *Izmedju Slave i Anateme: Politicka Biografia Slobodana Milosevica (Between Glory and Anathema: A Political Biography of Slobodan Milosevic)* (Belgrade: Filip Visnic), pp. 184–5.

iii   Misha Glenny, *The Fall of Yugoslavia* (London: Penguin, 1992), p. 37.

iv   Milovan Djilas, *Wartime* (New York: Harcourt Brace Jovanovich, 1977), p. 356.

v   Ibid.

vi   Ridley, *Tito*, pp. 292–3.

vii   West, *Black Lamb and Grey Falcon*, p. 1101.

viii   Alija Izetbegovic, *The Islamic Declaration* (republished 1990), p. 55.

ix   See e.g. Wijnaendts, *Joegoslavische Kroniek*, pp. 152–3.

x   George Kenney, 'How Many Have Died?', *New York Times Magazine*, 22 April 1995.

xi   Robert D. Kaplan, *Balkan Ghosts: A Journey through History* (New York: St Martin's, 1993, Vintage, 1994), p. 247.

xii   See Paul C. Szasz, 'Protecting Human and Minority Rights in Bosnia: A Documentary Survey of International Proposals', *California Western International Law Journal*, vol. 25, no. 2, Spring 1995.

Chapter 3   The Vance–Owen Peace Plan

i   See e.g. Noel Malcolm, *Bosnia: A Short History* (London: Macmillan, 1994), p. 248.

ii   *Newsweek*, 18 January 1993.

iii   *International Herald Tribune*, 2 August 1995.

iv   David Owen, *Personally Speaking to Kenneth Harris* (London: Pan, 1987), p. 137.

v   A/RES/48/143, 20 December 1993, and A/RES/49/205, 23 December 1994.

vi   Haris Silajdzic, Evidence to Hearing of Senate Foreign Relations Committee, Washington, 18 February 1993. (Congressional Information Service S381-15.2.)

vii   General Sir Michael Rose, speech to Royal United Services Institute, London, 30 March 1993.

viii   See Resolution (93) 6 on the Control of Respect for Human Rights in European States Not Yet Members of the Council of Europe, art. 1, at 5, European Comm. of Ministers, Doc. No. 93/222 Add. (1993) (adopted on 9 March 1993).

ix   Colin Powell, *A Soldier's Way* (London: Hutchinson, 1995), p. 576.

Chapter 4 Ditching the VOPP

i   Glenny, *Fall of Yugoslavia*, pp. 124–6.
ii   Elisabeth Drew, *On the Edge: The Clinton Presidency* (New York: Simon and Schuster, 1994), pp. 157–8.
iii Kaplan, *Balkan Ghosts*.
iv   Arthur Schlesinger, 'How to Think About Bosnia', *Wall Street Journal*, 3 May 1993.
v   Elaine Sciolino, *New York Times*, 21 May 1993.

Chapter 5 A Union of Three Republics

i   An account of the Principals' meetings on Bosnia is given in Drew, *On the Edge*, pp. 145–6, 148–52, 274.

Chapter 6 The EU Action Plan

i   Charles G. Boyd, 'Making Peace with the Innocent', *Foreign Affairs*, September/October 1995, pp. 28–9.

Chapter 7 The Contact Group

i   Alain Juppé, interview in *Nouvel Observateur*, 17 February 1994.
ii   Mira Markovic, *Night and Day: Diary December 1992–July 1994*.
iii Owen, *Time to Declare*, pp. 377–8.

Chapter 8 Soldiering On

i   Boyd, 'Making Peace with the Innocent', p. 34.
ii   Zlatko Dizdarevic, 'Divided We Stand', *INDEX on Censorship*, vol. 24, no. 5, September–October 1995, p. 55.
iii Arthur Schlesinger, Jr, in *Wall Street Journal*, 27 October 1993.

Chapter 9 Lessons for the Future

i   Laura Silber and Allan Little, *The Death of Yugoslavia* (London: Penguin/BBC, 1995), pp. 354–9.
ii   *The Times*, 10 August 1995.
iii Robert Blackwell, 'Engaging Russia', *Triangle Papers*, June 1995, p. 46.

CD-ROM References

1 London Conference speeches and papers.
2 London Conference Declaration of Principles.
3 UNSCR 776, September 1992.
4 UNSCR 743, February 1992.
5 Note on ICFY and list of countries on Steering Committee.
6 Audio recording of BBC Radio Four, *Today*, 30 July 1992.
7 Lord Carrington, statement to the London Conference, 26 August 1992.
8 Lord Carrington, statement to the parties, Brussels, 9 March 1992.
9 London Conference papers, August 1992.
10 Recognition of Croatia.
11 Film footage of the beginnings of the conflict 1990–1.
12 Comments on Dobrica Cosic, *Yugoslavia and the Serbian Question*, 1991, Alija Izetbegovic, *The Islamic Declaration*, republished 1990, Franjo Tudjman, *Nationalism in Contemporary Europe*, Columbia University Press, 1981.
13 UNSCR 743, February 1992.
14 UNSCR 727, January 1992.
15 UNSCR 757, May 1992.
16 Maps of the UNPAs.
17 UNPROFOR press release 9 September 1992.
18 UNSCR 713, September 1991.
19 UNSCR 761, June 1992.
20 UNSCR 764, July 1992.
21 UNSCR 758, June 1992.
22 Joint communiqué by President Cosic, Prime Minister Panic and ICFY Co-Chairmen, Belgrade, 11 September 1992.
23 Lord Owen, COREU on visit to Zagreb, Sarajevo and Belgrade, 9–12 September 1992.
24 Map of Sarajevo.
25 Map of Prevlaka.
26 For example, reports of the UN Secretary-General to the President of the Security Council on the International Conference on the Former Yugoslavia (UN Sec.-Gen. to UNSC) S/24795, S/25015, S/25050.
27 UNSCR 770, August 1992
28 UNSCR 776, September 1992.
29 COREU telegram and 'Note on Briefing for Ambassadors', 15 September 1992.
30 UNSCR 779, October 1992.
31 *Channel Four News*, 3 November 1992.
32 Lord Owen, 'Personal Note to Cy Vance on UN Trusteeship', 22 October 1992.
33 ICFY working paper on constitutional options, 4 October 1992; also, preliminary plan submitted to the parties, October 1992.
34 Constitutional principles of Cutileiro plan and map.
35 Position of the government of Bosnia-Herzegovina, 16 July 1992.
36 See UN Sec.-Gen. to UNSC, S/24795, 11 November 1992, pp. 12–23.
37 Military attitudes to safe areas.
38 UNSCR 780, October 1992.
39 Letter to Boutros Boutros Ghali, 18 September 1992.
40 UN Secretary-General's letter to the Security Council, 23 November 1992.
41 Lord Owen, speech to the Security Council, 13 November 1992.
42 Lord Owen, telegram to Douglas Hurd, 18 November 1992.
43 'Proposal on Arrangement of Bosnia-Herzegovina', Bosnian Serb paper, November 1992.
44 Briefing given to Co-Chairmen in Eastern UNPA on 18–20 November 1992, and comment on Croatian problem.
45 Possibilities for boundary changes.
46 Meeting with the OIC, Jeddah, 1–2 December 1992.
47 Map of Macedonia and Greece.
48 UNSC debate on the deployment of UN border monitors, 29 November 1992.

49 ICFY memo on electoral analysis, December 1992.

50 Co-Chairmen's message on Yugoslav elections, 15 December 1992.

51 Summary of Lord Owen's speech and answers to questions at NATO, Brussels, 4 December 1992.

52 Co-Chairmen, letter to Boutros Ghali, 8 December 1992.

53 'Brief Explanations of the Proposal of Thirteen Regions in Bosnia-Herzegovina', paper submitted to the ICFY by the State Delegation of the Republic of Bosnia-Herzegovina.

54 The International Criminal Tribunal for the Former Yugoslavia ('Yugoslav War Crimes Tribunal', YWCT).

55 UNSCR 827, May 1993.

56 Lord Owen and Cyrus Vance, reports to the Steering Committee, Geneva, 16 December 1992.

57 Lord Owen's visit to Croatia and Bosnia-Herzegovina, 17–21 December 1992.

58 Opening statements by the parties and the ICFY Co-Chairmen at plenary session, Geneva, 2 January 1993.

59 President Izetbegovic's objections to the first VOPP map, 2 January 1993.

60 Lord Owen, telegram to Douglas Hurd, 7 January 1993.

61 Meeting in Sarajevo between Co-Chairmen and President Izetbegovic and Prime Minister Akmadzic, 20 January 1993; meeting in Zagreb with President Tudjman, 21 January 1993.

62 Opening statements by the parties at plenary session, Geneva, 23 January 1993.

63 Aleksa Buha, letter to ICFY Co-Chairmen, 16 January 1993.

64 Lord Owen, memorandum to Prime Minister John Major's seminar, 22 January 1993.

65 Lord Owen, COREU, 29 January 1993.

66 Cyrus Vance, remarks at plenary session, Geneva, 30 January 1993.

67 Lord Owen, remarks at plenary session, Geneva, 30 January 1993.

68 Lord Owen, personal telegram to Sir Robin Renwick, 29 January 1993.

69 EU statement, 1 February 1993.

70 Reports on rape in Bosnia-Herzegovina.

71 Articles 2–5 of the Statute of the Tribunal. This Statute is set out in the Annex of UN Sec.-Gen. to UNSC, S/25704.

72 UN military briefing on humanitarian situation, early February 1993.

73 Warren Christopher, statement on US policy initiative, Washington, 10 February 1993.

74 Mile Akmadzic, letter to UN Secretary-General, 1 March 1993; letter to Senator Joseph Biden, Chairman of the European Affairs Subcommittee of the Senate Foreign Affairs Committee of the United States Congress, 24 February 1993.

75 Details of ICFY diplomatic activity, 1 February 1993–8 March 1993.

76 Annex on human rights to S/25221, 2 February 1993.

77 Lord Owen, COREU, 2 March 1993.

78 S/25497, 26 March 1993.

79 Assessment of Serbian economic vulnerability, March 1993.

80 Details of ICFY diplomatic activity, 26 March–16 April 1993.

81 Foreign Affairs, Spring 1993, no. 72201.

82 UNSCR 819, April 1993.

83 UNSCR 820, April 1993.

84 Film footage of BBC television, Breakfast with Frost, 18 April 1993.

85 Graham A. Messervy-Whiting, 'Options for Offensive Air Operations to "level the playing field" against the Bosnian Serb Army (BSA)', 18 April 1993.

86 Public statements by Foreign Ministers Hurd, Claes, Juppé and Kinkel, 17–19 April 1993.

87 Details of ICFY diplomatic activity, 20–24 April 1993.

88 Lord Owen, personal message to EC Foreign Ministers, 24 April 1993.

89 Lord Owen, COREU, 27 April 1993.

90 Analysis of political groupings in Serbia, April 1993.

91 ICFY Co-Chairmen's proposals for a settlement in Bosnia-Herzegovina, Athens, 2 May 1993.

92 Description of Lord Owen's meeting with NATO, Brussels, 5 May 1993.

93 Bosnian Serb Assembly Commission's nine conditions, Bijeljina, 5–6 May 1993.

94 UNSCR 824, May 1993.

95 UNSCR 815, March 1993.

96 Discussion within Foreign Affairs Council, Brussels, 10 May 1993.

97 UN Sec.-Gen. to UNSC, S/25855, Annex V, 14 May 1993.

98 Lord Owen, 'US–European Relations and the Conflict in the Former Yugoslavia', Basil Hicks Memorial Lecture, University of Sheffield, 8 November 1995.

99 Co-Chairmen's discussions in the US, 12–13 May 1993.

100 Situation between Croats and Muslims in central Bosnia, April–May 1993.

101 Nick Gowing, 'Deceit Devours Diplomacy in Bosnia Last Rites', The Times, 2 August 1993; Channel Four documentary, 2 August 1993.

102 Text of US/Russia/UK/France/Spain Joint Action Programme on Bosnia.

103 UNSCR 836, June 1993.

104 Cosic hit-back at Milosevic's 'self-will' and comments by Montenegro's President Bulatovic, 2 June 1993.

105 Lord Owen, statement to the Foreign Affairs Council, 8 June 1993.

106 Declaration on Former Yugoslavia, European Political Cooperation Press Release, 9 June 1993.

107 Global settlement with limited trade-offs, 9–11 June 1993.

108 Fred Eckhard, letter to The Guardian, 14 June 1993.

109 Discussions on creating a new map, 25 April–15 June 1993.

110 Lord Owen, COREU, 17 June 1993; report of Co-Chairmen's meeting of 15–16 June.

111 Lord Owen, letter to the Danish EC Presidency, 22 June 1993.

112 Discussion at Foreign Affairs Council, Copenhagen, 22 June 1993.

113 Serb–Croat constitutional principles, Geneva, 23 June 1993.

114 Discussions on Serb–Croat proposals, 23 June–9 July 1993.

115 Annex to Lord Owen's letter to President Izetbegovic, 1 July 1993.

116 UN Sec.-Gen. to UNSC, S/26260, 6 August 1993, p. 11.

117 Statement issued by Tudjman and Milosevic, Geneva, 10 July 1993.

118 COREU telegrams to EC Foreign Ministers.

119 Constitutional Agreement of the Union of Republics of Bosnia and Herzegovina, provisionally agreed draft, 30 July 1993.

120 Map of Neretva river.

121 Map of Neum.

122 Lord Owen, letter to NATO Secretary-General, 1 August 1993.

123 NATO Secretary-General, press statement, Brussels, 2 August 1993.

124 UN Sec.-Gen. to UNSC, S/26260, 6 August 1993.

125 Briefing of Steering Committee, 6 August 1993.

126 Lord Owen, reply by COREU of 10 August 1993 to COREU CPE/BON/526 of 8 August 1993.

127 UN Sec.-Gen. to UNSC, S/26260, 6 August 1993.

128 President Izetbegovic, letter to Ms Madeleine Albright, President of the UN Security Council, 11 August 1993, challenging Co-Chairmen's report S/26260 of 6 August 1993.

129 Discussions on map with the parties, 31 August–8 September 1993.

130 Proposed Serb–Muslim agreement discussed in Montenegro, 15 September 1993.

131 Actual Serb–Muslim agreement signed in Geneva, 16 September 1993.

132 Text of the agreement to the access to the sea on HMS *Invincible*, 20 September, 1993.

133 Co-Chairmen, letter to President Izetbegovic, 26 September 1993.

134 Co-Chairmen, letter to President Izetbegovic, 1 October 1993.

135 Lord Owen, letter to Belgian EC Presidency, 1 October 1993.

136 Lord Owen, letter to Charles Redman, 1 October 1993.

137 Discussions with the parties, 4–25 October 1993.

138 Lord Owen, paper to EC Foreign Ministers, 1 November 1993.

139 Lord Owen, 'Joint Action on the former Yugoslavia', personal paper to Foreign Affairs Council, 5 November 1993.

140 Klaus Kinkel and Alain Juppé, letter to Belgian EU Presidency, 7 November 1993.

141 Lord Owen, COREU, 14 November, of meetings with Susak in London and Milosevic in Belgrade, 11–12 November 1993.

142 Lord Owen, COREU, 18 November, on meetings in Geneva on Bosnia-Herzegovina.

143 Lord Owen, 'A Framework for Survival', Eighth Annual International Health Lecture, Royal College of Surgeons in Ireland, Dublin, 8 November 1993.

144 Lord Owen to EU Political Directors, 15 November 1993.

145 Discussion between Foreign Ministers on the political agenda, Foreign Affairs Council, Luxembourg, 22 November 1993.

146 Detailed account of EU Foreign Ministers' meeting with the parties in Geneva, 29 November 1993.

147 Lord Owen, COREU reports, 30 November, 1 December and 2 December 1993 on negotiations between 30 November and 2 December 1993.

148 Lord Owen, COREU report, 9 December 1993, on meetings in Belgrade, 9 December 1993.

149 President Tudjman, letter to Co-Chairmen, 20 December 1993.

150 Lord Owen, COREU report, 18 December 1993, on meeting with Serbs and Croats, Belgrade, 17 December 1993.

151 EU request to all the parties, Brussels, 20 December 1993.

152 Lord Owen, COREU to EU Foreign Ministers on talks in Brussels 22–23 December 1993, and account of bilaterals between EU Foreign Ministers and parties, 22 December 1993.

153 Lord Owen, COREU, 6 January 1994, on Co-Chairmen's talks on 5–6 January 1994.

154 Lord Owen, letter to Douglas Hurd, 7 January 1994.

155 Lord Owen, COREU, 13 January 1994.

156 Lord Owen, COREU, Bosnia Report, 11 January 1994.

157 UNPROFOR inter-office memo, 29 January 1994.

158 See Lord Owen, COREU on Mostar City opstina, 19 December 1993.

159 Lord Owen, COREU, 27 January 1994, on Arbitration Commission and COREU, 20 January 1994, on Bosnia talks of 18–19 January 1994.

160 Lord Owen, personal letter to Douglas Hurd and Sir David Hannay, 2 February 1994.

161 Description of meeting of Steering Committee in Geneva, 2 February 1994.

162 Lord Owen, COREU, 7 February 1994, on meeting of the Co-Chairmen with Karadzic, Krajisnik and Koljevic, Zvornik, 6 February 1994.

163 Six points circulated at Foreign Affairs Council and Lord Owen's speaking notes for Foreign Affairs Council, Monday 7 February 1994.

164 Lord Owen, letter to Douglas Hurd,
     8 February 1994.
165 Lord Owen, COREU, 12 February
     1994, on Bosnia: Geneva talks,
     11–12 February 1994.
166 NATO communiqué, 9 February
     1994.
167 Lord Owen, COREU, 11 February
     1994, on Bosnia: Geneva talks,
     11–12 February 1994.
168 Lord Owen, COREU, 12 February
     1994, on Bosnia: Geneva talks,
     10 February 1994.
169 Details of diplomacy in ICFY and
     national capitals, 11–14 February
     1994.
170 Lord Owen, COREU, personal for
     Foreign Ministers, 14 February
     1994.
171 Both texts annexed to letter dated
     3 March 1994 from the Permanent
     Representatives of Bosnia and
     Herzegovina and Croatia to the
     United Nations addressed to the
     Secretary-General, UN SCOR, 49th
     session, UN Doc. S/1994/255 (1994).
172 Extracts from the Federation
     Constitution Confederation of
     13 March 1994.
173 President Clinton's statement on
     Washington Accords, 18 March 1994.
174 Details of negotiations involving
     the US, Russia, the EU and ICFY,
     21 February–23 March 1994.
175 Lord Owen, COREU, 30 March
     1994, on meeting with President
     Milosevic, 27 March 1994.
176 Briefing of Steering Committee,
     Geneva, 30 March 1994.
177 UN–NATO disagreement over the
     use of air power.
178 Chronology of events, Gorazde,
     10–16 April 1994.
179 Lord Owen, COREU, personal for
     Foreign Ministers, 14 February 1994.
180 Lord Owen, COREU on establish-
     ment of Contact Group, 19 April
     1994.
181 Lord Owen, COREU, 20 April
     1994, on Co-Chairmen's talks in
     Moscow, 20 April 1994.

182 Contact Group negotiations,
     26 April–14 May 1994.
183 Communiqué of first ministerial
     Contact Group meeting, 13 May
     1994.
184 Discussions surrounding Contact
     Group map, 14 May 1994–6
     February 1995.
185 Lord Owen, COREU reports,
     19 May and 21 May, on Co-
     Chairmen's meetings, 17–18 May
     1994.
186 Conversation with General Mladic,
     Geneva, 3 June 1994.
187 Lord Owen's letter to three Contact
     Group Foreign Ministers, 4 June
     1994.
188 COREU, 7 June 1994, Co-
     Chairmen's talks with Croatian Serb
     leader, Martic, Geneva, 7 June
     1994.
189 ICFY paper, 'Possibilities of using
     air power in the context of the
     implementation of international
     agreements including the allocation
     of territory within Bosnia and
     Herzegovina', Geneva, 15 June 1994.
190 David Ludlow's Report to ICFY on
     Contact Group negotiations.
191 Direct negotiations by Stoltenberg,
     4 August–4 September 1994.
192 Note on ICFY Mission in Belgrade.
193 Lunchtime discussion during
     informal EU Foreign Ministers'
     meeting in Usedom, 11 September
     1994.
194 Note on Zagreb 4 plan.
195 Meeting between the ICFY Co-
     Chairmen and Ibrahim Rugova on
     the situation in Kosovo, Geneva,
     2 November 1994.
196 Lord Owen, COREU with letters
     and statements on Krajina economic
     agreement.
197 Film footage of BBC television
     Panorama interview with Haris
     Silajdzic, 23 January 1995.
198 Text of Krajina Serb–Croatian
     Economic Agreement, submitted
     to the UN Security Council,
     2 December 1994 (S/1994/1375).

199 Lord Owen, COREU, 20 December 1994.

200 Lord Owen, letter to President Mitterrand, 17 January 1995.

201 Lord Owen, letter to French EU Presidency on 'FRY Recognition of Croatia', 27 February 1995.

202 Lord Owen, record of meeting between Lord Owen and M. Alain Juppé, Paris, 30 January 1995.

203 Lord Owen, letter to French EU Presidency, 8 February 1995.

204 Lord Owen, letter to French EU Presidency, 10 February 1995, with maps.

205 Lord Owen, COREU, 27 February 1995, Zagreb/Belgrade/Moscow – visits and subsequent follow-up.

206 Lord Owen, letter to French EU Presidency, 17 February 1995.

207 Co-Chairmen's statement, 1 March 1995, on three months of Croatian economic agreement.

208 Lord Owen, COREU to EU Foreign Ministers, 25 March 1995.

209 Lord Owen, minute to Paris and London, 27 April 1995.

210 Lord Owen, letter to President Chirac, 29 May 1995.

211 Lord Owen, speech in House of Lords, 31 May 1995.

212 Lord Owen, COREU to EU Foreign Ministers on Former Yugoslavia, 6 June 1995.

213 Note on 'Succession Issues'.

214 Agreed Basic Principles, Part 1, Foreign Ministers of Bosnia-Herzegovina, Croatia, Federal Republic of Yugoslavia, Geneva, 8 September 1995; Agreed Basic Principles, Part 2, New York, 26 September 1995.

215 Guiding Basic Principles for Negotiations on a Settlement of Eastern Slavonia, Baranja and Western Sirmium, 3 October 1995.

216 Lord Carrington, letter to EC President of the Council of Foreign Ministers, Hans van den Broek, 2 December 1994; UNSG Perez de Cuellar, letter to Hans van den Broek, 10 December 1994; Hans-Dietrich Genscher, letter to Perez de Cuellar, 13 December 1994; Perez de Cuellar, letter to Hans-Dietrich Genscher, 14 December 1994.

217 Press release, French Embassy in London, Sp.St/LON/88/92, 'Debate on the Revision of the Constitution. Reply of M. Bérégovoy, Prime Minister, to a Parliamentary Question (National Assembly, 12 May 1992)'.

218 President Jacques Chirac, English translation of speech, 31 August 1995, on the Intergovernmental Conference 1996.

219 Note on ICFY Mission in Belgrade.

220 UNSCR 819, April 1993.

221 UNSCR 824, May 1993.

222 UNSCR 815, March 1993.

223 UNSCR 836, June 1993

224 UNSCR 844, June 1993.

225 UN–NATO disagreement over the use of air power.

226 Lord Owen, 'The Limits of UN Peacekeeping', Fourth Cornelis Van Vollenhoven Memorial Lecture, University of Leiden, 6 June 1995.

The Standard Edition of the CD-ROM contains all of these references, plus extensive video footage from the BBC, ITN and other international broadcasters. In addition to this, the Academic Edition contains all ICFY Co-Chairmen's reports to the Security Council from September 1992 until July 1995, all relevant UN Security Council Resolutions, key internal ICFY documents, the full texts of all peace plans and Lord Owen's personal communications with EU Foreign Ministers.

Enquiries should be directed to:
Balkan Odyssey CD-ROM
PO Box 9414
London SW1H 9ZA
Telephone 44 (0)171 222 2398
Facsimile 44 (0)171 233 0574
email odyssey.csa@eworld.com

Index